Legal Aspects of Nursing

PRENTICE HALL NURSING SERIES

A series of comprehensive textbooks and reference manuals for nurses and other health care professionals.

Other titles in the series include:

Teaching and Assessing in Clinical Nursing Practice
edited by Peter L. Bradshaw

Clinical Nursing Manual
edited by Jennifer E. Clark

Nursing Research: A Skills-Based Introduction
Collette Clifford and Stephen Gough

Nursing Care of Women
Dinah Gould

Drugs and Nursing Implications
Laura E. Govoni and Janice E. Hayes (adapted by Jill A. David)

Research and Statistics: A Practical Introduction for Nurses
Carolyn M. Hicks

Becoming a Staff Nurse: A Guide to the Role of the Newly Registered Nurse
edited by Judith Lathlean and Jessica Corner

Nursing Concepts for Health Promotion
Ruth Beckman Murray and Judith Proctor Zentner (adapted by Cindy Howells)

Body Image: Nursing Concepts and Care
Bob Price

Clinical Nursing Practice: The Promotion and Management of Continence
Brenda Roe

The Art and Science of Midwifery
Louise Silverton

Nursing the Patient with Cancer
edited by Verena Tschudin

Legal Aspects of Nursing

2nd edition

Bridgit Dimond MA LL.B. D.S.A. A.H.S.M.
Barrister-at-Law

Emeritus Professor
University of Glamorgan

PRENTICE HALL

London   New York   Toronto   Sydney   Tokyo
Singapore   Madrid   Mexico City   Munich

First published 1990

This 2nd edition, first published 1995, by
Prentice Hall Europe
Prentice Hall
A Pearson Education Company
Edinburgh Gate,
Harlow,
Essex, CM20 2JE, England

Typeset in 10/12 Times
by Mathematical Composition Setters Ltd, Salisbury, Wiltshire

Printed in Great Britain by
T J International Ltd, Padstow, Cornwall

Library of Congress Cataloging-in-Publication Data

A catalogue record for this book is available from
the Library of Congress

British Library Cataloguing in Publication Data

A catalogue record for this book is available
from the British Library

ISBN 0-13-190901-0

7 8 01 00

To Clare and Bec

Contents

List of figures and tables

Figures

Tables

Table of cases

Cases before British courts

Cases before courts in the United States of America

Cases before courts in Canada

Quasi-judicial proceedings

Industrial Tribunal

Health Authority Inquiry

Table of statutes

Statutory instruments

Abbreviations

The health services are awash with abbreviations and jargon. It would, however, be immeasurably tedious and unrealistic to ignore these and always use the full words. Some of the most commonly used abbreviations are therefore set out here. Where there is any possibility of confusion, words are spelt out in full.

ACAS	Advisory, Conciliation and Arbitration Service
A & E	Accident and emergency department
AID	Artificial insemination by donor
AIDS	Acquired immune deficiency syndrome
AIH	Artificial insemination by husband
AIP	Artificial insemination by partner
ARC	Aids-related complex
BID	Brought in dead
BMJ	*British Medical Journal*
BP	Blood pressure
CAB	Citizens Advice Bureau
CHC	Community Health Council
CICA	Criminal Injuries Compensation Authority
CPN	Community psychiatric nurse
CSSD	Central sterile supply department

D and C	Dilation and curettage
DHA	District health authority
DHSS	Department of Health and Social Security, divided in 1989 into
DH	Department of Health, and
DSS	Department of Social Security
ET	Embryo transfer
EWC	Expected week of confinement
FPC	Family Practitioner Committee
GIFT	Gamete intrafallopian transfer
GMC	General Medical Council
GP	General practitioner
GUM	Genito-urinary medicine
HFEA	Human Fertilisation and Embryology Authority
HSC	Health Service Commissioner
IV	Intravenous(ly)
IVF	*In vitro* fertilisation
LREC	Local research ethical committee
MHAC	Mental Health Act Commission
MPP	Maternity period pay
NAI	Non-accidental injury
NFR	Not for resuscitation
NHS	National Health Service
ODA	Operating department assistant
PCC	Professional Conduct Committee
PPE	Personal protective equipment
PRN	*pro re nata* (as required, whenever necessary)
QW	Qualifying week
RCN	Royal College of Nursing
RCP	Royal College of Psychiatrists
SEN	State Enrolled Nurse
SMP	Statutory maternity pay
T+P	Temperature and pulse
TUR & ER 93	Trade Union Reform and Employee Rights Act 1933
UKCC	United Kingdom Central Council for Nursing, Midwifery and Health Visiting
VD	Venereal disease

Foreword

The author, Bridgit Dimond, is well known to nurses working in Wales. She has assisted many of us in developing an increased awareness of the need for expert legal advice and knowledge of the law to inform our practice in the interests of our patients, our colleagues and ourselves.

The text of the book illustrates very graphically that she has skilfully drawn her material from frequent contact with nurses, midwives and health visitors working in a variety of settings. The topics are relevant to the work of the practitioner, the educator and the manager and presented in a form which encourages the reader to delve further into the subject. Although this book is seen by the author primarily as a work of reference, the very fact that many of the issues identified are at the centre of the profound changes taking place in the pattern and organisation of services and within the nursing profession itself, ensures that it will have wider interest and will assist nurses considerably with understanding their responsibilities in a period of significant development.

Bridgit Dimond has, through this publication, yet again provided valuable assistance for improving the practice of nursing – by encouraging nurses to acquire a deeper understanding of the relevant legal aspects of the work of nursing.

Miss M. Bull
Chief Nursing Officer
Welsh Office

Preface to first edition

I make no apologies for producing a book on law for nurses. It is apparent to me that nurses are increasingly aware of the need for up-to-date legal knowledge, that they realise that they practise their profession within the constraints and limitations of the law and very occasionally with the powers of the law, and that they are increasingly held responsible. The approach adopted here is, however, a practical one. I attempt to start with the problems and move outwards to the legal significance of the events described. The result is very different from the traditional textbook approach. My aim is not to teach the nurse the academic niceties of contract law, nor of the law of negligence but, rather, to take some everyday situations in which the nurse finds herself and examine the legal consequences of the situations so that she comes to an understanding of the legal principles which arise. In this way her legal understanding will develop and she will then be able to apply those principles to similar situations.

I am aware of the dangers of this approach. Any situation is of course very complex; there are considerable dangers of over-simplification. However, I am not of the persuasion that because a little knowledge is a dangerous thing law must be kept for the lawyers. It is essential that nurses understand the legal implications of their work so that they can protect both themselves and their patients. With a basic understanding of the law they should know when they need to seek expert legal advice and also to know what elementary precautions they should be taking to protect themselves. Where possible, actual wording of Acts of Parliament has been placed in Figures, so that it would not break the flow of the text, and so that the nurse can see the actual wording. It is antic-ipated that the book would be used as a source book to dip into rather than be read from cover to cover. The appendices thus include much reference information and the index has been designed with this purpose in mind. I have not flinched from including some of the technical legal terms and have given the case references so that the nurse who wishes to pursue the subject in more detail can follow the cases.

Many of the problems discussed here are ones cited to me by hundreds of nurses in seminars I have conducted throughout the country and this explains the apparent concen-tration on issues relating to negligence litigation. This is a field that nurses are consid-erably anxious about and constantly ask questions on problems relating to the extended role, responsibility for others, and aspects relating to resourcing.

A note of caution: there are many situations which arise where there are no clear legal guidelines; the dilemmas which arise are of an ethical rather than a legal dimen-sion. The law is both narrower and wider than the field of ethics. There are some prob-lems where ethical issues arise and where the law as yet provides no specific guidelines other than the basic legal principles, for example many issues arising from the devel-opments in reproductive technology have still not been covered by legislation although, following the Warnock Report, this situation is about to be changed. In other respects the law is wider than ethical issues: for example the need to register a birth, marriage or death raises no ethical issues other than that of obeying the law. Some of these ethical issues will be covered although, clearly, it is only where there is a breach of the law that specific guidance can be given. This is not to say that ethical issues are not important. It is simply that there is no space for their discussion here. However, reference is made in the extended reading list to books which deal solely with these issues.

Some of the discussion relates to nursing procedure and practice which does not have legal status. However, it is considered essential to include this in a work of this kind.

A word about terminology. I have used the term 'nurse' to cover all categories of nursing staff from auxiliary to nursing officer. When it is significant that the nurse has a partic-ular rank, then I have used the appropriate grade. I have also tended to refer to the nurse as she; this is not meant to be sexist: it simply covers the vast majority of nursing staff and is less clumsy than any contrived alternative such as 'he/she'. To illustrate prac-tical situations two different terms have been applied: **situation** to describe an imagi-nary series of events which could well occur but in fact the names are fictitious and not intended to refer to any actual persons living or dead; **case** to cover actual cases which were heard before the courts. Not all of these refer to nursing staff; indeed the actual number of cases in which nurses have personally been defendant or accused are compar-atively rare. Many of the cases involve medical staff or are not directly concerned with the health professions. However, the principles which arise are significant for nursing practice and on that account have been included. Because law even more than health care is a jargon-dominated profession, a Glossary has been included to explain those legal terms which could cause difficulties.

The aim is to provide some practical guidance to nursing staff on the many problems that they might encounter. Part I of the book deals with those general problems which face all nursing staff covering principles of professional negligence and the rights of the patient, and also those areas where the nurse herself is a victim of an accident or assault, etc. Part II deals with those specialist areas which are more likely to be encountered by nurses working in different fields but they may also be of general interest. Finally, certain areas which seem to require attention in their own right such as property matters, handling complaints, drugs and AIDS are considered separately, in Part III. Appendices provide additional useful information to which the nurse may wish to refer. I have endeavoured to state the law for England and Wales at 31 August 1989.

I am grateful for the support and encouragement of so many in the preparation of this book. I am considerably indebted to Tessa Shellens and Dr Sue Revel who painstakingly read through the draft and offered much advice and guidance and to Mrs Brenda Hall, my indexer, for her patience, tenacity and thoroughness. I also thank Ann Cross for her detective work. In addition, I am grateful to the following who read individual sections: Dawn O'Brien, Val Taylor, Margaret Winter, Anne Ryall-Davies, Sylvia Parker, Sue Bowers, Yvonne Peters, Gillian Davies, Helen Gray, Keith Weeks, Heather Anderson, Duncan Bloy, Helen Power, Jean Jones, and Jean Whyte. The responsibility, however, for the accuracy and contents of the book remains mine. I also acknowledge the support and encouragement of my publishers, particularly Cathy Peck and Mike Cash.

Finally I am conscious of the great debt I owe to my family whose delight in my work is encouragement in itself. I thank you all.

Preface to second edition

In the four years since the book was first published, major changes have taken place in the delivery of patient care within the NHS. This revision takes into account the legal implications of the UKCC Scope for Professional Practice and the changes to the constitution, function and powers of the UKCC and National Boards. It also includes the NHS and Community Care Act 1990, the Access to Health Records Act 1990, the 1992 Regulation on Health and Safety and numerous other changes. It is even more apparent that the registered practitioner needs to be vigilant of the many implications of the law for her professional practice and her personal accountability.

Acknowledgements

Permission to quote from the following sources is gratefully acknowledged:

Mr Burrows of S. Glamorgan Health Authority for Appendices 12 and 13;

Mr Geoff Davies of S. Glamorgan Health Authority for Appendix 14;

Mr R Pyne, Director of Professional Conduct of UKCC for Appendices 1, 2, 3, 4, 6, 7, 8, 9, and 10;

HMSO for extracts from Statutes, Statutory Instruments and Government circulars, in particular Appendices 5, 11, 15 and 16;

Butterworths for extracts from All England Law Reports.

Part I General principles affecting all nurses

1 Introduction: four arenas of accountability and the legal system

This book is about the accountability of the nurse, which means that it is concerned with how far the nurse can be held in law to account for her actions. No distinction is drawn in this context between responsibility and accountability. Responsibility is seen as being liable to be called to account, answerable for, accountable for. Space does not permit discussion of the moral or ethical dimensions. There may be circumstances where a nurse could be held morally responsible but there is no legal liability. For example, if a nurse fails to volunteer her services at the scene of a road accident the law at present recognises no legal duty to volunteer help and thus any legal action brought against the nurse would fail. However, many would hold that there is a moral duty to use her skills to help a fellow human being. Obviously, the law and ethics overlap, but each is both wider and narrower than the other. The list of extended reading on page 560 promotes further consideration of the moral dilemmas in health care. In this book we are concerned with the legal aspects of the accountability of the nurse. Many problems arise, however. Can a nurse, who does not have control over the resources, be held liable for harm suffered by a patient? Can a nurse be held responsible if she is ignorant, through lack of training, of certain procedures, and as a result the patient is harmed? Issues such as these are of significant concern to the nurse. In order to be responsible it is necessary to have knowledge and this includes legal knowledge. Ignorance of the law is no defence

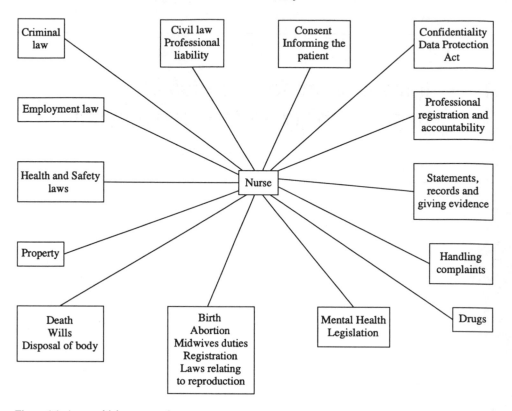

Figure 1.1 Areas which concern the nurse.

and the nurse should be aware of the limits which the law imposes upon her, and also of the power it gives her.

Four main arenas of accountability in law are identified and discussed in detail. It might be considered that the most important has been omitted, i.e. accountability to oneself. This, however, is the moral dimension. There are no legal means of enforcing this form of accountability, though many would recognise it as being at the heart of the best of professional competence and skill.

Figure 1.1 illustrates the many areas of law which concern the nurse and most of these topics are considered in this first part. Some of the more specialist areas, e.g. the Abortion Act, are considered in the second part of the book which deals with different specialties. In this introductory section the four fields of accountability which the nurse faces will be considered.

When a patient suffers harm or there is loss of or damage to property, the nurse may be called to account in four different courts and tribunals. Not all actions will be heard in all four but we shall give an example incident to illustrate the different procedures which could involve all four. Figure 1.2 illustrates the four arenas of accountability.

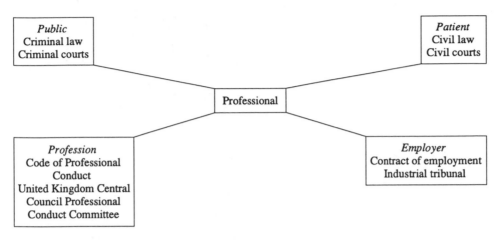

Figure 1.2 Arenas of accountability.

SITUATION 1.1 THE WRONG DRUG_____

Staff Nurse Greaves was under considerable pressure on the paediatric ward. A spate of very seriously ill patients being admitted and a few absences from 'flu put great strains on the ward. A junior house doctor wrote up a 4-year-old child with suspected meningitis for a high dose of antibiotics, and told the staff nurse that he was prescribing a higher dose than was usual because of the severity of the child's condition. Normally, Staff Nurse Greaves would have checked the dose in the *British National Formulary* (*BNF*), but since they were so busy she took the doctor's word for it and gave the child the dose indicated on the sheet. Not long afterwards, the child showed signs of kidney failure and despite efforts to save him, he died. Subsequently, the post mortem investigations revealed that the child had been given a 1,000-fold overdose of the antibiotic.

Criminal liability

Death in circumstances like that described above would have to be reported to the coroner, who would immediately take control of the whole case, would order a post mortem, which the relatives would have no right to refuse, and would probably hold an inquest to establish the cause of death. Details of the coroner's powers and the progress of an inquest are discussed in Chapter 29. The staff nurse is likely to be asked to provide a statement and may well be called to give evidence at the inquest. The Chief Officer of Police or the Director of Public Prosecutions can request the coroner to adjourn the inquest on the grounds that a person may be charged with an offence committed in circumstances connected with the death of the deceased. The coroner also has the power to adjourn the hearing.

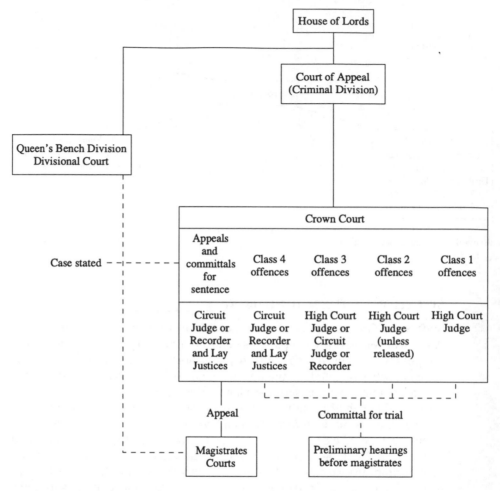

Figure 1.3 System of criminal courts.

In a case like this, it is highly likely that after investigation by the police a decision might be taken to prosecute the nurse and the doctor for a criminal offence in connection with the child's death. Offences are classified as indictable or summary. An indictable offence is one which is heard before a judge and jury in the Crown Court, such as murder, manslaughter, rape and very serious offences. A summary offence is one which is heard by the magistrates in the Magistrates Court such as driving without due care and attention and some parking offences. Many offences can be tried in either the Magistrates Court or the Crown Court. For further discussion on this see Chapter 2.

Figure 1.3 shows the system of our criminal courts. Even where a case is to be heard in the Crown Court because it concerns an offence which can be tried only on indictment, the magistrates will still hear the case as examining justices to decide if the case is to be committed for trial.

In a situation like the above it is quite likely that the inquest would be adjourned and that criminal proceedings would then take place against the staff. The prosecution have the burden of establishing to the satisfaction of the jury that the accused is guilty beyond all reasonable doubt of the offence.

Once the jury has found the accused guilty, the judge has considerable discretion over sentencing. Only where the accused has been found guilty of murder is the judge compelled to sentence him to life imprisonment. In other cases, the judge has a discretion which ranges from an absolute discharge to imprisonment. There is now a right of the prosecution to appeal against sentencing.

Criminal charges in relation to the care of the patient are rare, but when they do arise they attract considerable publicity. In recent years the trial of Dr Arthur in connection with the death of a severely handicapped Down's syndrome baby, and the committal proceedings of Dr Hamilton on a charge under the Infant Life Preservation Act, have raised serious issues in relation to the position of the doctor and the criminal law. The nature of criminal proceedings is considered at greater length in Chapter 2.

Professional liability

In the situation described above, Staff Nurse Greaves could be found guilty of causing the death of the child, though this obviously depends on the detailed facts of the case. The result would automatically be reported to the United Kingdom Central Council for Nursing, Midwifery and Health Visiting (UKCC), and it is highly likely that a Professional Conduct Committee (PCC) would hear the case to decide if Staff Nurse Greaves is guilty of misconduct and if so whether she should be removed from the Register. Information goes to the UKCC from a variety of sources about the conduct of a nurse, and in a case like this the police would also report it to the registration body. Non-criminal misconduct may also be reported.

The nurse is entitled to challenge the findings of the criminal court and to argue that she is not guilty of misconduct. Even if she fails in this she could argue that the special circumstances of the case do not warrant her being removed from the Register. The full details of the powers and procedures of the PCC are discussed in Chapter 11. In contrast to the criminal prosecution in the Crown Court there is no jury here and the members who make up the constitution of the PCC are concerned with protecting the public from an irresponsible nurse; their intention is not to punish the nurse. The powers of the PCC are set out in Fig. 1.4. Following any decision by the PCC, an appeal on a point of law can be made to the High Court which can instigate a judicial review. (The UKCC has recently issued a paper on accountability – see Appendix 7.)

Civil liability

The death of the child gives the child's personal representative the right to sue in the civil courts (see Fig. 1.5) for the negligence which led to the child's death. The action could be brought against the nurse and the doctor personally, or against the NHS Trust, which could be sued either for its direct responsibility for the death of the child or its

Following investigation by the Preliminary Investigation Committee and referral to the Professional Conduct Committee of the UKCC, the Professional Conduct Committee after a finding of misconduct by the nurse can take one of the following courses:

(i)   no action
(ii) refer respondent to the Health Committee
(iii) postpone decision
(iv) strike off the Register
(v)   issue a caution
(vi) suspend from registration.

Figure 1.4 Powers of the Professional Conduct Committee.

vicarious (indirect) liability for the negligence of its staff while acting in the course of employment. If the NHS Trust is found vicariously liable, then it has a right under the contract of employment to seek an indemnity from the negligent employee, although this right is rarely exercised. The vicarious liability of the employer is considered in Chapter 5. The plaintiff, i.e. the person who is bringing a civil action for negligence, must show fault on the part of the person or organisation he is suing. Figure 1.6 shows the elements which must be established by the plaintiff, and the importance of these elements in a claim for compensation for negligence is considered in Chapter 4.

Because of rising costs and awards of compensation, and due to the injustice to plaintiffs should they fail to obtain compensation, many associations are now urging the adoption of a system of no-fault liability. If this system is adopted, then a patient who is harmed will be able to obtain compensation without establishing that someone is to blame for the harm. New Zealand is one example of a country which operates a system of no-fault liability and in which this apparently works well. However, even with this system, the patient must show that the harm resulted from an untoward occurrence rather than as the natural course of an illness.

In the situation that Staff Nurse Greaves faces here it is particularly unlikely that the NHS Trust would defend an action for vicarious liability for her negligence if she had already been found guilty of a criminal offence. They would be more likely to offer a sum in compensation for the death of the child, the only likely dispute being over the appropriate sum of compensation. The problems of quantifying harm and putting a monetary figure on loss suffered are discussed in Chapter 6.

In the civil courts the plaintiff has to establish liability of the defendant on a balance of probabilities. This is an easier task than that facing the prosecution in the criminal courts, where proof is required beyond all reasonable doubt.

Accountability to the employer

Finally, the staff nurse has to account to her employer. There is an implied term (i.e. a term which may never even be discussed or written down but which is assumed by the courts to exist unless there is evidence to the contrary) in every contract of

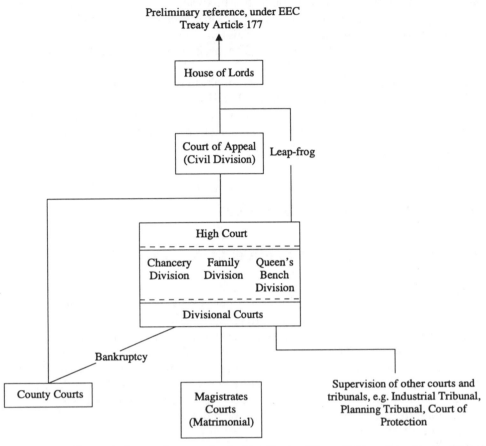

European Court in Luxembourg

Preliminary reference, under EEC
Treaty Article 177

House of Lords

Court of Appeal
(Civil Division)   Leap-frog

High Court

Chancery   Family   Queen's
Division   Division   Bench
Division

Divisional Courts

Bankruptcy

County Courts

Magistrates
Courts
(Matrimonial)

Supervision of other courts and
tribunals, e.g. Industrial Tribunal,
Planning Tribunal, Court of
Protection

The European Economic Community set up by the First Treaty of Rome 1957 was joined by the United Kingdom in 1973. Sovereign powers were surrendered and the supremacy of Community law over the national systems of law was accepted. There are four main institutions responsible for discharging the functions of the EEC

1. The Commission – the executive body
2. The Council of Ministers – one representative from each state
3. The Assembly or European Parliament directly elected by voting in member states
4. The Court of Justice – sits in Luxembourg

Figure 1.5 The civil courts.

1. A duty of care is owed by the defendant to the plaintiff.
2. There is a breach in the standard of the duty of care owed.
3. This breach has caused reasonably foreseeable harm.

Figure 1.6 Elements in an action for negligence.

employment that the employee will obey the reasonable instructions of the employer and will use all care and skill. In a case such as this where it is evident that the employee has been grossly negligent, then that employee is in breach of contract and the employer can take appropriate disciplinary action. This might mean a warning – oral or written, demotion, suspension, or even dismissal. The disciplinary powers of the employer are considered in Chapter 10.

In the case discussed here, the employer might initially suspend the staff nurse on full pay pending an inquiry, and then dismiss her. If she has the requisite length of continuous service the staff nurse would be able to apply to an industrial tribunal for a hearing of unfair dismissal. At this hearing the tribunal is concerned with the following issues:

1. What was the reason for the dismissal and was it one recognised by statute (i.e. Act of Parliament)?
2. Did the employer act reasonably in treating that reason as justification for dismissal?

This is considered in more detail in Chapter 10.

Relationship between the four arenas of accountability

In a situation such as the one described here, if the staff nurse has been grossly negligent, then consistent results for all four hearings are likely: she will be found guilty in the criminal courts; liable in the civil court; removed from the Register by the PCC and dismissed by the employer. However, this is not necessarily so and cases are on record where the employer dismisses the nurse but the UKCC keeps her on the Register, or where the employer does not dismiss the nurse but she is removed from the Register (in which case of course the nurse would lose her registered post). In addition, a criminal charge may fail where a civil charge succeeds. The reason for the lack of consistency is that the four forums are concerned with different aspects of the situation and have different standards of proof.

Sources of law

A brief word is appropriate on what is meant by the term 'law' and what is its origin. The law derives from two main sources:

1. *Acts of Parliament and Statutory Instruments which are enacted under the powers given by the former*: these are known as statutory sources, include the legislation of the European Communities, and take precedence over all other laws. Laws of the European Community automatically become part of the law of the United Kingdom (see Fig. 1.5). The Council and the Commission have law-making powers and this can be in the form of Regulations or Directions.
2. *The common law*: this is made up of the decisions by judges in individual cases which are often, but not always interpretations of statute law. The judge, in deciding a particular case, is bound by a previous decision on the law made by judges in an earlier case if it is relevant to the facts before him and if that decision was made

by a higher court than the one in which he is sitting. There is a recognised order of precedence so that, for example, a decision by the House of Lords is binding on all other courts except itself, but would be subject to relevant precedents of the European Court of Justice. The decisions are recorded by officially recognised reporters, so that in a case similar to a previous one the earlier decision can be put before the court. If the facts and the situation are comparable and the decision was made by a court whose decisions are binding, then the earlier precedent will be followed. If there are grounds for distinguishing the case then a different decision may follow.

Of vital importance to the system of precedence is a reliable procedure for recording the facts and decisions on any court case. Each court has a recognised system of reporting and the case is quoted by a reference which should enable the full report of the case to be found easily. An example is given in the Glossary.

Similarly, Acts of Parliament and Statutory Instruments have chapter numbers for each year, or a serial number.

There are recognised rules for interpreting Acts of Parliament in relation to the following of precedents. Ultimately, however, if the law is unsatisfactory and fails to provide justice the courts look to the Houses of Parliament to remedy the situation by new legislation. There is a right of appeal on matters of law to courts of higher jurisdiction, but unfortunately there has been a tendency in recent years to take many cases to the Court of Appeal and then to the House of Lords if permission is granted, so that until the House of Lords has pronounced on a particular point of law there is considerable uncertainty as to what the law in a given situation is. A considerable number of medical law cases have been referred to the House of Lords in recent years.

Department of Health (DH) circulars, Department of Social Security (DSS) circulars and UKCC codes of practice are not legally binding but they are recommended practice. Breach of these codes may be evidence of failure to follow the approved practice, but cannot in itself result in successful civil or criminal action. This does not apply to the Midwives Rules which do have statutory force.

Differences between civil and criminal laws

What is the difference between the civil law and the criminal law? The only safe answer is that a breach of the criminal law can be followed by prosecution in the criminal courts, whereas liability in civil law is actionable in the civil courts and may or may not be a crime. There is no necessary moral difference between the two. Prior to the Suicide Act of 1961, suicide and attempted suicide, for example, were crimes and as such the latter was subject to criminal proceedings. To many people, however, suicide may still be regarded as morally wrong irrespective of its non-criminal status and it is still a criminal offence to assist someone in a suicide attempt. Some acts may be both criminal and civil wrongs: thus to drive without due care and attention and cause harm can be followed by both criminal and civil proceedings.

How does one know if an act is a civil wrong? One way would be to consider previous cases to find if there is a precedent. The ultimate way would be to establish in the House

1. *Torts*
    Negligence
    Trespass to property
                to land
                and to the person
    False imprisonment
    Wrongful interference
    Breach of a statutory duty
    Nuisance
    Defamation
    Malicious prosecution
    Deliberate interference with interests in trade or business
2. Breach of Contract

Figure 1.7 Some forms of civil action.

of Lords whether a particular action gives rise to civil liability. There is, for example, an increasing acceptance by the courts that information given in specific circumstances can give rise to an action for breach of confidence. Liability in civil law is thus a growth area.

Civil actions

A civil action for negligence will be the main one considered here in relation to the liability of the nurse or NHS Trust, but there are other civil actions which will be considered briefly. The various forms of civil action are shown in Fig. 1.7. All these, except actions for breach of contract, are known as torts, i.e. civil wrongs.

The action for breach of a statutory duty arises when an Act of Parliament or Statutory Regulations place duties on organisations or individuals. In certain circumstances where an individual suffers harm as a result of the breach of these statutory duties an action for compensation may ensue in the civil courts. For example, many of the provisions of the Factories Acts give rise to such actions. In contrast, a breach of the general duties under the Health and Safety at Work Act does not give rise to such an action and this is considered in Chapter 12.

Defamation is another tort which is considered in Chapter 9. An action for nuisance is not considered and is unlikely to concern the nurse at work. An action for breach of contract will be briefly considered in Chapter 10 in connection with the nurse's contract of employment. An action for trespass to the person exists where a person alleges that they have been touched without their consent, and this is considered further in Chapter 7.

Legal personnel

At present we have a divided legal profession (although changes to the profession are planned): solicitors and barristers (counsel). There are about 50,000 solicitors and about 5,500 practising barristers. The former are the main link with the client. Thus in the situation quoted above, if the parents of the child decided to take civil action against the NHS Trust, they would consult a solicitor, who would give them advice and possibly prepare an application for legal aid. If the case were to proceed, he would probably instruct counsel (i.e. a barrister) to prepare the pleadings (see Chapter 6) and represent the client in court. Solicitors have not had full right of audience (i.e. presenting a case) in the Crown Courts, High Courts and Appeal Courts, but recent reforms now enable solicitors to become eligible for advocacy in the High Courts.

Although the initial training is the same (a law degree or Part 1 of the Common Professional Examination), would-be solicitors then serve articles with a firm of solicitors, and then take the Law Society's Part 2 examination, called the Legal Practice Course, while would-be barristers study for the Bar to which they are 'called'. They must join one of the Inns of Court and must dine there on a specified number of occasions. The barrister must then undertake pupillage where they are attached to a practising barrister. Barristers work together in Chambers managed by a clerk who negotiates and collects the fees from solicitors. Fees are at present negotiated in advance and include a brief fee for accepting a case and a refresher fee which is a daily fee for each day that the case is in court. Senior barristers are eligible 'to take silk', i.e. they become Queen's Counsel (QC) appointed by the Lord Chancellor.

The future

Major changes are now planned for the legal profession. The Marre Committee recommended significant changes to the structure and practices of the legal profession. Subsequently a White Paper was issued in July 1989 on *Legal Services: A Framework for the Future*. Legislation will be introduced shortly.

Questions and exercises

1 Consider any situation you know of where a patient (almost) suffered harm as a result of a careless act by a professional and analyse the potential consequences as far as the civil and criminal courts, the PCC and the industrial tribunal are concerned. Refer to Chapters 2, 3, 10 and 11 for more details.
2 What is the difference between statutory law and the common law?
3 Try to arrange a visit to one of the four forums described here, or a coroner's court (see Chapter 5) and draw up a plan for the procedure that you witness.
4 What is the difference between a solicitor and a barrister?

2 Actions in the criminal courts and defences to criminal charges

In this chapter we consider the course followed if criminal proceedings are brought against a nurse, and the ways in which she could defend herself. It must be emphasised that the burden is upon the prosecution to establish the guilt of the accused beyond all reasonable doubt. The accused still has a right of silence at all stages of the prosecution, but proposals to change this are currently being debated.

SITUATION 2.1 THEFT

A discrepancy is found between the ward drug control records and the stock. An investigation is initiated and suspicion falls upon Staff Nurse Jarvis. The police are brought in and after making their enquiries they decide that Staff Nurse Jarvis should be charged with the offence of theft.

A situation such as this involves several kinds of investigation. The NHS Trust will be concerned to determine whether there are grounds to discipline and possibly eventually dismiss the staff nurse. The fact that the police are brought in does not mean that the NHS Trust can abandon its own investigation, but clearly, its enquiries should not conflict with those of the police. The NHS Trust must allow the staff nurse to give a full explanation of what has occurred and she should be allowed a representative. Disciplinary proceedings by the employer are discussed in Chapter 10. There is also the possibility of a hearing before the PCC of the UKCC, but this may well be postponed

1. Initial stages of arrest and prosecution.
2. Magistrates Court.
3. Committal proceedings.
4. Crown Court proceedings.
5. Elements of a crime.
6. Defences.

Figure 2.1 Issues covered in Chapter 2.

pending the outcome of the police investigations and criminal charges. Here we are concerned only with the criminal proceedings, aspects of which are shown in Fig. 2.1.

Initial stages of arrest and prosecution

The staff nurse may well be asked to accompany the police to the station (see Fig. 2.2). A Code of Practice (C) prepared under the Police and Criminal Evidence Act 1984, provides guidance on the detention, treatment, and questioning of persons by police officers, and is intended to provide clear and workable guidelines for the police, while strengthening safeguards for the public at the same time. This Code of Practice must be readily available at all police stations. The Code applies both to those who have been arrested and those who have voluntarily attended the police station.

The staff nurse may have been arrested before she is taken to the police station, or she may be arrested there. In either case, she should be given a caution as soon as there are grounds to suspect her of the offence and before she is questioned about it for the

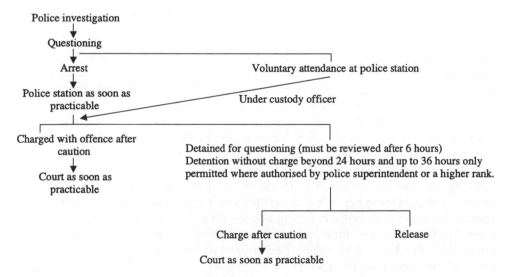

Figure 2.2 Initial stages of arrest and prosecution.

Custody records should be kept for each person who is brought to a police station under arrest or who is arrested at the police station after attending there voluntarily. He is entitled on request to be supplied with a copy when he leaves the police station.

The information must be recorded as soon as practicable and should include the following:

1. Grounds for a person's detention.
2. Detained person's property.
3. Request made for a person to be informed and action taken; any letters or messages sent, calls made or visits received and any refusal on the part of a person to have information about himself or his whereabouts given to an outside enquirer.
4. Any request for legal advice and the action taken on it.
5. Replacement clothing and meals offered.
6. Medical examination by a police surgeon, or request for one and the arrangements made; any medication the detained person is on.
7. An interview record should record
   (a) the times at which the detained person is not in the custody of the custody officer and why, and the reason for any refusal to deliver him out of that custody;
   (b) any intoxicating liquor supplied to a detained person;
   (c) any decision to delay a break in an interview;
   (d) a written record of the interview (unless tape recorded) signed by the detained person as correct;
8. Any action taken to call an interpreter and any agreement to be interviewed in the absence of an interpreter.
9. Grounds for and the extent of any delaying in conducting a review.
10. Anything a detained person says when charged, any questions put after the charge and answers given relating to the offence shall be contemporaneously recorded in full on the forms provided and the record signed by the detained person.
11. Details of any intimate or strip search: which parts were searched, by whom, who was present, reasons and the result.
12. Grounds for any action in delaying the notification of an arrest or allowing access to legal advice.

Figure 2.3 Documentation kept by the police (see Code of Practice C).

purpose of obtaining evidence which may be given to a court in a prosecution. The caution should be given in the following terms: 'You do not have to say anything unless you wish to do so, but what you say may be given in evidence.' Minor deviations do not constitute a breach of this requirement provided that the sense of the caution is preserved. The documentation that the police must retain is shown in Fig. 2.3. The Code sets out rules for the police in the interview. The usual procedure now is for the interview to be tape recorded and the guidelines and Code of Practice for tape recording should be followed.

When the officer considers that there is sufficient evidence to prosecute a detained person he should bring her before the custody officer without delay, who will then be responsible for considering whether or not she should be charged. A further caution must then be given. In addition, a written notice should be given showing the particulars of the offence with which she is charged and including the name of the officer in the case, their police station, and reference number for the case. Questions relating to an offence may not be put to a person after she has been charged with that offence, or after she has been informed that she may be prosecuted for it, unless they are necessary to prevent or minimise harm or loss to some other person or to the public, or to clear up an ambiguity in a previous answer or statement, or where it is in the interests of justice that she should have an opportunity to comment on some fresh information. Before these additional questions are put, the accused must be given another caution. Annex D to the Code of Practice gives rules on written statements given under caution.

Role of the Crown Prosecution Service

Since the introduction of the Crown Prosecution Service, the responsibility for the conduct of most criminal proceedings is on the Director of Public Prosecution and the Crown Prosecution Service. They have the responsibility of instituting criminal proceedings and appearing for the prosecution.

The Magistrates Court

If the staff nurse is charged with the offence of theft she would probably be given police bail and told to appear at the Magistrates Court. Almost all criminal cases begin in the Magistrates Court and 90 per cent are dealt with there. The remaining cases go before the Crown Courts before judge and jury or are dismissed by the magistrates at the committal proceedings.

Indictable-only offences can only be heard before a judge and jury in the Crown Court, summary offences can only be heard by magistrates but many offences are triable either way. Fig. 2.4 shows the classification of the offences.

When the staff nurse is brought before the magistrates on a charge of theft she has the choice of a hearing before the magistrates or of a jury trial in the Crown Courts. If she decides that the case should be heard before the magistrates, but wishes to plead not guilty, then there will probably be an adjournment and a date set for the hearing. The magistrates will hear the case for the prosecution and for the defence at the

---

1. Offences triable only on indictment (i.e. by judge and jury):
   murder; genocide; infanticide; causing death by reckless driving; robbery; treason; wounding with intent.
2. Offences triable only summarily (i.e. by magistrates):
   drunk and disorderly; careless driving; assault on police; and other offences set down by statute, such as the Road Traffic Act 1972 and Schedule 1 of the Criminal Law Act 1977.
3. Offences triable either way (by judge and jury or by magistrates) – case can be heard by magistrates in summary trial if the defendant agrees to be tried by them:
   theft; handling, obtaining property or pecuniary advantage by deception; assault occasioning actual bodily harm.

Figure 2.4 Classification of offences.

The Magistrates Courts hear

(a) offences which are only triable as summary offences, e.g. careless driving;
(b) offences which are triable either way (e.g. theft).

Hearing
1. Plea:
    a plea of guilty must be unequivocal;
    a plea of guilty may be made by post.
2. Summary trial
   Where the defendant pleads not guilty
   A. Prosecution
       1. Opening speech by prosecution.
       2. Examination in chief of prosecution witnesses.
       3. Cross-examination by defence.
       4. Re-examination.
   B. Submission by defence of no case to answer. Prosecution have the right to reply and Magistrates determine the question.
   C. Defence case
       1. Defendant can remain silent or give evidence. (The right to silence without adverse comment is under review.)
       2. Defence witnesses are called.
       3. Defence lawyer addresses the Magistrates.
   D. The finding: the Magistrates determine the guilt or innocence and determine the sentence if a guilty verdict.

Figure 2.5 Course of a hearing in a Magistrates Court.

adjourned hearing, and will determine the guilt or absence of guilt of the staff nurse (see Fig. 2.5). In the event of her being found guilty, the magistrates determine the sentence but if information is not available on her social and economic background there would be an adjournment for this information to be made available. The powers of the magistrates in sentencing are limited; if they find the accused guilty of an indictable offence the case may be referred to the Crown Court for sentencing if the magistrates consider their powers insufficient to deal appropriately with the offence.

Committal proceedings

If on the other hand, Staff Nurse Jarvis opts to have the case heard in the Crown Court, she must first face committal proceedings before the magistrates. Here they act as examining justices and decide if there is sufficient evidence for the case to be committed to the Crown Court. The two forms of committal proceedings are shown in Fig. 2.6.

Crown Court

Let us assume that Staff Nurse Jarvis's case is committed to the Crown Court for trial. The procedure followed is shown in Fig. 2.7. Recent changes have been made regarding

Before the Examining Justices in the Magistrates Court to determine if there is sufficient evidence to put the accused upon trial by jury for any indictable offence.

A. Short form of committal (S.1 of Criminal Justice Act 1967, as amended). The accused, legally represented (the representative need not be present in court) may agree that the Magistrates should formally commit him to the Crown Court without their considering the evidence against him at all.

    The prosecution must have available all their evidence in statements and must have given copies of those statements to the defence counsel, who must be satisfied that there is a case to answer.

B. Full committal proceedings
1. Address by prosecution.
2. Oral evidence: witnesses called by the prosecution, examined in chief, cross-examined by defence advocate, and then re-examined by the prosecution. The clerk records the evidence in the form of reported speech. This is read over to the witness, who signs it. This record is then known as the 'deposition'.
3. Written evidence: written statements taken by the police which the defence do not wish to challenge at the committal proceedings are admissible as a substitute for oral evidence.
4. Submission by defence: at the conclusion of the prosecution evidence, the defendant can submit that the evidence produced by the prosecution is not of sufficient weight to warrant committing the accused for trial.

    The Magistrates decide whether or not to uphold the defence submission. If it is upheld, the accused is discharged. If not, then the committal proceedings continue.
5. Defence case can be put: this will only be done where there is a chance that the Magistrates will refuse to commit. Otherwise it is preferable for the defence not to reveal the nature of the defence to the prosecution in advance.
6. Committal Crown Court for trial: Court decides on the types of witness, order (full or conditional).

    The defendant may apply for bail.

Figure 2.6 Forms of committal proceedings.

---

1. Attendance of the defendant to appear (or the governor of the prison if the defendant has been remanded in custody).
2. The indictment (the document embodying the charge(s) brought by the Crown against the defendant) is read by the clerk to the accused and he is asked whether he pleads guilty or not guilty. This is known as the Arraignment.

    The accused can
(a) plead guilty – if accepted, court proceeds to sentencing;
(b) plead not guilty – see below 3;
(c) stand silent – if mute of malice (this is determined by the jury) and plea of not guilty entered
    – if mute by visitation of God, Court will decide if accused is fit to plead (see insanity below);
(d) object on legal grounds – e.g. indictment is invalid and should be quashed; the accused has already been tried for the same offence (i.e. a plea of *autrefois* acquit or convict).

Figure 2.7 *(Continued)*

3. Empanelling of the Jury: if the defendant has pleaded not guilty to any count on the indictment, a jury must be empanelled. The jury is not present during the arraignment so that
   they are kept in ignorance if the accused has pleaded guilty to some offences and not guilty
   to others.

   The jurors are called in after the arraignment and the names of 12 are called out. They can
   be challenged by defence or prosecution for cause (see Fig. 2.8). They are then sworn and
   the clerk reads the indictment to them, tells them the defendant has pleaded not guilty
   and that their charge is to say, having heard the evidence, whether he be 'guilty' or 'not
   guilty'.

4. The trial
   A. Prosecution
      1. Opening speech by the prosecution.
      2. Prosecution evidence
         (a) attendance of witnesses whose depositions or statements were tendered at committal
             proceedings (see Fig. 2.6);
         (b) if use additional witnesses, defence must be informed and given a statement of
             evidence.
      3. Examination in chief: prosecution witnesses questioned by the prosecution.
      4. Cross-examination – to discredit witnesses, leading questions can be used and earlier
         inconsistent statements by the witness can be put to him.
      5. Re-examination – to offset the effects of cross-examination. It cannot be used to produce
         new evidence which should have been brought out in the examination in chief.
      6. Written statements or depositions of witnesses who were subject to a conditional
         witness order and whose evidence the defence does not wish to dispute will be read
         out.
      7. Challenges to admissibility of evidence: the defence can (in the absence of the jury)
         challenge the admissibility of evidence. The judge will rule on the admissibility and if
         he upholds the defence objections to the evidence, all reference to the evidence must
         be omitted.
   B. Defence
      1. Defence submission: after the conclusion of the prosecution evidence, the defence can
         ask the trial judge to direct the jury as a matter of law that they should acquit the
         defendant either
         (a) because the prosecution have failed to produce any evidence to establish some
             essential ingredient of the offence; or
         (b) because the evidence produced is so weak or so discredited by cross-examination
             that no reasonable jury could convict. If the defence submission is upheld, an acquittal
             is directed.
      2. Case for the defence: an opening speech can be made where the defendant and other
         witnesses are being called to give evidence as to facts (not where only the defendant
         is called or the other witnesses are only as to character).
             Procedure as above.
             Examination in chief.
             Cross-examination.
             Re-examination.
   C. Speeches: by prosecution and defence counsel.
   D. Summing up by judge.
   E. Verdict of jury.
   F. Sentencing following finding of guilt.

Figure 2.7 Procedure in the Crown Court.

Prosecution: can ask for any would-be juror to 'stand-by' until they have gone right through the panel.
Can challenge for cause (e.g. ineligibility, disqualification, presumed or actual bias).

Defence: has lost right to three peremptory challenges (i.e. challenging without having to give any reasons).
Can challenge for cause (e.g. ineligibility, disqualification, presumed or actual bias).

The effect of challenging for cause is that if either side can show that a juror is personally concerned in the facts of the particular case or closely connected with a party to the proceedings or with a prospective witness he can be removed. A challenge for cause should not succeed if the only ground for bias is so insubstantial as to be unlikely to affect the jurors' approach to the case.

The challenging party says 'challenge' immediately before the juror takes the oath. He then has the burden of satisfying the judge on a balance of probabilities that his objection is well founded and produce *prima facie* evidence of this.

Figure 2.8 Challenging the jury.

the right to challenge the jury (see Fig. 2.8). Once the jury have been sworn in, the hearing follows the same path as that in the Magistrates Court but only counsel or solicitor-advocate can represent the accused before the court and a barrister would therefore have been briefed by Staff Nurse Jarvis's solicitor.

The charges on the indictment must be put to Staff Nurse Jarvis. If she pleads not guilty the trial will then proceed as set out in Fig. 2.7. There will be an opening address by the prosecution counsel, setting out the elements which the prosecution have to prove and the standard of proof. This has no evidential value but can be an important scene setting for the jury. The prosecution then calls its witnesses who are examined in chief, which means that the witness cannot be asked leading questions. The witness can be cross-examined by the defence, and here leading questions designed to show the irrelevance of this evidence, or in some other way discredit it, can be asked (see Chapter 9 on evidence in court). After the cross-examination has finished, the party calling that witness can re-examine the witness on points arising from the cross-examination. The judge can call a halt to the case on completion of the prosecution evidence if he is not satisfied that there is sufficient evidence to go before the jury, in which case the jury is asked to bring in a not-guilty verdict.

If the case proceeds, the defence calls its witnesses. At present there is still a right of silence for the accused so Staff Nurse Jarvis would not have to give evidence if she chose not to do so. If she does give evidence she cannot refuse to answer a question which might incriminate her on the offence charged.

After all the evidence has been given the defence and prosecution conclude their cases in final speeches. The judge then sums up the case for the jury. He has the task of explaining to the jury the elements of the crime which the prosecution must prove the accused committed; the nature of the burden of proof which is upon the prosecution; and he analyses the evidence which both sides have put before the jury.

The foreman of the jury is then chosen and the jurors retire to decide their verdict.

Absolute/conditional discharge.
Bindover.

Adults
Fine.
Probation.
Probation and attendance at training centre.
Probation and attendance at mental hospital.
Community service.
Suspended sentence.
Suspended sentence and supervision.
Guardianship order.
Prison.
Extended sentence.
Hospital order Section 37 Mental Health Act 1983.
Hospital order and restriction order Sections 31 and 41 Mental Health Act 1983.

Figure 2.9 Sentencing in the Crown Court.

Initially, the jury is asked to return a unanimous verdict. If it is clear that they can never reach a unanimous verdict, then they can return to court and can be given instructions on returning a majority verdict.

If the jury decide that the staff nurse is guilty, evidence of previous convictions (until this moment usually kept secret from the jury) and the present social and economic circumstances she is in will be given before sentencing. Figure 2.9 sets out the powers of sentencing.

The staff nurse has the right to appeal against the finding of guilt on any matter relating to the way in which the judge directed the jury or in the decisions taken by the judge over the admissibility or inadmissibility of evidence. She also has the right to appeal against the sentence imposed. The prosecution can appeal against sentencing and it has the right to appeal on a point of law.

The elements of a crime

In order to establish guilt the prosecution must be able to show that each element of the crime charged is proved beyond all reasonable doubt. Each crime thus has its ingredients which make up that particular offence. Examples are given of the elements of some crimes in Fig. 2.10.

Mental and physical elements

There is a further breakdown of the elements which have to be established to prove that a crime has taken place, i.e. between the *actus reus* and the *mens rea*. The *mens rea*, or mental element, includes all those elements which relate to the mind of the accused. The *actus reus* is everything else. There are some crimes where there is no

---

1. Assault (common law offence)
   actus reus: an act which causes the victim to fear the immediate application of force against him;
   mens rea: an intention to cause the victim to apprehend the immediate application of force or recklessness as to whether the victim might apprehend immediate force.
2. Battery (common law offence)
   actus reus: an act which results in the application of force to the person of another;
   mens rea: an intention to apply force or recklessness as to whether force might be applied.
3. Wounding or causing grievous bodily harm. Section 18 Offences against the Person Act 1861
   actus reus: wound or cause any grievous bodily harm to any person;
   mens rea: maliciously and unlawfully with intent to do grievous bodily harm or an intent to resist or prevent lawful apprehension or detaining of any person.
4. Wounding or inflicting grievous bodily harm. Section 20 Offences against the Person Act 1861
   actus reus: to wound or inflict any grievous bodily harm upon any other person, either with or without any weapon or instrument;
   mens rea: unlawfully and maliciously (intentional or recklessly and without lawful justification).
5. Theft. Section 1(1) Theft Act 1968
   actus reus: appropriate property which belongs to another;
   mens rea: dishonest with the intention of permanently depriving the true owner of that property.

Figure 2.10 Examples of the definition of certain crimes.

---

requirement to show a mental element. For example, the sale of medicine by a person who was not qualified and while unsupervised by a pharmacist and which was contrary to Section 52 of the Medicines Act 1968 was held to be a strict liability offence (*Pharmaceutical Society of Great Britain* v. *Logan* 1982 Crim. LR 443). The law has now been changed. As a rule, however, there is a distaste for offences of strict liability, i.e. where there is no requirement for the prosecution to prove *mens rea*.

If there were no requirement for the prosecution to establish a mental element in the crime of theft, Staff Nurse Jarvis could be successfully prosecuted for theft in circumstances where someone had accidentally dropped a bottle of tablets in the staff nurse's open bag and she had therefore taken them home inadvertently. In order to secure a conviction, whether the prosecution takes place in the Magistrates Court or in the Crown Court, all the elements, mental and physical, must be shown to have existed at the time it was alleged that the crime was committed.

Defences

The main defences to a criminal act are shown in Fig. 2.11. They are all given here for completeness, but not all of them are relevant to Staff Nurse Jarvis's case.

Absence of any of the elements making up the offence

It will be apparent from what has been said above that if the accused can show that any of the required elements, either *actus reus* or *mens rea*, as defined in the Act of

1. Absence of any of the elements making up the offence: *mens rea* or *actus reus*
2. Infancy
    (a) Below 10 no crime;
    (b) Over 10 and under 14 mischievous discretion must be shown;
    (c) 14 and over as adults.
3. Insanity
    (a) unfit to plead and stand trial;
    (b) not guilty by reason of insanity at the time of the crime.
4. Diminished responsibility and provocation.
5. Mistake.
6. Drunkenness.
7. Necessity.
8. Duress and coercion.
9. Superior orders.
10. Self-defence.

Figure 2.11 Main defences to a criminal offence.

Parliament or the common law definition of the crime, are missing then there should be an acquittal. Even though it is usually for the prosecution to show they exist rather than for the defence to prove their absence, it would clearly be an advantage for the defence to show their absence. Thus, for example, in the offence of theft, one of the elements is that the property which has been taken belonged to another. If the defence can show that the property did not belong to anyone but had in fact been abandoned, then that would be a successful defence.

Infancy

Children under 10 years are exempt from criminal responsibility and cannot be found guilty of a crime. The infant is known as *doli incapax*.

Children over 10 and under 14 years are exempt from criminal responsibility unless it is proved not only that they caused an *actus reus* with *mens rea*, but also that they did so with a mischievous discretion.

Minors over 14 years are presumed to be responsible for their actions but there are considerable procedural differences from the way in which an adult is proceeded against.

Insanity

Insanity can be pleaded before or when the trial takes place so that the accused is held unable by reason of insanity to stand trial. Alternatively, it can be pleaded as a defence to the crime on the basis that at the time the crime was committed the accused was insane. The definition of insanity as a defence is based on the M'Naghten Rules, which were laid down in 1843. The basic propositions are:

> every man is presumed to be sane and to possess a sufficient degree of reason to be responsible for his crimes, until the contrary be proved;
> and that to establish a defence on ground of insanity, it must be clearly proved that at the time of the committing of the act, the party accused was labouring under such a defect of reason, from disease of mind, as not to know the nature and quality of the act he was doing, or if he did know it, that he did not know he was doing what was wrong.

Since 1843 there have been many interpretations and refinements of this definition but the substance has survived.

Diminished responsibility and provocation

These statutory defences are provided by the Homicide Act 1957, apply only to murder, and have the effect of enabling the accused charged with murder to be found guilty of manslaughter on grounds of diminished responsibility or provocation.

Mistake

This can be an effective defence where it prevents the accused from being able to form the required mental element (i.e. *mens rea*) to be guilty of the offence charged. Mistake of law is not sufficient, for knowledge that an act is a crime is not usually a necessary ingredient of the *mens rea*.

Drunkenness

This can be a defence if the effect of the drunkenness is to prevent the accused from having the *mens rea* required for that particular crime.

Necessity

There is considerable debate on the question as to whether there is a defence of necessity to a criminal charge. There are some examples where it has been accepted as a defence to a murder charge, but there is no recognised principle that necessity is a valid defence to any crime.

Duress and coercion

This will be a valid defence where it can be established that the force or compulsion was such that the accused had no choice. It is unlikely to be accepted as a defence to a charge of murder but has been invoked on other lesser crimes.

Superior orders

It is not a defence for the accused to argue that the crime was committed in obedience to the orders of a superior. However, it might be possible for her to show that as a result of the orders she lacked the required mental element for the crime and that she was acting reasonably in all the circumstances. The issue of obeying orders as a defence in the civil courts is considered in Chapter 4.

Self-defence

Reasonable force can be used to defend oneself or another person against an attack. However, greater force than is reasonable would result in the possibility of the defender being liable to prosecution for assault. This is considered further in Chapter 12.

The future

Recommendations by the Royal Commission on Criminal Justice in changes in criminal procedures are currently being discussed in Parliament.

Questions and exercises

1 In the case of Staff Nurse Jarvis, trace the course which would be followed if
   (a) she was tried in the Magistrates Court;
   (b) she was tried in the Crown Court;
   (c) she pleaded guilty in the Magistrates Court;
   (d) she pleaded guilty in the Crown Court.
2 What do you consider are the advantages and disadvantages of trial before the magistrates compared with a jury trial for an offence which is triable either way?
3 What are the differences in committal proceedings between the short form of committal and the full proceedings?
4 What evidence do you consider that the prosecution would require in a case similar to that of Staff Nurse Jarvis and what evidence would the defence seek? (Consider also Chapter 9.)
5 Visit your Magistrates Court and Crown Court and analyse the difference between the two in terms of formality, procedure, and justice to the accused.

3 The professional liability of the nurse in a civil court case for negligence

If the patient is harmed, when is the nurse liable in the civil courts? Accidents to patients are infinite: they range from incidents where the patient falls out of bed, pressure sores develop, the wrong dose of medication is given, it is given at the wrong time or at the wrong site by the wrong method, or the expiry date is passed, the wrong limb is amputated, the treatment is given to the wrong patient, the patient dies as a result of a mistake. Not all accidents, however, will end in the payment of compensation to the patient or relatives.

The elements that must be established by the plaintiff in a case of negligence before the civil courts are set out in Fig. 1.6. In this section we are concerned with four basic questions:

1. What is meant by the term 'duty of care'; when does the nurse owe a duty of care; and to whom is it owed?
2. What is the appropriate standard of care and what criteria determine whether the nurse is in breach of that duty?
3. What is meant by 'foreseeably caused' and why and how must the plaintiff prove this in an action for negligence?
4. What type of harm do the courts recognise as capable of being compensated?

This chapter will answer these questions by providing examples where patients have been harmed. The next two chapters will consider some specific problems of liability in relation to inexperienced staff, team responsibility, limits on resources, and also the liability of the NHS Trust.

The duty of care

Difficulties can arise as to whether a duty of care arises, especially outside the immediate employment situation. A duty of care is not owed universally and the plaintiff bringing the action has to show that a duty of care was owed to them personally.

The legal test of whether a duty of care exists was laid down in the case of *Donoghue* v. *Stevenson*. (In this case manufacturers were held to owe a duty of care to the ultimate consumer. The facts of this case were that a person who was bought a bottle of ginger beer discovered the decomposed remains of a snail when half the beer had been drunk.) In that case Lord Atkin stated that

> You must take reasonable care to avoid acts or omissions which you can reasonably foresee would be likely to injure your neighbour. Who then in law is my neighbour? The answer seems to be persons who are so closely and directly affected by my act that I ought reasonably to have them in contemplation as being so affected when I am directing my mind to the acts or omissions which are called in question.
>
> 1932 AC 562

In other words a duty of care can be said to exist if one can see that one's actions are reasonably likely to cause harm to another person.

Does one have a duty to volunteer help?

SITUATION 3.1 VOLUNTEERING HELP_____

A nurse on her way to work passes a road accident. She sees that a man is still trapped in a vehicle. Does she have an obligation to stop and render first aid? If she does stop and help and something goes wrong would she be liable?

Unless there is a pre-existing relationship between the parties (for example, if the nurse has caused the accident or if she is employed to assist people in such circumstances) she has no duty in law to stop and render first aid. So if, for example, someone saw her drive past and, knowing that she was a nurse believed that she could have saved the victim, she was consequently sued, the action would fail. Her failure to help is not actionable. There is in law no duty to volunteer help. There must be a pre-existing duty. However, once the nurse undertakes the duty of care she is then bound to follow the standard of care which would be expected of a reasonable person. So, for example, imagine that she moves the victim and causes spinal injury. If it can be shown that she should have anticipated the dangers of moving a person when a spinal injury was possible, and if there was no immediate danger in leaving the man where he was, then she could be sued for any further injuries she had caused him.

It could be argued, therefore, that no nurse would ever wish to go to anyone's help. Yet while it is not a duty in law, some may see it as a professional/moral/ethical/citizen's duty.

SITUATION 3.2 A FALL IN THE NIGHT

Mary Smith is in the post-operative ward following a gall-bladder operation. She becomes very disturbed during the night and Staff Nurse Janice Parker hears a crash and rushes to the ward. She finds Mrs Smith on the floor.

How is the civil liability of the staff nurse determined? The questions to be answered are:

1. Does Staff Nurse Parker owe a duty of care to Mrs Smith?
2. Is she in breach of the duty of care?
3. Has her breach of care led to reasonably foreseeable harm?
4. Has the patient suffered compensatable harm?

To win compensation in a civil case Mary Smith would have to show that the staff nurse failed to follow the approved accepted practice without good reason in carrying out her duty of care for her, and that as a reasonably foreseeable result she suffered harm.

Does a duty of care arise?

A nurse, by virtue of the nurse/patient relationship, does owe a duty of care to her patients. Whether a duty of care exists will be decided by established legal principles. However, once it is decided that a duty is owed, the next question is: has there been a breach of this duty? Before this can be answered, and it is of course a question of fact in each case, what standard of care is owed must be established.

The standard of care

The approved practice

CASE 3.1 BIRTH TRAUMAS

Stuart Whitehouse was born on 7 January 1970 with severe brain damage. His mother alleged that the brain damage was caused because the doctor pulled too hard and too long with forceps, as a consequence of which the baby was severely disabled. The doctor denied the allegations.

The House of Lords stated that whether an error of judgement was negligence or not depended on the facts of the situation. The test to be applied to determine if there was negligence was the Bolam Test, and in applying this test in this case, they decided that

Mr Jordan had not been negligent. The Bolam Test is as follows (from the earlier case *Bolam v. Friern Barnet HMC* 1957 2 All ER 118):

> When you get a situation which involves the use of some special skill or competence, then the test as to whether there has been negligence or not is ... the standard of the ordinary skilled man exercising and professing to have that special skill. If a surgeon failed to measure up to that in any respect ('clinical judgement' or otherwise) he had been negligent and should be so adjudged.
>
> (*Whitehouse v. Jordan* 1981 1 All ER 267)

In the last sentence the name of any other professional can be substituted for the word 'surgeon'. Thus the negligence of a nurse is to be determined by the standard of the ordinary skilled nurse.

Let's turn to the situation above of the patient falling out of bed and see how the court would decide whether or not Staff Nurse Janice Parker was in breach of care in relation to the patient Mary Smith.

What would the ordinary skilled nurse be expected to do in those circumstances? Was it reasonably foreseeable that this patient was likely to be restless? If so, what additional precautions should have been taken? Was she in the right location and was she adequately supervised? Had the patient called earlier for help or a bed pan and did that request go unheard or unmet? In the actual court hearing, expert evidence would be given (probably by both sides) as to what would have been expected of a nurse in that context, and the judge would decide what should be regarded as acceptable practice in that context.

Deviations from the approved practice

It does not follow that simply to fail to follow the accepted practice is in itself evidence of negligence since there may well be very strong reasons why the usual properly accepted practice was not followed in a particular case.

CASE 3.2 BIOPSY

A consultant physician and a consultant surgeon, while recognising that the most likely diagnosis of the patient's illness was tuberculosis (TB), took the view that Hodgkin's disease, carcinoma and sarcoidosis were also possibilities. Because Hodgkin's disease was fatal unless remedial steps were taken in its early stages, they decided that rather than wait several weeks for the result of a sputum test, the operation of mediastinoscopy should be performed to provide a biopsy. This involved some risk of damage to the left laryngeal recurrent nerve, even if correctly performed. The operation was carried out properly but that damage did in fact occur. The biopsy proved negative and it was subsequently confirmed that the patient did have TB and not Hodgkin's disease. The patient brought an action against the health authority, claiming that the decision to

perform the biopsy rather than wait for the result of the TB test had been
negligent.

At the trial a distinguished body of medical opinion was called approving of the action
of the consultants in carrying out the operation, but the judge said that he preferred
the evidence of an expert witness called for the plaintiff, who had stated that the case
had almost certainly been one of TB from the outset and should have been so diagnosed, and that it had been wrong and dangerous to undertake the operation. The trial
judge gave judgment for the plaintiff. The defendants succeeded before the Court of
Appeal and the plaintiff therefore appealed to the House of Lords. The House of Lords
held that in the medical profession there was room for differences of opinion and practice, and that a court's preference for one body of opinion over another was no basis
for a conclusion of negligence. Where it was alleged that a fully considered decision
by two consultants in their own special field had been negligent, it was not sufficient
to establish negligence for the plaintiff to show that there was a body of competent professional opinion that considered that the decision had been wrong if there was also a body
of equally competent professional opinion that supported the decision as having been
reasonable in the circumstances. The plaintiff therefore lost his appeal and the case
(*Maynard* v. *W. Midlands RHA* 1984 1 WLR 634).

While this decision might seem very hard for the patient, it is only fair to the professional staff where a decision has been made carefully and with great consideration and
is supported by substantial opinion, even if not everyone would have followed the same
practice. In applying this to nursing staff it can be said that in most circumstances the
nurse will be expected to follow the standards of practice laid down by her profession,
or the local policy of her employer, but there may be very exceptional circumstances
where it is justifiable not to follow the accepted practice.

The wording of the Congenital Disabilities (Civil Liability) Act 1976 (which does allow
right of action in cases of pre-natal infliction of harm) puts the point very clearly:

> Section 1(5) The defendant is not answerable to the child, for anything he did or
> omitted to do when responsible in a professional capacity for treating or advising
> the parent, if he took reasonable care having due regard to then received profes-
> sional opinion applicable to the particular class of case; but that does not mean
> that he is answerable only because he departed from received opinion.

(This Act is considered in detail in Chapter 14.) The situation is thus as follows:

1. There is no breach of the standard of care if the professional has acted in accordance with the practice accepted as proper by a responsible body of professional
   skill in that particular art, and this was appropriate in the circumstances of the
   case.
2. There is no breach of the standard of care if there is no acceptable body of opinion
   covering that situation but what the professional did was considered reasonable
   in all the circumstances.
3. There is no breach of the standard of care if the professional did not follow the
   accepted practice but his actions were reasonable in all the circumstances.

Reasonable foreseeability

Other criteria are considered in determining if the professional has been negligent. One of the basic principles of the law of negligence is that precautions can only be taken against reasonably known risks.

CASE 3.3 AMPOULES IN PHENOL

A local anaesthetic was given by injection in a hospital. The ampoule, which was stored in phenol to sterilise it, contained invisible cracks caused by some mishandling in the hospital, through which the phenol seeped into the ampoule and the injection caused paralysis.

The patient sued the anaesthetist and nurses and their employer. The patient, however, lost the case. The possibility of seepage through invisible cracks was not known at that time and precautions against an unforeseeable possibility are not required of the defendant. However, successful defence may of course mean that the next plaintiff has a greater chance of winning since such risks are now known. The standard of care thus increases (*Roe* v. *Minister of Health* 1954 2 QB 66).

The Judge, Lord Denning, said in this case:

> It is so easy to be wise after the event and to condemn as negligence that which was only a misadventure. We ought always to be on our guard against it, especially in cases against hospitals and doctors. Medical science has conferred great benefits on mankind, but these benefits are attended by considerable risks. Every surgical operation is attended by risks. We cannot take the benefits without taking the risks. Every advance in technique is also attended by risks. Doctors like the rest of us have to learn by experience; and experience often teaches in a hard way. Something goes wrong and shows up a weakness, and then it is put right . . . We must not look at the 1947 accident with 1954 spectacles.

Exactly the same could be said of practice today and of nurses as well as doctors. There may be many occasions when one looks back and says 'I would do things differently if I were to do it again' but that does not mean the professional has been negligent.

Keeping up to date

When one looks at the many professional journals which exist the question must arise as to what extent the professional can be expected to master all this knowledge. How up to date is one expected to be?

CASE 3.4 *CRAWFORD* v. *CHARING CROSS HOSPITAL*, *The Times* 8 December 1953

A patient developed brachial palsy during a blood transfusion. An article had appeared in the *Lancet* six months previously describing this hazard.

The patient lost the case on the grounds that, provided the professional staff were following the accepted approved practice at that time, then it could not be said that they were negligent in failing to apply or be aware of recent knowledge.

Articles in magazines and journals can be of very different status. Some are pure research articles, the lessons from which have not yet been absorbed into current accepted practice; others are controversial and their conclusions may never become part of the recognised procedure. Other instructions, however, would have immediate effect. Thus if a directive from the Committee of the Safety of Medicines warned against prescribing a particular drug to a patient, to ignore that instruction might well be evidence of negligence. Nursing staff who had received comparable instructions from their profession or senior nurse management would be expected to be aware of these orders and to comply. The instructions would become part of the accepted practice.

Balancing the risks

As the quotation from Lord Denning above points out, there are hazards in modern medicine and much of professional discretion is concerned with balancing the risks of taking action A compared with action B or compared with taking no action at all. Some nurses have argued that we should throw away the ward procedure books and rely entirely upon professional discretion. This would appear too foolhardy a gesture since established procedures are essential for the beginner and have their place in practice. It is equally true, however, that they will never be so comprehensive and detailed as to replace professional judgement and discretion. In using her judgement the nurse has to balance the risks to the patient against the benefits. She has to establish priorities between individual patients and consider the practicalities of preventing any reasonable foreseeable harm.

SITUATION 3.3 MENINGITIS

A patient was admitted with a provisional diagnosis of meningitis. She was immediately barrier nursed in a single room, even though that meant moving a very sick patient onto a four-bedded ward. The patient who was removed died in the night. There was criticism from relatives that the patient should not have been moved and also a suggestion that the death was accelerated. Was the nurse at fault if the next day it is discovered that the suspected meningitis patient was only suffering from a non-fatal virus?

Provided the nurse used her professional judgement in making the decision to give the single room to that particular patient, with the knowledge available to her at that time, then there should be no finding of negligence. In fact, if meningitis had been confirmed, then the nurse may well have been negligent in not taking precautions to prevent any danger of staff or patients being infected. She has to use her judgement in determining the degree of risk to both patients.

Causation

The third element in the plaintiff's case against the NHS Trust or the nurse is to establish that there is a causal link between the breach of the duty of care by the nurse and the harm suffered by the plaintiff. It is possible for the nurse to fail in her duty of care to the patient and for the patient to suffer harm yet the nurse not be liable in civil law. This is because one of the essential elements that the plaintiff must establish in an action for negligence is that there is a causal link between the failure of the defendant to follow the approved practice and the harm suffered by the patient. The possibility that this harm could occur must be reasonably foreseeable and must also take place.

Factual causation

CASE 3.5 CAUSATION

A patient attended the casualty department after drinking tea which unknown to him had been contaminated with arsenic and which caused prolonged vomiting. The doctor did not examine him but sent a message that he should see his own doctor. He died a few hours later.

The widow failed in her action because it was established that the patient would have died even if properly examined and treated. In this case the pathological evidence on the progress of arsenic poisoning and the projected timetable of events had the patient been examined and admitted was of vital importance (*Barnett* v. *Chelsea HMC* 1968 1 All ER 1068).

In such circumstances, although a civil action fails there are likely to be professional and disciplinary proceedings by the professional body and the employer.

Barnett's case was an example of a lack of factual connection between the breach of duty of care and the harm suffered by the patient.

Another example of a case that has recently been before the House of Lords is the following:

CASE 3.6 BLINDNESS BUT HOW CAUSED?

In the Wilsher case considered below (page 43) the House of Lords decided that the case should be reheard by a new High Court Judge on the issue of whether it was the defendant's negligence which had caused the harm to the child. In this case it was agreed that there were several different factors which could have caused the child to become blind and the negligence by the defendant was only one of these. The trial judge had failed to make a relevant finding of fact and could not presume that it was the defendant's negligence which had caused the harm (*Wilsher* v. *Essex Area Health Authority* CA 1986 3 All ER 801 HL 1988 1 All ER 871).

CASE 3.7 THE CAUSE OF DEAFNESS_____

A child suffering from meningitis was given 300,000 units of penicillin instead of 10,000 units. The mistake was discovered and remedial action taken. The health authority admitted liability and made an offer to the parents for the additional pain and suffering that the negligence caused the boy. However, the parents argued that the overdose had caused the boy to become deaf and they rejected the board's offer, claiming instead many thousands of pounds more because they held the health authority liable for the deafness.

The House of Lords eventually heard the case and decided that the parents had not made out the factual causation between the overdose and the deafness and thus that the boy was not entitled to the larger amount. It is a well-known fact that meningitis itself can cause deafness. (*Kay* v. *Ayrshire and Arran Health Board* 1987 2 All ER 417).

Reasonably foreseeably caused

In a civil case for negligence the plaintiff also has to establish that the harm that occurred was a reasonably foreseeable consequence of breach of duty by the defendant.

SITUATION 3.4 REASONABLE FORESEEABILITY_____

In breach of her duty of care a nurse failed to dispose properly of contaminated dressings which were left on a stainless steel trolley in the treatment area. By chance, two boys broke into the room looking for syringes and needles. When they heard footsteps approaching they grabbed as much as they could from the trolley and ran off, taking the dressing with them. Subsequently an outbreak of disease attributable to the dressing occurred in the neighbourhood. Was the nurse responsible in law for this?

The nurse was certainly at fault in not disposing correctly of the dressing. However, it could be argued that the subsequent events were not reasonably foreseeable and in any event the chain of causation between the nurse's action and the outbreak of the disease was broken by the action of the boys. This is sometimes known as a *novus actus interveniens* (i.e. a new act intervening).

Taking one's plaintiff as one finds him

There is one important exception to the rule that the harm resulting from the breach of duty is reasonably foreseeable, known as the thin skull rule or 'you take your plaintiff as you find him'.

SITUATION 3.5 THE THIN SKULL RULE_____

A nurse puts some drops in the wrong eye. They were meant to dilate the pupil in the other eye. They would not normally have caused any harm but because of an existing defect in that eye the patient became blind.

The nurse in this case is clearly negligent. However, in the majority of patients her error would have caused none, or very little, harm. In this case, however, even though she could not have predicted the outcome she would be liable for the harm that has occurred on the basis of the doctrine 'you take your plaintiff as you find him'.

CASE 3.8 THE THIN SKULL RULE

An accident occurred at work when a labourer was splashed with a piece of molten metal and his lower lip was burnt. The burn was treated and the labourer thought nothing more about it. However, the place where the burn had been began to ulcerate and get larger. He consulted his general practitioner who sent him to hospital where cancer was diagnosed. Treatment by radium needles enabled the lip to heal and destroy the primary growth. Subsequently, however, secondary growths were observed. He had six operations and died of cancer just over three years after the accident. His widow claimed compensation from the employers.

They admitted liability for the original accident but denied that they were responsible for the man's death. Lord Parker in the Queen's Bench Division held that the test was not whether the defendants could reasonably have foreseen that a burn would cause cancer and that Mr Smith would die. The test was whether these defendants could reasonably foresee the type of injury which he suffered, namely the burn. The amount of damage which he suffers as a result of that burn depends on the characteristics and constitution of the victim. The widow therefore won her case. (*Smith* v. *Leech Brain & Co. Ltd* QBD 1961 3 All ER 1159).

Harm

Not all forms of harm are compensatable by the civil courts. Grief itself is not a ground for a claim, although there is now a statutory right for compensation for bereavement. This is considered in Chapter 6 when the basis for the amount of compensation is discussed. The court recognises that harm which involves personal injury or death or loss or damage of property should be compensated if the other elements of negligence can be proved. However, the harm must be a reasonably foreseeable consequence of the breach of duty: it must not be too remote. This is a particularly difficult question when economic loss has occurred and the courts have limited the liability of the defendants to reasonably foreseeable economic loss. Similar difficulties arise over determining the liability for causing nervous shock.

CASE 3.9 NERVOUS SHOCK

Mr Thomas McLoughlin and his three children George (aged 17), Kathleen (aged 7) and Gillian (aged 3) were in a motor car driven by George when it was in collision with a lorry. George was not at fault. Mrs McLoughlin who was not in the vehicle was told by a friend who was in the car behind (with Michael, another McLoughlin child (aged 11), who was a passenger) that George had probably died and that he was uncertain of the condition of the husband or the other children. She was driven to the hospital and saw Michael who told her that Gillian was dead. She was taken down the corridor and through a window she saw Kathleen, crying with her face cut and begrimed with dirt and oil. She could hear George shouting and screaming. She was taken to her husband who was sitting with his head in his hands. His shirt was hanging off him and he was covered in mud and oil. He saw his wife and started sobbing. She was then taken to see George. The whole of the left face and left side was covered. He appeared to recognise her and then lapsed into unconsciousness. Finally, she was taken to see Kathleen who by now had been cleaned up. The child was too upset to speak and simply clung to her mother. As a result of this experience Mrs McLoughlin suffered from severe shock, organic depression and a change of personality. She was normally a person of reasonable fortitude. (*McLoughlin* v. *O'Brian* 1982 2 All ER 298).

Obviously, in a case like this damages would be payable to the husband and the children, but in addition to that, compensation was claimed by Mrs McLoughlin for nervous shock. The defendants argued that she was too remote from the defendants' negligence: she was not herself a direct victim of the accident, nor was she a bystander witnessing what happened. The House of Lords decided that she was entitled to receive compensation since she was so closely related to those injured, and the nervous shock that she suffered was close in both space and time.

Lord Wilberforce said:

> It is necessary to consider three elements inherent in any claim: The class of persons whose claims should be recognised; the proximity of such persons to the accident; and the means by which the shock is caused. As regards the class of persons the possible range is between the closest possible of family ties, of parent and child or husband and wife, and the ordinary bystander. Existing law recognises the claims of the first; it denies that of the second, either on the basis that such persons must be assumed to be possessed of fortitude sufficient to enable them to endure the calamities of modern life or that defendants cannot be expected to compensate the world at large.

Any persons wishing to claim compensation for nervous shock would have to show that they were actually suffering from an illness and not just grief and that they were sufficiently closely related to the objects of the defendant's negligence and also in time and space. The law has been further clarified by the House of Lords in the case of *Alcock* v. *Chief Constable S. Yorks. Police* 1991 4 All ER 407.

This relates to the practising nurse in two ways. Firstly, she herself may be the victim of nervous shock arising from another person's negligence, in which case she needs to know whether she is likely to obtain compensation. Secondly, in her own work she should be aware of the dangers of causing nervous shock in others, and the possibility of claims for compensation arising out of this.

Questions and exercises

1 Consider the duty of care possibly owed by the nurse or NHS Trust and discuss whether and upon what grounds you think a duty would be owed in the following circumstances:
   (a) an informal patient who wanders away from the hospital and damages cars in the vicinity of the hospital;
   (b) a detained patient who does likewise;
   (c) a patient in the accident and emergency department who after an attempted suicide insists on taking his own discharge and is shortly afterwards found dead on a railway line;
   (d) a doctor in a theatre who gives a person having a cardiac arrest the wrong treatment;
   (e) a community nurse who is caring for a neighbour, not on her list, and who accidentally leaves the door open and the neighbour is mugged and the house burgled.
2 How would you determine the standard of care that should be adopted in carrying out the following procedures:
   (a) lifting;
   (b) administering medication;
   (c) informing patients of their rights;
   (d) advising relatives on the procedures to be followed in dealing with death?
3 Why do you consider that causation is an important element in an action for negligence? Would it be fairer to the plaintiff if causation did not need to be proved?
4 If there has been a negligent act but no harm has occurred to the patient, what remedies are available (if any) for the patient to obtain compensation?

4   Specific problem areas in civil liability: the personal liability of the nurse

In this chapter we explore some of the particular difficulties which can arise in determining the liability of a professional in some specific situations (see Fig. 4.1), beginning with liability for negligence in communicating.

Negligence in communicating

It is possible to be negligent in failing to communicate with the appropriate person at the correct time and in the proper way.

CASE 4.1 CRUSHED FINGERS

Mr Coles suffered a crush injury to his finger. He went to the cottage hospital where the nurse cleaned the wound of dust and dirt and told him to go to a proper hospital where he would have an anti-tetanus injection. But neither she nor anyone else impressed upon him the purpose and importance of the visit and so he did not go. He later saw his general practitioner who believed that he had had the injection and so he did not give him one. He subsequently died of tetanus. (*Coles v. Reading HMC* 1963 107 SJ 115).

In this case there was negligence by all those professional staff (including the nurse) who had failed to communicate adequately with other professionals and with the patient.

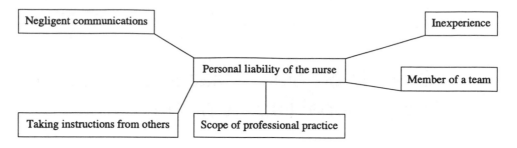

Figure 4.1 Issues covered in Chapter 4.

Failure to communicate, if it falls short of the required professional standard, can be regarded as negligence and is actionable if it causes reasonably foreseeable harm to the patient.

Failure to communicate rarely causes such devastating harm as in this tetanus case, but there are other well-known examples where it is vital that the patient receives certain information and it cannot be assumed that the patient is aware of the dangers. For example, in head injury cases there may be no detectable sign of head injury when the patient is seen in the accident and emergency department. However, it is essential that the patient is warned to return if certain symptoms appear. Comparable instructions must be given after plastering and in many other situations. In such circumstances it is advisable for a strict procedure to be implemented to ensure that the correct information is given both by word of mouth and in writing. If there is likely to be any dispute as to whether the information was given and/or where there are considerable dangers if the patient is not informed, it is possible to ask the patient to acknowledge in writing his receipt of that information. This procedure has the added advantage of making the patient aware of the importance of the information or instructions.

Negligence in instructing others is considered in further detail in Chapter 18 which deals with the law and the nurse educator.

Liability for a negligent mis-statement was found when a local authority recommended a registered childminder to a mother despite an earlier case of non-accidental injury by the minder. (*Harrison* v. *Surrey County Council and others*, TLR 27 January 1994).

Inexperience

Does a newly qualified nurse have to follow the same standard of care as an experienced nurse?

In practical terms it is of course impossible to expect the same standard of care from the junior nurse as from the experienced senior nurse. However, in practice that is what the patient is entitled to expect. You cannot say in defence to a patient 'The reason that you were given the wrong drug is that nurse X administered it and of course she has only just qualified.' The patient is entitled to receive the accepted standard of care whoever provides it. It is, however, essential that staff work within their field of competence and that work requiring greater experience is performed by those with the appropriate skills, or that those lacking in experience have adequate supervision to ensure the task is safely undertaken. This point is discussed in the Wilsher case which is considered below on page 43.

CASE 4.2 A LEARNER DRIVER

Mr Nettleship was teaching Mrs Weston to drive in her husband's car. On the third lesson he was helping her by moving the gear lever, applying the hand brake, and occasionally helping with the steering. In the course of the lesson they made a slow left-hand turn after stopping at a halt sign. However, Mrs Weston did not straighten up the wheel and panicked. Mr Nettleship got hold of the hand brake with one hand and tried to get hold of the steering wheel with the other. The car hit a lamp standard. Mr Nettleship broke his knee-cap. He claimed compensation and succeeded before the Court of Appeal.

The crucial question in the case was: since Mrs Weston was not a qualified driver, was the standard of care that she owed to him lower than would otherwise have been the case? The court decided not. They preferred to have one standard of driving, not a variable standard depending on the characteristics of the individual driver: 'The certainties of a general standard is preferable to the vagaries of a fluctuating standard' (Lord Justice Megaw).

This might seem irrelevant to the standard of the nurse but Lord Justice Megaw, in discussing the issue, used the example of the young surgeon:

> Suppose that to the knowledge of the patient, a young surgeon, whom the patient has chosen to operate on him, has only just qualified. If the operation goes wrong because of the surgeon's inexperience, is there a defence on the basis that the standard of care and skill was lower than the standard of a competent and experienced surgeon? In cases such as the present it is preferable that there should be a reasonably certain and reasonably ascertainable standard of care, even if on occasion that may appear to work hardly against an inexperienced driver.
>
> (*Nettleship* v. *Weston* 1971 3 All ER 581)

(Mr Nettleship obtained his compensation.)

SITUATION 4.1 NO EXPERIENCE

Ruth Evans is recently qualified and is a staff nurse at Roger Park Hospital. She is asked to work initially on the orthopaedic ward until a vacancy occurs on the paediatric ward, which is her chosen speciality. The orthopaedic consultant suggests that Fred Timms who has recently been taken off traction could start some mobility exercises. Ruth, following this advice, approaches Fred's bed with a nursing auxiliary and with a pair of crutches. She suggests that Fred should manoeuvre himself to the side of the bed and gently put his sound leg on the floor. Then when he feels steady enough he should take the crutches and start to walk. Fred shifts to the side of the bed, puts his sound leg on the floor, but as he stands up holding onto the crutches they slide away from him and he falls heavily to the ground. Subsequently, X-rays reveal a further fracture of the injured leg and a fresh fracture in the other leg. Where does Ruth stand as far as liability is concerned? Is the fact that she has only just commenced on the orthopaedic ward and has never specialised in it a good defence for her personally against any potential court action that Fred might bring?

It is quite likely that if this case were investigated it would be established that there was a recognised procedure for mobilisation of orthopaedic patients which would most likely involve the physiotherapist, and that Ruth had failed to follow this and probably was not even aware of its existence. This would be no defence against Fred. If he can establish the four elements of negligence – (a) a duty of care was owed to him, (b) Ruth was in breach of that duty by failing to follow the accepted approved practice and that (c) as a reasonably foreseeable consequence, he has (d) been caused harm – then he would succeed in his action. Ruth would be held to be negligent. Fred is, however, more likely to sue the NHS Trust as Ruth's employer on the grounds that it is vicariously liable for her negligence and is also directly liable for failing to ensure a system of supervision of unqualified staff. Other staff may also be held negligent. For example, who should have ensured that Ruth had the requisite training, that she was made aware of ward procedures, and that she had adequate support? Someone else should have ensured that she was aware of the role of the physiotherapist.

In practice, of course, the experience of individual staff varies greatly and, even where staff have had the same experience and training, their level of skill and manual dexterity may also vary greatly. However, the patient should be assured that he will receive the recognised approved standard of care. Occasionally, a patient may require a higher standard. For example, Mr Links may have held himself up as a specialist in a tricky ear operation which is often not performed because of its particular hazards and difficulties. A general practitioner might refer a patient to Mr Links because of his particular skill. If Mr Links then fails to perform the operation carefully and the patient suffers harm, it is no defence for Mr Links to claim that he knows he did not perform it correctly but no other ear surgeon could have done it. He has held himself up as having that particular skill. Of course, it would have to be shown that he had failed to perform the operation with the required level of care and skill. The fact that things go wrong does not in itself mean that there has been negligence.

Team liability and the apportionment of responsibility

Team liability

If harm is caused by another member of the team, is the nurse responsible?

Work in the health service is, above all, team oriented. Very few tasks are performed entirely on one's own. In the community, particular tasks are often allocated not purely on a professional basis but on a key worker basis which enables one person to take responsibility for a wide range of tasks.

SITUATION 4.2 THE TEAM

Jane is a third-year student who, together with other members of staff on the ward, is caring for orthopaedic patients. The nursing process is in operation. One day Jane is asked to work in the plaster unit where it is her task to bind the plaster bandage around the patients' limbs. One of the patients, a young boy called Sam, has a broken wrist and Jane is told to strap it up. She bandages the wrist and then calls the sister to look at it. The sister glances at it but does not touch it and the boy's mother is asked to bring him back in three weeks' time. No instructions are given about checking the tightness of the bandage or moving the hand. Three weeks later the boy returns with his mother and it is noticed that the bandage has been put on too tightly and it appears that permanent damage has been done to the boy's hand. What is Jane's responsibility?

Jane is of course the employee who actually bandaged his wrist and her liability will depend on such questions as: Had Jane been trained to plaster? Was such a task entirely within her competence? Was her level of expertise such that the sister should have checked her work? If, for example, it should have been quite clear that Jane was too inexperienced to undertake the task without supervision, the fact that she asked the sister to check over the work might be sufficient to relieve her of personal responsibility. The failure to communicate to the parent the need to check on the plaster is also a breach of duty and liability will depend upon who had the responsibility of ensuring that this was done. As has been noted in the first section of this chapter, failure to communicate can itself be grounds for an allegation of negligence.

The team may be a group of nurses working together – it might be a multidisciplinary group. In the following case the team is made up of doctors and nurses working under one consultant.

CASE 4.3 NO TEAM LIABILITY

A premature baby was placed in a special care baby unit staffed by a medical team consisting of two consultants, a senior registrar, several junior doctors and trained nurses. A junior doctor, while monitoring the oxygen intake, inadvertently put the catheter in a vein rather than in an artery. He asked the senior registrar to check what he had done. The registrar failed to see the mistake and several hours later made exactly the same mistake himself. As a result the catheter failed to monitor the oxygen correctly and it was alleged that the child suffered from an incurable condition of the retina resulting in near-blindness. (*Wilsher* v. *Essex Area Health Authority* CA 1986 3 All ER 801 HL 1988 1 All ER 871).

At the trial the judge awarded £116,199 to the child. The health authority appealed to the Court of Appeal on the grounds that (1) there had been no breach of care of duty owed to the child because the standard of care required of doctors in the unit was only that reasonably required of doctors having the same formal qualifications and practical experience as the doctors in the unit, and (2) the child had failed to show that the health authority's actions had caused or contributed to his condition since excess oxygen was merely one of several different factors, any one of which could have caused or contributed to the eye condition from which the child suffered. This last point is known as causation and is discussed in Chapter 3.

On the point of the standard of care the court held that there was no concept of team negligence, in the sense that each individual team member was required to observe standards demanded of the unit as a whole, because it could not be right, for example, to expose a student nurse to an action for negligence for her failure to possess the experience of a consultant. The standard of care required was that of the ordinary skilled person exercising and professing to have that special skill, but that standard was to be determined in the context of the particular posts in the unit rather than according to the general rank or status of the people filling the posts, since the duty ought to be tailored to the acts which the doctor had elected to perform rather than to the doctor himself. It followed that inexperience was no defence to an action for negligence. One judge, however, stated that an inexperienced doctor who was called on to exercise a specialist skill and who made a mistake nevertheless satisfied the necessary standard of care if he had sought the advice and help of his superior when necessary. The court in this case applied the same standard as the court in the Whitehouse and Jordan case (see pages 29–30), i.e. the 'Bolam Test'. The judges held that the junior doctor had not been negligent and had upheld the relevant standard of care by consulting his superior. His superior had, however, been negligent in failing to notice that the catheter had been mistakenly inserted in a vein rather than an artery and, accordingly, the health authority was vicariously liable for the registrar's negligence.

An additional finding was that there was no reason why, in certain circumstances, a health authority could not be directly liable to a plaintiff if it failed to provide sufficient or properly qualified and competent medical staff for the unit. The House of Lords has subsequently ordered a new trial on the issue of causation (see Chapter 3).

Apportioning responsibility

Although there is no concept of team negligence in law, each person is individually responsible for his/her negligence; it does not follow that there are no occasions of multiple liability, i.e. in a given situation several different professionals might be individually responsible for their own individual negligence. An example of this is given below. The case does not involve a nurse but if the situation was in a hospital context rather than in the home, one can imagine a nurse being involved.

CASE 4.4 HOME PRESCRIBING

It was alleged by Mrs Dwyer that Dr Roderick prescribed a particular drug (Migril) and was negligent in choosing the number and frequency with which the relevant tablets should be taken, so that within a relatively short time she had received a dangerous overdose. The manufacturers had warned that not more than four tablets should be taken for any one attack of migraine and that no more than 12 tablets should be taken in the course of one week.

Dr Roderick's prescription was for two tablets to be taken every four hours as necessary. He prescribed a total of 60 tablets. Dr Roderick admitted that this was utterly wrong: 'I have no satisfactory explanation. It was a mental aberration.' When the prescription was taken for dispensing there were two qualified pharmacists in the shop, neither of whom noticed the error and simply repeated Dr Roderick's instructions on the label. They in turn accepted some liability. Over the next six days Mrs Dwyer took 36 Migril tablets. As a result of this overdose she suffered serious personal injuries, i.e. irreversible ergotamine poisoning which resulted in constriction of the blood vessels and gangrene of her toes and lower limbs. As well as suing the chemists and Dr Roderick, Mrs Dwyer sued as second defendant Dr Roderick's partner, Dr Jackson, who saw her three days after the prescription had been given and who failed to discover the fact that his partner had overprescribed the drug and failed to stop her taking it. (*Dwyer* v. *Roderick* 20 June 1984 QBD).

The trial judge decided that each defendant was liable: Dr Roderick was 45 per cent liable, Dr Jackson was 15 per cent liable and the pharmacists were 40 per cent liable. The Court of Appeal held by a majority that Dr Jackson was not negligent. It accepted his evidence that it was his usual practice to enquire what medication a patient was on. Liability was thus divided between Dr Roderick and the pharmacists. Mrs Dwyer received £92,000 compensation.

One of the very interesting aspects of this case was that the incident occurred in November 1973 but did not come to court until 1982, thus the actual evidence of what happened was scanty and undoubtedly made Mrs Dwyer's case against Dr Jackson very difficult. The court commented adversely on the delay and suggested that the time may be ripe for changes designed to enable the court and the judiciary to play a greater part in encouraging the parties and their advisers to speed up the process of litigation. However, these changes have not yet taken place and considerable delays still occur before a case comes before the courts. This is an important point for nurses to appreciate, especially when keeping records, since in any such incident the nurse is likely to have very little personal recall of events but will be heavily dependent on the clarity and comprehensiveness of the records.

The scope of professional practice

In June 1992 the UKCC published the Scope of Professional Practice which can be found in Appendix 10. It marks a major development in the thinking underlying professional practice. Previously the concept of the extended role highlighted the distinction between the basic training that the practitioner received in order to become a registered professional and post-registration training. Under 'the extended role', professional development was seen as incremental, task orientated and often delegated from other professionals (usually medical). A circular in 1977 (CHC (77) 22) advised that, before a nurse was competent to perform an extended role task, the following circumstances must apply:

1. The nurse must be specifically and adequately trained for the new task and she must agree to undertake it.
2. This training must be recognised as satisfactory by the employing authority.
3. This new task must be recognised by this profession and by the authority as a task that may be properly delegated to a nurse.
4. The delegating doctor must be assured of the competence of the nurse concerned.

In 1986 a working party was set up by the Standing Medical Advisory Committee and the Standing Nursing and Midwifery Committee to review the extended role of the nurse. Its report was circulated under cover as a DHSS letter from the Chief Nursing Officer, dated 26 September 1989. Whilst it upheld the principles established in 1977, it recommended that they should be reinterpreted and re-expressed in the light of developments in clinical practice and changes in health service organisation. It paved the way for the publication of the UKCC's Scope of Professional Practice.

The UKCC emphasises that professional practice must be sensitive, relevant and responsive to the needs of individual patients and clients and have the capacity to adjust, where and when appropriate, to changing circumstances (see Appendix 10, paragraph 1). It sets out principles that should govern adjustment to the scope of professional practice (paragraph 9). These are laid out in Fig. 4.2.

The Scope of Professional Practice should be seen in the context of Post-Registration Education and Practice (PREP) which is the UKCC's framework for continuing education. It includes a duty on practitioners to have at least five refresher days every three years. Implementation commenced in April 1995. Undoubtedly there are opportunities for nursing, midwifery and health visiting to develop safely beyond the original boundaries. It will enable practice to develop naturally into areas that were once seen as delegated medical tasks; it moves development away from

---

The registered nurse, midwife or health visitor:

1. must be satisfied that each aspect of practice is directed to meeting the needs and serving the interests of the patient or client;
2. must endeavour always to achieve, maintain and develop knowledge, skill and competence to respond to those needs and interests;
3. must honestly acknowledge any limits of personal knowledge and skill and take steps to remedy any relevant deficits in order effectively and appropriately to meet the needs of patients and clients;
4. must ensure that any enlargement or adjustment of the scope of personal professional practice must be achieved without compromising or fragmenting existing aspects of professional practice and care and that requirements of the Council's Code of Professional Conduct are satisfied throughout the whole area of practice;
5. must recognise and honour the direct or indirect personal accountability borne for all aspects of professional practice; and
6. must, in serving the interests of patients and clients and the wider interests of society, avoid any inappropriate delegation to others which compromises those interests.

Figure 4.2 Principles for adjusting the Scope of Professional Practice.

new tasks to a more holistic view of practice relevant to a nurse, midwife or health visitor.

Practitioners have concerns, however, as a result of the move away from certified tasks, which include the following:

1. How do I know if I am competent?
2. How does my employer know if I am competent?
3. What happens if I undertake an activity which is outside my field of competence?
4. Where do I stand if a doctor/senior manager/other professional ignores my refusal to undertake an activity because I have not sufficient competence or experience to undertake that activity?

Some situations will be considered which highlight these dilemmas.

SITUATION 4.3 SCOPE OF PROFESSIONAL PRACTICE 1_____

Mavis, a staff nurse, was asked by the registrar to do the intravenous infusions. The registrar rushed away before she had the chance to explain to him that she had not developed the skills, competence and knowledge to undertake that activity safely. However, she decided that she would carry out his instructions as best she could. Unfortunately when she was adding a drug to Jimmy Price's intravenous infusion she failed to set the speed of his drip correctly and as a result Jimmy became very ill. Where do Mavis and the registrar stand in relation to the responsibility for the harm to Jimmy?

As far as Mavis was concerned, she was at fault in failing to mention her lack of competence for that activity to the registrar. No nurse should work outside her range of competence and skill unless a dire emergency arises when the risks in failing to act are greater than in acting. There is no suggestion that this was an emergency. The nurse ignored a fundamental principle of the Code of Professional Practice (see Appendix 1, paragraph 4): to 'acknowledge any limitations in your knowledge and competence and decline any duties or responsibilities unless able to perform them in a safe and skilled manner'.

The failure of Mavis to notify the doctor and the resulting mistake which caused harm to the patient could result in a civil action brought against her employer because of its vicarious liability for the negligent actions of an employee acting in course of employment (see pages 60–7). Mavis herself may be subject to professional disciplinary proceedings before the UKCC Professional Conduct Committee. Were Jimmy to die, she might also face criminal proceedings. Her employer, of course, would commence its own disciplinary inquiry and proceedings.

What of the registrar? Is he also at fault? If the addition of drugs to intravenous transfusions is seen as a task delegated by a doctor to a nurse practitioner, then he would be liable as delegator in failing to ensure that he was delegating to a competent person. However, under the Scope of Professional Practice, such activities are not seen as 'delegated tasks' and the duty was incumbent upon the individual nurse practitioner to ensure that, if she herself was not competent, another practitioner, whether medical or nursing, who was competent, performed the activity. The managerial responsibilities in ensuring appropriate supervision and allocation of activities are discussed on pages 58–9.

Can a nurse refuse to undertake training in new areas of competency?

It was a principle under the concept of the 'extended role' that nurses could refuse to undertake a new task or activity. However, this approach is probably no longer appropriate in relation to the Scope of Professional Practice. Clause 3 of the Code of Professional Conduct requires nurses to 'maintain and improve your professional knowledge and competence' (see Appendix 1). It would be entirely inappropriate for a practitioner to refuse to develop her professional practice beyond the level she reached when she became registered. In addition it is directly contrary to the principles of PREP. However, she probably could not be required to develop outside her current level of clinical grading (e.g. to move from an E to an F). There are other contractual considerations. In an interview for a job, for example, a nurse might be told that a contractual requirement for that particular post is that the nurse is competent in a specified area. If the nurse agrees to this condition then she is contractually bound to develop, with support from the employer, the appropriate skills, knowledge and competence. If she refuses the condition, she will probably not get the post.

The Scope of Professional Practice in primary care

SITUATION 4.4 SCOPE OF PROFESSIONAL PRACTICE 2

Practice Nurse Jenny Brown was asked by the GP to make a primary visit to a child whose mother had reported him too ill to come to surgery. Jenny Brown visited the child, took his temperature and blood pressure, and examined him. She told the mother that she thought he was suffering from the flu that was going round at present, to keep him warm with lots of drinks and, if he worsened or failed to improve within a few days, to let the surgery know. She reported the results of the visit to the GP, who approved of her action. Unfortunately, that same night an emergency call was made by the mother to the locum who was on duty and the boy was rushed to hospital, where he was diagnosed as suffering from meningitis. He eventually died. The mother is now demanding that action be taken against both the nurse and the doctor. What is the responsibility of the nurse and the doctor?

If the nurse had acted outside her competence, been negligent and caused harm as a consequence, then she will be liable. The doctor will be vicariously liable for the actions of a negligent nurse employee. The competence of a nurse in making a primary visit will become of increasing importance when nurse prescribing is implemented.

Taking instructions from others: refusal to obey

The general principles

When we looked at the Scope of Professional Practice, we considered the possibility that the nurse might have to refuse to undertake a task where, for example, she was not trained to perform it or where she had insufficient time to undertake it safely. In this section we look at the wider field of obeying orders.

SITUATION 4.5 ORDERS ARE ORDERS_____

A house officer decides that Margaret Brown should be prescribed a new drug which has only just been released onto the market and writes her up for it. The staff nurse on that ward is not familiar with the drug and says that she would like to check it with the pharmacist before she administers it. The doctor is furious with this insolence and says that if he has written it up then she should administer it without questioning his competence. The nurse says that she needs some understanding of the drug before she gives it to the patient. The doctor insists she gives it. Where does the nurse stand?

This is a simplified version of situations that often confront the nurse. This particular example raises the issue of what is the nurse's responsibility in relation to the administration of drugs, but examples could be given from other fields such as obeying the orders 'not for resuscitation', not passing certain information on to a patient, etc.

It is impossible to give an answer that would apply to every situation. In an emergency, for example, certain risks have to be taken which would not be appropriate in non-urgent circumstances. In the above situation the nurse would be quite correct in obtaining further information about the drug in question. When she administers a drug she must be sure that she is administering the right drug, at the right time, in the right place, at the right dosage, in the right way, to the right patient. She should not administer a drug of which she has no knowledge without taking all reasonable steps to ascertain that it is appropriate for that particular patient. If in the above situation she were to go ahead and administer the drug on the orders of the doctor and the patient were to die or suffer harm as a result, she could be liable for civil action since she failed to follow the reasonable standards of care expected of a nurse. She could also face professional disciplinary proceedings before the PCC and disciplinary proceedings before her own line manager because she failed to use all care and skill in carrying out her contract of employment. If the patient died the nurse might have to appear in the coroner's court and there may also be criminal proceedings brought against both her and the doctor. (See the UKCC advisory paper *Exercising Accountability* on this issue, in Appendix 7).

In all these courts and hearings, the phrase 'but I was only carrying out orders' will not be sufficient defence on its own. In the civil courts, the professional proceedings and the employer's disciplinary proceedings, the nurse would have to show that what she did was reasonable having regard to the approved accepted practice to be expected from any qualified nurse. In the criminal courts she would have to show that her acts did not constitute the ingredients of the particular charge and/or that she lacked the required mental state.

Obeying orders in an emergency

In certain circumstances time does not permit the usual practice to be followed, but the risks taken must be balanced against the risk of the patient dying.

SITUATION 4.6 EMERGENCY

A patient has been brought into the accident and emergency department with severe bleeding. A blood sample is taken for cross-matching and he is immediately put on an intravenous infusion of plasma. The doctor erects the intravenous infusion and asks the nurse to set up a saline solution straight away. Staff Nurse Bryant takes the bag that the doctor is holding out to her and attaches it to the IV line. She does not check the bag. The patient's condition worsens and he eventually dies. It is then discovered that the doctor inadvertently gave the nurse a bag containing a substance other than saline. What is the nurse's liability?

It is clear that a quick check of the label on the bag would not have delayed the patient's treatment and could have been done by the nurse without any difficulty. It is most likely that she would be found personally liable in these circumstances and any defence of 'but that was the bag the doctor gave me' would be unlikely to succeed. There could be other circumstances where emergency life-saving measures are required and the nurse would be unable to make the same checks. Very rarely, however, would the defence of 'obeying orders' succeed, since as a professionally qualified person the nurse would be expected to act responsibly and carefully and to ensure that her own personal actions are safe. Nurses sometimes complain that the misgivings they express to doctors are ignored. What do they do then? Obviously, it depends upon the circumstances. Where her misgivings concern treatment that could be harmful to the patient and if one doctor ignored her concern, then the nurse should express her misgivings to her own line manager and, if necessary, the advice of a more senior doctor should be sought. Much depends upon the approach made by the nurse and the nature of the relationship and understanding which exists between the nurse and the doctor. Undoubtedly, encouragement of a team approach to patient care could prevent many unnecessary confrontations of this kind. It should of course be stressed that a nurse should not disobey the instruction of a doctor lightly; she should have compelling reasons from the patient's point of view. She should ensure that she has detailed records indicating the reasons for her actions and that her nurse manager is brought in at the earliest opportunity. If it should happen that the nurse's attitude was unreasonable then she would of course face disciplinary action and, if the patient has been harmed as a result of the nurse's action, civil proceedings and professional misconduct proceedings.

Questions and exercises

1 There can be liability for failure to communicate. Apply this principle to your particular post and consider how and to what extent communication with the patient could be improved.
2 Consider any work you undertake as a member of a team and assess the extent to which it is clear where the boundaries of individual responsibility lie.
3 Study a copy of your NHS Trust's policy on the scope of professional practice duties and the principles contained therein.
4 There are times when it is essential that a nurse obeys the orders of a doctor without question, and others where it is imperative that she checks that the instructions are appropriate. What distinguishing features would decide whether an order falls in the first category or in the second?

5   More specific problems in negligence liability

The areas to be covered in this chapter are shown in Fig. 5.1.

Pressure from inadequate resources

Unfortunately, harm to the patient can occur due to shortage of staff, inadequate equipment and unsafe premises. This section deals with the liability of those concerned. Refer to the UKCC advisory paper *Exercising Accountability* (Appendix 7) and, in particular, paragraphs relating to the environment of care.

General principles

SITUATION 5.1 RESOURCES

Pauline Cross is working on a busy geriatric ward with only two staff. The patients are severely confused and can do little for themselves. As she is transferring a patient from a wheelchair into bed the patient falls to the floor and breaks her hip bone. Is Pauline likely to be held responsible in law for the patient's injuries?

Figure 5.1 Issues covered in Chapter 5.

It could be argued that this incident took place because there was inadequate staffing. However, there are many factors to be considered. Were they so short staffed that even when priorities were set it would have been impossible for another member of the staff to help Pauline? Was such an incident reasonably foreseeable such that additional precautions should have been taken, or was it an inevitable accident and therefore unavoidable? If the conclusion is that the accident was avoidable and another nurse should have been assigned to assist Pauline, then this will not automatically relieve Pauline of responsibility, especially if she was in charge of the ward. The question arises whether it would not have been possible to have put the patient to bed later when more help would have been available. Alternatively, could the tasks that were occupying the other nurses have been given a lower priority?

Even if all the questions could be answered negatively, i.e. they were so short staffed that they could not take the necessary foreseeable precautions to ensure the patient was put to bed safely, Pauline may still be responsible. If she was in charge of the ward, had she warned her senior nurse management of the staffing difficulties and suggested remedial action such as discharging patients to other wards or home, or suggesting the use of agency nurses if nurses could not be transferred from other wards? Failure to take such action where her management role requires it would mean that Pauline would have to share some measure of responsibility for the occurrence (see the section on nurse as manager below on page 58).

Employer's responsibility?

If a patient is harmed because of an accident which would not have occurred had reasonable resources been available, then the patient would have a valid action to recover compensation in the civil courts. It is no defence to say to a patient 'We are sorry we amputated the wrong leg but Wednesday is our busiest day and we had a lot of staff off with influenza.' A patient is entitled to the approved standard of care. Even in an emergency situation, staff would be expected to take additional precautions to prevent further harm arising on the basis of a clear order of priorities. In such circumstances the patient would be able to sue the NHS Trust for its vicarious liability for the negligence of the staff. However, it is probable, too, that an action of direct liability also might succeed against the Trust because harm was caused to the patient as a result of inadequate resources.

CASE 5.1 INADEQUATE RESOURCES 1

A casualty officer, through pressure of work, made only a brief examination and treated a major head injury on the assumption that it was a minor one.

Both he and the health authority were held liable. The judge held that pressure of work was no defence to the patient's claim (*McCormack* v. *Redpath Brown*, *The Times* 24 March 1961).

CASE 5.2 INADEQUATE RESOURCES 2

In a more recent case several allegations were made by a patient that she was not treated with proper professional care and skill during the delivery of her first child. A Shirodkar suture had been fitted at an earlier stage because of an incompetent cervix. It was important that the suture should be removed promptly once labour had commenced, otherwise there was a danger that the cervix could be damaged. The patient claimed that the staff had failed to act speedily and as a consequence her cervix was damaged. The defendants claimed that the ward was very busy that night and the patient received appropriate care.

At the defendants' request the judge directed that the notes of the other patients should be made available to show what was going on in the labour ward that evening. He did so with reluctance because he did not wish a breach of the duty of confidentiality owed to the patients and the defendants had not pleaded any special emergency which prevented speedier attention to the patient. These patients were referred to by code names. Their notes were exhaustively examined in the course of the evidence. 'In summary they showed that the doctors were busy and that the patient bringing the action was not the only patient who presented problems. But they did not show there was anything to prevent the doctors performing a vaginal examination or removing the suture sooner than they did.'

One of the criticisms was that the doctors had failed to give the patient sufficient priority. The doctor in his defence said that on a busy labour ward the doctors do not sit down and work out a list of priorities. The judge, however, had to decide if the patient had been kept waiting too long. He said: 'I appreciate that one must not be too critical of what goes on in a busy ward but it is difficult to understand why the patient did not have a vaginal examination until two hours after admission. Other ladies were admitted at about the same time as she was and whose cases were of no greater urgency had their examinations far sooner.'

The judge commented on the statement of one of the experts for the defence who had said 'I think the time scale is within the pattern of what occurs in a busy ward.'

That may well be, but it does not resolve the question whether this particular patient was given proper care ... I do not pinpoint any particular moment when a particular doctor did something wrong. It was rather a case where there was a lack of sufficient sense of urgency on all sides. In these circumstances I hold that the second defendants (Leicester Health Authority) did not treat the patient with proper professional care and skill.

The patient was awarded £1,500 (*Deacon* v. *McVicar and another* 7 January 1984 QBD). Several important points emerge from this case.

1. The assessment of priorities can be carried out negligently or not at all and can itself form the basis of a claim for compensation.
2. To ascertain the work load and other demands, it is possible with the approval of the judge for the records of other patients to be made available. It is essential that comprehensive records are always kept.

Coping under pressure

One question often asked by nursing staff in relation to shortage of resources is 'What happens if we are dangerously short of staff and yet we cope? What is the situation then?' This is a frequent situation. Yet if no person suffers harm as a result of the inadequate levels, then there can be no action for negligence, since harm must be established. However, it would be part of the duties of the nurse, both in her professional duties and as a manager, to ensure that senior levels are notified of any dangers or hazards so that harm does not eventually occur. An inadequate number of trained staff in proportion to the demands of patients could lead to inexperienced people administering drugs, using specialised equipment or assisting doctors in complex treatments and patients could therefore suffer overdoses or other forms of harm.

Legal requirements on staffing

Another question which is raised is 'What are the legal staffing levels or of what legal significance is a particular staffing ratio which has been recommended by different researchers?' Minimum staffing levels or ratios are unlikely to be laid down by Act of Parliament or by the courts. Under the principles relating to liability in negligence sufficient resources must be provided to ensure that the patients being cared for are provided with the approved accepted standard of care. All circumstances must be taken into account in determining whether this has been provided in respect of a given patient who has suffered harm. Obviously, evidence could be given of the extent to which the staffing levels had fallen below the levels considered by experts in the field to be the minimum consistent with good practice, but this is evidence, not law.

Failures by management

What does the nurse do if she has drawn the attention of management to a situation which she considers dangerous and nothing is done about it? Whatever the situation, whether it is concerned with inadequate resources or incompetent staff, the nurse should not give up if she feels her concern about a dangerous situation is being ignored. She has a duty to ensure that the patients are cared for appropriately. She should there-fore put her concerns in writing with evidence of hazards which have occurred. Her report would need to be a detailed account which is meaningful to management of the levels of staffing and the needs of the patients. If nothing is done she should then be prepared to refer the matter to a higher level of management. Eventually, if she is still concerned that the dangers are being ignored she should take the matter to her NHS Trust or national board or the UKCC. This is preferable to bringing the local or national press into a field that should be sorted out internally.

Whistle blowing

Nurses have feared victimisation as a result of bringing hazards to the attention of management, as they are required to do under the Code of Professional Practice. To allay such fears and prevent victimisation the NHS Management Executive issued 'Guide-lines for Staff on Relations with the Public and the Media' (1993). This emphasised that under no circumstances are employees who express their views about health service issues in accordance with this guidance to be penalised in any way for doing so (paragraph 6). Each NHS employer has a duty to establish a procedure for employees to raise concerns. An employee who has exhausted the locally established procedures can take his/her concerns to an outside body. Note the future statutory protection given to employees against dismissal when the employer is alerted to health and safety dangers (page 156).

The 1993 guidance emphasises the duty of confidentiality owed by staff to patients but recognises that disclosure may be justified in the public interest. Where this may be the case, staff should obtain specialist advice before making any disclosure. The local procedure for dealing with staff concerns should be set up after full consultation with staff, and should aim at resolving these issues informally. Managers should take concerns seriously, consider them fully and sympathetically, recognise that raising a concern can be a difficult experience for some staff and seek advice from health care professionals where appropriate. The procedure may identify a designated officer to whom matters unresolved by immediate line managers could be referred directly by the member of staff concerned.

Waiting times for admission

What if a patient is waiting for a long time before admission? There is an interesting distinction in the following two situations.

1. Where the treatment has commenced it must be carried out according to the accepted approved standard. If a negligent act occurs which causes harm to the patient, then this is actionable by the patient.
2. Where treatment has not commenced and the patient has to wait on a waiting list then even though the patient's condition might deteriorate this is not actionable provided the health authority has carried out its purchase of health services rationally.

CASE 5.3 INADEQUATE RESOURCES 3

Orthopaedic patients at a hospital in Birmingham who had waited for treatment for periods longer than was medically advisable, brought an action against the Secretary of State, the regional health authority and the area health authority. They were seeking a declaration that the defendants were in breach of their duty under Section 1 of the National Health Service Act 1977 to continue to promote a comprehensive health service designed to secure improvement in health and the prevention of illness, and under Section 3 to provide accommodation, facilities and services for those purposes.

The judge held that it was not the function of the court to direct Parliament as to what funds to make available to the health service and how to allocate them. The Secretary of State's duty under Section 3 to provide services 'to such extent as he considers necessary', gave him discretion as to the disposition of financial resources. The court could only interfere if the Secretary of State acted so as to frustrate the policy of the Act or as no reasonable minister could have acted. No such breach had been shown in the present case. The court could not grant mandamus or a declaration against area or regional authorities since specific remedies against them were available by Section 85 and Part V of the 1977 Act. Nor if a breach were proved did the Act admit of relief by way of damages. The application was therefore dismissed. (*R. v. Secretary of State for Social Services ex parte Hincks and others, Solicitors' Journal* 29 June 1979 436).

The reasoning behind the above ruling was confirmed in the following case.

CASE 5.4 POSTPONED OPERATION

Mrs Walker's baby son required a heart operation and was on the waiting list. A date was fixed for the operation to be performed but was postponed by the Birmingham Health Authority. She applied to the court for a judicial review of the decision of the health authority. The High Court judge refused her application. She appealed to the Court of Appeal who upheld the earlier decision.

The Health Authority had accepted that the regional district health authorities could be subject to judicial review where there was reason to believe that they might be in breach of their public duties. There would always be individuals who believed that treatment was not provided quickly enough, but the financial resources were finite and always would be. The court held that it was not for the court to substitute its own judgement for that of those responsible for the allocation of resources. It would only interfere if there had been a failure to allocate funds in a way which was unreasonable or where there had been breaches of public duties. Mrs Walker's application was refused (*In re Walker's application, The Times* 26 November 1987).

The nurse as manager

Managerial responsibility and professional conduct

This section looks at the nurse's responsibility as a manager of a ward or department.

SITUATION 5.2 ON HOLIDAY

Marion is ward sister of an acute surgical ward of 30 patients. When she is on holiday a patient is given a premedication prior to the form of consent for his operation being signed. The mistake is discovered and because it was felt that there was no doubt that the patient wanted to have the operation he was still asked to sign the form. He was then taken to theatre. Subsequently, he disputed the extent of his operation as he understood that the operation was only exploratory, but he received radical surgery including the provision of a colostomy. He argued that had he known that this was a possibility he would not have agreed to have the operation and he could not remember signing any form of consent. The circumstances of his signature then were discovered. Since the ward sister was on holiday at the time is there any possibility of her being liable?

It would be cheering for ward sisters and managers if the question could be answered with a definite 'No'. However, this is not possible. A manager has a continuing responsibility to ensure that procedures and policies are designed and implemented to prevent any likelihood of harm to the patient. A vital question to be answered would be: had a procedure been established to ensure that the nursing staff checked that the consent form had been signed before administration of premedication? It would be the ward sister's responsibility to ensure that those procedures which come under the responsibility of the nursing staff are carried out competently and diligently, even when she is not there. In this example the doctor would be liable for failing to obtain consent. In addition, as far as the immediate responsibility is concerned, the manager in charge of the ward at the time would also share liability for the events but if, for example, it were established that there was no clear system for ensuring a correct procedure in relation to the checking of consent forms prior to the premedication being given, then the ward sister who should have implemented and supervised such a procedure would share some responsibility for the events. It is likely, too, that evidence of similar events in the past would be used to show the deficiencies in overall ward management in this particular context. In this context the ward sister's liability is not vicarious (see next section), i.e. it does not concern taking responsibility for the fault of others. It is direct, her own personal liability for failing in her management role. If of course it can be shown that a sound practice had been implemented and was not followed on that occasion due to the negligence of the staff on duty at that time, then there is less likelihood that the ward sister would be held liable.

Her failings in her responsibilities as manager could result in her being sued in the civil courts and, in addition, it could result in her facing a hearing for professional misconduct before the PCC of the UKCC. The definition of misconduct which may justify removal from the Register is sufficiently wide to cover mismanagement by a nurse. It is thus an increasing feature of the PCC hearings that as well as hearing a case against an individual nurse who has been at fault in the care of patients, that nurse's manager or managers may also appear before the PCC to answer the charge of misconduct in failing to take responsibility for the situation and having shown a failure in management. Similar principles would apply if, for example, a nurse was known to be on drugs or under the influence of drink at work. If this was known or should have reasonably been known to the managers (they cannot simply turn a blind eye and pretend to be ignorant) and they failed to take appropriate action, then they may well face a hearing for professional misconduct.

Delegation and supervision

Management also involves the responsibilities of delegating and supervising staff. Those for whom she is responsible may include not only the other trained staff, learners, and nursing assistants, but also volunteers. On some occasions these volunteers may be very unwilling helpers as, for example, where youth training schemes include an attachment to a hospital. If such persons are assigned to work on a ward or department and the nurse manager is responsible for them, then she would have to ensure that their training and the tasks delegated to them are appropriate, and that adequate supervision is provided (see also discussion of the extended role of the nurse in Chapter 4).

As manager, the nurse would be responsible for ensuring that the resources were effectively used and were sufficient for treating patients according to the approved standard of care. If harm is caused by inadequate resources and it is established that she failed to take the appropriate measures to prevent unreasonable risks arising, then she may well be liable (see above).

Pressure upon the manager

SITUATION 5.3 MANAGER'S NIGHTMARE_____

Nursing Officer Janice Clarke is on duty and is informed by the staff in the surgical ward that although they are on intake and have three empty beds, due to illness and the failure to fill vacancies they are so far below their establishment that the situation is dangerous and the present staff cannot cope with any more patients.

Obviously, the nursing officer would ensure that the facts are correct and that the nurses on that ward are using their time appropriately and not undertaking tasks which could safely be left, in order to give priority to the work which is most important. Having assured herself that the situation is critical she would then look internally at other wards and decide whether staff could be transferred. She might also have to consider bringing in agency nurses. If necessary, she would consider the situation on a district basis which might mean that she would have to discuss the possibility of another hospital taking over the intake at the present. Ultimately, she might have to bring in other districts or at least refer the problems to a more senior manager. The decision might be made that waiting list admissions are cancelled for the time being. Clearly, at all stages in this decision the evidence of the individual ward staff on the dangers and hazards is vital for informed decisions to be made. Like the ward sister or staff nurse the nursing officer herself should keep records of the reasons behind the actions she has taken since this information may well be relevant to a court or PCC hearing.

Covering several wards

Another difficulty which can arise in this context is where a ward sister is in charge of her own ward and also holds the drug cupboard keys for another ward because there is no trained nurse on that ward. In such a situation the ward sister would have the same responsibilities for both wards. Her tasks of delegation and supervision become extremely difficult and if something goes wrong on one ward in her absence she may well be liable if that task required her personal supervision. If such problems were likely, then she would obviously have to ensure that this was made known to the senior nurse management and ultimately the NHS Trust whose duty it is to take reasonable steps to provide the appropriate facilities.

The liability of the employer

Vicarious liability

The NHS Trust or employer has two forms of liability in negligence: one is known as direct liability, i.e. the Trust itself is at fault; the other is known as vicarious liability or indirect liability, i.e. the Trust is responsible for the faults of others, mainly its employees. In this first section we look at the vicarious liability of the employer, which could be a health authority, an NHS Trust, a private hospital, a company, or even a general practitioner who employs his own staff.

SITUATION 5.4 ASSAULT ON BEHALF OF THE EMPLOYER

Kate was a staff nurse in casualty where at weekends there tended to be a problem with drunks. The hospital was close to the town centre and to several pubs and not infrequently people needing some assistance were accompanied by friends who were incoherent and abusive. One evening Kate was very busy and therefore extremely annoyed to find some very obstreperous men accompanying a man with a cut head. She asked them to leave him and wait outside.

> They refused to go. She said she would have to summon the police if they did not leave quietly. One particularly aggressive visitor moved towards the treatment trolley and Kate, fearing that he would knock it over, raised her arm to prevent him. He was taken by surprise at her actions and fell heavily to the ground catching his head on the side of the trolley. Kate has subsequently learnt that he intends to sue her and her employer.

In a personal action against her for assault Kate would have to prove that she took reasonable action in self-defence or in protecting her employer's property or in evicting on behalf of the occupier a trespasser who refused to go. In such cases it is more likely that the plaintiff would sue the NHS Trust responsible for the wrongs of its employees. The plaintiff does not have to choose whether to sue the employer or the employee. He can sue both. The obvious advantage of suing the employer is that funds will be available to pay him should he win the case. To win against the employer he has to establish the following:

1. Kate was negligent or was liable for a civil wrong (see below).
2. Kate was an employee (see below).
3. Kate was acting in course of her employment (see below).

There is no problem with the second element in this case. Kate was an employee, but there may be cases where this is not so clear, for example if Kate were an agency nurse it might not always be obvious whether Kate is considered to be an employee of the authority to which she is sent or whether she continues to be an employee of the agency.

In practice, the first element could cause some considerable difficulty. Much would depend on the circumstances of the assault: whether she had lost her temper, the level of provocation she was subjected to, etc. Let's assume, for the purposes of this discussion, that it was established as a matter of fact that Kate had acted unlawfully and that personal action against her would therefore succeed.

In course of employment

In the employer's interests
The third element now needs to be considered. Was the nurse acting in course of her employment when she assaulted the visitor? The test used to answer this question is as follows: what was she employed to do and when she carried out that act was she acting for the benefit of her employer? In this case she was clearly not employed as a bouncer but she was trying to prevent a trolley from being upset by an obstreperous visitor (or even trespasser). This could certainly be seen as being in the interests of the employer's business. Even if there were a clear policy that nursing staff should not attempt to deal with aggressive visitors on their own, this should not necessarily prevent the act from being in course of employment. The performance of a prohibited act does not on its own mean that the employee has ceased to be acting in course of employment. All the facts have to be considered. If it can be shown that all three elements were present, the NHS Trust could be held vicariously liable for the harm caused by the nurse.

The term may cover

1. Acts authorised by employer.
2. Acts not authorised by employer, but
   (a) performed for the purpose of the employer's business;
   (b) prohibited acts, but the prohibition does not take the conduct outside the sphere of employment (*Rose* v. *Plenty* 1976 1 All ER 97);
   (c) acts incidental to the employment, undertaken for the employee's benefit whilst the employee is working on the employer's business (e.g. smoking on duty) (*Century Insurance Co. Ltd* v. *Northern Ireland Road Transport Board* 1942 1 All ER 491);
   (d) acts for the protection of the employer's property and business (*Poland* v. *Parr and Sons* CA 1926 All ER 177);
   (e) dishonest or fraudulent acts of the employee, if the employer is under a duty to the person suffering the loss (*Lloyd* v. *Grace Smith & Co.* 1912 AC 716; *Morris* v. *C. W. Martin & Sons Ltd* 1965 2 All ER 725).

Figure 5.2 Definition of 'in course of employment'.

The difficulties in establishing whether an act is in course of employment are shown in the following cases. See Fig. 5.2 for examples of criteria used by the courts to decide if an act is in course of employment.

When is an assault considered to be in course of employment, and when is it not?

CASE 5.5 A BAG OF SUGAR

Hall, a carter, employed by the defendants, honestly and reasonably believed that the plaintiff, a boy of 12, was pilfering or about to pilfer from a bag of sugar on the defendant's wagon. He hit him on the back of the neck, causing him to fall under one of the wheels of the wagon, which injured his foot.

The court held that Mr Hall was acting within the class of acts which the servant (i.e. employee) is authorised to do in an emergency. In this case he was protecting his masters' property, which was, or which he reasonably thought was, being pillaged. His mode of acting was not such as to take it out of the class. The masters were therefore held vicariously liable for the act of Mr Hall (*Poland* v. *Parr and Sons* CA 1926 All ER 177).

CASE 5.6 PETROL PROBLEMS

Beaumont was employed as a petrol pump attendant by the defendants. He wrongly accused the plaintiff, in violent language, of having tried to drive away without paying for petrol which had been put into the tank of his car. The plaintiff paid his bill, called the police and told the pump attendant that he would be reported to his employers. The attendant assaulted and then injured the plaintiff who then sued the employers for their vicarious liability for the actions of their employee.

The court held that the act of the attendant was not of the class of acts that he was authorised to perform. It was performed entirely on his own account. The employers were therefore not liable for it (*Warren* v. *Henley's Ltd* KBD 1948 2 All ER 935).

The differences between these two cases are clear. Had the attendant used reasonable force on the basis of a reasonable belief that the car driver did not intend to pay, then there may well have been a different result. He was hardly acting in the employer's interests. Similarly, in Kate's case: both the timing of her assault and also the reasonableness of what she did would be taken into account in determining if the act was in course of employment.

Outside the job description

SITUATION 5.5 HELPING OTHERS

Ann Barrett was a staff nurse on a medical ward and was concerned that the kitchen had not sent up the diets. She telephoned for them and was told that she would have to wait since there were no porters available. Rather than wait she decided to fetch them herself. She went to the kitchen, passing the notice saying 'No admission, kitchen staff only'. She went across to the diet bay and as she did so she knocked into a cook who was removing a pan of gravy from the stove. The gravy splashed over the cook and also over Ann. What remedies do the cook and Ann have in this situation and is the employer vicariously liable for Ann's negligence?

The cook could of course sue Ann personally. Ann owed a duty of care to the cook, and by her carelessness she caused reasonably foreseeable harm to the cook. However, is the employer liable for Ann's actions? There is no doubt that she is an employee. There is also no doubt that she was negligent in knocking into the cook. However, is the third element satisfied, i.e. was she acting in course of employment when she went to the kitchens and when she knocked into the cook? She was employed as a nurse, not as a kitchen porter but she was acting in the care of the patients (her employer's business) when she went to the kitchens. Even if there was a clear prohibition on non-kitchen staff entering the kitchens this would not in itself remove the act from the course of employment. The crucial point would be whether she was acting on the employer's business when she entered the kitchen, and the answer to that in this case is yes. It would be very different if she entered the kitchen to have a chat on non-hospital business with a friend of hers who worked there.

It is not of course uncommon for staff in the health service to step outside the strict confines of their job descriptions. If the employer is aware of this and turns a blind eye to it then it could be said that he condones it and accepts that the employee's duties have been expanded to include the additional tasks. In such cases if the employee acts negligently while carrying out these duties it could be argued that he or she is acting within the course of his or her employment. In addition, particularly during times of industrial action, employers specifically authorise staff to cover for the strikers or those working to rule. In such cases the employees are acting in the course of their employment: they have the express authorisation of the employer.

Activities incidental to the work

SITUATION 5.6 SMOKING ON DUTY

There was a clear and enforced policy at Roger Park Hospital that there was no smoking except in authorised areas. One of the nurses ignored these instructions and regularly smoked with the patients in the ward area. On one such occasion she accidentally dropped the cigarette and burned a patient's foot. He threatened to sue the NHS Trust. Was the nurse acting in course of employment?

The answer is probably yes, based on the following case.

CASE 5.7 LIGHTING UP

A tanker driver ignored his instructions not to light matches when loading or unloading his vehicle and as a result the tanker, a vehicle belonging to the garage, and several nearby houses were destroyed.

In this case the court held that even though the act of lighting a cigarette is for the employee's own comfort and even though it is prohibited, the act could not be separated from the circumstances of his employment. The driver was held to be negligent in the course of performing his authorised work and the employers (and therefore their insurers) were liable (*Century Insurance Co. Ltd* v. *Northern Ireland Road Transport Board* 1942 1 All ER 491).

In our example of the smoking nurse, it is highly likely that she will face disciplinary proceedings and possibly even dismissal, yet she may still be held to be acting in course of employment and therefore the employer is liable.

What if a nurse is off duty?

There can be no easy answer. It depends entirely on what she is doing and in what way she has been negligent. In a recent case the Court of Appeal allowed an appeal with costs against the decision of the PCC who found that a nurse was guilty of misconduct when she refused to answer a heart patient's call for help because she was having her tea-break. The decision was based on the fact that it had not been established that the nurse knew it was an emergency. However, this case was before the PCC and different principles might apply in a civil case.

In one case, for example, some employees in their employer's van left the authorised route and went to a café to have a snack. On the way back they had an accident and the court held that they were not acting in course of employment (*Hilton* v. *Thomas Burton (Rhodes) Ltd* 1961 1 WLR 705). It might have been different if they had deviated from their route to collect goods for the employer. In the Hilton case the employees had only just stopped off for lunch in a pub. If they had not had lunch but were driving to one, the decision might also have been different. The determination of whether an employee is or is not acting in course of employment can be a very difficult question. A recent case illustrates the problems.

Employed for what purpose?

CASE 5.8 CHEAP CALLS

A cleaner was employed by a firm of cleaning contractors to clean some offices. It subsequently became apparent that she had run up a bill of over £1,000 for telephone calls. The managers of the offices claimed this sum from the cleaning contractors, arguing that they were responsible for the cleaner's acts and that she was acting in course of her employment when she made those calls. The cleaning firm denied liability: they employed her to clean the offices and the telephones, not to use them. She was not acting in course of employment when she made the calls. They were therefore not liable.

The Court of Appeal decided in favour of the cleaning firm. This decision has major implications for the liability for independent contractors who operate the privatised services of the NHS. It is, however, always possible to provide, as a term of the contract for the privatised services, the extent of the contractor's liability, and this could well exceed the extent under the common law.

Non-employees

It will be recalled that in order to establish vicarious liability it must be established that the negligent person is an employee of the defendant. Figure 5.3 shows some of the criteria used by the courts to decide if an individual is an employee. The following case illustrates this principle.

CASE 5.9 CLASSROOM CHAOS

A deputy headmistress was injured when she fell over a tricycle which had been negligently placed near a classroom door by a 10-year-old boy in the course of carrying out his assigned task of distributing milk in the classrooms. There was a strict rule that tricycles were not to be removed from their safe position in the middle of the assembly hall.

---

1. The employee agrees that in consideration of a wage or other remuneration he will provide his own work and skill in performance of some service for the employer.
2. He agrees, expressly or impliedly, that in the performance of that service he will be subject to the other's control in a sufficient degree to make that other the employer.
3. The other provisions of the contract are consistent with its being a contract of service.

'Control in itself is not always conclusive'. *Ready-Mixed Concrete (South-East) Ltd* v. *Ministry of Pensions and National Insurance* 1968 1 All ER 433.

Figure 5.3 Criteria used to define an employee.

The Court of Appeal held that the boy was not an employee of the authority, that he was doing those duties as part of his education, and that the authority was therefore not vicariously liable. (*Watkins* v. *Birmingham City Council, The Times* 1 August 1975).

Liability for the negligence of volunteers

What about volunteers? Do the same principles apply? Is the NHS Trust liable for the negligent acts of the volunteer? If we follow the basic principles of vicarious liability, it could be argued that since the volunteer is not an employee, then the NHS Trust should not be liable. However, the philosophy that underlies the concept of vicarious liability is one of public policy, i.e. the person or organisation that has set in motion a particular activity which has caused harm should bear the loss rather than an innocent victim. In addition, one of the essential elements in the principle of vicarious liability is that the master is in control of the servant's activity. Unfortunately, there is no decided case on whether the NHS Trust would be liable to a third person for the negligence of a volunteer. Much would of course depend on the circumstances of the volunteer's negligence. It may be that the NHS Trust or its staff are themselves at fault in failing to provide adequate training or supervision, or have delegated an entirely inappropriate task to the volunteer. DHSS circular HM (72)6 states the following:

1. The Department's [i.e. the Department of Health] view is that hospital authorities should accept responsibility for the activities of all voluntary workers who are providing services for the hospitals. Arrangements should therefore be made between the hospital and volunteers or voluntary organisations which clearly define the scope and limits of the volunteers' activities and authorities should accept liability for the results of all such activities. Where voluntary workers are carrying out in good faith work in accordance with such arrangements the authority should act towards them as it would towards its paid staff, subject to any arrangement which the volunteers themselves or the voluntary organisation may prefer to make for personal insurance.
2. Some voluntary organisations insure their members against personal liability arising out of their work in hospital. This is a welcome precaution; but, for others and for individual volunteers, hospital authorities should not require an indemnity against liability arising out of such work. This could be an obstacle to the provision of voluntary service.

In applying the principle of this circular, much hangs on the meaning of 'in good faith'. It could be claimed, for example, that a volunteer who wilfully disobeyed the orders of the NHS Trust staff was not acting in good faith and therefore the NHS Trust should not be liable for his negligence. This would result in a considerable narrowing of the scope of liability which would not necessarily be so in the case of negligence by an employee. This circular has been replaced by HSG (92)15 which advises providers to define clearly the scope or limits of volunteers' activities and accept liability for the results of such activities.

Independent contractors, i.e. self-employed persons or company employees

SITUATION 5.7 AGENCY LIABILITY

Mary Downs is employed by a nursing agency and is often sent to work in National Health Service hospitals who call on the agency for additional staff to cover any crises. While she is assisting on the ITU she fails to notice that one of the monitoring machines has ceased to function and she then discovers that the patient has died. The relatives wish to bring a complaint or even take the NHS Trust or the agency to court.

In a case like this there may well be direct responsibility of the NHS Trust for failing to provide a machine that had an effective alarm system or had been satisfactorily maintained. If there is also negligence on the part of the agency nurse, does it make any difference that she is not an employee of the NHS Trust but is employed by the agency? Could the NHS Trust still be liable for her negligence? The answer would depend to a considerable extent on the agreement between the NHS Trust and the agency on the terms of employment of their staff. In the unlikely event that this has not been predetermined, the control test would be applied. The general or permanent employer has to shift the presumption of responsibility for the negligence of the employee on to the hirer. He can do this by showing that the control of the employee has passed to the hirer. In a health service context this should be relatively easy since an agency staff nurse sent to help out at an NHS hospital would automatically become part of the ward/department, would be under the control of the ward sister or departmental head, and would be subject to their supervision. In most cases, unless there is a clear agreement to the contrary, the NHS Trust would probably be vicariously liable for the negligence of the agency staff.

Direct liability

The Secretary of State has a statutory duty (i.e. one laid down by Act of Parliament) under the NHS Act 1977 to provide medical services throughout England and Wales and to direct the regional health (in England) and the district health authorities to exercise his functions. It has been argued that if any employee or independent contractor or agency person is negligent, then there is a breach of the duty under the Act and the NHS Trust is primarily liable, without having to establish all the elements of vicarious liability. This was the opinion of Lord Denning in the case described below.

CASE 5.10 A HAND OPERATION

The patient lost the use of his left hand and had severe pain and suffering as a result of negligent treatment following an operation on his hand. The evidence showed a *prima facie* case of negligence on the part of the persons in whose care the plaintiff was, although it was not clear whether this was to be imputed to Dr Fahrni, the full time assistant medical officer, or to the house surgeon, or to one of the nurses.

The Court of Appeal held that the hospital authority was liable. Lord Denning said:

> Whenever (hospital authorities) accept a patient for treatment, they must use reasonable care and skill to cure him of his ailment. The hospital authorities cannot, of course, do it by themselves. They have no ears to listen through the stethoscope, and no hands to hold the knife. They must do it by the staff which they employ, and, if their staff are negligent in giving the treatment, they are just as liable for that negligence as is anyone else who employs others to do his duties for him. ... I decline to enter into the question whether any of the surgeons were employed only under a contract for services, as distinct from a contract of service. The evidence is meagre enough in all conscience on that point, but the liability of the hospital authorities should not, and does not, depend on nice considerations of that sort. The plaintiff knew nothing of the terms on which they employed their staff. All he knew was that he was treated in the hospital by people whom the hospital authorities appointed, and the hospital authorities must be answerable for the way in which he was treated.
>
> (*Cassidy* v. *Ministry of Health* 1939 2 KB 14)

This suggests that the NHS Trust cannot delegate its duty by providing competent trained staff. It will always be primarily responsible for any negligence to the patients whether the negligent person is an employee, a volunteer, an independent contractor or an agency employee.

A recent case on this point is that of *Wilsher* v. *Essex Area Health Authority* CA 1986 3 All ER 801, discussed in full in Chapter 4. In this case it was held that there was no reason why, in certain circumstances, a health authority could not be directly liable to a plaintiff if it failed to provide sufficient or properly qualified and competent medical staff for the unit.

It must be pointed out, however, that even where it is possible to hold the NHS Trust directly liable for the harm caused to the patient under the principle set out by Lord Denning above, those individuals who were negligent could still face an action for their personal liability. In addition, if the NHS Trust pays out compensation as a result of its negligence it would be possible for it to seek an indemnity from the negligent person. At present this indemnity is rarely sought.

Indemnity from the employee at fault

This indemnity arises as a result of an implied term in the contract of employment, that the employee will indemnify the employer as a result of any losses caused by a breach of contract by the employee. In these circumstances this would be a breach of the term to use all reasonable care and skill.

CASE 5.11 FAMILY TROUBLE

Lister was employed as a lorry driver who worked with his father. He negligently ran down his father while backing the lorry in a yard. The father recovered damages from the employers on the grounds of their vicarious liability for the negligence of their employee. The employers' insurers then brought an action against the son for damages for breach of an implied term in his contract of employment that he would exercise reasonable care and skill in his driving. The son in his defence claimed that he was entitled to the benefit of any insurance which his employer either had or should have taken out. Therefore they could not claim an indemnity from him.

The House of Lords held by a majority decision that they could claim an indemnity from the employee and they refused to imply a term in the contract of employment that the employer would not seek to claim an indemnity from the negligent employee (*Lister* v. *Romford Ice and Cold Storage Co. Ltd* HL 1957 1 All ER 125).

CASE 5.12 ANAESTHETIC

The widow of a patient who died as a result of negligent hospital treatment sued for damages. The hospital board claimed an indemnity from Dr Wilkes, an inexperienced physician, who had administered the fatal anaesthetic under the instructions of Dr Sejrup, a house surgeon.

The Court of Appeal rejected this claim for an indemnity partly because the hospital itself was at fault (*Jones* v. *Manchester Corporation* CA 1952 2 All ER 125). In 1954 medical staff and health authorities agreed a procedure (set out in HM (54)32) whereby doctors and dentists would be personally accountable for their own negligence and would be members of defence organisations which would meet claims for compensation. The health authority would accept liability for the negligence of all other employees and in the event of a dispute between health authority and doctor/dentist, over the extent of liability, it would be split on a 50 : 50 basis.

A new scheme was introduced for claims lodged on or after 1 January 1990 (see HC (89)34). Health authorities became formally responsible for handling and financing claims of negligence against their medical and dental staff. Arrangements were introduced at regional level to share the legal costs and damages of large settlements between districts. Guidance in relation to NHS Trusts is contained in EL (90)195, EL (91) 19 and EL (92) 8.

As the size of awards increases, there are likely to be a variety of experiments in providing cover for exceptionally large settlements, which individual Trusts would be unable to meet from the revenue funds without serious reductions to the levels of patient care.

Questions and exercises

1 Assess the different forms of liability for negligence which could arise where harm is caused to a patient by a nurse who complains that the error was the result of pressure of work.
2 What is the difference between direct and vicarious liability?
3 Obtain a copy of your NHS Trust's policy on the use of volunteers and study in particular those parts which relate to liability for the negligence of volunteers.

4 In what way do you think that the liability of the NHS Trust for the safety of the volunteer differs from its liability for the safety of staff (see, in addition, Chapter 12)?

5 An employee can be liable for the negligent actions of another person if the employee should not have delegated a task to him or, having correctly delegated it, has failed to provide the appropriate level of supervision. Apply this principle to the role of the nurse manager in relation to junior trained staff, learners, volunteers and untrained assistants.

6 What is meant by the employer's right of indemnity from a negligent employee?

6   Progress of a civil claim: defences and remedies

This chapter answers questions relating to the likely course that any civil case against a nurse and/or NHS Trust might follow, the ways in which compensation in the civil courts is assessed, and the defences which may be available (see Fig. 6.1).

Civil proceedings: stages, hearing and outcome

Two issues

In any civil case there are two separate issues:

1. Is the defendant liable?
2. How much compensation is payable?

It is sometimes possible that one of these issues has been agreed, e.g. the defendant accepts liability but disagrees with the amount of compensation claimed by the victim, or that the amount of compensation which would be payable is agreed but the defendant refuses to accept liability for that sum. Sometimes both issues are disputed. Evidence will therefore be required on both issues.

A nurse is first likely to be asked by management to provide a statement on the events. Care should be taken in the completion of this and guidelines are given in Chapter 9.

Civil proceedings
  1. Stages followed.
  2. Hearing.
  3. Outcome.
Res ipsa loquitur
Compensation
  1. Special damages.
  2. General damages.
Defences
  1. Denial of facts.
  2. A missing element.
  3. Contributory negligence.
  4. Willing assumption of risk.
  5. Exemption from liability.
  6. Limitation of time.

Figure 6.1 Issues covered in Chapter 6.

1. Pre-action discovery.
2. Issue of writ.
3. Service of writ.
4. Statement of claim.
5. Defence.
6. Interrogatories and discovery.
7. Pre-trial review.
8. Payment in to court.
9. Hearing.
10. Outcome.
11. Enforcement of judgment.

Figure 6.2 Stages in civil proceedings.

If the victim has sought advice and has decided to commence an action, the next stages are set out below (see Fig. 6.2). These are stages in the High Court. The County Court, which deals with claims up to £50,000, is less formal and speedier but the stages are similar (see Chapter 1 for civil courts).

Pre-action disclosure of information (discovery)

The victim's representative will attempt to obtain all the relevant documents which can include medical and nursing case notes, X-rays and any other relevant evidence in order to ascertain if there is any justification for the action. Such documents are obtainable under the Supreme Court Act 1981, Section 33 (see Chapter 8). The nurse may well not be aware of this activity unless she herself is being personally sued or unless good communication ensures that she is kept in the picture. In *Harris* v. *Newcastle HA* 1989 2 All ER 273, the court allowed pre-trial disclosure of records relating to events 26 years before even though the Health Authority intended to plead that the case was out of time.

Writ is issued

This marks the beginning of the case. There are important time limits (discussed below) within which the writ is issued. The writ indicates that action is now being commenced. It is preceded by what is known as a letter before action, i.e. a warning by the plaintiff (usually the solicitor) that if there is no acceptance of the claim, then the legal battle will commence. The writ usually names the NHS Trust as the defendant but it is possible for an individual employee to be named as a party in the writ.

Service of the writ

This must be sent to the defendant within four months of its issue. (In the past there was a requirement for personal service, i.e. the writ had to be handed to the defendant personally. Now, however, the writ is sent to a known address.)

Statement of claim

This is the document which sets out the basis of the claim against the defendant and the main allegations, though not the evidence.

Defence

The allegations in the statement of claim will then be answered by the defence. This enables the plaintiff to decide whether he should proceed, and also what basic defences are being put forward.

Questions and disclosure of information (interrogatories and discovery)

By this stage the parties should have a good idea of the issues between them. However, some of the allegations in the statement of claim may not be clear and some of the defence contentions might similarly not be understood or may require expansion. In this case each party is entitled to put written questions to the other to clarify the issue. At this stage in the procedure it is also the practice for there to be discovery of documents (which have not been disclosed in a pre-action discovery), where each side produces a list of the relevant documents for the other's inspection. Those documents which are not privileged (i.e. exempt from disclosure) are then available for examination by the other side.

The drafting of the above documents, known as pleadings, is arranged by the respective parties' solicitors who often instruct counsel (i.e. barristers). A litigant may, however, represent himself personally. Strict time limits are laid down for the service and response to the documents.

Pre-trial review

Eventually there will be an assessment of the situation by the parties, together with a registrar or judge, account taken of the number of witnesses to attend, exchange of any experts' medical reports and, finally, the case will be set down for hearing. Because of these stages, several years may elapse between the negligent act and the court hearing.

Payment in to court

In some cases where there is dispute over the amount of compensation but liability is accepted, the defendant will probably be advised to pay a sum in settlement of the case in to court. If the plaintiff accepts this payment in then the defendant will be liable for the plaintiff's costs up to that point. The court will be notified that there has been a settlement of the case. A payment in may also be made where the defendant does not accept liability but he is not confident of winning the case and rather than risk losing and having to pay the costs of both sides he offers a sum in full and final settlement.

If the plaintiff decides that the payment in is not acceptable, the case will continue. In these circumstances the judge is not told that there has been a payment in. He will not therefore be influenced by that in determining the case and deciding what compensation to award. If he awards less than the payment in or if he decides there is no liability by the defendant, then the plaintiff will have to pay both the defendant's costs from the time of the payment in as well as his own, since, of course, had the plaintiff accepted that sum deemed reasonable in comparison with the judge's award, there would have been no time-consuming and costly court hearing. These costs may well exceed the amount of the award.

The hearing

Plaintiff's case

Examination in chief (questions put to the witness by the party that has called him to give evidence)
The plaintiff has the burden of establishing to the satisfaction of the judge, on a balance of probabilities, that there has been negligence or some other alleged civil wrong. The plaintiff will therefore be asked to give evidence first.

His witnesses will be sworn in, in turn, and will then give evidence under examination of the plaintiff's legal representative. This will usually be a barrister (counsel), instructed by the solicitor; but in the County Court a solicitor may conduct the case. Sometimes the plaintiff appears personally. This initial questioning is known as examination in chief. The witness cannot be asked leading questions when being examined in chief. Counsel will have before him the proof of the witness's statement to the solicitor and will take him through this to bring his evidence to the court.

Cross-examination

Counsel for the defence is then able to question the witness, i.e. cross-examine. Here the task is to discredit the evidence by showing that it is irrelevant, or that it is unreliable, or for some other reason is of no weight against the defendant. Leading questions are allowed when the witness is under cross-examination. The judge will, however, intervene to protect the witness from harassment (see Chapter 9 on giving evidence in court). At this stage the judge may wish to question the witness to clarify points on which he is not certain.

Re-examination

Finally, the side calling that witness has the chance of repairing any damage that the cross-examination has inflicted but the re-examination is confined to points which have arisen during cross-examination or under questioning by the judge. All the plaintiff's witnesses give evidence in this way. When the case for the plaintiff has ended the judge has the opportunity of ending the case at this point and of finding against the plaintiff on the grounds that he has not established a *prima facie* case and therefore the defence is not required to give evidence. He cannot, of course, decide at this point against the defendant because he has not as yet given evidence.

Defendant's case

If the case proceeds, the defence must put forward its witnesses who are examined in chief, cross-examined and then re-examined as previously described. If it is alleged that the nurse has been negligent, she will be called as a witness for the defence. Several years may have elapsed since the events and her recall may be limited or even nil. She is able to refresh her memory by referring to contemporaneous records and therefore she should refer to the case notes. In this situation she will appreciate the value of detailed, accurate, clear information of those events. Counsel who examines her in chief will have a copy of statements she has previously given. She should ensure that she has help in making this statement and prior to the court hearing she should be instructed on the procedure to be followed and some of the pitfalls she may encounter. Most of those who have appeared in court describe the event as particularly harrowing, and preparation is essential. Giving evidence in court is discussed further in Chapter 9.

Judge's summing up

After summaries by counsel the judge then has the task of making his judgment. This may be reserved, i.e. the parties are notified that they will be informed of the outcome, or it might be given immediately. The judge will determine both liability and damages (whichever are in dispute). The party having to pay costs will usually depend upon the outcome, i.e. the loser pays the costs of both sides. There is no jury in a civil case (except very rarely in defamation cases).

Res ipsa loquitur

In certain cases inferences can be made from the facts about the existence of negligence. If the plaintiff can establish that it is a *res ipsa loquitur* situation ('the matter speaks for itself'), then the defendant can be asked to show how the incident occurred without negligence on his part. The plaintiff would have to show the following factors to raise a presumption of *res ipsa loquitur*:

1. What has occurred would not normally occur if reasonable care were taken.
2. The events were under the control or management of the defendants.
3. The defendant has not offered any reasonable explanation for what occurred.

The most obvious example is leaving a swab inside a patient, or amputating the wrong limb. This procedure gives the plaintiff a technical advantage which is very necessary when he is ignorant of the actual events which caused harm. Further examples are considered in Chapter 12. If the defendant fails to give a reasonable explanation of the events, then the court can draw the inference that there was negligence.

Compensation in civil proceedings for negligence

Nurses who work with the victims of road accidents or on orthopaedic wards may often find themselves being questioned by the longer-stay patients who are claiming compensation for their injuries. This question also arises where the nurse herself is the victim of an accident at work and she is considering bringing a court action. Nurses sometimes meet patients who are hesitant to undertake all the necessary physiotherapy lest the compensation will be reduced because they are seen to have made a full recovery.

SITUATION 6.1 LESLIE'S LEG

Leslie was travelling on his motorbike when a car started to overtake him. Unfortunately, a lorry was coming in the opposite direction and the vehicle pulled in to the side, knocking Leslie off. Leslie was admitted to the orthopaedic ward from accident and emergency. He suffered a serious compound fracture. The prognosis was that he was unlikely to make a complete recovery but could anticipate further problems with the leg, a slight limp and a vulnerability to arthritis later on. He had been advised not to expect to return to his existing job (a PE instructor) for at least nine months. How will his likely compensation be calculated?

1. Special damages: expenses and losses to the date of judgment.
2. General damages
   (a) non-pecuniary loss
          pain and suffering;
          loss of amenity;
   (b) pecuniary loss
          loss of earnings;
          loss of earning capacity;
          cost of future care and expenses;
          interest.

Figure 6.3 Headings of compensation.

Special damages

Leslie will first be entitled to receive special damages. These are amounts to cover specific losses which have already been suffered and where the amount can therefore be accurately stated. For example, the loss and damage to his motor bike, damage to his clothing, loss of wages up to the present day. Interest is allowed on the items.

General damages

The headings under which such damages are calculated are shown in Fig. 6.3.

Non-pecuniary loss (i.e. non-financial loss)

1. *Pain and suffering*: this is to cover the pain from the injury itself, as well as from any consequential medical treatment and worry about the effects of the injury on the patient's lifestyle. It could also include damages for the mental suffering resulting from the fact that the person's life has been shortened. (Administration of Justice Act 1982, Section 1(1) (a) introduced this form of compensation since there is no longer any compensation for the actual shortening of life itself. This used to be known as 'loss of expectation of life' and was abolished by this Act.)
2. *Loss of amenity*: Leslie will be able to recover additional compensation if it is established that his activities will be restricted because of the injuries to his leg. Clearly, if his leg had to be amputated then he would recover an additional sum for that loss.

These non-pecuniary losses are notoriously difficult to calculate. How can money ever be an adequate compensation for blindness or loss of the ability to have children or to enjoy normal activities? The answer is that it cannot be. However, since there is no other form of compensation the non-pecuniary loss has to be converted into pecuniary form. Judges follow precedents in calculating the awards. They examine decisions in preceding cases, taking into account any relevant differences between the present case and the earlier cases and allowing for inflation. A judge's award is subject to appeal.

Pecuniary loss

1. *Loss of earnings*: Leslie's loss of future earnings would be calculated by determining his net annual loss multiplied by a figure to cover the number of years the disability will last. The figure takes into account the fact that the compensation will be paid out all at once rather than each week or month over the next few years.
2. *Loss of earning capacity*: because of his injury Leslie may never be able to work as a PE instructor again. Alternatively, he may retain his job initially but with the risk that if he loses it he might never get similar paid work again because of his disability. He is entitled to be compensated for this risk.
3. *Expenses*: Leslie would also be entitled to recover reasonable expenses in getting to and from hospital, medical and similar expenses (e.g. physiotherapy) and, in some circumstances, domestic help.
4. *Interest*: interest is payable on the pecuniary loss already suffered at half the present rate and on the non-pecuniary loss at 2 per cent.
5. *Deductions*: deductions are made in respect of the value of certain social security benefits which are paid to the compensation recovery unit.

Interim payments can be made by the Court under Order 29 of the Rules of the Supreme Court. The plaintiff can apply for an interim payment at any time after the writ has been served on the defendant. Thus where the defendant has admitted liability but disputes the amount of damages payable, the court could make an order for an interim payment to be made. Because of the uncertainty of prognosis there is the power for an order of provisional damages for personal injuries to be made if there is a chance that at some time in the future the injured person will, as a result of the act or omission, develop some serious disease or suffer some serious deterioration in his physical or mental condition (Supreme Court Act 1981, Section 32A and Rules of Supreme Court 0.37, pp. 7–10). Provisional damages in relation to exposure to asbestos were awarded in *Hurditch* v. *Sheffield HA* 1989 2 All ER 869. Where large settlements are to be paid, parties often agree a structured settlement whereby an annuity is purchased with part of the lump sum, thus providing an income to the plaintiff for life.

CASE 6.1 A LIVING NIGHTMARE

Sally Kralj was admitted to hospital for the expected birth of twins. In the course of delivery without the use of anaesthetic, the consultant obstetrician put his arm inside Mrs Kralj in an effort to turn the second twin, who was lying in a transverse position, by manual manipulation of its head. There was expert opinion that such treatment was horrific and wholly unacceptable and must have caused the patient excruciating pain. The obstetrician's efforts were unsuccessful and the baby was later delivered by caesarian section. The child was born with severe disabilities which resulted from the obstetrician's attempt to turn it and it died eight weeks later. Liability was admitted and the only issue was how much compensation should be paid.

The court held that the concept of aggravated damages was not appropriate to claims arising out of medical negligence. Nevertheless, the compensatory damages could be increased if the impact of what had happened to the patient was such that it would be more difficult for the patient to recover. She was also entitled to damages for nervous shock as the result of learning what happened to the child and of seeing it, and was further entitled to have those damages increased if because of her grief at the loss of the child it would be more difficult for her to recover from her own injuries. If medical negligence resulted in the death of a child during pregnancy the financial loss suffered by the mother in replacing the dead child was not too remote to be recoverable as damages. General damages of £10,500 were awarded (*Kralj* v. *McGrath* 1986 1 All ER 54).

An example of the assessment of compensation is shown in Fig. 6.4.

Defending the nurse

There are many situations in which allegations made against the nurse are completely unjustified and against which the nurse can exonerate herself. In other situations the nurse may be at fault but the patient may still be unable to obtain compensation for

---

A boy aged 10 at the date of hearing was born suffering from asthetoid spastic quadriplegia. The defendants were held liable for his condition as a result of negligence at the time of his birth when he suffered from cerebral hypoxia during a prolonged labour. He had a normal expectation of life but was permanently paralysed in all four limbs and suffered almost continuous movements of the limbs and spasms of the trunk. He could see and hear, but not speak.

Damages were agreed at £347,546 made up as follows:

		£
1.	Loss of amenity	60,000
2.	Future loss of earnings	30,000
3.	Future care	
	(a) Accommodation (removal and conversion)	35,000
	(b) Motoring expenses (converted van and running expenses)	22,400
	(c) Medical supplies, equipment and aids	22,760
	(d) Additional heating	4,200
	(e) Holidays, special clothing, cleaning	5,516
	(f) Personal and domestic	121,170
4.	Physiotherapy	14,000
5.	Gadgetry (microcomputer)	15,000
6.	Special damages	7,500
7.	Administration expenses (private trust)	10,000
		347,546

Taken from Kemp and Kemp, *The Quantum of Damages.*

Figure 6.4 Example of an assessment of compensation (*Krishnamurthy* v. *East Anglia Regional Health Authority* 23 January 1985).

various reasons. This section looks at the defences open to a nurse in civil actions for negligence.

Denial of facts

It often happens that when things go wrong it is one person's word against another. The patient might complain that the nurse has been negligent but the nurse might be able to show that the events were not as the patient describes. Many court cases are simply disputes over facts. Where only two people are involved, with no other witnesses and no other circumstantial evidence, then if such a case comes before the courts the judge will have to decide on the basis of the evidence in court and the way the parties stand up to cross-examination which account of the events is acceptable.

In civil cases the burden is on the plaintiff to establish, on a balance of probabilities, that the defendant has been negligent.

Negligence: the elements

Even where the facts are not disputed it might still be possible for an action for negligence to be defended on the grounds that one of the essential elements is missing. From Chapter 3 it will be recalled that to succeed in a negligence case it is necessary for the plaintiff to establish that a duty of care was owed by the defendant, that the defendant was in breach of this duty, and that this breach caused reasonably foreseeable harm to the plaintiff.

Contributory negligence

SITUATION 6.2 WALKING AIDS

Fred, who has recently had an operation for a fractured leg, has been receiving help from the physiotherapist in walking with crutches. Fred asks a nursing auxiliary who has only just come onto the ward for help in going to the toilet. She is not aware that Fred has been told not to try to walk yet unless he is accompanied by a qualified person. She assists him out of bed and onto the crutches. As she does so the crutches slip from under Fred and he falls to the ground, sustaining another fracture.

In this situation the nursing auxiliary or the ward management are clearly at fault in allowing Fred out of bed in these circumstances. However, Fred is also at fault. He should have followed instructions. Fred's liability depends to a large extent on his level of understanding, how clear the instructions were to him, and how reasonable it was to expect him to have waited for experienced help in using the crutches. If he were to sue the

Section 1 (i) Where any person suffers damage as the result partly of his own fault and partly of any other person or persons a claim in respect of that damage shall not be defeated by reason of the fault of the person suffering the damage, but the damages recoverable in respect thereof shall be reduced to such an extent as the court thinks just and equitable having regard to the claimant's share in responsibility for the damage.

Figure 6.5 Law Reform (Contributory Negligence) Act 1945 Section 1.

NHS Trust and its staff they may well defend themselves on the grounds that he was partly at fault in not taking care of himself. This defence is known as a defence of contributory negligence. The defendant is saying to the plaintiff: you failed to take care of yourself and that has led to or increased the harm that you have suffered. If the judge is satisfied that the defendant has succeeded in this defence he is able to reduce the compensation by the extent to which he considers the plaintiff's fault has contributed to the harm. The wording of Section 1 of the Law Reform (Contributory Negligence) Act 1945 is shown in Fig. 6.5.

CASE 6.2 NO SEAT BELT

Mr Froom was driving his car carefully at a speed of 30–35 mph with his wife sitting beside him and his daughter in the back seat. The front seats were fitted with seat belts, but neither Mr nor Mrs Froom were wearing them. Unfortunately, Mr Froom's car was struck head on by a car travelling at speed in the opposite direction and on the wrong side of the road as it had pulled out to overtake a line of traffic.

The trial judge decided that failure to wear a seat belt was not contributory negligence. The defendant appealed to the Court of Appeal and won his appeal. Lord Denning emphasised that where the damage to the plaintiff would not have been reduced by failure to wear the seat belt, then there should be no reduction of compensation, but where, as here, the injuries would have been reduced by wearing a seat belt there should be a reduction of compensation. In Mr Froom's case the injuries to the head and chest would have been prevented by wearing a seat belt. His finger would have been broken anyway and therefore there was no reduction on that account. The overall deduction of compensation for Mr Froom's contributory negligence was held to be 20 per cent (*Froom* v. *Butcher* 1975 3 All ER 520). (This case was heard before the wearing of front seat belts was compulsory.)

Reductions of compensation on grounds of contributory negligence can vary from 95 per cent to 5 per cent. When it is larger, then there is held to be no liability on the part of the defendant; when it is smaller it is considered to be too insignificant to count. To succeed, the defendant has to establish that the plaintiff failed to take reasonable care of himself and that this failure contributed to the harm he suffered, or increased it.

Contributory negligence and children

Lord Denning has said:

> A very young child cannot be guilty of contributory negligence. An older child may be; but it depends on the circumstances. A judge should only find a child guilty of contributory negligence if he or she is of such an age as reasonably to be expected to take precautions for his or her own safety: and then he or she is only to be found guilty if blame should be attached to him or her.

In the same case Lord Justice Salmon said:

> The question as to whether the plaintiff can be said to have been guilty of contributory negligence depends on whether any ordinary child of 13½ years could be expected to have done any more than this child did. I say 'any ordinary child'. I do not mean a paragon of prudence; nor do I mean a scatter-brain child; but the ordinary girl of 13½ [the age of the child in that case].
>
> (*Gough v. Thorne* CA 1966 3 All ER 398)

Willing assumption of risk (*volenti non fit injuria*)

Sometimes, where there is a known risk, the possibility of this taking place is accepted and the defendant is not liable. The most obvious example is dangerous sports where both players and spectators are at some risk. If that risk occurs it is assumed that there will be no court action but that the risk has been willingly accepted. For example, in a rugby match it is possible that a player may be seriously injured, even though no rules have been broken and there is no criminal act. This is a risk of the game and is accepted by the players. If, of course, the rules have been broken and thus resulted in injuries, then the injured player may well have an action for assault.

In the health service context, the agreement by the patient that treatment can proceed counts not only as consent to what would otherwise count as a trespass to the person, but it is also an acceptance of the possibility that those hazards which are an inextricable risk of that particular treatment could occur. Consent, however, does not imply consent to the risk that the professional will be negligent (see Chapter 7 on consent).

SITUATION 6.3 BLOOD DONOR

Rachel had been giving blood for many years. She was summoned on one occasion to the session. As the needle was inserted and the canula put in place she felt an appalling pain. She shrieked and the needle was quickly withdrawn and a new painless site was found. After the session Rachel found that it was very difficult to move her hand, arm and fingers. She was examined by a doctor who sent her for tests and eventually she was told that a very rare damage to the nerve had occurred. However, she was assured that with physiotherapy she would soon recover full function. Unfortunately, this did not prove to be true, she was eventually forced to take early retirement on the grounds of ill health, and did not recover full arm or hand movement. She sought advice about suing the doctor and was given an expert's report that such a rare event could occur without any negligence on the part of the doctor, so that there was no point in suing either the doctor or the health authority. However, Rachel argued that if she had known of the risk she would not have agreed to give blood unless she had been given an assurance that in the event of the risk taking place she would have received compensation.

As the law stands at present, unless Rachel can show negligence by the professional staff or the employer, she would be unable to recover compensation in court. We do not have a system of no-fault liability. As a volunteer she can be assumed to have accepted the possibility of those risks occurring, although she may well be able to show that there was a breach of the duty owed to her as a volunteer if certain risks were not pointed out to her. The Pearson Report on compensation for personal injuries recommended that there should be an acceptance of no-fault liability for volunteers in medical research. These recommendations have not yet been implemented and it could be argued that if they ever are they should be extended to cover such situations as donation of blood. In such situations, many NHS Trusts would make an *ex gratia* payment, i.e. a payment without any acceptance or implication of liability on its part.

To establish a defence of willing assumption of risk the defendant has to show that the plaintiff knew of the risk, willingly consented to run it, and waived any right to sue for compensation. If it is successfully pleaded it operates as a total defence.

Sometimes employers have tried to rely on this defence when sued by an employee for injuries at work. For example, it has been said that back injuries are an occupational hazard for nurses; all psychiatric nurses accept the risk of physical violence; CSSD assistants are likely to suffer from 'sharp' injuries as an occupational hazard. However, it is quite clear that where there is a failure of the employer in his duty to care for the employee's safety, then the defence of willing assumption of risk will not prevail.

Exemption from liability

NHS Trust premises are a blaze of exemption notices: 'no responsibility is taken for cars parked in this area'; 'the "X" NHS Trust accepts no liability for patients' property'. How effective are these notices if the NHS Trust or its employees are negligent? Can a patient be persuaded to sign a form saying that he will not hold the 'X' NHS Trust liable in any respect? Sometimes an NHS Trust responds to a complaint by asking for a declaration that if the complaint is to be pursued and an investigation conducted, then the NHS Trust requires an assurance that there will be no civil action. Can such a declaration be held against the person who signed? The answer to these questions is to a considerable extent given by reference to the Unfair Contract Terms Act 1977. This Act prevents anyone in the course of any business activity (and this covers professional, local, and public authority activity) from exempting himself from negligence if that negligence gives rise to personal injury or death. Any agreement, notice or clause to that effect is void (see Fig. 6.6).

SITUATION 6.4 NO LIABILITY

A surgeon said 'I am prepared to carry out upon you a very risky operation and I want you to sign that you will exempt me from all blame if anything goes wrong.' The patient, in his desire to have the operation, signed the form but unfortunately the surgeon made a very careless error which no competent surgeon would have made, leaving the patient severely crippled.

Is the patient bound by that form? The answer is no. The Act prevents the surgeon relying upon that form as a defence against the patient. He cannot exclude or restrict his liability for death or personal injury resulting from his negligence. What about damage to or loss of property – do the same principles apply? The answer is no. Under the Unfair Contract Terms Act 1977 an exemption for damage to or loss of property is valid if it is reasonable (see Fig. 6.6).

For further discussion upon this see Chapter 25.

Limitation of time

Civil case of negligence: the general principles

Most civil court actions must be brought within a certain length of time. The time limit for actions concerning personal injury and death is three years from the cause of action arising. The issue of the writ marks the beginning of the court action and it is the time that elapses from the cause arising to the day the writ is issued which is critical.

Knowledge of the harm

What, however, if a patient did not even realise that he was suffering from the effects of someone's negligence in that time? It used to be law that this was the patient's hard luck and if he was out of time for whatever reason then he was barred from proceeding with the case. The injustice of this rule is very easy to see from cases involving such long-term diseases as pneumoconiosis, asbestosis, and similar conditions. The law was therefore amended so that the period did not start to run until the plaintiff had knowledge of the facts shown in Fig. 6.7.

The potential plaintiff cannot, however, simply turn a blind eye to knowledge which any reasonable person would acquire from the facts around him. If, however, he had no knowledge of the facts then he is not barred from proceeding.

SITUATION 6.5 DELAY

Claire French was admitted for an appendectomy. The operation was performed successfully and she was discharged. From time to time, however, she complained of violent stomach pain for which she took very strong pain killers. Some six years after the first operation she was admitted to hospital in intense agony and no pain killer could relieve it. The consultant was reluctant to operate since he could not identify any possible cause for which surgery was the solution.

1. Scope of Part I

1. For the purposes of this part of this Act, 'negligence' means the breach:
   (a) of any obligation, arising from the express or implied terms of a contract, to take reasonable care or exercise skill in the performance of the contract;
   (b) of any common law duty to take reasonable care or exercise reasonable skill (but not stricter duty);
   (c) of the common duty of care imposed by the Occupiers' Liability Act 1957 or the Occupiers' Liability Act (Northern Ireland) 1957.
2. This part of this Act is subject to Part III; and in relation to contracts, the operation of sections 2 to 4 and 7 is subject to the exceptions made by Schedule 1.
3. In the case of both contract and tort, sections 2 to 7 apply (except where the contrary is stated in section 6 (4)) only to business liability, that is liability for breach of obligations or duties arising
   (a) from things done or to be done by a person in the course of a business (whether his own business or another's); or
   (b) from the occupation of premises used for business purposes of the occupier; and references to liability are to be read accordingly.
4. In relation to any breach of duty or obligation, it is immaterial for any purpose of this part of this Act whether the breach was inadvertent or intentional, or whether liability for it arises directly or vicariously.

2. Negligence liability

1. A person cannot by reference to any contract term or to a notice given to persons generally or to particular persons exclude or restrict his liability for death or personal injury resulting from negligence.
2. In the case of other loss or damage, a person cannot so exclude or restrict his liability for negligence except in so far as the term or notice satisfies the requirement of reasonableness.
3. Where a contract term or notice purports to exclude or restrict liability for negligence a person's agreement to or awareness of it is not of itself to be taken as indicating his voluntary acceptance of any risk.

11. The 'reasonableness' test

3. In relation to a notice (not being a notice having contractual effect), the requirement of reasonableness under this Act is that it should be fair and reasonable to allow reliance on it, having regard to all the circumstances obtaining when the liability arose or (but for the notice) would have arisen.
4. Where by reference to a contract term or notice a person seeks to restrict liability to a specified sum of money, and the question arises (under this or any other Act) whether the term or notice satisfies the requirement of reasonableness, regard shall be had in particular (but without prejudice to subsection (2) above in the case of contract terms) to:
   (a) the resources which he could expect to be available to him for the purpose of meeting the liability should it arise; and
   (b) how far it was open to him to cover himself by insurance.
5. It is for those claiming that a contract term or notice satisfies the requirements of reasonableness to show that it does.

14. Interpretation of Part I

In this part of this Act:
'business' includes a profession and the activities of any government department or local or public authority;...

Figure 6.6 Unfair Contract Terms Act 1977.

(a) that the injury in question was significant;
(b) that the injury was attributable in whole or in part to the act or omission which is alleged to constitute negligence;
(c) the identity of the defendant; and
(d) the identity of any other defendant.

The term 'significant' is further defined as where 'the person whose date of knowledge is in question would reasonably have considered it sufficiently serious to justify instituting proceeding against a defendant who did not dispute liability...' Limitation Act 1980.

Figure 6.7 Limitation Act 1980: definition of 'knowledge'.

However, he eventually did so and it was then discovered that a swab had been left behind in the previous operation. The consultant was completely open with Claire about his findings and assured her that from now on she should not get any pain. She felt that she should be compensated for the fact that she had already suffered much pain and had had to endure the risks, pain and suffering of a second operation. Is she entitled to obtain compensation?

As a result of the changes to the Limitation Act she would not be barred on the grounds of exceeding the time limit which would run from the time she was informed of the cause of her suffering.

Judge's discretion to extend time limit

In addition the judge has the discretion to allow a case to proceed which would otherwise be outside the time limit where it would be just to the plaintiff to permit him to continue.

Extension on other grounds

Where minors under 18 years of age have suffered personal injury there is no time barrier to bringing an action until they reach the age of 21 years (see Chapter 13 on paediatrics). The same principle applies to the mentally disordered whose disorder prevents them from bringing an action within the appropriate time limits. The time limits do not commence until the disorder ceases.

Questions and exercises

1 Take any of the cases or situations on liability in negligence described in this book and work out the stages which the case would follow and the nature of the evidence which would be required at the hearing.
2 What is meant by *res ipsa loquitur*? In what situations in health care do you think it could apply?

3 What is the difference between pecuniary loss and non-pecuniary loss as a result of a civil wrong? How is compensation for the latter calculated?

4 What is meant by contributory negligence? What are the principles upon which the judge works in deciding the level of deduction of compensation? (see Fig. 6.5).

5 Are there any tasks that you perform which are likely to cause harm to you? Do you consider the principle of *volenti non fit injuria* applies to any of them and if so why?

6 Examine the notices in your hospital which disclaim any responsibility for loss or damage. Consider any ways in which they might not be completely effective in the light of the Unfair Contract Terms Act 1977.

7 Consent to treatment and informing the patient

The basic principles

Any adult, mentally competent person has the right in law to consent to any touching of his person. If he is touched without consent or other lawful justification, then the person has the right of action in the civil courts of suing for trespass to the person – battery where the person is actually touched, assault where he fears that he will be touched. The fact that consent has been given will normally prevent a successful action for trespass. However, it may not prevent an action for negligence arising on the ground that there was a breach of the duty of care to inform the patient. This chapter explores both these aspects of consent and looks at the information which must be legally given to the patient and other questions which arise on informing the patient. Reference should be made to Chapter 13 on consent in relation to minors – those under 18 years, to Chapter 20 on consent in relation to the mentally disordered, to Chapter 19 on consent in relation to the elderly, and to Chapter 17 in relation to consent to operations.

How should consent be given?

Figure 7.1 illustrates the different forms of giving consent. As far as the law is concerned there is no specific requirement that consent for treatment should be given in any

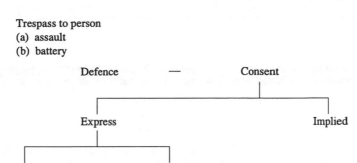

Trespass to person
(a) assault
(b) battery

Figure 7.1 Various forms of consent.

particular way. They are all equally valid. However, they vary considerably in their value as evidence in proving that consent was given. Consent in writing is by far the best form of evidence and is therefore the preferred method of obtaining the consent of the patient when any procedure involving some risk is contemplated. Advice and model forms are provided by the Department of Health (HG (90) 20). Reference should also be made to the NHS Management Executive's 'Guide to Consent for Examination and Treatment'.

Consent, it should be noted, is not a defence to an offence of causing actual bodily harm under the Offences Against the Person Act 1861 (see *R. v. Brown and others* House of Lords TLR 12 March 1993).

Consent in writing

Some specimen forms of consent to an operation, currently used in the health service, are shown in Fig. 7.2. They give the surgeon the right to undertake other procedures which are deemed necessary. However, unless these are related to the operation for which consent has been expressly given, or can be justified out of necessity, they will not be covered by this consent. For example, liability has been accepted for a surgeon who, while operating on the patient's abdomen, saw that the patient had an ingrowing toe nail and remedied that. The surgeon had not received the patient's consent for this and it was thus a trespass to the person.

If, on the other hand, the surgeon had noticed a life-threatening tumour while performing an operation for a hernia, to remove that may be justifiable if it is of urgent necessity to save the patient's life.

Nurses are often aware that the patient who has put his signature to a consent form has very little idea of what he has given consent to. Often the ward round where the doctor obtains the signature of the patients to operations is followed by the nurse's round explaining what the patient has agreed to. Where does the nurse stand if she is aware that the patient has signed a form without realising what is involved?

CONSENT FORM

For medical or dental investigation, treatment or operation

Health Authority	Patient's Surname . . . .
Hospital	Other Names . . . .
Unit Number.	Date of Birth . . . .
	Sex: *(please tick)* Male ☐ Female ☐

DOCTORS OR DENTISTS *(This part to be completed by doctor or dentist. See notes on the reverse)*

TYPE OF OPERATION INVESTIGATION OR TREATMENT

I confirm that I have explained the operation investigation or treatment, and such appropriate options as are available and the type of anaesthetic, if any (general/regional/sedation) proposed, to the patient in terms which in my judgement are suited to the understanding of the patient and/or to one of the parents or guardians of the patient

Signature. . . . .   Date . . . /. . . /. . . . .

Name of doctor or dentist . . . .

PATIENT/PARENT/GUARDIAN

1. Please read this form and the notes overleaf very carefully.

2. If there is anything that you don't understand about the explanation, or if you want more information, you should ask the doctor or dentist.

3. Please check that all the information on the form is correct. If it is, and you understand the explanation, then sign the form.

I am the patient/parent/guardian *(delete as necessary)*

I agree	■ to what is proposed which has been explained to me by the doctor/dentist named on this form.
	■ to the use of the type of anaesthetic that I have been told about.
I understand	■ that the procedure may not be done by the doctor/dentist who has been treating me so far.
	■ that any procedure in addition to the investigation or treatment described on this form will only be carried out if it is necessary and in my best interests and can be justified for medical reasons.
I have told	■ the doctor or dentist about any additional procedures I would <u>not</u> wish to be carried out straightaway without my having the opportunity to consider them first.

Signature   . . . .

Name   . . . .

Address   . . . .

(if not the patient)   . . . .

. . . .

NOTES TO:

Doctors, Dentists

A patient has a legal right to grant or withhold consent prior to examination or treatment. Patients should be given sufficient information, in a way they can understand, about the proposed treatment and the possible alternatives. Patients must be allowed to decide whether they will agree to the treatment and they may refuse or withdraw consent to treatment at any time. The patient's consent to treatment should be recorded on this form (further guidance is given in HC(90)22 *(A Guide to Consent for Examination or Treatment.)*

Patients

- The doctor or dentist is here to help you. He or she will explain the proposed treatment and what the alternatives are. You can ask any questions and seek further information. You can refuse the treatment.

- You may ask for a relative, or friend, or a nurse to be present.

- Training health professionals is essential to the continuation of the health service and improving the quality of care. Your treatment may provide an important opportunity for such training, where necessary under the careful supervision of a senior doctor or dentist. You may refuse any involvement in a formal training programme without this adversely affecting your care and treatment.

Figure 7.2 Specimen forms of consent. Appendix A(1) medical or dental investigation, treatment or operation.

CONSENT FORM

For sterilisation or vasectomy

Health Authority . . . .   Patient's Surname . . . .

Hospital . . . .   Other Names . . . .

Unit Number. . . . .   Date of Birth . . . .

Sex: *(please tick)*   Male ☐   Female ☐

DOCTORS *(This part to be completed by doctor. See notes on the reverse)*

TYPE OF OPERATION: STERILISATION OR VASECTOMY

Complete this part of the form

I confirm that I have explained the procedure and any anaesthetic (general/regional) required, to the patient in terms which in my judgement are suited to his/her understanding.

Signature. . . . .   Date. . . . /. . . /. . . . .

Name of doctor . . . .

PATIENT

1. Please read this form very carefully.

2. If there is anything that you don't understand about the explanation, or if you want more information, you should ask the doctor.

3. Please check that all the information on the form is correct. If it is, and you understand the explanation, then sign the form.

I am the patient

I agree	■ to have this operation, which has been explained to me by the doctor named on this form.
	■ to have the type of anaesthetic that I have been told about.
I understand	■ that the operation may not be done by the doctor who has been treating me so far.
	■ that the aim of the operation is to stop me having any children and it might not be possible to reverse the effects of the operation.
	■ that sterilisation/vasectomy can sometimes fail, and that there is a very small chance that I may become fertile again after some time.
	■ that any procedure in addition to the investigation or treatment described on this form will only be carried out if it is necessary and in my best interests and can be justified for medical reasons.
I have told	■ the doctor about any additional procedures I would <u>not</u> wish to be carried out straightaway without my having the opportunity to consider them first.
For vasectomy I understand	■ that I may remain fertile or become fertile again after some time.
	■ that I will have to use some other contraceptive method until 2 tests in a row show that I am not producing sperm, if I do not want to father any children.
Signature	. . . .

NOTES TO:

Doctors

A patient has a legal right to grant or withhold consent prior to examination or treatment. Patients should be given sufficient information, in a way they can understand, about the proposed treatment and the possible alternatives. Patients must be allowed to decide whether they will agree to the treatment and they may refuse or withdraw consent to treatment at any time. The patient's consent to treatment should be recorded on this form (further guidance is given in HC(90)22 *(A Guide to Consent for Examination or Treatment.)*

Patients

■ The doctor is here to help you. He or she will explain the proposed procedure, which you are entitled to refuse. You can ask any questions and seek further information.

■ You may ask for a relative, or friend, or a nurse to be present.

■ Training health professionals is essential to the continuation of the health service and improving the quality of care. Your treatment may provide an important opportunity for such training, where necessary under the careful supervision of a senior doctor. You may refuse any involvement in a formal training programme without this adversely affecting your care and treatment.

Figure 7.2 Specimen forms of consent. Appendix A(2) sterilisation or vasectomy.

CONSENT FORM

For treatment by a health professional other than doctors or dentists

Health Authority . . . .   Patient's Surname . . . .

Hospital . . . .   Other Names . . . .

Unit Number . . . .   Date of Birth . . . .

Sex: *(please tick)*   Male ☐   Female ☐

HEALTH PROFESSIONAL *(This part to be completed by health professional. See notes on the reverse)*

TYPE OF TREATMENT PROPOSED

Complete this part of the form

I confirm that I have explained the treatment proposed and such appropriate options as are available to the patient in terms which in my judgement are suited to the understanding of the patient and/or to one of the parents or guardians of the patient.

Signature. . . . .   Date. . . . /. . . /. . . . .

Name of health professional . . . .

Job title of health professional . . . .

PATIENT/PARENT/GUARDIAN

1. Please read this form and the notes overleaf very carefully.

2. If there is anything that you don't understand about the explanation, or if you want more information, you should ask the health professional who has explained the treatment proposed.

3. Please check that all the information on the form is correct. If it is, and you understand the treatment proposed, then sign the form.

I am the patient/parent/guardian *(delete as necessary)*

I agree   ■ to what is proposed which has been explained to me by the health professional named on this form.

Signature . . . .

Name . . . .

Address . . . .

(if not the patient) . . . .

. . . .

NOTES TO:

Health Professionals, other than doctors or dentists

A patient has a legal right to grant or withhold consent prior to examination or treatment. Patients should be given sufficient information, in a way they can understand, about the proposed treatment and the possible alternatives. Patients must be allowed to decide whether they will agree to the treatment and they may refuse or withdraw consent to treatment at any time. The patient's consent to treatment should be recorded on this form (further guidance is given in HC(90)22 *(A Guide to Consent for Examination or Treatment.)*

Patients

■ The health professional named on this form is here to help you. He or she will explain the proposed treatment and what the alternatives are. You can ask any questions and seek further information. You can refuse the treatment.

■ You may ask for a relative, or friend, or another member of staff to be present.

■ Training health professionals is essential to the continuation of the health service and improving the quality of care. Your treatment may provide an important opportunity for such training, where necessary under the careful supervision of a fully qualified health professional. You may refuse any involvement in a formal training programme without this adversely affecting your care and treatment.

Figure 7.2 Specimen forms of consent. Appendix A (3) treatment by health professional other than doctors or dentists.

Medical or dental treatment of a patient who is unable to consent because of mental disorder

Health Authority . . . . Patient's Surname . . . .

Hospital . . . . Other Names . . . .

Unit Number . . . . Date of Birth . . . .

Sex: *(please tick)*   Male ☐   Female ☐

NOTE   If there is any doubt about the ability of a mentally disordered patient to give consent to treatment, the Registered Medical Practictioner in charge of the patient should be asked to interview the patient. If, in his or her opinion, the patient is able to give valid consent to medical, dental or surgical treatment, he or she should be asked to do so and no-one further need be involved.

If the patient is considered unable to give valid consent it is considered good practice to discuss any proposed treatment with the next of kin.

For surgical or dental operations the form should also be signed by the Registered Medical or Dental Practitioner who carries out the treatment.

DOCTORS/DENTISTS

Describe investigation, operation or treatment proposed.

_____

(Complete this part of the form)

In my opinion . . . . is not capable of giving consent to treatment. In my opinion the treatment proposed is in his/her best interests and should be given.

The patient's next of kin have/have not been so informed. *(delete as necessary)*

Date: . . . .

Signature   Signature

. . . .

Name of Registered Medical Practitioner   Name of Second Registered Medical/Dental
in charge of the patient: Practitioner who is providing treatment:

. . . .

Figure 7.2 Specimen forms of consent. Appendix B medical or dental treatment of a patient who is unable to consent because of mental disorder.

SITUATION 7.1 IGNORANCE IS BLISS

Susan Smith had signed the form to consent to an operation for the investigation of a lump in her breast. She was very distressed to be undergoing surgery and ever since she had come into hospital had been able to understand and take in very little of what was said to her. The doctor had explained that a biopsy would be carried out and if that was positive further surgery would be undertaken. It was apparent to Staff Nurse Rachel Bryant that Susan had very little awareness that a radical mastectomy could be in the offing.

Where does Staff Nurse Bryant stand in relation to the proposed operation? The staff nurse has a legal duty to the patient and if she knows that the patient did not understand what she signed or failed to take in the information given by the doctor she should arrange for the doctor to return and give the patient more information. From the court's point of view the fact that the patient has signed the form and expressly agreed that the 'nature and extent of the operation has been explained to me' would be very strong evidence to defend any action for trespass to the person. There is a possibility, however, of a successful action in negligence if the patient has not been given relevant information (see below). There is a clear duty on the doctor to take reasonable care that a patient receives the appropriate information before any consent form is signed and treatment proceeds; the nurse should, as far as possible, take appropriate steps to inform the doctor if she discovers that this duty has not been carried out. The DH has recently expressed concern about the way in which consent for treatment for breast cancer is obtained and is advocating the design of a new form of consent.

Consent by word of mouth

Many of the less risky treatments are carried out without any formal signature of the patient. Consent by word of mouth is valid but it may be far more difficult to establish in court, since it might be one person's word against another. Many of the day-to-day treatments and tests are, however, carried out on this basis.

SITUATION 7.2 CONSENT TO TESTS

Mary Spratt, a patient on the medical ward, is asked by the pathology laboratory technician if she will agree to give some blood for tests. She agrees and he proceeds to apply a tourniquet and to take some blood in several small test tubes. He does not explain the tests that he will be doing on the blood. Mary is subsequently told that she is HIV positive. She says that she had never agreed to be tested for AIDS and would have refused consent had she known that was one of the tests.

This situation is discussed in Chapter 26. AIDS has presented new problems in law. Normally when blood is taken for tests, it is not practice to explain to the patient why the blood is being taken or for details of the many tests to be explained to the patient. There is an underlying assumption that the tests are in the interests of the patient and will enable the appropriate treatment to be given. Knowledge by the patient that she has AIDS or is HIV positive is not necessarily in her interests (for example, insurance cover or mortgage may be refused), at least until a cure is found so different legal principles may apply. Apart from an AIDS test, consent to give blood for testing implies consent to all those tests which are in the patient's interests.

Implied consent

It is sometimes said that the fact that a patient comes into hospital means that he is giving his consent to anything that the consultant deems appropriate. That, however, is not supported in law. There are many choices of available treatment and when care is provided there must be evidence that the patient has agreed to that particular course. Similarly, it is said that when an unconscious patient is treated in the accident and emergency department, then he implies consent to being treated. This, however, is not so. An unconscious patient implies nothing. The professionals care for him in the absence of consent as part of their duty to care for the patient out of necessity in an emergency, and would defend any subsequent action for trespass to the person on that basis.

Implied consent is better reserved for situations where non-verbal communication by the patient makes it clear that he is giving consent. Nurses are familiar with the signs: the patient rolls up his sleeve for an injection; the patient opens his mouth as the nurse waves the thermometer in the air. Such actions indicate to the nurse that the patient agrees to the treatment/care proceeding. No words are spoken, there is no signature, but it is clear that the patient is in agreement. The weakness of implied consent is, however, that it is not always clear that the patient is agreeing to what the nurse intends to do. Thus the patient who moves over to receive a pressure sore area rub when he sees the nurse approaching with the trolley would get a nasty shock when the nurse gave him an injection, yet that is how the nurse interprets his non-verbal actions. To avoid such misunderstandings it is preferable if the nurse obtains a spoken consent from the patient. The problems in giving day-to-day care to the confused elderly are considered in Chapter 19.

The right to refuse treatment

It is a basic principle of law in this country that an adult, mentally competent person has the right to refuse treatment and take his own discharge contrary to medical advice. This can be upsetting for staff as in the following situation.

SITUATION 7.3 THE PATIENT'S AUTONOMY

A 25-year-old unmarried man has severe vascular disease and it is recommended that his left foot be amputated to below the knee. He is advised that if he refuses to agree to this operation his chances of survival are very remote. He is adamant that he would rather die than be one-legged. He is strongly counselled and his

family all advise him to have the operation. The ward sister arranges for a patient
of similar age, who had the operation several years ago and who has since
completed the marathon and adjusted very well to the amputation, to visit the
patient and he shows him how he is enjoying life. The patient is not persuaded
and still refuses to sign the consent form. Legal advice is taken that in the absence
of any mental disorder he cannot be compelled to undergo the operation. A
psychiatrist who visits him concludes that the patient is not mentally disordered
and has decided on rational grounds that he would prefer death to an
amputation.

In this situation the patient has a right to refuse treatment. It must be clear, however,
that he is mentally competent. The situation clearly brings out the clash between the
patient's autonomy and the professional duty of care. Clearly, it would be essential for
those in charge of the patient to take all reasonable precautions to ensure that the patient
has appropriate counselling and help in facing the future, but if this fails it is the patient's
right to refuse. Similarly, an adult Jehovah's Witness is able to refuse a blood
transfusion. Different principles apply in relation to children and these are discussed
in Chapter 13.

The Court of Appeal has recently emphasised the importance of ensuring that, when
a patient refuses treatment, the patient has the mental capacity to make a valid decision and has not been subjected to the undue influences of another.

In re T. (an adult) (refusal of medical treatment) 1992 4 All ER 649 a young woman
was injured in a car accident and told the staff nurse that she did not want a blood
transfusion. Her mother was a Jehovah's Witness. At the time it was unlikely to be
necessary. However, subsequently she went into labour and a Caesarean was necessary.
She told medical staff that she would not want a transfusion and had signed a form to
that effect. She was not told that it might be necessary to save her life. After the
operation she required blood as a life-saving measure and her father and co-habitee
applied to court. The judge authorised the administration of blood on the ground that
the evidence showed that she was not in a fit condition to make a valid decision.
(See the case of *In re S. (an adult) (refusal of medical treatment)* 1992 4 All ER 671,
discussed on page 224. For a case on refusal of treatment by a 16-year-old, see *In re W.*
on page 207.)

It should be noted that the presence of a mental disorder does not automatically
mean that a person is incapable of making a valid decision in relation to treatment.
In re C. (an adult) (refusal of medical treatment) Family Division 1994 1 All ER 819
the patient, a 68-year-old man, suffered from paranoid schizophrenia and was
detained at Broadmoor Hospital. He developed gangrene in one foot and doctors
believed an amputation to be a life-saving necessity. He refused to give consent and
sought an injunction restraining the hospital from carrying out an amputation without
his express written consent. He succeeded on the grounds that the evidence failed to
establish that he lacked sufficient understanding of the nature, purpose and effects
of the proposed treatment. Instead the evidence showed that he had understood
and retained the relevant treatment information, believed it and had arrived at a clear
choice.

Taking one's own discharge

It follows from what has been said above that the adult, mentally competent patient is able to take his own discharge. However, this principle causes concern for staff in practice.

SITUATION 7.4 SELF-DISCHARGE

Don Pritchard was admitted from the accident and emergency department with a suspected head injury. Before X-rays had been taken he insisted on leaving the hospital, contrary to medical advice. The nursing staff knew that he was still very confused and it seemed likely that his aggression was a result of a brain injury.

This is a difficult situation because it could be argued here that as a result of the brain injury the patient was not mentally competent and therefore his decision to discharge himself was an irrational one. If there is clear danger to the patient's life if he is allowed to leave, then it could be argued that these are circumstances in which the staff would be justified in acting in an emergency to save the patient's life. If this does not apply, then the patient has the right to go. If possible, he should be persuaded to sign a form that he took his own discharge contrary to medical advice. However, it is not always possible to get this signature and therefore it is necessary to ensure that another member of the staff can act as a witness to what occurred. In either case it is essential that full records are made of the circumstances leading to the patient's discharge and the efforts made to persuade him to stay. If harm eventually befalls the patient as a result of his taking his own discharge contrary to medical advice, and there is evidence that the staff did all they could to persuade him to stay, there is unlikely to be a successful action for negligence against the staff.

The mentally incompetent patient

This is considered in Chapter 20. There are two possible courses: detention under the Mental Health Act 1983 or use of common-law powers to act in an emergency to save life. The latter could be used only if temporary restraint is justified in the interests of the patient.

The unconscious patient

It has been mentioned above that the doctors and nurses in their duty of care for the patient may take life-saving action. If there is no consent by the patient, relatives are sometimes asked to give their consent. However, if the patient is an adult, the validity of the relatives' consent is open to doubt and it is preferable if the doctors and nurses act in the patient's interests as part of their duty of care. If, for example, the spouse of an unconscious patient said to the doctor 'my husband is a Jehovah's Witness, you must

1. Consent.
2. Necessity.
3. Making a lawful arrest.
4. Acting under a statutory power, e.g. Mental Health Act 1983. (See Chapter 20.)
5. Parental powers. (See Chapter 13.)

Figure 7.3 Defences to an action for trespass to the person.

not give him any blood' the doctor would be wise to save the life of the patient and give him blood if that is essential, and defend himself against an action of trespass to the person in any subsequent court case on the grounds of acting in an emergency and out of necessity to save the life of the patient. In such situations the courts do not recognise the relatives as having any right to give or refuse consent. This topic is also considered in relation to the care of the elderly in Chapter 19.

In a Canadian case (*Malette* v. *Shulman* 1991 2 Med LR 162) an unconscious patient was given a life-saving blood transfusion in spite of the fact that she was carrying a card refusing such treatment. She was awarded C$20,000 for assault.

Other defences to an action for trespass to the person

While consent is the main form of defence to an action for trespass to the person, it is not the only one and Fig. 7.3 illustrates other defences.

Necessity

Where a practitioner takes measures to save the life of an unconscious patient, that is not a situation of implied consent, but a situation of necessity. In such circumstances the common law recognises the power of a professional to take action out of necessity in the best interests of the patient following the accepted standard of care of the reasonable professional. The House of Lords established this principle in the case of *F.* v. *West Berkshire Health Authority* 1989 2 All ER 545, which concerned the sterilisation of a woman who suffered from severe learning disabilities and was incapable of giving consent. However, the principle of acting out of necessity where an adult was incapable of giving consent, also applies to day-to-day care. Recommendations have been made by the Law Commission No. 119 and No. 129 for a statutory duty to replace this common-law power, with specific requirements depending on the seriousness of the treatment to be undertaken. Legislation is awaited.

Giving information to a patient prior to consent being obtained

As has been mentioned, there are two main actions in relation to consent:

1. an action for trespass to the person;
2. an action in negligence for a breach of the duty of care to inform the patient.

We now turn to the action for negligence. The courts have made it clear that if the patient has given a willing consent for a procedure, then an action for trespass to the person cannot proceed. If the patient alleges that he was not given significant information about possible side-effects, then the action will be one of negligence. This raises the question of how much information must be given to the patient. The leading case on this question is the following.

CASE 7.1 THE SIDAWAY CASE

Amy Sidaway suffered from persistent pain in her neck and shoulder and was advised by a surgeon to have an operation on her spinal column to relieve the pain. The surgeon warned her of the possibility of disturbing a nerve root and the possible consequences of doing so, but did not mention the possibility of damage to the spinal cord, even though he would be operating within 3 millimetres of it. The risk of damage to the spinal cord was very small (less than 1 per cent), but if the risk materialised the resulting injury could range from mild to very severe. Amy consented to the operation, which was performed with due care and skill. However, in the course of the operation, she suffered an injury to her spinal cord which resulted in her being severely disabled. She sued the surgeon and the hospital governors, alleging that the surgeon had been in breach of a duty owed to her to warn her of all possible risks inherent in the operation, with the result that she had not been in a position to give an informed consent to the operation. Amy lost the case before the trial judge and her appeal to the Court of Appeal. She then appealed to the House of Lords (*Sidaway* v. *Bethlem Royal Hospital Governors and others* 1985 1 All ER 643).

The House of Lords held that her appeal should fail. Three of the judges held that the test of liability in respect of a doctor's duty to warn his patient of risks inherent in treatment recommended by him was the same as the test applicable to diagnosis of treatment, i.e. the doctor was required to act in accordance with a practice accepted as proper by a responsible body of medical opinion. (This is known as the 'Bolam Test' and is discussed on page 30.) Since the surgeon's non-disclosure of risk of damage to the plaintiff's spinal cord accorded with a practice accepted as proper by a responsible body of neuro-surgical opinion, the defendants were not liable to the plaintiff.

The other two judges (Lord Scarman and Lord Templeman) were also of the opinion that Amy's appeal must fail since she had not proved on the evidence that the surgeon (who had died since the operation) had been in breach of duty by failing to warn her of the risks. Lord Scarman alone of all the judges held that a patient had a right to give informed consent and he followed an American case, *Canterbury* v. *Spence* 1972 464 F 2d 772, where the 'prudent patient' test was applied to decide on the information a patient should be given prior to any consent, i.e. 'What would a reasonable prudent patient think significant if in the situation of this patient?' He concluded that

> English law must recognise a duty of the doctor to warn his patient of risk inherent in the treatment which he is proposing, and especially so if the treatment be surgery. The critical limitation is that the duty is confined to material risk. The test of materiality is whether in the circumstances of the particular case the court is satisfied that a reasonable person in the patient's position would be likely to attach significance to the risk. Even if the risk be material, the doctor will not be liable if on a reasonable assessment of his patient's condition he takes the view that a warning would be detrimental to his patient's health.
>
> (Lord Scarman)

Comment on the Sidaway case

While the case was concerned with treatment by a doctor, the same principles would apply to treatment by any other professional. The situation at present is not entirely clear since although all the judges turned down Amy's appeal, their reasons for doing so were extremely varied. The majority applied the 'Bolam Test' of the accepted approved professional practice.

Even Lord Scarman, who used the 'prudent patient' test, still agreed that there may well be exceptions where the doctor is entitled to use 'therapeutic privilege' in deciding what to tell or what not to tell the patient prior to any procedure. This exception means that in the end the professional must follow the accepted approved practice in so far as it is applicable to the particular needs of that specific patient.

The Sidaway case was cited and followed in the case of *Blyth* v. *Bloomsbury Health Authority*, *The Times* 11 February 1987. In this case a patient had been given an injection of depo-provera and claimed that she had suffered harm as a result of it and that knowledge which was possessed by hospital researchers about some of the side-effects of the drug was not made known to her at the time that she was prescribed it. The Court of Appeal applied the Bolam Test and the Sidaway case to the facts and decided that there was no negligence by the doctors who cared for her in the information they gave to her. They emphasised that the extent of the duty to give information is to be judged in the light of the state of medical knowledge at the time and one must avoid the danger of being wise after the event. In addition, they refused to interpret the Sidaway judgments as implying that where the patient asked specific rather than just general questions this meant that the doctor is under an obligation to tell the patient all he knows about the subject. 'The amount of information to be given must depend on all the circumstances, and as a general proposition it is governed by what is called the Bolam Test' (Lord Justice Neill).

Another important point is that in subsequent cases the courts have held that the professional's duty is not divisible. Diagnosis, treatment, carrying out that treatment and informing the patient are all part of the doctor's duty of care and cannot be separated into different boxes. Informing the patient of risks is as much a part of the clinical judgement of the doctor as all his other tasks.

Giving information to the terminally ill patient

If a patient is terminally ill, should the nurse tell the patient contrary to medical advice? What is the position if the relatives do not wish the patient to be told?

SITUATION 7.5 SILENCE OR LIES?

Paul George has been operated on for 'ulcers'. Unknown to him the surgeons actually found an inoperable tumour with wide spreading of the malignancy throughout the body. It is estimated that death is likely to occur in a few months. The consultant who normally is in favour of a very open approach to patients believes that Paul, who is 54, would not be able to cope with this news yet and he discusses this with Paul's wife, who agrees. The nursing staff are advised accordingly.

This kind of situation is in substance not unfamiliar to nursing staff and is repeated in different guises on many occasions. Unfortunately, however, it is the nursing staff who are most frequently with the patients and who are most likely to be asked: 'I don't have cancer, do I nurse?' or 'When am I likely to get out of here?' or 'Is it worth my while booking for this holiday next year?' and other direct or indirect questions designed to obtain a little more information for the patient as to where he stands. The questions which then arise in the nurse's mind are: Where does the patient stand in law? Does the patient have a legal enforceable right to obtain this information? What is the nurse's position in regard to the patient, the doctor, and the relative?

The patient's rights

As has been seen in the discussion above, there is a duty on professional staff when advising certain forms of treatment to ensure that the patient is notified of any significant risks of substantial side-effects. However, this duty on the professional is qualified by the power to withhold information if it is deemed to be in the patient's interest not to know. This is known as therapeutic privilege. Informing the patient that he is terminally ill may well come under this heading. Thus if in the opinion of the doctor it would be harmful to tell a patient such disturbing news then the doctor can withhold such information on the grounds that he is acting in the patient's best interest. A doctor cannot withhold information about risks because he believes the patient would refuse consent if he was aware of them. There must be other reasons to justify withholding this information. There is no clear right in law for the patient to insist on being told and even where the patient is exercising his right under the Data Protection Act (see Fig. 7.4) there is the power to withhold such data from him.

The consultant or general practitioner has clinical responsibility for the patient. If in the doctor's opinion the patient would be harmed by any disclosure and he has exercised his judgement on this in accordance with the approved professional practice, then that decision must be accepted and implemented by the rest of the team of professionals. The nurses might disagree with the decision and of course they may well have the opportunity of persuading the doctor to change his mind, based on their own personal knowledge of the patient, his needs and his own understanding. Ultimately, however, they would be obliged to defer to the clinical decision of the doctor. Any nurse who flagrantly went against the doctor's view on this may well face disciplinary proceedings. What is clear at the present and in the absence of any Bill of Rights for patients is that there is no clear right in law for the patient to obtain this information.

The court has yet to deal directly with the question as to whether the patient has a right to be told and whether the doctor has a duty to tell. It is quite likely that if this is put before the courts, the court will apply the Bolam Test and leave it to the approved professional practice in relation to that particular patient.

Even if the patient is ultimately held to have such a right it does not follow that the nurse can ignore the instructions of the doctor.

The relatives' rights

It is not uncommon for relatives on hearing of a particularly upsetting diagnosis to ask for the patient not to be informed of that 'because he could not cope with that yet'. Often, perhaps, it is not the patient's inability to deal with the information but the relatives' inability to cope with the patient's knowledge of it. The conspiracy of silence thus begins. As far as the law is concerned this should not arise. The patient is entitled to have information about him kept confidential (see Chapter 8). It is a breach of this duty to the patient when the relative is told first. It is always open to the patient to say to the doctor 'I would rather that my wife was not told about my diagnosis yet.' That is his right. Yet when terminal illness or chronic sickness are concerned the rules of confidentiality are broken and the relative is informed first. Obviously, there are exceptions to this duty of confidentiality when the patient is too ill to be told and decisions have to be made which therefore involve the relative. However, that should be the exception.

Let's return to the situation of Paul George above. If the nurse has received clear instructions that Paul should not be told that he is terminally ill, then the nurse should not act contrary to these instructions. Nor, however, should she lie to Paul. If Paul makes it clear that he is seeking more information, then the nurse should arrange for Paul to speak with the doctor concerned and express to the doctor her own views of Paul's needs. Ultimately, the wife has no right to insist that information is withheld from Paul. Obviously, because of her knowledge of Paul she should be involved in any discussions on the correct approach.

Notifying the patient of negligence by a colleague

If a colleague has been negligent, should the nurse inform the patient?

Unfortunately this is not an entirely hypothetical question and it sometimes happens that a nurse is aware that a mistake has been made, and that neither patient nor relatives have been made aware of this, although they may realise that all has not gone according to plan. What is the nurse to do in these circumstances? Does she have a duty to inform the patient?

The nurse's duty to the patient is to ensure that the patient receives all the appropriate care and treatment. If a mistake has been made, for example a colleague administers eye drops to the wrong eye, it is essential for the nurse to ensure that this is made known so that the patient can be given any necessary antidote. She should also ensure that steps are taken to prevent such an error occurring again and should therefore check that a report has been made to senior nurse management. Hopefully, if a nurse is at fault, she herself will have reported it. Good practice should ensure that a full disclosure is given to the patient and it would be the consultant's responsibility to see that this was done and to reassure the patient about any future effects.

Good practice dictates that there should be a full disclosure to the patient. The nurse should take every action that she can to ensure that the patient is fully informed. Some NHS Trusts have established codes of practice to ensure that this is carried out. Reference must also be made to the Code of Professional Conduct (Appendix 1) and the practitioner's duty.

Access to medical records

Does the patient have a legal right to see his medical records? The answer is yes. If the records are in computerised form, the Data Protection Act 1984 applies. Otherwise the Access to Health Records Act 1990 applies.

The Data Protection Act sets out eight principles which apply to the keeping of computerised data (see Fig. 7.4). These principles are designed to ensure that computerised personal data shall be accurate, relevant, held only for specific defined purposes for which the user has been registered, not kept for longer than is necessary, and not disclosed to unauthorised persons. In addition, a right of subject access is given, i.e. the individual should be able, on payment of a small fee, to see what is contained about him and have a right to rectify that if it is not correct. The registrar has the power to enforce the duties under the Act and offenders can be prosecuted. The individual data subject has the right to apply to the courts for compensation for damage and any associated distress caused by a breach of these principles by the data user.

Access to health service records (for example, medical and nursing records):
Data Protection Act 1984

From 11 November 1987, there has been a right of access by a subject to any health records held in computerised form. This right of access is, however, modified by Statutory Instrument (1987) No. 1903. The data user can withhold data from the subject if seeing the information is likely to cause serious harm to the physical or mental health of the data subject or would be likely to disclose to the data subject the identity of another individual (who has not consented to the disclosure of the information).

Only a health professional can exercise the right of disclosure under the Act. The

1. The information to be contained in personal data shall be obtained, and personal data shall be processed, fairly and lawfully.
2. Personal data shall be held only for one or more specified and law purposes.
3. Personal data held for any purpose or purposes shall not be used or disclosed in any manner incompatible with that purpose or those purposes.
4. Personal data held for any purpose or purposes shall be adequate, relevant and not excessive in relation to that purpose or those purposes.
5. Personal data shall be accurate and, where necessary, kept up to date.
6. Personal data held for any purpose or purposes shall not be kept for longer than is necessary for that purpose or those purposes.
7. An individual shall be entitled
   (a) at reasonable intervals and without undue delay or expense
       (i) to be informed by the data user whether he holds personal data of which that individual is the subject; and
       (ii) to access to any such data held by data user; and
   (b) where appropriate to have such data corrected or erased.
8. Appropriate security measures shall be taken against unauthorised access to, or alteration, disclosure or destruction of, personal data and against accidental loss or destruction of personal data.

Figure 7.4 Principles of the Data Protection Act 1984 Schedule 1.

appropriate health professional is the medical practitioner or dental practitioner currently responsible for the clinical care of the patient, or if there is more than one, the most suitable from the point of view of the information required, or if there is no such practitioner, then the health professional who has the necessary experience and qualifications. The schedule contains a list of the health professionals which includes registered nurse, midwife or health visitor. A similar statutory instrument (1987/1904) provides similar restrictions on the disclosure of information held in connection with the provision of personal social services. Here, however, the exemption from disclosure is based on the fact there would likely be prejudice to carrying out social work by reason of the fact that disclosure would cause serious harm to the physical or mental health or emotional condition of the data subject or any other person, or that the identity of another individual would be disclosed.

The procedure for access to computerised health records is now as follows: if a patient wishes to see his computerised medical and nursing records he may apply to the holder of these records, most likely the NHS Trust or general practitioner or possibly the Family Practitioner Committee. He pays the required fee, £10, and within 40 days he should be given the required information or informed that there are grounds for withholding it.

The information can only be withheld on the two grounds listed above.

It must be stressed that this Act only applies to computerised records. Social services manual records are, however, covered by the Access to Personal Files Act 1987 which enables individuals to have access to and require amendment to certain manually held records. Manually held records are covered by the Access to Health Records Act 1990 (see below).

If a patient uses his right of access under the Data Protection Act to the health records and discovers that they are inaccurate he can ask for them to be rectified. He also has the right to seek compensation for any harm that he has suffered as a result of the inaccuracy. Some say that the modifications to the right of access have taken much of the power out of the data access provisions. In addition, the data need not necessarily be supplied as a printout. The data user may choose to write or type the information to be supplied with any accompanying explanation. Much needs to be interpreted. What, for example, is meant by 'serious harm to the physical or mental health'? It is not defined in the order. How will the courts define what is appropriate for compensation and how will that be measured?

Where records are computerised it should be remembered that it is not just the medical records which are covered: the term 'health record' would include nursing records, physiotherapy records, pathology laboratory records and all other records relating to the patient's health. How costly and how frequently these rights are used will remain to be seen.

Access to Health Records Act 1990

This Act, which came into force on 1 November 1991, parallels the access rights under the Data Protection Act 1984. The 1984 Act covers automated processed data, the 1990 Act manually held personal health information. It is not retrospective, but if records made prior to 1 November 1991 are required to make sense of later records then access to those can be given. Similar exclusion provisions prevent access being permitted if serious harm would be caused to the physical or mental health of the patient or of any other individual or would identify an individual who has not consented to the application for access. (This latter provision does not cover a health professional who has been involved in the care of the patient.) The patient can apply for inaccurate records to be corrected and where the information is expressed in terms which are not intelligible without explanation, then an explanation must be provided. The term 'health professional' includes a wide variety of professions (plus osteopaths after the Osteopaths Act 1993) but does not include social workers.

The rights of access have been modified as a result of the human fertilisation and embryology treatment services. Access to Health Records (Control of Access) Regulations 1993 prevents access being given if it would disclose that an identifiable individual was, or may have been, born in consequence of treatment services within the meaning of the Human Fertilisation and Embryology Act 1990 (SI 1993/746).

Access to Medical Reports Act 1988

This Act came into force on 1 January 1989. It gives an individual a right of access to any medical report relating to him which has been supplied by a medical practitioner for employment purposes or insurance purposes. Before any such medical report can be supplied, the individual must be notified that it is being requested and the individual must give his consent to that request. The medical practitioner must not supply the report unless he has given the individual access to it and he has been allowed to correct any errors, or 21 days have elapsed since the practitioner notified him of his intention to provide a report. The medical report must be retained by the medical practitioner for at least six months from the date on which it was supplied.

There is an exemption from individual access where the medical practitioner is of the opinion that disclosure would be likely to cause serious harm to the physical or mental health of the individual or would indicate the intentions of the practitioner in respect of the individual or where the identity of another person would be made known.

Questions and exercises

1 What is meant by implied consent to treatment? Consider examples of implied consent from your own practice.
2 Obtain a copy of the standard consent-to-treatment form. How appropriate do you think it is to cover the wide range of treatments for which it is used?
3 Refer to the specialist subject areas in Part II and consider the principles that apply to consent by minors under 16, consent by minors of 17 and 18, consent by the mentally disordered and by the unconscious patient.
4 Relatives have no legal right to give consent or withhold consent on behalf of an adult. Do you think the law should be changed to give them this right and how should the interests of the patient be protected from unscrupulous relatives?
5 What is the difference between the 'Bolam Test' and the 'prudent patient' test so far as consent to treatment is concerned?
6 Do you consider that all patients should have a right of access to their medical records? What exceptions, if any, would you see as essential?
7 There is in this country no Bill of Rights which sets out certain inalienable rights. If you were asked to draw one up in relation to health care, what would you include?

8   The law on confidentiality, and the exceptions

The duty of confidentiality

The patient is entitled to confidentiality of the information about him. There is therefore a duty on every professional and indeed every employee of the authority to ensure confidentiality of information. The duty arises

1. from the duty of care in negligence discussed in Chapter 1;
2. from the implied duties under the contract of employment (see Chapter 10);
3. from the duty to keep information which has been passed on in confidence, confidential, even when there is no pre-existing relationship or legally enforceable contract between the parties. (This is a duty based on equity and only recently recognised by the courts, and was discussed in the case of *Stephens* v. *Avery and others*, 1988 2 All ER 477.)

Under the duties implied in the contract of employment, the employee has a responsibility to the employer to keep information acquired from work confidential. For the nurse, too, that duty is also spelled out by the Code of Professional Conduct (see Fig. 8.1).

While this code is not enforceable in a court of law, it reflects what the law upholds and is used by the PCC as a guideline in determining whether the nurse is guilty of professional misconduct.

Respect confidential information obtained in the course of professional practice and refrain from disclosing such information without the consent of the patient/client, or a person entitled to act on his/her behalf, except where disclosure is required by law or by the order of a court or is necessary in the public interest.

Figure 8.1 Paragraph 9 of the Code of Professional Conduct.

Difficulties arise not in understanding the duty of confidentiality, but in knowing when the exceptions arise and in what circumstances breaking the duty is permissible. Because of these problems the UKCC has issued an advisory paper elaborating on Clause 9, which can be found in Appendix 2. The DH is also in the process of preparing a code on confidentiality and a draft has been circulated for consultation.

Exceptions to the duty of confidentiality

See Fig. 8.2.

The consent of the patient

The duty is owed to the patient and it is therefore in the patient's power to authorise disclosures to be made. Thus announcements to the press, notification of relatives and spouses, and provision of information to a solicitor or to an insurance company are all legitimate disclosures with the consent of the patient. If the patient is unconscious and an adult, the consent of the relatives is often used to justify disclosure on behalf of the patient, but there may well be little justification for this in law unless the patient has appointed that relative as his agent and given him that authority.

1. Consent of a patient.
2. Interests of patient.
3. Court orders
   (a) subpoena;
   (b) Supreme Court Act 1981.
4. Statutory Duty to disclose
   Road Traffic Act 1972;
   Prevention of Terrorism Act;
   Public Health Acts;
   Misuse of Drugs Acts.
5. Public interest.
6. Police.

Figure 8.2 Exceptions to the duty of confidentiality.

SITUATION 8.1 SPOUSE'S CONFIDENCE

Annabel was involved in a serious road accident and admitted to hospital. While on the orthopaedic ward a telephone request came in asking for information on her progress. The nurse taking the call asked who the caller was. The answer was 'her husband'. The nurse then gave the caller full details of Annabel's progress. She then told Annabel that her husband had phoned asking for information about her; the nurse was surprised at Annabel's fury. It appeared that she had recently separated from him, she had not notified him of where she was now living, and did not want any communication with him because of his violence.

The difficulties of the nurse's position in a situation like the above are easily understood. In 99 out of 100 cases, Annabel would be delighted to receive a message of concern and interest. However, it is the hundredth case which causes concern and procedures have to be established to prevent any unauthorised information being disclosed. Annabel is entitled to withhold information of her condition from her relatives and friends. In some cases, even an acknowledgement that a patient is on a particular ward, e.g. psychiatric or gynaecology (abortion) might be an unwarranted disclosure. In the above situation the nurse was at fault in not checking with Annabel first, and it is now standard practice not to disclose information over the phone unless checks on the caller have been made and the patient is agreeable to the information being given.

There can often be a problem in caring for elderly patients where the patient has made a special request to the nurses that the relatives should not be told about his condition. However, it can give rise to additional problems for staff. 'Where do I stand if I do not contact the relatives regarding the condition of the elderly patient because the elderly patient has asked me not to do so?' is a not infrequent question. Applying the principles discussed here the patient does have the right to refuse to allow this information to be passed on. However, if the relatives are to care for the patient eventually, there may well be information which they need to know for the patient's own safety and thus disclosure is justified in the interests of the patient (see below).

Disclosure to the press

Exactly the same principles apply when the press are asking for information about a patient. If the patient consents, the information can be given. If the patient refuses, then no information should be given and this includes a condition check, where the press phone up to find out the latest condition of the patient. Where the patient is unconscious the same principles should prevail.

Disclosure in the interests of the patient

Disclosure between professionals caring for the patient is justified on the basis that if information obtained by the doctor and relevant to the care of the patient is not passed on to the appropriate professional, then the patient might suffer. An obvious example is the patient's history of allergy to certain medication: if the pharmacist and the nurse were not told of a known allergy or allowed to see the records, they would be unable to ensure that the patient was given appropriate medication. Traditionally nurses have not usually had difficulties over access to the patient's records. Other professional groups have encountered difficulties: occupational therapists, physiotherapists, social workers and other groups have sometimes been refused access to the patient's records on the grounds that it is unnecessary and also a breach of confidentiality. This is a difficult problem. On the one hand, the wider the range of people who have access to the medical records of the patient, the more difficult it is to maintain the duty of confidentiality. On the other hand, there are many situations where a professional caring for the patient, in ignorance of certain facts known to the doctor, could do the patient considerable harm. The problem becomes even more complex when we consider the question of how much confidential information should be given to a volunteer who is taking the patient out. For example, if the volunteer is taking a patient with learning disabilities out for the day, it might be vital in the interests of the safety of the patient to advise the volunteer that the patient is epileptic and to ensure that the volunteer would know how to cope should the patient have an attack. On the other hand, the fact that the patient had an abortion five years ago would be irrelevant and thus would be a disclosure which would not be justified in the interests of the patient.

In conclusion it could be said that disclosure of confidential information to others is justified if it is necessary in the interests of the health and/or safety of the patient or the professional. AIDS has raised many significant problems in this field and these are discussed further in Chapter 26.

Court orders

Subpoena (an order made by the court, which must be obeyed under threat of punishment for contempt of court)

The court has the power to subpoena any relevant evidence or witnesses in a case in the interests of justice. There are only two exceptions to this power and these are known as being privileged from disclosure.

Privilege on grounds of public interest
An example of public interests protected from an order for disclosure is national security.

Legal professional privilege
This second exception to the power of the court to order disclosure covers communications between client and legal adviser where litigation is envisaged or is taking place. In the interests of total disclosure between client and lawyer, and in the advancement of justice, these communications are free from an order of discovery or disclosure. Difficulties have arisen over the disclosure of statements taken from witnesses to any

accident which might be used later in any court proceedings. Are such statements protected from disclosure on the grounds of legal professional privilege? In the case of *Waugh* v. *British Railway Board* 1980 AC 521 it was held that where a document comes into being after an accident and where there are two purposes for its use (e.g. management purposes to ensure that the accident does not happen again, and legal purposes to defend any potential action), then if the dominant purpose is for management purposes, the document is not privileged from disclosure under the rules of professional legal privilege. This ruling by the House of Lords was upheld in the following case:

CASE 8.1 DISCLOSURE

Marlon Lee, a young boy, was severely scalded and was initially treated in a hospital run by one health authority, then subsequently transferred to a burns hospital run by another district authority. Shortly afterwards he developed breathing problems and was transferred to the first hospital by the ambulance which came under the South West Thames Regional Health Authority. He suffered brain damage which was considered to be due to lack of oxygen. The mother asked for disclosure of the ambulance report produced by the Regional Health Authority for the first hospital but was refused it. Her application to the court for disclosure failed on the basis that the report was prepared in contemplation of litigation and to assist the legal advisers, and disclosure could not be ordered even though it had been initiated as a result of the request by the first hospital authority, not by the authority responsible for the ambulance service. (*Lee* v. *South West Thames Regional Health Authority* 1985 2 All ER 385).

This case shows the disadvantages faced by potential litigants since the health authority or NHS Trust is of course both custodian of the records and also a potential defendant, and can use its first function to enable it to have immediate access to all the relevant records.

The test to decide whether communication between a solicitor and his client was privileged from disclosure was to consider whether it was made confidentially for the purposes of legal advice, constructing such purposes broadly (*Balabel and another* v. *Air India*, *The Times* 19 March 1988).

Apart from these exceptions the judge has the power to order the production of any evidence relevant to the case. There is no recognition of the privilege of confidential medical information, nor do the courts recognise the secrecy of the confessional or press informants. It will be remembered from the case of *Deacon* v. *McVicar* (see page 55) that the judge ordered the production of the records of other maternity patients in the ward at that time as they were relevant to the argument that the ward was undergoing several crises at that time.

Health visitors are more likely than any other group of nurses to be summoned by subpoena to appear in court. They have adopted a procedure whereby they will normally require service of a subpoena before giving evidence in court. In this way they are able to make it clear to their clients that they have no option but to attend court and are obliged to disclose confidential information. The Children Act 1989 has led to health visitors giving evidence in the interest of the child without waiting for a subpoena.

On the application, in accordance with rules of court, of a person who appears to the High Court to be likely to be a party to subsequent proceedings in that Court in which a claim in respect of personal injuries to a person, or in respect of a person's death, is likely to be made, the High Court shall, in such circumstances as may be specified in the rules, have power to order a person who appears to the Court to be likely to be a party to the proceedings and to be likely to have or to have had in his possession, custody or power any documents which are relevant to an issue arising or likely to arise out of that claim:

(a) to disclose whether those documents are in his possession, custody or power; and
(b) to produce such of the documents as are in his possession, custody or power to the applicant or, on such conditions as may be specified in the order
  (i) to the applicant's legal advisers; or
  (ii) to the applicant's legal advisers and any medical or other professional adviser of the applicant; or
  (iii) if the applicant has no legal adviser, to any medical or other professional adviser of the applicant.

Figure 8.3 Supreme Court Act 1981 Section 33.

1. This section applies to any proceedings in the High Court in which a claim is made in respect of personal injuries to a person or in respect of a person's death.
2. On the application, in accordance with the rules of court, of a party to any proceedings to which this section applies, the High Court shall in such circumstances as may be specified in the rules, have power to order a person who is not a party to the proceedings and who appears to the Court to be likely to have in his possession, custody or power any documents which are relevant to an issue arising out of the said claim:
   (a) to disclose whether those documents are in his possession, custody or power; and
   (b) to produce such of those documents as are in his possession, custody or power to the applicant or, on such conditions as may be specified in the order
     (i) to the applicant's legal advisers; or
     (ii) to the applicant's legal advisers and any medical or other professional adviser of the applicant; or
     (iii) if the applicant has no legal adviser to any medical or other professional adviser of the applicant.

Figure 8.4 Supreme Court Act 1981 Section 34.

Disclosure in personal injury cases

Supreme Court Act 1981, Section 33
This section is set out in Fig. 8.3. It gives a party likely to be involved in an action for personal injury or death the right to seek a court order requiring a party to the case to disclose any relevant documents.

Disclosure is now restricted to the applicant's medical and legal adviser. As a result of pressure from the Health Service Commissioner and also from judges in several cases where there has been evidence of unnecessary delay in the production of medical records,

NHS Trusts nowadays rarely wait to be issued with an order for disclosure, but are more likely to produce the relevant documents when the solicitor requests them.

Supreme Court Act 1981, Section 34

This section enables an order for disclosure to be made against a person who is not likely to be a party to the proceedings, and is set out in Fig. 8.4. In this situation it is necessary for the writ to have been issued and thus the case to have commenced. Again, it refers to personal injury and death cases. The situation envisaged is as follows:

CASE 8.2 A ROAD ACCIDENT

Mr McIvor was injured in a road accident and brought an action against the defendant, Mr Reid, for damages for personal injuries. One of the medical issues in the case was whether Mr McIvor's alleged total incapacity for work since the accident was caused by the injuries sustained in the accident or by a pre-existing cardiac or vascular condition. Medical records and notes were in the custody of the Southern Health and Social Services Board. The defendant applied for production of the records by the hospital. (*McIvor* v. *Southern Health and Social Services Board* 1978 1 WLR 757)

The judge made an order restricting disclosure to the legal advisers of the defendant and the hospital wished to restrict disclosure to the medical advisers nominated by the plaintiff and the defendant. The House of Lords decided that there was no such power under the predecessor to the Supreme Court Act 1981. Section 34 now gives this power (see Fig. 8.4).

Disclosure before trial

In addition to the rules under the Supreme Court Act, the rules of the High Court enable an order for relevant information to be made once the writ has been issued and the case commenced. This order for the production of documents is part of the pleadings and the exchange of information which takes place between the parties before the hearing takes place in the court. The aim is to ensure that the parties understand the main points in dispute and are not surprised when the oral hearing takes place. The days in court should thus be kept to a minimum and should only take place when there really is an outstanding issue between the parties. Recent court decisions have emphasised that there is wide discretion for the court to grant disclosure, including the disclosure of expert's reports (*Naylor* v. *Preston Area Health Authority* 1987 2 All ER 353). In exceptional circumstances, the court could order disclosure to a person who was neither a party to the case nor a lawyer. Thus, in the case over the alleged harm caused by the drug Opren, the Court of Appeal allowed disclosure to the medical and scientific journalist and writer who was assisting the many plaintiffs in their case against Eli Lilly (*Davies and Eli Lilly and Co.* 1987 1 All ER 801).

Disclosure to the patient

The Data Protection Act and the Access to Health Records Act gives the right of subject access to health records, subject to several exceptions. In the case of health records, the professional can refuse production of the records to the patient on the grounds that it would adversely affect their physical or mental well-being. There is no absolute legal right for the patient to see his medical records. See Chapter 7 for a discussion of this. The changes of law brought about by the Supreme Court Act have meant that disclosure of the relevant records is kept to the medical or legal adviser. The patient has no right to see them under that Act of Parliament.

Nurse and disclosure by order of the court

A nurse is likely to be affected by these provisions since the records include not only the medical records but all records held by the NHS Trust which are relevant to an issue arising in the case. Of course, in the McIvor situation the health authority was not the defendant but it is quite possible that the health staff could still have been called as witnesses to explain any queries relating to those records. It will be appreciated from the chapter relating to compensation and causation that a plaintiff who had a pre-existing medical condition which was the main cause of his disability could only recover from the defendant who had injured him the losses following from the defendant's acts and not those that would have occurred anyway.

Statutory duty to disclose

Whatever the views of the patient there are certain circumstances in which disclosure of otherwise confidential information must be made by law. The following are the main provisions.

1. Road Traffic Act 1972 S 168(2)(b): this requires any person to give information to the police relating to a road traffic accident involving personal injuries. A doctor was prosecuted under its provisions for failing to disclose the relevant information and was fined £5 (*Hunter* v. *Mann* 1974 1 QB 767). His claim that he should not be required to give information which would be a breach of the patient's confidence was not accepted either by the trial judge or by the Divisional Court (see also Chapter 21).
2. The Prevention of Terrorism Act (Temporary Provisions Act 1988), Section 11 (Continuous Order SI 1993/747), makes it an offence for any person having information which he believes may be of material assistance in preventing terrorism or apprehending terrorists to fail without reasonable cause to give that information to the police. This therefore places a burden on staff, for example, in accident and emergency departments to disclose the existence of wounds which may have resulted from terrorist acts.
3. The Public Health (Control of Disease) Act 1984 requires a medical practitioner attending a patient who appears to be suffering from a notifiable disease to notify the medical officer of the district of the name and whereabouts of the patient and the disease. Notifiable diseases include cholera, plague, smallpox, and typhus.

4. Misuse of Drugs Act 1971 and the Regulations under it require the Home Office's Drug Branch to be notified by a doctor of any patient who appears to be drug dependent (see Chapter 28).
5. The Abortion Act 1967 requires doctors to inform the Chief Medical Officer of the DH of detailed information relating to the termination of pregnancy (see Chapter 15).

Public interest

Unfortunately, many of the difficulties relating to the exceptions to the duty of confidentiality come under the broad heading of 'public interest' where there is little guidance from the courts. Let's look at some of these controversial areas.

SITUATION 8.2 AN EPILEPTIC LORRY DRIVER

Bill, a long-distance lorry driver, is diagnosed as having epilepsy which is not yet under control through medication. The doctor has advised him to notify his employers and cease driving until the epilepsy is under control. Bill does not wish to do this since he has just been interviewed for the job of coach driver on the continent and he has been hoping for this chance for years. April, a nurse in the neurology ward, recognises Bill as a neighbour and is horrified when she hears from Bill's wife that Bill has been given the job of driving a coachload of school children to France. She knows several children who will be on that trip.

There must be many who would argue that in these circumstances a breach of the duty of confidentiality owed to Bill is justified on grounds of the public interest. Obviously, there are advantages in Bill himself being persuaded of the dangers of driving on the trip, but if he fails to disclose this and continues with his plans, then many would justify the doctor making the disclosure. If the doctor is adamant that he will not breach that confidence, does the nurse have any right to do so? There is no specific answer but it could be argued that in these exceptional circumstances the employers should be notified in the public interest. Some doctors argue very vigorously against this and it is true that they have no duty in law to inform the licensing authority of any condition which affects the patient's ability to drive. However, nor is there any authority which states that such a disclosure is an unjustifiable breach of confidence. In fact, it is possible to imagine an action for negligence being brought by people injured in a road accident, caused because a driver was not medically fit, against the doctor who knew of this condition and yet failed to take the appropriate action. The success of such a hypothetical case would depend upon establishing the following:

1. The doctor (or the nurse or other professional) owed a duty of care to the person who was eventually injured.
2. There was a breach of this duty in that the relevant information was not passed to the appropriate authority.

3. The personal injuries or death were a reasonably foreseeable result of that failure and were caused by that failure.

Until such a case is heard, or a law is enacted, a firm decision cannot be made. In its Advisory Paper the UKCC states (see Appendix 2, Paragraph 5) 'In all cases where the practitioner deliberately discloses or withholds information in what he/she believes is the public interest he/she must be able to justify the decision. These decisions can be particularly stressful, especially where vulnerable groups are concerned, as disclosure may mean the involvement of a third party as in the case of children or the mentally handicapped.' The paragraph continues by emphasising the need to consult with other practitioners and professional organisations before making a decision and eventual careful recording of the action taken and why. This advice is not law of course but in the absence of any clear legal duty in these circumstances it is the best that can be offered. Ultimately, it is for the professional concerned to exercise her own discretion according to the general principles. April should in any case be advised to notify her consultant neurologist of her information. He may well then consult with his professional organisation.

The Court of Appeal has recently given guidance on the public duty of confidence. In this case (*W.* v. *Egdell* 1989 1 All ER 1089 HC, 1990 1 All ER 835 CA) W., a psychiatric patient, brought an action against an independent psychiatrist, the health authority, the mental health review tribunal and the Secretary of State for breach of confidentiality. The psychiatrist had sent a copy of his report on W.'s mental condition to the hospital on grounds of public interest on the basis of W.'s particular circumstances. The High Court judge held that no distinction should be drawn between a psychiatrist who was independent and one employed by the health authority. The report did not come under the heading of legal professional privilege (see page 113). The judge relied on the General Medical Council's Advice on Standards of Professional Conduct and Medical Ethics and refused an injunction against the use on disclosure of the report and dismissed his claims for damage. The Court of Appeal dismissed W.'s appeal and held that the balance came down in favour of the public interest in the disclosure of the report and against the public interest in the duty of confidentiality owed to the patient. Unlike the trial judge, the Court of Appeal considered the General Medical Council's rules as inappropriately relied upon by the judge, since Dr Egdell did not have clinical responsibility for W. The Court of Appeal quoted Article 8(2) of the European Convention on Human Rights which permits intervention by a public authority in the duty of professional secrecy (see Article 8(1)) in the interests of public safety and the prevention of crime. The same considerations justified Dr Egdell's actions.

SITUATION 8.3 OCCUPATIONAL HEALTH

Brenda works as a nurse in the occupational health department and is horrified to discover that a paediatric nurse, Karen, has an unusual bacterial infection which makes it very dangerous for her to work in the unit, particularly with the premature babies. However, she knows that Karen has exhausted all her sick pay allowance from the authority and would be dependent on DSS benefits. She is bringing up two children on her own and would have great difficulty managing without her NHS pay. Karen herself is not ill: she appears to be a carrier rather than a sufferer of this particular germ and is anxious to continue to work and does not want her nursing officer to be notified.

An occupational health department is sometimes caught in the clash between its duty to keep information acquired from its clients/patients confidential and the interest of the employer in being aware of that information, especially where there is danger to the health or safety of other employees as a result of the person's medical condition. (AIDS is considered separately in Chapter 26.) Exactly the same principles apply as in the situation described above, with the additional dimension of the employers' duty to other employees in the workplace. There is a clear duty owed by the employer to his employees under an implied term in the contract of employment (see Chapter 10), whereas the duty owed in the law of negligence in the situation of the epileptic lorry driver described above is not at all clear. In Brenda's case there is clear justification for advising Karen that the information cannot be withheld. The dangers to the patients and to other staff are such that she cannot continue to work until she is free of the germ. Karen may have the right to claim the statutory right of payment on the grounds of medical suspension (see Chapter 10). This breach of confidentiality can be justified by reference to a preceding agreement, namely the contract of employment and the implied terms in it (see Chapter 10). Some authorities may well have an express term in their contract of employment authorising the occupational health department to notify the employer of any condition which would be dangerous to patients or other employees.

Disclosures to the police (see Appendix 13 for a health authority policy on disclosure)

There are very few occasions on which the citizen is obliged as a duty by Act of Parliament to provide the police with information. The main statutes requiring disclosure are cited above. Many quandaries arise outside those areas and concern the powers of the police to require a professional to disclose confidential information during police investigations. Another difficulty is the position where, by chance, particularly through work in the community, the professional obtains evidence that a crime has been committed or is being committed: for example stolen goods are seen in a client's home; there is evidence of drug abuse; there is evidence that a child is being physically or mentally ill-treated, or sexually abused; there is evidence that a patient has had an illegal abortion; there has been an attempt to conceal the birth of a stillborn child; a wife has suffered a severe battering by the husband.

The police powers are now contained in the Police and Criminal Evidence Act 1984. Medical records and human tissue or tissue fluid which has been taken for the purposes of diagnosis or medical treatment and which a person holds in confidence are subject to special procedures (see Fig. 8.5). A suggested procedure for disclosure to the police can be found in Appendix 13.

Police and Criminal Evidence Act 1984 Section 9. A constable may obtain access to excluded material or special procedure material by making an application under Schedule 1 Section 11. Excluded material means

(a) personal records which a person has acquired or created in course of any trade, business, profession ... and which he holds in confidence;
(b) human tissue or tissue fluid which has been taken for the purposes of diagnosis or medical treatment and which a person holds in confidence
(c) ....

Section 12. Personal records means documentary or records concerning an individual (whether living or dead) who can be identified from them and relating

(a) to his physical or mental health;
(b) to spiritual counselling or assistance given or to be given to him

Section 14. Special procedure material means material other than items subject to legal privilege and excluded material in the possession of a person who

(a) acquired or created it in course of any trade, business, profession or other occupation ...; and
(b) holds it subject to an express or implied undertaking to hold it in confidence

A circuit judge can make an order that the person who appears to be in possession of the specified material should produce it to a constable for him to take it away or give a constable access to it, not later than the end of the period of 7 days from the date of the order. The judge must be satisfied that specific access conditions are fulfilled before making the order.

Figure 8.5 Police and Criminal Evidence Act 1984.

Disclosure where a criminal offence is believed to have taken place

SITUATION 8.4 RAPE?

The police arrive at the accident and emergency department one night enquiring about the possibility of a young man in his twenties having been admitted with severe lacerations to his face and neck. About two hours earlier a girl of 15 years had been found in a serious condition having suffered an attack. She tried to defend herself by hitting the assailant in the face with a mirror. There was blood on the mirror and she believed she had cut him severely. The police arrive in the department and ask the duty nurse if they can go through the admissions during the last two hours.

The information required by the police is related to the medical records and thus comes under the special procedure. The police can make an application to a circuit judge for an order for the production of special procedure material. He will only do so if he is satisfied that certain conditions are present. However, these are the ultimate powers. It is unlikely that the police would be obliged to go to this length against a health authority. If it is known that the police can ultimately seek an order for disclosure, then the NHS Trust policy is likely to be one of cooperation with them. In a case such as the rape case above, the nurse would be advised to call the medical officer in charge of the accident and emergency department who would identify any patients who come within a fairly detailed description of the likely assailant. Giving the police the admission book would be beyond this duty.

In a recent case, *R. v. Cardiff Crown Court ex parte Kellam, The Times* 3 May 1993, an order for disclosure to the police of the social security records giving dates of admission and discharge to the hospital was held not to come within the provisions of Schedule 1 of the Police and Criminal Evidence Act 1984.

SITUATION 8.5 LET ME KNOW!

The police are investigating a burglary in which the householder came back early and surprised the burglar, who fell from a first floor window but still managed to escape. The police have enquired at the various accident and emergency departments in the vicinity. At one hospital they heard of an admission following a road accident where a man said he fell from a motorcycle when it crashed against a tree. There were no witnesses. They believe that the injuries are comparable to those the burglar might have sustained. Since the patient is not yet fit for interrogation as he has just come from the operating theatre, the police ask the ward sister:

1. to let them know when he can be questioned; and
2. not to let him go until the police arrive.

What is the ward sister's position? Must she obey this order?

1. *Notifying the police of the patient's fitness for questioning*: it is not clear whether the police have a legal right to insist that this is done. For example, if the ward sister decides that her duty is to the patient, not to the police and thus fails to notify the police, could she then be prosecuted for obstructing the police in the execution of their duty? The answer is probably not, unless it can be shown that they had express legal powers to demand the information from her. In practice, of course, staff often rely on the help of the police when they have aggressive visitors, or even aggressive patients, and are therefore prepared to reciprocate. What we are concerned with here is the legal duty on the ward sister to provide this information, and it is unlikely that this power exists.
2. *Keeping the patient until the police arrive*: the citizen does have wide powers of arrest, though they are of course more limited than police powers. The sister would have no statutory power of keeping the patient (which would, in fact, be arresting him) until the arrival of the police unless either she knows that an arrestable offence has been committed and the patient is guilty of this, or she has reasonable grounds for suspecting that he is guilty. In the circumstances described above it would not appear likely that the ward sister has those grounds since as far as she knows the patient could well have fallen from his motorcycle. She would therefore be on very shaky grounds if she refused to allow him to take his own discharge other than on the basis that she was acting out of her duty of care to save his life. In this situation the police would have to provide a watcher to wait until

such time as the patient could be questioned or taken to the police station under arrest.

Reporting crime to the police

SITUATION 8.6 DISCOVERY IN THE COMMUNITY_____

Jane, a health visitor, goes to enquire at a house where there is a young child of 18 months, since she has not seen her in the clinic and the child is due for several vaccinations and tests. While in the house she notices the following: small burn marks on the child who looks very undernourished; four brand new video recorders in the corner of the room; and a pipe from the electricity supply which by-passes the meter. One might question her imagination over the last item but if this is in fact what she spotted, does she have any duty in respect of them?

1. *Non-accidental injury*: Jane's duty is to the child so there can be no doubt that if she has reasonable grounds for suspecting that there is any abuse, then she must take the appropriate action to safeguard the child. There is a clear procedure for action if such a situation exists and Jane would have the responsibility to set it in motion. Even if Jane were a district nurse and visiting the mother rather than the child she would still have a duty to ensure that the appropriate care was taken.
2. *Suspected stolen goods*: there is no duty upon Jane to act as police informer in such circumstances. If of course the goods were subsequently found to be stolen and Jane was summoned to court as a witness she would have to give evidence of what she had seen. What, however, if the goods were NHS Trust property? Does she have a duty to inform her employer that goods are being stolen? The answer depends upon whether a term can be implied into the contract of employment that any employee must inform the employer of any thefts from the workplace. There is no case which has decided the point but it would appear to make business sense of the contract of employment if such a duty could be seen to be implied (see Chapter 10 on implying terms into a contract of employment).
3. *Electricity*: it could be argued that the system for by-passing the meter is simply another case of stolen goods and theft. However, there are additional problems here since a considerable public danger in risking fire or (if it were gas) explosion might be caused. It could therefore be argued that Jane did have a public duty to notify the police since her client and others could be in considerable danger.

It is obvious that the present law on disclosure to the police in the public interest is unsatisfactory. Much is left to the discretion of the individual nurse in walking the tightrope between keeping the patient/client's information confidential and ensuring the public is not harmed. The UKCC's elaboration of Clause 9 should be closely followed and the DH consultation document on disclosure studied with great care. It must of course be emphasised that neither of these documents have the force of law and it is ultimately up to the courts to determine how the Police and Criminal Evidence Act should be interpreted and to set guidelines for the future.

Questions and exercises

1 Prepare guidelines for a new employee on the duty of confidentiality.
2 Do you consider that there is a breach of confidentiality if a nurse returns home and tells her husband that they are treating a patient with AIDS on the ward? She does not mention the patient's name.
3 Consider the exception to the duty of confidentiality entitled 'public interest' and consider examples from your own experience which may come under that heading. What justifications could you give for and against disclosure?
4 Do you consider that the patient should have an absolute right of access in law to health records held in manual form? Justify your answer.
5 Hospitals are often seen as the most difficult institutions in which to keep personal matters secret. What action do you think could be taken to enforce the duty of confidentiality in practice?

9   Statements, medical record-keeping and evidence in court

The topics to be covered in this chapter are set out in Fig. 9.1.

Statements

Figure 9.2 illustrates some of the many occasions on which staff may be required to produce a statement. The statements produced on different occasions have very different purposes and effects. For example, where a statement is taken by the police it can be used as formal evidence in criminal proceedings and the person who made the statement can be questioned on it. Where it has been made under caution, it can be used in evidence against an accused. In civil proceedings the statement is not regarded as formal evidence, though the civil court now has the power to order disclosure of witnesses' statements.

The purpose of this section is to explore the principles of statement-making and highlight some of the dangers.

Does one have to make a statement?

The one occasion on which one can refuse to make a statement is if it criminally implicates one. There is still a right of silence both in court (at present this is under review)

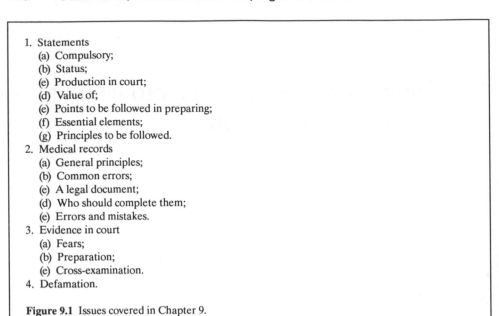

1. Statements
   (a) Compulsory;
   (b) Status;
   (e) Production in court;
   (d) Value of;
   (e) Points to be followed in preparing;
   (f) Essential elements;
   (g) Principles to be followed.
2. Medical records
   (a) General principles;
   (b) Common errors;
   (e) A legal document;
   (d) Who should complete them;
   (e) Errors and mistakes.
3. Evidence in court
   (a) Fears;
   (b) Preparation;
   (e) Cross-examination.
4. Defamation.

Figure 9.1 Issues covered in Chapter 9.

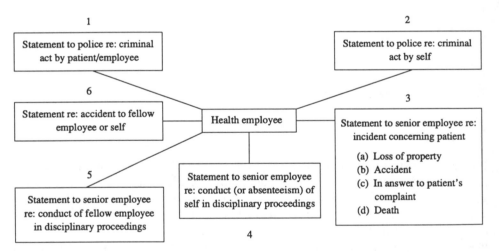

Figure 9.2 Occasions when a statement might be requested: [1 and 2 criminal proceedings; 3(a–c) and 6 civil proceedings; 4 and 5 tribunal proceedings; 3d coroner's proceedings].

and out of court. No one can be forced to answer a question if the effect of the answer is to incriminate them. Even in these circumstances, however, there are considerable advantages in setting out exactly what took place as a record, though help and guidance are clearly essential. In general, a statement is required not for self-defence but as evidence of the events to which one was a witness. There have been examples where hospital staff have refused to participate in an inquiry set up by the health authority.

For example, in the Shewin case where a patient went into hospital for a gall-bladder operation and suffered irreversible brain damage, the doctors initially refused to take part in the health authority inquiry. They eventually did so and were exonerated (1979 *BMJ* 1232).

In general, it could be argued that provided a member of staff is given appropriate guidance in making a statement, then the statement should be a valuable reminder at a later date of the details of what took place. It has not been tested out in court as to whether the employer could insist upon a statement being made by an employee as a result of an implied term in the contract of employment. However, it could be argued that the National Health Service employee would be expected to cooperate with the police and the coroner's court, and in addition that the employee would give a statement and information relevant to civil claims.

What is the status of a statement as evidence in court?

In criminal proceedings

Where the statement forms part of a police investigation and a caution has been given as to its effect, it could be used in evidence against the person who gave it, especially where the account they are now giving is entirely different from the statement.

Where the statement has been given by a person who is a witness of the events, then the statement, if it was made contemporaneously with the events described, can be used as an aid to memory. It must be emphasised that the statement is not in itself proof of the truth of the events therein described. Any number of lies or exaggerations can be recorded in a statement. However, except for certain exceptions, the person who made the statement would be expected to give evidence in court and could be cross-examined on the statement, from which the court could deduce the weight to be attached to the statement. Documentary evidence is permissible under Criminal Justice Act 1988 Ss. 23–28.

In civil proceedings

The statement can be used by its maker to refresh his memory. The court now has access to the statement; it can order disclosure of the witnesses' statements. Written documents can now be entered as evidence under the provisions of the Civil Evidence Act 1968.

Can the court always insist on the statement being produced?

In Chapter 8 the occasions on which documents are regarded as privileged were discussed. Where the statement, document, letter, etc., have come into existence as a result of and for the purposes of proposed or existing litigation, then they are covered by professional legal privilege and their disclosure cannot be enforced by the courts.

Should one make a statement?

A distinction must again be made between the criminal and the civil courts. Where the police are investigating a crime and seeking information from witnesses, then it could be an offence to refuse to cooperate with them. There is, however, no duty to incriminate oneself.

In potential civil cases there is no duty to make a statement, except possibly under the contract of employment (see above).

However, if one considers the time it takes for a case to come to court – in the civil courts sometimes as long as five or six years – it is highly unlikely that anyone would have a detailed recollection of the facts when they finally come under cross-examination or are giving evidence in chief. A detailed comprehensive statement of the events is essential to refresh one's memory. Many people have survived the ordeal of acting as witness in court and are thankful that their records and statement covering the events were so clear and detailed.

In addition, a detailed sensibly prepared statement may eliminate the chance of a nurse being called as a witness and thus save a needless attendance in court.

What points should be followed in making a statement?

Purpose?

Before a statement is made it is always advisable for its maker to have an idea of the purposes for which it is being made. Is it going to the coroner's office? Is it for internal information only? Is it to be used in a criminal prosecution? The purpose will affect the detail, style and content of the statement. The maker should therefore find out from the person who has asked for the statement who will read it and to what varied purposes it will be put. If there is any danger that the maker would incriminate herself she should ask for legal advice before making the statement. It is not necessary to wait for a request before writing a statement about a certain occurrence. In some situations it may be wise for a witness or participant to write down a brief account of the events immediately.

Guidance?

Even in circumstances where there is no question of self-incrimination it is always advisable to seek advice in making the statement. An objective reader can see gaps, ambiguities and confusion in a statement and give much valuable assistance.

Who should provide the guidance?

Normally this help should be given by a senior nurse manager. There will be occasions, however, where advice from a union officer is required. In disciplinary proceedings this depends on how far the proceedings have been taken. It would, for example, be contrary to the guidelines for good practice for management to refuse to allow an employee to receive the advice of the union representative prior to any formal disciplinary action being taken.

The essential elements in a statement are shown in Fig. 9.3.

Principles to be followed (see Fig. 9.4)

Accuracy

It is essential that only those facts which took place should be recorded. There should be no exaggeration or minimisation. Read through the statement to check if there are any inconsistencies.

Factual

The maker should, if at all possible, avoid value judgements and should keep to the facts. For example, a health visitor might have formed the opinion that one of her clients was lazy. If this is relevant to the statement it is of far more value if she were to write down a description of the facts which led her to that opinion than to make value judgements. Thus 'there were 12 dirty milk bottles on the living room floor and piles of papers on every seat, etc.' is more useful than expressing an opinion which may or may not be acceptable and is not on its own very meaningful. The facts on which those opinions are based are more useful. There are occasions where it is necessary to express opinions, especially where they led one to act in a particular way. Even here, however,

---

(a) date and time of incident;
(b) full name of maker, position, grade and location;
(c) full name of any person involved, e.g. patient, visitor, other staff;
(d) date and time the statement was made;
(e) a full and detailed description of the events which occurred;
(f) signature;
(g) any supporting statement or document attached.

Figure 9.3 Essential elements in a statement.

---

1. Accuracy.
2. Factual.
3. Avoid hearsay.
4. Conciseness.
5. Relevance.
6. Clarity.
7. Legibility.
8. Overall impact.
9. Keep copy.

Figure 9.4 Principles to be followed in preparing a statement.

it is still necessary to record the facts which led to those opinions. For example: 'Because I felt she was a danger to herself I put the cot sides up.' This statement needs to be amplified in order to expand on what has caused the nurse to believe that the patient was a danger to herself, for example had she fallen out of bed? Had she tried to leave the ward? Was she in a confused state and if so, how did she show it?

Where it is possible to check facts before making the statement this should be done. For example, a statement that a patient had a high temperature should be checked against the patient's record; similarly a description that the patient had been written up for a particular form of medication should be checked against the drug card. Sometimes it is helpful to draw a sketch of the ward layout or where the patient was found or where there is a need to identify the exact location, but only if the plan is a help rather than a further source of confusion.

Avoid hearsay

This is the recording or repetition of what someone else has seen or heard. If possible, it is best to avoid this as the person making the statement is only repeating what someone else has said and cannot give first-hand evidence of what was heard or seen. Imagine a situation where a nurse hears a fall in the night and runs in to the ward to find a patient on the floor. It is better for her statement to cover what she herself saw and heard rather than to repeat what another employee heard and saw. This other person should be asked to provide a statement of what she witnessed at first hand. Where the only witness to the events may have been another patient, it may be possible to obtain a statement from that patient but that does depend upon his physical and mental condition.

Concise

The statement must not ramble. It must be to the point in a logical sequence. Padding, waffle, meaningless generalisations should all be avoided. However, essential detail should not be sacrificed on the altar of brevity. The amount of detail required will of course depend on the facts described.

Relevance

It is a useful exercise to question oneself on the events to establish what detail a stranger to the situation would require. This questioning would have to take place in the context of the purpose for which the statement is required. In some circumstances it may be important to describe the colour, material, and style of the patient's clothes – in other circumstances this may be entirely irrelevant. If there is any doubt as to what is relevant or not, one should err on the side of inclusion. What is in can always be omitted on the grounds of relevance at a later stage; what is left out is left out for good.

Clarity

It is essential that the maker should read through the statement to ensure that it is clear and meaningful. If there are any doubts as to what is meant it should be rewritten until one is sure that it is an exact clear record of what happened. Substitutes for any misleading or ambiguous words or phrases should be found. The use of clichés should be avoided. Any abbreviations which are used should only have one meaning or the context should be so clear that there can be no mistake as to what they stand for. The readers should be ascertained so that the relevant level of technical language can be used. In some circumstances it will be necessary to explain technical procedures in full. In others there will be no need. Emphasis should be on the side of simplicity rather than complexity. One should make sure one understands it oneself.

Legibility

If the statement is handwritten it should be legible. If it is typed at a later date, ensure that the typed copy is checked for errors.

Overall impact

When reading through the statement assess its overall impact. Does it give sufficient detail? Is it clear exactly what happened? Is it accurate? Is there any further information that should be included? Is it internally consistent? Have any facts been checked?

Be prepared to make any necessary changes. The statement should not be signed unless its maker is 100 per cent satisfied with it. Never let it go if you are dissatisfied with any aspect. Never allow yourself to be browbeaten into including something which is not within your knowledge or which you know is not entirely accurate. This is your statement which you will sign as accurate in every detail and your reputation and integrity might depend upon this accuracy. A copy should be kept.

SITUATION 9.1 SCOPE OF PROFESSIONAL PRACTICE

The facts: The Roger Park District Health Authority had agreed with the National Board, Royal College of Nurses, and other nursing professional organisations that registered general nurses employed by the District Health Authority would be able to carry out certain clinical tasks formerly considered to be the sole responsibility of the medical staff. One of these tasks was inter-nasal gastric feeding by clinifeed tube, a very small tube which usually has to be X-rayed to ensure that it is correctly sited. Margery Broome, who had been employed by the District Health Authority for three years as a staff nurse on a surgical ward was off sick when the course for clinifeed tubing was held (on which she had been selected to go). She thus missed the intense tuition for this skill. No alternative course was suggested to her.

One weekend in December, when Margery was on duty and in charge of the ward, the consultant surgeon, Mr Browne, was on intake and the ward was under heavy pressure. The difficulties were aggravated by the fact that Mr Browne had had a long list on Saturday in an effort to reduce the waiting list (increased as a result of recent industrial action) and to prevent any further build-up before Christmas. Extra beds had been put up in the centre of the ward and the nursing team were particularly harassed because their numbers were reduced by a flu epidemic.

Mr Browne's registrar decided that Peter Price, a young man who had been operated on earlier in the week and had been drip-fed for several days, should be tube-fed experimentally to see how he coped. He recommended that a clinifeed tube be fitted. He did not ask Margery if she was eligible to undertake the procedure, nor did she attempt to tell him that she had not yet been on the training course.

Margery initiated the feed by inserting the tube down Peter Price's nose into the stomach and commenced pouring in the liquid feed. As she was doing this a state enrolled nurse came to ask if another extra bed could be put up for another emergency admission patient who had just been brought in. As Margery Broome indicated where she wished the bed to be placed, she heard a spluttering and coughing behind her and realised that Peter was in considerable distress. She immediately stopped the feed and removed the tube. He was gasping for breath, Margery requested that a doctor be called and initiated resuscitative measures. Despite an emergency operation on the lungs, however, Peter Price died. Peter's widow brought an action under the Fatal Accidents Acts and the Law Reform (Miscellaneous Provisions) Act 1934 against Margery Broome, Mr Browne, the registrar and the Health Authority alleging that their negligence caused the death of her husband. Damages are agreed as being over £100,000. Liability is denied.

Margery Browne's statement: (how many errors can you spot based on the principles already discussed?)

The Death of Peter Price

I certainly remember the day it happened. The morning began with a row with Mr Browne's registrar, Danladi Singh – I'm not racially prejudiced but I knew from the moment he started that he would be difficult. He never understood the nursing difficulties. He was always admitting patients, never minding how the nursing staff would cope, and since Mr Browne's illness Singh had made all the decisions. Well that morning we were on intake, Mr Browne was doing an additional list and Singh wanted me to ask Medical Records to send a telegram to ask the patient to come in the afternoon. Sister was off. I was in charge and I really blew my top. I told him of the difficulties we were in with the flu outbreak and the union dispute. I told him it wasn't fair on the patient – to call her in on a Saturday afternoon. He said it did not matter if it was Christmas Day or Saturday. That's partly the trouble with these foreigners. They don't make any attempt to understand the patients and their ways. Anyway, Singh agreed that he would not call her. I'm sure that it was because of this he then asked me to do the drip feed with the clinifeed tubes. I knew I had missed the course but I had seen it done many times by Sister and the principles seemed to be the same as the nasal gastric feeds I did in training. Singh was too bad-tempered to stay and help me so I started to set it up on my own. I knew that we would soon be having patients back from theatre so I wanted to get started.

Peter Price was making very good progress. He had had carcinoma of the stomach and I don't think they left much stomach after the operation. The one advantage of the clinifeed was that he would be on a permanent feed which Mr Browne believed was much better for the patients post-operatively. Singh always regarded Peter as an aggressive patient but I never had much trouble with him.

I started introducing the tube with the introducer. It was a bit difficult pulling it out, but I had often seen Sister straining to get it out. I checked to ensure that the tube was in the stomach by aspirating it, but the tube was too fine to get any result. Just as I had started pouring in the feed, the SEN, Janet Pritchard, called me about an extra bed that Singh wanted for another emergency patient. I was really incensed. We were too overworked to have extra beds. Peter Price made a gurgling noise and Pritchard and I rushed to him. I took out the tube and Pritchard went to get Singh. It seemed as though he had a cardiac arrest or a fit of some sort. He was very blue and I started to do mouth-to-mouth resuscitation. Singh then came and took over. I am sure that the feed had nothing to do with his death.

There can seldom be a statement as bad as this, not only for the irrelevancies that it contains but also the essential information which is missing. The time and date of the events, as well as the time and date of the statement being made, are all missing. The staff on the ward who are potential witnesses should also be named with their appropriate grade. Far more information is required as to what exactly she did with the feed when her attention was diverted as well as more information about patient numbers and more specific information about the pressures: 'too overworked' is meaningless. Specific facts relating to the work pressure should be given along with any information relating to formal or informal complaints to senior nursing staff or medical staff about the pressures. In addition, it is clear that the whole style of the statement is wrong and unprofessional.

Medical record-keeping

General principles

Most nurses are now using the nursing process as a system of patient care and record-keeping. Kept properly, the records should be meaningful, clear accounts of the patients' care. 'Had a good day', which is one of the most unhelpful statements, should not feature in the new records. Why did she have a good day? Had her appetite returned? Had she spent most of the time sleeping? Alternatively, had she spent most of the day awake? Had she been of minimal trouble to the nursing staff? Had she in contrast been lively and interacted with the nursing staff? All these situations, many of them incompatible, are within the meaning of those words.

Some nurses might see this paperwork as a distraction from the real task of nursing, i.e. caring for the patient. However, these records are not just for the protection of the nurse. They are an integral part of the nursing care. Failure to record an important item, e.g. administration of a drug, may mislead other professionals such as those on a later nursing shift, and the patient could consequently be given an overdose. Accurate, comprehensive information relating to the care and the condition of the patient is a vital part of the professional role of the nurse. In addition, the information could be used for many other purposes of which the nurse may not be aware at the time.

On some occasions, records may be looked at in a matter unconnected with the treatment of that particular patient. For example, in the *Deacon* v. *McVicar* case (see pages 54–5) there was a dispute as to the priority that a particular patient should have been given and the judge ordered the records of the other patients on the ward at the time to be disclosed in order to assess whether or not they would have been making demands upon medical and nursing time at a particular point in time.

The preceding chapter considers the rules relating to the disclosure of medical records in cases of personal injury litigation, and the powers of the court to order the discovery of any relevant documents with only privileged records being exempt from disclosure.

Again it must be repeated that medical records are not proof of the truth of the facts stated in them but the maker of the record must be called to give evidence as to the truth of what is contained in them. There are exceptions under the Civil Evidence Acts which permit the records to be used in evidence without the presence of the maker (where, for example, the maker is dead, or overseas) but due warning of the intent to use the records in evidence must be given to the other side.

UKCC: standards for records and record-keeping

This document was issued in April 1993 and is an invaluable guide to all practitioners. A copy can be found in Appendix 9. It provides guidelines for recording patient information and summarises the principles underpinning records and record-keeping.

Common errors noted in record-keeping

These are listed in Fig. 9.5 and are the most common errors noted by a group of health visitors in record-keeping.

It is clear that any weakness in record-keeping will hamper the professional when it comes to giving evidence in court and will render her vulnerable in cross-examination, especially when there has been a considerable delay between the events recorded and the court hearing.

times omitted;

illegible handwriting;

lack of entry in the record when an abortive call has been made;

abbreviations which were ambiguous;

record of phone call (e.g. to social services) which omitted the name of the recipient (e.g. social worker);

use of Tippex and covering of errors;

no signature;

absence of information about the child;

inaccuracies, especially of the date;

omission of date of medical check up and hearing test and records for immunisation;

delay in completing the record; sometimes more than 24 hours elapsed before the records were completed;

record completed by someone who did not make visit;

inaccuracies of name, date of birth, and address;

unprofessional terminology, e.g. 'dull as a door step';

meaningless phrases, e.g. 'lovely child';

opinion mixed up with facts;

reliance on information from neighbours without identifying the source;

subjective not objective comments, e.g. 'normal development'

Figure 9.5 Common errors in record-keeping.

What constitutes a legal document?

The nurse is often concerned as to what is a legal document. For example, are the nursing care plans legal documents? The answer is that any document requested by the court becomes a legal document. The court could subpoena the disclosure of Kardex or the nursing process documents, medical records, X-rays, pathology laboratory reports, social workers' records, any document in fact which may be relevant to the case. If they are missing, the writer of the records could be cross-examined as to the circumstances of their disappearance.

Who should sign or write the records?

Any individual, and this would include untrained staff or learners who have first-hand knowledge of any events regarding the care of the patient, should write up the relevant record and initial or sign it. Countersigning might be required by trained staff in certain circumstances and the procedure for this would be laid down locally. Any member of staff, trained or not, could be summoned to court to give evidence of what took place.

What about errors and mistakes?

If it is necessary to change what has been written it is good practice for a line to be put through the incorrect statement and the correct statement made underneath rather than heavily scoring out the incorrect sentence or using correction fluid. If the records are ever used in evidence, it is then clear what was originally written and why it was changed. It must be repeated that these records are not proof of the truth of what they contain but the writer of the records could be summoned to court to give direct evidence as to their accuracy and reliability. Reference should be made to Paragraph 13.4 of the UKCC guidelines (see Appendix 9).

Evidence in court

(Reference should be made to Chapters 2 and 6 for procedures followed in criminal and civil courts.)

Fears of giving evidence in court

There are few health professionals who relish the possibility of being required to give evidence in court. Preparation and guidance in facing the ordeal are essential, whether it is a criminal court, coroner's court, civil court, professional conduct hearing, or industrial tribunal. Of equal importance, however, are comprehensive, clear and accurate records. Figure 9.6 sets out some of the fears expressed by health visitors (probably the most likely of the nursing profession to face a court appearance).

---

fear of the unknown;
hearing the client call one a liar;
publicity;
waiting and the build-up in tension which can arise;
remembering the detail of what took place;
fear of being made to look a fool;
being unable to express oneself concisely;
contradicting oneself;
omissions in one's statement upon which one could be cross-examined;
being made to feel guilty;
downright rudeness and offensiveness of the others in court, especially the barristers;
tension and nerves;
being turned into the betrayer of the client;
waste of time;
being cross-examined by the client when he is not represented but is conducting his case personally;
failure to understand the legal jargon, the procedure and the gestures;
manipulation under cross-examination and being forced to change one's evidence.

Figure 9.6 Fears over a court appearance.

Preparation for a court appearance

Experience in giving evidence in court will undoubtedly clear some of the anxieties illustrated in Fig. 9.6. Many can be solved by a private visit to a court hearing (they are all open to the public except for the few cases such as juvenile and matrimonial proceedings which are heard in camera), and going on one's own or in a group without any personal involvement gives one a sense of the procedure and language used and provides a chance of familiarising oneself with the process.

Preparation for the appearance with the solicitor who should explain the procedure and the context in which one would give evidence is also essential. Considerable expertise can often be built up within a department and the lessons learnt passed from one to another.

Confidence in the records that have been kept and the statements made should ensure that nerves are kept in control. The nurse should know the contents of the original records and where the entries appear so that there is no fumbling through the original records in the course of giving evidence.

Cross-examination

As far as the cross-examination is concerned it should be remembered that following a few guidelines should limit the damage to one's evidence in chief:

> Go prepared to the court hearing with the relevant records and documentation; read through the contemporaneous notes beforehand; go through the evidence with a senior nurse manager.
> *In court:*
> Be honest; do not exaggerate; do not be drawn into saying something that is not true; do not rush the answers; take time to think.
> Be aware of the 'Catch 22' type question:
> > *Q.* You are a nurse?
> > *A.* Yes.
> > *Q.* You are therefore observant?
> How do you answer this? If you say 'yes' the next questions could be:
> > *Q.* How fast was the car going?
> > *A.* Er ... I'm not sure.
> > *Q.* But I thought you said you were observant.
> If you say 'no' the next question could be:
> > *Q.* Then your observations in this case are entirely useless?
> > *A.* Er.
> If you answer the original question: 'sometimes it depends on what I am observing' it is likely to lead to a question or comment such as 'then we cannot rely on your evidence in this case'.

Such tactics are unlikely to have any effect on the judge's view but they can sometimes influence the jury's thinking (it must be remembered, however, that there is usually no jury in the Civil Court and the nurse's involvement in a jury trial in the Crown Court is likely to be rare). What is more likely, however, is that the tactics used unnerve the person being cross-examined and cause difficulties for the future. The witness feels discredited. One way of avoiding the Catch 22 question is to expand on the answer so that one is answering fully and accurately.

Q. You are therefore observant?
A. My training has taught me to observe a patient's condition.

It is important under such pressure to avoid becoming angry or upset.

It is important to avoid commenting on the relevance of the question: 'do I have to answer that question, my Lord?' is fine on a TV drama but unnecessarily dramatic in court. In most circumstances one can rely upon one's own lawyer or the judge to protect one from unnecessary harassment.

It must be remembered that in cross-examination there are two purposes. One is to discredit the witness's potentially hostile evidence against a client by showing the witness to be unreliable, dishonest, exaggerated, given to imagination, inconsistent (either internally, i.e. within her own evidence, or externally, i.e. in contrast to what another witness has said or what other evidence shows), unclear, confused, suffering from amnesia, or (and this may be the most effective) irrelevant.

The other purpose of cross-examination is to build up the strength of the side undertaking the cross-examination. Thus the witness being cross-examined can be used to bolster the good character and reputation of the defendant. 'What were his good qualities?' 'Was she a good mother?' 'Did you see her show any kindness to the child?' 'Did you like her?' is another Catch 22 question since once again to answer negatively implies that the witness being cross-examined is prejudiced; to answer affirmatively shows that the client has likeable qualities.

It is important in this context for the professionals to remember that in cases where they are giving evidence as witnesses as a result of their professional work, they are not on a particular side. They are called to give evidence of facts that they themselves witnessed. Their reputation does not hang upon getting a particular outcome in a negligence case or in a non-accidental injury case. Where the client is personally cross-examining the professional there should be no sense of betrayal since the professional would have been subpoenaed to attend court and is not there voluntarily.

Defamation

One concern of anyone asked to provide a statement or give evidence is that he or she could face an action for defamation. The main principles of such an action will be discussed very briefly here.

Defamation is either libel or slander. Libel is usually in writing or at least in a permanent form. Thus broadcasting or a record would be considered to be libel. Slander is the spoken word. The main difference is that to succeed in an action for slander it is necessary to show that harm has occurred as a result of the slander, whereas in an action for libel is not necessary to establish harm. There are four main exceptions to having to show harm resulting from a slander: imputation of a criminal offence; imputation that the individual suffers from a contagious or infectious disease; accusation of unchastity in a woman; imputations in respect of profession, business or office.

To be defamatory the statement must tend to injure the reputation of the person to whom it refers, i.e. it tends to lower him in the estimation of right-thinking members of society generally. The statement must be untrue. Truth is a complete defence to an action for defamation. In addition it must be 'published', i.e. spoken or made to an individual other than the plaintiff. Thus if when we were alone together I accused you incorrectly of having AIDS this would not be defamatory since there is no publication. On the other hand, if I said this to someone else about you it could be actionable.

There are certain occasions which are said to be privileged, i.e. even though the statement is untrue and defamatory it is not actionable since it is made in privileged circumstances. Some occasions are regarded as absolute privilege, for example statements made in the Houses of Parliament or in judicial proceedings. Other occasions are considered to have qualified privilege. These include statements made in the performance of duty, in the protection of an interest, professional communications between solicitor and client or reports of parliamentary, judicial and certain other public proceedings. A statement which is subject to absolute privilege is not actionable, even though the speaker knows that what he is saying is untrue or he is acting out of malice. In contrast an untrue statement made on a qualified occasion which is actuated by malice is actionable. Malice means the presence of an improper motive, or even gross and unreasoned prejudice. The effect of malice is to destroy the privilege and if the statement is untrue and defamatory then it is actionable.

SITUATION 9.2 REFERENCES

A ward sister is asked to provide a reference for an SEN who has been working on her ward. The SEN came under suspicion of theft shortly before this request and the ward sister felt that she would not be honest or accurate if she omitted this fact. The SEN failed to get the job she was applying for and subsequently learnt of the contents of the reference. In the meantime a cleaner was charged and found guilty of the theft. The SEN is threatening to sue the ward sister for defamation. Would she succeed?

There is no doubt that to say someone is guilty of theft would be a defamatory statement if it were untrue. However, writing a reference would probably be regarded as an occasion of qualified privilege. If the ward sister wrote the reference without any improper motive she should have a good defence in an action for defamation. If, on the other hand, she made that statement for some other purpose, then the privilege is destroyed by malice. What if she merely stated that the nurse was under suspicion for theft which would be true? If the words conveyed the impression that there were grounds for considering the nurse to be guilty of theft then they could be regarded as defamatory and therefore actionable unless protected by qualified privilege. The Defamation Act 1952 provides defences where an innocent defamation is made.

Questions and exercises

1 Prepare a statement concerning an incident which has recently occurred. Read it through and consider the errors which have been made.
2 What errors have you noticed in record-keeping?
3 What is meant by hearsay? Give several examples of it.
4 Arrange a visit to your local Magistrates Court, County Court, Crown Court or industrial tribunal and write up the points that any potential witness should be aware of in relation to the procedure, formality and language used. If you have the chance to visit more than one court draw up a list of the differences between them.
5 What most concerns you about the possibility of giving evidence in court? Prepare a list of your concerns, then consider ways of meeting some of these anxieties.
6 In defamation, information given on a privileged occasion without malice is not actionable, even though it is untrue and defamatory, provided that there is no malice. What is meant by this statement? What occasions do you consider could be privileged in this way?

10   The nurse and employment law

The nurse is often bewildered by the complexities of employment law, yet she needs to know her way through the maze for two basic reasons: on the one hand, she is an employee and therefore should be acquainted with the rights of an employee; on the other hand, she may be or become a manager in which case she will need to be able to advise her staff on their rights and also to understand the relevant employment law covering her role as manager. The areas discussed in this chapter are set out in Fig. 10.1.

The legal relationship of employee/employer is composed of many terms drawn from a variety of sources. These are shown in Fig. 10.2. First we look at how the contract of employment comes into existence.

The contract of employment

Formation and content

Stages leading to the formation of a contract of employment

When a nurse accepts the offer of a post, a contract then comes into existence and the nurse will be bound by its terms. In this sense the contract is an abstract concept; there

1. The contract
   A. Formation and contents
      (a) formation;
      (b) failure to declare a particular medical condition or criminal record;
      (c) are terms agreed at interview binding?
      (d) content of the contract
          (i)   express terms;
          (ii)   express terms already agreed;
          (iii) future terms;
          (iv)   statutory terms;
          (v)   implied terms;
          (vi)   terms resulting from custom and practice.
   B. Can an employee see or have a copy of the contract?
   C. Changes in the contract.
   D. Breach of contract
      (a) by employee;
      (b) by employer.
2. Statutory rights
   A. Rights of the pregnant employee.
      (a) right not to be unfairly dismissed;
      (b) right to return to work;
      (c) ante-natal visits;
      (d) maternity pay;
      (e) maternity leave.
   B. Time-off provisions.
   C. Unfair dismissal
      (i)   general principles;
      (ii)   constructive dismissal;
      (iii) the procedure;
      (iv)   the hearing.
3. Trade union rights.
4. Public and private employees.
5. Discrimination by sex or race.
6. Equal pay.

Figure 10.1 Issues covered in Chapter 10.

Figure 10.2 Sources of a contract of employment.

may be nothing in writing but the relationship of the parties is radically altered by that agreement.

In any negotiation leading up to a contract of employment there may be many documents circulated: an advertisement, an application form, perhaps a job description, certainly an interview.

All these stages are known as an invitation to treat. Neither party is bound by them and can pull out of the negotiations at any stage. Thus an employer is not bound to appoint after advertising a post. Similarly, someone who has sent in an application form can withdraw at any stage from the field prior to acceptance of an offer. A contract only comes into being once an offer has been accepted. The offer is usually made by the employer. This could be in writing (for example, after holding interviews the applicants could be sent away without knowing the results and be told that they will be notified) or it could be at the actual interview when the applicants wait until the successful one is summoned and offered the post. Sometimes this might be a conditional offer: it might, for example, be an offer dependent on a satisfactory medical examination or references, or the selection panel might not have the power to offer the post but can only recommend to the authority that X be appointed. The candidate should be absolutely clear as to the nature of the offer since if it was subject to approval by a higher authority who did not agree to that appointment, or indeed to any appointment, then the candidate would have no remedy if she has undergone expenses believing that she had a contract, or has even terminated her existing job. If the candidate accepts an unconditional offer then and there she is bound by that contract.

SITUATION 10.1 BETTER PROSPECTS

A ward sister applies for, is offered and accepts a post in a neighbouring NHS Trust. She then sees a nursing officer post advertised in her own Trust, applies and is accepted before she has commenced work in the new post. What is her position in law?

Technically she is in breach of contract. She is bound by the contract to the first Trust. In practice, it is unlikely to take action against her; certainly the publicity that would arise would do little to enhance the reputation of that Trust and the courts are unlikely to order the ward sister to commence work with the new Trust, preferring to compensate by an order for damages to be paid rather than make what is known as an order for specific performance of the contract. The amount payable would be minimal and it may be difficult to obtain payment from an individual.

Failure to declare a particular medical condition or criminal record

It is for the prospective employer to ascertain the good and bad about any prospective employee. There is no obligation upon the candidate to present her inadequacies. However, if the applicant is questioned about medical history or criminal record and lies or fails to disclose relevant information, then if this information is later discovered after the applicant has been offered the post and accepted, the employer is entitled to terminate the contract on the grounds of the misrepresentation provided that he would not have offered the post had he known of the facts. In addition a lie can also be a criminal offence.

The Rehabilitation of Offenders Act 1974 protects those who have a past criminal record from being compelled to disclose it (for example, someone who has been imprisoned for between 6 and 30 months can regard this record as spent after a rehabilitation period of 10 years). However, this Act does not apply to most health service posts and thus the applicant would have to disclose a criminal record when asked.

SITUATION 10.2 UNDISCLOSED EPILEPSY

An applicant for a post of nursing auxiliary is not asked and fails to disclose that she suffers from epilepsy. This is discovered subsequently when she has a fit at work. The employers sent her a letter dismissing her. What are her legal rights?

The employers can either give her the requisite notice or they could dismiss her instantly on the grounds that she is not capable of performing the job safely. (For her rights to apply for unfair dismissal see below.)

Are terms agreed at an interview binding?

It sometimes happens that an applicant at an interview is given certain assurances about the conditions of work: shifts, hours, days off, holiday dates, location of the work place, etc. These terms can be made conditions of the contract. Thus an applicant who had already booked a holiday can obtain an agreement that one of the terms of the contract is that these dates can be retained. Failure to keep to this agreement would constitute a breach of contract by the employer. However, it is a question of fact as to whether the discussion leads to an agreed term or is merely a working arrangement which can be changed by the employer at a later date. In order to safeguard her position, the nurse, in accepting the post in writing, could confirm that certain terms have been agreed as part of the contract.

Content of the contract

Figure 10.2 shows sources of the various terms which comprise a contract of employment.

Express terms agreed between employer and applicant
These would include the starting date, the grade and title of post, the point on the salary scale at which the employee would start and many others. It is a matter of interpretation as to how much of the details in the advertisement become terms of the contract.

Express terms already agreed for the post
The bulk of the terms and conditions of posts in the National Health Service are nationally agreed and contained in the Whitley Council Agreements, and the health authority

was bound by these. They comprise the General Council Conditions and conditions relating to particular staff groups. The employee's contract should make it clear that it is subject to these nationally negotiated conditions. They should be available for inspection by any employee or applicant. NHS Trusts have power to negotiate terms locally.

Future terms agreed by Whitley Council

Even though an employee is not a member of a trade union and not represented on the Whitley Council the changes and modifications to these terms will be binding on all employees and will usually be incorporated into the individual's contract of employment. At present, the Nurse Pay Review Body recommends revisions to the nurses' pay. In the future, NHS Trusts will negotiate terms locally with their employees and there is likely to be a reduction in the number of NHS employees under Whitley Council conditions of service.

Statutory terms

Additional terms are added by Act of Parliament and are discussed below. These are binding on the employer.

Implied terms

Additional terms are also implied in a contract of employment which place obligations upon the employer or employee. Past court rulings by judges have decided whether certain specific terms should be implied and also what tests should be used to decide if a particular term is implied.

Figure 10.3 sets out implied terms placing obligations on the employer. Figure 10.4 sets out implied terms placing obligations on the employee.

SITUATION 10.3 IMPLIED TERMS

An emergency arises in Y Hospital following a multiple pile-up on the nearby motorway. A call is put out to those off duty in the nurses' home, which is on site, that help is urgently required. Mavis, a staff nurse who has just come off

---

(a) a duty to care for the health and safety of the employee;
(b) a duty to pay and provide work;
(c) a duty to treat the employee with consideration and support him.

Figure 10.3 Implied terms binding on the employer.

(a) a duty to obey the reasonable orders of the employer;
(b) a duty to act with care and skill;
(c) a duty not to compete with the employer's enterprise;
(d) a duty to keep secrets and confidential information.

Figure 10.4 Implied terms binding on the employee.

duty after an eight-hour shift, is asked to return. She refuses, saying she is too tired. She has actually arranged to go out with her boy friend. Her absence is noted and she is subsequently disciplined. She argued that her off duty was her own time and she had no obligations to the employer during it. Also she was far too tired to be of any assistance and in fact would have been positively dangerous to the patients. The employers, in contrast, might argue that there is an implied term in the contract that even when the employee is off duty she can still be summoned to assist in an emergency. The outcome of such a case will hinge on whether such a term should be implied and also whether a nurse is correct in refusing to help when she is tired and therefore a potential hazard to the patient.

What tests are used to determine if a term will be implied? The courts have decided that the following tests are appropriate in determining whether a term will be implied. One is known as the Officious Bystander Test. Imagine the following situation: nurse and NHS Trust are discussing the possibility of establishing a contract between them. They are outlining the terms: hours, pay, holidays, etc., and someone overhearing them asks what happens in an emergency. Does the employer have the right to summon any nurse to return to work? If the negotiating couple were to turn to the questioner and say 'Of course that goes without saying', then the term would be implied. Another test used is whether the term is necessary to make business sense of the contract. There is no decided case on the question here but I think most nurses would agree that such a term would be implied subject to the question of the physical and mental fitness of the nurse to continue to work.

What about Mavis's fitness to work? It is true that an employee who is unfit to work and a likely danger to fellow employees and patients should stay away. However, in an emergency situation risks might have to be taken and the risk of potential harm to the patient balanced against the value of that additional pair of hands. It would be a question of fact.

Terms resulting from custom and practice

This overworked phrase has been used by trade unionists to give contractual force to certain work practices and privileges which were not original terms of the contract. However, the judicial meaning is much narrower and is confined to special trades and works where the nature of the work has led to special terms being implied. To be legally recognised by the courts a custom must be 'reasonable, certain and notorious'.

Can an employee see or have a copy of her contract?

A statutory right is given to employees to receive a statement of written particulars of the contract. Previously NHS employees, as crown employees, were excluded from these provisions. However, by Section 60 of the NHS and Community Care Act (see page 188), health service bodies lost the status of being crown bodies and all NHS employees now have this statutory right. Employers are required within two months of the commence-

(a) Name of employer and employee.
(b) Date when employment (and the period of continuous employment) began.
(c) Remuneration and the intervals at which it is to be paid.
(d) Hours of work.
(e) Holiday entitlement.
(f) Sickness entitlement.
(g) Pensions and pension schemes.
(h) Notice entitlement.
(i) Job title or brief job description.
(j) Period of employment, or date of ending fixed term, if post not permanent.
(k) Place of work or locations if more than one, and the employer's address.
(l) Details of collective agreements affecting employment.
(m) Additional detail if employee is expected to work abroad.
(n) Details of disciplinary and grievance procedures.

Figure 10.5 Written particulars of the contract of employment.

ment of employment, and as soon as possible after any change in the contract, to give written particulars of the terms set out in Fig. 10.5. This statement is not the contract itself but provides *prima facie* evidence of the contractual terms. This right is given to all employees working eight hours a week or more, provided that they are employed for at least a month (Section 26, Schedule 4, Trade Union Reform and Employee Rights Act 1993).

Changing the contract

SITUATION 10.4 JOB TITLE

A staff nurse was appointed on the basis that she worked on the surgical ward at Roger Park Hospital. After two years she was asked to work on the medical wards at Green Down Hospital. She was unwilling either to change her speciality or to move from the present hospital. Could she refuse to move?

The answer depends upon whether the location and the speciality are terms of the contract. If they are, then it would be a breach of contract for the employer to change the contract unilaterally. This is because one of the basic principles of contract law is that one party cannot change the terms without the agreement of the other party to the contract. Thus if these issues are seen to be contractual conditions, then the nurse is entitled to retain them. However, care must be taken in insisting on legal rights since it may be that a redundancy situation exists in which case a nurse who refused unreasonably to accept suitable alternative work would lose both her job and the right to obtain compensation. In addition, if someone has been unfairly dismissed she has a duty to mitigate the loss (see section on unfair dismissal, page 156).

Often, however, the location and ward are not contractual terms but simply a working arrangement, in which case they can be reasonably altered by the employer without the consent or the right of refusal of the employee. How does one know if the issue in dispute is a contractual term or not? This would depend upon the nature of the agreement between them, on the letter (if any) offering the post, and on other evidence of the understanding between the parties as to the nature of the contract.

SITUATION 10.5 NIGHT OR DAY

Jane Jarvis decided to return to work part-time when her two children commenced play school. She decided initially to work a few nights a week, taking advantage of the children's absence to get some sleep. After a few months the NHS Trust decided to rearrange the shifts and all staff were to be employed on a day/night rota. Jane protested that this was in breach of contract. Is she right?

As in the above case on location, it depends on what was agreed when Jane accepted the post. If the post was advertised as a night sister post and at the interview there was no suggestion that she would be expected to work days and a letter offering her the post described it as a night sister's post, it would be reasonable to say that she has a contractual right to work nights only. An attempt by the employer to change this without her consent would be a breach of contract. She might therefore be able to negotiate compensation for waiving her contractual rights to stay on nights. If she were to claim unfair dismissal she might find her compensation reduced should she fail to take alternative work since she has a duty to mitigate her loss in an unfair dismissal situation.

The employer: NHS Trust

Most NHS nurses now work for provider units known as NHS Trusts. These were set up under the NHS and Community Care Act 1990 and contracts have been transferred from health authorities and their directly managed units. Protection is given by Sections 6 and 7 of the 1990 Act to staff who are transferred to NHS Trusts. In addition, Section 33 of the Trade Union Reform and Employee Rights Act 1993, in implementing the Transfer of Undertakings (Protection of Employment) Regulations 1981, makes it clear that protection is provided to the employee whatever the nature of the business or undertaking, and there is a duty to consult with the employees. Contracts cannot be changed unilaterally. Where, however, the employee seeks to obtain promotion or change her post she may be asked to accept new contractual provisions which may not be based on Whitley Council Terms and Conditions of Service.

Breach of contract

By employee

The employee, as has been seen, has an implied duty to take reasonable care and skill in his work and to obey the reasonable orders of the employer. If he is in breach of these terms he can be disciplined. An example of a disciplinary procedure can be seen in

Appendix 14. In extreme cases the employee's actions may justify summary dismissal by the employer. Other rights of the employer include suspension, demotion, warnings, etc.

By employer

The duty to abide by the contractual agreement is reciprocal and the employee is therefore entitled to expect that he will be treated with consideration and that there will be no unilateral change of contract conditions. If it is apparent that the employer is in fundamental breach of contract, then the employee may be able to consider himself constructively dismissed. This is considered below.

Statutory rights

Certain Acts of Parliament provide additional rights to employees. The most significant Act is the Employment Protection (Consolidation) Act 1978. Further consolidation has taken place under the Trade Union and Labour Relations (Consolidation) Act 1992 and additional rights given by the Trade Union Reform and Employee Rights Act 1993. Table 10.1 sets out some of the statutory rights and the minimum time of continuous service which the employee must have in order to claim these rights. They include medical suspension payments, guaranteed pay, rights for the pregnant employee, time off work provisions, rights in relation to trade unions, and many others.

Rights of the pregnant employee

These rights have been strengthened by the Trade Union Reform and Employee Rights Act 1993 (TUR & ER 93) in its implementation of the EC Pregnant Workers Directive. No continuous service is required to obtain these rights. These include:

Table 10.1 Statutory rights

Right	Period of continuous employment
Guarantee payment	4 weeks
Not to be dismissed because of medical suspension	4 weeks
Written statement of terms and conditions of employment	4 weeks
Written reasons for dismissal	2 years
Not to be unfairly dismissed	2 years
Maternity rights	
1. Paid time off work to receive ante-natal care	No minimum period
2. Right to return to work after pregnancy	No minimum period
3. Not to be unfairly dismissed on grounds of pregnancy	No minimum period
Redundancy pay	2 years
Not to be dismissed because of trade union activities	No minimum period
Time off for trade union duties, trade union activities and public duties	No minimum period

1. the right not to be dismissed on grounds of pregnancy;
2. the right to receive maternity pay;
3. the right to return to work after confinement;
4. the right to attend ante-natal classes;
5. the right to be offered suitable alternative work or be paid during suspension from work on maternity grounds.

Table 10.2 sets out the conditions of entitlement for these benefits.

In addition to the statutory rights, Whitley Council conditions covering the same field often exist. The employee usually has the right to choose whichever benefits are more favourable to her.

Right not to be unfairly dismissed on grounds of pregnancy

SITUATION 10.6 MORNING SICKNESS

Barbara is two months' pregnant and suffering very badly from morning sickness and hypertension. Her absence from the ward is causing considerable difficulties and she is not popular with the other staff. She has worked with the authority for three years. It has been agreed that she should be dismissed because of the continual absences. What are her rights?

She is pregnant, a full-time employee for three years and is therefore able to claim the right of not being unfairly dismissed on the grounds of pregnancy. The authority might argue that her pregnancy is making it impossible for her to do her job adequately, there is no suitable alternative work and therefore they are justified in dismissing her. This

Table 10.2 Entitlement for maternity benefits (as amended by TUR & ER 93)

Right	Special conditions	Continuous service
Right to attend for ante-natal care with paid time off	After first visit, produce a certificate of expected date of confinement or appointment card	Not required
Right to receive maternity pay	See Fig. 10.7	See Fig. 10.7
Right to have maternity leave	14 weeks' statutory maternity leave with 2 weeks' compulsory leave after birth. Must give notice	Not required
Right to have maternity absence	To have up to 29 weeks' absence after birth. Must comply with notification requirement	2 years' continuous service
Right to return to work after maternity leave	Notice requirements must be satisfied. Suitable alternative employment may be offered	Not required
Right not to be dismissed on maternity-related grounds		Not required
Rights in relation to suspension from work on maternity grounds	Right to be offered suitable alternative work. Right to be paid normal remuneration during suspension	Not required

is, however, no longer an acceptable defence to an application for unfair dismissal on grounds of pregnancy and the employee would probably succeed in her application. No continuous service is required. Furthermore, since October 1994 the employee is entitled to receive pay during a time of suspension from work on maternity grounds, if suspension results from a health ground specified by statute (i.e. pregnancy, birth or breast feeding) or to be offered suitable alternative work. If suitable alternative work is not available, the employee can claim pay during the time of suspension from work. Claims in relation to dismissal on grounds of pregnancy can also be brought under the Sex Discrimination Act (see pages 162–4).

The right to return to work after confinement

SITUATION 10.7 WARD SISTER OR STAFF NURSE?

June Brown was a full-time ward sister and decided that after her baby was born she would like to return to work part-time as a ward sister. She made her wishes known to the nursing officer who said she would always be pleased to see June return. Three weeks before she was due to leave she duly gave her notice of intention to return to work after the confinement. Seven weeks after the baby was born she received the formal enquiry in writing asking if it was her intention to return to work and telling her the procedure to follow if she did. Otherwise, the letter said that she would lose her right to return. She replied to the letter stating the date she intended returning and that she wanted to work part-time but was prepared to continue as ward sister.

The reply stated that there was a vacancy for a part-time staff nurse on nights but she would be unable to be a part-time ward sister. She was upset by this reply since she had always understood that she had a statutory and a contractual right to return to the same post.

Both the Whitley Council conditions of service and the statutory right under the Employment Protection Act and TUR & ER Act 1993 are that the pregnant employee may return after the confinement on the same conditions that she left. June could thus return as a full-time ward sister but she has no right to insist on being a part-time ward sister. It is up to the discretion of the employer as to whether she is allowed a part-time post. She cannot insist on returning to the same location or even exactly the same duties, only that her terms and conditions of service are the same. (If the employee can show discrimination on the grounds of sex, she may have a remedy – see below.)

The procedural rules on giving notice of intention to return to work are strictly enforced; thus to fail to give the requisite notice at least three weeks before commencing maternity leave, of the fact that she is pregnant and notice of the date she intends to begin the leave, may involve loss of the right to return (see Fig. 10.6).

Dismissal of maternity leave replacement

The European Court in Luxembourg has recently ruled (*Webb* v. *EMO Air Cargo (UK)* TLR 15 July 1994) that, where an employee who was taken on to replace an employee

---

Maternity leave
1. Applies to all pregnant employees regardless of length of service or hours of work.
2. Gives entitlement to 14 weeks' maternity leave.
3. Two weeks of maternity leave must be after the birth.
4. All normal terms and conditions of employment apply during leave period except for wages or salary.
5. Also entitled to be offered a suitable alternative vacancy, where available, if employee would have been made redundant during the period of leave.
6. Employee must give 21 days' notice, before she begins leave, of the fact that she is pregnant and the date of confinement.
7. Employee must give 21 days' notice of the date on which she intends to begin leave.

Maternity absence
1. Applies to pregnant employees with two years' continuous service.
2. Employee must comply with the above notification requirements and also notify her intention of exercising the right to a longer absence.
3. Within 14 days of request by employer she must give written confirmation of her intention to return.
4. Must give at least 21 days' notice of the date on which she intends to return.
5. Date of return must be no later than 29 weeks after the actual week of childbirth.
6. If not permitted to return to employer, this counts as unfair dismissal unless it is not reasonably practicable and there is no suitable alternative work.

Figure 10.6 The right to return to work after maternity leave or maternity absence.

---

during maternity leave, herself became pregnant and was dismissed, it was unfair dismissal on the grounds of pregnancy. The facts were that Mrs Webb was recruited with a view initially to replace Mrs Stewart who was to take maternity leave, but following a probationary period would probably continue when Mrs Stewart returned to work. Mrs Webb had not known that she was pregnant when the employment contract was entered into. When the pregnancy was confirmed, she was dismissed. Her application on the grounds of direct or indirect discrimination on the grounds of sex failed before the industrial tribunal. Her appeals to the employment appeal tribunal and the Court of Appeal also failed. She then appealed to the House of Lords, which referred her case to the European Court of Justice for a preliminary ruling on the effect of Council Directive 76/207/EEC of 9 February 1976 on the implementation of the principle of equal treatment for men and women as to access to employment, vocational training, promotion and working conditions. The European Court took into account the general context of the measures taken under Council Directives 92/85/EEC of 19 October 1992 to encourage improvements in the safety and health at work of pregnant workers and workers who had recently given birth and were breast feeding, and for special protection to be given to women, by prohibiting dismissal during the period from the beginning of their pregnancy to the end of their maternity leave. The European Court held that this protection of women could not be dependent on whether her presence at work during maternity was essential to the proper functioning of the undertaking in which she was employed. Any contrary interpretation would render ineffective the provisions of the directive. Its decision was therefore that EEC Directive 76/207 precluded dismissal of an employee, who had been recruited for an unlimited term with a view initially to replacing another employee during maternity leave, and could not do so because, shortly after her recruitment, she was herself found to be pregnant.

Ante-natal visits

This right was added to the existing maternity rights by the Employment Act 1980. It is a right to attend ante-natal examinations with paid leave. For the first visit there is no requirement to show the certificate for the expected date of confinement or the appointment card, but for subsequent visits the employer can insist on seeing both. The right is not absolute, however. It depends on the reasonableness of the request and it may be reasonable to refuse such time off if an employee can reasonably make arrangements for an appointment outside normal working hours.

Maternity pay

Statutory Maternity Pay Scheme (see Fig. 10.7): this came into force on 6 April 1987 and applies to women whose babies are due on or after 21 June 1987. This is in addition to any rights that the woman has from her employer, but payment under the state scheme will be regarded as part payment by the employer. An employee who has been continuously employed by the same employer for at least 26 weeks continuing into the 15th week before her baby is due (i.e. the qualifying week) and whose average earnings are not less than the lower earnings limit for the payment of National Insurance contributions and who is still pregnant or has had the baby and has stopped working by that time is eligible to receive SMP.

She must start her maternity pay period at any time from the start of the 11th week before the expected week of confinement (EWC). The maternity pay period is 18 weeks but it cannot start earlier than the 11th week before the EWC.

Commenced 16 October 1994. An employee whose baby is due on or after 16 October 1994 is entitled to statutory maternity pay if:
(a) her average weekly earnings are above the lower earnings limit; and
(b) she has been employed continuously for 26 weeks into the qualifying week.

SMP is payable at:
(a) 90 per cent of average weekly earnings for the first 6 weeks; and
(b) £52.50 for the rest of the maternity pay period.

If the 90 per cent of the average weekly earnings is less than £52.50, £52.50 is payable for all the maternity pay period.

Changes have been made in the recovery of SMP payment by employers from funds due to the Inland Revenue. From 4 September 1994 only 92 per cent of SMP can be recovered. There is an exemption for small employers who are able to recover 100 per cent provided that they pay less than £20,000 total gross Class 1 National Insurance contributions.

Figure 10.7 Statutory maternity pay.

SITUATION 10.8 STILLBIRTH

Brenda Fox was pregnant ard working as a staff nurse on the surgical ward. She intended to take her full maternity leave and return to work eventually. When she was 26 weeks' pregnant and while still at work she miscarried. She claimed her statutory maternity pay. Was she successful?

The answer is yes. Statutory maternity pay is payable where there is a miscarriage or stillbirth after the 24th week of pregnancy. SMP is payable just as if the birth was live. What if she had twins? There is no extra payment.

SITUATION 10.9 DISMISSAL AND SMP

Ruth Harris worked in the operating theatre. She became pregnant and was initially given work in the recovery room, away from the anaesthetic gases. However, this work became too heavy for her and eventually, since there was no suitable alternative work, she was dismissed. Her dismissal took place before she had reached the qualifying week for SMP. Is she entitled to receive SMP?

Yes; if she has been dismissed because her condition makes it impossible for her to do the job adequately, then the 26-week continuous employment rule is satisfied (if, had it not been for the dismissal, she would have otherwise worked into the qualifying week and completed 26 continuous weeks). Her average weekly earnings are calculated over the period of X weeks ending with the last day immediately before her employment ended. There is no need for Ruth to give notice of the day she will stop work because of pregnancy. Under the new protection provided by TUR & ER 93 the dismissal is automatically unfair, and salary during suspension from work on maternity grounds is payable if suitable alternative work cannot be provided.

What happens if the baby arrives early?

1. If the maternity pay period has started, the statutory maternity pay is not affected.
2. Before or during the qualifying week: the employee must give notice if reasonably practicable to the employer of the confinement within 21 days. The 26-week rule is satisfied if it would have been satisfied were it not for the early confinement.
3. Before the MPP is due to start but after the qualifying week: as above but there is no requirement to give notice.

How does SMP end?

1. after the 18 weeks maximum for which SMP is payable;
2. if the employee works after the confinement;
3. if the employee goes outside the EEC;
4. if the employee is taken into legal custody;
5. if the employee dies.

Maternity leave

Although the maximum time of the state maternity pay is 18 weeks, it is possible for a pregnant employee to take much longer than that, though any excess may be without pay. June gives notice of her intention to take maternity leave and leaves work 11 weeks before the expected date of confinement. Her total leave could be as follows:

Leave prior to the expected date	11 weeks
The baby is born 2 weeks late	2 weeks
She is then entitled to take 29 weeks off after the birth	29 weeks
She delays the return by 4 weeks as she is entitled to do	4 weeks
	46 weeks

Time-off provisions

Paid or unpaid time off (depending on the benefit) is also a statutory right and can be seen in Fig. 10.8. Again, there are comparable Whitley Council rights and the employee is entitled to choose whichever is more advantageous.

(NB: New NHS Trusts' contracts may not be based on Whitley Council agreements.)

SITUATION 10.10 REARRANGING A TIMETABLE

Mary Briggs was a nurse tutor. She also was very involved in local government and had recently been elected as leader of the opposition on the County Council. She was appointed to several sub-committees. She applied for time off to attend the meetings. The principal was extremely helpful and rearranged her timetable so that she would not have to teach in the afternoons when the council meetings took place. Mary complained that her work load had not decreased and she now found that she was having to spend several evenings doing work which normally she would have done during her free periods which had now been lost.

She took the case to an industrial tribunal and won since it was held that rearranging a timetable was not giving time off. However, Mary was still receiving her full pay and

---

Time off for

1. Trade union duties (officer): reasonable paid time off to carry out duties in connection with industrial relations and for training relevant to carrying out those duties (reasonable defined in ACAS Code of Practice No 3).
2. Trade union activities (member): reasonable unpaid time off during working hours to take part in TU activities (see ACAS Code of Practice No 3).
3. Public duties – local authority member, school governor, JP: reasonable unpaid time off (take into account time off given in relation to 1 or 2 above and other public duties).
4. To seek job in redundancy situation: reasonable paid time off to seek work or seek retraining.
5. Jury service: unpaid time off.
6. Health and safety representative: reasonable paid time off to perform function and train for it.

Figure 10.8 Time-off provisions.

the time-off provisions were only for unpaid time off. (The school could have reduced her work load, reduced her salary accordingly, and then employed a locum to teach in Mary's place with the money saved. Mary may have preferred the existing arrangements!)

Unfair dismissal

General principles

One of the most important of the statutory rights is the right not to be unfairly dismissed. Every employee has a right by virtue of his contract, statute or the common law (see below) to receive notice unless the employee is himself in breach of contract and is summarily dismissed. Thus a nursing officer who has worked for 20 years with that employer could lawfully be given her requisite notice under the contract with no particular reasons for the notice being specified and be lawfully dismissed. This would be contractually acceptable but highly unjust. The right not to be unfairly dismissed protects employees who meet certain conditions against this unjust treatment. The Trade Union Reform and Employment Rights Act 1993 Section 28 and Schedule 5 have introduced a right not to suffer a detriment or dismissal in health and safety cases. It will be unfair to dismiss an employee in circumstances arising out of health and safety matters, e.g. carrying out health and safety activities at the request of the employer, being a safety representative or a member of a safety committee, bringing the employer's attention to harmful circumstances, refusing to work in dangerous conditions, or taking appropriate steps to protect himself or others from damage. Section 29 of TUR & ER 93 entitles all employees, irrespective of their length of service, hours of work and age, to apply to an industrial tribunal if they are dismissed or selected for redundancy because they have sought to assert one of their statutory employment protection rights by bringing proceedings against the employer to enforce the right or by alleging that the employer had infringed the right.

The conditions which the employee must satisfy to bring an action for unfair dismissal are set out in Fig. 10.9. If these conditions are met the employee can then, within three months of the dismissal, apply to the industrial tribunal for an unfair dismissal hearing. The three months' time limit can be extended if the tribunal considers that it was not reasonably practicable for the employee to comply with it.

Constructive dismissal

SITUATION 10.11 DANGEROUS CONDITIONS_____

Kay was a nursing officer in charge of the acute wards of Roger Park Hospital. She had warned the senior managers that the situation was dangerous since, due to an acute shortage of nurses which coincided with a vigorous attempt to reduce the waiting lists, with extra beds being put up on all the wards, there was a danger that accidents could happen. No notice was taken of her warnings and in fact more patients were admitted. She advised the consultants that nurses would not be able to carry out certain tasks normally undertaken by

(a) 2 years' continuous service with that employer (except in cases of trade union activity or discrimination) and dismissal on grounds of pregnancy or childbirth;
(b) be eligible under the legislation;
(c) be below retirement age;
(d) be dismissed (i.e. termination by employer, expiry of fixed-term contract or constructive dismissal).

Figure 10.9 Conditions for bringing an unfair dismissal action.

doctors and that the junior doctors would be expected to add the drugs to intravenous transfusions. Her senior nurse manager was advised by the consultants that this was unacceptable and Kay was asked to withdraw that instruction and notify the nurses that they must continue to undertake such tasks. She pointed out that they did not have the time to do these. She was warned that she would face disciplinary proceedings if she continued to defy the managers. She said she would prefer to leave than endanger the lives of patients and stated that the managers were in breach of contract in failing to support her attempt to maintain professional standards. She left and subsequently brought an action for unfair dismissal.

Assuming that she qualifies as far as the conditions set out in Fig. 10.9 are concerned, she needs to establish as a preliminary point that she was dismissed and did not resign. The employers are likely to argue that they did not dismiss her, that she left work of her own free will, and that she is therefore ineligible to bring an unfair dismissal action.

The question is: have the managers acted in such a way that she is entitled to see the contract as at an end? It will be remembered that one of the implied terms in a contract of employment is that the employer will act reasonably towards the employee and support him. It could be argued here that in failing to support Kay's endeavours in this situation the employers are in fundamental breach of contract. If this can be established, then Kay can argue that there is a constructive dismissal, she is entitled to bring her action before the tribunal and it is then for the managers to establish that the dismissal was fair. On the other hand, the employers will be arguing that Kay was not dismissed, that she had failed to do all she could to work with them, and that she had defied reasonable orders from them. Ultimately, the outcome will depend upon the evidence from both sides: Kay would have to show evidence, both documentary and through witnesses, of earlier attempts to persuade management that the situation was dangerous and that the managers were acting in fundamental breach of contract.

CASE 10.1 FAIR DISMISSAL

The Court of Appeal heard a case where a senior nurse had been dismissed for failure to wear the appropriate uniform. They held that the dismissal was fair. (*Atkin* v. *Enfield Group Hospital Management Committee* 1975 I RLR 217)

Procedure in an application for unfair dismissal

The employee is normally expected to exhaust the internal appeal machinery set up by her employer before an application to an industrial tribunal is heard. But due to time limits the employee should instigate the application in any case and ask for an adjournment pending the outcome of the internal appeal. In this way she will not be out of time.

The stages which follow an application to the tribunal are shown in Fig. 10.10.

The hearing

If the employee is able to show that she satisfies the conditions set out in Fig. 10.9 the burden will be on the employer to show that the dismissal was based on a statutory reason. These are set out in Fig. 10.11. The tribunal must then decide if the employer has acted reasonably in treating this reason as sufficient to justify dismissal. The criteria which have been considered by the tribunals in determining the reasonableness of employers' actions are set out in Fig. 10.12. Every circumstance must be taken into account, and the fact that the tribunal might not have acted in the way in which the particular employer acted is not relevant. The crucial question is: was *that* employer acting reasonably? One important point is whether the disciplinary code of practice and the guidelines prepared by ACAS were followed.

The outcome

If the employee's application for unfair dismissal is upheld, the following remedies are available to the tribunal:

(a) reinstatement/re-engagement;
(b) compensation – basic award; compensatory award; special award.

---

1. Internal appeal application to health authority.
2. Application to industrial tribunal – obtain from IT.
3. Copy sent by industrial tribunal to the respondent (i.e. employer) asking him to complete a Notice of Appearance stating whether he intends to contest the application and if so, the grounds. This is sent by IT to applicant.
4. Conciliation: copies of all relevant documents are sent to a conciliation officer of the Advisory, Conciliation and Arbitration Service (ACAS), who will try to assist the parties to reach a settlement.

If he fails

5. Notice of hearing: sent at least 14 days before date of hearing.
6. Preliminary hearing: held where tribunal is not certain it has the power to consider the application (e.g. out of time, whether there was a dismissal, etc.).
7. Pre-hearing assessments: used where either party appears to have a case which has no reasonable chance of succeeding.
8. The hearing.

Figure 10.10 Stages in an application for unfair dismissal.

(a) capability or qualifications;
(b) conduct;
(c) some other substantial reason;
(d) redundancy;
(e) statutory prohibition;
(f) lock out or participation in strike or industrial action;
(g) national security.

Figure 10.11 Statutory reasons to dismiss.

(a) code of practice (a recent case has emphasised the importance of following the code of practice, even if following it would make no difference to the outcome);
(b) nature of employment situation, e.g. size and resources of organisation, type of work;
(c) consistency of employer;
(d) timing of dismissal;
(e) length of service of employee;
(f) in cases of dishonesty and other misconduct
   (i) the employer must show that he genuinely believes the employee to be guilty of the misconduct in question
   (ii) he must have reasonable grounds on which to establish that belief
   (iii) he must have carried out such investigation into the matter as was reasonable in all the circumstances
   British Home Stores v. *Birchell* 1980 I RLR 379;
(g) principles of natural justice.

Figure 10.12 Criteria for the reasonableness of the employer.

In assessing compensation, the tribunal will take into account any fault on the part of the employee.

Statutory sick pay scheme

Most NHS employees enjoy six months' full pay and six months' half-pay while absent on grounds of sickness. The employer is able to recover some of this from the statutory sick pay scheme. The operation of the scheme is illustrated in Fig. 10.13.

Employers whose National Insurance bill is less than £20,000 per week can recover the full cost of SSP from their payments on National Insurance and PAYE. Other employers can only recover 80 per cent of their SSP. All employers can offset any contractual liability to pay sick pay against their payments under SSP.

Redundancy

The NHS has its own redundancy scheme set out in the Whitley Council general conditions of service. It broadly follows the statutory scheme from the point of view of

---

Eligibility – employees with average gross pay being eligible for National Insurance contributions
Qualifying period – off sick for at least 4 days (including weekends, holidays and days off).
   First 3 days off sick are waiting days – statutory sick pay is not given for these.
   Payable for 28 weeks.
   Links between spells of sickness – any spells of sickness of 4 or more days in a row with less
   than 8 weeks between are linked for SSP.
Amount payable – two rates of SSP depending upon earnings
   (a) earnings of £55–£195 – payment of £46.95;
   (b) earnings of £195 and over – payment of £52.50.
Link with Whitley Council sick pay (depending on length of service) or NHS Trust contractual rights
   NHS pay for first 3 days – no SSP;
   SSP + NHS pay up to full salary for 28 weeks;
   NHS pay for further 6 months – half-pay.

Figure 10.13 Statutory sick pay scheme.

---

consultation when redundancies are envisaged. However, the NHS has a much wider definition of suitable alternative work. The main aspects of the scheme are shown in Appendix 17.

Trade union rights

It is impossible in a work of this nature to be other than superficial in relation to the status and powers of trade unions. Reference should be made to the bibliography on special books in this field. Figure 10.14 illustrates some of the present rights of the independent trade union. The principal Acts are the Employment Protection (Consolidation) Act 1978, and the Trade Union and Labour Relations (Consolidation) Act 1992 as amended by the Trade Union Reforms and Employment Rights Act 1993.

Over the last ten years the power of the unions and employers to enforce a closed shop situation has decreased so that since the Employment Act 1988, the dismissal of a non-unionist in a closed shop situation is now automatically unfair. The 1992 Act gives protection to employees against exclusion or expulsion. The employer cannot prevent anyone from joining an independent trade union. The unions have the right to obtain information relevant to collective bargaining and also to receive notice of any redundancies. A union member should be allowed the presence of a union officer at any disciplinary proceedings. Under health and safety legislation, safety representatives appointed by trade unions have the right to visit the workplace and to inspect the site of any accident. Officials of trade unions have the right to reasonable paid time off for the purposes of their activities in relation to collective bargaining or representing their members, and for training for such purposes. The members, however, only have the right of reasonable unpaid time off work for union activities.

The trade union officers do not have any management rights: they have no power as part of their function as union officials to give orders to the employees. Obviously,

1. A union is independent if it is not under the domination or control of an employer, and not liable to interference by an employer. Its independence can be certified by the certification officer, and his certificate is conclusive evidence that the union is independent.
2. Independence is an essential feature if the union is to enjoy the following statutory rights
   (a) to take part in trade union activities;
   (b) to be given information and be consulted over 'Transfers of Undertaking';
   (c) to gain information for collective bargaining;
   (d) to secure consultation over redundancies;
   (e) to insist on time off for trade union duties and activities;
   (f) to appoint health/safety representatives.
3. A trade union is fully liable for any of its acts which constitute a tort (civil wrong) EXCEPT where it acts in contemplation or furtherance of a trade dispute. The meaning of these words has been narrowed since 1980 so that in general secondary action (e.g. where employees of A go on strike to support the employees of B) is not covered, and therefore the union would be liable for the damage that results from the unlawful action.
4. Safety representatives appointed by a recognised trade union from among the employees.
   Names to be notified to the employer in writing shall represent employees in consultation with the employer under Section 2(4) and (6) of the Health and Safety at Work Act 1974. Functions set out in Regulation 4 of Section 1. 1977 No. 500.
   (a) Investigate potential hazards and dangerous occurrences at workplace and examine cause of accidents at work.
   (b) Investigate complaints of employees relating to health, safety or welfare at work.
   (c) Make representations to employer under (a) and (b).
   (d) Make representations to employer on general matters affecting health, safety or welfare.
   (e) Carry out inspections under Reg. 5, 6 and 7.
   (f) Represent employees in consultation with Health and Safety Inspectorate.
   (g) Receive information from inspectors under Section 28 (8).
   (h) Attend meetings of safety committees.
   No function given to a safety representative by this paragraph shall be construed as imposing any duty on him.

Figure 10.14 Trade union rights and the role of safety representatives.

they might advise their members to follow a particular course but it is up to the members' own judgement whether they follow the advice or not. The Employment Act 1988 gave additional protection to the employee: he has the right not to be denied access to the courts by union rules; the right not to be unjustifiably disciplined by a union; the right to complain to an industrial tribunal and obtain compensation if this latter right is infringed. The Act also provides for the Secretary of State to appoint a Commission for the rights of trade union members. Under the Trade Union and Labour Relations (Consolidation) Act 1992 a trade union may lay down certain requirements for membership, but otherwise must admit any person seeking to join. The member cannot be unjustifiably disciplined by the union and has a right to resign and a right not to be expelled from the union.

Sections 1–22, Part 1 of the Trade Union Reform and Employment Rights Act 1993, has provided further regulation of trade union elections and ballots, of the financial affairs of the trade union, rights in relation to trade union membership and regulations covering ballots on industrial action.

Public and private employees

Those nurses who work as employees in the private sector enjoy much the same rights as those who work in the NHS. There are, however, some major differences. If the nurse is only one of a few employees, then she may not enjoy all those statutory rights enjoyed by those working for employers of large concerns. This also applies to those NHS nurses who work for single-handed general practitioners or group practices.

In addition they may not be subject to Whitley Council conditions of service. In this case there will be other provisions relating to holidays, pay, sick pay, pensions, time off, etc., which will either have been laid down in advance or which will have to be agreed with the employer. The nurse should make sure that she is aware of these provisions before she accepts the post.

Discrimination by sex or race

The Race Relations Act 1976 and the Sex Discrimination Acts 1975 and 1986 outlaw discrimination in employment, education, housing or the provision of goods, facilities, and services on grounds of race, colour, nationality, or ethnic or national origins, sex, and marital status.

Direct discrimination

This is where one person treats another less favourably on the grounds of sex, race or marital status than he would treat another person of another sex, race or marital status. The two questions which the tribunal would have to determine under the Act are: has the person been discriminated against? And is the cause of that discrimination one of the forbidden grounds?

Indirect discrimination

This is where a condition is applied to persons so that the following prevail:

1. The proportion of people of one race or sex who can comply with it is considerably smaller than the proportion of another.
2. The employer cannot show the condition is justifiable on other than racial or sexual grounds.
3. The condition is to the detriment of the complainant because he cannot comply with it.

Victimisation

This indirect form of discrimination is also prohibited under the legislation and covers the situation where a person is treated less favourably because he brings proceedings, gives evidence or information, alleges a contravention or otherwise under the Acts, or intends to do any of these things.

Segregation

It is unlawful to maintain separate facilities for members of different races. There is no such law in relation to different sexes.

The areas covered by the laws against discrimination are shown in Fig. 10.15.

The discrimination laws are wider than much of the employment legislation. For example, they cover an applicant for a post, as well as independent contractors and the self-employed. Along with employers, the following are subject to the laws: trade unions, partnerships, qualification bodies for trades and professions and vocational training, employment agencies, the Manpower Services Commission, and the Crown.

Exceptions to laws on discrimination

These are listed in Fig. 10.16 for discrimination on grounds of sex and Fig. 10.17 for discrimination on grounds of race. One of the most important is 'the genuine occupational qualification', i.e. that the employer can justify discrimination because of the particular characteristics of the post. For example, the employment of Chinese people in a Chinese restaurant may be justifiable.

Applications for compensation for discrimination on grounds of sex or race can be made to the industrial tribunal. In the case of discrimination on grounds of sex, the European Court held in the case of *Marshall* v. *Southampton AHA* (No. 2) 1993 4 All ER 586 that the upper limit fixed by statute on the payment of compensation infringed the European Equal Treatment Directive which, since November 1993, applies to both public and private sector employees. Subsequently substantial sums have been awarded to women who have lost their jobs through dismissal on grounds of pregnancy. On 29 July 1994 the Employment Appeal Tribunal held, in the case of the Ministry of Defence's appeal against the decision in *Cannock* (awarded £172,000 by a tribunal) (*Minister of*

Arrangements for recruitment.
Advertisements.
Refusal or deliberate omission to offer employment.
Terms and conditions of service.
Access to transfer or promotion.
Access to training.
Fringe benefits.
Dismissal.
Any other detriment, e.g, full-time working is made a requirement.

Figure 10.15 Areas covered by discrimination.

Sex
1. Sex of a person is a genuine occupational qualification for the job:
   (a) The essential nature of the job calls for a man because of his physiology.
   (b) A man is required for authenticity in entertainment.
   (c) The job needs to be held by a man or woman in order to preserve decency or privacy because
      (i) it is likely to involve physical contact with a person in circumstances where that person may reasonably object to it being carried out by a person of the opposite sex;
      (ii) persons of one sex might reasonably object to the presence of the other sex because they are in a state of undress or using sanitary facilities (e.g. lavatory attendants).
   (d) Job is at a single-sex establishment – hospital, prison, etc.
   (e) Holder of post provides individuals with personal services promoting their welfare or education which can most effectively be provided by one sex.
   (f) Job needs to be held by a man because of restriction imposed by laws regulating the employment of women.
   (g) Job likely to involve work abroad which can only be done by men (e.g. Middle East).
   (h) Job is one of two which are to be held by a married couple.
   (i) Employee is required to live on premises.
2. Other exceptions
   (a) Acts done to safeguard national security.
   (b) Undertakings with less than five employees.
   (c) Ministers of religion.
   (d) Sports and sports facilities.
   (e) Special treatment afforded to women in connection with pregnancy or childbirth.
   (f) Provisions in relation to death or retirement (subject to 1986 Act).

Figure 10.16 Exceptions to unlawful discrimination on grounds of sex.

A genuine occupational qualification requires a particular race, e.g.:
(a) authenticity in entertainment;
(b) employee provides personal services towards the welfare or education of others;
(c) a member of a particular race is required for reasons of authenticity in art or photography;
(d) a bar or restaurant has a particular setting (e.g. Chinese restaurant) for which a person of that racial group is required for reasons of authenticity;
(e) immigration rules, civil service regulations which restrict those eligible for Crown employment;
(f) acts done to safeguard national security.

Figure 10.17 Exceptions to unlawful discrimination on grounds of race.

Defence v. *Cannock* TLR 2 August 1994) and other similar awards, that the assessment of awards in the future by industrial tribunals should assess the chances of a woman returning to work and make a percentage award on that basis.

However, the European Commission has not made comparable directives in relation to discrimination on race-related grounds and the upper ceiling on compensation still applies to those claims.

Male midwives

Originally midwifery was one of the exemptions to the Sex Discrimination Act 1975 and the employment and training of men as midwives was restricted. However, under Order 1983 SI No. 1202 the exemptions were brought to an end. The health authorities were notified that when implementing these legislative changes they must make appropriate arrangements to ensure that:

1. women have the freedom of choice to be attended by a female midwife;
2. where male midwives are employed, provision is made for them to be chaperoned as necessary.

Equal pay

The Equal Pay Act 1970, as amended by subsequent legislation, aims at preventing discrimination as regards terms and conditions of employment between men and women. Central to its provisions is the concept of an equality clause which is to be implied into the contract of a woman who can show she is either employed in like work with a man at the same establishment, or at an establishment where similar terms and conditions are applied, or has been the subject of a Job Appraisal scheme or performs work of equal value.

The Act and Article 119 of the Treaty of Rome enable an employee to claim equal pay in comparison with a person of the opposite sex who is employed by the same employer at the same establishment if she or he is doing the same job or a job of equal value. Thus men as well as women can bring a claim under these provisions.

Questions and exercises

1 If you have a letter which purports to be your contract of appointment, compare it with particulars set out in Fig. 10.5.
2 Obtain a copy of your employer's disciplinary procedure and apply the procedure to any of the situations of alleged negligence by a nurse set out in this book.
3 Take any statutory right and contrast it with the comparable rights given under Whitley Council conditions. Which right would be of most benefit to the employee?
4 Visit an industrial tribunal and prepare a brief guide for a potential applicant on the procedure and formalities.
5 A manager is both an employee and the representative of the employer. In what way, if any, is there likely to be a conflict between these two roles?
6 If you were preparing to interview prospective employees, what questions do you consider would be unlawful under the sex and race discrimination legislation?

11   The nurse as a registered professional

It will be recalled from Chapter 1 that there were four fields of accountability to be faced by the nurse: the civil and criminal courts; the disciplinary proceedings of the employer and the Professional Conduct Committee (PCC) of the United Kingdom Central Council for Nursing, Midwifery, and Health Visiting (UKCC). This chapter considers the procedure for a hearing before the PCC. First, however, the constitution of the UKCC and the National Boards will be considered. Figure 11.1 sets out the topics to be discussed.

The Nurses, Midwives and Health Visitors Act 1979 sets up the framework for the Central Council, the National Boards and the Professional Register. Statutory instruments passed in the exercise of powers conferred by the principal Act fill in the flesh. Rules are laid down in the principal Act on the practice of midwifery, local supervision of midwifery practice, and on re-enacting the offence of an unqualified person attending a woman in childbirth. These are considered in the section dealing with midwifery. The 1979 Act was amended by the Nurses, Midwives and Health Visitors Act 1992. By this Act, the UKCC became a mainly elected body and the National Boards became appointed executive bodies with changed functions.

The United Kingdom Central Council

The constitution of the UKCC is given in Fig. 11.2 and its functions can be seen in Fig. 11.3. The regulations require the UKCC to have specific standing committees and these can be seen in Fig. 11.4.

1. United Kingdom Central Council
   (a) constitution;
   (b) functions;
   (c) standing committees.
2. National Boards.
3. Registration
   (a) false representation;
   (b) removal from Register
       (i) on grounds of misconduct
           1. The hearing:
                Is there misconduct?
           2. The outcome:
                postponement of judgement;
                no action;
                striking off Register;
                refer to Health Committee;
           3. criminal misconduct.
       (ii) Removal on grounds of health
           1. Constitution of Health Committee.
           2. Procedures:
                professional screeners;
                action following reports;
                notice of referral.
           3. Restoration to Register.
4. Professional standards and codes of practice.
5. Education and training.

Figure 11.1 Issues covered in Chapter 11.

The United Kingdom Central Council for Nursing, Midwifery and Health Visiting: consists of not more than 60 members, two-thirds elected by the profession and the others appointed by the Secretary of State from amongst nurses, midwives, health visitors or registered medical practitioners or have such qualifications and experience in education or other fields as in the Secretary of State's opinion will be of value to the Council in the performance of its functions. He must especially have in mind the need to secure that members of council include registered nurses, midwives and health visitors living or working in each part of the United Kingdom and that qualifications and experience in the teaching of nurses, midwives and health visitors are adequately represented on the Council.

Figure 11.2 Constitution of the UKCC.

The National Boards

These corporate bodies are appointed for England, Scotland, Wales and Northern Ireland. The original constitution under Section 5 of the Nurses, Midwives and Health Visitors Act 1979 has been amended by the 1992 Act. Originally each Board consisted of a majority of elected members: about two-thirds. The remainder

(a) to establish and improve the standards of training and professional conduct for nurses, midwives and health visitors;

(b) to ensure that the standards of training meet any Community obligation in the United Kingdom;

(c) to determine. by means of rules, the conditions of a person's being admitted to training, and the kind and standard of training to be undertaken with a view to registration;

(d) the rules may also make provision with respect to the kind and standard of further training available to persons who are already registered;

(e) the powers of the Council shall include that of providing, in such manner as it thinks fit, advice for nurses, midwives, and health visitors on standards of professional conduct;

(f) the Council, in the discharge of its functions, shall have proper regard for the interests of all groups within the professions, including those with minority representation.

Figure 11.3 Functions of the UKCC.

A Midwifery Committee and Finance Committee shall be constituted by the Secretary of State as standing committees. The Council shall consult the Finance Committee on all financial matters. If the Council (having regard to the duty to have proper regard for the interests of all groups within the profession) requests the Secretary of State to constitute standing committees then he may by order constitute other standing committees and require the Council to consult them on or empower them to discharge functions of the Council.

The Midwifery Committee must have a majority of practising midwives and the Council has a duty to consult the Committee on all matters relating to midwifery. In addition, the Committee must discharge such functions of the Council as are assigned to them either by the Council or by the Secretary of State by order. The Midwifery Committee also has the function of considering any proposal to make, amend, or revoke rules relating to the practice of midwifery and reporting back to the Council. The Secretary of State will not approve rules relating to midwifery practice unless satisfied that they are framed in accordance with recommendations of the Council's Midwifery Committee.

Figure 11.4 Standing Committees of the UKCC.

---

1. To approve institutions in relation to the provision of:
   (a) courses of training with a view to enabling persons to qualify for registration as nurses, midwives or health visitors or for the recording of additional qualifications in the register and
   (b) courses of further training for those already registered;
2. To ensure that such courses meet the requirements of the Central Council as to their content and standard;
3. To hold or arrange to hold such examinations as are necessary to enable persons to satisfy requirements for registration or to obtain additional qualifications;
4. To collaborate with the Council in the promotion of improved training methods; and
5. To perform such other functions relating to nurses, midwives or health visitors as the Secretary of State may by order prescribe.

Figure 11.5 Functions of the National Boards.

were appointed by the Secretary of State. The maximum in total for each Board was 45 (35 for Northern Ireland). The Secretary of State had a statutory duty to ensure that the qualification and experience in the teaching of nurses were adequately represented.

Following the changes effected by the 1992 Act, the new Boards were appointed by and accountable to the Secretary of State and must be made from among persons who

(a) are registered nurses, midwives and health visitors; or
(b) have such qualifications and experience in education or other fields, as in the opinion of the Secretary of State, will be of value to the Board in the performance of its functions.

He has a duty in exercising these powers to ensure that a majority of the members of the Board are registered nurses, midwives or health visitors. The functions of the National Boards are shown in Figure 11.5. In addition they have a statutory duty (Section 6(2) of the 1979 Act, as amended by Section 5 of the 1992 Act) to 'discharge their functions subject to and in accordance with any applicable rules of the council and shall take account of any difference in the consideration applying to the different professions'. The National Boards no longer have a duty to conduct preliminary investigations into misconduct allegations. This function has been taken over by the UKCC.

Registration and removal

The Central Council has the duty of preparing and maintaining a register of qualified nurses, midwives, and health visitors and setting out rules in relation to the entry on to, removal from, and restoration to the Register. These rules are set out in a Statutory Instrument (1993 No. 893).

The Vice-Chairman shall be chairman of the Preliminary Proceedings Committee.

The Council shall appoint two of its members to be deputy chairmen of the Preliminary Proceedings Committee and each may act as chairman at the Vice-President's request or in her absence.

The Committee is quorate if at least three members of the Council constitute a majority of those considering a particular case. Members must be selected with due regard to the professional field in which the practitioner under consideration works or has worked.

It shall meet in private.

It shall not be necessary for the Preliminary Proceedings Committee when meeting to consider a particular case to be composed of the same members who considered that case on any previous occasion.

Figure 11.6 Composition of Preliminary Proceedings Committee.

False representation

SITUATION 11.1 FALSE QUALIFICATIONS_____

Brenda had always wanted to be a nurse but lacked the educational background. When she left school she worked as a nursing auxiliary for many years and was given much responsibility. She then left the district when her husband moved jobs. She applied for the job of a night nurse in a private nursing home. At the interview she was asked where she trained and she gave false information about her background. Because of her great experience they were very impressed with her and failed to take up her references. After she had worked there for two years a former colleague from her previous hospital came to visit a relative in the home and was surprised to discover that Brenda was referred to as 'Sister'. The colleague made some enquiries and realised that Brenda was being treated as a registered nurse when in fact she was not one. She felt that it was her duty to point this out to the owners of the home because of the possibility that a patient could suffer harm. When the owners discovered the truth Brenda was dismissed on the spot.

In a situation like this, as well as a loss of job, Brenda could face a criminal charge of falsely representing that she was on the Register or falsely representing that she possessed qualifications in nursing, midwifery or health visiting. These are offences under Section 14 of the Nurses, Midwives, and Health Visitors Act 1979. The matter would not be one for the Central Council or National Boards since she is not registered but would be a matter for the criminal courts.

However, the Council would be required to provide evidence of the fact that she was not on the Register. Of course, if she was on the Register for one purpose, e.g. a general nurse, it would be an offence under the Act for her to pretend that she was a midwife. This would then be a matter which could be heard before the PCC since, as she is already registered, the Committee could decide if she should remain on the Register or if any other action should be taken against her.

The Statutory Instrument also sets out rules relating to nurse training: the age of entry, educational requirements, interruption of training, admission to parts 1–8 of the Register, the examinations, and student index and health visitor training rules (see section on the midwifery rules).

Removal from the Register

Under Section 12 the Council has the responsibility of determining the circumstances and the means by which a person may, for misconduct or otherwise, be removed from the Register or part of it. These rules are set out in a Statutory Instrument (1993 No. 893).

The circumstances in which a person can be removed from the Register are:

1. that she has been guilty of misconduct; or
2. that her fitness to practise is seriously impaired by reason of her physical or mental condition.

Suspension from the Register

This power was introduced in 1993 and can be exercised where a person's fitness to practise is seriously impaired by reason of her physical or mental condition; or where it appears necessary to suspend as an interim measure

(a) for the protection of the public; or
(b) in the practitioner's interests.

Removal on grounds of misconduct

SITUATION 11.2 MISSING AMPOULE

Janice Lane was a ward sister on a busy surgical ward. One day she was preparing the mid-day medications on her own and while preparing a morphine injection for a patient dropped the ampoule which broke. Ashamed of what had happened, she locked up the cupboard and pretended that it had not happened instead of following the correct procedure and writing the loss in the correct book and getting a witness. Subsequently the loss of the ampoule was noticed by the following shift, and a search and an inquiry commenced which revealed nothing. The police were brought in and eventually Janice confessed.

The 1992 Act transferred the function of carrying out a preliminary investigation into any misconduct from the National Boards to the UKCC. Professional Conduct Rules now provide for a Preliminary Proceedings Committee to be constituted by the UKCC. Its constitution is shown in Figure 11.6. It has the function of

(a) carrying out investigations of cases of alleged misconduct;
(b) determining whether or not to refer a case of alleged misconduct to
 (i) the Conduct Committee with a view to removal of a practitioner from the Register; or
 (ii) the professional screeners with a view to consideration of a practitioner's fitness to practise;
(c) determining whether a practitioner is guilty of misconduct and, if so, whether it is appropriate to issue a caution as to her future conduct.

After an allegation of misconduct which the council officer considers may lead to removal from the Register, the Registrar shall send the following, in writing, to the practitioner concerned:

(a) a summary of the allegation;

(b) notice that the preliminary proceedings will in due course consider the matter; and

(c) confirmation that if a Notice of Proceedings is issued by the Preliminary Proceedings Committee, the practitioner will be invited to respond in writing to the Notice, but that if the practitioner wishes to submit a preliminary response to the summary of allegations, such response will be made available to the Preliminary Proceedings Committee, provided that it is in time.

Council can conduct, through the solicitor or otherwise, an investigation before the matter is first considered by the Preliminary Proceedings Committee and if such an investigation indicates that the practitioner may be removed from the Register, the Registrar should send copies of the statements and other documents to the practitioner and notify her that she is entitled to submit a preliminary response for consideration by the Preliminary Proceedings Committee.

The Preliminary Proceedings Committee may

(a) decline to proceed with the matter;
(b) require further investigation to be conducted;
(c) adjourn consideration of the matter;
(d) refer the matter to the professional screeners;
(e) take the advice of the solicitor and may instruct him to obtain such documents, proofs of evidence and other evidence in respect of the allegations as he considers necessary;
(f) require the complaint to be verified by statutory declaration.

Rules relating to the procedure of the Preliminary Proceedings Committee require a Notice of Proceedings to be sent to the practitioner together with statements and a request that the practitioner respond in writing.

After receipt of any written response by the practitioner, the Preliminary Proceedings Committee can, in addition to the powers outlined above:

(a) refer the case to the Conduct Committee (where removal from the Register might be justified);
(b) refer the case to professional screeners (where the physical or mental condition of the practitioner may seriously impair her fitness to practise);
(c) determine if the practitioner has been guilty of misconduct and, if so, whether it is appropriate to issue a caution.

Professional Conduct Committee

It may be that, after scrutiny of the evidence in Janice's case, the Preliminary Proceedings Committee decides that the case should be referred to the Professional Conduct Committee. The composition of the Professional Conduct Committee is shown in Fig. 11.7.

After referral of the case to the Conduct Committee, the Registrar must send to the practitioner a Notice of Inquiry in writing in the form set out in the First Schedule to

All members of the Council are eligible and may be required to serve on the Conduct Committee. The quorum is three. The composition for any particular case must be chosen with due regard to the professional fields in which the respondent works or has worked. The President of the Council is the Chairman of the Committee but the Council shall appoint a panel of not more than nine persons from whom a deputy chairman may be chosen who shall then take the chair in the absence of the Chairman. Any person who has participated in the preliminary consideration of a case as a member of the Preliminary Proceedings Committee or as a professional screener shall not be permitted to be a member of the Conduct Committee dealing with that case.

Figure 11.7 Composition of the Professional Conduct Committee.

the Statutory Instrument. This notice must be sent by recorded delivery to the registered address or to any later address known to the Registrar. Twenty-eight days must elapse between the day on which the Notice is posted and the date fixed for the hearing unless the practitioner agrees otherwise. If there is a complainant, that person, too, must be sent a copy of the rules and the Notice of Inquiry. The Notice of Inquiry must not include any charge inconsistent with the substance of allegations set out in the Notice of Proceedings.

The hearing

The charge(s) shall be read in public and in the presence of the parties to the proceedings by an officer of the Council. If Janice failed to turn up the hearing could still take place but the solicitor would be called upon to satisfy the PCC that Janice had received the Notice of Inquiry. Even if there were no evidence that it had been received, the inquiry can still proceed if the PCC is satisfied that all reasonable efforts in accordance with the rules have been made to serve the Notice of Inquiry on her.

Procedure differs initially if a conviction is alleged. The procedure to be followed in such circumstances is considered below.

Is there misconduct?

This is the first issue to be considered. Two different issues arise: first are the facts upon which the charge of misconduct is based to be accepted by the PCC; and, secondly, if they are admitted by the respondent or accepted as true after a hearing by the PCC, do these facts constitute misconduct? Misconduct is defined in the Rules as 'conduct unworthy of a registered nurse, midwife or health visitor as the case may be and includes obtaining registration by fraud'.

The Chairman would ask Janice if she admits the facts alleged in the charges. If she does not or if she has failed to attend the proceedings, the solicitor or the complainant will open the case and adduce evidence of the facts alleged. Witnesses would be summoned to give evidence before the Committee and the defendant (or her representatives) is able to cross-examine any witnesses. At the close of the case against her, she may if she wishes make either or both of the following submissions:

1. that no sufficient evidence has been adduced upon which the PCC could find the facts alleged on the charge to have been proved;
2. that the facts alleged in the charge are not such as to constitute misconduct.

The Committee retire and discuss in camera whether either or both of these submissions should be upheld. If they decide that the submissions are not upheld Janice herself can give evidence to contradict the allegation that her conduct was misconduct.

Janice can address the Committee whether or not she calls witnesses. After she has finished, the solicitor for the complainant may, with the leave of the PCC, adduce evidence to rebut (contradict) any evidence that Janice has put forward. She would then be entitled to address the Committee further to contradict this evidence. The PCC would then consider in camera what allegations have been proved in relation to each charge.

Different procedures apply if the respondent does not appear and if the respondent admits the facts on which the charges are based.

In Janice's case it is likely, depending upon the evidence of the witnesses and the establishment of the facts upon which the charge of misconduct is based, that they would find Janice guilty of misconduct; more for her failure to confess her mistake and her attempt to cover up than for the actual breaking of the ampoule.

If, however, they decided that either there were no facts from which they could deduce there had been misconduct or that the alleged facts did not constitute misconduct, the Chairman would announce the finding that the respondent is not guilty of misconduct in respect of the matters to which the charge relates. This decision must be announced by the Chairman in public and he must also declare the respondent not guilty of misconduct.

Where, however, the PCC has found the alleged facts proved to their satisfaction, the respondent is able to put further argument forward as to why these facts do not constitute misconduct. Where the Council has found the respondent guilty of misconduct the solicitor or complainant can give evidence as to the respondent's previous history. Janice could also give evidence in mitigation and as to her character.

The outcome

Once there has been a decision that the nurse is guilty of misconduct the Committee then has to decide what sanction to adopt. There are several choices (see Fig. 11.8).

1. *Postponement of judgment*: if the PCC decides to postpone judgment it will decide on the month and year when the hearing will resume and the Chairman will announce, in public, the decision and the recommendations that the PCC has decided upon.
2. *No action*: if it is decided not to remove the respondent from the Register this will also be announced in public.
3. *Striking off the Register*: this is announced in public and the Registrar will remove the respondent's name from the relevant part of the Register either for a specified period or not. The respondent will be required to send to the Registrar within 21 days any document or insignia issued by the Council or its predecessor which indicates registration status and the Registrar's letter will warn her of her

(a) postponement of judgement;
(b) no action;
(c) striking off the Register;
(d) referral to the Health Committee;
(e) suspension (added by 1992 Act);
(f) caution (added by 1992 Act).

Figure 11.8 Outcomes available to the Professional Conduct Committee.

liability to proceedings if she holds herself out as being a practitioner in a part of the Register from which her name has been removed.

4. *Refer to the professional screeners* (see below).
5. *Suspension for a specified period from the Register*: on expiry of this time she shall be restored to the Register.
6. *Caution as to the practitioner's future conduct*: the letter must record the caution. The Council shall keep a record for five years of each caution and the existence of a caution must be taken into consideration by the Preliminary Proceedings Committee and the Conduct Committee.

The professional screeners, the President or the Health Committee can refer a case back to the Conduct Committee.

In all cases the respondent must be notified by recorded delivery of the decision of the PCC.

Criminal misconduct

If the charge relates to criminal misconduct, then slightly different rules apply. Evidence as to a conviction on a criminal charge can be put before the PCC and the respondent can adduce evidence to prove beyond all reasonable doubt that she is not the person referred to in the certificate of conviction or that the offence referred to in the certificate of conviction was not that of which she was convicted (this prevents a second trial on the actual charge which was before the criminal courts).

The PCC will determine whether any conviction has been proved and after that the validity of the conviction will not be questioned. Proof of a conviction alone will not be determined to be misconduct. However, proof of the conviction is evidence of the commission of the offence. It then has to be decided whether that offence constitutes misconduct.

SITUATION 11.3 BREACH OF THE PEACE

A district nurse was very angry to discover that a traffic warden was standing by her car as she returned from visiting a patient. She pointed out her nurse's sticker and explained that she was only visiting for a few minutes just to give an injection. The traffic warden was unimpressed by her pleading and took no notice of what she was saying. The nurse became very heated and an argument

> broke out during which the traffic warden said 'You nurses are all the same. You all think the law does not apply to you.' The nurse lost her temper and pushed the warden. She was subsequently charged with conduct likely to cause a breach of the peace. She was found guilty and fined. She eventually found herself facing PCC proceedings.

A case like this would be conducted under the procedure to be followed where a conviction is alleged. Once evidence of a conviction was produced, the nurse could adduce evidence to show that she was not the person convicted or that she was convicted of a different crime. If the PCC determined that the conviction had been proved, it is then open to the nurse to submit that the charges are not in themselves evidence of misconduct.

Obviously, the outcome would depend upon the circumstantial evidence and the attitude of the Committee to such conduct. The statutory definition of misconduct given above does not offer much help in this respect and gives considerable discretion to the PCC to define conduct unworthy of a registered nurse, etc., in terms of current conventions of behaviour.

Removal on grounds of health

At any time the Preliminary Proceedings Committee, when investigating a case of apparent misconduct or a complaint against a nurse, can refer the case to the Health Committee of the UKCC.

The Health Committee is constituted to determine whether or not:

1. a practitioner will be removed from the Register or part of it;
2. a person who has been removed from the Register or part of it may be restored;
3. a practitioner's registration shall be suspended;
4. the suspension of a person's registration shall be terminated.

The constitution of the Health Committee can be seen in Fig. 11.9.

No case can be considered by the Health Committee unless it has been referred by professional screeners. These professional screeners are appointed from a panel of Council members. A group of three are to be selected to consider any matters referred to them. Regard must be had to the professional field in which the professional is working.

Twenty-five members are to be appointed by the Council from among its members who shall be eligible and required to serve on the Health Committee. The members are to be chosen with regard to the need to represent a wide range of fields of professional work. Any ten members constitute the Health Committee. The President of the Council will be the Chairman of the Health Committee and there is a panel of Deputy Chairmen. The quorum is three.

Figure 11.9 Constitution of the Health Committee.

Procedure

Information in writing and received by the Registrar, that raises any question of the practitioner's fitness to practise being seriously impaired by reason of her physical or mental condition, shall be submitted to the professional screeners. Anyone wishing to lay information before the Registrar may make a statutory declaration.

1. If the professional screeners decide there is no reasonable evidence to support the allegations they shall direct the Registrar to inform the complainant and, if they consider it necessary or desirable, the practitioner. The professional screeners may obtain the opinion of a selected medical examiner on the information and evidence that they have received.

2. If they feel that the matter should proceed further they shall direct the Registrar to write to the practitioner by recorded delivery:
   (a) notifying her that information has been received which appears to raise a question as to whether her fitness to practise has become seriously impaired by reason of her physical or mental condition, and indicating the symptomatic behaviour which gives rise to that question;
   (b) inviting the practitioner to agree within 14 days to submit to examination at the Council's expense by two medical examiners to be chosen by the professional screeners and to agree that such examiners should furnish reports to the Registrar on the practitioner's fitness to practise;
   (c) informing the practitioner that it is open to her to nominate other medical practitioners to examine her at her own expense and to report to the Registrar on the practitioner's fitness to practise; and
   (d) inviting the practitioner to submit to the Registrar any observations or other evidence which she may wish to offer as to her own fitness to practise.

If the two medical practitioners are not able to agree, a third can be appointed at the Council's expense.

The professional screeners can make their own enquiries before giving any of the above directions.

Action following reports received from the medical examiners

1. If the medical examiners are unanimously agreed that she is not fit to practise then the Registrar shall refer the information, together with the medical examiners' reports, to the Health Committee. The solicitor may be directed to take all necessary steps for verifying the evidence to be submitted to the Health Committee and for obtaining any necessary documents and the attendance of witnesses;

2. If there is considered to be no sufficient evidence of illness the practitioner and the complainant shall be informed.

Referral of case to professional screeners by Preliminary Proceedings Committee, President or Conduct Committee

The practitioner is invited:

1. to submit to examination by at least two medical examiners to be chosen by the professional screeners;

2. to agree that such examiners should furnish to the Health Committee reports on the practitioner's fitness to practise; and
3. the Registrar informs the practitioner that it is also open to her to nominate another medical practitioner at her own expense to examine her and report to the Health Committee.

If she refuses to submit to such an examination or nominate her own medical examiner, the professional screeners shall decide whether or not to refer the information received to the Health Committee, indicating the reason why no medical report is available.

Notice of referral

Sent by the Registrar to the practitioner which shall:

1. indicate the grounds for the belief that her fitness to practise is seriously impaired; and
2. state the day, time, and place at which the Health Committee will meet to consider the matter.

Twenty-eight days must elapse between the date of posting the notice and the day of the hearing unless the practitioner agrees otherwise. The notice must be sent by registered post or recorded delivery. She must be notified that she can be represented at the hearing and can also be accompanied by her medical adviser.

The Health Committee

The Committee sits in private. At least one of the medical examiners selected by the Preliminary Proceedings Committee to examine her shall be in attendance. The practitioner may be present while her case is heard and may also be represented.

Witnesses may be called and at least one of the medical examiners who has examined the practitioner should be present throughout the inquiry except where the Health Committee decide to meet in camera. The practitioner shall be entitled to representation while her case is heard and may be represented by a friend or by counsel or by a solicitor or officer of a representative organisation or by any other person of her choice and may be accompanied by her medical adviser.

The Chairman opens the proceedings by drawing attention to the grounds for the belief that the practitioner's fitness to practise is seriously impaired as set out in the Notice of Referral and the documentation which has been circulated. If the practitioner has requested that oral evidence be given, the relevant persons are called as witnesses. Even if the requisite notice has not been given, the Health Committee can consult the legal assessor to decide if, in the interests of justice, there should be an adjournment to allow for witnesses to be called. At the conclusion of the practitioner's case the Chairman shall invite the practitioner or her representative to address the Health Committee and to adduce evidence of her fitness to practise.

The Committee can:

1. adjourn for further medical reports;
2. find that the fitness to practise is not seriously impaired by reason of the practitioner's physical or mental condition;

3. postpone judgment;
4. find that the fitness to practise is seriously impaired by the practitioner's physical or mental condition (it can direct the Registrar to remove the practitioner from the Register and can specify a period or not).

In the event of a finding under point 2 above, the Committee must refer the matter back to the committee from which the case was referred or to the President (if she referred it) who shall refer it to the Conduct Committee.

Restoration to the Register

This is governed by Rule 22 which does not set any minimum time before which an application to be restored to the Register is not possible. If suspension from the Register has been for a specified time, then on the expiry of that time the practitioner is restored to the Register. The applicant for restoration must apply in writing to the Registrar detailing the grounds for the application. The Registrar will then send details of the procedure, the recommendations of the Committee at the time of removal from the Register, an application form requiring the applicant to cite two persons who can give evidence for her, require her to state that she has not been convicted of a criminal offence since removal from the Register, require her to testify that she has not held herself out as registered, and request the fee for restoration. Procedure for the hearing is laid down in Rules 15, 16, and 17 and is otherwise as determined by the Committee.

The proceedings of the PCC and the Health Committee are subject to review by the High Court. For example, in *Slater* v. *United Kingdom Central Council for Nursing, Midwifery and Health Visitors*, *The Times* 10 June 1987, the Queen's Bench Division quashed the decision of the PCC in removing Mr Stephen Slater's name from the Register of nurses and remitted the case to a freshly constituted Committee for a rehearing on the grounds that the practitioner's case had not been fully considered by the Committee and an injustice might therefore have been done. In a later case, *Hefferon* v. *Committee of the UKCC*, *Current Law* May 1988 221, the High Court quashed the decisions of the Committee on the grounds that there had been a breach of natural justice.

Professional standards and codes of practice

The Chairman of the UKCC emphasised in an opening address at a conference in May 1983 that

> the professional conduct function should be seen in positive terms – as one of the means through which a regulatory body, acting on behalf of the profession, honours the contract between the profession and society by ensuring that any member of the profession who has failed to meet the trust which society has placed in him or her is not permitted to continue to practise, or if the failure has not been a serious one, is reminded of the standard which professional practitioners are expected to meet.

The functions of the UKCC set out in Fig. 11.3 include that of establishing and improving standards of training and professional practice, and also providing, in such manner as it thinks fit, advice for nurses, midwives and health visitors on standards of professional conduct. In fulfilment of this duty the UKCC has issued and revised a code of professional conduct and many guidelines on different aspects of professional practice, many of which are included here in the appendices. In addition, the Council has decided that, in the future, all nurses (and not just midwives, who have had this requirement since 1936) will be required to maintain their professional competence to enable them to practise. Many of the codes and advisory papers produced by the UKCC are to be found in the appendices here and are frequently referred to in the text.

Education and training

The statutory duty to establish and improve standards of training falls on the UKCC and the National Boards. A team of professional officers works with members through specialist committees including the Educational Policy Advisory Committee, the Midwifery Committee and a Committee on Research. New rules for the education of students, known as Project 2000, are now in place. The 1992 Act ended the duty of National Boards to provide pre-registration training courses. It is now their function to approve institutions in relation to the provision of training, etc.

Post-registration development

The UKCC has set standards for the Future of Professional Practice (UKCC March 1994). This will require the following:

(a) a minimum of five study days every three years;
(b) a Notification of Practice Form;
(c) a Return to Practice programme if they have been out of practice for five years or more; and
(d) a personal professional profile.

New standards have been set for specialist post-registration education. It is anticipated that these provisions will be implemented in April 1995.

Questions and exercises

1 The PCC sits in different parts of the country and is open to the public and members of the profession. Next time it meets in your vicinity try to attend and write up the hearing from the point of view of the formality, the procedure followed, justice to the nurse defendant, and justice to the general public.
2 In what ways does a hearing before the PCC differ from a hearing before a civil court?
3 How would you define misconduct by a nurse? Would any of the following count as misconduct by your definition?:

    (a) A nurse has an illegitimate child.

    (b) A nurse is convicted of shop-lifting.

    (c) A nurse is found guilty of a breach of the peace after being involved in an argument with a traffic warden.

    (d) A nurse is fined for speeding.

    (e) A nurse borrows money from a junior member of staff on her ward.

    (f) A nurse is discovered to be drunk when off duty but still in her uniform.

4 Since the decision as to whether there is misconduct or not depends upon the detailed circumstances, what additional information would you need to answer question 3 above and how would that information affect your answer?

5 Arrange a visit to your National Board and prepare a chart showing the relationship of the National Board to the UKCC.

6 Do you consider that there should be a time limit within which the nurse who has been struck off cannot apply to be reinstated?

12 Health and safety and the nurse

Unfortunately, injuries at work to nursing staff are not uncommon. It is now recognised that back injuries are almost an occupational hazard; publicity has recently been given to the number of staff who are injured by violence at work, including work in the community; the hazards that a nurse faces in administering carcinogenic substances such as cytotoxic drugs are only now being appreciated and precautions (such as protective clothing and masks) are being laid down. The nurse has always faced the problem of contamination from infectious diseases and the particular problems relating to AIDS are considered in Chapter 26. In this chapter the remedies available to the nurse for injuries at work will be considered. They can be seen in Fig. 12.1.

If the nurse has been injured at work she may be able to bring several of the actions set out in Fig. 12.1 and can sue several different defendants.

Occupiers' Liability Act 1957

General principles

If a nurse is injured as a result of the state of the premises she may be able to bring an action against the occupier who has a duty under the Occupiers' Liability Act 1957 to ensure that the premises are safe. The statutory duty is set out in Fig. 12.2.

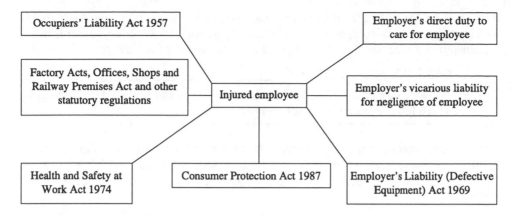

Figure 12.1 Remedies to an injured employee.

Section 2(1) An occupier of premises owes the same duty, the 'common duty of care', to all his visitors, except in so far as he is free to and does extend, restrict, modify or exclude his duty to any visitor or visitors by agreement or otherwise.

Section 2(2) The common duty of care is a duty to take such care as in all the circumstances of the case is reasonable to see that the visitor will be reasonably safe in using the premises for the purposes for which he is invited or permitted by the occupier to be there.

Figure 12.2 Occupiers' Liability Act 1957 Sections 2 (1) and (2).

The duty is owed to the visitor. This term 'visitor' includes the person who has expressed permission to be on the premises as well as the person who has implied permission to be there. Thus in the hospital context the term 'visitors' will include employees, patients, friends and relatives visiting patients, contractors and suppliers, and others who have a genuine interest in being there. If any of these persons were to be injured, for example when plaster fell off the wall, they could claim compensation from the occupier.

Who is the occupier?

The occupier is the person who has control over the premises. This will usually be the owner of the premises, but not necessarily. There could be several occupiers, each having control over the premises and responsibilities for the safety of the building. For example, contractors might be working on hospital premises and both the NHS Trust and the contractor could be regarded as occupiers for the purpose of the Act. A private house visited by a community nurse may be owner-occupied, in which case that person will be the occupier for the purposes of the Act; alternatively it could be under a tenancy agreement, in which case the landlord and the tenant will have different duties under this agreement regarding the upkeep and maintenance of the premises and could there-fore be regarded as occupiers under the statutory provisions. Which occupier is liable for harm to a visitor will therefore depend upon the cause of the injury.

CASE 12.1 SLIPPERY FLOOR

A visitor slipped on polish which had been put on the floor but not wiped off, which left the floor excessively slippery.

The visitor succeeded in obtaining compensation for the harm. The occupier had failed to take reasonable care for the safety of the visitor (*Slade* v. *Battersea HMC* 1955 1 WLR 207: this was a case decided before the 1957 Act, but the result would be the same after 1957).

Privatisation of cleaning and catering services

What is the effect of the privatisation of services upon the occupier's liability?

This is likely to lead to some complications since where services are contracted out there is likely to be dual occupation of premises, i.e. by the NHS Trust and by the private company. Thus in the case of a contract for cleaning services, if an injury is caused to a visitor by the conditions of the premises, e.g. an uneven surface or falling plaster, and the NHS Trust has retained responsibility for such conditions, then the NHS Trust would be responsible for the visitor's injuries. If, on the other hand, the injuries are caused by the carelessness of any of the contractor's employees, then the contractor would be responsible for compensating the person injured as a result of the negligence under the principles of vicarious liability previously discussed in Chapter 5. If, therefore, the employee of the cleaning firm has left the floor in a dangerous state and there are no warning notices and a nurse is injured as a consequence, she would sue the cleaning company because its employee had been negligent in the course of employment and had caused her foreseeable harm.

What is the effect of a warning notice?

Section 2 (4) (a) of the Occupiers' Liability Act 1957 is set out in Fig. 12.3. The warning is not conclusive: if compliance with it is sufficient to prevent any harm to the visitor, then it will be effective as a defence in an action under the 1957 Act.

SITUATION 12.1 WARNING

An NHS Trust is undertaking major renovation work to a corridor and puts up a warning notice saying 'Danger'. As a nurse walks along, she is struck by a piece of plaster falling from the ceiling.

If there were other precautions that the NHS Trust could reasonably have taken, e.g. a safety net cordoning off the work area, then the NHS Trust would probably be seen to have been in breach of its duty of care to the visitor subject to the possibility

Section 2 (4) (a) in determining whether the occupier of premises has discharged the common duty of care to a visitor, regard is to be had to all these circumstances, so that (for example): where damage is caused to a visitor by a danger of which he had been warned by the occupier, the warning is not to be treated without more as absolving the occupier from liability, unless in all the circumstances it was enough to enable the visitor to be reasonably safe.

Figure 12.3 Occupiers' Liability Act 1957 Section 2 (4) (a).

of contributory negligence by her. If on the other hand, the notice said 'corridor closed – diversion' and indicated a different route which was practicable, then the occupier would have satisfied the duty under the Act. If, of course, the nurse ignored the notice, continued along the dangerous corridor, and was injured, then it is probable that there would be no breach of duty by the NHS Trust since the notice was in all the circumstances enough to enable the nurse to be reasonably safe.

Independent contractors

Where independent contractors are brought onto site the usual occupier and employer of the firm will not normally be liable for their safety (see Fig. 12.4).

Liability for children

It is expressly provided that all the circumstances must be taken into account in deciding whether the occupier is in breach of his duty of care under the Act (see Fig. 12.5). The

Section 2(4b) when damage is caused to a visitor due to the faulty execution of any work of construction, maintenance or repair by an independent contractor employed by the occupier. The occupier is not to be treated without more as answerable for the danger, if in all the circumstances he had acted reasonably in entrusting the work to an independent contractor and had taken such steps (if any) as he reasonably ought in order to satisfy himself that the contractor was competent and that the work had been properly done.

Figure 12.4 Liability for independent contractor.

Section 2(3) the circumstances relevant for the present purpose include the degree of care, and of want of care, which would ordinarily be looked for in such a visitor, so that (for example) in proper cases: an occupier must be prepared for children to be less careful than adults.

Figure 12.5 Liability for children.

occupier can expect a lower standard of care from children and therefore additional precautions have to be taken where the presence of children can be foreseen.

Trespassers

The Occupiers' Liability Act 1957 does not cover any duty towards trespassers. The courts recognised a limited duty of the occupier towards trespassers, particularly children, and statutory provision was made in the Occupiers' Liability Act 1984.

A duty of care only arises when the occupier knows or has reasonable grounds to know of a danger and the risk if the trespasser comes into the vicinity of the danger. The standard of care is to take such care as is reasonable in all the circumstances of the case to see that injury is not suffered. The duty can be discharged by warnings or discouraging persons from incurring the risk. Clearly there is more likely to be a duty of care to child rather than adult trespassers.

Injuries caused by another employee

Where a nurse has been injured as a result of the negligence of another employee, she can either sue the employee for compensation or she could bring an action against the NHS Trust under the principles of vicarious liability.

SITUATION 12.2 WHEELCHAIR CHAOS

Two nurses, Mary and Jean, are working together in a ward for elderly mentally infirm patients. They are moving a patient from a chair into a wheelchair. As they do so, the wheelchair moves and Mary, in her endeavour to save the patient, takes the full weight and falls to the floor. She suffers a severe injury to her back and shoulder. An investigation reveals that Jean was responsible for ensuring that the brake was safely on the wheelchair and her carelessness was responsible for Mary's injuries.

Mary can take one of the following paths.

1. She could sue Jean personally, since Jean is probably in breach of the duty of care she owes to Mary to ensure that reasonable steps are taken to prevent foreseeable harm to Mary. However, such an action is likely to be pointless unless Jean is insured for such liability or has sufficient funds to pay compensation to Mary.
2. She could sue the NHS Trust for its vicarious liability for harm caused by the negligence of an employee. Jean is an employee, has been negligent, and is acting in the course of employment. Mary would still have to establish that Jean was personally negligent, but this action has the advantage over suing Jean personally since the NHS Trust should have the funds to pay compensation.
3. In addition, Mary could sue the NHS Trust for breach of its duty of care to look after her safety as an employee. In this action Mary would have to establish that

At common law the employer has an implied term in the contract of employment to look after the safety of the employee:

1. To ensure the premises, plant and equipment are safe.
2. To provide competent staff.
3. To establish a safe system of work.

Figure 12.6 Employer's direct duty of care.

Every employer carrying on any business in Great Britain shall insure against liability for bodily injury or disease sustained by his employees and arising out of and in course of their employment.

Business includes a trade or profession, and includes any activity carried out by a body of persons, whether corporate or unincorporate. Penalty for failure to insure.

Figure 12.7 Employer's Liability (Compulsory Insurance) Act 1969.

the NHS Trust itself was at fault, e.g. if it had failed to provide Jean with adequate training in carrying out such a manoeuvre (see below).

In all three actions, it will of course be a defence, complete or partial, that Mary was herself contributorily negligent (see Chapter 6).

The direct duty of care for the safety of the employee

It is an implied term of the contract of employment that an employer will take reasonable care for the safety of his employees. The obligation is set out in Fig. 12.6. If there is a breach in carrying out this threefold duty and as a consequence the employee is foreseeably injured, then he may be able to obtain compensation from the employer.

There is an overlap between the direct duty of care of the employer for the safety of the employee and the duty of the employer as occupier under the Occupiers' Liability Act 1957. Thus in a case where a nurse is injured as a result of defects in the NHS Trust's premises, she may have a cause of action under the Occupiers' Liability Act, and also because of breach of the employer's common law duty to care for the employee.

Insurance by the employer

The Employer's Liability (Compulsory Insurance) Act 1969 (see Fig. 12.7) obliges all non-Crown employers to be covered by an approved policy of insurance against liability for bodily injury or disease sustained by an employee and arising out of and in course of employment. By Section 60 of the NHS and Community Care Act 1990, health authorities ceased to enjoy Crown immunity. However, Schedule 8 of the Act preserves immunity from this Act for health authorities and NHS Trusts. The employers of a nurse working in the private sector or a practice nurse working for general practitioners are, however, bound by the Act.

Health and Safety at Work Act

General principles

How does the employer's duty to care for the safety of the employee relate to the Health and Safety at Work Act 1974?

The employer has two parallel duties – one under the civil law and enforced through the civil courts, the other under the criminal law and enforced through the criminal courts. The Health and Safety at Work Act is an Act which is enforceable through the criminal courts and places upon both employer and employee considerable duties in relation to health and safety. Figure 12.8 sets out the general duties under Section 2 of the Act. Figure 12.9 sets out the duties of the individual employee. A glance will show how comprehensive they are. Until 7 February 1987, while the general duties were binding upon a health authority, they could not be enforced against it. This was because the health authority enjoyed the privileges of Crown immunity. Employees could, however, be prosecuted under the Act. It is specifically provided under the Health and Safety at Work Act that a breach of the general duties does not give rise to an action in tort. However, a breach of the specific regulations may do so. This provision is unlikely to hamper a prospective litigant since an action could be based on a breach of the duties at common law set out in Fig. 12.6.

Abolition of Crown immunity

Health authorities used to enjoy protection from the enforcement provisions of much legislation on the grounds that, as Crown bodies, they were immune from prosecution. However, this immunity was removed by the National Health Service (Amendment) Act 1986 Sections 1 and 2 in respect of the food legislation and Health and Safety at Work Act 1974. Section 60(1) of the NHS and Community Care Act 1990 states that 'no health service body shall be regarded as the servant or agent of the Crown or as enjoying any status, immunity or privilege of the Crown'. Thus the health authority and family health services authority lost their status as Crown authorities, and in Schedule 2 Paragraph 18 an NHS Trust is not to be regarded as a Crown servant or agent. (The NHS (Amendment) Act 1986 Sections 1 and 5 were repealed.) Some immunities were, however, retained under Schedule 8 of the Act, including Employer's Liability (Compulsory Insurance) Act 1969 (see above).

General duties of employers to their employees

(1) It shall be the duty of every employer to ensure, so far as is reasonably practicable, the health. safety and welfare at work of all his employees.

(2) Without prejudice to the generality of an employer's duty under the preceding subsection, the matters to which that duty extends include in particular:

    (a) The provision and maintenance of plant and systems of work that are, so far as is reasonably practicable, safe and without risks to health;

    (b) arrangements for ensuring, so far as is reasonably practicable, safety and absence of risks to health in connection with the use, handling, storage and transport of articles and substances;

    (c) the provision of such information, instruction, training and supervision as is necessary to ensure, so far as is reasonably practicable, the health and safety at work of his employees;

    (d) so far as is reasonably practicable as regards any place of work under the employer's control, the maintenance of it in a condition that is safe and without risks to health and the provision and maintenance of means of access to and egress from it that are safe and without such risks;

    (e) the provision and maintenance of a working environment for his employees that is, so far as is reasonably practicable, safe, without risks to health, and adequate as regards facilities and arrangements for their welfare at work.

(3) Except in such cases as may be prescribed, it shall be the duty of every employer to prepare and as often as may be appropriate revise a written statement of his general policy with respect to the health and safety at work of his employees and the organisation and arrangements for the time being in force for carrying out that policy, and to bring the statement and any revision of it to the notice of all of his employees.

(4) Regulations made by the Secretary of State may provide for the appointment in prescribed cases by recognised trade unions (within the meaning of the regulations) of safety representatives from amongst the employees, and those representatives shall represent the employees in consultations with the employers under subsection (6) below and shall have such other functions as may be prescribed.

(5) (Repealed)

(6) It shall be the duty of every employer to consult any such representatives with a view to the making and maintenance of arrangements which will enable him and his employees to co-operate effectively in promoting and developing measures to ensure the health and safety at work of the employees, and in checking the effectiveness of such measures.

(7) In such cases as may be prescribed it shall be the duty of every employer, if requested to do so by the safety representatives mentioned in subsections (4) and (5) above, to establish, in accordance with regulations made by the Secretary of State, a safety committee having the function of keeping under review the measures taken to ensure the health and safety at work of his employees and such other functions as may be prescribed.

Figure 12.8 Health and Safety at Work Act 1974 Section 2.

Section 7   (a) to take reasonable care for the health and safety of himself and of others who may be affected by his acts or omissions at work.

        (b) as regards any duty or requirement imposed on his employer or other person by or under any of the relevant statutory provisions to co-operate with him in so far as is necessary to enable that duty or requirement to be performed or complied with.

Figure 12.9 Health and Safety at Work Act 1974 Section 7.

Powers of the health and safety inspector

These are set out in Section 20 of the Act (see Fig. 12.10) and are extensive. The inspector is able to issue improvement or prohibition notices which order the recipient to make equipment or premises safe or to cease a particular activity until the danger is removed. He also has the power to prosecute the authority in the Magistrates or Crown Court for a breach of the duties or regulations or to comply with the notice.

The nurse and the abolition of Crown immunity

How does the abolition of Crown immunity affect the nurse? In theory there should be no effect since the duties under the Act have always been binding and enforceable against employees, even if they were not enforceable against the health authority. In practice, however, if environmental health officers and health and safety inspectors take full advantage of their new powers against the NHS Trusts, one can expect the consequences set out in Fig. 12.11.

An example of an area where there has been some confusion over responsibilities is the ward kitchen. Any area where food is prepared for serving to others as a business is covered by the Food Act and its regulations. Those involved in preparing and serving food are regarded as food handlers and come under the provisions of the regulations. Local policies are required to determine whether the ward sister is responsible for the implementation of the Food Act 1984 and Food Safety Act 1990 and regulations in the ward kitchen and for the work of the servers, or whether such managerial responsibility is assigned to the catering officer or domestic superintendent.

Could the nurse be prosecuted?

Yes, in two respects. Firstly, under the Health and Safety at Work Act 1974 Section 7 (see Fig. 12.9) which places a duty on all employees in respect of health and safety. A nurse who, for example, failed to follow the correct practice in disposing of pressurised cans as a result of which an incinerator blew up, injuring a porter, could be prosecuted for breach of her duty under Section 7 of the Act. Secondly, the nurse as manager will have responsibilities in advising on and implementing the health authority's duties under the Act and if she neglects these she could be prosecuted personally.

SITUATION 12.3 WARD BOILER

A ward kitchen has a water heater which is not fixed according to the regulations. The boiler is moved to a more convenient location. A lead from the boiler runs to a point a few feet away. A domestic trips over the lead, the boiler falls on her, and she is severely scalded. The health and safety inspectorate investigate and consider prosecuting the ward sister and others responsible.

An inspector may, for the purpose of carrying into effect any of the relevant statutory provisions within the field of responsibility of the enforcing authority which appointed him, exercise the powers set out in subsection (2) below.

(2) The powers of an inspector referred to in the preceding subsection are the following, namely:
   (a) at any reasonable time (or, in a situation which in his opinion is or may be dangerous, at any time) to enter any premises which he has reason to believe it is necessary for him to enter for the purpose mentioned in subsection (1) above;
   (b) to take with him a constable if he has reasonable cause to apprehend any serious obstruction in the execution of his duty;
   (c) without prejudice to the preceding paragraph, on entering any premises by virtue of paragraph (a) above to take with him:
      (i) any other person duly authorised by his (the inspector's) enforcing authority; and
      (ii) any equipment or materials required for any purpose for which the power of entry is being exercised;
   (d) to make such examination and investigation as may in any circumstances be necessary for the purpose mentioned in subsection (1) above;
   (e) as regards any premises which he has power to enter to direct that those premises or any part of them, or anything therein, shall be left undisturbed (whether generally or in particular respects) for so long as is reasonably necessary for the purpose of any examination or investigation under paragraph (d) above;
   (f) to take such measurements and photographs and make such recordings as he considers necessary for the purpose of any examination or investigation under paragraph (d) above;
   (g) to take samples of any articles or substances found in any premises which he has power to enter, and of the atmosphere in or in the vicinity of any such premises;
   (h) in the case of any article or substance found in any premises which he has power to enter, being an article or substance which appears to him to have caused or to be likely to cause danger to health or safety, to cause it to be dismantled or subjected to any process or test (but not so as to damage or destroy it unless this is in the circumstances necessary for the purpose mentioned in subsection (1) above);
   (i) in the case of any such article or substance as is mentioned in the preceding paragraph, to take possession of it and detain it for so long as is necessary for all or any of the following purposes, namely:
      (i) to examine it and do to it anything which he has power to do under that paragraph;
      (ii) to ensure that it is not tampered with before his examination of it is completed;
      (iii) to ensure that it is available for use as evidence in any proceedings for an offence under any of the relevant statutory provisions or any proceedings relating to a notice under section 21 or 22;
   (j) if he is conducting an examination or investigation under (d) to require any person ... to answer any questions as the inspector thinks fit and to sign a declaration of the truth of his answers ...
   (k) to require production of, inspect and take copies of any entry in any books or documents ...
   (l) to require any person to afford himself such facilities and assistance within that person's control or responsibilities as are necessary for him to exercise his powers;
   (m) any other power which is necessary for the purpose of exercising any of the above powers.

Figure 12.10 Health and Safety at Work Act 1974 Section 20.

1. Health authorities, NHS Trusts and health premises are subject to the enforcement provisions of the Food Act and Health and Safety at Work Act and relevant regulations.
2. Enforcement officers, i.e. environmental health officers and health and safety inspectors, have statutory powers to enforce the relevant legislation. This might lead to
   (a) more visits of inspection, use of enforcement notices and prosecutions;
   (b) requirements of greater capital investment in the premises and equipment, which could result in
       (i) an impetus towards privatisation
       (ii) an impetus towards rationalisation and centralisation of services;
   (c) greater involvement of the health authority and NHS Trust in establishing codes of practice and ensuring their implementation through tighter managerial controls;
   (d) more specific definition of managerial and individual responsibilities;
   (e) more training.

Figure 12.11 Consequences of the abolition of Crown immunity.

Control of hazardous substances

The Control of Substances Hazardous to Health (COSHH) Regulations 1988 came into effect in 1989 and aim to control activities where exposure to substances could lead to disease or ill health, i.e. substances that are toxic, harmful, corrosive or irritant; the Regulations also cover those that have delayed effects or are hazardous in conjunction with other substances. The employer must assess the risks and take appropriate action, including protective clothing, information and training of staff.

Notification of accidents

Regulations require the notification to the appropriate authority, usually the health and safety inspectorate, of all fatal accidents, major injuries and dangerous occurrences. Accident reports should, however, be kept of all accidents occurring at work, whether notifiable or not. Documentation of the details of the incident is often vital to the success of any claim for civil compensation. A detailed comprehensive account of how the accident occurred is of extreme benefit to any potential litigant (see Chapter 9).

Health and Safety at Work Regulations 1992

In compliance with the EC Directive, Health and Safety Regulations were issued in 1992, which came into force on 1 January 1993. They include the following:

(a) Management of Health and Safety at Work Regulation 1992;
(b) Manual Handling Operations Regulations 1992;
(c) Personal Protective Equipment at Work Regulation;
(d) Provision and Use of Work Equipment Regulation;

(e) Workplace (Health, Safety and Welfare) Regulation;
(f) Health and Safety (Display Screen Equipment) Regulation.

These regulations are enforceable against all employers and employees (whether NHS or not). Codes of Practice have been issued by the Health and Safety Commission. Failure to comply with the Code is not in itself an offence, but can be used in evidence in criminal proceedings.

For protection of the employee against dismissal in health and safety cases, see page 156. The Environmental Protection Act 1990 creates duties in relation to waste management.

Defective equipment

If an employee has been injured as the result of defective equipment, an additional remedy may be available under the Employer's Liability (Defective Equipment) Act 1969. This is set out in Fig. 12.12. The Act is binding upon the Crown and enables the employee to obtain compensation from the employer if the injury has been caused by defective equipment supplied by the employer where a third party is to blame. Instead of the employee having the cost and hassle of obtaining compensation from the third party, that burden falls upon the employer from whom the employee can obtain direct compensation.

SITUATION 12.4 FAULTY BED

A nurse is injured when a recently supplied bed, which she is raising by the foot pedal, breaks and falls on to her leg. It is discovered that there was a defect in the bed mounting which should have been spotted by the manufacturers before it left the factory.

Factors which must be present
1. Personal injury by employee in course of employment.
2. As a consequence of a defect in equipment.
3. Equipment provided by his employer for purposes of his business.
4. Defect attributable wholly or partly to the fault of a third party (whether identified or not).

Action
1. Injury deemed to be also attributable to negligence on part of employer, i.e. employee can recover compensation from employer.
2. Contributory negligence by employee may be raised as a defence (either full or partial).
3. Employer can recover contribution from third party (in contract or negligence).

Applies to the Crown.

Figure 12.12 Employer's Liability (Defective Equipment) Act 1969.

The nurse could claim compensation from the NHS Trust under the provisions of the Employer's Liability (Defective Equipment) Act 1969. The costs, problems and time associated with suing the manufacturers would then fall upon the shoulders of the NHS Trust.

Product liability

In all the above forms of action the injured person has to show that someone was at fault in causing the accident. However, a recent innovation in the law of liability came into force on 1 March 1988. The Consumer Protection Act 1987 (Part 1) gives a right of compensation against the producers and suppliers of products if a defect in the product has caused personal injury, death, loss or damage to property, without the requirement of showing that the defendant was at fault. This has been introduced into this country following an EEC directive dated 25 July 1985 (No. 85/3741/EEC). The Act applies to the Crown. The NHS Trust itself could be a defendant in a product liability action since it is a producer of many products; it could also be liable as a supplier.

Defect

The definition of defect is shown in Fig. 12.13. It is still to be seen how easily the plaintiff will be able to show the existence of a defect in the product. The defendant can rely on the fact that the state of scientific knowledge at the time was such that the defect could not have been discovered (i.e. 'the state of the art' defence).

How does product liability affect the nurse?

SITUATION 12.5 NEEDLE INJURY_____

A nurse is giving an injection to a patient when the needle snaps and she is injured.

_____

She would ask whoever supplied the needle in the NHS Trust (probably the CSSD) who was the producer of that particular needle. The supplier has a duty under Section 2 (3) to inform her of the name of the producer who will then be strictly liable to the nurse for causing her harm. If the CSSD is unable to provide her with that information, the CSSD could itself be liable to her. The nurse herself would have to show that there was a defect in the needle, i.e. that the safety was not such as persons generally are entitled to expect. This is defined in Section (2) as including the manner in which and purpose for which the product has been marketed, the instructions and warnings accompanying it, and what might reasonably be expected to be done with or in relation to it at the time it was supplied (see Fig. 12.13).

3. (1) Subject to the following provisions of this section, there is a defect in a product for the purposes of this part if the safety of the product is not such as persons generally are entitled to expect; and for those purposes 'safety', in relation to a product, shall include safety with respect to products comprised in that product and safety in the context of risks of damage to property, as well as in the context of risks of death or personal injury.

(2) In determining for the purposes of subsection (1) above what persons generally are entitled to expect in relation to a product all the circumstances shall be taken into account, including:

(a) the manner in which, and purposes for which, the product has been marketed, its get-up, the use of any mark in relation to the product and any instructions for, or warnings with respect to, doing or refraining from doing anything with or in relation to the product;

(b) what might reasonably be expected to be done with or in relation to the product; and

(c) the time when the product was supplied by its producer to another;

and nothing in this section shall require a defect to be inferred from the fact alone that the safety of a product which is supplied after that time is greater than the safety of the product in question.

4. (1) In any civil proceedings by virtue of this part against any person ('the person proceeded against') in respect of a defect in a product it shall be a defence for him to show:

(a) that the defect is attributable to compliance with any requirement imposed by or under any enactment or with any Community obligation; or

(b) that the person proceeded against did not at any time supply the product to another; or

(c) that the following conditions are satisfied, that is to say:

(i) that the only supply of the product to another by the person proceeded against was otherwise than in the course of a business of that person's; and

(ii) that section 2(2) above does not apply to that person or applies to him by virtue only of things done otherwise than with a view to profit; or

(d) that the defect did not exist in the product at the relevant time; or

(e) that the state of scientific and technical knowledge at the relevant time was not such that a producer of products of the same description as the product in question might be expected to have discovered the defect if it had existed in his products while they were under his control; or

(f) that the defect

(i) constituted a defect in a product ('the subsequent product') in which the product in question has been comprised; and

(ii) was wholly attributable to the design of the subsequent product or to compliance by the producer of the product in question with instructions given by the producer of the subsequent product.

Figure 12.13 Definition of defect and defences in product liability.

Timing

There is a ten-year time limit from the date of the supply of the product. The individual plaintiff must bring the action within three years of suffering the harm or having knowledge of the relevant circumstances.

Naming the producer

What if the NHS Trust department which supplied the goods cannot name the producer? The person who suffered the harm must ask the supplier to identify the producer or importer of the product in the EU and must make that request within a reasonable period after the damage has occurred and at a time when it is not reasonably practicable for the person making the request to identify those persons. If the health department supplying the goods fails to comply within a reasonable period after receiving the request, then the claimant is entitled to recover damages from the supplying department. All departments in an NHS Trust which supply products to persons who suffer damage from them could thus become liable: the supplies department, pharmacy, cleaning, catering, CSSD, office equipment, works and buildings.

   The implications of this are that department records must be sufficiently comprehensive and clear to provide the appropriate information to the person injured by the defect, in order that the claim can be made against the actual producer of the product rather than the supplier.

The nurse as supplier

Could the nurse ever be a supplier? In the course of her duty a nurse certainly supplies many products to patients, other staff, visitors, and contractors: drugs, food/drink, equipment, syringes, etc. Could she be a supplier for the purposes of this Act?

> ### SITUATION 12.6 SUPPLYING DEFECTIVE PRODUCTS_____
>
> The nurse gives a patient a high protein food to take home with him, which is defective, e.g. it has glass in it and the patient is injured.

In most similar circumstances it will be clear to the person suffering harm, who are the producers or trademark user and it will therefore be reasonably practicable for the person suffering harm to identify the potential defendant. In other cases, the nurse will have obtained the goods from another department in the hospital, which would become the supplier for the purposes of the Act.

Product liability and the Employer's Liability (Defective Equipment) Act 1969

The relationship between these two Acts is shown in Fig. 12.14. The right of the employee to claim from the employer under the 1969 Act is unaffected by the provisions of the

1. The injured employee can obtain compensation from the employer under the 1969 Act only if there has been negligence by a third party.
2. The injured employee can obtain compensation from the employer as supplier only if he has not identified the producer under the 1987 Act.
3. The 1987 Act covers all persons suffering damage, i.e. patients, employees, visitors etc. The 1969 Act only relates to employees.
4. The 1987 Act covers damages in the form of personal injury, death, loss or damage to property, the 1969 Act only covers loss of life, impairment of a person's physical or mental condition and any disease, not loss or damage to property.
5. Fault need not be established under the 1987 Act – only a defect in the product. However, the defence of what is known at the time is available.

Figure 12.14 Product and defective equipment liability.

1987 Act. Clearly, any person who has been injured by a defective product can use whichever remedy is likely to be most successful and in fact can bring an action using several different causes of action.

Back injuries

Unless a nurse can establish that she has injured her back as a result of a defect in a product (e.g. hoist, or bed), to claim compensation from the NHS Trust, she must show that the NHS Trust is liable to her for breach of its direct duty of care to look after her safety or for its vicarious liability for the negligence of an employee in course of employment.

CASE 12.2 BACK INJURY

The injured nurse was one of a team of four. The patient was obese, elderly and uncooperative, hence four nurses were engaged to lift her. Evidence was given in court, and was accepted by the judge that a proper method of lifting this known awkward patient was used at the relevant time. Nevertheless, the patient was said variously to 'lurch' or 'flop'. At this time the injured nurse cried out in pain and the patient was lowered again to the bed, and lifting not resumed until another nurse was called. Examination showed a prolapsed disc (quoted by Ivor Abelson in *Aspects of Health Service Law*, Ravenswood Press 1981).

Industrial injury payment of 30 per cent together with an exceptional hardship allowance were awarded, the nurse having now retired. However, her claim in the High Court for damages failed as, quite clearly, on the facts accepted by the judge, it was correct to prefer evidence that lifting was carried out properly to that alleging there was 'a muddle'. The nurse therefore failed to establish fault.

A recent spate of back injury claims has highlighted the importance to the NHS Trust of establishing that the nurse has at some stage received appropriate training in lifting. The legal aspects of this are considered in Chapter 18.

Manual handling

From 1 January 1993 the Manual Handling Operations Regulations 1992 have been in force. These require employers to undertake a risk assessment on manual handling and, where possible, manual handling should be avoided. If this cannot be done, then employers should take measures to reduce the risk of injury, assessing both the movements required of the employee and the nature of the loads to be removed. Schedules provide checklists for undertaking assessments. The Health and Safety Commission has issued guidance on manual handling of loads in the health service (1992). This includes a section on lifting in the community.

On 24 July 1994 a nurse was awarded £205,000 for a back injury (*Boag* v. *Hounslow and Spelthorne Health Authority, The Times* 25 July 1994). The circumstances were that in November 1988 she and a colleague were trying to lift an elderly woman from a commode to a chair, when the patient's legs gave way. Due to the lack of space, Mrs Boag was forced to twist her back to place the woman in the chair. The Health Authority, which admitted liability, agreed the out-of-court settlement shortly before the case was due to be heard. She was forced to give up her job and is regularly confined to bed. She attends a pain relief clinic and will probably never work again. Her husband has had to take time off work to help with the two children.

Carrying weights

What if an injury occurs as the result of a nurse carrying too heavy a load? The nurse is protected generally by the employer's direct duty of care for her health and safety and by his duty under the Health and Safety at Work Act. Unlike employees in offices, shops and railway premises, she does not have protection in relation to specific weights.

Violence

Suing the NHS Trust

The employer's duty extends to protecting the employee against reasonably foreseeable attacks from violent patients or even from violent visitors and trespassers.

SITUATION 12.7 MIXED WARD

A psychiatric nurse is on an acute mixed ward. Complaints have been made that although this is a mixed ward, there are insufficient numbers of male nurses and thus the female nurses are often dealing with male patients on their own. A known aggressive male patient, without any warning or provocation, suddenly produces a razor and cuts a nurse badly on the face.

To obtain compensation from the NHS Trust the nurse must establish that another employee has been negligent in course of employment and therefore the NHS Trust is vicariously liable, or that the NHS Trust was itself directly at fault. To establish this she would need to show that inadequate precautions were taken for her safety: that there were reasonable precautions that the authority could have taken and failed to take, e.g. male staffing; training in the handling of violent patients; special facilities for dealing with known aggressive patients; a special wing; an alarm system; a safe system for control of dangerous items. The injured nurse would also have to show a causal connection between the injuries she suffered and these failures on the authority's part, i.e. if she would still have been injured even had these precautions been taken, then the NHS Trust would not be liable.

In its defence the NHS Trust would have to establish either that such reasonable precautions had been provided – a dispute on the facts – or that even if such precautions had been taken the injury would still have occurred. In addition it might be able to show that the nurse was contributorily negligent. Some employers have argued that being injured by aggressive mentally disturbed patients is an occupational hazard for the nurse working with the mentally ill or handicapped and that there is a voluntary assumption of the risk of injury by the staff concerned (see Chapter 6). However, it is not thought that this would provide a successful defence for an employer who was clearly at fault in respect of reasonable precautions in protecting the nurse from harm.

Suing the patient

Could the nurse sue the patient if she has been injured by an assault? Yes, the nurse would have a right of action against anyone who assaults her but there are difficulties where the defendant is mentally disordered. The Magistrates Courts have thrown out such cases as being inappropriate. If the defendant is prosecuted, then the magistrate or judge can make an order for compensation to be paid by the defendant to the injured person. If the nurse decides to bring civil proceedings for trespass to the person, the defendant may not have the resources to pay any compensation awarded by the civil courts. Alternatively (and probably preferably), the nurse could seek compensation from the Criminal Injuries Compensation Authority (see below).

Violence by a visitor or employee

SITUATION 12.8 INJURIES IN THE ACCIDENT AND EMERGENCY DEPARTMENT

A patient with lacerations to the face and severe bruising is brought into the department by two friends. All three have been drinking heavily. Two nurses take the injured man into the treatment room and ask the others to stay in the waiting room or leave the hospital. They insist on following the patient and in the ensuing fracas a nurse is injured. The various possible remedies are set out in Fig. 12.15.

1. Obtain compensation from the criminal courts following a successful prosecution of the assailant.
2. Sue the aggressor personally for trespass to the person (there is little point if they have no assets or income to pay the damages awarded).
3. Sue the employer if she can establish that there has been a breach of the employer's duty of care to her.
4. Claim compensation from the Criminal Injuries Compensation Authority (see Fig. 12.16).
5. She could receive, if eligible, statutory sick pay, Whitley Council sickness pay and DSS benefits.

Figure 12.15 Remedies following violence.

Self-defence

Can the nurse defend herself if attacked by a patient, visitor, trespasser or employee?

Every citizen has the right of self-defence. In the above example, therefore, the nurse could use reasonable means to defend herself against an aggressor. What is meant by reasonable?

SITUATION 12.9 REASONABLE MEANS

A nurse is faced by a patient who is approaching her with a knife. He is a 6 feet tall, stockily built man of 35 years. There are no other staff or competent patients in the room and there is no call system available. As he comes forward she picks up a chair and hits him over the head with it. He is severely concussed and requires stitches. Could she successfully defend an action for assault brought by the patient? Has she acted reasonably in defending herself?

Reasonableness means, firstly, that the force used should be no more than is necessary to accomplish the object for which it is allowed (so retaliation, revenge and punishment are not permitted) and, secondly, the reaction must be in proportion to the harm which is threatened. Thus all the circumstances must be taken into account: the contrast between the strength, size, expertise of the assailant and the defendant, and the type of harm with which the person is being threatened. Obviously, the greater the severity of the threatened danger, the more reasonable it is to take tougher measures. In assessing the reasonableness of the defence, account is taken of the fact that the defendant may only have a brief period to make up his mind what to do. Turning back to the above situation, if the nurse in question is tiny with no training in self-defence, the odds do seem to be stacked against her, and may justify her use of the chair. All the circumstances must be taken into account, including the possibility of her retreating from the assault.

Criminal Injuries Compensation Authority

The Criminal Injuries Compensation Authority was given a statutory basis by the Criminal Justice Act 1988 but the provisions were not implemented. A tariff scheme was introduced in April 1994. The elements required to obtain compensation from the Authority are shown in Fig. 12.16.

1. Scheme came into force on 1 April 1994.
2. Applies to all applications on or after that date irrespective of when the incident took place.
3. The applicant must have been:
   (a) a victim of a crime of violence or injured in some way covered by the scheme;
   (b) physically and/or mentally injured as a result;
   (c) injured seriously enough to qualify for at least the minimum award.
4. The tariff scheme is from £1,000 (Bond 1), e.g. multiple minor injuries/fractured tooth, to £250,000 (Bond 25), e.g. quadriplegic/permanent serious brain damage.
5. The applicant must have reported the matter to the police.
6. The applicant must apply within one year to the CICA.

Figure 12.16 Compensation from the Criminal Injuries Compensation Authority.

SITUATION 12.10 INJURY FOLLOWING AN EPILEPTIC FIT_____

A nurse working with the mentally handicapped is preparing a resident for bed, when he suddenly has an epileptic fit. The nurse is pushed off balance and the resident falls on her. She breaks her collar bone and is off work for several weeks. She claims criminal injury compensation from the Authority but her claim is turned down since to be a victim of an individual having an epileptic fit is not the same as being a victim of a crime of violence.

Exactly the same problem confronted those train drivers who suffered considerable nervous shock after persons had committed suicide on the railway line before their trains. The decision not to award them compensation was upheld by the courts (*R. v. CICB ex parte Warner* 1986 2 All ER 478). However, the Authority now recognises such claims.

The fact that the aggressor is a mentally disturbed patient against whom a prosecution may not succeed on the grounds of insanity will be left out of account in deciding whether compensation should be paid.

The Authority has considerable discretion. At present the minimum level of payment excludes many potential claimants from receiving compensation under the scheme. Many of the injuries suffered by an NHS Trust's employees following violence would be excluded on the grounds that they are below the minimum level of payment.

The future of the Criminal Injuries Board (compensating victims of violent crime)

A white paper published in December 1993 put forward proposals to replace the discretionary scheme operated by the CIB by establishing a tariff system of fixed awards for different kinds of injuries at levels likely to be less than most currently paid out. The proposals have been attacked (see letter to *The Times*, 17 December 1993, by a former member of the Board, Martin Thomas QC) and may be considerably modified before legislation is passed. However, they were implemented in April 1994.

Opponents lost an application to the court to declare the new non-statutory scheme illegal as being contrary to the provision in the Criminal Justice Act 1988. The Court of Appeal overruled that decision on 9 November 1994 (see *R. v. Secretary of State for the Home Department, ex parte Fire Brigades Union and others*, TLR 10 November 1994). It held that the Secretary of State had acted illegally in ignoring the provisions of the Criminal Justice Act 1988 which placed the existing criminal injuries scheme on a statutory basis, at a date to be appointed by the Secretary of State, by setting up a radically different scheme on a tariff basis instead. The tariff scheme, which has been in force since 1 April 1994, will now be set aside and the previous scheme reinstated, unless an appeal by the Secretary of State to the House of Lords succeeds.

Questions and exercises

1 Who is the occupier of premises owned by the NHS Trust and used by general practitioners?

2 All the circumstances must be taken into account in deciding whether the occupier is in breach of his common duty of care. What is meant by this? Explain the statement in relation to an accident caused to an infant patient who slipped on a pool of water on the floor in the ward.

3 A nurse is injured while lifting a patient because the nurse assisting her suddenly let go and the injured nurse was left supporting the whole weight. What remedies, if any, does the injured nurse have and how could she claim compensation?

4 If a nurse is injured as the result of defective equipment, in what ways could she obtain compensation?

5 Ask to see (if you have not already received one) a copy of your NHS Trust's or employer's health and safety policy. How is this policy reflected in your working environment?

6 The Health and Safety at Work Act 1974 is enforced through the criminal courts. The employer's duty to care for the safety of his employee exists at common law. What is meant by these two statements and what is the difference in the enforcement provisions of each?

7 What records would it be advisable to keep as a result of the provisions of Part 1 of the Consumer Protection Act 1987?

Part II Specialist areas

13   Paediatric nursing

In addition to the basic principles of law discussed in the first part of this book, paediatric nurses, because they care for minors (i.e. persons under 18 years), must also be aware of several special provisions which apply. (In some hospitals minors over 16 years are cared for in adult wards.) These are shown in Fig. 13.1 and are the subject of this chapter. The Children Act 1989 has provided a framework for the provision of services for children in need and sets out the basic principles to be followed in determining the welfare of the child.

Consent to treatment

At age 18 and over, adults, if mentally competent, are able to make all decisions in relation to their medical care. They can also consent to being participants in research programmes and this applies whether the research is seen as being in their therapeutic interests or not. Prior to 18 years, several different provisions apply.

The 16- and 17-year-old

Treatment

Under Section 8 of the Family Law Reform Act 1969 the minor of 16 or 17 can give a valid consent to treatment. The provisions of this section are set out in Fig. 13.2.

1. Consent to treatment
   (a) 16- and 17-year-old
       (i) treatment
       (ii) consent to research
       (iii) refusal
       (iv) emergencies
       (v) parallel consent.
   (b) Children under 16
       (i) parental rights
       (ii) children's rights
       (iii) overruling the parent
       (iv) transplants
       (v) withholding consent by parents
       (vi) childhood euthanasia.
2. Non-accidental injury.
3. Parental care and the nurse.
4. Disciplining a child.
5. Education of children in hospitals.

Figure 13.1 Issues covered in Chapter 13.

1. the consent of a minor who has attained the age of 16 years to any surgical, medical, or dental treatment, which in the absence of consent would constitute a trespass to his person will be as effective as it would be if he were of full age; and where a minor has by virtue of this section given an effective consent to any treatment, it shall not be necessary to obtain any consent for it from his parent or guardian.

Treatment is defined very widely, Section 8(2). In this section, 'surgical, medical, or dental treatment' includes any procedure undertaken for the purposes of diagnosis and this section applies to any procedure (including in particular the administration of an anaesthetic) which is ancillary to any treatment as it applies to that treatment.

Figure 13.2 Family Law Reform Act 1969 Section 8.

These two sub-sections, set out in Fig. 13.2, cover most eventualities as far as consent to treatment is concerned for the 16- and 17-year-old.

Consent to research

It should be noted, however, that the above does not cover consent to take part in research unless it can genuinely be considered to be part of the treatment. Thus a 16-year-old suffering from a disorder where there is no clearly proven successful method of treatment might well be asked to consent to a new untried form of treatment as part of a research project. If this is clearly in the patient's therapeutic interests and if there are no undue risks, then such a proposal would be covered by the words of the section. If, however, there was at hand a proven successful method of treatment but the minor was approached to see if he would agree to take part in a research programme where there were considerable risks which may or may not be of benefit to him, it is likely that such a treatment would not be covered by the Act.

Refusal to have treatment

A 16-year-old girl under local authority care suffered from anorexia nervosa. She refused to move to a specialist hospital. The Court of Appeal held that the Family Law Reform Act 1969 Section 8 did not prevent consent being given by parents or the court (*In re W. (a minor) (medical treatment)* 1992 4 All ER 627).

Emergencies

The Act does not prevent any emergency action being taken to save the life of a minor who is unconscious and unable to give consent. Thus a 16-year-old who is wheeled into the accident and emergency department in an unconscious state can be given emergency treatment in the same way that a patient of any age could be treated. This is because such treatment would not constitute a trespass to the person. The professional providing it is protected against any such allegation by the defence of acting in an emergency out of necessity to save life.

Parallel consent

Section 8 of the Family Law Reform Act can also be interpreted as giving power to parents to give a valid consent on behalf of their child of 16 or 17. This is because a third subsection of this section states:

Section 8 (3): Nothing in this section shall be construed as making ineffective any consent which would have been effective if the section had not been enacted.

One interpretation of this is that the fact that the minor of 16 or 17 can now give a valid consent to treatment does not mean that consent by the parents on behalf of the minor ceases to be effective. Prior to the 1969 Act a parent could give a valid consent on behalf of his child up to the age of 18 and this right is not affected by the Act. Thus there could exist a parallel right to consent: both the parents and the minor of 16 or 17 could give consent. This is unlikely to cause difficulties except in those rare occasions where there is a dispute between the minor and the parent. Whose views does the doctor or nurse take?

SITUATION 13.1 CLASH BETWEEN PARENT AND MINOR

A girl of 17 who had recently become a Jehovah's Witness was involved in a car crash. She was just conscious as she was wheeled into the accident and emergency department and made it clear that she did not wish to be given a blood transfusion. Her parents were notified of the crash and told of her statement. However, not sharing her religious views, they said they would give their consent if blood was necessary to save her life. The consultant wishes to know the legal situation.

The fact that Section 8 (3) preserves the right of the parent to give consent means that, legally, the doctor could rely on that consent as a defence against any action for trespass to the person subsequently brought by the girl. Prior to the Section being passed, parents had the right to give consent and this right continues. Another interpretation of this section is that the new statutory powers do not remove the mature minor's ability in law to give a valid consent to treatment. This is considered below. Both interpretations could exist side by side.

What, however, if the doctor took notice of the girl's refusal, did not give blood and as a consequence the girl died? Could the parents then sue the doctor for negligence? The answer is that probably such a case would be unsuccessful but much would depend on the circumstances – for example the mental competence of the daughter in refusing blood; whether she understood the full implications; her general and specific capacity to give a valid consent.

Where there is a clash the doctor has the choice of following the wishes of the minor or the parents: if the position were reversed and the parents were Jehovah's Witnesses and the daughter consented to having blood, there would be no difficulties; he could rely on her consent under Section 8 (1) and if the girl were unconscious he could act in an emergency to save her life, whatever the views of the parents. However, where it is the minor of 16 or 17 who is withholding consent and the parents wish to give it, many would argue that it is the doctor's duty to save life and he should rely on the parents' consent under Section 8 (3). The point was considered by the courts in *Re W. (a minor) (medical treatment)* 1992 4 All ER 627 where the court overruled the minor's refusal.

Children under 16 years

The Children Act 1989 requires the court to have regard to 'the ascertainable wishes and feelings of the child concerned considered in the light of their age and understanding' (Section 1 (3)(a)) in deciding whether to make specific orders under the Act. Certain sections require, if the child has sufficient understanding, the child's consent to be given, before the child can be asked to submit to a medical or physical examination.

Parental rights

The parents or guardian of a child under 18 have the right to give consent to treatment for their child.

The Children Act 1989 Section 3(5) provides that a person who (a) does not have parental responsibility for a particular child, but (b) has care of the child, may (subject to the provision of this Act) do what is reasonable in all the circumstances of the case for the purpose of safeguarding or promoting the child's welfare. It is suggested that this would include giving consent to necessary emergency treatment in the absence of the parents. In addition, professional staff would have a duty of care to take action to save life in such circumstances. *In re R.* (1991 4 All ER 177) the court gave permission for psychiatric medication to be given to a girl aged 16 against her will.

Children's rights: can children give consent themselves?

If the minor is mature and capable of understanding the situation and it is not possible to contact the parents, the child can give a valid consent and this principle is emphasised in the Children Act 1989. This issue was considered in the Gillick case on the narrow issue of advice and treatment for family planning. However, the principles established by the House of Lords cover a much wider area.

CASE 13.1 THE GILLICK CASE

Mrs Gillick questioned the lawfulness of a DHSS circular HN (80) 46 which was a revised version of part of a comprehensive *Memorandum of Guidance* on family planning services issued to health authorities in May 1974 under cover of circular HSC(IS)32. The circular stated that in certain circumstances a doctor could lawfully prescribe contraception for a girl under 16 without the consent of the parents. Mrs Gillick wrote to the acting administrator formally forbidding any medical staff employed by the Norfolk AHA to give 'any contraceptive or abortion advice or treatment whatever to my ... daughters whilst they are under 16 years without my consent'. The administrator replied that the treatment prescribed by a doctor is a matter for the doctor's clinical judgement, taking into account all the factors of the case. Mrs Gillick, who had five daughters, then brought an action against the AHA and the DHSS seeking a declaration that the notice gave advice which was unlawful and wrong and which did or might adversely affect the welfare of her children, her right as a parent and her ability properly to discharge her duties as a parent. She sought a declaration that no doctor or other professional person employed by the Health Authority might give any contraceptive or abortion advice or treatment to any of her children below the age of 16 without her prior knowledge and consent (*Gillick v. West Norfolk and Wisbech AHA and the DHSS* 1985 3 All ER 402).

She failed before the High Court judge, succeeded in her appeal before the Court of Appeal and the DHSS and Health Authority, and appealed to the House of Lords. The Lords decided by a majority of three to two against Mrs Gillick. The majority held that in exceptional circumstances a doctor could provide contraceptive advice and treatment to a girl under 16 without the parents' consent. The circular was therefore upheld.

Lord Fraser stated the exceptional circumstances which are set out in Fig. 13.13.

Many questions still remain uncertain. Can it be assumed that a mature minor under 16 can give a valid consent to any form of treatment and research or only when his life is in danger? What efforts must be made to obtain the parents' consent? For what can a child give consent: a few stitches; an anaesthetic; an abortion?

What is the position where the minor is a mother? If she has the mental capacity, does she have the legal capability of giving consent for her child to be treated or is it necessary to obtain the consent of her own parents, i.e. the baby's grandparents? As an example many health visitors treating a minor's child protect themselves by obtaining both the consent of the underaged mother and also of a grandparent. From the cautious words of the majority judges sitting on the Gillick case in the House of Lords it would

1. The girl would, although under 16, understand the doctor's advice.
2. He could not persuade her to inform her parents or allow him to inform the parents that she was seeking contraceptive advice.
3. She was very likely to have sexual intercourse with or without contraceptive treatment.
4. Unless she received contraceptive advice or treatment her physical or mental health or both were likely to suffer.
5. Her best interests required him to give her contraceptive advice, treatment or both without parental consent.

Figure 13.3 Exceptional circumstances set out in the Gillick case.

appear that, provided the underaged mother had the requisite mental capacity to consent to treatment on the child's behalf, this would be a valid consent.

Overruling the parent

While parents have the power in law to give consent to the treatment of the child, this is not an absolute power. If their consent or their refusal to give consent is considered to be against the interests of the child then the court can intervene.

CASE 13.2 STERILISATION OF A MENTALLY HANDICAPPED GIRL

A girl of 11 years suffered from Sotos syndrome, the symptoms of which included accelerated growth during infancy, epilepsy, general clumsiness, an unusual facial appearance and behaviour problems including emotional instability, certain aggressive tendencies and some impairment of mental function. The mother, taking the advice of the consultant paediatrician that her daughter would remain substantially handicapped and that she would always be unable to care for herself or look after any children, discussed with the obstetrician the possibility of her daughter being sterilised. An operation was arranged. However, before it was performed the educational psychologist applied for the girl to be made a ward of court. Mrs Justice Heilbron who heard the case was not convinced that the operation was in the best interests of the girl and so ordered that the operation should not proceed (*In re D. (a minor) (wardship, sterilisation)* 1976 1 All ER 327).

It can be seen from this case how fortuitous it was that the case ever came before the courts. Had it not been for the strongly held views of the educational psychologist, the operation could well have gone ahead. This should not be so in the future. In a recent House of Lords case, *In re B. (a minor) (wardship, sterilisation)* 1987 2 All ER 206, where the judges agreed to a sterilisation proceeding upon 'Jeanette', they made it clear that, in future, every such case of a sterilisation upon a mentally handicapped minor should receive the approval of the court before it proceeded. In that case they did not make the distinction between therapeutic and non-therapeutic sterilisation which Mrs Justice Heilbron had made *In re D*. In theory, every case of sterilisation on a minor should come before the courts, even though the operation is performed because of the presence of a malignancy. This is further discussed in Chapter 15.

The important point for paediatric nurses is that if they feel that a particular procedure or treatment agreed between the parents and the medical staff is not in the interests of the child, then the nurse should raise it with her senior management who could if necessary arrange for the matter to be brought before the courts.

Transplants and the interests of the child

SITUATION 13.2 SISTERLY TRANSPLANTS

Mary, aged 7 years, had an incurable blood disease and was found to be compatible only with her younger sister Janet who was 4 years old. It was therefore agreed by the parents that Janet would provide a bone marrow transplant for Mary. Staff Nurse Bryant was concerned by the legalities of the proposed transplant.

The parents have the right to consent to any treatment which is in the interests of the child. However, in this case there is a clash between the interests of Mary and the interests of Janet. Any operation, no matter how small, involves some risk to the patient and Janet would be put at risk for the benefit of Mary. In the case of a bone marrow transplant it could be argued that the risk is so small and the psychological benefit for Janet when she becomes older so immense that it would be inhuman not to allow Janet to be a donor. If she is asked, she would probably agree herself, though her capacity to understand would be very limited. It would probably be lawful for the transplant to proceed, though there are no statutory or common law guidelines on the question in this country. However, as the risks to the donor increase, so do the problems. Imagine that in the last example Mary requires a kidney and tests show that Janet is an ideal match: do the parents have the power to give consent on Janet's behalf to such a donation? Again, there is no legal precedent but it could be argued that there is no way in which such an operation can be considered to be in Janet's interests.

Would it make any difference if Janet were mentally handicapped and in an institution? The answer is that it should make no difference and the sole question for the courts is what is in the interests of the donor where the donor lacks the mental capacity or capability in law to give consent in his own right. This situation arose in the American case of *Hart* v. *Brown* where the donor and recipient were identical twin girls. The court approved the parental request to transfer a kidney from one to the other. One of the main justifications was that, medically, such a graft was more likely to be successful, and another justification was that if they refused to allow the donation the donor might in later life feel guilty at not being allowed to be a donor (*Hart* v. *Brown* 289 A 2d 386 Conn. 1972). In another American case (*Strunk* v. *Strunk* 445 SW 2d 145 (Ky App. 1969)), a kidney transplant was authorised to proceed from an institutionalised adult with the mental capacity of a 6-year-old to his brother who was terminally ill with kidney trouble.

The court accepted the medical evidence that there was a strong emotional bond between the brothers and the mentally incompetent would suffer a severe traumatic experience if the brother died.

There are no comparable cases in the English courts and it is probable that they would take as their guiding line what was in the interests of the donor child, considering psychological as well as physical factors in reaching their decision, as they did in Jeanette's case. It can be a criminal offence for parents to fail to take appropriate action for the care of their children.

It was reported in *The Times* (29 October 1993) that a couple who refused to allow their diabetic daughter to receive modern medicine because of their religious beliefs were convicted of manslaughter.

In 1993 the court held that a blood transfusion should be given to a premature baby girl who suffered from respiratory distress syndrome and whose parents were Jehovah's Witnesses. The order authorising medical treatment was to be made under the court's inherent jurisdiction rather than pursuant to the Children Act 1989 (*In re O. (a minor) (medical treatment)* 1993 4 Med LR 272).

Withholding consent by parents

Where the parents refuse to consent to treatment which the doctors determine is in the interests of the child, then there is a well-tried procedure for taking the appropriate action. No child should die because the parents have unreasonably refused their consent to a necessary treatment.

SITUATION 13.3 BLOOD TRANSFUSION

Eric, aged 3 years, is admitted with an operable tumour. The neurologist reassures the parents and says that Eric can be saved. The parents say that on religious grounds they could not agree to Eric having a blood transfusion. Mr Sharpe, the neurosurgeon, replies that he would not be prepared to carry out such an operation with such a restriction, as it is highly likely that blood would be required in the operating theatre. The parents therefore refuse their consent to the operation. The neurosurgeon cannot let the child die so he has two options. He can either proceed and justify his action on the basis that he is acting in the best interests of the child in an emergency; or he can arrange through the administration for an application to be made to the court for Eric to be made a ward of court, and for the operation to be ordered to proceed.

The official guidelines recommend that the former option be followed but it seems less stressful to doctors if they know that they are acting under the umbrella of the courts in the absence of parental consent.

CASE 13.3 DOWN'S SYNDROME

A child who was born suffering from Down's syndrome and an intestinal blockage, required an operation to relieve the obstruction if she was to live for more than a few days. If the operation were performed, the child might die within a few months but it was probable that her life expectancy would be 20–30 years. Her parents, having decided that it would be kinder to allow her to die rather than live as a physically and mentally handicapped person, refused consent to the operation. The local authority made the child a ward of court and, when a surgeon decided that the wishes of the parents should be respected, they sought an order authorising the operation to be performed by other named surgeons. The judge in the High Court decided that the wishes of the parents should be respected and refused to make the order. The local authority took the case to the Court of Appeal which said that the operation should proceed (*In re B. (a minor)* 1981 1 WLR 1421).

The court decided that the question before it, was whether it was in the best interests of the child that she should have the operation and not whether the parents' wishes should be respected. Since the effect of the operation might be that the child would have the normal life span of a person with Down's syndrome, and since it had not been demonstrated that the life of such a person was of such a nature that the child should be condemned to die, the court would make an order that the operation be performed.

This case and that where the sterilisation operation was refused by the court illustrates that, whether it is a question of the parents giving or withholding their consent, the court will review the decision and decide whether the treatment should be given in the light of what is in the best interests of the child. It is open to any interested party to ask the court to determine this question when he is not happy at what is proposed or not proposed.

Parents have a legal duty to care for their children. Where they fail to obtain medical treatment they could be guilty of a criminal offence. Recently a father was imprisoned for failing to give his diabetic daughter insulin (see page 212).

Childhood euthanasia

The Down's syndrome case above raises the issue of whether it is permissible in law to allow a severely handicapped child to die or even assist him to die. In what circumstances does the doctor cease to have a duty to care for the child? Certainly, as the case of *In re B.* above shows, the views of the parents are not the deciding factor. The point was raised in the case of Dr Arthur who was prosecuted for murder (later changed to attempted murder) since he prescribed, with the consent of the parents, the substance DF 118 for a Down's syndrome baby who also suffered from severe abdominal abnormalities. He was acquitted by a jury.

The law does not recognise any form of euthanasia but in practice it is left to the discretion of the medical staff to determine the extent of heroic medicine which is justified for severely handicapped babies. This discretion is reviewable in the criminal courts. It is not an easy situation for medical staff, and certain centres have attempted to devise guidelines for when treatment is or is not appropriate. This issue is discussed further in Chapter 14 in the section on special care baby units.

Non-accidental injury

The paediatric nurse needs to be aware of the possibility that injuries or illness in a child may have been caused by another person. This applies not just to bruising or lacerations but also to undernourishment and other ailments including psychological damage. The possibility of sexual abuse must also be borne in mind if the relevant symptoms are present. The parents have a legal duty to provide care for their dependent children under Section 1 (1) of the Children and Young Persons Act 1933.

In this situation the nurse is confronted by the following problems. What action should she take if she suspects a child of being the object of abuse of any kind? What are the potential consequences for her if she is mistaken? What powers does she have to prevent a parent removing a child from the ward when the child has been placed on the Non-Accidental Injury Register? What would her position be in relation to a court hearing? Does she have to make a statement to the police?

> ### SITUATION 13.4 COT DEATH OR ABUSE?
>
> Jane, a girl of six months, was admitted to the paediatric ward with a suspected chest infection. She was immediately placed on antibiotics and sputum samples taken. While the nurse was changing her she noticed some bruising to the upper legs and a possible burn mark on her back. The nurse pointed these marks out to the senior house officer who suggested that the registrar should be called in as it was possible that these marks were the result of abuse.

A procedure for dealing with suspected child abuse should be available on every ward. If child abuse is suspected, the nurse should be particularly vigilant in not leaving the child unattended with the parents. In addition, it is quite likely that she could be called upon to give evidence to the court as to the nature of the relationship and interaction between the parents and the child in hospital and also as to the physical and mental

---

A Part IV   Care and supervision order, Sections 31–42
B Part V   Protection of children, Sections 43–52
C Part XII   Miscellaneous and general, Section 100 Restriction of wardship; jurisdiction of High Court still exists in emergency situations

Section 43   Child assessment order
Section 44   Orders for emergency protection of children
Section 45   Duration of emergency protection orders
Section 46   Removal and accommodation of children by police in cases of emergency
Section 47   Local authority's duty to investigate
Section 48   Powers to assist in discovery of children who may be in need of emergency protection
Section 49   Abduction of children in care
Section 50   Recovery of abducted children
Section 51   Refuges for children at risk
Section 52   Risk and regulation relating to emergency protection order

Figure 13.4 Children Act 1989: protection of children.

state of the child on admission. It is essential, therefore, that her record-keeping should be detailed and clear to enable her to answer questions at some later time.

The social service department of the local authority could apply for a child assessment order or an order for the emergency protection of the child under Part V of the Children Act 1989 to care for the child initially pending the outcome of the full proceedings for the care of the child.

The orders which can be made in respect of a child suspected of being abused are contained in the Children Act 1989, set out in Fig. 13.4.

Other issues which arise in relation to non-accidental injury include disclosure of confidential information (this is covered in Chapter 8) and giving evidence before the court (covered in Chapter 9).

Parental care and the nurse

SITUATION 13.5 MUM KNOWS BEST_____

The paediatric ward at Roger Park Hospital introduced a scheme for mothers and other relatives to undertake some of the tasks in caring for the children. This had many advantages: on the one hand, it put the child at ease since the person most familiar to him was taking care of him as usual, albeit in a strange place; at the same time there were savings in staff time. Originally, the scheme covered only the day-to-day routine care of dressing, feeding, bathing and amusing the child. Subsequently, however, it was extended to nursing and extended-role tasks including the care of nasal-gastric feeding and intravenous medication. The reason for this extension was that several of the mothers of long-term chronically ill children undertook all these tasks in the community. The nurse or doctor had the task of ensuring that the mother had the appropriate training and the necessary equipment. Mrs Tait agreed to give her 4-year-old child, Robin, who had a chronic lung condition, the appropriate drugs intravenously every six hours. She had undertaken several such treatments on her own before and was familiar with the routine and procedure. On the ward she was given the keys to help herself to the necessary drugs. This was contrary to the accepted practice but was permitted because it was felt that she could be trusted. She gave Robin the 8.00 a.m. treatment without problems. She had to leave the hospital in the afternoon but told another parent that she would be back for the afternoon treatment. Unfortunately, she did not return until 3.30 p.m. because of an unexpected traffic holdup. Robin was with some other children watching Play School. She immediately went to the staff nurse to get the keys to draw up the drugs for the next treatment. She took the boxes from the cupboard and started to make up the syringes. She then took Robin into the single room to give him his treatment. As she was giving the medication Robin became very ill and she called for help. It was then discovered that the afternoon dose had already been given to Robin and although this had been written up into his notes, the nurse who did so was at tea when Mrs Tait returned and she herself did not check Robin's notes as it was never her practice to do so. Robin suffered severe renal failure as a result of an overdose of an antibiotic. Is the accident entirely the mother's fault or does the nurse carry some responsibility?

What is the situation where responsibilities like this are divided between several people? In legal terms it is probably true to say that the care of the child in hospital is primarily the responsibility of the nurse under the clinical supervision of the medical staff. In a sense, the nurse is delegating to the mother those duties which she is capable of performing and probably performs on her own at home. The nurse should only delegate those tasks that she feels the mother is competent to perform and in addition she should ensure that the mother (or, of course, any other relative, friend or volunteer) has the correct amount of training and supervision to undertake the task safely. The nurse would be responsible in negligence if she delegated an unsuitable task to the mother or failed to provide her with the appropriate instructions or gave her inadequate supervision. If, however, the nurse has satisfied all those requirements and something still goes wrong because the mother makes a silly mistake, then it would be the mother's responsibility for any harm caused to the child as a result of the mistake. In the above situation there is clearly a failure in communication between nurse and mother. It would have been preferable to set up a procedure whereby the mother was told to look at the drugs chart, to fill it in when she gave the drugs to the child and also to check that the drugs had not already been given. She should also be supervised in her administration of the drugs. Clearly, the nurse would be at fault in failing to set up this procedure and the supervision, and the mother would bear some responsibility for failing to check that they had been given, though in mitigation it could be said that the person responsible for the ward at the time she returned should have known the child had already had his medication and informed the mother accordingly. The problems relating to supervision and instructing others are dealt with more fully in Chapter 5.

Disciplining a child

SITUATION 13.6 THE NURSE *IN LOCO PARENTIS*_____

Adam was a bright 7-year-old who appeared totally undaunted by his stay in hospital for a hernia operation. Unfortunately, his mother could spend very little time with him as she had two younger children and her husband was overseas. Once Adam had recovered from the immediate effects of his operation he was uncontrollable. He wandered around the wards into the single-bed wards, ignoring all the nurses' instructions and delighting in disobeying them. In one of the single rooms a child was being barrier nursed with suspected meningitis. Staff Nurse James saw Adam about to enter this room and in her anxiety and her impatience with him she hit him hard on the leg. Adam screamed and other nurses came running. Staff Nurse James was disciplined by the nursing officer and Adam's mother said that she was going to make a formal complaint against the nurse and the hospital. Staff Nurse James argued that in the circumstances there was little else she could have done to prevent Adam entering that room, and in any case she had the powers of a parent to discipline a child who needed to be controlled.

It is true that parents do have in law the right to control and discipline their child by any reasonable means and that at present this includes using corporal punishment. School teachers have argued that they have the same powers by virtue of their acting *in loco parentis*. This has been challenged by a parent in Scotland before the European Court of Human Rights and has led to a campaign to declare any corporal punishment in school illegal. Provision has been made for corporal punishment to be illegal in state schools in the Education No. 2 Act 1986 Section 47. Although in the above example Staff Nurse James argued that she had this right, its basis in law is very uncertain and it would seem that other methods of control are preferable. There were other ways of stopping him entering the room other than hitting him and in the circumstances it seems more likely that she lost her temper and was unreasonable.

The issue becomes particularly important in the care of the mentally handicapped where there is only a thin line between what could be termed justifiable corporal punishment and abuse of the resident. Good nursing practice would advocate no use of physical force against a patient and it would seem preferable to follow this rather than rely on very uncertain legal justification. The implications of this for staffing levels are clear and the degree of unruliness in children and the extent of parental help could affect the level of staffing required.

Education of children in hospital

The special education of children in hospitals was provided for in the National Health Service Act 1946. Section 62 empowered regional hospital boards and teaching hospitals to arrange with a local education authority or voluntary body to use as a special school any premises forming part of the hospital. By 1955 there were 120 hospital special schools providing teaching for 8,476 pupils in addition to 1,425 children receiving individual or group tuition. In 1971, responsibility for the education of children in hospitals for the mentally handicapped was transferred to the education service (1975 Scotland). Home tuition is an important part of the education service for ill or handicapped children and there are signs that demand is growing. The nurse should be aware that every child has a right to education, even when in hospital, and that, provided his medical condition permits it, every effort should be made to ensure that the child is receiving schooling, preferably off the ward area. The nurse has a positive role to play in encouraging the child to take part.

Questions and exercises

1 What is the difference between a minor of 15 and one of 16 as far as consent to treatment is concerned?

2 What is the effect of the Family Law Reform Act 1969 Section 8?
3 Obtain a copy of your NHS Trust's procedure on the care of suspected non-accidental injury cases and familiarise yourself with it.
4 The occupier's duty of care for the safety of the visitor should take into account the possibility that children require greater care (see Chapter 12, Fig. 12.5). What is meant by this and how does it affect the work of the paediatric nurse?
5 Consider the extent that your department allows parents to take part in the care of children in hospital. What additional responsibilities does this place on the nurse?
6 If you were faced with a very disobedient child, how would you control him?

14   Midwifery

The midwife has always been in a special position compared with the general nurse in relation to her powers and duties. She has long been recognised as an independent practitioner with considerable powers in the prescribing and administration of certain drugs not possessed by the general nurse (see Chapter 28). This section considers the special position of the midwife in law, as well as the effects of some recent cases on midwifery practice.

The areas to be covered are set out in Fig. 14.1.

Midwives rules and code of practice

Under the Nurses, Midwives and Health Visitors Act 1979 the UKCC must make rules regulating the practice of midwives. Figure 14.2 indicates the purpose of these rules. The rules are set out under Statutory Instruments 1986 No. 786, 1990 No. 1624, 1993 No. 1901 and 1993 No. 2106, and can be seen in Appendix 5.

Rule 40 has been the subject of considerable debate and is set out in Fig. 14.3. It is at the heart of the debate of the respective roles and relationship of midwife and doctor.

In addition, the Central Council has produced a Midwife's Code of Practice. This is complementary to the practice rules but, unlike the practice rules, it does not have the force of law. The Code of Practice is to be found in Appendix 6. Of course, the midwives

1. Midwives Rules and Code of Practice.
2. Compulsion and consent
   (a) opposition to the midwife;
   (b) criminal offence;
   (c) compulsory powers of admission;
   (d) choice of treatment by mother;
   (e) consent to caesarian section.
3. Liability of mother for harm caused to baby
   (a) civil liability;
   (b) criminal liability.
4. Taking into care.
5. Midwifery practice and standard of care
   (a) midwife and doctor;
   (b) community midwife.
6. Congenital Disabilities Act
   (a) liability of midwife to unborn child;
   (b) professional standards;
   (c) child's action is derivative;
   (d) mother's liability under Act;
   (e) action for wrongful life.
7. Nurseries.
8. Special care baby units.
9. Registration of births and stillbirths.
10. Use of foetal tissue.
11. AIDS and the midwife.

Figure 14.1 Issues covered in Chapter 14.

(a) determine the circumstances in which and the procedure by means of which midwives may be suspended from practice;
(b) require midwives to give notice of their intention to practise to the local supervising authority in the area in which they intend to practise (in addition if the midwife practises in an emergency outside her normal authority she has to notify the new health authority within 48 hours); and
(c) require registered midwives to attend courses of instruction in accordance with the rules.

Figure 14.2 Aims of the Midwives Rules.

---

1. A practising midwife is responsible for providing midwifery care to a mother and baby during the antenatal, intranatal and postnatal periods. In any case where there is an emergency or where she detects in the health of a mother and baby a deviation from the norm a practising midwife shall call to her assistance a registered medical practitioner, and shall forthwith report the matter to the local supervising authority in a form in accordance with the requirements of the local supervising authority.
2. A practising midwife must not, except in an emergency, undertake any treatment which she has not been trained to give either before or after registration as a midwife and which is outside her sphere of practice.

Figure 14.3 Rule 40: responsibility and sphere of practice.

would also be expected to comply with the Code of Professional Conduct. It is not the intention to consider every one of these rules and codes in detail but, rather, to consider some of the more common problems concerning the midwife.

Compulsion and consent

Opposition to the midwife

SITUATION 14.1 HIPPIES

An encampment of hippies was established in the hills overlooking the town of Llanseid. They supported themselves by rearing hens and goats and depended upon social security benefits. For the most part they kept themselves to themselves and had little contact with the people from Llanseid. There were rumours that drug-taking was rife and that they grew their own plants for drugs. Sheila Armstrong, a community midwife, visited one of the hippies, Sharon Keene, who was six months pregnant. Sharon was aggressive and hostile. She made it clear to Sheila that she did not want to be confined in hospital but wanted her cohabitee, Jason, to deliver the baby. On one visit, Sheila found Sharon heavily under the influence of drugs and was anxious to arrange for admission to hospital to protect Sharon's life and that of the child. Jason made it clear that he would never allow Sharon to be taken away. Where does Sheila stand in relation to the law?

The actual facts of this situation may appear farfetched (though such problems can arise in rural areas), but in fact they are merely an extreme form of a problem frequently faced by midwives where an incalcitrant husband/cohabitee wishes to control the confinement and is unwilling for the wife/cohabitee to be admitted.

While a hippy commune may not be the experience of many midwives, unfortunately the refusal of a woman to attend ante-natal and post-natal clinics is not so rare. The woman might agree to attend just for the confinement. Often, the midwife might suspect that the woman's unwillingness is due to opposition from the husband or cohabitee. There is little that the midwife can do in this case other than continue to try to obtain the mother's confidence and trust.

The example also raises the much wider problem of where the midwife stands when the mother refuses to have a form of treatment which the midwife considers essential for the health and wellbeing of the mother and the baby. This wider issue will be considered later.

Criminal offence

One important strength that Sheila Armstrong has in the above situation is that Section 17 of the 1979 Act makes it a criminal offence for a person other than a registered midwife or a registered medical practitioner to attend a woman in childbirth except in an emergency. Thus if Jason delivered the baby himself he would be committing a crime. The only exception would be if there were an emergency and the baby arrived before they were aware of it. It is of course very difficult to prove that it was not an emergency and that there was no intention to call the midwife. Sheila would be able to warn the couple of the law and she would of course record this warning in her notes and also inform her supervisor of midwives. There have been some prosecutions under this section and its predecessor. For example, Rupert Baines from Bristol was found guilty of delivering a baby without assistance and Brian Radley from Wolverhampton was charged with attending a woman in childbirth otherwise than under the direction and personal supervision of a duly qualified practitioner and was fined £100 (August 1983). The difficulty confronting the midwife is in ensuring that she is aware of when the baby is imminent, since the aim is to protect the mother and child rather than take proceedings after the birth.

If she is obstructed by an aggressive partner during a home confinement the midwife would be able to call upon police powers to assist her.

Compulsory powers of admission

Could the midwife insist that a woman unwilling to be taken into hospital be admitted? There are no specific powers given her to take such action under the Act or the rules. However, in a life-or-death situation it could possibly be argued that the midwife would have the right to insist that a mother was admitted to save the life of herself or the foetus. Refer, however, to the case of *In re S*. (1992) on page 224 and the response of the Royal College of Obstetricians and Gynaecologists to this use of compulsion against a woman.

Choice of treatment by mother

SITUATION 14.2 CONSENT

Glenys Brown was expecting her first child. From the first moment the pregnancy was diagnosed, she was totally absorbed in her condition and the forthcoming event. She joined the local childbirth group and was very soon the local secretary. She attended psychoprophylactic and yoga classes and avidly read books, journals, leaflets, and all available information. She had clear ideas on how her own baby was to be born and while she would have preferred total immersion in water she accepted the fact that this would not be available in her local hospital. She was, however, adamant that she would not agree to an epidural, gas, an episiotomy or any other unnatural procedures. She was admitted to the delivery ward and after 12 hours of contractions the doctor set up a drip to speed the delivery as it was feared that the foetus was in danger. Glenys was eventually given an episiotomy despite her protests. She is now threatening to sue the midwife and doctor. Where do the midwife and doctor stand in law?

The basic principles relating to consent to treatment (set out in Chapter 7) apply to midwifery. There are no separate statutory laws covering the situation. However, while the general principle is that the patient has the right to refuse treatment, and any touching or treatment without her consent is a trespass to her person, in midwifery there is also a duty to the unborn child and this duty may clash with the desires of the mother. Thus, although Glenys had refused to have an episiotomy, it is quite possible that in a certain situation there could be damage or harm to the foetus if an episiotomy were not performed. The midwife could justify her actions on the grounds that she was acting in the interests of the unborn child. If the mother were to sue the midwife for assault it could be argued that, while it was technically an assault, it was justifiable. The court is unlikely to be sympathetic to the mother who might only obtain nominal damages, if any, in such an action.

However, to establish this defence the midwife would require very comprehensive records of the reasons for her actions and the situation at the time. The same principle would apply to any other contentious treatment, even a caesarian operation. In the above example, therefore, depending on the facts which are proved, it is possible that Glenys would lose her court action if the midwife could show that the action she took was essential to save the life of Glenys, or the child, or that it was taken to prevent serious harm.

This issue of consent and the respective liability of the midwife and mother for any harm to the child is becoming increasingly important. The midwives in particular are concerned at the possibility of the mother asking for and insisting upon a form of delivery of which they have had no experience. What happens if something goes wrong in such cases? For example, what if the baby inhales water when the mother has insisted upon an underwater confinement in which the midwives have had no training and experience? The midwife can refer to Midwives Rule 40 (2): she must not, except in an emergency, undertake any treatment which she has not been trained to give. This general rule embraces a principle which applies to all nurses.

Consent to caesarian section

The problem of consent to treatment often arises when it is necessary for the mother to have a caesarian section. If this possibility had not been considered at an earlier stage and the mother asked in advance to consent to a caesarian section in the unlikely possibility that this might become necessary, then it is quite possible that the mother's consent is being sought at a time when she is confused by drugs and the ordeal of the delivery. It is quite likely that she does not have the mental competence to know what she is giving consent to. Should this situation arise it is preferable for the professionals to treat her on the basis of the duty of care they owe her at common law rather than to rely on a form giving a dubious consent to treatment and signed at a time when the mother is incapable of giving a valid consent, i.e. they should accept that they are acting in an emergency to save the life of the mother and child. *In re T.* (1992, discussed on page 99) the Court of Appeal emphasised that professionals had a duty to check on the validity of a patient's refusal to have treatment.

What if the mother has made it clear that she refuses to give consent to a caesarian and there is no doubt about her capacity to make that decision? These were the facts *In re S. (an adult) (refusal of medical treatment)* 1992 4 All ER 671). The court made a declaration that the operation could proceed to save the life of the mother and unborn child. Even though there was no doubt about the mother's competence to refuse treatment, the interest of the unborn child appears to have been given priority. This case would appear to place pregnant women in a different legal category from other adults in the right to refuse treatment. It is only a decision at first instance and a Court of Appeal or preferably a House of Lords decision is required to resolve the issue of the rights of pregnant women to refuse treatment. (For the law on consent see Chapter 7.)

The Ethics Committee of the Royal College of Obstetricians and Gynaecologists has issued a paper on 'A Consideration of the Law and Ethics in Relation to Court Authorised Obstetric Intervention' (1994). Its conclusions are that 'It is inappropriate, and unlikely to be helpful or necessary to invoke judicial intervention to overrule an informed and competent woman's refusal of a proposed medical treatment, even though her refusal might place her life and that of her fetus at risk.' If this advice is accepted, the circumstances of *In re S.* are unlikely to be repeated.

The liability of the mother for harm caused to the baby

Civil liability

In the situation described above, if Glenys had refused to have the episiotomy, as a consequence of which the midwife did not carry this out and the baby was born brain damaged, could Glenys herself be liable to the child?

Legally the child's representative would have to argue that the mother owed a duty of care to the baby, that she was in breach of this duty by failing to take the advice of the midwife to have the episiotomy and as a consequence of her failure the child was born brain damaged. It is theoretically possible that such an action could arise at common law. There are no precedents and the implications are enormous. For example, it could be argued that a child who is underweight and suffers harm because the mother smoked or was on drugs or attempted to abort the foetus should be able to claim compensation because the mother has not cared adequately for the baby during the ante-natal period. Such an action is not maintainable under the Congenital Disabilities (Civil Liability) Act 1976, since under those provisions the mother can only be sued by the child's representative if she was driving a motor vehicle when she knew or ought reasonably to have known that she was pregnant and failed to take care for the safety of the unborn child. This Act would not explicitly prevent the action described above from being recognised but its existence makes it less likely that the judges at common law would recognise the rights of the child to sue a mother for harm caused to it during the pregnancy.

Criminal liability of the mother

The mother could be liable in the criminal law under the Infant Life Preservation Act 1929. This makes it a criminal offence for any person who, with intent to destroy the life of a child capable of being born alive, by any wilful act causes a child to die before it has an existence independent of its mother (Section 11). There is a defence if the act which caused the death of the child was done in good faith for the purposes only of preserving the life of the mother. There are also criminal provisions relating to attempting to procure an abortion by administering drugs or using an instrument or supplying the same under the Offences Against the Person Act 1861 Sections 58 and 59. For further discussion on this see Chapter 15. However, in the context we are considering here, i.e. where a pregnant woman is smoking or addicted to drugs or drink, it is not thought that she would have the necessary intent to be found guilty of a criminal act under these provisions. Similarly, a pregnant woman who refused to consent to an episiotomy in the circumstances outlined above would not be committing a criminal offence unless this refusal was made with the intention of causing the death of the child and unless this refusal to give consent could be defined as an act under the 1929 Act.

Taking the newly born into care

A recent phenomenon is the provision of an order whereby the child is taken into care as soon as it is born. This is usually because of the woman's conduct in relation to other children in the family. In a recent case an order was obtained where a woman was pregnant and where her two previous children had died in early infancy. The parents' appeal against the decision was halted when the child, the subject of the order, was stillborn.

CASE 14.1 PRE-BIRTH CONDUCT

At birth (12 March 1985) the child was suffering from symptoms caused by withdrawal from narcotics. The mother had been a registered drug addict since 1982, had continued to take drugs in excess of those prescribed during her pregnancy and had known that by taking drugs while pregnant she could be causing damage to the child. The child was kept in intensive care in hospital for several weeks immediately following the birth. A place of safety order was obtained on 23 April 1985, followed by successive interim orders.

The House of Lords, in a unanimous judgment, stated that the provisions of Section 1.2 (a) of the Children and Young Persons Act 1969 (which stated that if the court is satisfied that the child's 'proper development is being avoidably prevented or neglected or he is being ill-treated ... and also that he is in need of care and control then ... the court may if it thinks fit, make such an order') should be given a broad and liberal construction that gives full effect to their legislative purpose. They saw no reason why the courts should not look back to the time before the child had been born. However, in this case the mother was still a drug addict and there was thus a continuum between the pre-natal and post-natal period. The decision of the House of Lords against the mother cannot be used as a precedent for arguing that if the mother has failed to take care of herself and the foetus during pregnancy, this will constitute grounds for a care order irrespective of her post-natal care of the child. The law does not yet recognise the legal recognition of a child's right to receive, pre-natally, a responsible standard of care from its mother (*In re D. (a minor)* v. *Berkshire County Council and others* 1987 1 All ER 20). In a recent case the Court of Appeal has said that a care order is not available in respect of an unborn child (see page 230 below).

Midwifery practice and the standard of care

Midwife and doctor

All that has been said in relation to the duty of care and the principles relating to negligence apply to the practice of midwifery. However, a recent spate of cases in relation to birth trauma have special interest for the midwife. In particular, issues such as the following arise: the legal relationship between midwife and registered medical practitioner in regard to the care of the mother and child and the recording of information relating to the ante-natal confinement and post-natal care.

> **CASE 14.2 MIDWIFE AND DOCTOR MIX-UP**
>
> A 25-year-old woman was delivered of a normal baby by caesarian section in a small district hospital. The general practitioner who gave the anaesthetic had no specialist anaesthetic qualifications. The procedure lasted for two hours and was technically difficult because of adhesions from a previous caesarian section. In the immediate post-operative period the patient developed peripheral cyanosis with a drop in blood pressure (88/60) and was treated with intravenous fluids and oxygen. When she seemed to have improved, the doctor left the hospital.
>
> An hour later the patient developed a cough and tachycardia and the nurses gave linctus pholcodine. Ninety minutes later the doctor was informed by telephone that the patient had a persistent cough and he ordered oral aminophylline. After another 90 minutes he was summoned urgently because the patient had severe progressive respiratory distress and cyanosis. An X-ray confirmed Mendelssohn's syndrome and the patient was transferred to the main hospital where she required intensive resuscitation; she had sustained brain stem infarction with pseudobulbular palsy, spastic quadriparesis and cortical blindness. The Medical Defence Union (MDU) considered the claim for damages to be indefensible.

Although the time of gastric aspiration was uncertain, it was felt that the nursing staff had not adequately appraised the doctor of the patient's deteriorating condition, and on this basis the hospital's solicitors accepted a proportion of liability. The inadequate attention paid to the patient by the general practitioner in the early post-operative period was thought to be of major significance. The MDU paid two-thirds of the agreed damages (*Medical Defence Union Annual Report* 1982, 30). The acceptance of the nurse's partial liability in this case shows how important communication between the practitioners is in the care of the patient and the degree of responsibility which falls on the nurse's shoulders in ensuring that the doctor is adequately informed of the patient's progress or deterioration. The case also shows the importance of detailed and accurate records. In other circumstances it could well be that the nurse appreciated the severity of the patient's condition but that the doctor failed to respond to the entreaties to come. Accurate recordings of the times that phone calls were made, together with their content, will be partial evidence of the nurse's understanding of the situation. In serious cases it may not be sufficient to rely on the judgement of the one doctor and it may be necessary to take alternative action, which is a difficult dilemma for junior nursing and midwifery staff.

Community midwife

SITUATION 14.3 COMMUNITY MIDWIFERY

A very active community midwifery service existed in Roger Park District Health Authority. The midwives were proud of the fact that there was a much higher proportion of community confinements than in the rest of the country. In the community, medical support was provided by those general practitioners who had opted to care for obstetrical cases. Not all these GPs had received recent training in obstetrical practice. One such GP was Dr Marks, a 65-year-old doctor who had not attended a revision course in the last 30 years. He was a doctor of very fixed ideas. Grace Edwards had been practising midwifery for 18 years and had recently undertaken her statutory revision course at a large London hospital. She was called to Brenda Rice's home at 3.00 a.m. Grace realised that the birth was imminent. She phoned Dr Marks, advising him to come immediately and giving him details of the mother and foetal condition which was giving her cause for concern. On arrival Dr Marks disagreed with Grace's view of the severity of the situation and refused to agree to an ambulance being called. He considered that a forceps delivery could be performed safely. Unfortunately, this proved not to be so and the baby was stillborn.

In a situation such as this the midwife cannot avoid responsibility for her actions by saying that she obeyed the GP. If it is clear that his advice is mistaken and she fears for the health of the mother or baby, then she has a personal professional duty to them and would have to take further action. In extreme circumstances this might mean summoning an ambulance or calling out an obstetrician from the hospital despite the objections of the GP. This example also illustrates the importance of ensuring that the community midwife should be experienced.

Congenital Disabilities (Civil Liability) Act 1976

Liability of the midwife

Mention has already been made of this Act in connection with the liability of the mother. It will now be considered in relation to the liability of the midwife to the unborn child. The Act is set out in Appendix 11.

If it can be shown that the midwife has failed without justification to follow the approved accepted practice, then the mother has a right of action against her and also against the NHS Trust for the injury she has personally suffered. In addition, she can bring a claim in the name of the child for any harm suffered by the child. This latter action can be brought under the Congenital Disabilities Act 1976. It was enacted because, following the thalidomide tragedy, it was not clear in law whether the child, once born, had a claim in respect of pre-birth injuries. The legal status of the foetus was uncertain. While the Act was being debated, however, an action brought at common law (*Williams* v. *Luff, The Times* 14 February 1978) established that this was possible. In the case of *Burton* v. *Islington Health Authority* 1991 1 All ER 325, the mother was given a D and C in 1966 while she was pregnant and the baby was born with several disabilities. The baby subsequently sued in her own right for the harm, and on a preliminary point of law, the court held that if there had been parental negligence, which caused harm, then on her birth she would have a legal right to sue.

The Act enables a child who is born alive to sue any person (except the mother, apart from in one situation – see below) who has caused him to be born disabled as a result of an act of negligence. It must be established that the defendant's act would have made him liable to the parent.

Professional standards

There is a special provision covering professionals in Section 1 (5) of the Act which is set out in Fig. 14.4.

The working of the Act can be seen in another context. Imagine that another thalidomide-type situation were to occur. It might be possible that the mother had asked the midwife's advice in relation to a particular medicine/food during pregnancy. The midwife might reassure her that the particular product was fine. If in fact it then caused defects to the baby, would the midwife be liable to the baby under the Congenital Disabilities

---

The defendant is not answerable to the child for anything he did or omitted to do when responsible in a professional capacity for treating or advising the parent, if he took reasonable care having due regard to then received professional opinion applicable to the particular class of case; but this does not mean that he is answerable only because he departed from received opinion.

Figure 14.4 Congenital Disabilities (Civil Liability) Act 1976 Section 1 (5).

Act? The answer is that, if at the time her advice was reasonable in relation to what was known about the product and she was following the approved practice in recommending it, she would be unlikely to be found negligent.

It must be stressed that in order for an action to succeed under the Act it must be established that the harm that occurred was caused by the wrongful act. For example, a pregnant woman could be assaulted and subsequently go into premature labour. The child might suffer from some mental and physical handicaps. It must be established that these disabilities were caused by the assault. Causation in brain damage is particularly difficult to trace, as vaccination cases show.

Child's action is derivative

It must be emphasised that the child's right of action is derivative, i.e. only if the defendant would have been liable to one of the parents is the defendant then liable to the child. The father can be sued by the child. If the action concerns an occurrence that took place prior to conception the defendant is not answerable to the child if at that time either or both of the parents knew of the risk of their child being born disabled. If, however, it is the child's father who is the defendant, the action can continue if he alone knew of the risk but not the mother. To explain this provision, consider the following circumstance.

SITUATION 14.4 VD

Bill was aware that he was suffering from VD. He was unwilling to allow the special clinic to inform his wife and he refused to give them his address. However, he continued to have sex with her and she became pregnant. She was not aware that she might have contracted VD. Eventually the baby was born but suffered from an eye defect as a result of the infection.

In this situation it is possible that the child could maintain a successful action against the father under the provisions of the Act. Bill was in breach of the duty of care owed to the mother in that he failed to warn her of the VD and as a consequence the baby was born handicapped. It could be argued, however, that the father's negligence was in failing to prevent the baby from being born, not in actually causing harm to the child, and therefore the child would have no claim under the Act. This is discussed below in connection with the McKay case.

If both parents are aware of the possibility of the child being born disabled, no action can be commenced.

The mother's liability under the Act

The mother is only liable to the child under the Act if (Section 2) she is driving a motor vehicle when she knows (or ought reasonably to know) herself to be pregnant. Under this provision she is to be regarded as being under the same duty to take care for the safety of her unborn child as the law imposes on her with respect to the safety of other people; and if in consequence of her breach of that duty her child is born with disabilities which would not otherwise have been present, those disabilities are to be regarded as damage resulting from her wrongful act and actionable accordingly at the suit of the child.

Clearly, this provision is possible because the mother must by law be insured and the action would in reality be against the insurance company. It is thus of very limited scope and certainly does not lay down any general principle of liability of the mother to the child for the standard of pre-natal care. However, this may be possible under the *Williams* v. *Luff* and *Burton* v. *Islington Health Authority* precedents at common law. The following recent case has made it clear that the courts have no power to make an unborn baby a ward of court.

CASE 14.3 THE RIGHTS OF THE UNBORN

The mother was aged 36 and had suffered from severe mental disturbance since 1977. Throughout 1982 she had led a nomadic existence, wandering around Europe. She had returned in 1983 and had been settled in a flat in south London. Her only means of support was supplementary benefit. The local authority was concerned about the baby expected towards the end of January. Early in January the mother disappeared. The local authority instituted wardship proceedings (*In re F. (in utero)* 1988 2 All ER 193).

The Court of Appeal were of the opinion that if they had the power to institute wardship proceedings they would do so, but did they have the power? They concluded that they did not. There was no jurisdiction for the court to make a foetus a ward of court. They pointed out the difficulties of enforcing such an order against the mother: 'If the law was to be extended so as to impose control over the expectant mother, where such control was necessary for the benefit of the unborn child then it was for Parliament to decide whether such controls could be imposed and, if so, subject to what limitations. In such a sensitive field affecting the liberty of the individual it was not for the judiciary to extend the law' (per Lord Justice Balcombe).

The foetus cannot have a right of its own until it is born and has a separate existence from its mother. Once born it does then have the right to sue under the Congenital Disabilities Act and also at common law in respect of pre-natal negligence resulting in harm.

Action for wrongful life

CASE 14.4 GERMAN MEASLES

Mrs McKay was pregnant and suspected that she had contracted German measles in the early weeks of her pregnancy. Blood tests were arranged to see if she had been infected. Unfortunately, she was wrongly informed that she had not been infected. When the baby was born it was found to be disabled as a result of the effect of German measles (*McKay* v. *Essex AHA* 1982 2 All ER 771).

The Court of Appeal held that the child's claim for wrongful life (i.e. if there had been no negligence the child would have been aborted) could not be sustained. Although this child was born before the Congenital Disabilities Act 1976 was passed, the Court still held that an action for wrongful life could not stand, even under the provisions of the Act. This decision does not of course affect the rights of the mother to sue for damages resulting from the negligence in informing her of the results of the tests and Mrs McKay brought her own action on that point. The former decision was concerned solely with the rights of the child. In the VD case discussed above, the child, in suing the father, would have to prove that the father, knowing that he had VD, failed to undertake effective therapy to cure the VD or wrongly and carelessly believed that he was cured, and that as a result of this negligence the child was born disabled.

Nurseries within midwifery departments

Problems can sometimes arise within the midwifery department over the responsibility for the nursery nurse staff and those who are caring for the babies. It is essential that clear lines of accountability and responsibility are laid down so that there is no confusion on this point: local practices might differ.

Special care baby units

These units may or may not be under the control of the midwifery department. Some may be under the paediatric department. The nature of the control should not affect the standard of care.

Care of the grossly handicapped

One difficulty which faces special care baby units is the problem of determining the extent to which grossly underweight or severely handicapped babies should be given 'heroic' measures. In addition, the shortage of staff in these units has received much publicity and undoubtedly the pressure on resources has created difficulties for staff. The legal implication of this has been considered in detail in Chapter 3 and will not be repeated here. We shall consider the problems where the duty of care requires the doctor to provide all possible assistance.

CASE 14.5 FOETAL ACCIDENT INQUIRY IN GLASGOW

The parents of a girl born at 26 weeks' gestation, weighing 675 grams, requested an inquiry to discover why a paediatrician had made no attempt to resuscitate her. They alleged that the Royal Maternity Hospital operated a ban on resuscitating infants of less than 700 grams.

The Sheriff ruled that the doctor had behaved in a correct professional manner by assessing the weight, gestation and general condition of the infant before deciding not to resuscitate (quoted in the *Bulletin of the Institute of Medical Ethics*, February 1988, page 3).

It would be illegal, however, for the doctors to prescribe, either intentionally or recklessly, a substance to bring about the infant's death. The British Medical Association has recently issued a report on euthanasia (BMA, *The Euthanasia Report*, May 1988) which includes a discussion of child euthanasia. It says: 'There are circumstances where the doctor may judge correctly that continuing to treat an infant is cruel, and that the doctor should ease the baby's dying rather than prolong it by the insensitive use of medical technology.' It opposes any move towards liberalising the active termination of such an infant since this would herald a serious and incalculable change in the present ethos of medicine. Reference should also be made to the discussion on viability and the aborted foetus in the next chapter. The Court of Appeal has recently made a declaration (*In re C. (a minor) (wardship, medical treatment)* 1989 2 All ER 782) that an infant ward of court who was terminally ill, suffering irreversible and severe brain damage, was to be treated in accordance with the specialist's advice. The paragraph included by the trial judge relating to details of the treatment permitted, preventing the prescribing and administering of antibiotics, and preventing the setting up of intravenous fusions or nasal-gastric feeding regimes, was deleted by the Court of Appeal.

In the case of *In re J. (a minor) (wardship, medical treatment)* 1990 3 All ER 930, the baby suffered from severe disabilities and was likely to develop serious spastic quadriplegia and be both deaf and blind. He was not, however, on the point of death nor dying. In deciding whether he should be put back onto a mechanical ventilator, the Court of Appeal held that the test to be applied 'must be whether the child in question, if capable of exercising sound judgement, would consider the life tolerable'.

In the case of *In re J. (a minor) (wardship, medical treatment)* 1992 4 All ER 614, the baby suffered from a severe form of cerebral palsy with cortical blindness and severe epilepsy. The Court of Appeal held that the court will not exercise its inherent jurisdiction over minors by ordering a medical practitioner to treat the minor in a manner contrary to the practitioner's clinical judgement. In the practitioner's view, intensive therapeutic measures such as artificial ventilation were inappropriate.

Registration of births and stillbirths

Births

There is a duty on the doctor or midwife attending a woman in childbirth to notify the prescribed medical officer of the birth or stillbirth within 36 hours. This applies whether the birth is at home or in an institution.

Under the Births and Deaths Registration Act 1953 it is the duty of the father or mother to give information to the Registrar within 42 days. If either of them cannot, then there is a duty to do so on the occupier of the house, or any person present at the birth, or any person having charge of the child. This provision might well involve the midwife. If there is a failure to register within 42 days the Registrar can compel any qualified informant to attend to give information and sign the Register. The Registrar must give

7 days' notice in writing. There are additional powers if there is no registration after that date.

Stillbirths

A stillbirth is a child which is stillborn, which issued forth from its mother after the 24th week of pregnancy, and which did not at any time after being completely expelled from its mother breathe or show any signs of life (Section 41 1953 Act as amended by the Stillbirth Definition Act 1992 Section 1). The stillbirth has to be registered and the informant has to deliver to the Registrar a written certificate that the child was not born alive. This would be signed by the registered medical practitioner or a certified midwife who was in attendance at the birth or who has examined the body.

A stillbirth should be disposed of by burial in a burial ground or church yard or by cremation at an authorised crematorium.

What if the foetus is of less than 24 weeks' gestation?

If the foetus was delivered without any sign of life, then no registration is necessary. The foetus may be disposed of without formality in any way which does not constitute a nuisance or an affront to public decency. However, it is clear that even though the foetus is under 24 weeks the bereaved parents should be given the sympathy and care which would be given if the baby was full term.

If the foetus is under 24 weeks' gestation and initially shows signs of life and breathing and then dies, it should be treated as a neo-natal death and be registered as a birth and death.

Use of foetal tissue

This has recently come into public debate with the news that transplanted foetal brain tissue has been used in operations for Parkinson's disease. There would appear to be no legal grounds to prevent such use, provided that the consent of the mother was given to the use and that the foetus was not aborted for the purposes of obtaining foetal tissue. The British Medical Association has issued guidelines which forbid the possibility of a human brain transplant, but which approve the controlled use of brain cell implants from aborted foetal tissue. These guidelines are in keeping with the recommendations made by the Peel Report (HMSO, 1972) which put forward a recommended code of practice for the use of foetal materials. These recommendations are summarised in the *Bulletin of the Institute of Medical Ethics* No. 35, February 1988. The Polkinghorne Committee has reviewed the guidance on the use of foetuses and foetal material (1989 HMSO Cmd 762).

The recent announcement that eggs could be taken from dead foetuses and used to grow embryos for implantation has caused considerable concern and is currently before the Human Fertilisation Embryology Authority (for which see Chapter 22).

AIDS and the midwife

The possibility of a midwife contracting AIDS from an HIV positive patient is a growing problem, and midwives are concerned at the possibility of protecting themselves by equipment, gloves, clothing, and screening of patients so that midwives are warned of the potential dangers. These anxieties are part of the general dilemmas in relation to AIDS and are considered in Chapter 26.

Future developments in midwifery

In April 1991 the House of Commons initiated an inquiry into maternity services because concerns had been expressed that the services did not meet the wishes of women. Its report was published in February 1992 (House of Commons Health Committee Session 1991–92 Maternity Services). It concluded that 'the policy of encouraging all women to give birth in hospitals cannot be justified on grounds of safety'. It made wide-ranging recommendations covering the development of midwife-managed units, involvement of midwives in junior doctors' training, and emphasis on the rights and involvement of the mother. A joint committee supported its recommendations. The government set up an expert committee chaired by Lady Cumberlege to review policy on NHS maternity care and this committee reported in 1993 (*Changing Childbirth: Report of the Expert Maternity Group*, Department of Health, HMSO). It identified three key principles which should underlie effective woman-centred maternity services: the woman must be the focus of maternity care; maternity services can be readily and easily accessible to all; services must be effective and efficient. Recommendations were made on action to implement these principles. Legislation may be required to implement some of the suggestions. The government has set up an Implementation Committee and the NHS Management Executive has required purchasers and providers to include plans for implementation in their future purchasing agreements (see Executive Letter (94)9, issued 24 January 1994 by the NHS Management Executive). As a result the midwife will have an enlarged scope of professional practice and a challenging future as the mother's involvement in decision-making will continue to develop.

Questions and exercises

1 Plans agreed between midwife and expectant mother for her ante-natal and post-natal care and confinement are an increasingly accepted part of midwifery practice. In what circumstances can a mother refuse consent to any deviation from this care plan?

2 What are the implications of the Congenital Disabilities (Civil Liability) Act 1976 for the midwife?
3 What statutory duties does a midwife have in relation to the registration of a birth or stillbirth?
4 Does the law require that every effort must be made to save every child no matter how handicapped?
5 What specific powers and rights does the midwife have in relation to drugs which are not possessed by the registered general nurse? (See Chapter 28 and Appendices 5 and 6).

15   The nurse on the gynaecology ward

Figure 15.1 sets out the areas of particular concern to the nurse who works in the gynae-cology ward which will be considered in this chapter. In addition, the nurse should refer to the chapter on the law relating to fertility (Chapter 22) for further discussion of the legal implications of sterilisation.

Abortion laws

The general principles

The Abortion Act 1967 amended by the Human Fertilisation and Embryology Act 1990 enables an abortion to be carried out but only after the legal requirements are satis-fied. If these requirements are not satisfied, then abortion is an offence which carries a maximum sentence of life imprisonment. The provisions of the Act as amended are set out in Fig. 15.2.

Account may be taken of the pregnant woman's actual or reasonably foreseeable envi-ronment in deciding whether there is a risk of injury to health under paragraph (a).

The abortion must be carried out in an NHS hospital or a place specifically approved by the Secretary of State or Minister of Health for the purposes of the Act. Emergency provisions are set out in Fig. 15.3.

1. Abortion
   (a) general principles;
   (b) conscientious objection;
   (c) nurse's participation in prostaglandin abortion;
   (d) when is an abortion illegal?
   (e) capable of being born alive;
   (f) negligence in failing to detect abnormality;
   (g) challenge by father;
   (h) husband's attempt to stop abortion;
   (i) abortion refused;
   (j) other related offences;
   (k) confidentiality;
   (l) notification under regulations;
   (m) consent by under 16-year-old;
   (n) abortion of mentally handicapped;
      (i) of the under 18-year-old
      (ii) of the adult.
2. Sterilisation
   (a) of mentally handicapped minor;
   (b) of the mentally handicapped adult;
   (c) rights of the spouse.

Figure 15.1 Issues covered in Chapter 15.

A person shall not be guilty of an offence under the law relating to abortion when a pregnancy is terminated by a registered medical practitioner if two registered medical practitioners are of the opinion, formed in good faith

(a) that the pregnancy has not exceeded its 24th week and that the continuance of the pregnancy would involve risk, greater than if the pregnancy were terminated, of injury to the physical or mental health of the pregnant woman or any existing children of her family; or
(b) that the termination is necessary to prevent grave permanent injury to the physical or mental health of the pregnant woman; or
(c) that the continuance of the pregnancy would involve risk to the life of the pregnant woman, greater than if the pregnancy were terminated; or
(d) that there is a substantial risk that if the child were born it would suffer from such physical or mental abnormalities as to be seriously handicapped.

Figure 15.2 Abortion Act 1967 as amended by the Human Fertilisation and Embryology Act 1990.

The Provisions set out in Fig. 15.2, including the requirement to have two registered medical practitioners, do not apply in an emergency when a registered medical practitioner is of the opinion, formed in good faith, that the termination is immediately necessary to save the life or to prevent grave permanent injury to the physical or mental health of the pregnant woman.

Figure 15.3 Emergency provisions of the Abortion Act.

Conscientious objection to participation in an abortion

The Abortion Act is one of the few examples where it is possible for a professional to refuse to take part in an activity. Thus Section 4 states that 'no person shall be under any duty, whether by contract or by any statutory or other legal requirement, to participate in any treatment authorised by this Act to which he has a conscientious objection: Provided that in any legal proceedings the burden of proof of conscientious objection shall rest on the person claiming to rely on it.' This right is, however, subject to Section 4 (2): 'Nothing in subsection (1) of this section shall affect any duty to participate in treatment which is necessary to save the life or to prevent grave permanent injury to the physical or mental health of a pregnant woman.'

The extent of the protection from being involved in an abortion was recently considered by the Court of Appeal.

CASE 15.1 THE LETTER

Mrs Janaway, a medical secretary, refused to type a letter referring a patient from a general practitioner to a consultant with a view to a possible termination of pregnancy. She was a Roman Catholic who believed strongly that abortion was morally wrong. The genuineness of her belief was never in dispute. She was asked to type the letter and refused on the basis that she was protected by Section 4 of the Abortion Act. She was dismissed by the Health Authority and subsequently applied for judicial review of the Health Authority's decision. This was refused and she therefore appealed (*R. v. Salford Health Authority ex parte Janaway, The Times* 2 December 1988).

The Court of Appeal held that she was not entitled to claim the protection of Section 4 of the Act. It could not be said that by typing the letter she was participating in any treatment authorised by the Act, nor could typing such a letter be regarded as a criminal offence prior to the Abortion Act so that it could be regarded as now being protected by the provisions of the Act.

Nurses' participation in prostaglandin abortions

CASE 15.2 PROSTAGLANDIN DRIP

The Royal College of Nursing brought a case on behalf of its members against the DHSS because members had complained that they were often left on wards to supervise (sometimes for several days) a patient who was having a prostaglandin-induced abortion. The doctor would set up the drip and then the nurse would undertake the care of the patient. The RCN queried the legality of this in the light of the wording of the Act that the pregnancy should be terminated by a registered medical practitioner. The RCN questioned, in particular, advice given in a DHSS letter and circular relating to the procedures that might be performed by an appropriately skilled nurse or midwife (*Royal*

College of Nursing v. *The Department of Health and Social Security* 1981
1 All ER 545).

The House of Lords decided on a majority of three to two that the DHSS advice did
not involve the performance of unlawful acts by members of the RCN. Lord Diplock's
views are set out in Fig. 15.4.

When is an abortion illegal?

The simple answer is: under any circumstances other than those permitted under the
1967 Act as amended by the 1990 Act. It is specifically provided that no offence is
committed under the Infant Life Preservation Act 1929 if the provisions of the 1967
Act are followed (Section 5 as amended by the 1990 Act).

The Infant Life Preservation Act 1929 provides that any person who, with intent to
destroy the life of a child capable of being born alive, by any wilful act, causes a child
to die before it has an existence independent of its mother, shall be guilty of felony, to
wit, of child destruction. A person is, however, protected from the effect of these provisions if the act is done in good faith for the purpose only of preserving the life of the
mother, and if the amended provisions of the Abortion Act 1967 are followed.

Evidence that a woman had at any material time been pregnant for a period of 28
weeks or more shall be *prima facie* proof that she was at that time pregnant of a child
capable of being born alive (Section 1 (2)). This sub-section is the origin of the 28-week
guidelines that were once used. However, it is only a presumption and advances in medicine have in practice clearly lowered the viability stage to 24 weeks or less. David Alton's
Bill sought to lower this to 18 weeks. If medical progress continues and viability remains
the test, this might have to be reduced until one can imagine that the lower limit of viability

In the context of the Act what was required was that a registered medical practitioner – a doctor –
should accept responsibility for all stages of the treatment for the termination of the pregnancy. The
particular method to be used should be decided by the doctor in charge of that treatment; he should
carry out any physical acts, forming part of the treatment, that in accordance with accepted medical
practice were done only by qualified medical practitioners, and should give specific instructions as
to the carrying out of such parts of the treatment as in accordance with accepted medical practice
were carried out by nurses or other hospital staff without medical qualifications. To each of them the
doctor or his substitute should be available to be consulted or called in for assistance from beginning to end of the treatment. In other words, the doctor need not do everything with his own hands;
the subsection's requirements were satisfied when the treatment was one prescribed by a registered
medical practitioner carried out in accordance with his directions and of which he remained in charge
throughout.

Figure 15.4 Lord Diplock's view in the case of *Royal College of Nursing* v. *The Department of Health
and Social Security* 1981 1 All ER 545.

outside the womb could link up with the length at which a test tube embryo could be kept alive.

The amendments to the 1967 Abortion Act limit termination to 24 weeks or less but only for sub-sub-section 1(1)(a). Sub-sections b, c and d give no time limit (see Fig. 15.2).

Capable of being born alive

SITUATION 15.1 BIRTH OR ABORTION

Mavis Spencer was 15 and her pregnancy was only discovered at a late stage. From the information provided by her and from his own medical examination the doctor judged her to be about 22 weeks' pregnant. He agreed that a termination should proceed and he arranged for her to see a second doctor who agreed with him. Mavis was immediately admitted for a termination. However, because of unforeseeable delays on the ward this was not commenced for another week. When the foetus was expelled it appeared to cry out and the nurse felt that it was breathing. She did not know what to do. The doctor told her to put the remains in the bucket for incineration. She was reluctant to do this, however, since she felt it to be a child capable of surviving. Where does the law stand?

As has been pointed out, the Infant Life Preservation Act 1929 only presumes that a foetus of 28 weeks is capable of being born alive. If it is clear that a foetus of a younger age *is* alive then all reasonable steps should be taken to preserve its life, otherwise there could be a prosecution for an offence under the 1929 Act as well as one for murder or manslaughter. A prosecution was brought against Dr Hamilton when an abortion produced a live foetus. However, the case did not proceed beyond the committal proceedings. In the above situation, if it is apparent that the aborted foetus is breathing and viable, then it should be transferred to a special care baby unit. Failure to do so could be grounds for a charge of attempted murder. In addition, of course, even if the child were to die shortly afterwards it would still have to be registered as a live birth (see registration provisions under the midwifery section). A coroner recently considered whether an aborted foetus which showed signs of life should be the subject of an inquest (see *Times Law Report*, 5 May 1988).

Negligence in failing to detect abnormality

In a recent case (*Rance and another* v. *Mid Downs Health Authority and another* 1991 1 All ER 801), the plaintiff had an ultrasound scan when she was about 26 weeks' pregnant. The radiographer queried a possible abnormality of the spine, but the consultant decided that there was no firm evidence of abnormality justifying further action. The baby was born and found to be suffering from spina bifida. The mother claimed that the defendants were negligent in not ascertaining the possibility of abnormality and thus enabling her to have an abortion. Her claim failed since (under the Abortion Act 1967, i.e. prior to the 1990 amendments) it would have been illegal to have carried out an abortion at that stage, since the baby would have been capable of being born alive within the meaning of the 1929 Act.

Challenge by the putative father

CASE 15.3 FATHER'S INTERVENTION

An Oxford student whose girlfriend become pregnant sought to stop the abortion on the grounds that the foetus, of between 18 and 24 weeks, was viable and that the abortion would thus be an offence under the Infant Life Preservation Act 1929. In this case the pregnant woman was given medication to terminate the pregnancy shortly after the time that conception must have occurred. It was assumed that the medication had been effective. She subsequently took anti-depressant drugs and underwent two chest X-rays, one of which was taken without any shielding to protect a foetus. Any of these treatments could have harmed the foetus. When she discovered that she was still pregnant she obtained the two necessary signatures for abortion. The father brought the court action (*C. v. S.* 1987 1 All ER 1230).

The Court of Appeal decided that the foetus was not capable of being born alive and therefore the termination of the pregnancy would not constitute an offence under the 1929 Act. The medical evidence showed that the cardiac muscle would be contracting and that there would be signs of primitive movement. It was said that these were real discernible signs of life. But the foetus would never be capable of breathing, either naturally or with the aid of a ventilator.

Husband's attempt to stop an abortion

CASE 15.4 HUSBAND'S RIGHTS

In the case described above the putative father was not married to the mother but it might be asked whether, if he were married, it would give him any rights to prevent the abortion going ahead. This point came before the courts when Mr Paton asked the court to prevent his wife going ahead with a termination. Two doctors had signed that the termination should proceed. Mr Paton claimed that as the father of the child he had a right to apply to the court for the termination to be stopped (*Paton* v. *Trustees of British Pregnancy Advisory Service* 1978 2 All ER 987).

The court, however, disagreed. It held that, provided the requirements of the Act were met, then the husband did not have any right in law to prevent it proceeding. He had no *locus standi* before the court.

An abortion refused

SITUATION 15.2 AN ENFORCED CHILD_____

After having two children Beryl Edwards considered her family to be complete.
They moved to a larger house with a huge mortgage and Beryl took a part-
time job to help pay for the additional loan and the extras: meals out and holidays. She was horrified when she discovered that she might be pregnant. Beryl
became severely depressed and visited her GP. He was very reassuring, stating
that she could have an abortion, and within a few days she was referred to a
consultant obstetrician. He listened to her case and then informed her that he
did not consider that she satisfied the requirements of the Abortion Act and
that he would therefore be unable to write a medical recommendation. Beryl's
depression became worse and she was unable to work. Eventually, her husband
suggested that she should seek another opinion. She was reluctant to do so,
not believing that it would be of any value. Eventually, however, under pressure from her husband she paid privately to see another specialist, who informed
her that in his opinion she did meet the Act's requirements. However, since
she was now 23 weeks' pregnant he would be unwilling to propose an abortion since the pregnancy was too far advanced for an abortion to be performed
safely and at this late stage he believed that it could constitute an offence under
the 1929 Act. Beryl eventually had the child but is seeking compensation against
the first specialist. Is she likely to succeed?

Beryl does not have an absolute right to an abortion. To obtain compensation she would
have to prove that in making his assessment of her present or foreseeable physical or
mental health the specialist was negligent in failing to take into account factors that
approved medical practice would have expected him to have taken into account, and
that his assessment had been made negligently. She may get some support from her GP
but, of course, it was open to him to refer her to another doctor at an earlier stage. Indeed,
the GP's failure to refer her to a second consultant might in itself give rise to a claim
of negligence against the GP. However, if the first consultant's report had been adamant
that there was no greater risk in proceeding with the pregnancy, then the GP could argue
that there was no negligence on his part in accepting that view as the likely prevailing
one and therefore a further referral was not justified. Where an abortion is performed
according to the provisions of the Abortion Act 1967 (as amended) this is a defence to
a charge of an offence under the Infant Life Preservation Act 1929.

Other related offences

The Offences Against the Person Act 1861 Section 58 makes it an offence to administer drugs or use instruments to procure an abortion. When a woman is charged it must
be shown that she is pregnant. This is not necessary when another person is charged
with an offence. Section 59 of the 1861 Act makes it an offence to supply or procure

any poison or any instrument or any other thing knowing that it is to be used with intent to cause a miscarriage whether or not the woman is with child. However, if the requirements of the Abortion Act are complied with, these provisions would not apply. Section 60 of the 1861 Act makes it an offence to conceal the birth of a child.

Dr Bourne, a gynaecologist, was prosecuted under Section 58 of the 1861 Act after he had terminated the pregnancy of a girl who had been raped. He was found not guilty on the ground that his action was taken to preserve the life of the mother. This situation is now covered by the 1967 Abortion Act.

Confidentiality and illegal abortions

SITUATION 15.3 TO TELL OR KEEP QUIET_____

Pam Reynolds is admitted in an emergency to the accident and emergency department with severe bleeding. She is transferred to the gynaecology ward where it is clear to nursing and medical staff that she had probably tried to obtain an illegal abortion, though Pam herself is silent as to what happened. It is the third case this month that there has been such an admission and the gynaecologist suspects that one person may be responsible. Does he or the nursing staff have any duty in law to inform the police?

The simple answer is that there is no statute which places a duty on anyone to report a crime of causing a miscarriage or an offence under the Infant Life Preservation Act. If, of course, the police had heard of the illegal abortion and had begun to investigate, then they would be able to subpoena witnesses or obtain information for their enquiries under the procedures laid down under the Police and Criminal Evidence Act. What about notifying them before they are aware of the possible crime? Some would argue that the doctor has a public duty to inform the police in such circumstances but until the law is changed this is not obligatory. For those offences which must be reported to the police see Chapter 8.

Notification

The Abortion Regulations 1968 as amended by the 1976, 1980 and 1991 regulations place a duty on the practitioner to notify the chief medical officer on the appropriate forms but restricts disclosure to anyone other than an authorised officer of the DHSS; the Registrar General; the Director of Public Prosecutions; the police; for the purposes of criminal proceedings; *bona fide* scientific research; to any practitioner with the consent of the woman; or at the request of the President of the General Medical Council for the purpose of investigating whether there has been serious professional misconduct.

Consent by a pregnant person under 16 years

If a young girl of 14 seeks an abortion, do her own parents have to consent on her behalf? This has not been tested out in law. Assuming that the girl is not in the care of the local authority and is seeking an abortion, then provided that she has the capacity to make the decision, she could give a valid consent under the Gillick case principles discussed in the section relating to paediatric nursing. What, however, if the girl's own parents wanted her to have the child and promised that they would care for it; could they refuse to allow the termination to proceed?

CASE 15.5 WHOSE CHOICE?

The mother was 15. She already had a son of 12 months and had been in care since she was 13 following a conviction for theft. She lived in a mother-and-child unit with schooling facilities and was then 12 weeks' pregnant. Her own parents objected to the abortion (as they had done during the first pregnancy). Her father offered to take care of his grandson and leave the daughter with the new baby. On religious grounds, as a Seventh Day Adventist, he opposed the termination of life. He also thought that the girl would live to regret the decision she had taken. He was convinced that she was still a child and that she should not be allowed to take a decision that she could subsequently regret (*In re P. (a minor)* 1981 80 LGR 301).

The child was placed under the wardship jurisdiction of the court and Mrs Justice Butler-Sloss ordered that the termination of the pregnancy should proceed. The judge was clearly influenced by the wishes of the girl, who had set her mind on the termination and had not in fact contemplated that it might not proceed. She discussed the matter with the girl and formed the opinion that she was of a strong personality and mature views. The judge also held that, on the facts, the risks to the health of the mother and the interests of the existing child satisfied the requirements of the 1967 Act. The grandparents' objections were thus overruled and they were accorded no rights in the matter. In this case, of course, the child was already in the care of the local authority. Where this is not so, it may be the practice for the parents of the pregnant girl to sign the consent form for a termination. Probably, too, if there is a clash between the rights of the mother and the grandparents the latter may put pressure on the girl to agree to an abortion since she may well be dependent on their help in bringing up the child.

Abortion of the mentally handicapped

Under 18 years old

The parents have the right to make decisions on behalf of the minor provided that they are acting in the interests of the child. The principles discussed in relation to the sterilisation of the minor by the House of Lords *In re B.* which is considered below would thus apply. It is considered necessary to obtain the approval of the court.

The adult mentally handicapped person

CASE 15.6 THE MENTALLY HANDICAPPED MOTHER_____

The defendant was a woman aged 19 who was epileptic and severely mentally handicapped. She was totally dependent upon others and was cared for by her mother. She became pregnant and termination of pregnancy was recommended by the medical advisers on the ground that it would be impossible for her to understand the concept of pregnancy or to cope with the difficulties and complications associated with that condition, and that she would be incapable of providing and caring for a child. The doctors also recommended that she should be protected from any further pregnancies by being sterilised. The doctors were, however, unwilling to carry out the abortion or sterilisation operation without authorisation. The mother thus applied to the court for a declaration that the procedures could be carried out lawfully (*T. v. T.* 1988 1 All ER 613).

The court held that the situation was not covered by the Mental Health Act 1983 consent to treatment provisions (see Chapter 20), nor did a guardian under the Act have the power to give consent. They also held that the court no longer had its power to act as *parens patriae* (a kind of wardship jurisdiction) and the court could therefore not give consent itself. (It held that this power had been repealed in 1959 and should be reinstated.) However, the court was prepared to grant the declaration requested and declared the proposed treatment lawful and therefore a defence to any action for trespass to the person. The doctors would be carrying out the treatment in the interests of the patient as part of their duty of care to the patient.

Sterilisation

Sterilisation of a mentally handicapped minor

CASE 15.7 STERILISATION_____

Jeanette was 17 years old but was described as having a mental age of 5 or 6. Her mother and the local authority, who held a care order on her, advised by the social worker, the gynaecologist and a paediatrician, considered it vital that she should not become pregnant. She had been found in a compromising situation in her residential home. She could not be relied upon to take or accept oral contraceptives. Jeanette was likely to move to an adult training centre at the age of 19 and it would not be possible to provide her with the degree of supervision she had at present (*In re B. (a minor) (wardship, sterilisation)* 1987 2 All ER 206).

The House of Lords decided that the paramount consideration was the interests of the girl and, taking account of all the medical evidence, decided that it was in her interests to be sterilised. They made no distinction between non-therapeutic and

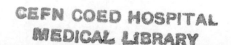

therapeutic care of the child and recommended that in future all such cases should come before the courts.

Sterilisation of a mentally handicapped adult

The House of Lords in the Jeanette case discussed above declared their decision before Jeanette reached 18 so they did not consider the law in relationship to the adult mentally handicapped person. This was considered in the case of *T.* v. *T.* considered above but that decision was taken in the High Court. The view of the House of Lords on this situation was given in the case of *In re F.* v. *West Berkshire Health Authority*.

In this case the court had to decide whether the sterilisation of a mentally handicapped woman, F., aged 35 would be unlawful because of her lack of capacity to give her consent to the operation. Mr Justice Scott Baker in the Family Division granted a declaration that it was in the best interests of F. to have the operation. He stated that there was a problem when, because of a mental condition, a patient was unable to give any meaningful consent to treatment for a physical condition. If he did nothing, a doctor could be said to be negligent; if he operated, he, *prima facie*, committed the tort of battery. The law's answer to this was that a professional was not liable if he acted in good faith and in the best interests of the patients. The Court of Appeal upheld this decision. The House of Lords (1989 2 All ER 545) confirmed the power at common law for a doctor to act in the best interests of the patient incapable of giving consent. The court also had an inherent jurisdiction to make declarations on the lawfulness of such treatment. Court involvement in cases of sterilisation was highly desirable as a matter of good practice.

The Law Commission has made recommendations on decision-making on behalf of the mentally incapacitated adult (Reports 119 (1991), 128, 129 and 130 (1993)) which are under consideration.

Sterilisation and the rights of a spouse

There is considerable confusion over the rights of each spouse in relation to the other being sterilised. Many hospitals still have forms where if a sterilisation is proposed, then the other spouse must consent in writing before the operation can proceed.

SITUATION 15.4 THE HUSBAND SAYS 'NO'

Audrey Rich was expecting her seventh child. Her eldest child was 10 years old and they lived with the husband in a four-bedroomed council house. She felt she could not cope with any further pregnancies and sought advice as to the possibility of being sterilised after the birth of the seventh. An appointment was arranged with the obstetrician for Audrey and Steve but Steve refused to attend, claiming that he would never give his consent to Audrey being sterilised. Audrey went on her own to see the obstetrician who told her that he could not carry out the operation without her husband's consent.

There is no longer any duty in law to obtain the consent of the spouse before sterilising the partner. In the past there was a legal duty when the husband had a right of consortium and could sue any person who caused him to lose this right. However, this right to sue for loss of consortium was repealed by the Administration of Justice Act 1982 Section 2 (a). The woman has never enjoyed such a right; the House of Lords refused to extend it to women in 1952 (*Best* v. *Samuel Fox and Co*. 1952 2 All ER 394). There may be considerable advantages in obtaining a signature to say that the spouse knows of the intended operation, since if this is obtained the doctor is less likely to be summoned as a witness in divorce proceedings where one spouse is alleging that the operation was performed without his/her knowledge. However, a form signifying knowledge of the operation is very different from a form of consent.

In the situation outlined above Audrey could obtain a solicitor's letter confirming the law but this of course does not place any duty on the doctor to perform the operation. She could request referral to a doctor who would perform the operation or even apply to the health authority for assistance. Ultimately, she could seek a declaration from the court that such an operation could proceed without the husband's consent.

Other issues relating to negligence in sterilisation operations and damages for unwanted children are considered in Chapter 22.

Questions and exercises

1 Obtain a set of the documentation which has to be completed when an abortion is performed and examine the legal requirements as shown in these forms.
2 What is the situation if an aborted foetus is found to be breathing?
3 What forms are completed in your hospital when an operation for sterilisation is performed? Can you see any significant difference in the form completed by the patient and the form completed by the spouse?
4 What information do you consider should be given to a patient before her consent to an operation for sterilisation? What are the legal requirements? (See also Chapter 7 and Chapter 22.)

16 Intensive care and transplant surgery nursing

The areas considered in this chapter are set out in Fig. 16.1. Definition of death is of such concern to the intensive care nurse in relation to requests for organs for transplantation that it was thought best to discuss it here. Further aspects relating to death are considered in Chapter 29. Other concerns for the transplant nurse are the decision not to resuscitate a patient and consent for the use of organs and tissues. Intensive care nurses are also frequently confronted by the issues relating to the switching off of machines. This chapter seeks to clarify the main principles which arise.

Definition of death

The traditional method for the determination of whether life has ceased was to check whether breathing had stopped by checking the pulse, the heart beat, and placing a mirror in front of the mouth, i.e. the cessation of circulatory and respiratory functions as evidenced by an absence of heart beat, pulse, and respiration. For most cases this was satisfactory. However, if the patient was on a ventilator where breathing was maintained artificially, this traditional definition was inappropriate. In addition, the advance in medical technology, particularly in transplant surgery, meant that it was essential to use the organs as soon as possible after respiration had ceased, and if there was likely to

1. Definition of death: brain death.
2. Importance of exact time of death.
3. Cause of death.
4. Legality of switching machines off.
5. Not for resuscitation.
6. Relatives and the treatment of patient.
7. Refusal of treatment by patient.
8. Organ transplantation.

Figure 16.1 Issues covered in Chapter 16.

The diagnosis of brain death should be made by two medical practitioners who have expertise in this field. One should be the consultant who is in charge of the case and one other doctor (or in the absence of the consultant, his deputy who should have been registered for 5 years or more with adequate previous experience in the care of such cases and one other doctor). The two doctors may carry out their tests separately or together. If the tests confirm brain death they should still be repeated. It is for the doctors to decide how long the interval between the tests should be. It may not be appropriate for the doctors to carry out all the recommended tests. The criteria are guidelines, not rigid rules.

These criteria are as follows:

1. All brain-stem reflexes are absent.
2. The pupils are fixed in diameter and do not respond to sharp changes in the intensity of incident light.
3. There is no corneal reflex.
4. The vestibular-ocular reflexes are absent.
5. No motor responses within the cranial nerve distribution can be elicited by adequate stimulation of any somatic area.
6. There is no gag reflex or reflex response to bronchial stimulation by a suction catheter passed down the trachea.
7. No respiratory movements occur when the patient is disconnected from the mechanical ventilator for long enough to ensure that the arterial carbon dioxide tension rises above the threshold for stimulation of respiration.

Additional recommendations are made as to how some of these tests should be undertaken.

Figure 16.2 Definition of brain death.

---

be a delay to keep the body ventilated, i.e. artificially breathing until such time as the organs required for transplant could be taken. In these cases 'brain death' became the criterion for whether death had taken place. If the traditional definition of death was used there was an 88 per cent incidence of post-operative renal failure in kidney transplants, whereas if the criterion of brain death was used on a patient maintained on a ventilator, the post-operative failure rate was 10–20 per cent. The same percentage occurs when kidneys from living donors are used.

What is brain death?

A conference of the Royal Colleges in 1976 set out the diagnostic tests to be used for the determination of brain death; these were circulated in 1978 and also included in the code of practice 'The removal of cadaveric organs for transplantation' which was distributed to doctors in January 1980. A subsequent conference in 1981 made the recommendations set out in Fig. 16.2.

The possibility of brain death is recommended where the patient is deeply comatose (but where depressant drugs, primary hypothermia, and metabolic and endocrine disturbances can be excluded) or where the patient is being maintained on a ventilator because spontaneous respiration had previously been inadequate or had ceased (relaxants or other drugs should be ruled out as a cause of respiratory failure), or where there is no doubt that the patient's condition is due to irremediable structural brain damage.

The importance of the exact time of death

The actual timing of death can be a significant feature in a variety of court actions. A few examples are set out in Fig. 16.3.

Criminal law

To constitute murder the victim must die within a year and a day of the act. If the victim is kept on a machine for longer than that, is it murder?

CASE 16.1 TIMING

Dyson, on 13 November 1906, seized his 3-month-old child by the legs, flung him down and beat him until he became unconscious and his skull had been fractured. On 29 December 1907 he again beat the child, causing severe bruising

---

1. *Criminal law*: definition of murder and suicides – death must be within a year and a day of the act.
2. *Civil law*:
   A. Survivorship. The rules of inheritance depend upon the order in which people die. If, therefore, there are incidents leading to multiple deaths, which victim died first can be very significant for inheritance. There are certain presumptions in law relating to the order of deaths in such circumstances, i.e. the oldest died first. However, if one of the victims is supported on a life support machine and kept 'alive' longer the presumption would no longer operate.
   B. Insurance policies often require that where death follows an accident it must be established that the death occurred within a fixed time limit in order to claim under the policy.
   C. Where the machine is switched off this could lead to claims for compensation for negligence by professional staff especially where organs are used for transplantation.

Figure 16.3 Causes of action where the time of death has considerable significance.

to the face and head. On 17 February 1908, by which time the bruises inflicted on the first two occasions had disappeared, the child was admitted to hospital and later died. The medical evidence showed that the fracture was the main cause of death. In his summing up, the trial judge told the jury that they should convict if they were satisfied that the death was caused by the violence of 13 November 1906 or accelerated by that of 29 December 1907. Dyson was convicted. On appeal it was held that the conviction should be quashed on the ground that no person can be convicted of murder unless the death occurred within a year and a day after the injury was inflicted and therefore the judge's summing up amounted to a misdirection (*R. v. Dyson* 1908 2 KB 454).

A recent case applied this 'year and a day' principle to the coroner's court. The passage of more than one year and a day between the act of the deceased, which caused his death, and his death itself, precluded a coroner from giving a verdict that the deceased had killed himself (*R. v. Coroner for Inner West London ex parte De Luca, The Times* 9 April 1988). A recommendation has been made by the Law Commission (1994) that the time limit in the definition of murder should be ended.

Cause of death

There must be a causal link between the act of violence and the death of the patient. Did the act of violence cause the death or was it caused by the switching off of the ventilator? If the latter, is the doctor criminally responsible for the death?

CASE 16.2 CAUSAL LINK

Malcherek was convicted of the murder of a victim of assault who had been connected to a life support machine which had been disconnected by medical practitioners. He was sentenced to life imprisonment. In a similar case, Steel was also convicted and sentenced to life imprisonment. Malcherek appealed against this decision and Steel applied for leave to put in further medical evidence as to the sufficiency and adequacy of tests by the doctors to determine brain death. They were both effectively challenging that there was causal link between the assaults and the deaths of the victims. The judge in each case had withdrawn the issue of causation from the jury (*R. v. Malcherek*; *R. v. Steel* CA 1981 2 All ER 422).

The Court of Appeal held that in each case it is clear that the initial assault was the cause of the grave head injuries in the one case and of the massive abdominal haemorrhage in the other. In each case the initial assault was the reason for the medical treatment being necessary. In each case the medical treatment given was normal and conventional. The court looked in detail at the tests carried out by the doctors and stated: 'It is not part of the task of this court to inquire whether the criteria, the royal colleges' confirmatory tests, are a satisfactory code of practice. It is not part of the task of this

A. *The unconscious dying patient*
1. The machine can be switched off if the patient is brain dead.
2. If the patient can breathe without it but weakly, then the decision to put the patient back on the machine depends on the medical prognosis. If treatment is futile then there is unlikely to be an obligation to put the patient back on again.
3. Where the patient can breathe on his own and the respirator is not needed, then the machine can be switched off. If the patient needs to have assistance again and the prognosis is hopeless, then there is unlikely to be a legal obligation to reconnect the respirator.

B. *The chronically dependent patient such as a polio victim*
1. If the patient requests discontinuation, as the law stands at present, it would be a criminal offence for anyone else to disconnect it. See the Suicide Act in Fig. 16.5. Euthanasia is not recognised in English law.
2. If the machine is turned off against the wishes of the patient this would of course be murder.

C. *Temporarily dependent emergency patient*
If the ultimate prognosis is a recovery and improvement, then switching off the machine would be murder. However, if the ultimate prognosis is extremely poor and hopeless, then the considerations in A1 above would apply.

Figure 16.4 Switching off a life support machine.

court to decide whether the doctors were, in either of these two cases, justified in omitting one or more of the so called "confirmatory tests". The doctors are not on trial: the applicant and the appellant were.' The Court of Appeal concluded that all the evidence suggested that at the time of death the original wound or injury was a continuing, operating and, indeed, substantial cause of death. The fact that the victim's life support treatment had been discontinued did not break the chain of causation between the initial injury and death. The issue of causation had therefore properly been withdrawn from the jury. The convictions were confirmed.

The legality of switching machines off

An article by Ian Kennedy (*Criminal Law Report*, 1977, page 443) describes three different circumstances where a professional might be concerned about the legality of switching off a life support machine. These are set out in Fig. 16.4. He also makes the point that there should be no difference in law between the legality of switching on the machine and of switching it off. The law does not expect a doctor to place every dying patient on a life support machine, only where there is a hope of recovery and the facilities exist.

Persistent vegetative state

CASE 16.3 ENDING TUBE FEEDING

Tony Bland was crushed in the Hillsborough football tragedy and for three and a half years was in a persistent vegetative state, being artificially fed but breathing

unaided. He could not see, hear, taste, smell, speak or communicate in any way.
The Trust, in agreement with the parents, applied for the withdrawal of nasal-
gastric tube feeding. The House of Lords held that medical treatment, including
artificial feeding, could be withdrawn from a patient in a persistent vegetative
state, if this was in the patient's best interests and it did not amount to a criminal act (*Airedale NHS Trust* v. *Bland* 1993 1 All ER 821).

Another application to the courts in similar circumstances was made in January 1994
in respect of a patient in Bristol (*Frenchay NHS Trust* v. *S.* TLR 19 January 1994 CA).
A court declaration is required in such circumstances, but the right to end treatment
is still subject to controversy.

Not for resuscitation

Obviously, in intensive care units it is usually the consultant who will decide if a ventilator is to be turned on or off. However, it is sometimes the practice for doctors to mark
the patient's notes 'NFR' and the nurse is then in a quandary as to what she should do.
She may feel that she is in an impossible, no-win situation: if she does not initiate resuscitation procedures following a collapse, then she could possibly be criticised by relatives or even face criminal charges; if, on the other hand, she ignores the letters 'NFR'
and starts resuscitation procedures, then she could be criticised by the medical staff and
face disciplinary proceedings. It is vital in these circumstances that the nurse is involved
in the discussions over the patient's prognosis so that she can understand the likely
outcome and the reasons for the doctor's decision. If she is in any doubt she should seek
expert advice and always err on the side of saving life. Unfortunately, the nurse is sometimes informed orally of the doctor's wishes, which are not written down, and this places
the nurse in an even more vulnerable situation.

Relatives and the treatment of the patient

SITUATION 16.1 THE RELATIVES SAY 'NO'

Katy Brown was 85 and just recovering from a particularly serious hiatus hernia
operation. She was very weak and there was considerable likelihood that she
would not survive. The relatives discussed her case with the doctors and asked
that in the possible event of a collapse she should not be resuscitated since they
did not want her to continue as an invalid and felt sure that this is what Katy
would have wished. What is the doctor's position?

Ultimately, the relatives, even a spouse, have no right in law to refuse consent to any
life-saving treatment required by the patient. Their motives can never be certain: perhaps
they have designs on the patient's property. The sole criterion which will determine whether
treatment can proceed is the medical prognosis. In this country we do not yet recognise

the legality of a 'living will' which is in use in some states of the USA. This document, signed and witnessed under strict procedures, enables the patient to state what he wishes to happen to him in the event of his requiring resuscitation, and the doctor can rely on this document as a defence in any action for failure to treat the patient. This procedure is not recognised by statute but is recognised by the common law. The only criterion which can determine whether or not treatment should proceed is the ultimate prognosis of the patient unless the patient has clearly expressed his views in advance. Obviously, the relatives' views should be made known to the doctor but they should not be the deciding factor. The Law Commission (Report 129, 1993) has recommended legislation covering advance directives. These recommendations were supported by the House of Lords Select Committee on Medical Ethics (1994) and legislation is awaited.

Refusal of treatment by the patient

Since 1961 suicide has not been a crime (see Fig. 16.5).

The position is clear for professional staff. Even though they sympathise with a patient's wish to die, they are prohibited by the criminal law in taking any steps or giving any advice to the patient to help him carry out this wish. Where a patient is clearly refusing medication because of this desire, it is essential for staff to record detailed accounts of the patient's attitude, his level of competence, the advice given to him, and, preferably, where the patient takes his own discharge contrary to professional advice, to obtain the patient's signature to that effect.

Euthanasia is not legally recognised in this country. The question is hotly debated among doctors, nurses, and others. It is accepted that in practice the decisions which have to be made in special care baby units and in intensive care or renal dialysis units, or over transplants, effectively means that those not selected for treatment may eventually die. This is, however, a very different matter from taking an action which will bring about or assist in bringing about another person's death. The House of Lords Select Committee on Medical Ethics (1994) did not make any proposals to change the law that makes euthanasia illegal.

Section 1 of the 1961 Suicide Act states that 'the rule of law whereby it is a crime for a person to commit suicide is hereby abrogated'. This, coupled with the right for a person to consent to treatment, means that it is possible for a seriously ill person to refuse consent to, say, antibiotics and staff have to accept that refusal. Only where there is a doubt over the person's mental competence to refuse treatment could the medication be given out of necessity to save the person's life (see the chapter in Part I on consent to treatment). While it is no longer a crime for a person to decide upon and bring about their own death, it is still, however, a crime for anyone to aid and abet in the suicide of another.

Section 2(1) states: 'A person who aids, abets, counsels or procures the suicide of another or an attempt by another to commit suicide, shall be liable on conviction on indictment to imprisonment.' (Up to 14 years.)

Figure 16.5 Suicide Act 1961.

SITUATION 16.2 TO LET GO

Harry Judd, aged 84 years, had told his daughter that if he became ill and suffered a cardiac arrest, he did not want to be resuscitated. His wife had died two years before and he had become increasingly depressed and frail with failing eyesight caused by his diabetes. He was still managing to cope on his own with a home help, but it was becoming more and more of a struggle. One day the home help found him in a coma and he was rushed into hospital. He remained seriously ill for several days and then slowly improved. His consultant physician, Dr Jones, discussed Harry's prognosis with his daughter and son-in-law. It appeared unlikely that he would be able to manage on his own. The daughter reported Harry's views about not being resuscitated. The next evening Harry suffered a cardiac arrest. The staff nurse summoned Dr Jones, who was unwilling to use resuscitative machinery. Is he obliged to do so?

From the above discussion it will be evident that there is no need provided it is absolutely clear that Harry's prognosis is hopeless. If there is any chance that Harry could recover, then Dr Jones's duty would require him to resuscitate him. Legislation on Advance Directives would clarify the situation.

Organ transplantation

SITUATION 16.3 A TRANSPLANT OPPORTUNITY?

A youth of 23 years is knocked down in a road traffic accident. He has no identification on him and appears to be unaccompanied. He is brought into hospital by the ambulance crew and is resuscitated. He is maintained on the ventilator but the prognosis is poor. Transplant teams are anxious to remove his lungs, heart, kidneys and liver and an ophthalmologist would like to make use of his eyes. The police are asked to notify the relatives as soon as possible. They are advised by the surgeon that the organs should be removed within half an hour of death. The youth is kept on a positive pressure ventilator. Can his organs be used for transplant on diagnosis of death before the relatives are contacted? What difference would it make if he was found to be carrying a donor card?

The law covering these circumstances is the Human Tissue Act 1961 (see Fig. 16.6). In addition, the case would automatically become a coroner's case because death occurred following an accident. The coroner's consent would therefore be required for any use of the organs (see Chapter 29).

There is no definition of what is considered to be 'such reasonable enquiry as may be practicable'. It could be argued that if after a day or so there is still no identification of the deceased, then the organs could be taken with the approval of the coroner. If, on the other hand, the deceased is identified and the parents, sister or indeed any relative expresses an objection to the organs being used, then this will effectively prevent their use. 'Any surviving relative' may in fact cover a very wide field.

What if the youth is carrying a donor card? (See Fig. 16.7.) Where a card is present the relatives have no right of veto under the Act unless of course they can prove that the deceased had changed his mind; not an easy task where he is still carrying the card. However, it would be rare in practice for the hospital management to give consent to the removal of the organs if the relatives objected. It would, of course, still be necessary for the coroner's consent to be obtained.

There has been a recent debate over the need to increase the number of organs available for transplant. One suggestion is that there should be an opting-out system, rather than an opting-in one, i.e. you carry a card if you do not want your body used for transplant purposes, and the absence of a card implies an agreement to the organs being transplanted. This suggestion has not met with wide acceptance. An alternative suggestion is that there should be a legal duty for the professionals to request an organ transplant from the relatives of the deceased or prospective deceased. This is described as the required request system. It has the advantage of removing some of the embarrassment that professionals feel when they have to broach the matter with relatives. They are able to say 'I hate having to ask you this, but I have no option as it is my legal duty to do so; would you agree to the possibility of X's organs being used for transplant?' It is thought that such a statutory request would lead to more organs being forthcoming without the

---

Under Section 1(2) of the Human Tissue Act the person lawfully in charge of the body of a deceased person may authorise the removal of any part from the body for use for the said purposes (therapeutic, or medical education, or research) if having made such reasonable enquiry as may be practicable, he has no reason to believe: (a) that the deceased had expressed an objection to his body being so dealt with after his death, and had not withdrawn it: or (b) that the surviving spouse or any surviving relative of the deceased objects to the body being so dealt with.

Figure 16.6 Donation of organs where there is no consent.

Under Section 1(1) of the Human Tissue Act: If any person, either in writing at any time or orally in the presence of two or more witnesses during his last illness, had expressed a request that his body or any specified part of his body be used after his death for therapeutic purposes, or for the purposes of medical education, or research, the person lawfully in possession of his body after his death may, unless he has reason to believe that the request was subsequently withdrawn, authorise the removal from the body of any part or, as the case may be, the specified part, for use in accordance with the request.

The presence of the donor card will count as evidence that the deceased agreed to the use of his body. The card may constitute a general consent or it may be specific. Under this section the person lawfully in charge of the body does not have to carry out reasonable enquiries to ascertain if the deceased had changed his mind. All that is necessary is that he has no reason to believe that the request was withdrawn. In practice, the same reasonable enquiries will be made whether or not the donor was carrying a card.

Figure 16.7 Donation of organs where the deceased has consented.

necessity for a change in the Human Tissue Act itself. The relatives would still have the freedom to refuse but they would also have the opportunity to agree.

Other provisions of the Act require the parts of the body to be taken by a registered medical practitioner who must have satisfied himself by personal examination that life is extinct. The procedure requires death to be certified also by a doctor who is not involved with the transplant team.

There is no statutory definition of the person lawfully in possession of the body. This would normally be the next of kin or occupier where the relative died at home, and the hospital manager where the person died in hospital or was brought in dead. The Act specifically prohibits those entrusted with the body for the purposes of interment or cremation from giving authority for the removal of any parts.

The Human Organ Transplant Act 1989 regulates the use of human organs between living persons. Section 1, prohibiting the buying, selling or advertising of human organs, came into force on 27 July 1989. The definition of organs (Section 7 (2)) covers any part of the human body, which if wholly removed cannot be replicated by the body. Bone marrow transplants or blood donors are therefore excluded from the Act. Restrictions are placed upon transplants between those who are not genetically related (Section 2). Regulations have been passed under the Act: Human Organ Transplant (Unrelated Persons) Regulation 1989/2480, Human Organ Transplants (Establishment of Relationship) Regulation 1989/2017 and the Human Organ Transplants (Supply of Information) Regulation 1989/2108. Further guidance is provided in circular HC(90)7. Health authorities and Trusts can be liable for any offences on their premises (Section 4 of the 1989 Act).

An Unrelated Live Transplant Regulatory Authority (ULTRA) has been set up and all proposals for transplants between persons who are not genetically related must be referred to it. Central records are maintained by the UK Transplant Support Services Authority, Southmead Road, Bristol, BS10 5ND (Department HOT A).

Other major concerns of relevance to the intensive care nurse include definition of her extended role, for example she may be placed in a situation where she is asked to undertake work that she has not been trained to do. In addition she is also faced with problems over resources and staffing, e.g. where do I stand if I have to leave a patient to attend to another? Both these issues are considered in Chapter 4 and the same basic principles which are discussed there apply to the intensive care nurse. Other aspects relating to death are considered in Chapter 29.

Questions and exercises

1 What are the main provisions of our present laws relating to consent to donate organs? What are the advantages and disadvantages of retaining the present system?
2 What is meant by brain death? What problems arise from recognising this as opposed to the traditional definition of death?
3 An intensive care nurse often has to undertake tasks which are regarded as expanded-role duties. What safeguards should exist before the nurse undertakes such duties? (See also Chapter 4.)

4 Over a period of two weeks list the legal problems that you have encountered in your work in an intensive care unit and refresh your memory of the basic principles.

5 Relatives often have very fixed views on the outcome they wish for the seriously ill patient. Prepare a short paper outlining the basic principles of consent which apply in order to clarify the situation for relatives.

6 A patient on positive pressure ventilation asks you to assist him in discontinuing his treatment. What is the legal position?

7 Look back over the records that you have made on a patient who was in hospital several weeks before. If you were now to be challenged on any aspect of your care in that case, how useful and comprehensive would your notes be? Are there any obvious gaps on which you should have kept a record?

17   Theatre nursing and the recovery ward

Like the ward nurse, the theatre nurse is constantly concerned with the possibility of litigation and also with the problems of her role in relation to the surgeons and the anaesthetists. These areas and the others to be covered in this chapter are set out in Fig. 17.1. Another area which is often of particular concern to the theatre nurse is the possibility of a patient dying on the table or shortly after the operation. This would automatically have to be reported to the coroner. The rules relating to this situation and the nature of the inquest are considered in Chapter 29. Another concern for theatre staff when an aborted foetus shows signs of life is considered in Chapter 15.

Civil liability procedures and practices in theatre

Professional liability

SITUATION 17.1 LOST SWAB

Staff Nurse French was the scrub nurse for a hernia operation performed by a registrar. They were running late and still had two patients left on the morning list. The afternoon list was due to start in ten minutes. Just before the registrar sutured the patient's wound he asked for a swab count. Staff Nurse French checked the thirty-four used swabs, which had been hung on the rack, and six unused swabs and two unopened packs with the operating department assistant. She confirmed that those were the only ones in use and the patient was sewn up. A few days later, just before the patient would normally have been discharged he reported violent pains and became seriously ill. It was decided to X-ray the patient prior to returning him to theatre. The X-ray showed up a swab. The relatives of the patient were told what had happened and they made it clear that they would seek compensation. An internal investigation was commenced to see if the cause of this error could be found. The conclusions were that there was an extra swab in one of the packs and this had not been spotted when the staff nurse opened and counted them. A dispute then ensued between the registrar and the staff nurse over liability for the incident. The staff nurse claimed that as she had checked the swabs in front of the registrar, he should accept responsibility for it; the registrar stated that as the staff nurse had clearly counted wrongly, it was entirely her responsibility and, in addition, the unscrubbed runner nurse had made a second check.

In a dispute like this the patient would be able to argue that this is a case of *res ipsa loquitur* and the burden should pass to the NHS Trust to show that they were not negligent. (This is discussed in Chapter 6.) It will be recalled from the case of *Wilsher* v. *Essex Area Health Authority* that the courts do not accept any concept of team liability (see page 43). The NHS Trust itself could be directly liable and in addition each individual professional could be liable for what he personally did or failed to do and would be judged according to the standards expected of them, but the employer would accept vicarious liability.

The actual proportion of responsibility in a case like the above would obviously depend on the actual facts of what went wrong. When the swabs were unpacked, were they properly checked to ensure that none were stuck together? What was the accepted approved practice that the doctor and the nurse should have followed? Were there any justifiable reasons why this need not have been followed? In addition, there might be some liability on the part of the manufacturer as well. Since 1 January 1990 health

---

1. Civil liability procedures and practice
   (a) professional liability;
   (b) policies and practices.
2. Theatre nurse and the scope of professional practice.
3. Accidents in the theatre.
4. Consent in the theatre
   (a) after premedication;
   (b) consent refused.
5. Drugs and the operating department practitioner.
6. Recovery room nursing.

Figure 17.1 Issues covered in Chapter 17.

authorities have accepted responsibility for the negligence of doctors and dentists whilst acting in course of employment. This also applies to NHS Trusts (see page 69). It is therefore less important how liability between nurse and doctor is shared, since the compensation will be paid to the patient by the employer. It is important, however, to allocate responsibilities through procedures and policies to ensure that similar harm does not occur again. It is essential that procedures are in place to prevent such incidents arising.

There have been some very rare cases where, although the scrub nurse points out that a swab is unaccounted for, the surgeon still proceeds with stitching up the patient. This may be justifiable in particular cases if the patient's condition is deteriorating and there is a greater risk in keeping him under the anaesthetic than in taking the risk of the swab still being inside him. It would be very different if the surgeon was simply ignoring the nurse's count without any justification.

The proportion of liability between nurse and surgeon thus depends entirely on the individual facts of the case.

Policies and practices

The situation illustrates the importance of having clear policies and codes of practice as to the responsibility of each person in theatre, so that there is no overlap. In a situation where the patient is unable to correct any wrong assumptions it is essential that these codes cover every possible danger. The responsibility for the identification of the patient, the nature of the operation to be performed, including the identification of the part of the body or limb to be operated upon, must all be clearly allocated so that there can be no errors. Many of these procedures may be repeats of checks already made at ward level but they cannot be omitted on that account in theatre. If any such cases came to court the judge would expect evidence on what the procedure should have been and what in fact took place.

Allergies not marked on notes.
Units of blood not checked.
Nerves over bony surfaces damaged.
Eyes exposed to harm.
Sharp and powered tools used dangerously.
Faulty gauges on pneumatic cuffs, faulty monitors.
Tourniquets left on too long and skin necrosis beneath tourniquet cuffs.
Spirit solutions used with cautery.
Hot instruments and hot water in tubing.
Water mattresses overheating.
Diathermy burns.
Uninsulated electrodes.
Misplaced footswitch.
Faulty alarms and faulty equipment.

Figure 17.2 Potential hazards in the operating theatre.

There are many implications for theatre nurses: they should clearly be familiar with the procedures and implement them, resisting any unjustifiable short cuts whatever the pressure. In addition, their records should be detailed and meaningful so that if there is a query about the care in the theatre, then they are able to refer to a comprehensive account of what took place. Booklets produced by the defence societies, the Royal College of Nursing and the National Association of Theatre Nurses on theatre safeguards cover procedures for admission, labelling and ward procedure, lost swabs and instruments, and other causes of potential hazards (see Fig. 17.2).

The theatre nurse and the scope of professional practice

There is little uniformity in the tasks which nurses are expected to perform in theatre. The duties of a scrub nurse can depend upon the personal preferences of an individual surgeon and on whether the hospital is a teaching hospital. Anaesthetic nurses may also have a variety of duties: for example, in some theatres they may be expected to draw up the drugs in syringes for the anaesthetist to check; in others the anaesthetist might do this himself. The nurse's role will also depend on the existence of and the duties performed by the operating department practitioner. Some of the tasks she performs will be regarded as expanded-role duties in which she might have been trained on a post-registration training course.

In some hospitals the theatre nurse might be asked to act as the surgeon's assistant. What is her position? Should she refuse on the grounds that she has not been trained to fulfil this role? What if this request comes at night where there is only a registrar on his own and it is an emergency case? The basic principle is that, whatever duties she is called upon to perform, she should undertake no work that she is not competent to undertake. Reference should be made to the booklet prepared by the National Association of Theatre Nurses (see Recommended Further Reading).

In an emergency situation when the harm to the patient of her acting is outweighed by the harm to the patient of her not acting, the balance might be in favour of her acting as assistant (but these occasions are likely to be rare).

To refuse to perform certain tasks is not pleasant for the nurse but it is her duty both in civil law and also as part of the rules of her profession. Only in this way can the safety of the patient be ensured. If such situations arise where the nurse is expected to undertake tasks for which she is not trained this must ultimately be referred to nurse management. Unfortunately, they are often not notified of such problems as soon as they arise and in their ignorance cannot take appropriate action.

Accidents in the theatre

Unfortunately, there can be accidents in the theatre and an incident book should be kept to record such mishaps. There may be opposition from some medical staff over the necessity to record untoward incidents but the nurse has a duty to ensure that records are maintained on incidents which cause harm: diathermy burns, an unintentional cut, and the more serious incidents such as operating on the wrong side of the patient or even on the wrong patient. A policy of disclosure to the patient should be encouraged. However, it is not for the nurse to notify the patient; this is the consultant's duty.

Consent in the theatre

Some particular problems arise in relation to consent in the theatre. One is the failure of ward staff to ensure that the appropriate forms have been filled in before the patient is sent to theatre. Consider the following situation.

Consent after premedication

SITUATION 17.2 VALIDITY OF CONSENT

Paula Green was admitted to hospital for a biopsy of the breast. It was intended that, should there be any malignancy, then a mastectomy would be carried out immediately. Paula was given the premedication by the ward staff and brought to theatre. When the theatre sister was checking through the records she noticed that there was no consent form. The anaesthetist, who had begun to prepare Paula for the operation, said that he had seen Paula on the ward the previous day and knew there was no doubt that she wanted this to be carried out and that she might still be able to put her signature to a form. The theatre sister was very unhappy about this. The surgical registrar then apologised and said that he had spoken to Paula about the operation and that she knew the implications of it. However, when he had visited the ward he had run out of consent forms. He had intended returning to the ward to get Paula's signature but had been distracted and had completely forgotten about it. He saw no reason not to proceed with the operation and argued that Paula would be far more upset if the operation did not proceed and she returned to the ward without it than for the operation to go ahead without her signature. What should the theatre sister do?

It will be recalled from the discussion on consent to treatment in Chapter 7 that consent can be given in a variety of forms: in writing, by word of mouth, by implication. These are all equally valid in law. It could be argued, therefore, that the fact that Paula had given her consent to the registrar means that that can be relied upon and therefore the operation can proceed. However, consent in writing is infinitely superior as a form of evidence. Imagine that Paula's operation proceeded. When the biopsy was analysed a malignancy was discovered and the surgeon therefore proceeded with a mastectomy. On recovery, however, Paula denied that she had any idea that this was a likely possibility and had she known she would have preferred to have had radiotherapy. This possibility cannot be discounted and in such a situation it would be far better for Paula to return to the ward and, when the premedication has worn off, to agree in writing that the operation can proceed. One can imagine certain circumstances where there would be such considerable risks in postponing the operation that on balance the advantages to the patient are in favour of proceeding rather than returning the patient to the ward. In such cases there could be an action for negligence if harm were caused by this delay. However, these would be unusual circumstances. In general, it would be wiser to ensure that the patient has signed a consent form and has had all the risks and implications explained to her. Sending the patient back to the ward, although undoubtedly leading to a furious complaint from a rightly indignant patient, has several long-term advantages: the ward staff will be less likely to give the patient a premedication before checking whether the consent forms have been signed and the doctors will know that they cannot get by with a casual approach to patients' rights.

A more difficult situation which occasionally occurs is where the patient himself, after premedication and prior to the general anaesthetic, asks the surgeon if something else could be 'sorted out', e.g. an ingrowing toe nail; a cyst, etc. What is the surgeon to do? It would seem churlish for him to say 'No. I must have your consent in writing for that and since you have been premedicated you are incapable of giving a valid consent.' On the other hand, if he agrees to proceed and undertakes the additional task and there are some unforeseen or unmentioned side-effects, then the surgeon could be in serious difficulties.

Consent refused

SITUATION 17.3 WHAT THE EYES DON'T SEE ..._____

Take the situation of an adult Jehovah's Witness patient who makes it clear that he will only agree to a particular operation on the understanding that he will not be given blood (see Fig. 7.2). The surgeon agrees to operate on that basis but does intend that, if blood is needed, the patient will be given it anyway and will be none the wiser. The operation proceeds. The patient begins to haemorrhage and the surgeon instructs that blood should be given. Somehow the patient discovers what has happened and sues the NHS Trust for trespass to the person.

There has to my knowledge never been such a case. It is not clear how the judge would tackle it. On the one hand, he could say that there has quite clearly been a trespass to the person since the patient was given blood contrary to his express instructions and any deliberate intention to mislead the patient by the surgeon was a professional breach. The patient should therefore be entitled to substantial damages. Alternatively, the judge could take the view that although there is in theory a trespass to the person, if there had not been one the patient would not now be standing before the court suing the health authority. Therefore only nominal damages should be awarded and, perhaps more significantly these days, there would be no award for costs. To avoid the possibility of court action a surgeon could advise that he is not prepared to operate with restrictions upon his discretion and if the patient refused to give an unrestricted consent then he would not be operated upon. (Note the case of *Malette* v. *Shulman* where blood was given to an unconscious card-carrying patient (see page 101).

Other restrictions which the patient may also wish to impose upon the surgeons are often refused; thus it should be made clear that the operation will not be performed by a particular surgeon or that there will be a specified anaesthetist or that any particular procedure will be followed.

Even though the patient has consented to a particular operation and is therefore prevented from bringing an action for trespass to the person, it might well be that when things go wrong the patient complains that he has not been informed of these possibilities and side-effects and that, had he known, he would not have gone ahead with it. This possibility is discussed in connection with the Sidaway case (see Chapter 7).

One important point must be emphasised, however. The patient, in signing the consent form, is consenting to an action which without his consent would count as a trespass to his person. He is also consenting to undergo the risks of those unforeseen chances which, no matter how much care is taken, can still occur. He is not consenting to negligence nor to the possibility that harm could occur to him because a nurse or doctor is careless, or because the procedures are not followed correctly or inadequate precautions are taken to ensure that he will be safe.

Sometimes it might be pointed out to the patient that a particular operation is experimental, and he might expressly agree to undergo the additional risk of this unknown procedure but he still does not consent to the possibility of a failure to follow approved accepted practice.

Other difficulties in relation to consent to operations are considered in the sections relating to paediatric nursing, gynaecology (sterilisations), psychiatric nursing, and accident and emergency departments.

There have recently been successful claims by patients who have brought action on the grounds that whilst under the anaesthetic they were conscious of activities around them and suffered agonising pain but were unable to move. A report in the journal of the Royal College of Anaesthetists (see *The Sunday Times*, 31 July 1994) on a survey of doctors suggests that at least 7,750 patients are conscious during operations each year. Of these about 250 feel their bodies being opened and internal organs manipulated by doctors. In 1985 £15,000 was awarded to Margaret Acters from Wigan. Clearly nurses should be vigilant for any sign that the patient is not properly anaesthetised.

Drugs and the operating department practitioner

The profession of operating department practitioner, separate from the nursing profession, is a relatively new phenomenon still with many areas of responsibility and job description to be clarified. There is still a great diversity across the country over the role of the operating department practitioner *vis-à-vis* the nurse and the anaesthetist. One of the most frequently debated issues is whether the operating department practitioner is allowed by current law to hold the keys to the Controlled Drugs cupboard. Practice varies. In some hospital theatres the theatre sister has jealously guarded control over the keys: in other hospitals the operating department practitioner holds the keys and this is often accompanied by much wider duties in relation to the anaesthetist. The legal niceties have been debated in an article (*Technic*, March 1987) and the conclusions reached were that if the provisions of the Misuse of Drugs Act are given a wide definition, then the operating department practitioner can be a key holder in carrying out tasks under the overall responsibility of one of the named professions in the Act. If, on the other hand, the Act is given a restricted interpretation, then the control of the keys, and therefore the possession of the drugs, must remain with the professions named in the Act. There is no doubt that the situation is unsatisfactory and can only be resolved by either a court case on the point or by more specific legislation.

Recovery room nursing

This is often under the control of the consultant anaesthetist. The nurses should have extended-role training for their tasks since it is essential that they should have the expertise and knowledge to detect possible adverse side-effects resulting from the anaesthetic drugs. They must be trained to act speedily in an emergency and staffing ratios assume even greater importance than elsewhere in the hospital. It is essential that what they are or are not qualified to do is expressly spelt out.

Another interesting facet of the law in this area is the fact that nurses may hear confidential information from the semi-conscious patient which would come under the principles discussed in Chapter 8. Similarly, it is essential that the nurses do not discuss the patient or any other patient in front of any of the semi-conscious patients in the recovery room since there are many accounts of patients who have overheard what staff have said and have been very upset by this. The nurse's duty of care obviously includes the duty of foreseeing what could harm a patient in this context and taking reasonable precautions to prevent that occurring.

Questions and exercises

1 How do the provisions of the Health and Safety at Work Act (see Chapter 12) affect the theatre manager?
2 Procedures do not provide the solution to every eventuality. In what circumstances do you consider a nurse would be justified in deviating from a specified procedure (see Chapter 3)?
3 How do the basic principles of consent to treatment affect the work of the theatre nurse?
4 How do the principles relating to the scope of professional practice affect the theatre nurse (see Chapter 4)?
5 Obtain a copy of the incident book which is kept in the theatre in which you work and consider how some of these incidents could have been avoided.

18 Nurse educator and researcher

It might surprise some people that a chapter is devoted to the legal aspects involved in teaching and research, but tutors have recently been involved in litigation both in respect of what they have taught, how it was taught and when. In addition the contract of employment for the learner is different from that of the ordinary employee and nurse tutors should be familiar with the differences and implications. Of course they are also concerned with all the general aspects of the law covered in the first part: not only in relation to their own position but also because they might have to teach some of it! The topics to be considered in this chapter are set out in Fig. 18.1.

Record-keeping by teachers

SITUATION 18.1 INSTRUCTION IN LIFTING – THE EVIDENCE_____

Beryl Sharp, a nurse tutor, received a request from her hospital administrator to provide her with the information she had given to a staff nurse on a lifting course. It appeared that this staff nurse had sustained a serious back injury at work and was suing the NHS Trust for a breach in its direct liability to take care of her safety. The claim was likely to amount to a considerable sum since the prognosis was poor and she was unlikely to be able to return to work in the foreseeable future. The NHS Trust was defending the claim on the grounds that the ward was adequately staffed and that the staff nurse had been given instruction in lifting. It now required evidence of that fact from Beryl. Fortunately, Beryl was a hoarder – a fact frequently greeted with derision by her colleagues. She never threw anything out and was able to go through her records and find the series of seminars which had been organised on lifting. She had both the dates and the names of participants including the names of those who had failed to attend. She had not given the seminar herself: a physiotherapist had done the teaching. Beryl had simply organised it as part of her work as an organiser for continuing education. She checked her records and could find no record that the particular staff nurse had attended. In fact she was able to see that she was included in the list of those who were supposed to attend but was not present at a seminar and that 'sick' had been written against her name. There was no evidence that she had been invited to attend a subsequent seminar, although another three were held in the following months.

One can imagine that this information would disappoint the hospital administrator in providing information to defend the staff nurse's claim. However, it is not completely fatal to any defence of the claim since it might well be that the staff nurse had received appropriate training in lifting during her basic training. In addition, there may be some element of contributory negligence in that the staff nurse herself failed to ensure that she was included on another seminar once she had returned from sick leave.

Such a request must worry nurse tutors and give rise to many further questions. How long must my records be kept? What sort of detail do I need to keep? It will be recalled from the section in Chapter 6 dealing with the time limits for bringing a court action that in a case of negligence the action must be brought within three years of the negligent incident unless the victim is under 18 years old, under a disability or in cases where the relevant information was not available within the three-year period. A period of

---

1. Record-keeping by teachers.
2. Liability for instructing others.
3. Hearing about unsound practices.
4. Employment law
   (a) employees – yet students, fixed-term contracts;
   (b) dismissal on grounds of absenteeism and course failure;
   (c) clinical placements.
5. Legal aspects of research
   (a) control of a research programme;
   (b) confidentiality;
   (c) consent;
   (d) liability for volunteers in research;
   (e) health and safety of the researcher.

Figure 18.1 Issues covered in Chapter 18.

(a) the names of those who should have attended the sessions;
(b) the names of those who did attend;
(c) times and dates of the sessions;
(d) the content of the sessions and who did the teaching;
(e) the grades of achievement where there was any assessment.

Records are of course kept of the content, standard, and timetable of learners and it is not difficult to extend this to the post-basic courses.

Figure 18.2 Information which should be kept by the nurse tutor.

retention of seven years is therefore likely to cover most eventualities. In addition it could be argued that in those areas where regular retraining and revision study days are necessary, if several years have elapsed since the opportunity to go on to a course then the authority is at fault in not providing a revision course. The information which should be retained is set out in Fig. 18.2.

Liability for instructing others

It will be recalled from the general law section that there is also a duty of care owed by those who are instructing others so that if harm occurs as a result of negligent instruction the instructor can be sued by the person who has suffered the harm. This applies not just to the classroom situation but to all those situations where advice is given in circumstances where the person receiving it can be expected to act upon it. If the advice has been given negligently, then an action in negligence for breach of a duty of care may follow.

SITUATION 18.2 NEGLIGENT INSTRUCTIONS

Beryl Sharp acted as the course tutor on some of the post-basic courses. She ran one course, that of training nurses in the adding of drugs to IVs and failed to mention that the first dose of the drug to be added to the IV should always be given by a doctor. One of the staff nurses who had been at that session and had been deemed competent to give IV drugs returned to the ward and was instructed that a patient who was already on an intravenous drip had been written up for an IV drug. At the appropriate time the staff nurse prepared the drug, checked it with another nurse, and added it to the drip according to the instructions she had been taught on the course. The patient reacted violently against the drug and a doctor was summoned urgently. An inquiry was then held to find out why the first dose of this drug had been administered by a nurse and not by a doctor. It was the local policy for the doctor to administer the first dose of a drug intravenously. It then emerged that Beryl Sharp had failed to point out this requirement in her teaching on the course.

In this situation the victim is a patient. In other cases the victim could be the person who received the negligent information or advice. Where a patient is the victim the claim is relatively simple: he would show that he has suffered harm as a result of a negligent act of an employee acting in course of employment and therefore that the employer is vicariously liable for the harm. Alternatively, the individual employee could be sued as personally liable for the harm. In such a case the employee may bring her own action against the tutor who was negligent in the instructions that she gave. In this type of action the following facts would have to be shown:

1. A duty of care was owed by instructor to the instructee.
2. There was a breach of this duty since the instructions were given negligently.
3. As a foreseeable consequence of this breach the person has suffered harm (this might be personal injury but it could also include financial loss or loss or damage to property).

Hearing about unsound practices

It is not unknown for tutors in the school of nursing to discover from their learners about staff who are guilty of unacceptable practices or ill-treatment of patients. What should the nurse tutor do? Should she investigate the allegation and, if challenged, say why? Should she keep her source secret? Should she report her suspicions to nurse management? Obviously, there can be no single answer since much depends upon the circumstances. If, for example, the learner has witnessed ill-treatment of a patient by a member of staff on a ward, then she should be encouraged to write a statement setting out exactly what she has seen and the nurse tutor should ensure that appropriate action is taken by nurse management, at the same time protecting the learner from any victimisation. On the other hand, if the nurse witnesses a procedure being carried out on the wards which is not in line with present-day safe practices the nurse tutor could arrange appropriate revision courses with the in-service training officer colleagues.

Conflicts could also arise where the school has been teaching learners the basic principles of patients' rights, e.g. consent to treatment, and as a result the learner encounters difficulties with some medical staff. There could be a come-back on the school for its teachings. Such a situation indicates the importance of very close contact between the school and the NHS Trust. The school of nursing should not, however, be seen as a policing machine for the hospital. On the other hand, it has an essential part to play in maintaining the highest standards of nursing care in cooperation with the managers. Hopefully the successful implementation of Project 2000 should promote integration of nurse clinical teaching and practice.

Employment law

Students

Learners were once both employees and students. Now with the introduction of Project 2000 learners are students, usually attached to a college of education. They are entitled to receive student bursaries, and the college negotiates an agreement with accredited hospitals for the clinical placements. In theory they are supernumerary to the workforce, but inevitably, especially in the last years of training, the hospitals and community services may exploit their services. There is no right in the learning contract for the student to insist on employment once she is qualified.

Dismissal on grounds of absenteeism or course failure

Since the Project 2000 student is not an employee, if she should be dismissed during the course on the grounds of absenteeism or failing course assessments or examinations then the student's remedy is an appeal through the appeal mechanisms of the college. These should have clear guidelines on the rules that operate in these circumstances and these procedures should be carefully followed.

Clinical placements

There is normally an agreement between colleges providing Project 2000 training and provider units for clinical placements. This agreement should cover the issue of liability for the actions of the students if they cause harm to others through negligence. Since the students are not employees of the provider unit, the latter can argue that they are not vicariously liable for the actions of students. Prior agreement between college and provider unit can resolve such issues and also cover the topic of supervision of the student and clinical instruction.

Legal aspects of research

It is increasingly expected that the nurse will undertake research. Often it is an integral part of a management course or post-registration qualification and she will be expected to prepare a dissertation or project which shows some original material and analysis. In addition, there may well be researchers coming into her department or ward: she should in either case be aware of the many legal issues which arise. Some of the basic problems relate to consent by the patient, confidentiality and disclosure of the findings, safety of the researcher, and liability for any volunteer in a drugs research programme.

Control of a research programme

SITUATION 18.3 GAGGED

Ann Jones, a ward sister, was on a management course which required her to complete a dissertation. She chose as her subject the consequences of the privatisation of cleaning services and studied one hospital where the services were

contracted out to a private firm and another hospital where direct labour ancillary staff were used. Her conclusions were that privatisation led to a lower standard of cleaning, a less hygienic environment for patients, and nursing staff
undertaking more cleaning work because the private firm only sent cleaners
to the wards for a short proportion of the day. Just before she was due to submit
the dissertation for her diploma, her divisional nursing officer heard of it and
asked to see it. She has now been told that her findings are politically unacceptable, that she cannot present it to the college, and that she must commence
a totally different topic of research.

Many points arise in a situation like this which is not entirely unbelievable. Firstly, here
the researcher is also an employee. She therefore has responsibilities to her employer.
Even if she were an independent researcher funded from outside the institution which
is the subject of the research, she might well have had to agree to a clause that the research
findings have to have the prior approval of the institution before the research results
can be published. As an employee she would be expected to obey the reasonable orders
of the employer. Is it reasonable in these circumstances for the researcher to be silenced?
The answer would depend on more detailed facts: for example, was it only because the
results were unwelcome that they are being suppressed? Was the basis of her data collec-
tion and statistical analysis sound? If there is no criticism to be made of her method
and findings other than that they are embarrassing, it could be argued that the same
principles apply here as apply in the situation discussed in Chapter 7 relating to reporting
on negligence by a colleague or some other form of unacceptable practice. Where
management itself fails to take action, i.e. when all the internal procedures for improving
the situation have been used to no avail, then it would not be considered unreasonable
to take the matter to a higher authority, initially within the organisation and, if necessary, ultimately outside, but this obviously depends on the findings and the reasons for
prohibiting publication.

Clearly, many difficulties can be avoided if the research receives the proper approval
before it is begun. In some cases this might mean obtaining the approval of an ethics
committee. Where this authority is received it would be more difficult to prohibit publication of the results purely on the grounds of embarrassment at the findings. The Department of Health issued advice on the establishment and operation of local research ethics
committees, and any research involving NHS patients, access to their records or use
of NHS premises or facilities must be referred to the LREC (HSG (91) 5).

Confidentiality

Where use is made of computerised personal information, access to it and disclosure
of it in such a form that the individuals can be identified is subject to the provisions of
the Data Protection Act (see Chapter 7). This means that if the data is not exempt from
any of the provisions of the Act, and if it is to be used in addition for research, then it
must also be registered for research use. Even where the data is not automated it would,
in most health service cases, be subject to the rules of confidentiality. This means that

it can only be disclosed in those exceptional circumstances outlined in Chapter 7. Difficulties can arise for the researcher where information is obtained which has nothing to do with the research: i.e. it is simply doing the research that has given the opportunity to gain this information.

SITUATION 18.4 SILENCE OR DISCLOSURE?_____

Sandra James, a staff nurse, was conducting a research project into the care of the post-operative surgical patient. She was interested in the rate of infection, length of stay, convalescent care and the nature of community care. Her research therefore required visits to the patients' homes. One of her patients, Glenda Mitchell, had been operated on for gallstones. She was in hospital for 7 days and was then discharged to her home. Her cohabitee had taken a few days off work to care for their 3-year-old daughter. While Sandra was visiting the home, she was surprised to see that the child was very frightened of her and was withdrawn and hostile. Sandra tried to talk to her and touch her and noticed severe bruising and pinch marks on the child's legs.

In a suspected case of non-accidental injury there would be few who would maintain that the duty of confidentiality must be maintained in preference to the interests of the child. In a case like this Sandra might try to persuade the mother to explain the child's bruising and if this were unsatisfactory, she should ensure that appropriate action is taken to protect the child: e.g. arranging for the health visitor to visit, initiating the non-accidental injury procedure or even bringing in the NSPCC. Whatever action she takes along these lines would be protected from any action for breach of confidentiality on the grounds that the public interest justified it. If the facts of this situation are changed slightly and instead of a potential NAI case a potential crime against property is suspected, e.g. stolen goods are seen in the house, many professionals would feel that their duty of confidentiality must ensure that there is no disclosure. In the case of the *In re D.* v. *NSPCC* 1977 1 All ER 589, the House of Lords stated that the NSPCC was entitled to maintain the secrecy of the names of its informants, even if they had been malicious. This decision is based on public policy because it is essential that people are prepared to report potential incidents of child abuse.

Consent

Unfortunately, not all research subjects are notified that they are to be included in a research project and their consent is not always obtained to the participation. Even in controlled drugs trials patients should be informed that they have the right to refuse to take part unless the treatment is therapeutic rather than research, in which case it could be argued that the doctor's right of therapeutic privilege (discussed by the House of Lords in the Sidaway case (see Chapter 7)) applied and there are special circumstances to justify not informing the patient of that fact.

The basic legal principles would appear to be as follows: consent to participate in research should be given freely by an adult, mentally competent person and should be preceded by sufficient relevant information about serious harmful side-effects, as approved practice would require the professional to give the patient. Where research is contemplated upon minors, the mentally handicapped, or others who lack the competence to give a valid consent, it should only proceed if it is in the subject's interests and the benefits substantially outweigh any potential harm. The question as to whether parents have the right to consent to non-therapeutic research on their children is discussed in Chapter 13. Failure to obtain consent to research or to give the necessary information could render the researcher liable to action.

Liability for volunteers in research

SITUATION 18.5 GUINEA-PIG

Benjamin Robinson was a medical student who was very short of money because he sent part of his grant home to his family each week. He heard of a research project being undertaken in the pharmaceutical department and offered his services. Because he was anxious to be accepted he failed to tell the medical officer in charge of the research that he had suffered from glandular fever as a child. He subsequently took drugs to test out the toxicity of a drug for migraine. A few weeks later he had a heart attack and died. Is there any liability for his death by the NHS Trust and/or the research team?

At present there is no law that the volunteer should automatically obtain compensation for harm which occurs as a result of the research participation. The Pearson Report of 1978 recommended that volunteers in medical research should be compensated on a no-fault basis, but this has not been implemented. As the law stands at present the volunteer who is harmed as a result of participation in a research project can only obtain compensation on the basis of negligence, i.e. he must establish that a duty of care was owed to him; this has been broken and as a reasonably foreseeable result of this breach the subject has suffered some harm. Applying these principles here, Benjamin's family would have to show that in one way or another the researchers were negligent. For example, they failed to give him a proper medical examination or the design of the research was faulty and foreseeably dangerous to the volunteers. There is little evidence of that here and in addition, Benjamin, by concealing his previous illness, would have been contributorily negligent and therefore considered to a certain extent to be responsible for what happened.

It is now possible that if it can be established that Benjamin was harmed as the result of a defect in a product, then the Consumer Protection Act 1987 applies and Benjamin's family can obtain compensation under these provisions against the producer or supplier. This is considered at greater length in Chapter 12. Much of the debate on liability would hinge upon whether at the time of production the producer should have realised that there was a defect in the product.

Another possible defence against such a claim is the possibility of alleging that Benjamin, by volunteering willingly, assumed the risks of such an event occurring. This is known as the defence of *volenti non fit injuria* and is explained in more detail in Chapter 6. In order to rely on this as a defence it would have to be shown not only that Benjamin knew of the risks but also that he consented willingly to run them and agreed to waive all claim for compensation as a result.

Health and safety of the researcher

Exactly the same principles of health and safety apply to the researcher as apply to other employees, i.e. the employer owes a duty of care at common law to ensure that they are provided with a safe environment, a safe system of work and competent staff. Where the researchers are not employees, the occupier of the premises on which they are working would still be expected to uphold the duty of care for their safety under the Occupiers' Liability Act. It could be, however, that as specialists they would be expected to be aware of those risks which arise from their particular tasks, and the NHS Trust would not be liable for harm resulting from that. The provisions of the Health and Safety at Work Act 1974 would also apply (see Chapter 12).

Questions and exercises

1 How could a nurse tutor defend herself if a nurse who is accused of causing harm to the patient blamed the teaching that she had received in the nurse training school?
2 What records do you currently keep on your teaching programmes? Review the period for which you keep them and the content in the light of this chapter.
3 What records do you keep in respect of external lecturers who are invited to teach in your department?
4 In what ways does cooperation exist between the nurse training school and the wards and departments to ensure that the nurse's training meets the standards of approved accepted practice?
5 Prepare a procedure for initiating a research proposal, for obtaining the necessary approvals, for envisaging any possible difficulties in carrying it out, and for publishing the results.

19 Legal aspects of the care of the elderly

It is a truism that every elderly person is different. The fact that a person is over 60 or 70 or 80 or 90 says absolutely nothing else about them. Standards of health, loneliness, housing, finance, mobility and capability are as varied as with any other age group. All that can be said of them as a group is that it is more likely than not that they will be faced with some problems – social, economic, health or others – and that these are more likely to be multiple problems, interrelated, with one triggering off another. For example, it might be that an old person living on his own has limited mobility, and therefore finds it difficult to get to the shops. He thus does not feed himself properly and comes under the hospital's care as a result of lack of proper nourishment. It is equally true that in itself there are no basic principles of law purely for geriatric patients. All that has been said of the general principles of negligence and vicarious liability applies equally to the nurse who cares for the elderly. However, there are particular difficulties which the geriatric nurse is more likely to encounter than other nurses and it is to these that we now turn. In this section particular attention will be paid to the issues illustrated in Fig. 19.1.

There are, in addition, problems relating to the property and possessions of the elderly and these will be dealt with in Chapter 25. In Chapter 29 there is a discussion on the law relating to the making of wills and other aspects of dealing with death. Those nurses who care for the elderly in the community should refer to Chapter 24 for coverage of that topic.

1. Consent to treatment.
2. Force, restraint and assault.
3. Medication and the confused elderly patient.
4. Resistance to rehabilitation.
5. Standard of care.

Figure 19.1 Issues covered in Chapter 19.

Consent to treatment

SITUATION 19.1 AN OPERATION AT 90?

Amy Ash was admitted to a long-stay geriatric hospital because she had reached the stage where she could not care for herself. Her daughter was unable to look after her as she was coping with her mentally handicapped son. Amy was inter-mittently competent. There were days when she recognised Gwen, her daughter, and others where she did not but instead abused Gwen when she came to visit her. She had been complaining increasingly of a pain in her chest. The ward sister arranged for the physician to see her and he diagnosed a hiatus hernia. There was considerable debate over the best method of treatment. Initially a strict diet and medication were proposed but there were signs that this was not working when Amy started bleeding internally. The physician asked Gwen to come in and see him to talk about Amy's future care. He said that possibly the only long-term course of treatment was an operation. However, at Amy's age there were considerable risks in undertaking this. Although she was in a reason-ably good state of health she might not withstand the operation. Gwen was in a dilemma, not knowing whether to sign the form of consent on Amy's behalf. She attempted to explain the position to Amy. Amy grasped the fact that she would have to have an operation. She made it clear to Gwen that she had had a good life and did not want to be cut open now. Gwen also spoke to the ward sister who explained that Amy was in very good health and would probably survive the operation but of course one could not be 100 per cent sure. What should Gwen do?

There is no authority in law, apart from that given to the parent of a minor under 18, where a relative can give a valid consent for a patient. For example, what if Gwen refused, not because she felt that it was not in Amy's best interest to have the operation but because as the only child she would inherit Amy's possessions and she had built up consider-able debts while caring for her mentally handicapped son? On the other hand, if the doctor goes ahead and operates without any consent and Amy does not survive the oper-ation, is there any danger that the relatives would hold him responsible since a person of that age should not have been compelled to have an operation of this type?

The first question which arises is, of course, Amy's capability. It could well be that in her saner moments she is fully capable of understanding what is happening to her and of giving a valid consent or refusal. At other times she may well be far removed from reality. If the doctor persuades her to sign a form consenting to the operation in one of these sane spells can he rely on it when she becomes insane? The answer is probably yes. Supervening incapacity does not make a valid contract invalid provided the party had the capacity to contract at the time she agreed to the contract. While a consent form is not a contract, similar principles on capacity may prevail. It is essential, however, that only a reasonable time elapses between the signing of the form and the operation being carried out, and the operation must clearly be in the interests of the patient. What is reasonable? Certainly not as long as a year, but possibly up to three months. It depends upon the operation to be performed and whether the circumstances remain exactly as they were when the patient signed the form.

If Amy is incapable of signing the form at any time it could be argued that although it would be wise to discuss all the various options with Gwen to ascertain where Amy's best interests lie, in the last resort it must be the doctor's decision to decide clinically if the operation should proceed. In reaching his decision the doctor may well discuss Amy's standard of health and prognosis with the nurses. Ultimately, therefore, given this vacuum in law and the inability of the relative to give a valid consent, the doctor can only do what he considers to be in her best interests. In a case such as Amy's the relative would be consulted over what would be the best action but in the ultimate resort the relative does not have the power of consent or of refusal to consent.

The Law Commission has recommended laws recognising advance directives for treatment (see pages 254 and 282).

Force, restraint and assault

Refer also to the following chapter on caring for the psychiatric patient and also Chapter 25 on the compulsory removal of patients from the community to a place of safety.

Restless patients

SITUATION 19.2 THE WANDERER

One further difficulty that the staff had with Amy (described in the above situation) was that she could never stay in one place. She always liked to be on the move. Her restlessness took her all round the hospital where she was well known and those with time on their hands would eventually bring her back to the ward. Unfortunately, building work started on site and while the contractors were asked to take special care in crossing hospital roads with their plant, the nursing officer instructed Amy's ward sister to keep her on the ward because of the danger. The ward sister could not be sure that someone was always available to keep an eye on Amy and, rather than lock the ward door and imprison all the patients, she decided to use a restrainer on Amy so that every time Amy tried to get out of her chair a belt, which was fastened around Amy and to the chair, rang a bell and prevented Amy from leaving the chair. Gwen visited Amy and was distressed to see this form of restraint; Amy herself protested about it. What is the legal position?

To restrict a person's movement without lawful authority so that they have no way of escape is a form of false imprisonment. This effectively is what Amy is – imprisoned. Is there any legal justification? Temporary restraint could possibly be justified if it were on the grounds of preventing another person being injured by Amy or to prevent Amy harming herself. However, the form of restraint used by the ward sister is clearly not temporary. What alternatives are available to the ward staff, given that they have a duty to care for Amy and to prevent her exposure to danger? Adequate staffing to keep an eye on each person is obviously one possibility but given present-day economic constraints and nurse staffing levels it may not be an option. Another possibility is the use of more volunteers to supervise certain patients. One suggestion is to change the locks so that it takes some ingenuity to open the door without the help of the ward staff, though this is not a happy compromise. Even if there are no contractors on site there may be other dangers such as a main road nearby, a stream in the grounds, etc. The Royal College of Nursing has issued a booklet on the use of restraint in the care of older people. Reference should also be made to publications of the Social Services Inspectorate, such as *No Longer Afraid* (HMSO, 1993).

Control at night

At night cot sides are often used to prevent patients climbing or falling out of bed. In one sense, where the elderly person is clearly struggling against them, these represent a form of restraint. On the other hand, they may in some circumstances be justified and indeed necessary where the patient is very confused and restless. Failure to use them might lead to action against the authority for failing in its duty of care for the patient. However, the potential danger of the patient trying to climb over the cot sides and causing himself harm must always be borne in mind.

Daily care

SITUATION 19.3 CHIROPODY CARE

One form of treatment that Amy could not tolerate was having her toe nails cut. She was abusive to the chiropodist who found it very difficult to keep her nails in reasonable order. The chiropodist asked the ward sister if she would hold Amy down while she attempted to cut her nails. The ward sister was not happy with this suggestion and felt that they should first seek medical guidance as it might be preferable to cut the nails when Amy was mildly sedated. What is the legal position?

It will be clear from the section dealing with consent to treatment that touching another person without their consent or some other lawful authority is a trespass to their person. Does the fact that Amy needs to have her toe nails done constitute lawful authority? The answer to this is, in general, no. However, the fact that Amy lacks the capacity to give a valid consent may well justify the professionals taking some action to care for her. As has been seen earlier, professionals are justified in taking care of a patient in an emergency out of necessity to save his life. This is quite clear if the patient is unconscious. However, in considering chiropody we are not talking of something which is, at least initially (though it may well be ultimately), a life-saving procedure. In addition, there are numerous nursing tasks and social tasks such as bathing, hairwashing and brushing to which patients like Amy may well object. In theory of course, to brush Amy's hair without her consent is a trespass to her person. There may be occasions when Amy can be persuaded to have it done and will not struggle against it. However, inevitably, there may come a time when Amy needs to have something done despite her protests. In such cases it is possible that reasonable force could be used provided it is justifiable in her interests. Under the Mental Health Act 1983 treatment can only be imposed for mental disorder on long-term detained patients. The Law Commission is considering the wider issue. This is considered below. The House of Lords *In re F.* (see page 246) recognised the duty of a professional to care for an adult who was incapable of making decisions. It is not clear how far this would justify force and restraint.

Medication and the confused elderly patient

The above principles apply equally to the administration of medication. The majority of patients in psychiatric hospitals are on some form of medication but only a few of them are under a section (about 5 per cent). There are many occasions when, through a variety of reasons ranging from justifiable ones to pure cussedness or confusion, they reject the tablets, injections or liquid. What does the nurse do? Obviously where the patient is capable of making that decision his refusal should be respected. But this is rarely the case. Often the patient is in Amy's situation: intermittently or permanently confused and mentally infirm. It would be an abuse of the Mental Health Act to place all such patients under its compulsory provisions. Yet there is at present no interim legal stage between providing treatment under the Part 4 provisions of the Mental Health Act or providing life-saving treatment in an emergency and allowing the patient to make the decision. We have no system of guardianship where a guardian has the power of giving a proxy consent on behalf of the patient and, as explained above, the relative does not have this power for anyone of 18 or over. In this vacuum the only advice which can be given to nursing staff is: ensure that the medication is essential and in the patient's interests; that the patient is incompetent to refuse; use all possible means to ensure that the patient will take it willingly, considering the use of force only in the most extreme cases and even then only after discussion with the psychiatrist, the social worker and the nearest relative as to whether there should be an order under the Mental Health Act (see Chapter 20). The Law Commission's proposals are discussed below.

Resistance to rehabilitation

This is not an infrequent problem and what has been discussed in the preceding section applies here. Day-to-day management of Fred requires that he gets out of bed and is encouraged to move around. Indeed, the nurse would be failing in her care of the patient if she failed to do this. However, if Fred totally refuses he probably could not be coerced into rehabilitation training. If during these exercises Fred fell, exactly the same principles of negligence would apply as are discussed in Chapter 3. Account would be taken of whether the nurse was following the approved accepted practice, the purpose of what she was doing as far as Fred was concerned, and whether there were any additional precautions which she should have taken and failed to take. Compensation would only be payable if there were a causal link between anything the nurse may have done wrong and the harm suffered by Fred. Fred's own contributory negligence would be taken into account in determining both the nurse's liability and the extent of compensation. Obviously, in deciding whether Fred was contributorily negligent account would be taken of his mental and physical state.

Standard of care

It is not difficult to spot the bad practice in this case study. Even if the night nurse considered on reasonable grounds that there was no need to call the doctor out in the night, her failure to ensure that the incident was reported to the doctor on the following morning and her failure to arrange for a doctor to examine Fred was clearly not in accordance with approved practice. In addition, she failed to give to the day staff a full account of the night's events so that they were unable to ensure that the appropriate action was taken. The night sister compounded these omissions by failing to fill in an accident report. Unless there are any other mitigating factors in an incidence like this, Fred would undoubtedly have a possible claim for compensation against the night nurse and also against the NHS Trust for its vicarious liability for their employee. Compensation is unlikely to amount to very much since it would only cover the additional days of pain and suffering because the fracture had not been diagnosed earlier (unless of course the nurses were negligent in failing to put cot sides up and prevent the original fall). However, if it is discovered that those few days' delay have had considerable effects on the long-term prospects for Fred's recovery, then, clearly, compensation would be much more. The night sister would obviously face disciplinary proceedings and also possibly professional conduct proceedings.

The future

At present there is a vacuum in law in that no relative or professional has a legal right to give consent to treatment on behalf of a mentally incompetent adult. The House of Lords decision on *In re F* (discussed on page 246) enables a professional to act in the best interests of the patients according to the approved accepted standard of care (i.e. the 'Bolam Test') in the absence of consent. However, where major surgery or treatment is contemplated (e.g. sterilisation), reference to the courts is required.

The Law Commission in 1991 issued a Consultation Paper (No. 119, 'Decision Making and the Mentally Incapacitated Adult'). Following feedback, three further papers have been published covering private and public law issues and treatment decisions. The Commission recommends that legislation covering advance directives should be passed in order to clarify their validity, formation, revocation and status. It also recommends that there should be a statutory power to treat those who lack the mental capacity to make their own decisions. Its proposals have been considered by the House of Lords Select Committee on Medical Ethics (1994) and draft legislation is expected shortly.

Questions and exercises

1 Liability in negligence takes into account what the professional person should have
    foreseen about the personality and likely acts of the patient. To what extent are you
    analysing the level of competence and degree of confusion of the patient in deciding
    on the care to be provided?

2 What particular precautions should you take when caring for disturbed elderly patients?

3 To what extent do you consider the nurse should be the advocate for the patient, and to what extent do you think that this role can be left to relatives?

4 Obtain a copy of your NHS Trust's summary of accidents to patients and analyse those relating to elderly patients. To what extent do you consider some of these accidents could have been prevented if different procedures had been adopted by the carers or by the NHS Trust itself?

20 Nursing the mentally disordered

This section cannot cover all the law relevant to the nursing of the mentally ill and mentally handicapped. The intention is to deal with some of the more common dilemmas faced by these nurses through the case study approach, and to include in the diagrams a summary of some of the main points of the Mental Health Act 1983. This Act is the main legislation covering the mentally disordered and for the most part replaces the Act of 1959 which by the end of the 1970s was seen as failing to protect the rights of the mentally disordered. This chapter will cover the areas illustrated by Fig. 20.1. Reference should be made to the Code of Practice of the Department of Health on the Mental Health Act which was revised in 1993.

The holding power

SITUATION 20.1 TO STOP OR LET GO

Bill Smith, an informal patient in a psychiatric hospital, admitted three weeks ago, wakes up at 3.00 a.m. and starts abusing nursing auxiliary Mavis Jones who is on her own, Staff Nurse Rachel Robinson having just gone for her break. Bill starts throwing furniture around and is threatening to leave the ward. Mavis contacts the night operator and asks for immediate help. What is her legal position in relation to Bill? Rachel Jones returns with a charge nurse. They telephone for the responsible medical officer and are informed that he will not be able to arrive until 9.30 a.m. What are their legal powers?

Figure 20.2 sets out the main points of the holding power of the nurse laid down by Section 5 (4) of the Act. As a nursing auxiliary, Mavis is not a prescribed nurse for the purposes of using the holding power under the Mental Health Act. The only nurses designated as prescribed nurses under the Act are those who have been trained in mental illness or mental handicap. She does, however, have the health carer's duty to act in an emergency to save life. She also has the powers of the citizen to effect an arrest on the limited occasions set out in the Police and Criminal Evidence Act. If she feared for the life of Bill were he to be allowed to leave hospital immediately, or for the life of anyone

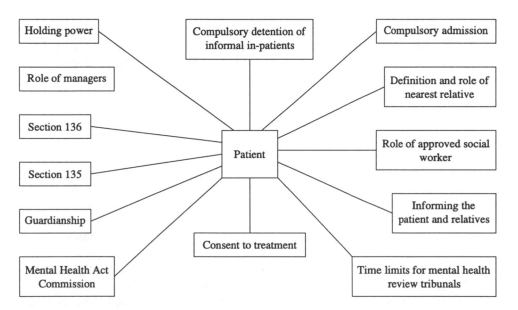

Figure 20.1 Issues covered in Chapter 20.

1. The patient is receiving treatment for mental disorder.
2. The patient is an in-patient.
3. It appears to the prescribed nurse that the patient is suffering from mental disorder to such a degree that it is necessary for his health or safety or for the protection of others for him to be immediately restrained from leaving the hospital.
4. It is not practicable to secure the immediate attendance of a practitioner who could exercise the powers under Section 5 (2).

Figure 20.2 The holding power: Mental Health Act 1983 Section 5 (4).

else, she could legally prevent his leaving the ward in an emergency. Rachel Robinson would be regarded as a prescribed nurse if she is either a registered mental nurse or a registered nurse for the mentally handicapped. She can exercise the holding power set out under Section 5 (4) of the Mental Health Act 1983 if the conditions set out in Fig. 20.2 are present.

If all these requirements are present then Rachel has the power to detain Bill for up to six hours. As soon as the appropriate medical practitioner arrives, however, the holding power will cease.

Rachel must fill in the appropriate forms and ensure that these are taken to the managers of the hospital immediately. Procedures vary: in some hospitals it is the practice for the hospital manager to be on call for such purposes; in others this duty is delegated to the nurse manager on duty at night and weekends. If the doctor arrives and decides that Bill should be detained under Section 5 (2) then whatever part of the holding power has elapsed before his arrival will become part of the 72 hours' detention.

From the situation described here it is apparent that the appropriate doctor will not be able to arrive within the six hours. In this case it is essential for the doctor to exercise his powers of nomination under Section 5 (3) so that another medical practitioner can act as nominee and see Bill at the earliest possibility.

This situation gives rise to other questions. Must Rachel remain with Bill personally even though she is due off duty at 7.30 a.m.? There is no requirement in the Act that Rachel should stay. The fact that Bill is under a holding power should of course be made clear to the senior nurse on the shift that takes over from Rachel. In particular, she should be informed of the time of commencement of the holding power and, if a doctor fails to arrive, the time when the holding power is due to end.

What powers does Rachel have in relation to Bill? Could Bill, for example, forcibly be given some medication for which he has been written up? The Act gives Rachel the power to restrain Bill from leaving hospital. She does not have power under the Mental Health Act to compel Bill to have treatment. Informal patients or those who have been placed under short-term detention orders covered by Sections 5 (2), 5 (4) and Section 4 are specifically excluded from the compulsory treatment provisions of Part IV of the Act. Many feel that it is kinder to control Bill through medication than through physical restraint. There is no power to do this under the Act, however, and any such use of compulsory treatment can only be lawfully justified under the common law powers to act out of necessity. The legality of using them for this purpose is in doubt and practice varies.

What if Bill runs off during the period of the holding power – can he be brought back? Section 18 (5) by implication allows Bill to be brought back as long as the time limit for the holding power has not elapsed. Section 18 (1) enables a patient who is absent without leave to be taken into custody and returned to the hospital by any approved social worker, by any officer on the staff of the hospital, by any constable, or by any person authorised in writing by the managers of the hospital.

Could the holding power be used if Bill was an in-patient in a general hospital? From the requirements listed above it is clear that Bill must be receiving treatment for mental disorder. It is, of course, possible for Bill to be admitted for surgery while still under treatment for a mental disorder and in this case the holding power could be exercised but only if the nurse had the appropriate registration.

Compulsory detention of informal in-patient

What would happen in a general hospital if a patient became severely mentally disordered? Temporary emergency measures could be taken to save life: either the life of the patient or of others. In addition, it is possible for any registered medical practitioner in charge of the patient to exercise the powers under Section 5 (2).

This section applies to an in-patient in a hospital. There is no requirement that he should be having treatment for mental disorder. The registered medical practitioner in charge of the patient's treatment must consider that an application ought to be made under the Act for the admission of the patient to hospital. He then furnishes the managers with a report to that effect and the patient may then be detained in the hospital for a period of 72 hours from the time the report is furnished. There is no requirement that the practitioner should be a psychiatrist but the Mental Health Commission has recommended that advice should be sought from a psychiatrist before this power is exercised.

In such circumstances on a general ward, it would also be possible to make use of the powers under Section 4 (see Table 20.1). In this case it would be necessary for the nearest relative or an approved social worker to make the appropriate application for admission.

Compulsory admission

Table 20.1 sets out the section numbers and requirements for each section which enables compulsory admission to take place and the length of detention. The requirements in relation to the two medical recommendations are set out in Fig. 20.3.

The role of the nearest relative

The nearest relative now has an important role to play and has to be given specific information; this task often falls on the nurse. The definition of nearest relative and the hierarchy is given in Fig. 20.4. This diagram also illustrates the powers of the nearest relative.

The role of the approved social worker

Table 20.2 sets out the main tasks of the approved social worker. Only social workers who have completed a specified training can be recognised as approved for the purposes of the Act. The approved social worker is more likely to be the applicant for the purposes of Sections 2, 3, 4, and 7.

Table 20.1 Compulsory admission provisions

Section	Duration (up to)	Applicant	Medical requirements	Other requirements
4 Emergency admission for assessment	72 hours	Approved social worker or nearest relative	1 recommendation only stating that patient is suffering from mental disorder and stating the provisions of Section 2 exist (see below)	Applicant must have personally seen patient within 24 hours before the application. Admission must be of urgent necessity
2 Admission for assessment	28 days	Approved social worker or nearest relative	2 medical recommendations (a) patient is suffering from mental disorder of a nature or degree which warrants detention in hospital for assessment and (b) he/she ought to be so detained in the interests of his/her own health or safety or with a view to the protection of others.	Applicant must personally have seen patient within the period of 14 days ending with the date of the application
3 Admission for treatment	6 months, renewable for a further 6 months, then for a period of 1 year	Approved social worker or nearest relative	2 medical requirements (a) patient is suffering from mental illness, (severe) mental impairment or psychopathic disorder and his/her mental disorder is of a nature or degree which makes it appropriate for him/her to receive medical treatment in hospital and (b) in the case of psychopathic disorder and mental impairment, such treatment is likely to alleviate or prevent a deterioration of his/her condition and	As above under Section 2. Approved social worker must consult with nearest relative before making an application unless this would not be reasonably practicable or would involve unreasonable delay. The application cannot be made if the nearest relative objects

Section	Duration	Conditions	Criteria
37 Hospital order without restrictions	6 months, renewable for a further 6 months, then for a period of 1 year	Order can be made by Crown Court in case of person convicted of an offence punishable by imprisonment or by magistrates (a) if convicted of offence punishable on summary conviction with imprisonment or (b) if person is suffering from mental illness or severe mental impairment and magistrates are satisfied that he committed the crime	(c) it is necessary for the health or safety of the patient or for the protection of others that he/she should receive such treatment and it cannot be provided unless he/she is detained under this section. 2 doctors required to give oral or written evidence that (a) offender is suffering from mental illness, psychopathic disorder or (severe) mental impairment of a nature or degree which makes it appropriate for him/her to be detained for medical treatment and (b) in the case of psychopathic disorder or mental impairment such treatment is likely to alleviate or prevent a deterioration of his/her condition and (c) the court is of the opinion, having regard to all the circumstances, that the most suitable method of disposing of the case is by means of a hospital order
41 Restriction order (imposed in conjunction with hospital order Section 37)	For a specified period or without limit of time	Crown Court which has made a hospital order can impose a restriction order. Magistrates Court cannot make a restriction order but can send offender over 14 to Crown Court for a restriction to be made	As for Section 37; at least one of the 2 doctors must give evidence orally before the court.

1. Practitioners must have personally examined the patient either together or separately, but where they have examined the patient separately not more than 5 days must have elapsed between the days on which the separate examinations took place.
2. One of the medical recommendations must be from a practitioner approved by the Secretary of State for such purposes as having experience in the diagnosis or treatment of mental disorder and unless that practitioner has previous acquaintance with the patient, the other practitioner should have, if practicable.
3. One (but not more than one) of the medical recommendations should be given by a practitioner on the staff of the hospital to which the patient is to be admitted.
4. 3 above does not apply, i.e. both medical recommendations can be given by staff of the hospital in question, if
   (a) compliance with 3 above would result in delay involving serious risk to the health and safety of the patient; and
   (b) one of the practitioners works at the hospital for less than half of the time which he is bound by contract to devote to work in the health service; and
   (c) where one of the practitioners is a consultant, the other does not work in a grade in which he is under that consultant's directives.
5. A medical recommendation cannot be given by
   (a) the applicant;
   (b) a partner of the applicant or of a practitioner by whom another medical recommendation is given for admission;
   (c) a person employed as an assistant by the applicant or by any such practitioner;
   (d) a person who receives or has an interest in the receipt of any payments made on account of the maintenance of the patient;
   (e) except as set out in 3 and 4 above a practitioner on the staff of the hospital to which the patient is admitted or by specified relatives of the other practitioner giving the medical recommendation.
6. A general practitioner who is employed part-time in a hospital shall not be regarded as a practitioner on its staff.

These provisions also apply to the two medical recommendations for guardianship.

Figure 20.3 Requirements for the second medical recommendation.

Informing the patient

The task of explaining his legal rights to the patient once a detention order has been imposed often falls on the nurse (see Fig. 20.5).

SITUATION 20.2 INFORMATION

Edna Johns, an informal patient in a psychiatric hospital, became very disturbed and aggressive in the early hours of the morning, threatening to kill herself and wishing to leave hospital. Staff Nurse Thomas, an RMN, on learning that the responsible medical officer would take at least 30 minutes to arrive on the ward decided to exercise the holding power under Section 5 (4). When the appropriate doctor arrived he decided to detain Edna under Section 5 (2). Within

Definition: the highest in the following hierarchy, Section 26(i)
Relative who ordinarily resides with or cares for the patient
   husband or wife
   son or daughter
   father or mother
   brother or sister
   grandparent
   grandchild
   uncle or aunt
   nephew or niece
Preference is given in relatives of the same description to the whole blood relation over the half-blood relation and the elder or eldest regardless of sex.

Husband and wife include a person who is living with the patient as the patient's husband or wife and has been so living for not less than six months. A person other than a relative with whom the patient ordinarily resides for a period of not less than 5 years shall be treated as if he were a relative. However such a person is at the bottom of the above hierarchy.

Power of nearest relative

1. To apply for the admission of the patient for assessment, for assessment in an emergency, for treatment and for guardianship.
2. To be informed about the approved social worker's application to admit patient for assessment.
3. To be consulted about the approved social worker's proposed application for treatment and to object to it.
4. To be given information about the details of the patient's detention, consent to treatment, rights to apply for discharge, etc. (but subject to the patient's right to object to this information being given).
5. To discharge the patient after giving 72 hours' notice in writing to the managers.
6. To apply to a Mental Health Review Tribunal under Sections 16, 25 and 29.

Figure 20.4 Definition and powers of the nearest relative.

the next 48 hours the approved social worker applied for admission under Section 3 on the recommendation of Edna's doctor and a second recommendation. What duties exist in relation to informing Edna?

The duties set out under Section 132 are illustrated in Fig. 20.5. Forms are available covering the information to be given under each section. Often the nursing staff have the task of giving out the forms and telling the patient about the provisions. It is vital that it is recorded that the patient has been informed since it is a statutory duty and there should be evidence that the statutory duty has been carried out.

In Edna's case she will have been placed under three separate sections in less than 72 hours. She must be given the relevant information each time the section is imposed and will be given a different form each time. Section 132 requires the information to be given as soon as practicable after the commencement of the section. 'Practicable' must take into account the patient's physical and mental ability to take in what is said. To stand over a screaming, or even unconscious, patient reading him his rights would not seem to be a proper fulfilment of the statutory duty.

Table 20.2 Role of the approved social worker and of any social worker

Duty	Details
Duties of the approved social worker	
Section 11(3) Inform nearest relative of admission of patient and of nearest relative's right to discharge	1. In admission for assessment (Sections 2 and 4). 2. Before or within a reasonable time after an application for admission for assessment is made 3. Such steps as are practicable to inform the person appearing to be the nearest relative
Section 11(4) Consult nearest relative on admission for treatment or guardianship and discontinue application if nearest relative notifies objection	1. Consultation with person appearing to be the nearest relative of the patient 2. Unless it appears that in the circumstances such consultation is not reasonably practicable or would involve unreasonable delay
Section 13(1) To apply for admission or guardianship order if satisfied application ought to be made and is of the opinion that it is necessary or proper for application to be made by him	1. In respect of patient within the area of local social services authority by whom he is appointed 2. Must have regard to wishes expressed by relatives of patient or any other relevant circumstances that are necessary or proper for application to be made by him
Section 13(2) To interview patient in suitable manner and satisfy himself that detention in a hospital is in all the circumstances of the case the most appropriate way of providing the care and medical treatment of which the patient stands in need	1. Before making application for admission to hospital
Section 13(4) To take patient's case into consideration with a view to making an application for admission. If decides *NOT* to make an application he will inform the nearest relative in writing of his reasons.	1. If nearest relative requires local social services authority of area in which patient resides, authority must direct approved social worker as soon as practicable
Duties of any social worker (approved social worker not specified)	
Section 14 To provide report on social circumstances	1. Where patient admitted to hospital an application by nearest relative other than Section 4 2. Managers must as soon as practicable give notice of that fact to local social services authority for area in which patient resided immediately before his admission

Table 20.2 *Continued*

Duty	Details
Duties of any social worker (approved social worker not specified)	
Section 117 Duty of district health authority and of local social services authority to provide after-care services	1. Applies to patients detained under Section 3 or admitted under hospital order (Section 37) or transferred under transfer direction (Sections 47 or 48) who cease to be detained and leave hospital 2. Authorities must cooperate with relevant voluntary agencies 3. After-care services to be provided until such time as the authorities are satisfied that the person concerned is no longer in need of such services

---

The managers of the hospital in which a patient is detained under the Act must:

1. Take such steps as are practicable to ensure the patient understands:
   (a) under which provisions of the Act he is for the time being detained and the effect of that provision; and
   (b) what rights of applying to a Mental Health Review Tribunal are available to him in respect of his detention under that provision;
   (c) the effect of certain provisions of the Mental Health Act including the Consent to treatment provisions, the role of the Mental Health Act Commission and other provisions relating to the protection of the patient.
2. The steps to inform the patient must be taken as soon as practicable after the commencement of the patient's detention under the provision in question.
3. The requisite information must be given to the patient in writing and also by word of mouth.

Figure 20.5 Informing the patient: Mental Health Act 1983 Section 132.

Informing the relatives

Where the patient is too disturbed to take in the information the statutory duty to inform the nearest relative assumes even greater importance. Section 132 (4) requires the managers to furnish the person appearing to them to be the patient's nearest relative with a copy of any information given to the patient, in writing, under the duty outlined above. The steps for this must be taken when the information is given to the patient or within a reasonable time thereafter. The patient has the right of veto and can request that this information is not given. Reasonable time here would seem to imply that it is not necessary to phone Edna's relative in the middle of the night to inform them of the exercise of the holding power but this should be done as soon as possible the next day.

Consent to treatment provisions

See Figs 20.6 and 20.7.

Long-term detained patients

Under the provision of Part IV of the Mental Health Act 1983 those patients who are detained under long-term detention provisions (e.g. Sections 2, 3, 37 and 41) can in certain circumstances be given compulsory treatment. For these patients the Act covers all possible treatments for mental disorder, both in emergency and non-emergency situations. The provisions are set out in Fig. 20.6.

---

1. Treatments involving brain surgery or hormonal implants can only be given with the patient's consent which must be certified and only after independent certification of the consent and of the fact that the treatment should proceed (Section 57).
2. Treatments involving electroconvulsive therapy, or medication where 3 months or more have elapsed since medication was first given during that period of detention can only be given either (a) with the consent of the patient and it is certified by the patient's own registered medical practitioner or another registered medical practitioner appointed specifically for that purpose that he is capable of understanding its nature, purpose and likely effects, or (b) the registered medical practitioner appointed specifically certifies that the patient has refused or is incapable of consenting but agrees that the treatment should proceed (Section 58).
3. All other treatments: these can be given without the consent of the patient provided they are for mental disorder and are given by or under the direction of the responsible medical officer (Section 63).

Figure 20.6 Consent to treatment: Mental Health Act 1983 Sections 57, 58, 63.

These can be given according to the degree of urgency and whether they are irreversible or hazardous. The table below illustrates the provisions.

Any treatment	which is immediately necessary	to save the patient's life
Treatment which is not irreversible	if it is immediately necessary	to prevent serious deterioration
Treatment which is not irreversible or hazardous	if it is immediately necessary	to alleviate serious suffering
Treatment which is not irreversible or hazardous	if it is immediately necessary and represents the minimum interference necessary	to prevent the patient from behaving violently or being a danger to himself or others

Irreversible is defined as 'if it has unfavourable irreversible physical or psychological consequences' and hazardous is defined as 'if it entails significant physical hazard'.

Figure 20.7 Consent to treatment: urgent treatments.

The role of nurse

What is the role of the nurse in consent to treatment provisions? Under the provisions of Sections 57 and 58 the independent registered medical practitioner, in determining whether the treatment should proceed, must consult with a nurse and another professional who have been professionally concerned with the patient's medical treatment. The independent doctor must record the fact that he has consulted these two persons. Interestingly, however, there is no requirement on the form that he should actually record their opinions, so it could well happen that both the nurse and the other professional counselled against, say, ECT but that the doctor still recommended ECT. A disagreement is unusual but it is advisable for the nurse, whether there is agreement or not with her views, to ensure that the advice she gave is recorded clearly and comprehensively.

Physical illness

These provisions on consent to treatment would thus appear to cover all eventualities concerning the long-term detained patient. However, there is a gap in relation to treatment for physical illness.

SITUATION 20.3 APPENDICITIS

Paul, a severely depressed patient, had been detained under Section 3 for two months. One morning he complained of severe stomach pains. He was sick, with a high temperature. Paul was taken to the 'sick' ward for the treatment of physical illnesses within the mental hospital and was diagnosed as suffering from appendicitis. It was recommended that an operation be performed immediately. When Paul heard this he immediately said there was no way in which he would agree to the operation. What is the legal position?

If Part IV of the Act is seen as applying only to the treatment of mental illness, then its provisions are irrelevant in these circumstances. Alternatively, it could be argued that if brain surgery can be undertaken under Section 62 to save the life of a patient (and this may cover informal patients since they are covered by the provisions of Section 57), where the treatment is given for a mental disorder, then the words 'any treatment' in Section 62 can cover not only treatment for mental disorder but also treatment for physical disorders. If the purpose is to save life, then Section 62 (1) (a) covers the situation. This is a logical view but it has not gained universal acceptance. The alternative is to say that the situation is not covered by Part IV of the Act and that the rules relating to acting in emergency under the common law to save life would apply. This would mean that treatment could be given without the patient's consent as part of the doctor's duty of care to the patient. *In re C.* 1994 (see page 99) a Broadmoor patient's refusal to have an amputation was upheld by the court. In the case of *B. v. Croydon Health Authority*, the Court of Appeal held that compulsory feeding by tube came under Section 63 (TLR 1 December 1994).

Short-term detained patients and informal patients

As far as the consent to treatment provisions of the Mental Health Act is concerned these patients are not covered by the provisions of Part IV. There is only one exception to this: informal patients are specifically covered by the provisions of Section 57 relating to brain surgery and hormonal implants, and by the relevant provisions of Sections 62, 59 and 60. As far as Section 57 is concerned this means that brain surgery for mental disorder or hormonal implants cannot be given without the safeguards set out above. The short-term detained patient is not explicitly covered but there would appear to be no reason why he should not receive the same protection.

As far as all other treatments are concerned, one has to look outside the Act for the law relating to consent to treatment and this is as set out in Chapter 7. This means that since only some 5 per cent of mentally ill and mentally handicapped patients are under detention the majority are outside the basic provisions of the Act and the common law rules relating to trespass to the person and the duty of care to inform the patient, plus the emergency powers of acting in an emergency to save life, apply to them.

SITUATION 20.4 RESISTANCE IN THE ELDERLY (1)

Maud, a frail 85-year-old, was a 'wanderer' and occasionally resisted the efforts of the nursing staff to give her her medication. She was an informal inpatient on a psychogeriatric ward. One day she attempted to wander off the ward and, because they were short staffed and could not keep an eye on her all the time, the ward door was locked. A visitor to another patient complained that it was illegal for the door to be locked when the patients were not under section. What is the legal position?

There is no doubt that to prevent patients leaving the ward when there is no justification in law could give rise to an action for false imprisonment. This is a civil action where the person bringing the action would simply have to show that they have been effectively detained against their will without any lawful justification. They would not be required to show that they had suffered any harm other than the loss of their liberty. In the example given above, there would appear to be no justification for locking the ward and preventing everyone leaving simply to control Maud. It could therefore be argued that this is a false imprisonment of everyone in the ward. What about Maud? There may be justification in detaining Maud because she is a danger to herself were she to be allowed to wander away. It could perhaps be argued that this is lawful under the emergency provisions at common law discussed above. However, the situation is not clear, especially when what is involved is detention over a long period. The issue is the subject of a discussion document produced by the Mental Health Act Commission in which the Commission suggests that detention outside the powers of the Act should only be used in circumstances which would be justified at common law.

It is not unknown for some wards to cope with the problem of the confused elderly or other groups who need to be detained by arranging the door bolts and locks to be fixed in such a way that, while they are not technically locked, the degree of synchronisation required to open them is such that a confused person could not manage and is effectively locked in in practice though not in theory. Advice is given in the revised Code of Practice on the Mental Health Act (DH 1993).

SITUATION 20.5 RESISTANCE IN THE ELDERLY (2)_____

On one occasion Maud made it clear that she would not have her medication which was prescribed as a sedative and for her heart condition. As an informal patient, could she be forced to take the medication since it was for her benefit and she lacked the mental capacity to make a reasoned judgement over whether she should be taking it?

Unfortunately, this is not an uncommon problem for those working in hospitals for the mentally ill and mentally handicapped. Given the comparatively small number of patients who are actually detained and the reluctance to place patients under the detention provisions of the Act (even if they complied with the conditions for compulsory admission, which not all of them would) there are substantial problems for staff in caring for these patients, ensuring they have the necessary medication, and are kept in a place of safety. Many patients are intermittently confused and on occasions lack the mental competence to make rational decisions about their treatment. Should they be forced to have the treatment? The answer as far as the common law is concerned is yes, if the treatment is out of necessity and in the best interests of the patient. However, this would not cover day-to-day care which, while it is not life saving, may well be invaluable as far as the quality of life is concerned.

Unfortunately, the problem is exacerbated by staffing difficulties, so that patients can sometimes be given medication which is not clinically indicated in order to control restlessness and aggression. There is certainly no legal justification for giving medication to patients compulsorily on the grounds of patient management and staff shortage.

It is clear that the present gap that exists in the law in relation to the informal patient and short-term admissions must be filled so that staff know where they stand in regard to the treatment of those who are incapable of making a rational choice but who are not under a detention order. Proposals are made by the Law Commission which are discussed on pages 246 and 282.

Guardianship

SITUATION 20.6 HOW MUCH CONTROL?_____

Paul has been under a guardianship order for three months. He lives with his mother, the guardian, and attends a day centre three times each week. He sees the community psychiatric nurse regularly, both at the centre and also at home, and is on substantial levels of medication. One day he decides not to take the drugs. His mother pleads with him but is unable to persuade him to take them. She informs the CPN who also attempts to persuade Paul but is unsuccessful. His behaviour deteriorates and he becomes more aggressive. His mother asks if there is any way in which he could be compelled to take the drugs as she fears that he will ultimately have to be readmitted. Is there a way?

(a) the power to require the patient to reside at a place specified by the guardian;
(b) the power to require the patient to attend at places and times specified for the purpose of medical treatment, occupation, education and training; and
(c) the power to require access to the patient to be given at any place where the patient is residing to any registered medical practitioner, approved social worker or any person specified.

Figure 20.8 Statutory powers of the guardian.

The answer is that the Mental Health Act 1983 excludes from its provisions relating to consent to treatment those patients on guardianship orders. There are three statutory powers in relation to guardianship and these are set out in Fig. 20.8.

There are no means of enforcing the guardianship powers over the patient other than the right of returning the patient to the specified place if he absconds. The ultimate sanction is possibly the knowledge that if the patient does not cope in the community, then he is likely to be admitted to hospital. It is not, however, good professional practice to use this as a threat. Apart from gentle coercion there is no way to force a patient to take drugs. Because of this dilemma it had been the practice to use Section 3 and keep the patient on a long leash in the community by using the leave of absence provisions under Section 17. Thus after a short initial admission under Section 3 the patient could be allowed back into the community on condition that he took his drugs, and if he failed to do this then he could be pulled back into hospital where he would remain under the section until he could be trusted to take his drugs in the community. This practice was declared illegal by the court in *R.* v. *Hallstrom and another ex parte W.* (No. 2) 1986 2 All ER 306 and it was decided that there was no power under Section 3 to do this since a requirement of Section 3 was that the patient was admitted as an in-patient.

Community Supervision Order

Concern has been expressed that many patients are being discharged prematurely and that there are inadequate powers to care for patients in the community. An earlier suggestion for a power for patients to be given compulsory treatment in the community was discussed in a report of the Royal College of Psychiatrists in 1987. No action resulted and in January 1993 the Royal College of Psychiatrists put forward proposals for a Community Supervision Order. In June 1993 the Health Committee of the House of Commons (session 1992–93) reported on Community Supervision Orders and considered that the RCP's proposals were fundamentally flawed. It recommended instead that the highest priority be given to making fully effective the present statutory and non-statutory provision for the care of people with a mental illness. In August 1993 an internal review, set up by the Department of Health, on legal powers for the care of mentally ill people in the community recommended changes to the Mental Health Act including amendments to extend guardianship, remove the time limit on Section 17, provide

(1) If it appears to a justice of the peace, on information on oath laid by an approved social worker, that there is a reasonable cause to suspect that a person believed to be suffering from mental disorder

(a) has been, or is being, ill-treated, neglected or kept otherwise than under proper control, in any place within the jurisdiction of the justice; or
(b) being unable to care for himself, is living alone in any such place

the justice may issue a warrant authorising any constable to enter, if need be by force, any premises specified in the warrant in which that person is believed to be, and, if thought fit, to remove him to a place of safety with a view to the making of an application in respect of him under Part II of this Act, or of other arrangements for his treatment or care. Section 135(4) In the execution of a warrant issued under Section 135(1) a constable shall be accompanied by an approved social worker and by a registered medical practitioner (as amended by Police and Criminal Evidence Act 1984 Schedule 6 para 26).

Figure 20.9 Mental Health Act 1983 Section 135.

extended leave and set up supervised discharge arrangements for special categories of chronic patients. Legislation will be required to implement some of the proposals. In January 1994 the Secretary of State published guidelines on the discharge of patients who are dangerous to themselves or others. From 1 April 1994 all providers have had to keep supervision registers for patients most at risk and who need most support. Authorities are required to identify such patients, provide a care plan and follow up their care after discharge. The Mental Health Act Commission has recommended that there should be a radical review of the provision of the Mental Health Act 1983 which is essentially institution-focused legislation. In the meantime concern continues about deficiencies in community care provision for the mentally disordered.

Removal to a place of safety, Section 135

Figure 20.9 sets out the basic provisions of this power of the approved social worker. The section has been amended by the Police and Criminal Evidence Act 1984 so it does not now have to be a named constable who accompanies the approved social worker to the house.

Removal from a public place by police, Section 136

The basic provisions of this section are set out in Fig. 20.10. There has been considerable concern over the use of the section since the documentation has been inadequate: the police have not always recorded the details as to when they have used this section, and when the patient has been brought to hospital the details have not always been recorded by the hospital staff and managers. Many hospitals have now designed their

(1) If a constable finds in a place to which the public have access a person who appears to him to be suffering from mental disorder and to be in immediate need of care or control, the constable may, if he thinks it necessary to do so in the interests of that person or for the protection of other persons, remove that person to a place of safety within the meaning of Section 135.

(2) A person removed to a place of safety under this section may be detained there for a period not exceeding 72 hours for the purpose of enabling him to be examined by a registered medical practitioner and to be interviewed by an approved social worker and of making any necessary arrangements for his treatment or care.

Figure 20.10 Police Powers Section 136.

1. To accept a patient and record admission (Section 140).
2. To give information to detained patient (Section 132).
3. To give information to nearest relative (Section 132(4)) and inform him of discharge (Section 133(1)) or of detention (Section 25(2)).
4. To discharge patient (Section 23(2) (b)). Powers may be exercised by any three or more members of the authority (Section 23(4)).
5. To refer patient to Mental Health Review Tribunal (Section 63(1) (2)).
6. To transfer patient (Section 19(3), Section 19(1a) Reg. 7(2) and Reg. 7(3)).
7. To give notice to local social services authority specifying hospitals in which arrangements are made for reception in case of special urgency of patients requiring treatment for mental disorder (Section 140).

Definition of managers
District health authority or special health authority responsible for the administration of the hospital (Section 145).
   All powers can be delegated by Manager to the officers except for 4 above: discharging the patient.

Figure 20.11 Role of the managers.

own forms for this purpose which record the date and time the patient arrives and the number and name of the constable who brings the patient in.

The Mental Health Review Tribunal

Table 20.3 illustrates the time limits for applying to the tribunal, the powers of the tribunal, and the applicants. A major innovation of the 1983 Act is that the managers must automatically refer a patient to the tribunal if he has failed to apply himself. Every child under 16 must be referred by the managers every year if he has not himself applied.

The role of the managers

The managers are given certain statutory duties under the Act. These are set out in Fig. 20.11. Of these all can be delegated by the NHS Trust Board except the duty to hear

Table 20.3 Applications to Mental Health Review Tribunals

Section	Patient	Nearest relative	Manager
2 or 4	Applications by patients within first 14 days of detention	No application by nearest relative	No application by manager
3	Application by patient within first 6 months of detention, once within second 6 months, then annually	Yes, within 28 days of being informed that responsible medical officer has issued report barring discharge of patient When an order is made appointing a nearest relative under Section 29 On reclassification of patient under Section 16	Automatic referral if tribunal has not considered case within first 6 months of detention, thereafter if tribunal has not considered case within previous 3 years (1 year if patient is under 16)
37	Yes, once within second 6 months of detention, then annually	Yes, once within second 6 months of detention, then annually	Automatic if the case has not been considered by tribunal within previous 3 years (1 year if patient is under 16)
41	Yes, once within second 6 months of detention, then annually	No application by nearest relative	Automatic referral by Home Secretary if tribunal has not considered case within the preceding 3 years

---

1. Composition: chairman and about 90 members (doctors, nurses, lawyers, social workers, academics, psychologists, other specialists and lay members).
2. Seven Commission visiting teams with headquarters in Nottingham.
3. Ten National Standing Committees.
4. Duty to draft and monitor Code of Practice.
5. Prepare a biennial report to Parliament.
6. Review any decision at a special hospital to withhold a postal packet or its content.
7. Carry out on behalf of the Secretary of State duties in relation to the review of the exercise of powers and discharge of duties under the Act, visiting and interviewing detained patients, and hearing complaints from detained patients.
8. Exercise duties and appointment of second-opinion doctors in relation to Part IV. Consent to treatment provisions.

Figure 20.12 Powers and constitution of the Mental Health Act Commission.

---

an application from a patient for discharge. In this case the NHS Trust is empowered to appoint a subcommittee for hearing such applications.

The Mental Health Act Commission

Figure 20.12 illustrates the powers and constitution of the Mental Health Act Commission.

Questions and exercises

1 What are the main differences in law between treating a patient who is severely mentally handicapped in a general hospital and treating a similar patient in a mental hospital?
2 Study the restraint and seclusion policy in your hospital and consider the extent to which its implementation can remain within the law.
3 Ask to see the latest report of the Mental Health Act Commission in your hospital.
4 In what ways would informal patients benefit from coming under the jurisdiction of the Mental Health Act Commission?
5 Do patients under long-term detention, and therefore under the consent to treatment provisions of the Act, stand in a more favourable position in law than the informal patient or those under short-term detention? (See also Chapter 7.)

21 Accident and emergency, out-patients and genito-urinary medical departments

Figure 21.1 sets out the main areas of concern to the nurse who works in these departments.

The accident and emergency department

Pressure of work

SITUATION 21.1 PRIORITIES UNDER PRESSURE

The accident and emergency department was unusually pressurised one weekend: staff shortages due to a flu epidemic and cut-backs because of an attempt to reduce overspending left only a skeleton staff. Unfortunately, there was a particularly horrific pile-up on the motorway in the fog. Twelve people were brought in with varying levels of seriousness. One of them, David Lewis, a boy of 10 years, appeared to be mainly suffering from shock and bruises. He complained of a sore wrist. His mother was advised to take him home and give him a few aspirin, a hot drink, and after a good night's sleep he would be fine. The next day, however, it was learnt that he had died during the night after inhaling vomit.

1. Accident and emergency department
   (a) pressure of work;
   (b) giving information to patients;
   (c) relationship between GP and the A & E dept;
   (d) extent of duty of care;
   (e) pressure to disclose confidential information.
2. Out-patients department
   (a) excessive waiting;
   (b) mistaken identity.
3. Genito-urinary medicine
   (a) confidentiality;
   (b) request for information by spouse;
   (c) tracing;
   (d) venereal disease regulations;
   (e) AIDS testing.

Figure 21.1 Issues covered in Chapter 21.

This type of situation is one which is dreaded by accident and emergency staff. However, the pressure they are under will not be a defence if it can be established that they failed to follow the approved accepted practice in relation to the care of the patient. Dealing with children is particularly difficult since they cannot always correctly identify the site of any pain and discomfort. The possibility of head injury does not appear to have been considered in this case and this would be subject to investigation. Was the mother told the correct way of caring for the boy? The legal position is as follows: there is a duty to care for the boy; it must be established by the parents that the staff failed to follow the accepted approved practice, and that this failure foreseeably led to the death of the boy.

The work load in an accident and emergency department is extremely erratic. One moment there can be few demands, and then there may be a major incident or a sudden bout of patients and the pressure is on. What is the standard of care in such circumstances? Even though the nurses and doctors are under extreme pressure, each patient is still entitled to expect the appropriate standard of care. Thus it would still be actionable if a fracture remained undiagnosed or if a head injury were to be missed. However, the courts would take into account the pressure on the staff if priorities had to be set over who should be treated first. It would be open to the court to examine the basis of these priorities. It might be recalled that in the midwifery case (Chapter 5) where one patient alleged that she should have been seen earlier, the court was prepared to examine the records of other patients who were in the ward at the time to see if they were making demands on the staff at that time. The policy of triage has not yet been brought before the courts but there is no reason to doubt that the above principles would apply, i.e. the professional staff have to take all due care in treating the patients and where priorities have to be decided upon this must be according to approved accepted practice. There is no doubt that, in general, pressure of work does not justify a lower standard of care for the patient. It may in addition lead to a successful action against the NHS

Trust itself if it can be established that the authority failed to provide adequate resources and training for the patients to be cared for safely. It may be necessary in emergencies for staff to undertake tasks that they are not properly trained to do. If so, it is a question of balancing one risk against another, i.e. the risk of not being treated at all against the risk of harm arising because the only available person to treat the patient has not had sufficient training.

Giving information to patients

Additional precautions must thus be taken to ensure that where the patient is not detained overnight he has sufficient information to recognise any signs and symptoms which suggest a return to the hospital or to the general practitioner for further consultation and examination. Most hospitals already have preprinted leaflets covering warnings in relation to head injuries, care of plaster, the need for anti-tetanus, and other potential dangers. There is a need to stress, by word of mouth also, the importance of a patient following these instructions. If a patient ignored the instructions, having had clear advice from the staff, there is unlikely to be any blame on the part of the staff and certainly there may be a large element of contributory negligence on the part of the patient. Where information is given by word of mouth to the patient, one frequent concern of the staff is 'How can I prove what I said since it is only the patient's word against mine?' This is always a dilemma in negligence cases, since no matter how strong the defendant's case would appear to be on paper it still has to be proved through witnesses to the satisfaction of the courts. It is here that good record-keeping can be very important. If the nurse notes that the patient was given the relevant information, this does not in itself prove that he was since any lies can be recorded, but it does indicate the existence of a system where the nurse is more likely than not to have given the requisite information. In addition of course, any witness who can recall the events and substantiate what the nurse was saying will undoubtedly help her. An additional precaution where it is essential to emphasise the importance of following the correct advice is for the patient himself to be asked to sign that he has understood the importance of obeying the instructions (see also Chapter 4).

Relationship between the duty of care owed by the GP and by the accident and emergency department

Another difficulty which arises in the accident and emergency department is the extent to which the department is used, inappropriately as far as the operational policy of the accident and emergency department is concerned, as a GP surgery or health centre.

SITUATION 21.2 MINOR AILMENTS

A patient came into the accident and emergency department complaining of a pain in his ear. He was registered by the admission clerk and seen by a nurse who then told him to wait to see the doctor. The doctor asked him how long he had had the pain and the man said that he had had it for about three days. He was asked if he had been to see his GP and he said that he was not sure who his GP was. The house officer suggested that he should go to see his GP and that he should not have come to the accident and emergency department which was for emergency treatment of a serious kind. The man was very reluctant to go and very upset. It was subsequently learnt that he was admitted to the District General Hospital with mastoid meningitis and an enquiry was established to find out why he had not been diagnosed in the accident and emergency department.

The general principle would appear to be that once a patient comes through the doors, then a duty of care is owed and the patient should not be sent away without an adequate examination. The words 'through the doors' are important since a duty of care is not owed in a vacuum. It is perfectly possible for a hospital to say 'we do not accept accident and emergency patients here' and refuse to treat a patient. However, once a hospital accepts a patient for attention, then a duty of care would arise to ensure that this patient receives the appropriate standard of care, even though it might mean arranging the transfer of the patient to another hospital.

Extent of duty of care

SITUATION 21.3 REFERRAL FOR WHAT?

A patient was referred to the accident and emergency department by the GP for X-ray because she had fallen and sustained a severe injury and considerable bruising to her leg. The house officer arranged for her to be X-rayed and it was found to be negative. The patient mentioned to the doctor that she was very short of breath and thirsty. However, only her leg was examined. She subsequently discovered that she was suffering from diabetes and claimed that the casualty officer should have diagnosed this.

This is another situation which raises the extent of the duty of care owed by the hospital staff to the patient. If the GP refers a patient for a very specific purpose which is carried out, can it then be said that the patient should have been given a full examination so that other significant defects could have been detected? The answer must obviously depend upon the particular circumstances and what is the reasonably accepted approved practice.

Pressure to disclose confidential information

The basic principles relating to the disclosure of confidential information have already been discussed in Chapter 8. In that chapter two examples are given of requests for information in accident and emergency departments. Staff are under particular pressure in this respect since they are likely to be hounded by both the police and the press in order that sensitive and personal information can be disclosed. The professions owe a duty to society which takes precedence over the duty owed to the patient. However, the codes of ethics are couched in general terms and do not cover specific examples. The advice is that, where in doubt as to where the individual's duty lies, advice should be taken from the professional associations and the UKCC. The statutory powers of the police under the Police and Criminal Evidence Act enable, in cases of serious arrestable offences, a special procedure to be followed to compel the production of personal information and human tissue which would otherwise be protected from disclosure. Some hospitals have different policies and procedures relating to disclosure in different circumstances and these vary in the degree of readiness with which this confidential information is disclosed (see Appendix 13 for an example of one policy). Whatever the policy, in the end it must be the individual professional's decision since that individual may have to justify to the patient why the duty of confidentiality was not maintained.

SITUATION 21.4 ROAD TRAFFIC ACCIDENTS

The police are entitled to know the names and addresses of those who have been involved in a road traffic accident. This does not mean, however, that the media are also entitled to know these names or to know the condition of the patient. If the patient gives consent (and possibly the relatives, though this is more doubtful), then the information can be disclosed. If, however, this consent is refused the hospital spokesman must remain silent as far as the disclosure of any confidential information is concerned. Once again, practice varies and there is an absence of court cases to settle the issue. For example, some hospitals allow a condition report to be given to the press without obtaining the consent of the patient, e.g. 'Of the ten persons injured in the motorway pile-up on Tuesday one has since died, three have been discharged, four are comfortable, and two are on life support machines.' There are few who would see this as a breach of confidence.

Where the patients' records have been computerised and now come under the provisions of the Data Protection Act, they are of course subject to close controls over disclosure. The duty of confidentiality at common law owed to the patient in relation to all the personal information held about him should be enforced with similar close controls.

Other areas of concern to the accident and emergency staff are the problems of dealing with aggressive drunken patients and the rights of the staff to claim compensation either from the criminal courts (if there is a successful prosecution of the assailant) or of claiming from the Criminal Injuries Compensation Authority. These topics have been fully dealt with in Chapter 12 and will not be repeated here. Problems relating to the unconscious patient and the patient who has attempted to commit suicide have been considered in Chapter 7 on consent to treatment.

The out-patients department

Excessive waiting

SITUATION 21.5 WAITING_____

Bruce was self-employed and time was money. He had been suffering from a severe pain and his doctor had referred him to the consultant surgeon querying gallstones or cholecystitis. He was sent an appointment to see the surgeon at 9.30 a.m. in out-patients. Because he had an important meeting that afternoon which could involve him in a lot of valuable work he phoned the clerk who assured him that the clinic ended at lunch time. When he got to the clinic he discovered that 30 people had been booked in for 9.30, most of whom had arrived before him. As he sat chatting he discovered that others who had been booked in for 12.00 a.m. had come early since they were seen in the order of arrival and not according to appointments. He settled down for a long wait and then was told at 1.00 p.m. that the surgeon had had to rush off to theatre to cover for a colleague who had been taken ill, but that if Bruce waited the doctor would see him when the operation was over. Bruce said that he could not wait as he had a very important meeting. The clerk replied that if he went away he would be treated as a 'did not attend' and would have to take his place in the queue being seen in out-patients. He would not be able to give him an appointment for at least another three months. Bruce insisted on seeing the sister in charge.

Oddly enough there seems to be no grounds for bringing an action against an NHS Trust for causing excessive waiting in out-patients departments. At least, one has not yet been tried. If it was private practice and there was therefore a contract between professional and client, then it could be more clearly argued that there was a breach of contract when a client was kept waiting an unreasonable length of time. However, in NHS care there is no contract between the patient and the NHS Trust or between the patient and the professional, and the patient who is aggrieved at having to wait an unreasonably long time would have to argue that there was a breach of the duty of care owed to the patient under the laws of negligence which has caused him some loss or harm – a loss or harm which is compensatable under the law. There have been actions when patients have waited excessively long periods of time for inpatient treatment. However, no action has been brought in relation to a long wait within the department itself. Such a complaint is more likely to be investigated by the hospital management and then, if the patient is not happy with the response, to end up on the desk of the Health Service Commissioner or ombudsman. He has investigated many complaints of unreasonable waiting times in accident and emergency, outpatients, and other departments. The procedure for handling complaints is considered in Chapter 27. The Patients' Charter and local charters set targets for maximum waiting times. Compliance with these targets cannot be enforced in a court of law but complaints can be made through the hospital complaints procedure.

In the above situation, when the sister is confronted by a very disgruntled patient, she should ensure that the facts given by the clerk are accurate. It is unlikely, for example, that a patient who has been kept waiting in the way in which Bruce has should be treated as a 'did not attend'. If so, the system is manifestly unjust. The sister should be able, with cooperation from the doctor, to arrange for Bruce to be seen much earlier. In addition, she may be able to arrange a compromise by arranging for Bruce to attend the meeting and to return that same day. Certainly, she should be able to take the heat out of the situation, explain the problems fully to Bruce, work out some acceptable solution, and, of course, apologise to him for what has happened. This is not law but it is good practice. However, there are many such occasions where the patient may or may not have a right of action in law where skilled counselling and cooperation with the patient prevents a situation developing into a court action or Health Service Commissioner's inquiry.

Mistaken identity

SITUATION 21.6 THE WRONG NOTES

Sister Bailey was short-staffed in the out-patients department and the situation was made worse by a strike among the coordinators. However, the consultants were adamant that the clinics should continue. She called out for one patient, Handel Thomas, to come to the diabetic clinic. She checked that he was from The Marina, Fish Street, and he said he was. He was asked if he had brought any samples with him and he replied 'No, no one told me to'. He was then taken in to see the consultant. He was given a very full investigation and was asked how often he injected his insulin. He was a little surprised at this and replied that he had never been told to use insulin.

After considerable confusion, during which time Handel was getting very disturbed, it emerged that there was another Handel Thomas in Fish Street. This Handel James Thomas lived at number 45 and was due to be seen in the eye clinic; the other Handel, Handel David Thomas from 2 Fish Street, should have been seen in the diabetic clinic.

In circumstances like this there has been clear negligence by the sister in failing to check that she was taking the right patient to be seen and also by the doctor who also did not check. However, apart from causing distress to the patient and a breach of confidentiality of information about the other patient, no harm has been caused to either, so it is not a case that is likely to end up in the courts. However, the potential implications of this type of mistake are terrifying and the tightest control must be kept over patient identification. Unfortunately, one cannot always rely on patients to point out the error since they become so institutionalised and frightened at the prospect of challenging the professionals that stories abound as to what they are prepared to submit to by mistake.

Genito-urinary medicine

Confidentiality

It is probably not until one has worked in a genito-urinary department (formerly known as the VD clinic, or the special clinic) that one really understands what is meant by the duty of confidentiality. This section will look at some of the problems and pitfalls that can arise over confidentiality in this context, and also at the statutory provisions.

SITUATION 21.7 A REASONABLE REQUEST

Mr Grey had just visited the GUM clinic and samples had been taken. He was told that the results would be available by the Thursday of the following week. He was naturally anxious and since he lived some 40 miles from the clinic he phoned up late Thursday morning to find out the results. He gave his name and the nurse asked for his clinic number. She explained that it was on his card. He said that he had lost his card. She therefore told him that she would be unable to give him the result over the phone. He asked if that meant that the results were positive. She said not at all but because of the principles of confidentiality she could neither confirm that someone of that name had attended the clinic nor could she give any results over the phone without the clinic number. He became very angry, pointing out the inconvenience that he would suffer if he had to drive the 40 miles there and back, especially if the results were negative. She told him that she could not change the rules. He threatened to complain about her attitude and report her.

There is no doubt that the nurse is correct in not divulging information without being absolutely certain that she is talking to the patient. There are possible ways out of this dilemma. One would be for the nurse to phone a number that had already been given by the patient to the clinic for the notification of the results. The other would be to ensure that all patients are warned of the strict rules of confidentiality from the outset of their care so that they know the rules are firmly adhered to for their own protection, even in circumstances which cause them great inconvenience such as the one above.

A similar difficulty is the following situation.

Requests for information by a spouse

SITUATION 21.8 SPOUSELY CONCERN

A man phoned the GUM clinic saying that he was the husband of Mrs Robinson, a patient who had an appointment at the clinic that afternoon. He said that she had lost her appointment card and forgotten the time, and since he was giving her a lift could they let him know the time of the appointment?

This is the sort of request that few staff in a general out-patients department would hesitate to respond to helpfully. Yet if confidentiality is to be preserved, then it is essential that the person answering the phone does not admit to the fact (if this is indeed the case) that there is a patient of such a name attending the clinic.

Tracing

Obviously it is essential that, as far as possible, any persons who have been in contact with someone who is infected should be traced and advised to have tests. It is important that this should be done without revealing the name of the contact. A form is completed to assist the clinic. Obviously, if original contacts can be persuaded to advise their contacts to have a check, this is preferable to their receiving a call out of the blue.

Venereal disease regulations

These regulations (National Health Service (Venereal Diseases) Regulations 1974 Section 1 No. 29 (as amended by SI 1982 No. 288)) ensure that any information about any sexually transmitted disease is kept confidential. They came into operation on 1 April 1974 and place a duty on every regional health authority and every district health authority to take all necessary steps to secure that any information capable of identifying an individual obtained by officers of the authority with respect to persons examined or treated for any sexually transmitted disease shall not be disclosed. The exceptions to this rule are disclosures: (a) for the purpose of communicating that information to a medical practitioner, or to a person employed under the direction of a medical practitioner in connection with the treatment of persons suffering from such disease or the prevention of the spread thereof; and (b) for the purpose of such treatment or prevention. It was suggested in the case of *X.* v. *Y and another* 1988 2 All ER 648 that AIDS came within the scope of these regulations.

AIDS testing

This problem has recently arisen and is concerned with such questions as to whether the patient's consent is needed for an AIDS test to be carried out and whether it is possible to test secretly without the patient being told the results. These questions are fully discussed in Chapter 26.

Questions and exercises

1 Does the nurse (or doctor) who works in the accident and emergency department have a duty in law to assess the priority to be given to a patient, and could she be held liable in the civil courts for failures in making that assessment?
2 Can a patient be lawfully refused treatment in an accident and emergency department and be referred instead to his GP?

3   What remedy does a patient who has waited an excessive amount of time in the accident and emergency department or the out-patients department have?

4   What remedies does a member of staff who has been injured by a drunken patient in the accident and emergency have? (See also Chapter 12.)

5   Do you consider that the spouse of a patient suffering from a sexually transmitted disease should have a right to be told of the spouse's medical condition? What is the law on this?

6   What precautions might be taken to preserve medical confidentiality in the accident and emergency department in relation to:

(a) the press;

(b) the police;

(c) other staff?

7   In what way does the duty of staff in accident and emergency departments differ from those on the wards in relation to the care of the patient's property? (Refer also to Chapter 25.)

8   A patient is admitted into the accident and emergency department with severe bleeding. His clothes have to be cut from him and because they are badly soiled they are sent for incineration. He subsequently complains that there was £300 in the pockets of his jacket. What is the liability of the hospital or of the accident and emergency staff? (Refer to Chapter 25.)

22   Reproductive medicine

Nurses are increasingly likely to be caring for patients in clinics and on the wards who are receiving treatment in connection with problems of fertility. Medical technology has made vast strides in this field and now outpaces the law. This section provides guidance on the current legislation relating to artificial insemination by donor, embryo implantation and surrogacy. Some of the legal problems which arise from sterilisation and family planning are also considered. The areas to be covered are set out in Fig. 22.1. The Human Fertilisation and Embryology Act 1990 introduced statutory controls in this field of medicine.

Artificial insemination

Artificial insemination by husband (AIH)

If a married couple require help in conception such that the husband's semen is artificially transferred to the wife, the law would see the outcome of this as being identical with natural conception. So as far as such aspects as inheritance, legal guardianship of the child, etc., are concerned there is no difference between the artificially and the naturally conceived child. However, the involvement of a third person raises the possibility of other legal issues. For example, it is possible that if a pathology laboratory is involved,

313

1. Artificial insemination
   (a) by husband;
   (b) by donor.
2. *In vitro* fertilisation.
3. Surrogacy.
4. Nurse's personal beliefs.
5. Confidentiality.
6. Sterilisation and contraception
   (a) unsuccessful sterilisation: compensation;
   (b) failure to warn of risk of pregnancy;
   (c) private health care.

Figure 22.1 Issues covered in Chapter 22.

there could be a mix-up over the semen and the woman could be given semen from someone other than her husband. With genetic coding it would now be possible to prove that the child is not the husband's, though of course it must be remembered that in order to succeed in a negligence action it must be established that there was a causal link between the negligent act and the harm caused (the woman could have had sex with a third person). Some have opposed AIH on moral grounds since it is an unnatural form of conception, but the Warnock Committee (Committee of Inquiry into Human Fertilisation and Embryology 1984 Cmnd. 9314) were of the view that it was an acceptable form of treatment except where a widow used semen that had been stored in a semen bank. They felt that insemination after the husband's death could lead to profound psychological problems for the child and the mother. They felt that there was no need or even practical possibility of formal regulation of AIH but recommended that it should be administered by or under the supervision of a medical practitioner.

No licence is required under the 1990 Act for artificial insemination by husband, or by the woman's partner's sperm. Nor is one required for AIP (artificial insemination of an unmarried woman with her partner's sperm). Neither AIH nor AIP require the use of donated gametes. GIFT (gamete intrafallopian transfer) does not require a licence if the egg and sperm come from the woman and her partner/husband.

Artificial insemination by donor (AID)

Where the donor is not the husband, problems over legitimacy, rights to inheritance and the duties of the husband in relation to the child arise. A report from the Archbishop of Canterbury in 1948 recommended that AID should be made a criminal offence. The Feversham report set up by the government in 1960 recommended that AID should be discouraged. The opposite has happened. In 1973 a panel under the chairmanship of Sir John Peel recommended the setting up of accreditation centres for AID but this has not taken place. An early case regarding the rights of the father was that of *A.* v. *C.* 1978 8 Fam Law 170 where the father and mother entered into an agreement that the girl would be artificially inseminated by him and then hand over the child on payment of £3,000. She refused to hand the child over and the trial judge gave the father limited rights of access. The Court of Appeal, however, gave him no rights of access.

Artificial insemination by donor is not unlawful, but in contrast to the child born from AIH, the child born as a result of AID is illegitimate and the husband of the mother has no parental rights and duties in relation to the child unless he accepts the child as a child of the family. The donor could be held responsible for the maintenance of the child and could apply to the court for access or custody. The provisions of the 1990 Act on AID are set out in Fig. 22.2.

1. Definition of terms 'embryo' and 'gamete'.
2. Specific activities prohibited:
    (a) bringing about the creation of an embryo or keeping or using an embryo EXCEPT in pursuance of a licence;
    (b) placing in a woman a live embryo other than a human embryo or any live gametes other than human gametes;
    (c) A licence cannot authorise:
        (i)   keeping or using an embryo after the appearance of the primitive streak, not later than 14 days after the gametes are mixed;
        (ii) placing an embryo in any animal;
        (iii) keeping or using an embryo in any circumstances in which regulations prohibit its keeping or use; or
        (iv) replacing a nucleus of a cell of an embryo with a nucleus taken from a cell of any person or embryo or subsequent development of an embryo.
    (d) (i) No person can store gametes, provide treatment services for women (other than AID, AIP or GIFT), or mix gametes with live gametes of an animal, unless in pursuance of a licence.
        (ii) A licence cannot authorise storing or using gametes in any circumstances prohibited by regulations.
3. Human Fertilisation and Embryology Authority established with the function of:
    (a) reviewing information about embryos and advising Secretary of State;
    (b) publicising services provided to public by HFEA or in pursuance of licences;
    (c) providing advice and information;
    (d) other functions specified in regulations;
    (e) monitor committees to grant licences;
    (f) to give directions.
4. Licences for treatment, storage, research and conditions of holding licence.
5. Code of Practice to be issued by HFEA subject to Secretary of State's approval.
6. Definition of 'mother' and 'father'.
7. Register of information to be kept by HFEA with restriction on disclosure.
8. Amendments to Surrogacy Arrangements Act 1985 by providing that no surrogacy arrangement is enforceable by or against any of the persons making it.
9. Changes to Abortion Act 1967 (see Chapter 15).
10. Protection of those with conscientious objection.
11. Powers of enforcement given to HFEA including power to enter premises.
12. Offences established.

Figure 22.2 Provisions of Human Fertilisation and Embryology Act 1990 (summary of contents).

A consultation paper was published by the government in 1986. As yet only a few of these recommendations have been implemented in law, one of which is the treating of a child born to a woman as the result of artificial insemination by someone other than her husband as the child of the parties of that marriage. This is enacted by Section 27 of the Family Reform Act 1987. The main condition is that the marriage must be in existence at the time. Proof to the satisfaction of the court that the other party to the marriage did not consent to the insemination will prevent this provision arising. This means that the burden is placed on the husband to show that the insemination was performed without his consent. This provision came into force in April 1988 and only applies to children born subsequently.

In vitro fertilisation

The external fertilisation of an egg, extracted from the ovary, with semen is a relatively new development and the Human Fertilisation and Embryology Act 1990 provides a framework for control, covering such issues as the disposal of unwanted embryos, their ownership, power to undertake research on these embryos, embryo donation to another woman, or genetic engineering to prevent hereditary disorders or to create a superhuman. Fertilisation outside the body coupled with transfer of the embryo into the uterus is, in its most simple form, a means of overcoming a fertility problem in a married couple. However, because of the possibility of egg and semen donation and subsequent transfer to a woman other than the provider of the egg, a complex situation can arise. In addition, it can be coupled with a surrogacy arrangement whereby a couple for whom the woman is unable to carry a child arrange for an embryo created from their egg and semen to be inserted into a host woman who will return the child to the genetic parents after birth. The surrogacy arrangements will be considered later. This part will deal with IVF and ET (embryo transfer to the uterus).

The majority of the Warnock Committee recommended a time limit of 14 days because at about the 15th day after conception the formation of the primitive streak can be identified. This is the first of several identifiable features which develop in and from the embryonic disc during the succeeding days.

Subsequently a consultation paper and a white paper were produced in 1986. In *R. v. Ethical Committee of St Mary's Hospital ex parte Marnot, The Times* 27 October 1987) the High Court refused an application for judicial review of decisions by consultants who decided that a woman should be refused IVF treatment. The provisions of the Human Fertilisation and Embryology Act 1990 on IVF are set out in Fig. 22.2. On 20 July 1994 the Human Fertilisation and Embryology Authority ruled that eggs from aborted foetuses could not be used in fertility treatment, but they could be used in research. The same ruling applies to the eggs of a dead woman, even though she is carrying a donor card.

Surrogacy

This might be thought of, like IVF, to be a result of the recent developments in medical technology. However, the Biblical story of Abraham resorting to the servant who could bear a child for him because Sarah was barren is an early example of one form of surrogacy. The possibility of embryo implantation has, however, increased the number of ways in which surrogacy can take place. The child that is born might have no genetic relationship with the ultimate parents but be the natural child of the bearing mother or even an embryo from two donors. More likely, however, is the situation where the child is genetically related to the father as a result of artifical insemination but not to the adopting mother. Prior to the Warnock Report the only legislation which covered a surrogacy situation was the child care legislation and rules relating to adoption. Section 50, for example, of the Adoption Act 1958 prohibits any payment in connection with adoption. Such surrogate cases as Baby Cotton revealed the gaps in the law and the uncertainties surrounding basic questions. Is a contract for surrogacy enforceable by either party, neither party, or only by the mother? What are the legal implications if the child is handicapped? What controls do the contracting couple have over the standard of life of the mother during the pregnancy, e.g. what if she smokes or drinks heavily? If she changes her mind and has an abortion, are damages then payable?

CASE 22.1 A SURROGACY DISPUTE

Mr and Mrs A. were unable to have children and because of their age had been refused as adoptive parents. They entered into a surrogacy arrangement with Mrs B. who wished to help the childless couple. Under the arrangement, it was agreed that Mr and Mrs A. would pay £10,000 to Mrs B. who would give up her job to have the child. In due course a child was conceived, but in the event Mrs B. accepted only £5,000 and refused the balance. It was clear that the amount did not cover Mrs B.'s loss of earnings and expenses. After the birth Mr and Mrs A. applied to court for an adoption order. The question arose (a) whether the payment of money had been a payment of reward for adoption within the meaning of the Adoption Act Section 50 (1) and (b) if there had been a contravention of the section, whether the court could make a retrospective authorisation in respect of the payment under Section 50 (3) of the Act and grant an adoption order (*In re an adoption (surrogacy)* 1987 2 All ER 826).

It was held that a payment to the mother in a surrogacy arrangement did not contravene the Act if payments made by those others to the natural mother did not include an element of profit or financial reward. Even if they were made for reward the court had a discretion under the Act to authorise the payments retrospectively. The court granted the adoption order.

The government made clear its attitude to the commercial aspects of surrogacy, even before the full details of the Warnock Report had been digested, and the Surrogacy Arrangements Act 1985 was passed. This Act prohibits the making of surrogacy arrangements on a commercial basis. Those companies that had come over from the United States and started to arrange surrogacy contracts were thus forced out of business in the United Kingdom. This approach had been recommended by the Warnock Committee, whose recommendations, however, went further and suggested that both profit- and non-profit-making organisations should be made illegal, and also that any professional who knowingly assisted in the establishment of a surrogacy pregnancy should be criminally liable. They recommended that all surrogacy arrangements should be held illegal and unenforceable in the courts. Section 36(i) of the 1990 Act amends the 1985 Act to make a surrogacy arrangement unenforceable. It does not make it illegal.

The 1990 Act Section 30 enables a court to order a child to be treated as a child to the parties of the marriage where another woman has acted as surrogate, provided that certain conditions are met.

The nurse's personal moral beliefs

Section 38 of the Human Fertilisation and Embryology Act 1990 provides a conscientious objection clause as follows:

1. No person who has a conscientious objection to participating in any activity governed by this Act shall be under any duty, however arising, to do so.
2. In any legal proceedings the burden of proof of conscientious objection shall rest on the person claiming to rely on it.
3. In any proceedings, before a court in Scotland, a statement on oath by any person to the effect that he has a conscientious objection to participating in a particular activity governed by the Act shall be sufficient evidence of that fact for the purpose of discharging the burden of proof imposed by subsection (2) above.

Confidentiality

Section 33 of the 1990 Act places tight restriction on the disclosure of information held by the HFEA or a licensing authority. The few exceptions to these restrictives were considered to be inadequate and the Human Fertilisation and Embryology (Disclosure of Information) Act 1992 was passed, amending Section 33 as follows: to enable the patient to give specific and general consent to disclosure; for information to be disclosed by a clinician to his legal adviser in relation to legal proceedings (the 1990 Act had only permitted disclosures in relation to action under the Consented Disabilities (Civil Liability) Act 1976); and for a couple to obtain information about the legal parentage of a child born to a surrogate mother. Statutory Instrument 1993 No. 746 restricts the right of access to health records which would disclose information showing that an unidentifiable individual was or may have been born in consequence of treatment services under the Human Fertilisation and Embryology Act 1990. This does not affect the right given by Section 31(3) which enables a person of 18 or over to obtain information from HFEA if that person was born in consequence of treatment services, but an opportunity for proper counselling must be provided before disclosure.

Sterilisation and contraception

An operation to sterilise a patient can give rise to several problems, some of which are considered elsewhere. Does the spouse have the right to give or withhold consent for such a procedure? This is considered in Chapter 15. What if the operation is unsuccessful? Does the patient have the right to sue for compensation? Can she obtain compensation for the birth of an unwanted child? If the child is handicapped, does that child have the right to obtain compensation? If the mother, on discovering herself to be pregnant, refuses to have an abortion, does this bar her claim to compensation? If the sterilisation is carried out in the private sector, does this give the parent any greater rights if the sterilisation operation is unsuccessful?

Unsuccessful sterilisations: compensation

CASE 22.2 UNWANTED PREGNANCY_____

Mrs Emeh, a mother of three children, underwent an operation for sterilisation in May 1976. In January 1977 she discovered that she was 20 weeks' pregnant. She refused to have an abortion. She then gave birth to a child with congenital abnormalities who required constant medical and parental supervision. She claimed damages for the unwanted pregnancy and the birth and upkeep of the child. The trial judge held that the operation had been performed negligently and she could therefore recover damages for the time before she discovered the pregnancy, but since she refused to have an abortion she was not entitled to the costs thereafter apart from the cost of undergoing the second sterilisation operation. Mrs Emeh appealed to the Court of Appeal and won.

The Court of Appeal held that since the avoidance of a further pregnancy was the object of the sterilisation operation, it was unreasonable after the period of pregnancy which had elapsed to expect the plaintiff to undergo an abortion. Her failure to do so was not unreasonable. She was therefore entitled to recover damages for her financial loss caused by the negligent performance of the sterilisation operation. She was awarded £7,000 loss of future earnings, £3,000 for pain and suffering up to the trial and £10,000 for future loss of amenity and pain and suffering which will occur during the life of the child (*Emeh* v. *Kensington and Chelsea and Westminster Health Authority* 1985 2 WLR 233).

This decision is to be welcomed since it reverses an earlier decision in *Udale* v. *Bloomsbury AHA* 1983 2 All ER 522.

The mother's refusal to have an abortion was not an unreasonable one and it could not be used as a reason to limit the damages payable. Even if the baby had been healthy there are no reasons why compensation might not be payable. It must be emphasised that the mother has to be able to establish that the operation was performed negligently.

In a recent case (*Allen* v. *Bloomsbury Health Authority and another* 1993 1 All ER 651) a woman was sterilised when she was four weeks' pregnant, a fact unknown to herself and the surgeon. The Health Authority accepted liability and damages of £96,631 were awarded which included the future cost of caring for and educating the child. A pregnancy test should have been carried out before the operation for sterilisation was performed.

Failure to warn of the risk of pregnancy

There have been cases, however, where no negligence in the performance of the operation has been proved but compensation has been claimed on the grounds that the patient was not warned that there was a possibility of the operation being reversed and the patient becoming fertile or pregnant. This occurred in the following case:

CASE 22.3 NO WARNING

Mrs Gold, who had two children, decided when she became pregnant again that she would not have any more children. She was referred to the consultant obstetrician who suggested sterilisation but did not discuss the possibility of the husband having a vasectomy which had a slighter lower failure rate, nor did he discuss the risk of failure with her. The sterilisation operation was performed the day after the birth of the child but was not a success and Mrs Gold gave birth to a fourth child. She sued the Health Authority for negligence because she had not been warned of the risk of failure and the statement that the operation was irreversible was a negligent misrepresentation.

Initially Mrs Gold was awarded £19,000 damages on the grounds that, although the operation had not been negligently performed, the defendants had been negligent in failing to warn her of the possibility of failure of the operation. The defendants appealed and the Court of Appeal allowed the appeal for the following reasons:

1. The standard of care required of the medical practitioner was the same as that required of members of the profession, i.e. the ordinary skilled member of that profession who exercised and professed that special skill (see Chapter 3 for further details on this standard). Where medical advice had been given the standard of care required did not depend on the context in which it was given but on whether there was a substantial body of doctors who would have given the same advice. Since in 1979 a substantial body of responsible doctors would not have warned her of the risk of failure of the sterilisation operation the Health Authority was not liable in negligence.
2. The statement that the operation was irreversible could not reasonably be constructed as a representation that the operation was bound to achieve its objectives. Mrs Gold therefore lost the case (*Gold* v. *Haringey HA* 1987 2 All ER 888).

The Court of Appeal made it clear that it did not accept any distinction between advice given for a therapeutic procedure and that for a non-therapeutic procedure. The same standard should be applied to both, i.e. the 'Bolam Test'.

Private health care

What if the case concerns an operation carried out in the private sector? Do any different principles apply?

CASE 22.4 A FAILED VASECTOMY

Mr Thake, a railway guard, and his wife and four children lived in a three-bedroomed council house. When a fifth child was expected Mr Thake discussed with a surgeon the possibility of undergoing a vasectomy. Because of the long NHS waiting list it was agreed that the operation would be performed privately at a cost of £20. It was made clear to him that he would become permanently sterile. Both husband and wife signed forms consenting to the operation and declaring that they had been told of its purpose and effects. Tests on Mr Thake subsequently showed him to be sterile. However, two years after the operation Mrs Thake became pregnant again but did not realise her condition until it was too late to have an abortion. They claimed compensation. There was no suggestion that the operation had been performed negligently but that suitable warnings had not been given.

The judge held as follows:

1. On the facts the contract was not merely a contract to perform a vasectomy but was a contract to make Mr Thake irreversibly sterile.
2. The defendant failed to give a warning or gave too vague a warning about the possibility of the plaintiff becoming fertile again and was therefore in breach of a warranty that Mr Thake would remain sterile. Alternatively, the absence of the warning meant that the wife failed to realise the possibility that she might be pregnant in time to have had an abortion.
3. There was no reason on grounds of public policy that damages should not be payable for the unwanted birth of a healthy child.
4. There would be no damages for the distress, pain and suffering undergone by the plaintiffs because that was cancelled out by the joy they had received from the child. They were entitled, however, to damages for the birth and the upkeep of the child but on a moderate basis in view of the humble household into which the child had been born (*Thake* v. *Maurice* 1984 2 All ER 513).

It is clear from the arguments in this case that the contractual rights were important. Similar arguments could not be used in an NHS context since there is no contractual relationship between an NHS patient and the health authority or doctor. However, this case has led to much more meticulous wording of the agreement and warnings in relation to the possibilities of failure.

The sterilisation of a child under 16 is considered in Chapter 13 on paediatrics and the law, and is also discussed in Chapter 15 on gynaecology. The law relating to contraceptive advice for the under 16-year-old is also considered in the chapter on paediatric nursing (Chapter 13).

The future

Scientific developments in the field of genetics have progressed faster than the law and discussion is currently taking place in the following areas:

1. *Gene therapy* The Clothies Committee (HMSO, January 1992) recommended that research should continue for somatic cell gene therapy where treatment is given to an individual patient to alleviate disease (e.g. cystic fibrosis). However, germ line gene therapy, where future generations are affected, should not as yet be lawful. The establishment of a supervisory body was recommended. The Gene Therapy Advisory Committee has now been established under the chairmanship of Professor Dame Jane Lloyd.
2. *Gender selection* A commercial organisation has been set up to assist couples in obtaining the gender of their choice for their child. Where this does not involve gametes of other persons it does not come under the provision of the 1990 Act. Some consider, however, that there should be controls in this field.
3. *Genetic screening* Concern at the possibility that insurers and employers would require compulsory genetic screening led to the Nuffield Council on Bioethics reporting on the ethical issues involved in genetic screening. It recommended safeguards in relation to consent, confidentiality and monitoring of genetic screening programmes.

Questions and exercises

1 Look at the daily papers and journals over the next month and collect details on the cases, debates, and articles on the topics discussed in this chapter.
2 To what extent do you think that parents should have the right to obtain treatment for their infertility?
3 Where a child is born as the result of a surrogacy arrangement so that an embryo from a woman and her husband is transplanted into the uterus of another woman, what legal rights do you believe that the woman giving birth to the child should have over the genetic mother? What legal rights does she have at present?
4 Can experimentation on an embryo and its replacement in the uterus to develop as a human being be justified?
5 To what extent do you think the law is an appropriate machinery to determine the choices of parents and professionals in the topics discussed here?

23   Community nursing

The development of community care has meant that the focus for many health professionals has switched from the institution to the community and those who have always been community workers such as the health visitor and the district nurse are now feeling the increased pressure from the recent implications of the policy to transfer patients from the institution to the community. Recent developments have seen an increase in specialist posts in the community: community nurses for the mentally handicapped and community psychiatric nurses are increasing in number and specialist posts for stoma care, incontinence and terminal illness are being established. Many liaison nurses are now seeking specialist training. There are increased appointments for occupational therapists, physiotherapists, and community paediatricians. This section will consider some of the different issues which arise for these workers. Figure 23.2 sets out the areas which will be discussed in this chapter and Fig. 23.1 illustrates some of the particular difficulties with which these workers are faced.

NHS and Community Care Act 1990

The community provisions of this Act came into force on 1 April 1993 and are summarised below. They follow the recommendations of the Griffiths Report and the white paper 'Caring for People'. The Act requires the following:

1. Community care plans. Under Section 46, local authorities in conjunction with health authorities and the voluntary and private sector must prepare plans for the provision of services in the community and revise them annually.

2. Assessment of needs for community care services. Section 47 requires local authorities to carry out an assessment of needs for community services on any individual in its catchment area who would appear to be in need of any services that it provides or for which it arranges the provision. Where appropriate the health authority and/or the housing authority may be required to be involved in the assessment. In urgent situations community care services can be provided temporarily and an assessment should take place as soon as possible.

3. Financial arrangements for nursing and residential accommodation. The local authority has the responsibility for purchasing accommodation for clients from 1 April 1993. Those in residence on 31 March 1993 will continue to receive means-tested higher-level Income Support from the Department of Social Security. For those residents who move in on or after 1 April 1993 the local authority, following an assessment, may purchase a place at a nursing home or residential home and recover the fees from residents, who can claim means-tested Income Support from the DSS but only at the ordinary level.

4. Inspection and powers of the Secretary of State. Persons can be authorised by the Secretary of State under Section 48 to inspect premises used for the provision of community care services. Local authorities have inspection units. The Secretary of State can issue directions as to the exercise of social services functions (Section 50) and has required all local authorities to establish a procedure for considering any representations, including complaints about a failure to discharge local authority social services functions.

5. The Act also makes provision for the transfer of health service staff to local authorities (Section 49).

Considerable guidance has been issued by the Department of Health and Social Service Inspectorate on the implementation of these statutory duties. The Audit Commission (*Taking Care: Progress with Care in the Community*, December 1993) reported that cautious but steady progress has been made with the community care changes. Community health professionals are finding that they are caring for a more acutely ill population as the number of day cases increase and shorter lengths of stay for major surgery become the norm. The 'hospital at home' phenomenon places increasing pressure on community nurses who must ensure that their competence, skill and knowledge develop to meet their new roles. All community health professionals, whether caring for acute, chronically sick, mentally disordered, elderly or disabled patients are finding that the demands upon them are increasing and there are greater pressures on resources. Waiting lists for occupational therapy services are increasing in length. Controversy has developed over the nature of assessment and the extent to which they should identify needs which cannot realistically be met. The practitioner who works in the community should ensure that she plays a full part in the preparation of community care plans and the identification of needs and in upholding the professional duties to the patient set out in the Code of Professional Conduct (see Appendix 1).

1. Negligence and standard of care
   (a) key worker;
   (b) foreseeability and standard of care;
   (c) to whom is the nurse responsible?
   (d) giving advice;
   (e) vaccination.
2. Safety of the community professional
   (a) defective premises;
   (b) aggression.
3. Consent to treatment
   (a) mentally disordered;
   (b) forcible entry;
   (c) compulsory removal
       (i) Mental Health Act 1983
       (ii) National Assistance Act 1948.
4. Protection of property.
5. Disclosure of information.
6. Criminal suspicion.

Figure 23.1 Issues covered in Chapter 23.

1. Isolation.
2. Vulnerability.
3. Sole responsibility.
4. Pressure to go beyond job description.
5. Health and safety hazard and occupier's liability.
6. Variable facilities and resources.

Figure 23.2 Difficulties faced by the nurse in the community.

Negligence

The standard of care

SITUATION 23.1 KEY WORKER

The Roger Park Community set up a series of location managers and teams of multi-disciplinary professionals for clients. Each client was assigned a key worker who would discuss with the team that particular client's difficulties and try to resolve them as far as possible on his own, thus preventing the client from being visited by a whole host of different professionals. This key worker could be any one of a variety of professionals but as far as possible it was one whose training was most relevant to the client's needs. Margaret Downs lived on her own and was recovering from a stroke. With the help of the physiotherapist she was making good progress and the district nurse, Angela Hide, was visiting her twice a week to dress a leg ulcer and also to give her a bath. The district nurse was Margaret's key worker. After a few weeks Angela decided that Margaret would be able to manage to bath herself on her own if she had a bath rail and support. She got in touch with the local authority department that provided home aids and ordered the appropriate devices to be fitted. She told Margaret that once they were installed she would not need any assistance to bath but that if she got into any difficulties she should let Angela know. A few days later Margaret, who had not been seen by neighbours for a few days, was found dead in the bath. A post mortem showed that she had slipped while trying to get out of the bath, that the hand rail was not in a suitable position and that she had probably died of exposure. The coroner held an inquest and Angela was asked to provide a statement, as was the occupational therapist in the team since the task of assessment for bath aids was normally that of the occupational therapist.

At the inquest it is possible that the relatives will be present and probably represented by a solicitor or barrister. The inquest might well be followed by a civil claim against the NHS Trust on the basis of its direct liability for the death of Margaret in failing to lay down an appropriate procedure for caring for patients in the community and also on the basis of its indirect or vicarious liability for Angela's negligence. Was Angela negligent? Obviously, there are very few facts given here on which the answer to such a question could be determined but at the heart of the negligence action will be the question: did Angela follow the accepted approved practice in making those recommendations about the bath aids? Or if she did not follow the approved practice, was there justification for her not doing so? The question of whether such a decision was within her competence or whether she should have brought in the occupational therapist whose training includes that type of assessment will be crucial. It does not of course follow that the mere fact that Angela strayed outside her competence will automatically mean that she is liable in negligence. The relatives will still have to establish that there was a causal link between the breach of duty by Angela and the harm caused to Margaret and that harm was reasonably foreseeable.

The most important feature in any team approach and key worker system is that each should know the limits of their competence and the point at which the patient's safety demands that another person be brought in to advise. In the Wilsher case (considered in detail in Chapter 6) the court has held that there is no concept of team liability. It is a question of individual liability and/or the liability of the NHS Trust.

To whom is the nurse responsible?

SITUATION 23.2 A CLASH OF DUTIES

Community nurses in the Roger Park Unit had been given instructions that they should not carry drugs in their cars, nor should they personally arrange for drugs on prescriptions to be collected from the chemists. Ruth Green was caring for a terminally ill patient who was being nursed by her husband at home. The GP had left a prescription on his last visit and the husband asked her if she would be kind enough to bring the drugs back from the chemist. He said that he did not have any transport or any neighbours who could help and he did not want to leave his wife on her own. Ruth said that she was not allowed to collect drugs from the chemist for patients. He was clearly distressed and offered to come with her if she could provide the transport but it would still mean leaving his wife on her own. She agreed to this and took him to the chemist and then home again – a round trip of about seven miles which took 20 minutes. The husband could not understand why he had to go with her, leaving his wife for such a long time and obviously in danger. Ruth herself felt that the rules were not appropriate to that situation and wondered whether there was any law which covered her duties.

This situation, where there is a clash between what the nurse is told to do and what she feels is her duty to the patient, is not unusual, nor is it confined to the community. Other situations, for example where the nurse is told not to take patients in her car, or where she is given instructions about lifting which she cannot carry out because the facilities or staff are not available, place the nurse in a dilemma. Is she to fulfil what she believes to be her duty to the patient or should she obey the NHS Trust's or nurse manager's instructions? The clash can be seen as a conflict between the Code of Professional Conduct set down by the UKCC and her employer's orders. She has a contractual duty to obey the latter since it is an implied term of her contract of employment that she obey the reasonable orders of her employer; on the other hand she has a professional duty to follow the Code of Professional Conduct. If provisions of the Code were included in the contract of employment (for example, it is suggested in the advisory paper on confidentiality that a recommended clause on confidentiality should be included in the contract of employment), then there would be no clash between the two. However, this is a long way away and in the meantime the nurse has to cope with instructions which she does not always see as being in the patient's interests.

The first task for Ruth Green in a situation like this is for the nurse management to be given the full facts of any potential hardship suffered by the patient as a result of their instructions and procedures. Case studies of the difficulties which have and will arise from following these instructions must be provided in detail. It may so happen that, when presented with this evidence, management might well feel that either the whole policy should be revised or that certain exceptions can be made in circumstances where the patient is likely to suffer harm. Alternatively, it may be possible for other arrangements to be made which will ensure the safety and well-being of the patient. If the management is adamant that the procedures must be followed without any exception, then the nurse has a duty to undertake those unless there is likely to be such harm to the patient that it is clearly contrary to her duty of care to the patient. In such a situation her records would have to be very comprehensive to justify her action.

Giving advice

One of the most important tasks of the health visitor is giving advice to clients, young and old, on all aspects of their health and ways of keeping healthy. One of the vexed questions these days is the extent to which the health visitor should encourage a mother to have her child vaccinated and the possibility of the health visitor herself being held liable for giving advice which turns out to cause harm. The topic of liability for communications was discussed in Chapter 4 where it was stated that exactly the same principles of liability apply in giving advice as apply in using skills. Thus if a health visitor, knowing that a child has a history of convulsions, fails to take this into account in advising the mother to have the child vaccinated, and also fails to ensure that the doctor is advised of this fact, then the health visitor may well share some responsibility for any harm that befalls the child as a result of undergoing the vaccination.

Vaccination

Compensation for vaccine damage can be obtained in two ways. Firstly, there is a statutory scheme of compensation under the Vaccine Damage Payments Act 1979. Under this scheme £30,000 is now payable to a person who can establish that they have been severely disabled as a result of a vaccination against the specified diseases of diphtheria, tetanus, whooping cough, poliomyelitis, measles, rubella, tuberculosis, smallpox, and any other disease specified by the Secretary of State. The severe disability must be at least 80 per cent. Whether the disability has been caused by the vaccination shall be established on a balance of probabilities.

This statutory scheme does not prevent a claim being made in the civil courts for negligence in relation to damage caused by vaccine. Clearly, if such a case could succeed, far more than £30,000 would be payable for severely disabled persons. However, civil action faces a further difficulty as well as having to establish a causal link between the vaccine and the disability. The plaintiff must also show that this occurred as a result of negligence by the professional: for example the professionals failed to take account of the person's present health condition or previous history and the vaccine was contra-indicated for that person. A claim could also be brought against the drug company if there were some defect in the vaccine, and this claim could now come under the Consumer Protection Act (considered in Chapter 12), under which it is no longer necessary to show negligence by a manufacturer but simply that there was a defect in the product. This would be extremely difficult if the victim was the only one from a particular batch who suffered harm. The civil cases so far have not overcome the problems of proving causation apart from a case in Ireland (see below):

CASE 23.1 VACCINE DAMAGE

Susan Loveday was vaccinated for whooping cough in 1970 and 1971, following which she suffered permanent brain damage. She claimed compensation from the Wellcome Foundation who made the vaccine and from the doctor who administered it.

The judge held that on a balance of probabilities the plaintiff had failed to show that pertussis vaccine could cause permanent brain damage in young children. The case therefore failed on this point of causation. The judge also said that even if he had found in favour of the plaintiff on this preliminary point the plaintiff would still face insuperable difficulties in establishing negligence on the part of the doctor or nurse who administered the vaccine. Such a claim would have to be based on the ground that the vaccination had been given in spite of the presence of certain contra-indications (*Loveday* v. *Renton and another, The Times* 31 March 1988).

In *Best* v. *Wellcome Foundation, Dr O'Keefe, the Southern Health Board, the Minister for Health of Ireland and the Attorney General* 1994 5 Med LR 81, £2.75 million was awarded in respect of brain damage following a vaccination. It was established that a particular batch of vaccine was below standard and should not have been released onto the market.

Safety of the community professional

Entering other people's homes can be dangerous. Unlike the NHS Trust, the occupiers have no obligations under the Health and Safety at Work Act 1974, but they do have obligations under the Occupiers' Liability Act 1957. This is discussed in detail in Chapter 12. The community worker faces problems in relation to both the standard of the structure and the fixtures and fittings. In addition, she might find difficulties caused by the client or the relatives.

SITUATION 23.3 DEFECTIVE PREMISES

Pam Hughes, a health visitor, had a large caseload in one of the poorer parts of the city. In one council house, conditions were very bad: the wallpaper was peeling off the walls and there were piles of empty milk bottles in the kitchen and a miscellaneous assortment of carpet pieces on the concrete floor. The local authority had been notified of certain defects to the roof and the fittings, but had said that because of the backlog of maintenance work and staff cuts it would be several weeks before they could repair the property. The occupiers, Mr and Mrs James and their seven children, could not cope with the situation. Mr James was unemployed and attempted to rectify some of the defects, including putting a new piece of glass in the front door to replace the pane that had been broken when the door was slammed shut. The door had swollen due to the guttering leaking onto it. Pam Hughes was well used to the family and had been visiting regularly because of her concern over the two youngest children. After one visit she let herself out – as was her usual custom – and had to pull hard on the front door to open it. As she pulled, the new pane fell out onto her hand, cutting her severely across the wrist. After medical treatment and the advice of a specialist, it appeared that the tendons were severed and she would have very little movement in the four fingers of her right hand. It is certainly questionable whether she will be able to continue her work as a health visitor. Since she is unmarried, and the sole bread winner, caring for her elderly mother, she

> is frightened at the prospect of losing her job. She is therefore anxious to recover financial compensation for the injuries.

This particular situation may be unique but it represents the many dangers with which a community worker is faced.

What are the practicalities of obtaining compensation? Is the NHS Trust liable? The answer is probably no unless it can be shown that it was aware of the danger that an employee was in and failed to take reasonable precautions to safeguard her. There is no evidence that this was so in this case. Mr and Mrs James are possibly liable. As occupiers they failed to ensure that the premises were safe for the visitor. Mr James may well have repaired the door negligently. However, unless they are insured the question is academic since they are unlikely to be able to pay any compensation.

Since it is a council house it may be that Pam could establish a case against the council in its capacity as landlord and therefore occupier of the building. However, to succeed it would be important to show that, from the obligations under the lease, the landlord had a duty to carry out repairs and his failure to do so had reasonably foreseeably caused the injury to Pam's arm. However, Mr James' repair work makes a break in this chain of causation. If Pam fails against all three potential defendants (and the NHS Trust's likely involvement is minimal) then all she can do is fall back on her own insurance cover. Some household insurance schemes also cover for personal injuries or she may have her own personal accident cover. If not, she is unlikely to obtain any compensation other than the usual statutory sick pay scheme and the DSS injury benefits which are considerably smaller than the level of compensation awarded in the civil courts.

The lesson is clear: because of the dangers of working in variable conditions it is probably essential that community workers have some form of insurance cover for personal accidents. Some local authorities, professional associations and trade unions have negotiated group schemes of cover. It is, however, the policy of the NHS not to take out insurance cover. If the professional is working on NHS Trust premises all the time, then the authority as occupier has a duty to ensure that he is safe, and if it fails in this duty then it could be held liable under the Occupiers' Liability Act.

CASE 23.2 AGGRESSION IN THE COMMUNITY

> Mrs Wyatt suffered from multiple sclerosis, could do nothing for herself and needed nursing assistance. The health authority had the duty to provide a home nursing service under Section 25 of the NHS Act 1946 (as amended by the 1973 Reorganisation Act). The husband, who was also an invalid, abused the nursing staff when they visited his wife and was aggressive and threatening. He was asked to give an assurance that he would cease to behave so but he refused. The authority told Mrs Wyatt's solicitors that because of Mr Wyatt's behaviour they could not continue the nursing service.

The Court of Appeal held that the authority was doing all that could be reasonably expected of it and the application to compel the authority to provide the service would be dismissed (*R.* v. *Hillingdon Health Authority ex parte Wyatt* CA, *The Times* 20 December 1977).

The principle established in the Wyatt case can be applied to other situations, including the dangerous nature of the premises. However, before any service can be justifiably withdrawn, the threat to the safety of the community worker must have reached a serious level and every possible precaution must have been taken. For example, it might be necessary for some nurses to be sent in pairs to clients where they face danger. One question which a community nurse sometimes asks is: can I refuse to go if I consider that I am in personal danger? If the employer's instruction to go to a particular place is unreasonable with regard to the danger with which the worker is faced and the lack of precautions that the employer has taken for the employee's safety, then the employee can refuse to obey them. What is meant by unreasonable? This is a matter of balancing all the options available, including other precautions which it is reasonable for the employer to take against the risks involved and the needs of the client. Where the danger to the professional is the neighbourhood itself it might, for example, be reasonable for the employer to arrange for an alarm/warning system to be carried by the employee or to ensure that they visit homes in pairs. Where the danger comes from aggressive clients or their relatives, then it might be sufficient if a senior nursing officer accompanies the nurse to ensure her safety.

SITUATION 23.4 COMMUNITY DANGERS

Albert was a mentally handicapped man of 32 who had been living in a community home for about six weeks. He had settled down well and provided that he took his medication he coped quite well, taking his share of the household chores. He was due for an injection but to the surprise of the community nurse he said that he was not going to take it. She pleaded with him but to no avail. She said she would return that night but he again refused the injection. She offered to provide it in tablet form but he said that he would not take it in any form. The nurse tried to give the injection to him again but he lost his temper, striking out and severely injuring her.

Several problems emerge from this: one is the issue of consent to treatment in the community which we shall return to later; the other is the question of the safety of community nurses for the mentally ill and mentally handicapped.

It is the employer's duty to safeguard the safety and welfare of his employee. If it is known that a particular patient is a danger to nursing staff, then the employer has a duty to take reasonable precautions to see that they will be safe. These precautions might mean ensuring that a female nurse never visits the patient on her own. There is quite likely to be a need for refuge to be provided so that if a client is particularly disturbed he can leave the community or family house and make use of a respite bed, i.e. providing respite for the family. In the situation above, in deciding whether the NHS Trust is liable for the injuries suffered by the community nurse, account would have to be taken of whether it was known that the patient was aggressive and if so, whether the appropriate precautions had been taken, whether the community nurse followed approved accepted practice in her dealings with the patient or whether she provoked the patient by what she did and was therefore, to some extent, to blame for what happened.

Consent to treatment

Mentally disordered

In Chapter 20, which deals with the psychiatric nurse, the problem of giving drugs in the community is discussed. The fact is that at present there are no means in law of giving a patient compulsory drugs unless it is under the common law powers to act in an emergency to save life. Neither the guardianship provisions of the Mental Health Act nor the long leash can be used to enforce the taking of drugs in the community. If a patient refuses to take medication and it is essential for the care of his mental disorder that he has these drugs, he would have to be treated as an in-patient since only then is there statutory provision for the drugs to be given compulsorily. In Albert's situation, described above, if he continues to refuse to take medication considered essential for the treatment of his mental disorder as defined in the Act, and there is no other way of persuading him to take it as the law stands at present, he would have to be admitted to a mental hospital as an in-patient in order to be treated compulsorily. This is not satisfactory for community workers or necessarily in the best interests of the patient, and the subject is currently under debate. Special difficulties arise in particular with mentally handicapped adults over 18 since there is no system of decision-making on their behalf by proxy. The Law Commission has made recommendations to provide such a system (1991 No. 119 and 1993 No. 129) and legislation is awaited.

Government proposals have been made for a supervised discharge order for specific mentally disordered persons and those are discussed on pages 298–9.

Forcible entry

Another point which often concerns the community nurse and the health visitor is whether they have any rights of entry. As far as the statutory law is concerned, the answer is no. There may be a power of entry at common law where it is feared that an old person is lying in need of help but it exists only in an emergency to save life.

SITUATION 23.5 A ROW OF BOTTLES

Neighbours drew the attention of the community nurse to a row of bottles outside the house of an elderly recluse. They feared for her safety and suggested that they should break into the house to check that all was well. The community nurse was hesitant.

In a case like this it is preferable from the practical, as well as the theoretical, point of view for the police to be summoned. Their entry would provide legal justification as well as providing the most realistic means of entry. On the district the social workers have statutory powers of entry under specific conditions but the health workers do not.

Compulsory removal

Under the Mental Health Act 1983

SITUATION 23.6 REFUSAL TO LEAVE

Laura Thomas, a community nurse for the mentally ill, was notified that two sisters who were regarded as recluses had not been seen for several days. Neighbours reported that a number of cats were howling around their home and that the curtains had not been drawn for three days. Laura was also informed that of the two sisters, Annie, the younger one, was considered to be mentally handicapped. Laura went to the house and the door was answered by Agnes. She was abrupt and unwelcoming. When asked about her sister she said they did not want nosey-parkers and was quite happy. From the doorway Laura could see that the house was in a dirty condition and Agnes herself was in a dishevelled state. She feared for the physical and mental well-being of Annie. What could she do?

As a community nurse Laura has no power to enter the house. However, powers do exist: under Section 115 of the Mental Health Act 1983 an approved social worker employed by a local social services authority may at all reasonable times after producing, if asked to do so, some duly authenticated document showing that he is such a social worker, enter and inspect any premises (not being a hospital) in the area of that authority in which a mentally disordered patient is living, if he has reasonable cause to believe that the patient is not receiving care. This power enables the approved social worker to inspect premises other than hospitals, where a mentally disordered person is living. It does not, however, give the right to enforce entry, but refusal to permit the inspection could constitute an offence under Section 129 of the Mental Health Act 1983. Premises are not defined but could include private premises, provided a mentally disordered person is living there, and provided there is reasonable cause to believe the patient is not under proper care. Laura would therefore have to arrange for an approved social worker to visit the home. If entry is obstructed under Section 115, the approved social worker would have to make use of her power to apply to the Justice of the Peace for a warrant to search and remove patients (see Chapter 20). The approved social worker would have to give information on oath that there is reasonable cause to suspect that a person believed to be suffering from mental disorder: (a) has been, or is being, ill-treated, neglected, or kept otherwise than under proper control, in any place within the jurisdiction of the justice; *or* (b) being unable to care for himself, is living alone in any such place. The justice may then issue a warrant authorising any constable to enter, if need be by force, any premises specified in the warrant in which that person is believed to be and if it is thought fit to remove him to a place of safety with a view to the making of an application for his care and treatment. An approved social worker must accompany a constable. If it is thought fit, Annie could be removed to a place of safety and kept there for up to 72 hours under Section 135 (3).

The persons must be (a) suffering from grave chronic disease or being aged, infirm, or physically incapacitated, are living in insanitary conditions; AND (b) are unable to devote to themselves, and are not receiving from other persons, proper care and attention. In order to use this section there must be certification by the community specialist after thorough inquiry and consideration that in the interests of any such person or for preventing injury to the health of, or serious nuisance to other persons, it is necessary to remove any such person. An application is made to Court. Seven days' notice must be given of the application. If granted the person can be kept in a place of safety for a period not exceeding 3 months. This period can be extended.

Figure 23.3 National Assistance Act 1948 Section 47.

Removal under the National Assistance Act 1948

The provision of the Mental Health Act described in the last paragraph can only be used in the case of a person believed within the meaning of the Act to be suffering from mental disorder. There are occasionally cases where those powers are not appropriate. In the above situation it may well be that although Annie is mentally handicapped and may well come within the definition of suffering from mental disorder, Agnes might not but she might equally be in need of help.

Section 47 of the 1948 Act authorises the removal to suitable premises of persons in need of care and control in order to secure the necessary care and attention. Its main provisions are set out in Fig. 23.3.

Because of the dangers to the health of the person in delaying an application, an emergency application can be made under the provisions of the National Assistance Act 1951 (Amendment) under which the period of detention is three weeks. These provisions provide no power to treat the person compulsorily. The Law Commission has recommended changes to these provisions which are under discussion (1993 No. 130).

Protection of property

If both Annie and Agnes were removed from the house, what happens to their home?

Under Section 48 of the National Assistance Act 1948 the council has a duty to provide temporary protection for the property of persons admitted to hospitals. The section gives the council power to enter the property at all reasonable times and to deal with any movable property in order to prevent or mitigate any loss or damage. The council can recover any reasonable expenses incurred in carrying out this duty from the person who is admitted or any person liable to maintain him.

These provisions cause considerable difficulty for community physicians who may be under considerable pressure from neighbours to make use of these statutory powers, but it is well known that such a removal can be fatal for the person concerned who may fail to thrive in institutional care. The dilemma between the rights of freedom of autonomy and the duty to act in the public interest and to safeguard the person's welfare is evident.

Disclosure of information

This topic is fully discussed in Chapter 8 where an example of the problems faced by community staff is considered. In Appendix 13 there is a suggested policy for disclosure to the police. The health visitor is more likely to be required to give evidence in court than any other community worker and the policy is that she should wait to be subpoenaed before giving evidence. This is changing because of her duty to the child under the Children Act 1989.

Criminal suspicion

SITUATION 23.7 SUSPECTED

Kate Giles was a community nurse who had long been visiting an elderly widow who appeared to have no family apart from two grandchildren who rarely visited and a few other visitors. One of Kate's tasks was to dress the client's leg. On one occasion the client was anxious to point out some of her treasures to Kate. They included some very fine pieces of bone china. It was suggested to Kate that she might like to have a tiny Spode cat as a small gift. Kate protested that she was not allowed to receive gifts from clients. Her protests were ignored and the old lady wrapped the gift up in an old paper bag and gave it to Kate. Kate forgot to mention it to her nursing officer the next day and after that it seemed too small a matter to be of any concern. Shortly after this the old lady died. The grandchildren discovered that the piece of Spode was missing. They made some enquiries and Kate stated that she had been given it by the elderly lady but that they would of course be entitled to have it back. Kate was severely reprimanded and the grandchildren said they did not believe her story since the old lady had never been known to give anything away; they suggested that Kate had in fact stolen the china.

Community nurses often work alone and if they are charged with theft it is one professional's word against that of the client or relative. In a case like this Kate could well have been accused of theft by the old lady herself if she was at all absent-minded and had forgotten what she had done. The safest rule is therefore never to accept gifts, even though this might distress the client. If the client is insistent and wishes to make a generous gift then a health service manager could be called in to give advice but the client should be represented since if there is any evidence of undue influence the gift would be voidable.

Questions and exercises

1 A patient appears to you to be incapable of caring for herself. What action would you take? Outline a procedure to cover the situation if the patient shows extreme reluctance to move from her home and there are no relatives to care for her.

2 You break an ornament while visiting a patient. The ornament is valued at £5,000. You are personally unable to meet the costs of replacing it. What remedies are available to the owner of the ornament? (See also Chapter 25.)

3 Obtain details of the procedures for assessment for community care as a result of the 1990 Act. What impact have these had on your practice?

4 What special concerns does the community professional have in relation to health and safety, and what specific precautions should be taken to protect her? (Refer also to Chapter 12.)

24   School, clinic and practice nurses

The problems facing these nurses will be considered together for convenience, though it is clear that they each face very different problems. The issues to be covered are set out in Fig. 24.1.

The school nurse

Professional liability

SITUATION 24.1 DIAGNOSIS

Brian Brown, a bully in Year 9, was involved in a fight in the playground and fell to the floor. He was shrieking with pain but the headmaster told Audrey, the school nurse, that he was a notorious coward and not to worry too much. Audrey took Brian to the sick room, put him on the couch and told him to stay there quietly. Half an hour later she returned and since he no longer seemed to be in pain said he could return to his class. The next day she heard from the school secretary that Brian's parents had taken him to hospital the night before and a fractured wrist had been diagnosed. The parents are now complaining to the school that the school nurse is incompetent, should be dismissed and that they are prepared to sue her and the education authority in the civil courts.

1. School nurse
   (a) professional liability;
   (b) extent of duty;
   (c) use of car.
2. Clinic nurse
   (a) obtaining consent;
   (b) minors.
3. Practice nurse
   (a) primary visits;
   (b) employment situation.

Figure 24.1 Issues covered in Chapter 24.

First, a small point of procedure: if Audrey is employed by the NHS Trust, as is usually the case in state schools, then it would be the NHS Trust that would be held vicariously liable for any negligence on the nurse's part. It could also be held directly liable if it were at fault in failing to provide adequate training for her or clearly established procedures. If, on the other hand, the nurse is employed by the school or education authority, then it would be vicariously liable if any fault were found on the part of the nurse. In either case if it can be shown that the school is itself at fault then there could be an action against those responsible. The questions that arise in a case like this are the following. Did the nurse follow accepted practice in dealing with Brian? Was she so influenced by the headmaster's words that she failed to take the usual precautions? What more is it reasonable to expect her to have done in caring for Brian? Even if her decision not to arrange for him to go to the accident and emergency department for an X-ray was a reasonable one, should she not have arranged for a note to be sent home to the parents advising them of what had happened and warning of the signs to look for? If these questions are answered and suggest that there was a failing by the nurse, this might still not mean that any action in negligence against her would succeed since Brian's parents would have to show that he suffered harm as a result of the delay in caring for him. It is unlikely that a delay of a few hours in the diagnosis of a wrist fracture would cause any harm. However, this would not mean that she would not be faced with disciplinary proceedings since she may not have followed the procedures set down by her NHS Trust.

Extent of duty

SITUATION 24.2 AN UNEXPECTED ATTACK

The deputy head teacher asked Audrey, the school nurse, if she would cover Form 9A for one lesson, since the school was having difficulty in providing sufficient staff to supervise and teach the children because of the teachers' industrial action and the cut-back on the provision of supply teachers. Audrey said that she was employed by the NHS Trust, not the education authority, and that her duty was to act as a school nurse, not a teacher or child minder. The deputy was adamant that she take the class and, protesting, Audrey did so. While she was supervising Form 9A, a child from Year 7, Justin Smith, had an epileptic fit. The form teacher, Kate Jay, sent a child to get the school nurse but unfortunately Audrey could not be found. Kate had no experience in how to handle an epileptic patient and tried to lift Justin. His tongue slipped into his throat, he choked and went blue. Kate told another child to get the head teacher to call an ambulance. Unfortunately, by the time the ambulance arrived Justin was dead and could not be resuscitated.

In this tragic situation many different questions arise. What is the role of the school nurse? Is she on call for the whole time of school hours, waiting for such an emergency to arise? Many would say no, but it does of course depend on the individual employment contract and job description. The role she plays as far as teaching is concerned also varies from school to school. In some she might take on the task of teaching such subjects as personal hygiene, health education, sex education, biology, etc. Where she is undertaking this role it can hardly be expected that she will be fulfilling an emergency first aid role as well. In such circumstances Audrey is not to blame for the death of Justin. A more likely action is possible against Kate and the education authority for failing to provide a basic first aid training for staff, especially when it would have been known that Justin was epileptic. Kate's action was the worst possible in the circumstances. An action is also possible against the local education authority, for using the school nurse in another capacity so that she was not available.

Use of car

SITUATION 24.3 CAR INSURANCE

A child, Mary Pugh, cut her head very badly in the gymnasium. The children had been told to trot around like ponies with their heads up high. Mary trotted straight into the teeth of another child. Blood gushed from the wound. Audrey, the school nurse, realised the importance of getting her to the accident and emergency department for stitches. She put the child in her own car and rushed to the local hospital. In her haste she came out of a side road too quickly and crashed into a motor cyclist coming along the main road. She got out of the car to see what could be done and, seeing that other people had gathered around, she decided that it was her duty to get Mary to hospital. Subsequently she was notified that the police were charging her with failing to report an accident, and having no adequate insurance cover. Relatives of the motor cyclist were also intending to sue her for causing the accident and failing to provide assistance since the ambulance had taken 20 minutes to arrive and the cyclist had bled to death.

Any employee who does not usually use their car for work, other than going to and from work, would be well advised to ensure that insurance cover is provided for the exceptional circumstance when a car might be needed. Clinic nurses other than peri-patetic nurses, school nurses, or out-patient nurses might all find that on very rare occa-sions they need to use their car for work purposes and then they are not covered. The effect is that, although the insurance company will pay out compensation to the victim, it has the right to claim this money back from the person whose insurance did not cover this use. If this exceptional use is foreseeable it is wiser for the nurse to ensure that the company is notified of this possibility.

As far as the failure to report the accident is concerned it is a duty under the Road Traffic Act 1972 to ensure that the police are notified of any accident in which personal injuries are caused. Audrey's failure to ensure that this was done could lead to a successful prosecution. Her failure to stop and help the cyclist is a difficult question. On the one hand, as was pointed out in Chapter 3, there is no obligation to volunteer help. However, in this case Audrey caused the harm and is under a legal obligation to mitigate it as far as possible. However, she also has a duty to Mary and it is a question of assessing who is in most need. From the facts given here it would appear that the cyclist was in most danger and Audrey should have checked that there was nothing she could do before she went away.

These situations have illustrated a variety of different problems with which the school nurse is likely to be faced. It is clear that she should ensure clarification of her duties and her relationship with the teachers where she is employed by the NHS Trust and is thus not on the staff of the school. It is clear that a procedure should be laid down regarding transporting children to hospital for X-rays, etc., and informing parents of events in school likely to affect the health of the pupils. The need for teachers to be informed on how to cope with children who become ill at school should also be identified and met.

The clinic nurse

Clinic nurses may spend their time in one clinic assisting at mother and baby clinics, or be attached to specialist clinics such as family planning clinics, or travel from school to school, assisting the school doctors in provision of medical, eye and other examinations for school children.

Obtaining consent

SITUATION 24.4 CONSENT TO RUBELLA VACCINATIONS_____

Brenda West provided nursing assistance to the medical team which carried out the school medical examinations. One of their tasks was to offer the Year 8 girls a rubella vaccination. Letters were sent to the parents in advance, advising them of the service and asking for their consent. Unfortunately, Brenda failed to notice that the parents of Rachel Tyne had not signed the consent form and Rachel was given an injection by the school doctor. Shortly afterwards Rachel came out in an all-over rash. Investigations were made and it appeared that Rachel had recently had a variety of drugs in anticipation of a holiday to Morocco and these had reacted with the rubella vaccination. The parents were threatening to sue since they did not want Rachel to have the vaccination as she had had German measles a few years before. They also felt that the doctor and nurse should have checked with them before they gave the vaccination to ensure that there were no contra-indications.

There are two separate issues here: the one is the consent of the parents; the other is the timing of the vaccination. As far as consent is concerned the basic principles are that parents have the right to consent to treatment for their children. As far as school health is concerned it could be argued that under the Education Acts the school can provide the care as long as the parents do not object. This may well cover medical examinations but is unlikely to cover the giving of injections. The point has not been determined in court.

However, if the vaccination is to proceed it is essential that actual consent should be obtained, that there should be no contra-indications, and that the parents advise the school of any recent events in the child's medical history which suggest that a vaccination would be inappropriate at that particular time or, indeed, at any time. Because of the importance of this it is advisable for the parents to give positive consent to the vaccination and reassure the staff about the non-existence of any contra-indications.

As far as responsibility between the nurse and the doctor is concerned much depends upon the local policy in relation to who has the duty of ensuring that the parents' consent has been obtained. In some authorities this would fall upon the doctor. However, this does not necessarily mean that the nurse is free of all liability.

Minors

SITUATION 24.5 FAMILY PLANNING AND THE UNDER 16-YEAR-OLD

Maureen was working as a clinic nurse in the family planning clinic. She recognised one of the patients, Denise Wright, as a friend of her eldest daughter, aged 15 years. She completed the forms and the girl told her she was 17. Maureen knew that this was a lie. She was uncertain whether to tell the doctor and decided against this. The doctor prescribed the pill and asked Denise the name of her family doctor. Denise said she did not have one. She said she did not want any communication with her family, and the doctor said that would not be necessary if she was over 16.

Several issues arise here. One is the question of the nurse's personal knowledge and the extent to which she should inform the doctor of this. The other is the question of the law relating to an under 16-year-old in this context. This latter point is considered in some detail in the section dealing with paediatric nursing (Chapter 13).

From the House of Lords decision in the Gillick case it can be seen that in exceptional circumstances treatment and advice can be given to a girl under 16 without the parents being involved. As far as the first issue is concerned it could be argued that even though the nurse has acquired information about the patient from a different source, if this is relevant to the doctor's care and treatment of the patient, then it should be disclosed, i.e. her duty of care to the patient would require her to tell the doctor that the girl was 15. Similarly, if she knew that the girl suffered from epilepsy, even though the girl had not told the doctor this, the nurse should pass on the information. It could be argued that this principle only applies to information which is relevant to the care of the child. Thus if she by chance knew that the girl had been charged by the police for shop-lifting this need not be passed on.

The Children Act 1989 requires decisions relating to children to take into account the wishes of the child where the child has the capacity (see Chapter 13).

The practice nurse

The legal situation of the practice nurse can vary, especially as far as employment rights are concerned. Some practice nurses may be employed by single-handed or group general practitioners, others are employed by health authorities. Practice nurses employed by health authorities are more likely to be part of a nursing hierarchy and to receive guidance and policies from the employer. The topics to be considered in relation to the practice nurse are set out in Fig. 24.1.

Primary visits

SITUATION 24.6 DELEGATED TASK

In one single-handed GP practice the nurse occasionally undertook the primary visit to a patient's house. Sister Ward was an experienced practice nurse and an invaluable help to the GP. One morning he asked her to visit a 6-year-old patient who was reported to have all the signs and symptoms of mumps. The mother just needed reassurance and guidance over care. Sister Ward visited the boy whose mother said that the symptoms appeared to be just like her other son's who had mumps three weeks ago and was now back in school. Sister Ward examined the boy, confirmed the mother's opinion that it was mumps, and gave her guidance over care. Two days later the mother called the deputising service out and the boy was admitted with suspected meningitis. The mother is now arguing that the doctor and not the practice nurse should have visited her son.

In any case where there is delegation of a task which is normally performed by a doctor, the doctor will remain liable in civil law for that task unless he has delegated it to a competent, trained person and provides the requisite supervision for the task to be done safely. Here one might question whether it was a suitable case for the practice nurse to undertake the primary visit. Has she the necessary training and skills to detect whether the patient was suffering from mumps or another condition? Once she had visited the patient, should she not have arranged for the GP to attend or ensured that a closer eye was kept on him? Did she make all the appropriate tests and checks when she visited the boy? If these questions are answered in such a way that the nurse is shown to be at fault, then the GP could well be liable for any harm that has consequentially befallen the boy (there may in fact be no harm suffered since the short delay in diagnosis may have had no effect) and the nurse would also be liable for undertaking a task that she was not competent to perform. In either event, the nurse would be held professionally accountable before the UKCC for her actions.

Employment situation

The legal position of the practice nurse as an employee differs according to whether she is employed by a practice or single-handed general practitioner or if she is employed by the NHS Trust. In the former case, as an employee of someone who employs only a few people, she may not have all the statutory benefits to which the NHS Trust employee will be entitled. If she is employed by a single-handed general practitioner she may find it more difficult to resist pressure for her to go outside her limits of competence and she lacks the back-up of a clear nursing hierarchy and nurse management support. Her professional standards should, however, be the same.

Questions and exercises

1 What difficulties, if any, arise from the fact that the school nurse is employed by the NHS Trust and works with education authority staff?
2 Could the school nurse refuse to undertake tasks allocated by the head teacher? What are the likely implications?
3 What differences exist in law between the clinic nurse who spends all her time in a clinic and the nurse who visits patients in their own homes?
4 Obtain a copy of your NHS Trust's safety policy and ascertain the extent to which it applies to the clinic nurse and the extent to which it is fully implemented.
5 What possible differences may exist in law between the practice nurse who is employed by a general practitioner and the practice nurse who is employed by an NHS Trust?
6 Consider the expanded-role tasks which are sometimes undertaken by the practice nurse and outline the legal requirements. (See Chapter 4.)

Part III General areas

25   The legal aspects of property

There are many aspects of property which may be of concern to the nurse. She may wonder if she is liable should the patient's property go missing. This becomes of particular concern in those situations where the patient is incompetent to take care of his own possessions. What legal devices exist in those circumstances to protect both the patient and the nurse? The nurse may also be concerned for her own property. Does the NHS Trust as employer have any duty to make arrangements to care for the nurse's property? What happens if the nurse's car is damaged in the hospital car park? Does it make any difference to the liability of the employer if a patient damages the car? Figure 25.1 illustrates the topics to be covered in this chapter.

Principles of liability

SITUATION 25.1 A CHRISTMAS CASUALTY

Dora Hardy, a widow of 72 years, was staying with her son James and his family over the Christmas holidays. On the Saturday night, the day before Christmas Eve, she complained of feeling very tired and retired to bed at 7.00 p.m. At 9.00 p.m. James suddenly heard his mother cry out and, rushing upstairs, he found her very pale, gasping for breath and clutching her heart. Ann, his wife, phoned for the ambulance and collected up her mother-in-law's handbag and toilet bag.

Dora, still in her nightdress with an overcoat over her shoulders, was taken to Roger Park Hospital within 15 minutes. She was wheeled straight in the admission unit and a staff nurse asked James and Ann to wait in the waiting room. After five minutes the staff nurse returned to ask them Dora's name, address and age. They then waited for over an hour without seeing any sign of anyone and then decided to find out what was happening. James walked into the admission unit and asked the sister on duty if he could see his mother. The sister explained that she had gone up to the medical ward about an hour before. She apologised but said that, owing to the change of shift, she had not realised that Mrs Hardy had relatives with her and that anyone was waiting. To make up for her oversight the sister phoned the medical ward and arranged for James and Ann to go straight up. James and Ann, who was still clutching Dora's possessions, were led to the medical ward. There were screens around Dora's bed and Dora seemed to be unconscious. Ann tiptoed to the head of the bed and placed Dora's handbag and toilet bag in the locker. Since it was clear that there was little that they could do, James and Ann left the bedside, calling in to the ward sister's office to make sure that the night nurse had their address and phone number.

Dora remained critically ill for three days but on the fourth day she seemed to start pulling through. James visited her the day after Boxing Day and for the first time was able to chat with her. He asked if there was anything she needed and she said that she would like some Kleenex and orange squash. The next day James and Ann took in the Kleenex and squash and £10 in cash to ensure that Dora could buy things from the ward trolley. Ann took the handbag from the locker and opened the purse to put the £10 inside. She noticed that there was already £60 in the purse. However, she added the £10 and replaced the purse in the handbag, which she put in the locker. Over the next few days a number of relatives visited Dora but on 3 January James had a phone call to say that she had taken a turn for the worse. James and Ann rushed to the hospital but Dora died later that night.

The next day James returned to the hospital to collect the death certificate. The ward sister gave him a white plastic bag with 'Patient's Property' written over it. She handed him a checklist of its contents which included 'handbag with purse containing 30 pence'. James glanced at the list and pointed out that the purse should have contained about £70. The ward sister stated that she had personally checked through the contents and that was all that there was. James explained that his wife had seen £60 there and had added £10. The ward sister advised him to see the unit administrator since there was nothing more that she could do. The unit administrator, on interviewing James, ascertained the following:

1. No warnings had been given at the time that Dora was admitted about the patient's property and hospital rules.
2. There was a notice in the ward about the hospital not being liable for patient's property unless it was handed in for safe custody but this notice

was not prominently displayed and James and Ann said that they had not seen it.

Sister Thomas was interviewed and said that she knew that there was a handbag in the locker but had not looked inside it until after Dora's death when she was drawing up the checklist of contents. The first issue to arise is: can it be said that the NHS Trust is liable for the missing property and is Sister Thomas personally liable?

In general, a person does not become liable for another person's property unless he or she can be shown to have assumed some responsibility for it. The person who undertakes to look after the property of another person is known as a bailee. The person whose property it is, is known as the bailor. Thus if a patient were to give a gold watch to the ward sister, the sister on behalf of the NHS Trust acts as bailee of that property entrusted to it by the patient, the bailor. It is the duty of the bailee to carry out the instructions of the bailor and to surrender the property of the bailor when requested to do so or as previously agreed. In most circumstances the relationship of bailor/bailee is a voluntary one and one person cannot force another into being the bailee of one's property. When the person agrees to act as bailee (and there may be no reward for doing so) a transfer of possession takes place so that the bailee then becomes liable. In contrast with the usual principles of negligence, once the existence of the bailment is established it is not for the bailor to establish negligence by the bailee but for the bailee to show that he exercised all reasonable care for the goods and was not negligent. This is a reversal of the usual burdens of proof.

Applying this law to the above situation it could be argued that at no time did the family or Dora ask the NHS Trust or its staff to become bailees of the property and take care of it. There was therefore no liability in law for the missing cash.

However, in the context of hospital care, another duty arises under the law of negligence. If an unconscious patient is brought into the accident and emergency department, the NHS Trust and the professionals have a duty to care for the patient and this would include caring for his property if he is unable to look after it. This is known as

1. Principles of liability.
2. Administrative failures.
3. Exclusion of liability.
4. Property of mentally incompetent.
5. Day-to-day care of money.
6. Power of attorney.
7. Court of Protection.
8. Protecting patients from relatives.
9. Returning the patient's property.
10. Staff property.

Figure 25.1 Issues covered in Chapter 25.

involuntary bailment. Looking at Dora's situation, were there any occasions when it could be said that the NHS Trust became an involuntary bailee of Dora's property and had a duty of care in relation to it? The answer is when she became unconscious and was unable to look after her property herself. However, we have Ann's evidence that the cash was still there after Dora had resumed consciousness, so it could be argued that the NHS Trust was no longer a bailee (whether or not it had ever been one). The next point at which an involuntary bailment may have arisen is Dora's death. At this point the ward staff should assume control and ensure that a list of the property is drawn up and properly witnessed. If this is what Sister Thomas did and the cash was not there at that time, then it could be argued that the NHS Trust was not liable for the fact that it is missing.

This is the law in relation to bailment and would mean that in these circumstances the relatives would have difficulty in winning a case against the NHS Trust or Sister Thomas.

Administrative failures

However, what is more likely to occur is that there will be a complaint about the administrative procedures in relation to Dora's property, which would be based on failure of the staff to point out to the relatives procedures for dealing with the property or even checking whether they had brought any in for Dora. Complaints of this kind, though they may not lead to a court action, may, however, lead to the NHS Trust making an *ex gratia* payment to the patient or relatives. This is not an admission of liability but an attempt to appease the relatives and make up for administrative shortcomings. Occasionally, complaints over lost property lead to investigations by the Health Service Commissioner who might well eventually recommend an *ex gratia* payment to be made by the NHS Trust because for one reason or another it has failed to follow accepted administrative procedures.

Exclusion of liability

What is the significance of the notice absolving the health authority of all responsibility for the patient's property? Under the Unfair Contract Terms Act 1977 (see Fig. 6.6) such an exemption or exclusion notice is effective in relation to the loss or damage of property provided that it is reasonable to exclude liability for the negligence which has led to such loss or damage. (Liability for negligence which leads to personal injury or death cannot be excluded.) How is reasonableness defined? The requirement of reasonableness is defined as 'it should be fair and reasonable to allow reliance upon it, having regard to all the circumstances obtaining when the liability arose or [but for the Notice] would have arisen' (Section 11 (3)). It is for the party claiming that a contract term or notice satisfies the requirement of reasonableness to show that it does (Section 11 (5)). Applying this to Dora's situation, if it could be argued that the NHS Trust's employees had been negligent in relation to her property then the NHS Trust might claim to rely upon the

I .... acknowledge
that the opportunity has been given to me to hand over my personal property to be placed in safe-
keeping, that I have been advised to do so and that I have declined the offer of safekeeping of my
personal property.

Signature of Patient ....
Witnessed by ....
(Member of Staff)
Designation ....
Date ....

To be filed in Patient's case notes folder

Figure 25.2 Patients' property: form of notice disclaiming liability.

notice to evade liability. It would then have to show that it was reasonable for them to
rely upon it.

Patients should be advised not to bring valuable property into hospital. If they do,
then it can be recommended to them that the property should be taken into safekeeping
by the nursing staff. If they are unwilling to part with the property, then they can be
asked to sign a form of disclaimer which has the added advantage of impressing upon
the patient the dangers of having valuable property in hospital (see Fig. 25.2).

The property of the mentally incompetent

What about the property of the mentally handicapped and the mentally ill or the elderly
infirm?

SITUATION 25.2 POCKET MONEY

The NHS Trust has the power to give its long-stay residents pocket money for
sweets, cigarettes and other small personal purchases. Jimmy Jones, a mentally
handicapped adult of 24, rarely spent his money and since he was a hard worker
and regularly earned himself substantial amounts he accumulated over £100.
The ward staff attempted to encourage Jimmy to put this in the bank. However,
he could not be persuaded and there were rumours that he slept with it under
his pillow at night. One morning he screamed with distress and it appeared that
all his money had been stolen from under his bed. A search revealed nothing
and there was no hint as to where it had gone. Is the NHS Trust liable for the
loss?

From the case study on Dora discussed above it will be apparent that in this situation
there was no transfer of possession from Jimmy to the NHS Trust so that the latter is

not *prima facie* liable. However, much depends upon Jimmy's competence and whether sufficient effort was made to persuade him to allow it to be taken for safe-keeping. A system of tokens can sometimes be devised to protect patients' property though care must be taken not to limit their purchasing power and to ensure that the funds are available for them when they want them. In addition in this case, it could be argued that the NHS Trust had a duty of care in relation to the security of the ward.

The Law Commission has made recommendations relating to decision-making on behalf of the mentally incapacitated adult. Its recommendations on property are contained in Report No. 128 1993. It recommends that the present system, whereby appointees can collect DSS moneys on behalf of those incapacitated, should be subject to monitoring and regular review.

Day-to-day care of money

SITUATION 25.3 SHOPPING

Increasingly in institutional care, and of necessity in community care, clients/residents are encouraged to shop and take part in community activities. In these circumstances moneys might be entrusted to staff to guide patients in making small purchases. On one such shopping expedition Gary White, the staff nurse, took three residents to the shops. Two were able to manage their own purchases but the third, Leonard, needed some guidance and Gary aided him in purchasing several small items – toiletries, sweets, etc. On their return, Leonard complained to another resident that Gary had spent all his money. This came to the attention of the charge nurse who asked Gary for an immediate explanation. Gary showed how the money had been spent but was unable to produce any receipts or supporting evidence. Nor was he able to remember exactly where the money had gone.

In a situation like this the member of staff is like a trustee for the patient's property and should be able to account for it in detail with supporting receipts. Of course, the receipts do not in themselves show that the money was spent on the patient but, together with evidence from other witnesses, it should be possible to record exactly how the money was spent and that it was spent in the interests of the patient. In a case like this the senior nurse management would discipline Gary for his failure to follow the correct procedure.

In the community many patients may have considerable sums to spend and the staff are therefore vulnerable to an accusation that they have spent the money on themselves. It is essential that staff be trained in good practices of book-keeping and that there should be, as far as possible, witnesses to give evidence as to how the money has been spent. The ultimate aim is of course that the patient should be the watch dog for his own funds but many residents/clients may never get beyond the stage of entrusting all such matters to others.

1. Came into force 10 March 1986.
2. Enables a power of attorney to continue in force after the maker of the power (called 'the donor') becomes mentally incapable of handling his or her affairs.
3. After 1 July 1988 the enduring power of attorney must be in the exact form prescribed in the Enduring Powers of Attorney (Prescribed Form) Regulations 1987.
4. The Enduring Power of Attorney may give
    (a) a general power – which authorises the Attorney to carry out any transactions on behalf of the donor; or
    (b) a specific power – which authorises the Attorney to deal only with those aspects of the donor's affairs which are specified in the power.
5. The donor can revoke or cancel the Enduring Power at any time while she/he remains mentally capable, but the power cannot be cancelled or revoked once it has been registered unless the Court of Protection confirms the revocation.
6. When the donor becomes mentally incapable, the Attorney must apply to register the Enduring Power of Attorney with the Court of Protection before he/she can act under it.
7. Once registered, the Attorney has the power to act on behalf of the donor – either general or specific, but has no power over the person of the donor, and cannot make a will on behalf of the donor.

Figure 25.3 Enduring Power of Attorney Act 1985.

Power of attorney

Patients who anticipate incapacity or require assistance during absence or illness can grant a power of attorney. This power is revoked (i.e. withdrawn) if the person granting it becomes mentally incapable. However, since this is often the very occasion when it would be useful to exercise the power on behalf of the patient an Enduring Power of Attorney Act 1985 was passed which came into effect in 1986. This power only comes into existence if the person wishes the power to continue after the time at which he becomes incapable; he must sign to this effect and indicate that he is aware of the significance of the enduring element. Figure 25.3 sets out some of the requirements for and the characteristics of an enduring power of attorney.

Court of Protection

Often, however, there is no enduring power of attorney in existence and the person is incapable of managing his affairs. In these circumstances the Court of Protection would appoint a receiver to manage the affairs. There is a short procedure which can be used where the assets are small. Otherwise a relative, or perhaps the authority, could apply for a receiver to be appointed to manage the patient's affairs and to allow money to be spent on the patient. The powers of the Court of Protection are considerable. The applicant will have to pay in to the Court a sum of money as a recognisance. Notice of the application is given to the patient, who has the opportunity of opposing it. Medical evidence will also be required to show that the patient is incapable of handling his affairs by reason of mental disorder. This medical evidence can be challenged by the patient.

The Court of Protection has the power of making a will in the name of the patient and can arrange for sums to be paid to other persons who would have been dependent upon the patient or would have looked to him for help, even though these obligations would not have been legally enforceable. Obviously there is a power to pay all debts. The details of the powers available are set out in Part 7 of the Mental Health Act 1983 and some of the most important ones are shown in Fig. 25.4.

---

95. (1) The judge may, with respect to the property and affairs of a patient, do or secure the doing of all such things as appear necessary or expedient:
  (a) for the maintenance or other benefit of the patient;
  (b) for the maintenance or other benefit of members of the patient's family;
  (c) for making provision for other persons or purposes for whom or which the patient might be expected to provide if he were not mentally disordered; or
  (d) otherwise for administering the patient's affairs.

(2) In the exercise of the powers conferred by this section regard shall be had first of all to the requirements of the patient, and the rules of law which restricted the enforcement by a creditor of rights against property under the control of the judge in lunacy shall apply to property under the control of the judge; but, subject to the foregoing provisions of this subsection, the judge shall, in administering a patient's affairs, have regard to the interests of creditors and also to the desirability of making provision for obligations of the patient notwithstanding that they may not be legally enforceable.

96. (1) Without prejudice to the generality of section 95 above, the judge shall have power to make such orders and give such directions and authorities as he thinks fit for the purposes of that section and in particular may for those purposes make orders or give directions or authorities for:
  (a) the control (with or without the transfer or vesting of property or the payment into or lodgement in the Supreme Court of money or securities) and management of any property of the patient:
  (b) the sale, exchange, charging or other disposition of or dealing with any property of the patient;
  (c) the acquisition of any property in the name or on behalf of the patient;
  (d) the settlement of any property of the patient, or the gift of any property of the patient to any such persons or for any such purposes as are mentioned in paragraphs (b) and (c) of section 95(1) above;
  (e) the execution for the patient of a will making any provision (whether by way of disposing of property or exercising a power or otherwise) which could be made by a will executed by the patient if he were not mentally disordered;
  (f) the carrying on by a suitable person of any profession, trade or business of the patient;
  (g) the dissolution of a partnership of which the patient is a member;
  (h) the carrying out of any contract entered into by the patient;
  (i) the conduct of legal proceedings in the name of the patient or on his behalf;
  (j) the reimbursement out of the property of the patient, with or without interest, of money applied by any person either in payment of the patient's debts (whether legally enforceable or not) or for the maintenance or other benefit of the patient or members of his family or in making provision for other persons or purposes for whom or which he might be expected to provide if he were not mentally disordered;
  (k) the exercise of any power (including a power to consent) vested in the patient, whether beneficially, or as guardian or trustee, or otherwise.

Figure 25.4 Powers of the Court of Protection: Mental Health Act 1983.

Protecting patients from relatives

SITUATION 25.4 GRASPING RELATIVES

Mary Bennet was visited regularly by her daughter Jean and each week the ward sister noticed that Jean brought the pension book in for her mother to sign. However, it was noticeable that Mary never seemed to have any money for purchases from the ward trolley and if the ward had not supplied her with squash, tissues, and soap she would not have had any of those items. Janice, the ward sister, mentioned it to Jean who flushed a little and said that she did not have anything to do with her mother's money and by the time she had personally paid for the bus fare to the hospital she did not have any funds for such purchases, and anyway the hospital provided that, did they not?

Many nurses would recognise this type of situation and the dilemma which arises for them is to what extent the nurse is a protector of the patient, even when she has to protect the patient from his own relatives. In one sense this type of situation will not continue for very long since certain benefits are reduced and ultimately end after several weeks. However, the same issue can arise in other circumstances, for example the signing of wills (considered in Chapter 29). In the above situation there is little that the ward sister can do. In any event, she cannot be sure that the money is not being used to meet Mary's bills at home and the sum is of course far too small to consider taking out a Court of Protection Order. However, the fact that the relatives are aware of her concern might be of some small influence. The Law Commission has recommended that the present system whereby the DSS recognises an authorised person to collect moneys on a person's behalf should be subject to monitoring and review.

The law relating to the care of a patient's property on the death of a patient and the making of wills is considered in Chapter 29.

Returning the patient's property

SITUATION 25.5 WEEKEND PROPERTY PROBLEMS

It was the accepted practice at Roger Park General Hospital for any patients who were brought in in an emergency and who had more than a small amount of money with them to hand it in to the general office for safekeeping during their stay. On discharge they were then able to obtain a cheque representing that amount of money from the general office. Most patients, except those with no bank accounts, accepted the system. Problems, however, arose at weekends when no general office staff were on duty or when discharge was sudden and the cheques could not be made available in time. On such occasions patients complained that the actual cash that was taken from them was not returned and since not all banks were open on Saturday they could not change the cheques and some had no cash with which to return home. What is the legal position?

The legal position depends to a certain extent on the circumstances of the money being taken by the NHS Trust. If the patient is fully conscious when the money is handed over, he should be told that he will be given a cheque for this amount on discharge. If he refuses to agree to this, then it is open to him to ask relatives to look after his money or to take the risk of keeping that sum on his person. If, however, the money has been taken from the unconscious patient after an emergency admission, then there is no chance of the terms of the bailment being agreed with him. In such circumstances the hospital holds the money as part of its duty of care to look after the patient. It could be argued that this duty requires the hospital to return to the patient exactly the same coins and notes which were taken from him. Alternatively, it could be said that the hospital carries out its duty of care by giving the patient the cheque equivalent of what was taken. Unfortunately, there is no decided case to clarify the position in law. As far as administrative practice is concerned, possibly the best solution is to discuss with the patient as soon as he is conscious and capable of handling his affairs what the patient would prefer and, if the patient is unhappy at receiving a cheque for the entire amount, to consider the possibility of providing part in cash for immediate needs. Where the discharge is contemplated for a weekend, then either the cheque should be prepared in advance or there should be an emergency scheme to provide the patient with a cash advance. Where the patient has no bank account the hospital should be able to make special arrangements either for the cheque to be cleared at a local branch or for the cash to be made available.

Staff property

SITUATION 25.6 LOST HANDBAG

Mavis Jarvis, a staff nurse, was going straight from work to a travel company to pay for her holiday to Greece. She was holidaying with a friend and had £500 in cash to pay for both of them. The money was contained in a wallet inside her handbag. At the hospital all nursing staff were provided with a locker in a staff room in their ward or department. The lockers were fitted with a padlock and key. Mavis locked her locker and carried the key around for the whole shift. Several people knew that she was going to the travel agent after work. At the end of the shift when she went to her locker she found that it had been broken into: the small padlock had been forced open and the money was missing from the wallet. The police were summoned but despite intensive questioning and search the money was never recovered or the thief discovered. Mavis feels that the NHS Trust should pay for the missing money since, she argued, the padlock was inadequate and a far tougher system should have been provided for taking care of staff property. Is she right in law?

Unfortunately, for Mavis it is highly unlikely that she would win in a court action against the NHS Trust. If we return to the terminology used in Dora's case above, the NHS Trust is not the bailee of Mavis's cash; she has not transferred it to its safekeeping. She has, so to speak, brought the property into the hospital at her own risk. If of course she had gone to the general office and said 'please take care of this for me since I have to go the travel agent straight after work' and it had done so, the situation would have been very different. In that case the NHS Trust would have become a bailee of her money and would be accountable to her for its return. What about the argument that the locker should have been stronger? The locker should be as strong as is compatible with the value of property which is reasonable to be kept in there. There must be few who would think that attempting to keep £500 is reasonable. Anyone who brings valuable goods to work and keeps them there cannot expect the NHS Trust to be held responsible for their loss unless of course it is a requirement of the job that such items are brought to work, or unless the employer has assumed responsibility for them. The employer can, through the contract of employment, take on a wider responsibility for the property of employees, though this would be unusual. The courts are unlikely to imply a term that the employer has a duty to take care of the property of the employee. There would have to be an explicit undertaking to that effect.

SITUATION 25.7 STAFF CAR PARK

Jean Jones, a staff nurse in the out-patients department, parked her car in the staff car park. When she came back she found that there was an enormous scratch along the side. No note had been left on the windscreen. A pathology laboratory technician whose office overlooked the car park came up to her as she was looking at the damage and said that she had seen the whole incident. A medical records clerk who had been trying to reverse into too small a place had scraped along the side of the car. She had taken the number and said she would be prepared to give evidence for Jean. If it turns out that the medical records clerk refuses to pay for the damage and has no insurance cover, could Jean Jones hold the NHS Trust responsible for the damage?

There are two possible causes of action. One is to consider the possibility of the NHS Trust's direct liability for what occurred (for example, negligent marking of the car park) – there is no such evidence here. The other possibility is to allege that the NHS Trust is vicariously liable for the negligent driving of the medical records clerk. To establish this it must be shown that the medical records clerk was negligent while she was acting in course of employment. If, for example, she was on her way home she would probably not be acting in course of employment. If, on the other hand, she was about to visit a neighbouring hospital as part of her job, then she is clearly driving in course of employment, in which case the NHS Trust would be vicariously liable for her negligence.

Would it make any difference if a patient damaged the car? In what circumstances can it be said that the NHS Trust is responsible for the acts of the patients? Certainly, if the NHS Trust has authorised the patient to carry out a negligent act, then it would be responsible to any foreseeable victim; also where the NHS Trust has a duty of care to the victim to prevent foreseeable harm to the victim arising. This issue is discussed in relation to the existence and extent of the duty of care in Chapter 3.

Questions and exercises

1 How many disclaimer notices or exclusion notices do you see around the hospital? Consider the extent to which reliance on each notice would be reasonable to exclude liability for damage or loss of property caused by the negligence of the NHS Trust or its staff.
2 Consider the liability of the NHS Trust, if any, if a patient should take her engagement ring off in the bathroom and when she discovered that she left it there, found that it was missing.
3 Examine the procedure followed in relation to property when patients are admitted to hospital.
4 You are working at a psychiatric hospital and one of the patients drags a nail along the side of your new car. Is the NHS Trust responsible? Would it make any difference if there were a notice by the car park exempting the NHS Trust from loss or damage to staff cars parked there?
5 The relative of a patient in your geriatric wards asks you if you would sign a power of attorney so that the relative can manage the patient's affairs on his behalf. You know that the patient is mentally disordered but is reputed to be quite wealthy. What advice would you give to the relative?
6 The Court of Protection has been appointed to manage the property of one of the patients on your ward. What powers does it have and who will administer the property?

26   Legal aspects of AIDS

In one sense this section should not be needed since all those general principles of law which have been discussed in relation to health and safety, consent, confidentiality and professional liability apply to the patient suffering from AIDS or who is HIV positive. There are very few specific laws and cases dealing with the AIDS patient. However, because AIDS is at present incurable, because a high proportion of HIV patients eventually suffer from AIDS itself, and because of the present hysteria that surrounds it (as can be seen from the way in which different professional groups have argued that the basic principles of law do not apply in relation to such sufferers) it is considered advisable to discuss a few of the dilemmas which arise. The term 'AIDS patient' will be used to cover both the person who has AIDS itself and also the HIV positive person.

This chapter looks at those legal aspects of AIDS which are shown in Fig. 26.1. The UKCC's most recent statement on AIDS can be found in Appendix 8.

Statutory regulations

The Government has made regulations (Public Health (Infectious Diseases) Regulation 1985) which came into force on 22 March 1985 and which gave the powers which are illustrated in Fig. 26.2. In addition there is the AIDS Control Act 1987 which provides

1. Statutory regulations
2. Characteristics of AIDS
3. AIDS and employment
   (a) pre-employment medical examination;
   (b) tests for AIDS during employment;
   (c) AIDS and health and safety at work.
4. The AIDS patient.
5. Consent to screening.
6. Blood donors.
7. Haemophiliacs and the recipients of blood.
8. Confidentiality.
9. AIDS Control Act 1987.

Figure 26.1 Issues covered in Chapter 26.

1. Gives to local authorities the power to apply to a Justice of the Peace for the removal of an AIDS sufferer to hospital to be detained there.
2. Gives to the Justice of the Peace the power to make an order for a person believed to be suffering from AIDS to be medically examined. There are also powers in relation to the disposal of the body of an AIDS sufferer.

Figure 26.2 Public Health Act (Infectious Diseases) Regulations 1985.

It is incurable at present.
It is passed through body fluid contact.
It is of very puny strength outside body fluids.
A high proportion of those who are HIV positive are thought likely to suffer eventually from AIDS itself.
Screening for HIV positivity is beset with difficulties: there are false negatives and false positives.
Early incubation over the first three months does not necessarily show up as HIV positive.
A person who is shown to be HIV negative could become exposed to and acquire the virus immediately after the test.

Figure 26.3 Characteristics of AIDS.

for periodical reports upon AIDS to enable the appropriate resources to be allocated and the plans to be made. This Act is considered further below.

Apart from these rules and the existing public health laws which would cover AIDS, there has been minimal legislation. Codes of practice have been issued by the DH and by many professional associations, but these do not have the force of law. Although the guidance should usually be followed, failure to do so would not necessarily involve any illegality or give rise to a cause of action in law. Section 23 of the Health and

Medicines Act enables the Secretary of State to make regulations on HIV testing kits and services.

Characteristics of AIDS

AIDS does of course appear to have some characteristics which, taken together, make the disease unique. These are shown in Fig. 26.3.

The combination of these characteristics could possibly justify the judges making the law relating to AIDS an exception to the general principles of law and, until more cases are heard, the situation in law is uncertain.

AIDS and employment

Some of the many questions which arise in employment are as follows:
Can I refuse to nurse an AIDS sufferer?
Can I be compelled to have a test for AIDS?
Can an employee insist that other employees are tested for AIDS?
Can I refuse to work with an employee whom I know is an AIDS sufferer or whom I
  suspect might be?
Can an employee who suffers from AIDS be fairly dismissed?

Pre-employment medical examination

Can an employer legally insist on a prospective employee being screened for AIDS prior to being taken on as an employee? The simple answer is yes. An employer's right to choose the most suitable, competent, capable person for the job, while not absolute, is extremely wide. He is constrained by the Sex Discrimination Act 1975 and the Race Relations Act 1976 and cannot choose a particular sex or race unless the exceptions to those Acts apply. He is also prevented from compelling an employee to divulge a criminal offence if that conviction is spent for the purposes of the Rehabilitation of Offenders Act 1974 (however, most health service employees are excluded from the provisions of this Act). The requirement that a prospective employee has a medical examination can either be insisted upon before the contract of employment commences or it can result in the contract ending after it has commenced since the medical results are not satisfactory. Many occupational health departments carry out this examination for the NHS Trust and considerable hardship can arise if the employee commences the new post, having given in his notice in his previous employment, and only after starting work does the medical examination find him unfit and therefore he loses the new job. This could apply to a person suffering from AIDS or who is found to be HIV positive. Many of the codes of practice which exist advise that such tests should not be insisted upon, but in the absence of an Act of Parliament which makes it illegal to test for AIDS in such circumstances or which makes discrimination against such persons illegal, the employer is free to request such tests pre-employment. There is no protection for the employee who either refuses the test or loses the possibility of work because of the refusal or the fact that the test proves positive. A suggestion has been made that an employer who subjected employees to an AIDS test could be guilty of a breach under the Sex Discrimination Act. This is on the basis that because the majority of sufferers are homosexual males, fewer men than women will be able to meet such requirements and therefore the test could be regarded as discriminatory. However, this is only speculation as to the way in which tribunals are likely to interpret the law (see Olga Aiken, member of ACAS, writing in the *Journal of Personnel Management*, May 1988).

Tests for AIDS during employment

Once the employee's contract of employment has commenced he has certain protection against unreasonable requests by the employer.

SITUATION 26.1 COMPULSORY TESTING

Eddie was a staff nurse in the operating theatre. It was well known that he was homosexual. His colleagues were concerned that he might be HIV positive and felt that he should not be allowed to act as a scrub nurse if there were any danger to the patients. They felt that he should be tested. A request was made to the Director of Nursing Services and she asked Eddie to undergo the test. Is this request unreasonable and can Eddie refuse to comply?

Where the employee's physical or mental capability to do the job is in doubt, the employer can suggest that the employee submits to an independent medical examination but there is no power to order this. If the employee has refused a medical examination and if subsequently, in consequence, the employee is dismissed on the grounds of the refusal, the industrial tribunal will consider whether the employer acted reasonably in all the circumstances. Under the 1985 Regulations the Justice of the Peace can make an order for a person believed to be suffering from AIDS to be medically examined by a registered medical practitioner (under the Public Health (Control of Disease) Act 1984 Section 34). This provision is for the purpose of preventing a danger to public health and could be used where a person suspected of being an AIDS sufferer is acting intentionally or recklessly in endangering public health. If the disease were confirmed, the powers of the local authority to apply to a Justice of the Peace for the removal of the sufferer and detention in hospital could then be used (Public Health Regulations 1985 and Public Health (Control of Disease) Act 1984 Sections 37 and 38). In extreme circumstances it could be argued that these powers are available where the employer is concerned about a danger to public health. It is extremely unlikely, however, that their use could be justified in the circumstances described in Eddie's case. It could be argued that in Eddie's case the request to be tested for AIDS would be unreasonable for two reasons. If the test proves negative it is only of value for the day of testing and it does not exclude the possibility that Eddie has recently been exposed to the virus which has not yet shown up in tests. Frequent tests would have to be carried out to cover this possibility. If the test proves positive, what is the significance of this? It shows that the individual has been exposed to the virus but there is little indication to show the course of events: it could be many years before Eddie contracts the disease itself (if ever). It does reveal that he is a potential source of infection but if good hygienic practices are followed there should be no danger to other employees or patients. It could be argued that, being a theatre nurse, he is a greater danger to patients but this does not follow if the proper procedures are complied with. In addition it could be said that since there is no obvious value to the employer in insisting upon such a test, such a request is unreasonable because of the harm it could cause the employee. As long as the disease is incurable and as long as it is impossible to tell which HIV positive patients will contract AIDS or ARC (AIDS-related complex) and when, the knowledge of an HIV positive result confers no benefit on the employee and in fact brings him considerable harm. It affects his eligibility for a mortgage and life insurance, and he may lose his job and be unable to obtain a new one. Tentative conclusions here are that at the present time such a request by an employer would be unreasonable unless very exceptional circumstances existed. However, if Eddie has been in continuous employment for less than two years and is dismissed because he has refused to take the test, he is ineligible to bring an action for unfair dismissal before an industrial tribunal and, provided he has been given the contractual period of notice to which he is entitled, he would probably have no remedy for wrongful dismissal. If he is an NHS employee he would be entitled to make an internal appeal against dismissal but his only protection then is the overall policy of the NHS Trust and the rules of natural justice.

In the case of *Bliss* v. *S.E. Thames RHA* 1985 1 RLR 308, the Court of Appeal held that an employee could not be required to submit to a medical examination unless there were reasonable grounds to believe that he might be suffering from physical or mental disability which might cause harm to the patients or adversely affect the quality of the treatment given to them.

CASE 26.1 FEAR OF AIDS

Mr Buck had been employed as senior projectionist at the Broadway cinema in Letchworth since 1969. Mr Jones and his son were employed as relief projectionists, taking over from Mr Buck on his days off, when he was ill or on holiday. The management knew Mr Buck to be homosexual, but took no action when he was convicted of importuning in a public lavatory in the early 1970s. On 12 November 1986, a local paper reported that Mr Buck had been fined for insulting behaviour in Oxford Circus toilets. Mr Jones and his son informed the cinema manager that they no longer wished to work with Mr Buck because 'his way of life was exposing him to a risk of contracting AIDS and they felt that they might catch it from him'. Mr Buck returned from holiday to find a letter of summary dismissal awaiting him. The grounds given in the letter were the refusal of the relief projectionists to work with him.

It was argued for Mr Buck that the dismissal was unfair: he did not have AIDS and the amount of time he spent with the relief projectionists was extremely limited. He 'agreed that he lost his job because of his conduct in a public lavatory and for nothing else'. The company thought Mr Buck's offence made him unsuitable for his work because the cinema was popular with children; the cinema manager thought that he had made himself unacceptable to other employees. (This is a consideration to be taken into account in deciding whether there should be a dismissal for criminal conduct outside work in the ACAS Code of Practice.) The tribunal's findings are given in Fig. 26.4 (*Buck* v. *Letchworth Palace Ltd* 7 April 1987).

The tribunal therefore concluded unanimously that the company had acted reasonably when they dismissed Mr Buck by reason of his conduct as reported in the newspaper. His dismissal was not unfair. (Report from the Institute of Medical Ethics, Bulletin No. 28, July 1987, page 5).

It would be wrong to conclude from this case that an employer can fairly dismiss an employee simply because he is homosexual. In this case the tribunal was applying the general principles of dismissal on the grounds of conduct outside employment. It could be argued that this case is not in fact about AIDS at all. The Institute of Medical Ethics' comment on the case is that the Department of Employment's booklet *AIDS and Employment*, designed to prevent discrimination at work, would seem to be failing and they hoped that an appeal would be taken to the House of Lords. The case does indicate that the only way to prevent discrimination against AIDS sufferers or homosexuals would be to have an AIDS/Homosexuality Discrimination Act.

Would the same principle apply in the health service?

SITUATION 26.2 THE UNWITTING VICTIM

Unknown to Mary Kemp her husband was bisexual and was infected with the AIDS virus and eventually she was infected as well. She was not aware of this initially but after being away from work for an intractable infection it was discovered that she had AIDS. She was considered fit to return to work for the immediate future. She told her nursing officer of the diagnosis and it was suggested that she should return home and not consider working again. The nursing officer justified her decision on the basis that she was a risk to the staff and the patients and that she was unlikely to perform her job competently anyway.

---

1. The relief projectionists had overreacted.
2. The company had not dealt well with the matter by failing to discuss it at all with any of those involved before the dismissal.
3. Nevertheless even if there had been full discussions, 'the result in all probability would have been precisely the same'.
4. Had Mr Buck been dismissed merely because he was a homosexual to whom other employees objected, the dismissal would have been unfair; but 'he was the sort of homosexual who frequented Oxford Circus Underground Station lavatory, which we are told is a notorious haunt of homosexuals' looking for sexual intercourse.
5. The company had not taken notice of unreasonable prejudices of their employees.

Figure 26.4 Tribunal findings in *Buck* v. *Letchworth Palace Ltd*.

This situation is likely to be very complex. It is not an established principle that the fact that an employee suffers from AIDS (or is HIV positive) is in itself justification for imme-diate dismissal. Nor can it be said that the employer's duty to safeguard the health of other employees would automatically require him to dismiss the sufferer or carrier. There may of course come a time when that employee is incapable, by reason of his physical or mental condition, of carrying out his duties and a dismissal in those circumstances may well be fair. However, provided a safe system of work is followed and good hygienic practices are implemented, the AIDS sufferer should not be a danger to his fellow employees or the patients and should not be dismissed on those grounds alone. Simi-larly, a pregnant employee cannot be dismissed just because she is pregnant but, unlike the AIDS sufferer, the pregnant employee has the additional protection of a specific statu-tory right not to be dismissed solely on the grounds of pregnancy. A similar statutory provision might be required for the protection of AIDS sufferers or HIV positive persons.

The recent discovery that a surgeon had died of AIDS led to an extended public debate on the extent to which any health worker should be permitted to continue in work and possibly endanger the lives of his patients. In this particular case death followed within a few weeks of the knowledge of the illness (the surgeon ceased working as soon as he was aware of the diagnosis) and the health authorities in which the doctor concerned worked made a vigorous effort to contact patients who had been operated upon by the surgeon and offer them AIDS tests. Interestingly, and perhaps not surprisingly, the take-up on the offer of tests was very low. The General Medical Council announced that doctors risked being struck off the medical register if they contract AIDS but ignore advice to stop practising. New guidelines were published for doctors which included the advice that doctors should inform the health authorities if they suspected that a colleague had the virus but was not following advice. The General Medical Council announced that it was unethical for doctors who know or believe themselves to be infected with HIV to put patients at risk by failing to seek appropriate counselling or to act upon it when given. It could be added that if a doctor, knowing himself to be HIV positive, infected a patient as a result of his own carelessness, then it could be not only uneth-ical but also a civil wrong. This is discussed below on the duty of the AIDS patient. The Department of Health has issued guidelines to doctors and health authorities which make provision for the protection of patients in the case of HIV infection of health workers (April 1993).

The Midwives Rules, Rule 39, oblige a practising midwife to allow herself to be medically examined if necessary for the prevention of the spread of infection, when requested by the local supervising authority.

Reference should also be made to the UKCC Registrar's letter dated 6 April 1993 (12/1993) which sets out the Council's position on the routine HIV testing of health care professionals and the individual responsibility of the practitioner (see Appendix 8).

AIDS and health and safety at work

As explained in Chapter 12 the employer has a duty both under the common law and under the Health and Safety at Work Act 1974 to take care of the health and safety of his employees. Under the common law duty he is required to ensure that the premises, plant and equipment are safe, that the staff are competent and that a safe system of work is implemented.

SITUATION 26.3 CARING FOR THE AIDS PATIENT

Ruth was a staff nurse in a ward which had been specially adapted for the care of AIDS patients. Unfortunately, because of the financial position of the health authority it was necessary to reduce revenue costs. The recommended practice was that gloves should be worn at all times when dealing with the bodily fluids of the patients. However, the original type of glove which was provided was replaced by a cheaper alternative which tore easily. Since Ruth suffered from eczema she was very nervous about working in the ward and asked if she could reasonably refuse to work there.

In carrying out its duty in relation to health and safety the employer must ensure that all reasonable practical precautions are taken to safeguard the employee. A written statement of safety policy is a statutory obligation under the Health and Safety at Work Act. In order to comply with its duties each employer should ensure that the policy covers potential dangers from the AIDS virus. The employer has a duty to ensure that the equipment and protective clothing which are reasonably necessary to ensure the safety of the employee are provided. If a code of practice requires that, in the circumstances outlined above, gloves should be provided, then it would also be reasonable to provide gloves which met the needs of staff safety. If Ruth can show that the gloves provided are useless in protecting her and others could be purchased which would be effective at reasonable cost, then it could be argued that Ruth would be justified in requiring these reasonable precautions to be made for her safety. If she were to be dismissed in such circumstances it could be argued that the employer was being unreasonable and that it was an unfair dismissal. The employee could not refuse to treat an AIDS patient simply because he had AIDS. There are no statutory grounds for refusing to take part in such care as is provided by the Abortion Act.

It is, however, unreasonable of the employer to endanger the safety of the employee when reasonable precautions could be taken and they are not. The employer's duty in this respect would include the laying down of safe codes of practice and ensuring that these were implemented, training of staff in safe systems of work, as well as the provision of reasonable equipment to ensure a safe environment. If, however, an employee failed to follow the safe practices and became infected, any claim for compensation against the employer may be reduced on the grounds of contributory negligence.

The guidelines of the UKCC have made it clear that it would regard the refusal by a registered nurse to treat an AIDS patient as professional misconduct. The UKCC advisory paper on *Exercising Accountability* (see Appendix 7) emphasises that the practitioner has no right to refuse to treat a patient suffering from AIDS or who is HIV positive. There are examples in the press of different professional individuals declaring that they would not treat AIDS patients but this has often been followed by condemnation from the professional body concerned.

If, in the above case, Ruth was provided with gloves which were considered suitable and yet she still refused to work on the AIDS ward it is highly likely (depending of course on the details of the situation) that such conduct would be considered to be unreasonable. It would follow that the employers could use such conduct in refusing to care for the AIDS patient as a statutory reason for a fair dismissal. Ruth might also face disciplinary proceedings from the Professional Conduct Committee.

The Personal Protective Equipment (PPE) at Work Regulations 1992 require employers to carry out a risk assessment to avoid risks and, where this is not possible, to provide suitable PPE free of charge to employees exposed to these risks. Protection against dismissal in health and safety situations is given by employment legislation (see page 156).

The AIDS patient

Gradually a clearer idea is emerging on the rights and duties of the AIDS sufferer. The issues are often concerned with the rights of consent to be tested and also the problems of confidentiality and to whom the information that X is suffering from AIDS be given. There are also some cases directly concerned with the AIDS patient in the criminal law. For example, a threat by an AIDS victim to harm another person can be a criminal offence.

In addition it would seem that there is no reason why a person who knows that he is suffering from AIDS and is therefore a potential source of infection should not owe a duty of care to any person who he can reasonably foresee would be likely to be harmed by his actions. This is the same duty of care that is owed by anyone in the civil law of negligence to take such precautions as are reasonable to ensure that reasonably foreseeable harm does not occur as the result of their actions or omissions (see Chapter 3).

What is the nature of the duty of care owed by an AIDS sufferer to those who might be contaminated by him? Should he inform those with whom he is in contact that he has AIDS or is HIV positive? Take, for example, a situation where an AIDS sufferer is involved in a road traffic accident; should he tell the ambulance crew and those who are helping him as he lies bleeding in the road to take special precautions? If he fails to do so (and he might well fail to do so for fear that the volunteers might suddenly disappear) and some of the helpers become infected, would he then be liable to them? If the general principles of law are applied there should be no reason why he is not under the duty to inform them but the point still needs to be settled in the courts.

Consent to screening

There has been considerable debate in the press over whether people could be tested for AIDS without their knowledge and consent; for example in epidemiological research when there is a need to establish the extent of the disease or the existence of HIV positivity in the country for the purposes of planning resources and future policies. Some have argued that if the tests are done on an anonymous basis and the individuals therefore not informed of the results, then such testing would be lawful. Others have stated that to take blood for such testing without obtaining the patient's consent is a trespass to their person.

One of the difficulties is that while the law requires the consent of an individual for any interference with his person, at present consent is given for blood to be taken and this seems to include consent to all the various tests which are to be carried out on the blood: few doctors or technicians would explain to a patient all the tests that are to be undertaken. For example, in pregnancy it is routine for a Wassermann test (for venereal disease) to be carried out on patients but very few would be aware of the existence of the test or its purpose. The reasons that consent to all these various tests can be implied from the fact that there is agreement for the sample to be taken is that such tests are undertaken as part of the duty of care for the patient, to enable a proper diagnosis to be carried out and the appropriate treatment given. The difficulty over testing for AIDS at present is that as long as AIDS remains an incurable disease it could be argued that it is not in the interests of the patient to be tested. The knowledge that he is HIV positive merely puts an uncertain burden over him with little knowledge of prognosis and timings. Insurance companies, for example, are refusing cover for persons who have received a test, not just for those who are HIV positive. However, a new scheme whereby insurance cover is not provided for AIDS-related illnesses might take away the need to make any declaration in relation to AIDS tests or to one's sexual preferences.

What are our conclusions? It has been pointed out that there is, under the public health legislation, power for a doctor to be authorised to examine a person suspected of having AIDS. Since this statutory power exists, no further powers that contradict the general principles of consent should be implied, i.e. if Parliament had wished to give wider powers it could have done so under this legislation. In all other cases the principle that the patient should give consent to the testing should be applied and there should be no secret testing without the patient's knowledge or consent. As the extent of the disease grows there may well be specific laws changing this position. For example, there has been a strong plea in favour of anonymous screening for epidemiological reasons, and the Government has supported the need. The Public Health Laboratory Service commenced a programme of anonymous HIV testing, using blood left over from other tests authorised by the patient. A UKCC Registrar's letter (12/93) dated 6 April 1993 sets guidelines for practitioners involved in such testing.

This field is of particular concern to midwives and operating theatre staff who wish to know whether it is possible to insist that all midwifery patients or all surgical patients be screened for AIDS. There is certainly no power to insist on such screening under the laws at present, though there is the power to order an AIDS test on an individual under the public health regulations discussed above. The difficult question is: if there were power to screen prospective surgical or midwifery patients and the tests were carried out and some were found to be positive, what happens then? Can the professional staff refuse to operate or to attend them in their confinements? Can additional precautions for the safety of the staff be taken? If the answer to the latter question is yes, then it gives the staff a false sense of security since, as was pointed out in the section on the characteristics of AIDS, there can be false negatives. It would be better practice for midwifery, operating theatre and other staff to maintain standards of practice which assumed that every patient was HIV positive.

Blood donors

The present practice is for blood donors to be asked to agree that their blood can be tested for AIDS and a leaflet is given to them to sign as to whether they are in any of the high-risk groups and which asks them not to give blood if they are. The donors should not of course run any risk of contracting AIDS as a result of giving blood.

Haemophiliacs and the recipients of blood

Before the disease of AIDS was recognised in this country as a possible killer many haemophiliacs were given contaminated blood and have since contracted AIDS. In order to succeed in an action for compensation in respect of the harm caused by being given contaminated blood, they would need to be able to show that those professionals providing the blood should have tested it for AIDS and were in breach of their duty of care in failing to do so and that this failure was contrary to the standard accepted practices of the time. It is unlikely that those who were originally infected could show this and therefore they have been dependent upon government *ex gratia* payments and charity to assist them. Any person receiving contaminated blood now, however, which has not been properly tested would have a *prima facie* case of negligence and might also be able to obtain compensation under the Consumer Protection Act (see Chapter 12).

Confidentiality

SITUATION 26.4 A JUSTIFIED DISCLOSURE?

Dr Jones, a general practitioner, was treating Ben James for an undiagnosed condition. He thought initially that it could be glandular fever. However, the blood tests revealed that he was suffering from AIDS. Dr Jones was uncertain as to whom he could inform about this result. Ben was anxious that no one should be told and that the information should be kept from his wife till much later on. Dr Jones wondered if the practice nurse and others working in the health centre who were likely to come into contact with Ben should be notified.

AIDS probably comes under the definition of venereal disease (see statement by judge in the case of *X*. v. *Y. and another* 1988 2 All ER 648) and the Venereal Disease Regulations would therefore apply. AIDS was not a notifiable disease under the Public Health (Control of Disease) Act 1984. It was included in the list of diseases made notifiable under Regulation 3 of the Public Health (Infectious Diseases) Regulations 1988, to which only certain provisions apply. The AIDS Control Act 1987 regulates the reporting of cases and in 1988 this was extended to HIV positive persons. The powers set out in Fig. 26.2 were given to local authorities and Justices of the Peace to prevent the spread of infection of AIDS (Public Health (Infectious Diseases) Regulations 1985). These were consolidated in the Regulations made in 1988. In addition in Chapter 8 the general exceptions to the principle of confidentiality were discussed and it will be recalled that one of the exceptions was where disclosure was justified on grounds of the public interest. This was one of the most difficult exceptions since there is no clear judicial or statutory definition over what are the limits and extent of the term 'public interest' in this context. In Ben's case, if Dr Jones also treats Ben's wife it could be argued that he is not fulfilling his duty of care to her if he fails to inform her that she is at risk of contracting AIDS and even if she is not his patient he should inform her GP (unless of course he can persuade Ben to tell her). This breach in the duty of confidentiality owed to Ben is therefore justifiable on the grounds of the public interest. The same argument could be applied to informing any person in the health centre who is likely to be at risk from infection from Ben. Thus the practice nurse should be informed but not the receptionist since the latter is not likely to acquire the disease from Ben. The fact that the law is uncertain makes for considerable difficulties and ultimately it is up to individual practitioners to decide whether in the specific circumstances of an individual case there should be disclosure. The balance between an action for breach of confidentiality or an action for breach of a duty to care for the safety of a fellow employee is a very fine one.

In the case of *X* v. *Y and another* 1988 2 All ER 648, the High Court held that public interest did not justify a newspaper publishing or using information disclosed by a health authority employee in breach of contract who admitted to a journalist that two identified doctors were being treated for AIDS at an identified hospital. The newspaper was fined £10,000 for contempt of a court order.

There are numerous articles and books available on the subject of AIDS and some for further reading are listed in the bibliography. The situation is changing faster than publications can cope with and it is essential, therefore, to refer to the current press and journals for the up-to-date position.

AIDS Control Act 1987

This Act requires district health authorities to report to the regional health authorities (or Welsh Office) and for the regional authorities to report to the Secretary of State, giving information set out in the schedule and other such relevant information as the Secretary of State may direct. The schedule includes the following:

1. the number of persons known to be persons with AIDS and the timing of the diagnosis;
2. the particulars of facilities and services provided by each authority;
3. the numbers of persons employed by the authority in providing such facilities;
4. future provision over the next 12 months.

It also requires details of the action taken to educate members of the public in relation to AIDS and HIV, to provide training for testing for AIDS, and for the treatment, counselling and care of persons with AIDS or infected with HIV.

A subsequent statutory instrument has extended the information required to include HIV positive persons (Aids (Control) (Contents of Reports Order) 1988 SI 117). Nurses are extremely likely to be involved in providing information to managers for the necessary returns to be made.

Questions and exercises

1   What is meant by 'reasonably practical precautions to safeguard the safety of other employees'? To what extent do you consider your present practice meets this requirement in relation to the dangers of infection from the AIDS virus? (See also Chapter 12.)
2   Obtain a copy of your authority's policy and guidelines on AIDS and discuss the extent to which these are fully implemented.
3   Do you consider that we require an AIDS Discrimination Act? What provisions do you think such an Act would contain?
4   What is meant by the duty of confidentiality in relation to AIDS? Are any exceptions to the duty justified? To what extent do you consider that the duty is carried out and what suggestion would you make for improvements for all staff to observe this duty? (See also Chapter 8.)
5   Many regard hepatitis B virus as an even greater danger to health service staff. What are the main differences in the law (if any) relating to AIDS and to hepatitis?

27   Handling complaints

It is highly likely that at some time in her career a nurse will be involved in a complaint either in relationship to her own conduct or in handling a complaint about someone else's. There is no doubt that there is an increase in the number of complaints made about the NHS. To some this is a very bad sign and indicative of a growing discontent with the health services. However, others see this as a positive and valuable sign: an opportunity to improve the service and at the same time a sign that patients are more prepared to raise their voices over their concerns. Certainly, the current emphasis on customer and consumer relations is encouraging patients, through consumer satisfaction surveys, to make their views known so that the service can be improved. Feedback from the patient is essential if the quality of care is to be improved. Unfortunately, as the reports of the Health Service Commissioner show only too frequently, whether or not a complaint is initially justified, the way in which the complaint is handled can itself be a cause for complaint. The Patients' Charter and local charters may also encourage patients to criticise the services they have received in comparison with the standards they were led to expect. This section will review the procedures for handling complaints and discuss the legal powers of those statutory bodies which can represent or investigate the grievances of the patient.

Methods of complaining

Figure 27.1 shows the variety of ways of making a complaint about the NHS. Private hospitals have their own system for handling complaints and these tend to be on an individual hospital basis.

Many different motives exist behind a complaint. Some of the reasons why patients complain are shown in Fig. 27.2, and the outcomes that they are seeking are shown in Fig. 27.3. However, it should be appreciated that, for many people, to make a formal complaint requires considerable courage and there are many reasons why justifiable grievances are not brought to the attention of management (see Fig. 27.4). It is very difficult for patients who are suffering from chronic conditions where they are dependent upon the continued support of a particular department to make a formal complaint.

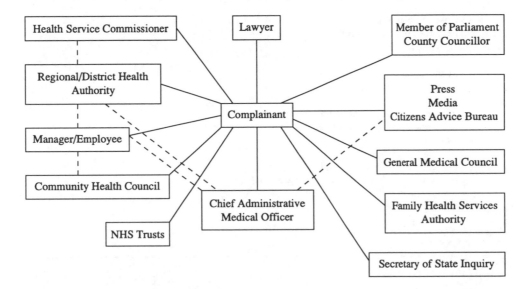

Figure 27.1 Various ways of making a complaint.

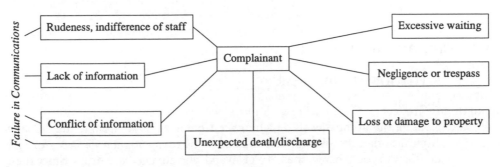

Figure 27.2 Why do people complain?

Apology.
Explanation.
Improvement.
Prevention of similar occurrences.
Compensation.
Punishment
   discipline;
   dismissal;
   striking off.
Criminal proceedings.

Figure 27.3 What do complainants seek?

1. No reason to complain.
2. No perceived reason to complain.
3. There is a perceived reason
   but
   A. Positive reasons
      (i) sympathy with staff;
      (ii) immediate apology/explanation offered;
      (iii) promise of rectification/improvement;
      (iv) immediate interview with consultant/senior manager.
   B. Negative reasons
      (i) apathy/indifference;
      (ii) ignorance of how to complain;
      (iii) acceptance that errors/inefficiency are inevitable;
      (iv) useless to complain – no point;
      (v) fear of retribution.

Figure 27.4 Why do people not complain?

A typical letter of complaint will be considered to illustrate how it should be handled and the role of the nurse.

Handling a complaint

SITUATION 27.1 DEAR SIR

Dear Sir

I was furious at the way my daughter was treated when we went to the diabetic clinic the other day. We waited two hours to be seen and then we saw a foreign doctor who could barely speak English and who changed her drugs. Since then she has had a diabetic coma and the GP has said that the dose should never have been changed. I think that that doctor should be prevented from practising again.

Yours sincerely

Valerie Machin

The above complaint is not untypical since, like many, it covers several different complaints, some of which relate to clinical matters and others to non-clinical matters, and often a lack of communication underlies the problem. This complaint is not directly concerned with nursing matters but the nurses in the clinic may well be asked to provide a statement as to what took place in the clinic and whether the parents complained at the time and what was done.

The above complaint raises the following issues:

waiting time in an out-patients' department clinic;

communication between doctor and patient;

the clinical practice of the doctor; and

the patient's current clinical condition.

The normal procedure would be for a letter of this kind to be referred to the hospital administrator. Many complainants are not always aware of the procedure and the letter could be sent to anyone. Staff should be aware of a procedure that ensures the letter is received by the administrator who can follow it up to ensure that the correct procedure is followed and an acknowledgement, and later a report, are sent to the complainant.

The administrator (or officer in charge of complaints) would be responsible for ensuring that every point raised by the complainant is investigated and reported upon satisfactorily.

1. The first task would be to refer the last two points listed above urgently to the consultant in charge of the patient to assess: it may be necessary for the consultant to discuss her present condition urgently with the GP to ensure that she is now on the appropriate medication.

2. Once her present clinical condition is satisfactory then the complaints relating to clinical matters would be investigated according to the appropriate procedure which is considered below.

3. An investigation into the waiting times would be initiated by asking the director of nursing services for a report and also asking for a report from the medical records officer or any administrative officer in charge of that department. It is an advantage if there is already a system for recording the times of the patients' arrival and departure and a system for pinpointing unreasonable delays. Some clinics do not operate an appointments system and block booking can often create unacceptable waiting times. Nursing staff will be required to provide information as to the usual way in which the diabetic clinic functioned, whether this could be improved and whether there were any extenuating circumstances on that occasion.

4. The consultant and director of nursing services would also be asked to report on the level of communication of the doctor in question, whether his English was at an acceptable level. It may be that that aspect of the complaint could be due to some form of racial prejudice, but it should never be assumed that the complaint is without foundation. A full inquiry must always be held.

The usual practice would be for the director of nursing services or his assistant to arrange for any individual nurse who was present at the time of the clinic visit to make a statement on what occurred. It is essential that the nurse receives guidance in preparing such a report and also checks with all the available documentation on the ward or department. Guidance is given in Chapter 9 on preparing statements. The nurse should never submit the statement unless she is 100 per cent satisfied with the contents and that she has, where possible, checked its accuracy. The administrator will probably be compiling his report to the complainant on the basis of what the nurse has said and if there are any inaccuracies in this which are not spotted by other hospital personnel, then the nurse could well be questioned by the Health Service Commissioner and criticism made in the report (see below).

When the administrator has received all the relevant reports, including at this stage the report by the consultant on the clinical complaints, he will respond to the complainant. This might be just a letter or it might be an invitation to attend a meeting; or both. It is vital that every single point raised by the complainant is answered fully and honestly. This might at this stage mean apologising for some shortcoming which has been revealed in the service.

In serious cases the NHS Trust might decide to set up an authority inquiry into the complaint. This might mean appointing some members to investigate the complaint.

Hospital Complaints Procedure Act 1985

A Hospital Complaints Procedure Act was passed in 1985 and requires the Secretary of State to issue directions on the complaints procedure to be initiated for hospital patients. (The limitation of the Act to hospital patients and not community patients seems to have been an oversight and the DHSS circular HC (88) 37 suggests that the same procedure should be used for complaints from the community.) A copy is to be found in Appendix 16. The Secretary of State's directives and the procedure for handling complaints concerning clinical judgements can be found in appendices to the circular. The key elements which must be present in a complaints procedure are set out in Fig. 27.5. The Department of Health has issued a consultation paper on an improved, more effective complaints system (see below).

Complaint or claim?

Difficulties arise where litigation is feared. This sometimes leads to an overcautious defensive approach such that the complainant is forced into the hands of solicitors in

1. A designated officer with responsibility for dealing with complaints in relation to a hospital or group of hospitals.
2. Duty of designated officer to receive and ensure action is taken on any formal complaint and assist in dealing with informal complaints.
3. Designated officer to investigate and report on the investigation of any formal complaint *except*
   (a) Matters relating to clinical judgement which cannot be resolved with consultant.
   (b) Serious untoward incidents involving harm to the patient.
   (c) Conduct of hospital medical or dental staff which should be the subject of disciplinary proceedings.
   (d) Criminal offences where police may be invited to investigate.
   These exceptions must be reported to the authority
4. Arrangements for dealing with informal complaints.
5. Formal complaints should be in writing and submitted within 3 months of matter complained of, though discretion over both. Complainant and hospital staff have opportunity to give information and make comments.
6. Report to Health Authority every 3 months for monitoring the progress on procedure, for considering the trends and taking remedial action.
7. Publicity over arrangements for dealing with complaints.

Figure 27.5 Key elements in a complaints procedure.

order to obtain satisfaction. This is a difficult area since initially it is not always known whether the complainant is seeking compensation. In theory the complainant's objective should not affect the nature and comprehensiveness of the investigation. In practice, there is a natural reluctance to admit fault where a legal remedy exists. However, many complaints do not become legal claims either because that is not the intention of the complainant or because for that particular complaint there is not remedy in law. For example, in Situation 27.1 above, there could be a potential negligence case over the change in medication if that resulted in a diabetic coma; but there is no legal remedy for the waiting time and possibly not for the difficulties in communication between doctor and patient, though this might be significant evidence in a negligence action.

Clinical complaints

Complaints relating to the exercise of clinical judgement by hospital medical and dental staff are subject to a different procedure. Figures 27.6 and 27.7 illustrate the recommended procedure in non-clinical and clinical matters respectively. The independent professional review that is allowed for by the clinical procedure is aimed at ensuring that the complainant receives a satisfactory explanation of what occurred. The procedure for the handling of clinical complaints can be seen in Appendix B to circular MC (88) 57; see Appendix 16.

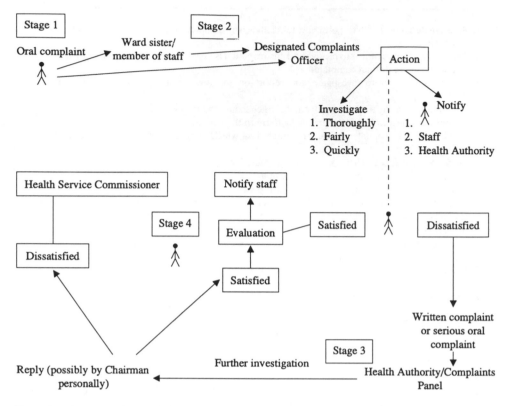

Figure 27.6 Procedure in non-clinical complaints.

The Health Service Commissioner

Jurisdiction

In 1974 the office of Health Service Commissioner (HSC) was established to provide an independent review of the complaints about the health service. There are, however, considerable restrictions on his jurisdiction which are shown in Fig. 27.8. The Health Service Commission Act 1993 provides for the consolidation of legislation relating to the HSC and came into force in February 1994.

Powers

The Health Service Commissioner has considerable powers. In the first place he is independent of any NHS Trust or Parliament. He is appointed by the Queen on the recommendation of the Prime Minister. There is therefore no reason why a complainant should fear any 'whitewash' by him. He can compel the production of documents from any person

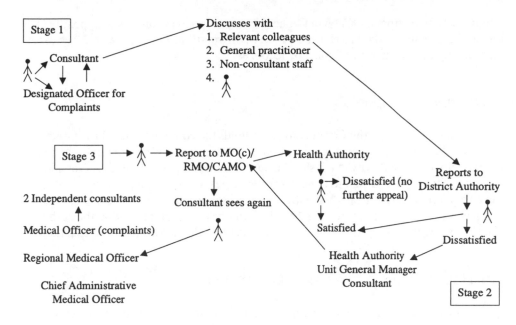

Figure 27.7 Procedure in clinical complaints.

The following are excluded from his investigation.

(a) complaints about services provided by family practitioners, dentists, opticians, and pharmacists;
(b) actions where there is already an existing remedy in law (but there is a discretion to hear such matters if the Commissioner is satisfied that it is not reasonable to expect the complainant to resort to this);
(c) personnel matters or contractual matters to do with the NHS;
(d) out of time complaints – there is a time limit of 12 months, though, again, there is discretion to extend this;
(e) complaints not yet reported to the authority. (This means that in the above case if the parent were to take her complaint straight to the Health Service Commissioner he would check to see if the authority had already had a chance of investigating the complaint and if not, the complainant would be asked to refer it there first);
(f) clinical judgement – the Health Service Commissioner is not entitled to investigate any complaint relating to the exercise of professional judgement by any professional, nurses as well as doctors. In the above situation if the result of the clinical investigation was not considered satisfactory by the complainant, even after the independent professional review, she could not take that aspect of her complaint to the Health Service Commissioner.

Figure 27.8 Jurisdiction of the Health Service Commissioner.

or authority apart from the Cabinet Office. He can subpoena witnesses to appear before him and they can be asked to testify on oath or affirmation. These powers are enforceable through the contempt of court procedures.

If a complaint is upheld

After an investigation, if the Commissioner upholds the complaint the following actions can take place: the authority might be asked to apologise to the complainant; he might recommend to the authority that it should make an *ex gratia* payment to the complainant; the authority might be asked to review its procedures. For example, if in the above case the complainant was not satisfied with the response of the authority to the complaint and it was therefore put before the HSC, the latter might recommend that the authority should review its waiting times in clinics and its procedures for attending to patients.

The House of Commons Select Committee

A final possibility, and this can be very effective, is for an inquiry to be set up by the Select Committee of the House of Commons, to whom the Health Service Commissioner reports. This committee has the power to investigate a matter further by summoning witnesses to appear before it and if in the report of the HSC it is clear that an authority has ignored its recommendations, the Committee can ask the authority to explain itself – an experience that few witnesses who have appeared before it will ever forget. In November 1987 the House of Commons Select Committee chose ten of the cases reported by the HSC to examine in Parliament. There is no secrecy. All these cases are fully reported and the proceedings of the Select Committee are themselves published.

There is no doubt that the fact that eventually an authority might have to explain how it dealt with any complaint is an important factor in ensuring that the complaint is properly, speedily and effectively dealt with.

The Mental Health Act Commission

Under the 1983 Mental Health Act there is a statutory duty placed on the Mental Health Act Commission to investigate complaints by detained patients. The jurisdiction could be extended to cover informal patients. Unlike the Health Service Commissioner, the Mental Health Act Commission is not precluded from hearing complaints of a clinical nature and in fact a high proportion of the complaints that it has investigated are concerned with clinical matters such as medication, medical, and nursing care. The MHAC has no power to subpoena witnesses nor to take evidence on oath and is itself one of the bodies whose administrative function can be investigated by the HSC (refer to the HSC report on MHAC 1992/93). From the five biennial reports of the MHAC so far produced, it is clear that the number and variety of the complaints which they are investigating are considerable. The Commission pointed out that it has complete discretion over how the complaints are to be investigated – methods range from a word to a ward sister to a full-scale investigation by Commissioners. It is also apparent that, while their terms of reference are so far only to cover the detained patient, many of their recommendations are wider and affect the care of the informal patient. For example, their procedure on the consent to treatment of the mentally disordered outside the provisions of Part IV of the 1983 Act has major implications for the care of the informal patient.

The Community Health Council (CHC)

Established in 1974, the CHC has the task of representing the interests of the patients. It has statutory powers of visiting health service premises and is entitled to information relevant to its functions. Increasingly, the CHC, and its Secretary in particular, has become 'the patient's friend' in relation to the handling of complaints. The new procedure on handling hospital complaints recommends that the hospital information booklet for patients should include the details of the local CHC so that any complainant can be advised as to the best method for dealing with the complaint. The CHC could, for example, advise a prospective complainant as to whether it would be better to refer the case to solicitors. The CHC has powers under the Community Health Councils (Access to Information) Act 1988 to obtain access to meetings and certain documents and information.

Secretary of State inquiries

Statutory powers are given in the NHS legislation for the Secretary of State to set up an inquiry into any case 'where he deems it advisable to do so in connection with any matter arising under this Act' (NHS Act 1977 Section 84). The powers of such an inquiry are extensive and include the power to summon witnesses and order the production of documents and the taking of evidence on oath. Any person who refuses to give evidence or attend or destroys documents is guilty of a criminal offence.

A public inquiry of this nature is kept for the most serious of complaints with very serious implications.

The Secretary of State also has statutory powers known as default powers: where he is satisfied after such inquiry as he thinks fit that a health authority has failed to carry out its statutory functions or is in breach of the regulations, then he can make an order declaring it to be in default. The effect of this is that the members of the authority in question must vacate their office and the Secretary of State can appoint new persons to undertake the functions. In addition he has emergency powers to give appropriate directions to ensure that the functions are properly performed. This control enables the Secretary of State to force the health authorities to comply with policies (e.g. keeping within their budgets) set by the government or the DH which they might otherwise be unwilling to do. Just as the DH can give directions to the regional health authority, so can the latter give directions to the district health authority. The DH also has the power to give directions to NHS Trusts.

Complaints about general practitioners and other services provided by the Family Health Services Authority

General practitioners (like opticians, retail pharmacists, and dentists) are independent practitioners who have a contract for services with the Family Health Services Authority. If there is a complaint about their work, then an application can be made to the relevant services committee. Thus the medical services committee would hear complaints about the work of a general practitioner, but only if it is alleged that there is a breach of the terms of service. For example, if it is alleged that the GP did not answer a night call or failed to visit a patient with no satisfactory justification for his failure, the services committee could decide after hearing all the evidence that there has been a breach of the terms of service. In this informal hearing the district nurse could well be asked by the patient or by the general practitioner to give evidence to the committee. This is not a formal hearing: evidence is not heard on oath and there are no powers of subpoena. Either side has the right of appeal to the Secretary of State.

The future

An expert committee was set up by the Department of Health to review the handling of complaints within the NHS under the chairmanship of Professor Alan Wilson. Radical recommendations have been made which take into account the effects of the 1990 Act in creating the purchaser/provider divide, the Patients' Charter and changes in primary health care organisation. Among its main recommendations are the following:

1. Establishing a common system for NHS complaints.
2. Encouraging rapid response by staff with power to deal with complaints immediately.
3. Stage 1 of the procedure should provide an immediate first-line response, on investigation and/or conciliation and action by the chief executive officer.
4. Stage 2 would be screening, followed by panel consideration.
5. The Health Service Commission should be empowered to investigate clinical complaints and those relating to general practitioners.

Consultation is currently taking place on the recommendations (*Being Heard*, Department of Health, May 1994).

Questions and exercises

1 Obtain a copy of the complaints procedure of your NHS Trust and familiarise yourself with it.

2 What do you consider to be the most appropriate system for recording informal complaints?

3 Ask the designated complaints officer if you can see the complaints book which is kept centrally and if you can see how an individual complaint has been followed up.

4 Complaints are one means of obtaining feedback from patients about their stay. Consider other means of a more positive nature to obtain information relating to patient satisfaction and consider the possibility of implementing them.

5 Complaints about clinical judgement are dealt with in a different way than those about non-clinical matters. Identify the main differences between the two procedures.

6 You are a staff nurse on a medical ward. A patient complains to you that he thinks that he is suffering from the side-effects of medication. How would you deal with this complaint?

7 In what ways does the power and jurisdiction of the Health Service Commissioner differ from that of the Mental Health Act Commission in the handling of complaints?

28 Legal aspects of drugs

The main legislation controlling the supply, storage, and administration of medicines is the Medicines Act 1968 and the Misuse of Drugs Act 1971 and many subsequent statutory instruments. Of particular importance are the Misuse of Drugs Regulations 1985. The Medicines Act 1968 set up a comprehensive system of medicines controls, as can be seen in Fig. 28.1. The main provisions of the Misuse of Drugs Act 1971 are seen in Fig. 28.2 and the 1985 Regulations in Fig. 28.3.

Figure 28.4 illustrates the main areas of control of drugs which are the concern of the nurse. The UKCC has published an advisory policy on the administration of medicines which can be found in Appendix 4. While this has no legal force in itself, its recommendations are firm guidelines to nursing staff who require clear evidence to justify any departure from these policies. Local policies may be drawn up which differ from the main guidelines and the advisory paper allows for this but it sets out principles which should be taken into account in the setting up of these local policies. Any local policy must of course comply with the statutory framework. The main areas to be covered in this chapter are set out in Fig. 28.5. Legislation has been passed to give nurses the power to prescribe, but at the time of writing, this has only been implemented in eight pilot areas in England.

Sets up a comprehensive system of medicine controls covering:
1. Administrative system
2. Licensing system
3. Sale and supply of medicines to the public
   (a) pharmacy only products;
   (b) general sales list;
   (c) prescription only list.
4. Retail pharmacies
5. Packing and labelling of medicinal products
6. British pharmacopoeia.

N.B. Exception to Part III Regulations on sale and supply of medicines to the public.
   Midwives – see Chapter 13.
   Hospitals: 'Prescription medicines may be sold or supplied by a hospital, provided they are in accordance with the written instructions of a doctor, although these instructions need not be contained in a formal prescription.'

Figure 28.1 Medicines Acts 1968 and 1971.

1. Lists and classifies controlled drugs.
2. Creates criminal offences in relation to the manufacture, supply and possession of controlled drugs.
3. Gives Secretary of State power to make regulations, and directions to prevent misuse of controlled drugs.
4. Creates advisory council on misuse of drugs.
5. Gives powers of search, arrest and forfeiture.

Figure 28.2 Misuse of Drugs Act 1971.

General principles

The nurse should have a good understanding of the classification of drugs. Under the Medicines Act, drugs are divided into categories for the purposes of supply to the public. The Part III regulations cover the following:

1. Pharmacy-only products, i.e. these can only be sold or supplied retail by someone conducting a retail pharmacy business when the product must be sold from a registered pharmacy by, or under the supervision of, a pharmacist.
2. General sales list, i.e. medicinal products which may be sold other than from a retail pharmacy so long as provisions relating to Section 53 of the Medicines Act are complied with, i.e. the place of sale must be the premises where the business is carried out; they must be capable of excluding the public; the medicines must have been made up elsewhere and the contents must not have been opened since make-up.
3. Prescription-only list, i.e. these medicines are only available on a practitioner's prescription. Schedule 1 of the subsequent Regulations lists the prescription-only products and Part II of the schedule lists the prescription-only products which are

covered by the Misuse of Drugs Act. Hospitals are exempt from these prescription-only provisions (see Fig. 28.1), as are midwives (see below).

The Misuse of Drugs Act and the 1985 Regulations make provision for the classification of controlled drugs and their possession, supply and manufacture. This is considered below.

Drugs are divided into five schedules, each specifying the requirements governing the import, export, production, supply, possession, prescribing and record-keeping.

Schedule 1 e.g. cannabis, lysergide. Possession and supply prohibited except in accordance with Home Office authority.

Schedule 2 e.g. diamorphine, morphine, pethidine, glutethimide, amphetamine – subject to full controlled drug requirements relating to prescriptions, safe custody, the need to keep registers.

Schedule 3 e.g. barbiturates, diethylpropion, mazindol – subject to special prescription requirements but not safe custody requirements (except for diethylpropion) nor to the need to keep Registers.

Schedule 4 includes 33 benzodiazepines which are subject to minimal control. In particular, controlled drug prescription requirements do NOT apply and they are NOT subject to safe custody.

Schedule 5 preparations which because of their strength are exempt from most controlled drug requirements, other than retention of invoices for two years.

Makes provision for:

1. Certain exemptions from the Misuse of Drugs Act 1971 in relation to the production, importation, exportation, possession and supply of controlled drugs.
2. Prescriptions, records and furnishing of information concerning controlled drugs and for the supervision of the destruction of such drugs.

Examples of the Regulations

1. *Persons entitled* to have controlled drugs in their *possession* include under Paragraph 6(7)(f): a person engaged in conveying the drug to a person who may lawfully have that drug in his possession.
2. *Administration of drugs* in Schedules 2, 3 and 4, Paragraph 7(3): any person other than a doctor or dentist may administer to a patient, in accordance with the direction of a doctor or dentist, any drug specified in Schedule 2, 3 and 4.

Production and supply of drugs

Paragraph 8 (2) (e)
In the case of Schedule 2 and 5 drugs supplied to her by a person responsible for the dispensing and supply of medicines at the hospital or nursing home, the sister or acting sister for the time being in charge of a ward, theatre or other department in such a hospital or nursing home as aforesaid ... may, when acting in her capacity as such, supply, or offer to supply any drug specified in Schedule 2 or 5 to any person who may lawfully have that drug in his possession, provided that nothing in the paragraph authorises:

(a) ...
(b) a sister or acting sister for the time being in charge of a ward, theatre, or other department to supply any drug otherwise than for the administration to a patient in that ward, theatre or department in accordance with the directions of a doctor or dentist.

Figure 28.3 Misuse of Drugs Regulations 1985 SI 1985/2066.

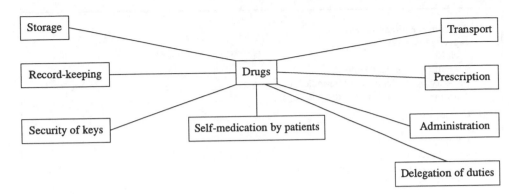

Figure 28.4 Areas which concern the nurse.

1. General principles.
2. Controlled drugs.
3. Problems in the administration of medication:
   (a) conflict with the prescriber;
   (b) sources of information;
   (c) illegible writing;
   (d) PRN medication;
   (e) instructions by word of mouth.
4. Supervision of administration of medication.
5. Self-administration by patients.
6. The nurse as prescriber.
7. Drug addicts.
8. Product liability and drugs.
9. Drugs and the midwife.

Figure 28.5 Issues covered in Chapter 28.

General principles in relation to the administration of drugs

Figure 28.6 shows a checklist that a nurse should go through before a drug is administered to a patient. There is no team liability for negligence, as was seen in the Wilsher case (page 43). Each professional must ensure that she fulfils her duties according to the approved standard of practice expected of her. If something goes wrong she is accountable in the criminal courts, the civil courts, before her employer and before the Professional Conduct Committee of the UKCC for her activities and would have to show that she followed the approved accepted practice.

A. *The correct patient. Consent?*
   capacity to consent:
      child
      mentally ill or handicapped
   pre-existing disability or contra-indications.
   warnings about side-effects; drowsiness, etc.

B. *Correct drug*
   side-effects
   timing
   special precautions
   any contra-indications
   expiry date

C. *Correct dose*
   type of patient
   physique of patient
   allergy frequency

D. *Correct site and method of administration*
   injection: skin, muscular, vein, artery, site on body.

E. *Correct procedure*
   level of competence of nurse
   skill, training
   appropriate delegation
   safe equipment, sound sterile procedure
   correct gauge of needle, form of drug and transport

F. *Correct record-keeping of dose, time, drug and method.*

Figure 28.6 Checklist for the administration of drugs.

Controlled drugs

The classification of controlled drugs by the Misuse of Drugs Regulations 1985 is shown in Fig. 28.3. Examples only are given here of the different schedules. The full list can be found in the *British National Formulary*. An example of the exemptions in relation to a nurse is shown in Fig. 28.3. The nurse should be familiar with the procedure for access to the controlled drugs stock and the record-keeping and also the way in which any destruction of the drugs is recorded.

Problems in the administration of medication

Conflict with the prescriber

SITUATION 28.1 CHALLENGING THE DOCTOR

Staff Nurse Johnson was a paediatric nurse with some two years' experience. One evening a child was admitted with suspected meningitis. The house officer on call wrote the child up for antibiotics after having given an injection. Staff Nurse Johnson was surprised at the dosage and queried this with the house officer who was surprised to find his treatment questioned by a nurse and confirmed that the nurse should administer that drug at the prescribed dose and at the intervals set out. Since Staff Nurse Johnson had not had many years' experience in paediatrics she was uncertain what to do since she knew that the child was seriously ill and that a higher dose than usual might be justified in the circumstances. She also knew that it was imperative that there were no delays in administering the drug. She was in charge of the ward.

The nurse is personally accountable for her actions in administering any drug. Only in the most serious emergency where speed is of the essence could she rely on the fact that a doctor ordered her to give the drug and she did not have the opportunity to question the dosage because of the seriousness of the situation. In any case where the nurse is not satisfied with some aspect of the drug she is instructed to administer, she must ensure the prescription is checked. She would have to do this despite considerable pressure brought by a junior doctor. The difficulties for Staff Nurse Johnson are that at night she may have to get someone in to check. She would inform her immediate nurse manager of her concern and would ask the registrar to confirm that the medication, dosage, frequency and route are correct. In extreme circumstances she is entitled to tell the doctor that she is refusing to administer the drug and the doctor then has the option of administering it himself or of rethinking the position. The nurse of course risks disciplinary action for her refusal but if she has good grounds for her belief that the drug or dosage is inappropriate, she should have the backing of her management. The UKCC advisory paper suggests that the practitioner will determine whether it is necessary or advisable to withhold the medicine pending consultation with the prescribing medical practitioner, the pharmacist or a fellow professional colleague (Para. 11.4 (c)). (See Appendix 4.)

Sources of information

The nurse should also be familiar with the *British National Formulary*. There should be an up-to-date copy on the ward and she should be familiar with it. There is some useful information at the beginning, giving guidance on prescribing.

Illegible writing

Nurses often complain that they are unable to read the doctors' writing on the drug charts. If they have any doubt about the drug prescribed they should not administer it unless they have checked it with the doctor who wrote it, his superior or, in certain circumstances, the pharmacist. If the nurse fails to double-check illegible writing she could herself become liable as the following case illustrates.

CASE 28.1 ILLEGIBLE WRITING

One of three items on a prescription was for 21 Amoxil tablets. The pharmacist misread this as Daonil. The patient suffered hypoglycaemia and sustained permanent brain damage. The pharmacist said that he had read the 'A' for a 'D' and the 'x' for an 'n'. There were other indications from which the pharmacist should have realised that his interpretation was for the wrong drug, i.e. the other drugs which were prescribed, the dosage and the fact that the patient paid for his prescription. Both doctor and pharmacist were held liable for the harm which befell the patient. The doctor was held 25 per cent liable. Damages totalled £137,547 (*Prendergast* v. *Sam Dee Ltd and others*, *The Times* 14 March 1989).

PRN medication

One major difficulty for the nurse is PRN medication (*pro re nata* – 'as required, whenever necessary'). This is the system where the doctor writes the patient up for a drug but leaves to the nurse the discretion as to when, if at all, the drug should be administered, depending on the patient's condition.

The value of the system is that it allows the patient to have a drug when necessary, without calling the doctor for the specific purpose of prescribing the drug for it to be administered immediately. Thus pain relief drugs, sleeping tablets, and indigestion drugs can be prescribed in case the patient might need such help. Unfortunately, the doctor does not always ensure that sufficient information is given on the drugs sheet. Thus he might fail to give the maximum amount that can be given in any 24-hour period. He might also fail to specify the dose and the intervals at which it can be given. The hospital pharmacist should ensure that the drugs sheets are regularly checked to ensure that all the relevant information is present and the nurse should not administer these drugs without first checking the limitations. It is also essential that every drug that is administered PRN should be recorded when given, as overdoses could easily occur if a record is not kept. Each hospital should have a policy relating to PRN medication.

Instructions by word of mouth

These also give rise to considerable concern for the nurse. Again the following situation is not uncommon.

SITUATION 28.2 NIGHT ORDERS

Ward Sister Dury was the night sister at a small geriatric hospital which was served by GPs. One night she was very worried about the condition of a frail patient whose blood pressure and temperature were raised. She telephoned the duty GP and expressed her anxieties to him. He was of the opinion that she need not be concerned and suggested that the patient should be given paracetamol. She was reluctant to take instructions over the telephone but decided that, since he would not visit, there was little else she could do for the patient. She gave the dose of paracetamol but unfortunately the patient's condition deteriorated and she again telephoned the GP, who did not visit until 9.00 a.m., by which time the patient had died.

What is the position of the ward sister? Should she have taken instructions over the telephone? The UKCC policy makes it clear that it is understood that, unless provided for in a specific protocol, instruction by telephone to a practitioner to administer a previously unprescribed substance is not acceptable, the use of facsimile transmission (fax) being the preferred method in exceptional circumstances or isolated locations (Para 6.11 Standards for the Administration of Medicines) (see Appendix 4). Paragraph 6.12 recommends that local protocols should be agreed between medical practitioners, nurses and midwives and the pharmacist 'where it is the wish of the professional staff concerned that practitioners in a particular setting be authorised to administer, on their own authority, certain medicines'. In Ward Sister Dury's dilemma described above it is clear that in the last resort it is her professional discretion as to what the patient should be given, but from the few facts described above it is not at all clear that she has exhausted all the possibilities of getting another doctor to see the patient. Similar problems can arise in a busy general hospital when junior medical staff, after very disturbed nights, are unwilling to come down again to the ward and expect nurses to take instructions over the phone. The situation is fraught with danger for the nurse and she would be well advised to follow the advice of the UKCC.

One of the biggest difficulties of taking any instructions over the telephone is the problem of proving what was said. If taking instructions over the telephone is essential, then the nurse receiving instructions should ensure that she repeats what has been said back to the doctor in the presence of a witness and then records it in writing so that if there is a dispute later as to what was said, there is some supporting evidence and an independent witness of her account. This should be contained within the protocol.

Supervision of administration of medication

One major problem which confronts nurses is the grade of nurse capable of administering drugs and whether supervision of the administration is necessary. Difficulties arise because not all local policies conform to the UKCC guidelines, many because earlier policies have not yet been revised to accommodate the suggested guidelines. Take the following situation.

SITUATION 28.3 LEVEL 2 NURSES AND DRUGS

There are few registered general nurses staffing the wards at night at Roger Park Hospital and therefore it has become customary for the SENs to take on much wider responsibilities than would otherwise be the case. Several of those who had been at the hospital for several years had long been responsible for the administration of drugs, using nursing auxiliaries to check the drugs. This policy ran counter to the UKCC guidelines in several respects: the SENs had not been specifically trained for this task and also the use of the auxiliaries in checking was in danger of giving a false sense of security to the SEN. If the wrong drug was administered and the patient suffered harm, who would be liable?

In the first place the SEN would be liable if it were her negligence which caused the harm according to the principles discussed in Chapter 3. The liability of the nursing auxiliary would depend upon the error made and whether it was reasonable to rely on the nursing auxiliary to have spotted that error and the type of error which occurred. The liability of the NHS Trust would of course be vicarious if it can be established that the SEN was negligent in course of employment, but in addition the NHS Trust could be directly liable if it can be established that the NHS Trust, knowing that its policy allowed SENs to administer drugs, had failed to provide the appropriate training.

Self-administration by patients

The involvement of the patient in his own medication is increasingly being adopted as a form of rehabilitation and as a move towards discharge and the assumption by the patient of responsibility for his own health and care. However, the retention by the patient of medication in his bedside locker puts additional responsibilities upon the nurse who needs to ensure that there is a clear policy in relation to the safety of the medicines, especially from other patients and visitors and also in relation to the training and supervision of the patient himself, and that these policies are implemented.

The nurse as prescriber

The midwife has the power of prescribing specific drugs once the consultant has given approval to them (see below). Legislation has been passed to give specified practitioners the power to prescribe specified medicines (Medicinal Products (Prescription by Nurses) Act 1992). A commencement date of 3 October 1994 was set, but only in eight pilot areas initially. The legislation followed the recommendations of the report of the advisory group on nurse prescribing (known as the Crown Report) to the Department of Health in December 1989. Earlier recommendations for nurse prescribing were made in the Cumberlege Report (*Neighbourhood Nursing: A Focus for Care*, 1986) and in the Edwards Report (*Nursing in the Community: A Team Approach for Wales*, 1987). The Crown Report was followed by a cost-benefit analysis undertaken for the Department of Health in 1991 by Touche Ross. The cost of the training in preparation for implementation led to a postponement of the original date of October 1993 for the Act coming into force. The implications for practitioners depend upon how extensively the power is given and the medicines that can be prescribed. The consultation document issued by the Medicines Central Agency on 1 July 1994 makes it clear that (a) employers will be able to decide whether or not a nurse, who is otherwise eligible, will be able to prescribe, and

(b) the power will not extend to nurses working in hospitals. Following the review of the eight pilot areas, nurse prescribing may be extended to other practitioners and other medical products.

Drug addicts

Nurses may sometimes encounter patients in their work who are registered addicts. They should know the law relating to such persons and how it affects their own position. For example, if a patient is a known addict, does that mean that any drugs he has brought into hospital with him should be returned at the end of his stay? The Misuse of Drugs (Notification of and Supply to Addicts) Regulations 1973 require a doctor to notify the Chief Medical Officer of the Home Office in writing if he knows or has reasonable grounds to suspect that a patient is addicted to certain specified drugs including cocaine and opium. Notification must be confirmed annually in writing if the doctor is still treating the patient. The names are contained in an Index and a doctor should check with the Chief Medical Officer all new cases of addiction or suspected addiction.

There are rules relating to the prescribing of these drugs by doctors: a special licence is required for the prescribing of some of the drugs as treatment for addiction.

Product liability and drugs

The case brought against the manufacturers of Opren has shown the difficulties and expense of suing a company for harm caused by medication. Initially a judge decided that a class action could not be brought on behalf of all those who claimed to have suffered side-effects, but each person claiming compensation would have to sue individually and contribute his share to the total costs. This has led to a demand for changes in the procedure in respect of such actions involving thousands of litigants which are currently being considered. Class actions have now been initiated in respect of several drugs products.

Under the present laws of negligence it is in any case difficult to show that a firm failed to take all reasonable care in testing and manufacturing its products. The victims of thalidomide did not establish negligence by the Distillers company in this country but agreed an *ex gratia* settlement. It is possible that the Consumer Protection Act 1987, Part I, which is now in force (applicable to damage suffered after the Act came into force) will make any action for liability by someone harmed by drugs easier on the basis that, provided the patient can prove that he has suffered injury as a result of a defect in a particular drug, it is then up to the manufacturer to show that one of the many defences open to him under the Act was present. This is further discussed in Chapter 12 and will not be considered further here.

Drugs and the midwife

Under the Misuse of Drugs Regulations 1985 a registered midwife who has notified the local supervising authority of her intention to practise may possess and administer any controlled drug in so far as is necessary for the practice of midwifery, and may surrender to her appropriate medical officer any stocks no longer required. A midwife may lawfully possess only those drugs that she has obtained on a midwife's supply order signed by the medical officer (Misuse of Drugs Act Section 1 1985/2066 Regulation 11). The midwife's supply order must specify in writing:

1. name;
2. occupation of midwife;
3. purpose for which the drug is required;
4. total quantity required.

The Midwives Rules, Rule 41, make further regulations on the administration of any medicines in respect of her training and the type and safety of any apparatus for the administration of inhalation analgesic. These Rules can be found in Appendix 5.

Questions and exercises

1 Review your practice in the administration of drugs. Are there any ways in which you consider that you might not be meeting the legal requirements?
2 A patient is concerned at the possibility of having suffered side-effects from medication. What is the relevant law?
3 In your hospital, when a patient is admitted, any drugs that he brings from home are immediately taken from him and destroyed. One patient complains about this practice because it is wasteful and because he paid the prescription price for those drugs. What do you consider should be the correct practice?
4 Design a policy for handling drugs to be learnt by a first-year learner.
5 What are the advantages and disadvantages of administering controlled drugs PRN?
6 If nurses were to be permitted to prescribe and administer specified drugs, what safe-guards do you consider should be laid down to protect the patient?

29   Legal aspects of death

The death of a patient can be upsetting for a nurse and even the fact that the patient is elderly does not necessarily mean that it is any easier for her to accept. Uncertainties surrounding legal issues and numerous questions from distressed relatives can add to the nurse's difficulties. It is important that the nurse should be acquainted with the procedures and the law so that she can cope at this distressing time with confidence in her knowledge. Figure 29.1 sets out the areas which will be considered in this chapter, again using the approach of 'where do I stand if "x" occurs?' In addition, reference should be made to appendices of sample leaflets giving information to relatives and to staff.

The certification and registration of death

Certification of death is a medical task. The complexities in dealing with brain death and organ transplants are considered in Chapter 16 which is concerned with law and the intensive care nurse, and which also deals with the definition of death and the importance of the exact time of death.

Here we consider the nurse's role and the procedures to be followed generally.

SITUATION 29.1 AN EXPANDED ROLE?

Night porters at Roger Park Hospital had clear instructions that no body should be taken to the mortuary unless it had been certified dead. This resulted from an unfortunate incident some time before when a body was taken to the mortuary but was seen to move and therefore quickly returned to the ward. An investigation revealed that the person had been certified dead by a nurse. The nurses were told always to call a doctor to certify death. However, house officers were not happy about being called out just to certify death and considerable pressure was put on the nursing staff. One night it was clear that one patient was extremely ill. There were no immediate relatives but a distant relative was notified of the situation. The patient died at 3 a.m. The nurse summoned the doctor who said that he would not come down but would see the patient in the mortuary and sign the certificate there in the morning. The nurse was asked by the Bed Bureau if she had a spare bed, as a GP had just phoned and was sending in an emergency case. The hospital had no spare beds at all except the one occupied by the dead person. Could the nurse certify death herself and arrange for the porters to remove the body?

---

1. Certification of death.
2. Disposal of the body.
3. Post mortems.
4. Notification to the coroner.
5. Inquests.
6. Property of the deceased.
7. Wills.

Figure 29.1 Issues covered in Chapter 29.

The medical certificate should be taken by the next of kin or, if not available, by any relatives living in the district or present at the death to the Registrar for Births, Marriages and Deaths within 5 days of the death. He will require the following information: the full name of the deceased; the last known address; date of birth; occupation; and whether the deceased was in receipt of a pension. The Registrar will give the person registering the death a certificate of disposal form which can be handed to the undertaker. If a cremation is intended, then certification by two doctors will be required. If the death has been referred to the coroner, then the relatives should be notified that they will not receive the certificate from the hospital. The coroner will issue his own disposal certificate.

The relatives will receive from the Registrar in addition to the certificate of disposal form a certificate of registration of death. This may be required by the DSS in order to claim any entitlements. (The death grant is no longer payable but other benefits are available to those who are eligible.) This certificate may also be required to obtain transfer of any bank accounts, etc., and further copies are available from the Registrar on payment of a fee.

Figure 29.2 Procedures for dealing with death.

There are numerous examples where pressure is placed upon nursing staff to go beyond their duties and powers and undertake additional activities. It is clear that the nurse does not have the power to certify death. She should not give way to any pressure, however reasonable it might appear.

Normally the General Office of the hospital or the medical records department deals with bereaved relatives. Sometimes there is a special office for dealing with the bereaved and during weekdays the relatives can be shown to this place. However, at night and during the weekends and bank holidays the nurse may be asked questions by the relatives. She should know the details relating to the registration of death and the disposal of the body. Figure 29.2 sets out the procedure to be followed. (See also Appendix 12.)

Disposal of the body

Different arrangements exist according to the local hospital facilities. Some hospital mortuaries also double up as the public mortuary and it is possible for the body to remain there until collected by the undertakers for the funeral. Before the body is taken from the ward, the nurse must ensure that it is properly labelled and that a receipt is signed and that any property on the body, e.g. rings, are carefully noted and signed for. Similar procedures to check identification and property on the body and the giving of receipts must also be followed when the body is handed over by the porters, administrators or even nurses to the undertakers. Unfortunately, mix-up between bodies still occurs and the wrong body is released.

Post mortems

The coroner might require a post mortem to ascertain the cause of death and can direct a legally qualified medical practitioner to carry out the post mortem. A post mortem ordered by a coroner may or may not precede an inquest. If the coroner orders a post mortem, then the person in possession of the body has no choice but to agree. Sometimes, however, medical staff may request the relative's permission to confirm the cause of death or for research purposes. They require the consent of the person in possession of the body (Human Tissue Act 1961 Section 2 (2)). This can be a distressing request to make to relatives and the request should be put to them with sensitivity (see Appendix 12 for leaflet for staff in dealing with death).

Deaths which have to be reported to the coroner

These are shown in Fig. 29.3.

If it is likely to be a coroner's case, no unofficial post mortem should be undertaken without the coroner's approval. The coroner can order a post mortem examination to be carried out before deciding to hold an inquest. A leaflet giving further guidance on dealing with death is included in Appendix 12.

(a) where there is reasonable cause to suspect a person has died a violent or unnatural death;

(b) where there is reasonable cause to suspect a person has died a sudden death of which the cause is unknown;

(c) the person has died in prison or in such place or under such circumstances as to require an inquest.

Those causes of death which should be reported to the coroner include: abortions; accidents and injuries; alcoholism; anaesthetics and operations; crime or suspected crime; drugs; ill-treatment; industrial diseases; infant deaths if in any way obscure; pensioners where death might be connected with a pensionable disability; persons in legal custody; poisoning; septicaemias if originating from an injury; and stillbirths where there may have been a possibility or suspicion that the child may have been born alive.

Figure 29.3 Deaths which have to be reported to the coroner.

Inquests

The Coroners Act 1988 covers the appointment of coroners, the holding of inquests, and post mortem examination.

SITUATION 29.2 AN UNEXPECTED DEATH

Bill Arthur was undergoing a stomach operation when the anaesthetist reported that his pulse was becoming very weak. Resuscitative procedures were undertaken but unfortunately Bill died. The death was reported to the coroner who decided that an inquest should be held.

What is the purpose of the inquest?

The purpose is to ascertain the following:

1. the identity of the deceased;
2. how, where, and when the deceased came by his death;
3. the particulars, for the time being required by the Registration Acts, to be registered concerning the death.

Section 11 (6) of the Coroners Act 1988 specifically states that the purpose of the proceedings shall not include the finding of any person guilty of murder, manslaughter, or infanticide.

Who should attend?

The coroner has a duty (Section 11 (2) Coroners Act 1988) to examine on oath all persons who tender evidence as to the facts of the death and all persons having knowledge of the facts whom he considers it expedient to examine. Under the Coroner's Rules (1984

Section 1 No. 552) the coroner has considerable discretion in deciding who should attend. He must notify the date, hour and place of an inquest to:

1. the spouse or a near relative or personal representative of the deceased whose name and address are known to the coroner; and
2. any other person who
   (i) in the opinion of the coroner is within Rule 20 (2), i.e. parent, child, spouse; any beneficiary under an insurance policy on the life of the deceased; any person whose act or omission or that of his servant or agent may have caused or contributed to the death of the deceased; any person appointed by a trade union to which the deceased belonged if the death may have been caused by an injury received at work or an industrial disease; an inspector appointed by an enforcing authority or government department to attend; the chief of police; any other person who in the opinion of the coroner is a properly interested person; and
   (ii) has asked the coroner to notify him of the particulars of the inquest; and
   (iii) has supplied the coroner with a telephone number or address for the purpose of so notifying him.

Examination of witnesses

Any of the persons listed under 2 (i) above is entitled to examine the witnesses either in person or through a solicitor or barrister. The coroner has the power to disallow any question which in his opinion is not relevant or is otherwise not a proper question.

The procedure is for any witness to be examined first by the coroner and, if the witness is represented at the inquest, lastly by the representative. No witness is obliged to answer any question tending to incriminate himself. Where it appears to the coroner that a witness has been asked such a question, the coroner must inform the witness that he may refuse to answer.

Any person whose conduct is likely to be called in question shall, if he has not been summoned to give evidence at the inquest, be given reasonable notice of the date, hour and place at which the inquest shall be held. If any such person has not been summoned or notified then the coroner must adjourn the hearing to enable him to be present. The inquest shall be adjourned by the coroner on notification by the clerk to the Magistrates Court that a person has been charged with an offence such as murder, manslaughter, infanticide, an offence under Section 1 of the Road Traffic Act 1972, or the offence of aiding and abetting a suicide under Section 2 (1) of the Suicide Act 1961. The Director of Public Prosecutions may also ask the coroner to adjourn the hearing. Where the coroner adjourns the hearing he shall send to the registrar of deaths a certificate stating particulars required for registration.

Nature of the inquest

The coroner's inquest is very different from the usual courts of law in this country. It is an inquisitorial hearing as opposed to the civil and criminal courts which are accusatorial. This means that in an inquest there are not two opposing parties with the coroner sitting back and hearing them argue out a case, intervening only to ensure fair play. At an inquest the coroner is in control. It is up to him to obtain answers to the questions set out above. He calls the witnesses and decides the order in which they are to give evidence and generally controls the court and hearing. There is not always a jury but where there is a point of public concern then the coroner will usually ensure that a jury is summoned.

Let's go back to Bill's case. The coroner's officer will have requested statements from relevant people who were present in theatre and who were concerned with Bill's treatment. It is helpful if those making a statement can keep a copy. The coroner will probably have requested a post mortem examination to ascertain the cause of death. He will decide which people he requires to summon as witnesses. Clearly, in Bill's case there will have to be evidence of identity and also of what took place in theatre. The surgeon, anaesthetist and the nurse are all likely to be called to give evidence. If detailed pathology laboratory results are not yet available there could well be an adjournment until they are ready. Bill's family will obviously wish to be present in order that they can ask the relevant questions to be put to prepare for a possible case of negligence in the civil courts. The coroner has the power to prevent any question that he does not consider relevant to the inquest.

Preparation for the theatre nurse before attending the inquest

The theatre nurse has, hopefully, kept a copy of the statement that she made for the coroner. The statement should have followed those guidelines discussed in Chapter 9. She should be advised by a senior nursing officer who has had some experience in such matters on the sort of questions she can expect and how to cope. (For further information on this aspect see Chapter 9.) The importance of comprehensive, meaningful record-keeping cannot, once again, be overstressed.

Property of the deceased

When a patient has died there is an obligation on the staff to ensure that the property is listed and accounted for. Usually the next of kin will arrange for clothes and small personal items to be taken away. However, any property which looks as though it might be of some value should only be handed over to the executor or personal representative on production of the grant of probate or letters of administration relating to the estate. This is the only way in which the NHS Trust can avoid being challenged for handing the property over to the wrong person. A form of indemnity may be required to protect the NHS Trust. (See Appendix 12, para. 18.)

Wills

The best advice to nursing staff in relation to the drawing up or signing of wills for patients is 'don't'! Ideally, if a patient makes it known that he wishes to make his will, the administrator should be advised and the patient's solicitor called. The nurse should not be involved. If there is likely to be any dispute as to the patient's competence to make a will it is worth getting medical opinion to check on this point since one of the grounds for challenging a will's validity is that the patient lacked the competence to sign it since he was unaware of the implications of his act. Another ground on which its provisions can be challenged is that the patient was subjected to undue influence at the time of signing it so that its provisions do not represent his real intent. Nursing and medical evidence thus becomes crucial in any such legal dispute and if there is mention in the medical records that the patient signed his will on such and such a day and that his state of mind was rational, clear and unconfused, while that is not in itself evidence of the truth of what is stated it should at least contain sufficient information to assist professionals in the recall of events, should they be subjected to cross-examination on the patient's competence or independent state of mind.

SITUATION 29.3 EXECUTION AT NIGHT

Florence Evans was convinced that she was dying. She fretted that she had not made her will and asked the night sister if she would sign a piece of paper declaring how she would like her property disposed of. The night sister was very reluctant to become involved, although she knew that Florence was in fact very ill. Florence showed her the paper on which everything was written and asked her to sign it with the auxiliary as a witness. Just to settle Florence the night sister agreed and she and the nursing auxiliary together watched Florence sign the piece of paper and then they signed their own names. Florence died that same week.

A few weeks later the sister was told that Florence's daughter was disputing the will which left everything to her two brothers and nothing to her. She said that the formalities were not complied with and that it was not a proper will.

This gives an example of one reason why nursing staff are well advised not to become involved with wills and many hospitals provide advice on what staff should do in this situation. In some hospitals it would be possible for a sister in this situation to summon the on-call administrator to take care of Florence's will. The actual signing and witnessing of the will is known as the execution of the will and strict rules are in force in relation to the validity of the process. These have been eased slightly since 1982 but the procedures must be strictly followed. Any major irregularity in the execution of the will can lead to the will being declared invalid. There are no special forms to be used although these are available. The legal requirements are set out in Fig. 29.4.

Any person who signs the will as a witness is prevented from being a beneficiary under the will and this applies to the spouse as well. (In one case where the solicitor allowed the beneficiary's spouse to sign the will the solicitor was liable for the lost inheritance.) If the testator intends leaving a gift to the NHS Trust or its staff, then no one from the NHS Trust should be involved in the drawing up or signing of the will. Otherwise the gift could be invalidated on the grounds of undue influence.

In the situation described above where the sister and the nursing auxiliary witnessed the will it is unlikely that the will could be declared invalid on the grounds of its actual

---

Section 17 Administration of Justice Act 1982 amending Section 9 of the Wills Act 1837
No will shall be valid unless

(a) It is in writing and signed by the testator, or by some other person in his presence and by his direction; and
(b) it appears that the testator intended by his signature to give effect to the will; and
(c) the signature is made or acknowledged by the testator in the presence of two or more witnesses present at the same time; and
(d) each witness either
  (i) attests and signs the will; or
  (ii) acknowledges his signature,
  in the presence of the testator (but not necessarily in the presence of any other witness), but no form of attestation shall be necessary.

Additional requirements:

(a) the testator must be over 18 (unless in the armed forces or the merchant navy);
(b) the testator must have the required mental competence at the time he signs the will.

Figure 29.4 Requirements for a valid will.

---

execution even though it might be challenged on other grounds (competence, undue influence, etc.). However, the possibility of involvement in litigation does illustrate the advantages of nursing staff ensuring that, where possible, the experts are involved.

Questions and exercises

1 Obtain a copy of the local policy and guidelines on dealing with death and familiarise yourself with it.
2 Consider any patient whose death you have witnessed and whose relatives you have had to comfort and assist. Was there any information of which you were ignorant? Could you answer all their questions? (Look at the leaflet in Appendix 12 and refresh your memory.)
3 In what ways would an inquest differ from a hearing in the criminal or civil courts?
4 Prepare a procedure for preparing a nurse who has been asked to give evidence at an inquest.
5 Obtain a copy of your NHS Trust's leaflet for the guidance of patients on the care of property. Does it consider the procedure to be followed at the death of a patient? What precautions would you as a ward sister take to ensure that the property of the deceased was cared for?

Appendix 1 Code of professional conduct for the nurse, midwife and health visitor[*]

Each registered nurse, midwife and health visitor shall act, at all times, in such a manner as to:

- safeguard and promote the interests of individual patients and clients;
- serve the interests of society;
- justify public trust and confidence and
- uphold and enhance the good standing and reputation of the professions.

As a registered nurse, midwife or health visitor, you are personally accountable for your practice and, in the exercise of your professional accountability, must:

1. act always in such a manner as to promote and safeguard the interests and well-being of patients and clients;
2. ensure that no action or omission on your part, or within your sphere of responsibility, is detrimental to the interests, condition or safety of patients and clients;
3. maintain and improve your professional knowledge and competence;

[*] Third edition, originally published as Code of Professional Conduct for the Nurse, Midwife and Health Visitor, by the United Kingdom Central Council for Nursing, Midwifery and Health Visiting, June 1992.

4. acknowledge any limitations in your knowledge and competence and decline any duties or responsibilities unless able to perform them in a safe and skilled manner;
5. work in an open and co-operative manner with patients, clients and their families, foster their independence and recognise and respect their involvement in the planning and delivery of care;
6. work in a collaborative and co-operative manner with health care professionals and others involved in providing care, and recognise and respect their particular contributions within the care team;
7. recognise and respect the uniqueness and dignity of each patient and client, and respond to their need for care, irrespective of their ethnic origin, religious beliefs, personal attributes, the nature of their health problems or any other factor;
8. report to an appropriate person or authority, at the earliest possible time, any conscientious objection which may be relevant to your professional practice;
9. avoid any abuse of your privileged relationship with patients and clients and of the privileged access allowed to their person, property, residence or workplace;
10. protect all confidential information concerning patients and clients obtained in the course of professional practice and make disclosures only with consent, where required by the order of a court or where you can justify disclosure in the wider public interest;
11. report to an appropriate person or authority, having regard to the physical, psychological and social effects on patients and clients, any circumstances in the environment of care which could jeopardise standards of practice;
12. report to an appropriate person or authority any circumstances in which safe and appropriate care for patients and clients cannot be provided;
13. report to an appropriate person or authority where it appears that the health or safety of colleagues is at risk, as such circumstances may compromise standards of practice and care;
14. assist professional colleagues, in the context of your own knowledge, experience and sphere of responsibility, to develop their professional competence, and assist others in the care team, including informal carers, to contribute safely and to a degree appropriate to their roles;
15. refuse any gift, favour or hospitality from patients or clients currently in your care which might be interpreted as seeking to exert influence to obtain preferential consideration and
16. ensure that your registration status is not used in the promotion of commercial products or services, declare any financial or other interests in relevant organisations providing such goods or services and ensure that your professional judgement is not influenced by any commercial considerations.

Notice to all registered nurses, midwives and health visitors

This Code of Professional Conduct for the Nurse, Midwife and Health Visitor is issued to all registered nurses, midwives and health visitors by the United Kingdom Central Council for Nursing, Midwifery and Health Visiting. The Council is the regulatory body responsible for the standards of these professions and it requires members of the professions to practise and conduct themselves within the standards and framework provided by the Code.

The Council's Code is kept under review and any recommendations for change and improvement would be welcomed and should be addressed to the:

Registrar and Chief Executive
United Kingdom Central Council for Nursing, Midwifery and Health Visiting
23 Portland Place, London, W1N 3AF

Appendix 2 Confidentiality: a framework to assist individual professional judgement[*]

The contents of this Advisory Paper apply to all persons whose names appear on any part of the Professional Register maintained by the UKCC and to those undertaking courses of education and training with a view to admission to the Register.

Although the list of contents is stated below it is essential that the document be read from its beginning to understand properly the issues addressed.

Contents

[*]A UKCC Advisory Paper originally published as *Confidentiality: An Elaboration of Clause 9 of the Second Edition of the UKCC's Code of Professional Conduct for the Nurse, Midwife and Health Visitor* by the United Kingdom Central Council for Nursing, Midwifery and Health Visiting, April 1987.

The UKCC members and officers responsible for the preparation of this document greatly appreciate the opportunity afforded them to discuss it in its formative stages with representatives of the General Medical Council.

Section D   Deliberate breach of confidentiality in the public interest or that of the
             patient/client
Section E   Summary of the principles on which to base professional judgement in
             matters of confidentiality

A Introduction

1. The Code of Professional Conduct for the Nurse, Midwife and Health Visitor (Second
Edition) published by the United Kingdom Central Council for Nursing, Midwifery and
Health Visiting is

  a statement to the profession of the primacy of the interests of the patient or client;

  one of the principal means by which the Council is seeking to comply with Section
    2(5) of the Nurses, Midwives and Health Visitors Act 1979 and give advice to its
    practitioners on standards of professional conduct;

  a portrait of the practitioner the Council believes to be needed and wishes to see
    within the profession.

2. In approving the terms of this edition of the Code the Council authorised the publication of key statements on a number of important professional issues.

3. One of these key statements (Clause 9) concerns 'Confidentiality'. It reads:

  'Each registered nurse, midwife and health visitor is accountable for his or her practice, and, in the exercise of professional accountability shall:
     Respect confidential information obtained in the course of professional
  practice and refrain from disclosing such information without the consent of
  the patient/client, or a person entitled to act on his/her behalf, except where
  disclosure is required by law or by the order of a court or is necessary in the public
  interest.'

4. It can be seen from the general description of the Code of Professional Conduct and
the particular contents of Clause 9 that breaches of confidentiality should be regarded
as exceptional, only occurring after careful consideration and the exercise of personal
professional judgement.

5. Any codified statements of this nature need continuous exploration, and on occasions a more detailed and authoritative elaboration. It is for the whole profession to
recognise its responsibility to share in such exploration, to use the respective knowledge and skill of practitioners to facilitate it and to recognise the important contribution
the professional press makes to this essential debate. The subject of confidentiality has
emerged as one on which the profession's practitioners need the relevant clause in the
Code of Professional Conduct to be developed more fully by the UKCC. It must be
said, however, that no exploration or elaboration by others alters the fact that the ultimate decision is that of the individual practitioner in the situation.
    The demand for elaboration of Clause 9 of the Code has focused particularly on deter-
mining the difficult boundary that applies in any case between the expectations of

patients/clients that information, whether recorded or not, obtained in the course of professional practice will not be disclosed, and the expectations of the public that they will not be put at risk because practitioners unreasonably withhold information.

It is not the purpose of this document to seek to provide answers to the many dilemmas which practitioners face. It is necessary, however, to provide examples of them since they have been a backcloth against which the discussions culminating in the publication of this document have taken place.

Correspondence on this point has come (for example) from:

a sister in a psychiatric day hospital who found a patient possessed of large quantities of controlled drugs that he cannot have obtained legally;

a medical practitioner concerned that a community midwife reported to her employers the fact that while visiting the wife of a hospital employee in a professional capacity she saw substantial quantities of stolen hospital property;

a health visitor who has been told by one child that another child is being sexually abused;

Accident and Emergency Department nursing staff who found that the unconscious patient they were treating had a gun on his person;

nurses working in the community who have been instructed by their managers (following approval by an ethical committee) to give researchers direct access to confidential information in respect of patients, but who knew that the consent of those patients had not been sought;

psychiatric nurses who fear that information revealed by a patient in a therapeutic group may be passed on by other patients and that the nurses will be held responsible;

occupational health nurses faced with requests from their managers for information about employees;

community psychiatric nurses who were reluctant to comply with the instruction to put full names and addresses of patients visited on their travel expense claims;

a health visitor who had become aware that information she shared with a social worker in a case conference had been given in evidence in a Magistrates Court;

practitioners who have chosen not to make a record of information given to them by patients in confidence, and who have later been worried about the propriety of their decision;

and

a health authority chairman who asks 'Who is to define the public interest?' and 'How is the nurse to recognise the authenticity of the claim of public interest?'

The Council has been left in no doubt that it has a responsibility to address this important subject in greater depth.

As already stated, the UKCC is not seeking to provide responses to those dilemmas since a judgement must be made by the individual practitioner concerned. It is instead seeking to provide guidance on disclosure of information:

(a) to assist development of understanding about the nature and scope of the dilemma which practitioners face, and to encourage those who employ nurses, midwives and health visitors to recognise the difficult and stressful situations encountered by practitioners and to offer support and guidance, stimulate discussion and develop and publicise policies on this important matter;

(b) to state certain principles which it is hoped will assist practitioners to consider situations which they encounter and to make sound professional judgements;

(c) to emphasise that the responsibility of whether or not information should be withheld or disclosed without the consent of the patient/client lies with the practitioner involved at the appropriate time and cannot be delegated;

(d) to stress that those who employ or supervise nurses, midwives and health visitors have an obligation to support these practitioners in discharging their responsibilities in respect of the right to disclose or withhold information using their professional judgement;

(e) to indicate the conditions which should be met before disclosure of information, so that the decision to either disclose or withhold information can be justified.

B Defining terms

1. What do we mean when we speak of something being 'Confidential'? Turn to almost any Dictionary and you find that the focal word in the definitions of 'confide', 'confidence' or 'confidential' is 'TRUST'. To trust another person with private and personal information about yourself is a significant matter. Where the person to whom that information is given is a nurse, midwife or health visitor the patient/client has a right to believe that this information, given in confidence in the expectation that it will be used only for the purposes for which it was given, will not be released to others without the consent of the patient/client. The death of a patient/client does not absolve the practitioner from this obligation.

2. Clearly it is impractical to obtain the consent of the patient/client every time that health care information needs to be shared with other health professionals, or other staff involved in the health care of that patient/client. Consent in these instances can be implied provided that it is known and understood by the patients/clients that such information needs to be made available to others involved in the delivery of his/her care. Patients/clients have a right to know the standards of confidentiality maintained by those providing their care, and these standards should be made known by the health professional at the first point of contact. These standards of confidentiality can be reinforced by the additional use of leaflets and posters where the health care is being delivered.

3. When an individual practitioner considers that it is necessary to obtain the explicit consent of a patient/client before disclosing specific information, it is the responsibility

of the practitioner to ensure that the patient/client can make as informed a response as possible as to whether that information can be disclosed or withheld.

4. It is essential that nurses, midwives and health visitors recognise the fundamental right of their patients or clients to information about them being kept private and secure. This point is sharply reinforced by only brief consideration of the personal, social or legal repercussions which might follow unauthorised disclosure of information concerning a person's health or illness.

5. Disclosure of information occurs in the following ways:

(a) with the consent of the patient/client;
(b) without the consent of the patient/client when the disclosure is required by law or order of a court;
(c) by accident;
(d) without the consent of the patient/client when the disclosure is considered necessary in the public interest.

It is the latter two categories that this Advisory Paper is particularly addressing, for a breach of confidentiality occurs if anyone deliberately or by accident gives information, which has been obtained in the course of professional practice, to a third party without the consent of the patient/client.

6. The public interest, in the context of this Advisory Paper, is taken to mean the interests of an individual, of groups of individuals or society as a whole, and would (for example) encompass matter such as serious crime, child abuse and drug trafficking.

C Ownership and care of confidential information

1. The organisations which employ professional practitioner staff who make records (whether in the National Health Service or in other spheres of practice) are the legal owner of such records, but such ownership does not give them any legal right of access to the information contained in those records. The patient also is involved in the ownership. The ownership of a record is therefore irrelevant to the patient's right to confidentiality and his/her expectation that identifiable personal health information will not be disclosed without consent.

2. In many situations genuine difficulties can be experienced in preventing the leakage of confidential information or its inadvertent spread into management layers leading to possible misuse. There is need for particular caution where a system of shared records is employed, it being incumbent on the author of any particular entry to satisfy himself or herself that other people with access to that shared record will respect the confidentiality of the information and will place neither the patient/client nor the author of the entry at risk by its release without consent.

3. The task with which individual professional practitioners are faced is not limited to that of exercising a judgement as to what information can be or should be disclosed. It also includes that of ensuring or helping to ensure that record keeping systems are

not such as to make the release of information possible or likely. Neither technology nor management convenience should be allowed to determine principles. Each practitioner has a responsibility to recognise that risks exist, and to satisfy himself or herself in respect of the system for storage and movement of records operated in the health care setting in which he or she works and to ensure that it is secure. The concern for the environment of care for which each practitioner is held accountable under the terms of clause 10 of the Code of Professional Conduct for the Nurse, Midwife and Health Visitor extends to include this.

4. The practitioner should act so as to ensure that he/she does not become a channel through which confidential information obtained in the course of professional practice is inadvertently released. The dangerous consequences of careless talk in public places cannot be overstated.

5. Where access to the records of patients or clients is necessary so that students may be assisted to achieve the necessary knowledge and competence it must be recognised that the same principles of confidentiality stated earlier in this document extend to them and their teachers. The same applies to those engaged in research. It is incumbent on the practitioner(s) responsible for the security of the information contained in these records to ensure that access to it is closely supervised, and occurs within the context of the teacher and student undertaking to respect its confidentiality, and in knowledge of the fact that the teacher has accepted responsibility to ensure that students understand the requirement for confidentiality and the need to observe local policies for the handling and storage of records. It is expected that the student or teacher who is active in giving care as a practitioner will apprise the patient of their role, thus enabling the patient who is so capable to control the information flow. Where deemed necessary the recipient of confidential information from a patient/client will advise him/her that the information will be conveyed to the nurse, midwife or health visitor involved in his/her care on a continuing basis.

6. It is advisable that the contracts of employment of all employees not directly involved with patients/clients but who have access to or handle confidential records contain clauses which emphasise the principles of confidentiality and state the disciplinary consequences of breaching them. Paragraph 3.20 of the Report from the Confidentiality Working Group of the DHSS Steering Group on Health Services Information suggests a form of words worthy of consideration as follows:

> 'In the course of your duties you may have access to confidential material about patients, members of staff or other health service business. On no account must information relating to identifiable patients be divulged to anyone other than authorised persons, for example medical, nursing or other professional staff, as appropriate, who are concerned directly with the care, diagnosis and/or treatment of the patient. If you are in any doubt whatsoever as to the authority of a person or body asking for information of this nature you must seek advice from your superior officer. Similarly, no information of a personal or confidential nature concerning individual members of staff should be divulged to anyone without the proper authority having first been given. Failure to observe these rules will be regarded by your employers

as serious misconduct which could result in serious disciplinary action being taken against you, including dismissal.'

The circumstances in which a nurse, midwife or health visitor chooses to disclose or withhold confidential information are explored in Section D.

D Deliberate breach of confidentiality in the public interest or that of the individual patient/client

1. The examples given in paragraph A5 remind us that we live in a real world, and that sometimes there are a range of interests to consider.

Pressure is often exerted on practitioners to breach the principle of keeping confidential and maintaining the security of information elicited from patients/clients in the privileged circumstances of a professional relationship. This should not be regarded as surprising, since 'Confidentiality' is a rule with certain exceptions. There is no statutory right of confidentiality; but there is also no bar to an aggrieved individual bringing a common law case before a civil court alleging breach of confidentiality and seeking financial recompense.

It is essential that before determining that a particular set of circumstances constitute such an exception, the practitioner must be satisfied that the best interests of the patient/client are served thereby or the wider public interest necessitates disclosure.

2. The needs of the community can, on occasions, take precedence over the individual's rights as for example in those situations where a Court rules that the administration of justice demands that a professional confidence be broken or the law requires that patient confidence be breached.

3. In many other situations sharing of confidential information occurs by intention. This is the case where information obtained in the course of professional practice is shared with other professionals in the health and social work fields in the belief that to do so is in the interests of the patient/client. Legislation concerned with data protection and its associated codes is not intended to prevent the exchange of information between professional staff who share the care of the patient/client. It is, however, the duty of the practitioner who obtains and holds the information to ensure, as far as is reasonable, before its release that it is being imparted in strict professional confidence and for a specific purpose. The same duty applies where the practitioner is contributing to a shared record. Wherever possible the consent of the patient/client to the sharing of information should first be obtained.

4. The situations that are the most exceptional and problematic for the practitioner are those where the deliberate decision to withhold confidential information or disclose it to a third party can have very serious consequences. The information can have been given to the practitioner in the strictest confidence or the practitioner may have obtained the information inadvertently in the course of his or her professional practice. The decision as to whether to make a record of such information, like the decision as to whether or not to disclose, poses many dilemmas, for the situations are invariably complex. In

some instances the practitioner can be under pressure to divulge information but it must be emphasised that the responsibility lies with him or her as an individual. This responsibility cannot be delegated.

5. In all cases where the practitioner deliberately discloses or withholds information in what he/she believes the public interest he/she must be able to justify the decision. These situations can be particularly stressful, especially where vulnerable groups are concerned, as disclosure may mean the involvement of a third party as in the case of children or the mentally handicapped. Practitioners should always take the opportunity to discuss the matter fully with other practitioners (not only or necessarily fellow nurses, midwives and health visitors), and if appropriate consult with a professional organisation before making a decision. There will often be ramifications and these are best explored before a final decision as to whether to withhold or disclose information is made.

Once having made a decision the practitioner should write down the reasons either in the appropriate record or in a special note that can be kept on file. The practitioner can then justify the action taken should that subsequently become necessary, and can also at a later date review the decision in the light of future developments.

E Summary of the principles on which to base professional judgement in matters of confidentiality

1. That a patient/client has a right to expect that information given in confidence will be used only for the purpose for which it was given and will not be released to others without their consent.

2. That practitioners recognise the fundamental right of their patients/clients to have information about them held in secure and private storage.

3. That, where it is deemed appropriate to share information obtained in the course of professional practice with other health or social work practitioners, the practitioner who obtained the information must ensure, as far as is reasonable, before its release that it is being imparted in strict professional confidence and for a specific purpose.

4. That the responsibility to either disclose or withhold confidential information in the public interest lies with the individual practitioner, that he/she cannot delegate the decision, and that he/she cannot be required by a superior to disclose or withhold information against his/her will.

5. That a practitioner who chooses to breach the basic principle of confidentiality in the belief that it is necessary in the public interest must have considered the matter sufficiently to justify that decision.

6. That deliberate breaches of confidentiality other than with the consent of the patient/client should be exceptional.

Appendix 3 Advertising by registered nurses, midwives and health visitors: an elaboration of clause 14 of the code of professional conduct*

Introduction

Clause 14 of the Second Edition of the UKCC Code of Professional Conduct for the Nurse, Midwife and Health Visitor states that the registered nurse, midwife and health visitor shall:

> 'Avoid the use of professional qualifications in the promotion of commercial products in order not to compromise the independence of professional judgement on which patients/clients rely.'

Like the preceding 13 clauses, this must be read within the context of the introductory paragraph of the Code, which states:

> 'Each registered nurse, midwife and health visitor shall act, at all times, in such a manner as to justify public trust and confidence, to uphold and enhance the good

---

* Originally published as *Advertising by Registered Nurses, Midwives and Health Visitors: An elaboration of Clause 14 of the Code of Professional Conduct* by the United Kingdom Central Council for Nursing, Midwifery and Health Visiting, March 1985.

This notice applies to all persons whose names appear on the professional register maintained by the United Kingdom Central Council for Nurses, Midwives and Health Visitors.

414

standing and reputation of the profession, to serve the interests of society, and above all to safeguard the interests of individual patients and clients.'

The purpose of this notice is to indicate the parameters within which the citing of registration status is not regarded as objectionable. Persons who advertise in ways not authorised by this paper either specifically or in principle may be found guilty of misconduct.

1 Advertising general availability for professional work as a nurse, midwife or health visitor

A registered nurse, midwife or health visitor may state his/her registration status in any published advertisement for professional employment, provided that any such advertisement:

(a) is not ostentatious; and
(b) does not make claims that the practitioner is to be preferred over others.

This authority extends to any statement of registration status in business cards, letter headings, or advertisements placed in the press or other places.

2 Advertising availability for a specific type of professional work as a nurse, midwife or health visitor

A registered nurse, midwife or health visitor who has successfully completed a specific post-basic course and thus obtained specialist knowledge and skills (e.g. in stoma care) may state his/her registration status (and recorded qualification status) in advertising his/her availability for care, advice or teaching in that specialty. The principles stated in 1 above apply.

3 Use of registration status in respect of a business owned or managed by the registered nurse, midwife or health visitor

A registered nurse, midwife or health visitor may indicate his/her registration status in connection with any business (associated with professional practice) of which he/she is the proprietor or manager. This authority applies to letter headings, business cards, advertisements, wall plates, etc., but the general principles of clause 1 above again apply.

4   Use of registration status in respect of employment by a person or company in a field related to nursing, midwifery or health visiting

A registered nurse, midwife or health visitor employed by another person or company in any capacity which requires him/her to correspond with or call on medical practitioners, pharmacists, hospitals, clinics etc. to promote particular products may indicate his/her registration status in association with his/her name on letters, or on business cards of modest size and design.

5 Use of registration status in promotional films or literature

Any registered nurse, midwife or health visitor who becomes involved in providing advice for, writing for or featuring in any films or other material, a purpose of which is to promote a commercial product or brand name must ensure that, if his/her name appears in any acknowledgements or credits, it should not be accompanied by any indication of registration status.

6 Use of registration status in respect of educational or documentary films or literature

Publication of an individual registered nurse, midwife or health visitor's registration status in association with his/her name is regarded as acceptable in educational or documentary films or literature provided that the purpose is not and could not be construed as to advertise the practitioner in his/her professional capacity other than as authorised elsewhere in this document.

7 Use of registration status in respect of writing for publication, participation in radio or television programmes and participation in conferences, seminars etc.

Indication of an individual's registration status with his/her name is regarded as acceptable, provided that the purpose is not and could not be construed as to advertise the practitioner in his/her professional capacity other than as authorised elsewhere in this document.

8 Use of nurse, midwife or health visitor registration status in advertising for professional work outside nursing, midwifery and health visiting

Advertising for professional work within the province of other professions should not be undertaken by persons on the UKCC register under any circumstances where registered practitioners of the profession in question are not allowed to advertise their services.

A registered nurse, midwife or health visitor who is also a registered practitioner of another profession which does allow advertising, and who wishes, in advertising his/her availability for work in that other profession, to indicate his/her status on the UKCC register should seek permission from the statutory body for that other profession before proceeding.

Some registered nurses, midwives and health visitors obtain non-registerable qualifications in other areas of health care, fully qualified practitioners in which are subject to regulation by registration. Such registered nurses, midwives and health visitors must not, in any circumstances, indicate their status in the UKCC register when advertising for work in another professional sphere on the basis of a non-registerable qualification unless permission has first been obtained from the UKCC.

9 Advertising outside the tolerances indicated in Clauses 1 to 8 above

The indication of a person's registration status as a nurse, midwife or health visitor outside the above stated tolerances may be regarded as unacceptable and result in charges of misconduct.

Any registered nurse considering using or authorising the use of his/her registration status in ways not referred to in this notice should seek specific advice from the Professional Conduct Division of the UKCC before proceeding.

Appendix 4 Standards for the administration of medicines*

Introduction

1. This standards paper replaces the Council's advisory paper 'Administration of Medicines' (issued in 1986) (1) and the supplementary circular 'The Administration of Medicines' (PC 88/05) (2). The Council has prepared this paper to assist practitioners to fulfil the expectations which it has of them, to serve more effectively the interests of patients and clients and to maintain and enhance standards of practice.

2. The administration of medicines is an important aspect of the professional practice of persons whose names are on the Council's register. It is not solely a mechanistic task to be performed in strict compliance with the written prescription of a medical practitioner. It requires thought and the exercise of professional judgement which is directed to:

2.1 confirming the correctness of the prescription;

2.2 judging the suitability of administration at the scheduled time of administration;

---

* Originally published as *Standards for the Administration of Medicines*, by the United Kingdom Central Council for Nursing, Midwifery and Health Visiting, October 1992.

2.3 reinforcing the positive effect of the treatment;

2.4 enhancing the understanding of patients in respect of their prescribed medication and the avoidance of misuse of these and other medicines and

2.5 assisting in assessing the efficacy of medicines and the identification of side-effects and interactions.

3. To meet the standards set out in this paper is to honour, in this aspect of practice, the Council's expectation (set out in the Council's 'Code of Professional Conduct') (3) that:

'As a registered nurse, midwife or health visitor you are personally accountable for your practice and, in the exercise of your professional accountability, must:

3.1 act always in such a manner as to promote and safeguard the interests and well-being of patients and clients;

3.2 ensure that no action or omission on your part, or within your sphere of responsibility, is detrimental to the interests, condition or safety of patients and clients;

3.3 maintain and improve your professional knowledge and competence;

3.4 acknowledge any limitations in your knowledge and competence and decline any duties or responsibilities unless able to perform them in a safe and skilled manner;'

4. This extract from the 'Code of Professional Conduct' applies to all persons on the Council's register irrespective of the part of the register on which their name appears. Although the content of pre-registration education programmes varies, dependent on the part and level of the register involved, the Council expects that, in this area of practice as in all others, all practitioners will have taken steps to develop their knowledge and competence and will have been assisted to this end. The word 'practitioner' is, therefore, used in the remainder of this paper to refer to all registered nurses, midwives and health visitors, each of whom must recognise the personal professional accountability which they bear for their actions. The Council therefore imposes no arbitrary boundaries between the role of the first level and second level registered practitioner in this respect.

Treatment with medicines

5. The treatment of a patient with medicines for therapeutic, diagnostic or preventative purposes is a process which involves prescribing, dispensing, administering, receiving and recording. The word 'patient' is used for convenience, but implies not only a patient in a hospital or nursing home, but also a resident of a residential home, a client in her or his own home or in a community home, a person attending a clinic or a general practitioner's surgery and an employee attending a workplace occupational health department. 'Patient' refers to the person receiving a prescribed medicine. Each medicine has a product licence, which means that authority has been given to a manufacturer to market a particular product for administration in a particular dosage range and by specified routes.

Prescription

6. The practitioner administering a medicine against a prescription written by a registered medical practitioner, like the pharmacist responsible for dispensing it, can reasonably expect that the prescription satisfies the following criteria:

6.1   that it is based, whenever possible, on the patient's awareness of the purpose of the treatment and consent (commonly implicit);

6.2   that the prescription is either clearly written, typed or computer-generated, and that the entry is indelible and dated;

6.3   that, where the new prescription replaces an earlier prescription, the latter has been cancelled clearly and the cancellation signed and dated by an authorised registered medical practitioner;

6.4   that, where a prescribed substance (which replaces an earlier prescription) has been provided for a person residing at home or in a residential care home and who is dependent on others to assist with the administration, information about the change has been properly communicated;

6.5   that the prescription provides clear and unequivocal identification of the patient for whom the medicine is intended;

6.6   that the substance to be administered is clearly specified and, where appropriate, its form (for example tablet, capsule, suppository) stated, together with the strength, dosage, timing and frequency of administration and route of administration;

6.7   that, where the prescription is provided in an out-patients or community setting, it states the duration of the course before review;

6.8   that, in the case of controlled drugs, the dosage is written, together with the number of dosage units or total course if in an out-patient or community setting, the whole being in the prescriber's own handwriting;

6.9   that all other prescriptions will, as a minimum, have been signed by the prescribing doctor and dated;

6.10 that the registered medical practitioner understands that the administration of medicines on verbal instructions, whether she or he is present or absent, other than in exceptional circumstances, is not acceptable unless covered by the protocol method referred to in paragraph 6.11;

6.11 that it is understood that, unless provided for in a specific protocol, instruction by telephone to a practitioner to administer a previously unprescribed substance is not acceptable, the use of facsimile transmission (fax) being the preferred method in exceptional circumstances for isolated locations; and

6.12 that, where it is the wish of the professional staff concerned that practitioners in a particular setting be authorised to administer, on their own authority, certain medicines, a local protocol has been agreed between medical practitioners, nurses and midwives and the pharmacist.

Dispensing

7. The practitioner administering a medicine dispensed by a pharmacist in response to a medical prescription can reasonably expect that:

7.1 the pharmacist has checked that the prescription is written correctly so as to avoid misunderstanding or error and is signed by an authorised prescriber;

7.2 the pharmacist is satisfied that any newly-prescribed medicines will not dangerously interact with or nullify each other;

7.3 the pharmacist has provided the medicine in a form relevant for administration to the particular patient, provided it in an appropriate container giving the relevant information and advised appropriately on storage and security conditions;

7.4 where the substance is prescribed in a dose or to be administered by a route which falls outside its product licence, unless to be administered from a stock supply, the pharmacist will have taken steps to ensure that the prescriber is aware and has chosen to exceed that licence;

7.5 where the prescription for a specific item falls outside the terms of the product licence, whether as to its route of administration, the dosage or some other key factor, the pharmacist will have ensured that the prescriber is aware of this fact and, mindful of her or his accountability in the matter, has made a record on the prescription to this effect and has agreed to dispense the medicine ordered;

7.6 if the prescription bears any written amendments made and signed by the pharmacist, the prescriber has been consulted and advised and the amendments have been accepted and

7.7 the pharmacist, in pursuit of her or his role in monitoring the adverse side-effects of medicines, wishes to be sent any information that the administering practitioner deems relevant.

Standards for the administration of medicines

8. Notwithstanding the expected adherence by registered medical practitioners and pharmacists to the criteria set out in paragraphs 6 and 7 of this paper, the nurse, midwife or health visitor must, in administering any medicines, in assisting with administration or overseeing any self-administration of medicines, exercise professional judgement and apply knowledge and skill to the situation that pertains at the time.

9. This means that, as a matter of basic principle, whether administering a medicine, assisting in its administration or overseeing self-administration, the practitioner will be satisfied that she or he:

9.1 has an understanding of substances used for therapeutic purposes;

9.2 is able to justify any actions taken and

9.3 is prepared to be accountable for the action taken.

10. Against this background, the practitioner, acting in the interests of the patients, will:

    10.1   be certain of the identity of the patient to whom the medicine is to be administered;

    10.2   ensure that she or he is aware of the patient's current assessment and planned programme of care;

    10.3   pay due regard to the environment in which that care is being given;

    10.4   scrutinise carefully, in the interests of safety, the prescription, where available, and the information provided on the relevant containers;

    10.5   question the medical practitioner or pharmacist, as appropriate, if the prescription or container information is illegible, unclear, ambiguous or incomplete or where it is believed that the dosage or route of administration falls outside the product licence for the particular substance and, where believed necessary, refuse to administer the prescribed substance;

    10.6   refuse to prepare substances for injection in advance of their immediate use and refuse to administer a medicine not placed in a container or drawn into a syringe by her or him, in her or his presence, or prepared by a pharmacist, except in the specific circumstances described in paragraph 40 of this paper and others where similar issues arise and

    10.7   draw the attention of patients, as appropriate, to patient information leaflets concerning their prescribed medicines.

11. In addition, acting in the interests of the patient, the practitioner will:

    11.1   check the expiry date of any medicine, if on the container;

    11.2   carefully consider the dosage, method of administration, route and timing of administration in the context of the condition of the specific patient at the operative time;

    11.3   carefully consider whether any of the prescribed medicines will or may dangerously interact with each other;

    11.4   determine whether it is necessary or advisable to withhold the medicine pending consultation with the prescribing medical practitioner, the pharmacist or a fellow professional colleague;

    11.5   contact the prescriber without delay where contra-indications to the administration of any prescribed medicine are observed, first taking the advice of the pharmacist where considered appropriate;

    11.6   make clear, accurate and contemporaneous record of the administration of all medicines administered or deliberately withheld, ensuring that any written entries and the signature are clear and legible;

    11.7   where a medicine is refused by the patient, or the parent refuses to administer or allow administration of that medicine, make a clear and accurate record of the fact without delay, consider whether the refusal of that medicine compromises the patient's condition or the effect of other medicines, assess the situation and contact the prescriber;

    11.8   use the opportunity which administration of a medicine provides for emphasising, to patients and their carers, the importance and implications of the prescribed treatment and for enhancing their understanding of its effects and side-effects;

11.9   record the positive and negative effects of the medicine and make them known to the prescribing medical practitioner and the pharmacist and

11.10 take all possible steps to ensure that replaced prescription entries are correctly deleted to avoid duplication of medicines.

Applying the standards in a range of settings

Who can administer medicines?

12. There is a wide spectrum of situations in which medicines are administered ranging, at one extreme, from the patient in an intensive therapy unit who is totally dependent on registered professional staff for her or his care to, at the other extreme, the person in her or his own home administering her or his own medicines or being assisted in this respect by a relative or another person. The answer to the question of who can administer a medicine must largely depend on where within that spectrum the recipient of the medicines lies.

Administration in the hospital setting

13. It is the Council's position that, at or near the first stated end of that spectrum, assessment of response to treatment and speedy recognition of contra-indications and side-effects are of great importance. Therefore prescribed medicines should only be administered by registered practitioners who are competent for the purpose and aware of their personal accountability.

14. In this context it is the Council's position that, in the majority of circumstances, a first level registered nurse, a midwife, or a second level nurse, each of whom has demonstrated the necessary knowledge and competence, should be able to administer medicines without involving a second person. Exceptions to this might be:

14.1 where the practitioner is instructing a student;

14.2 where the patient's condition makes it necessary and

14.3 where local circumstances make the involvement of two persons desirable in the interests of the patients (for example, in areas of specialist care, such as a paediatric unit without sufficient specialist paediatric nurses or in other acute units dependent on temporary agency or other locum staff).

15. In respect of the administration of intravenous drugs by practitioners, it is the Council's position that this is acceptable, provided that, as in all other aspects of practice, the practitioner is satisfied with her or his competence and mindful of her or his personal accountability.

16. The Council is opposed to the involvement of persons who are not registered practitioners in the administration of medicines in acute care settings and with ill or dependent patients, since the requirements of paragraphs 8 to 11 inclusive of this paper cannot
then be satisfied. It accepts, however, that the professional judgement of an individual
practitioner should be used to identify those situations in which informal carers might
be instructed and prepared to accept a delegated responsibility in this respect.

Administration in the domestic or quasi-domestic setting

17. It is evident that in this setting, on the majority of occasions, there is no involvement of registered practitioners. Where a practitioner engaged in community practice
does become involved in assisting with or overseeing administration, then she or he must
observe paragraphs 8 to 11 of this paper and apply them to the required degree. She
or he must also recognise that, even if not employed in posts requiring registration with
the Council, she or he remains accountable to the Council.

18. The same principles apply where prescribed medicines are being administered to
residents in small community homes or in residential care homes. To the maximum degree
possible, though related to their ability to manage the care and administration of their
prescribed medicines and comprehend their significance, the residents should be regarded
as if in their own home. Where assistance is required, the person providing it fills the
role of an informal carer, family member or friend. However, as with the situation
described in paragraph 17, where a professional practitioner is involved, a personal
accountability is borne. The advice of a community pharmacist should be sought when
necessary.

Self-administration of medicines in hospitals or registered nursing homes

19. The Council welcomes and supports the development of self-administration of medicines and administration by parents to children wherever it is appropriate and the necessary security and storage arrangements are available.

20. For the hospital patient approaching discharge, but who will continue on a prescribed
medicines regime following the return home, there are obvious benefits in adjusting
to the responsibility of self-administration while still having access to professional support.
It is accepted that, to facilitate this transition, practitioners may assist patients to administer their medicines safely by preparing a form of medication card containing information transcribed from other sources.

21. For the long stay patient, whether in hospital or a nursing home, self-administration can help foster a feeling of independence and control in one aspect of life.

22. It is essential, however, that where self-administration is introduced for all or some

patients, arrangements must be in place for the appropriate, safe and secure storage of the medicines, access to which is limited to the specific patient.

The use of monitored dosage systems

23. Monitored dosage systems, for the purpose of this paper, are systems which involve a community pharmacist, in response to the full prescription of medicines for a specific person, dispensing those medicines into a special container with sections for days of the week and times within those days and delivering the container, or supplying the medicines in a special container of blister packs, with appropriate additional information, to the nursing home, residential care home or domestic residence. The Council is aware of the development of such monitored dosage systems and accepts that, provided they are able to satisfy strict criteria established by the Royal Pharmaceutical Society of Great Britain and other official pharmaceutical organisations, that substances which react to each other are not supplied in this way and that they are suitable for the intended purpose as judged by the nursing profession, they have a valuable place in the administration of medicines.

24. While, to the present, their use has been primarily in registered nursing homes and some community or residential care homes, there seems no reason why, provided the systems can satisfy the standards referred to in paragraph 25, their use should not be extended.

25. In order to be acceptable for use in hospitals or registered nursing homes, the containers for the medicines must:

25.1 satisfy the requirements of the Royal Pharmaceutical Society of Great Britain for an original container;

25.2 be filled by a pharmacist and sealed by her or him or under her or his control and delivered complete to the user;

25.3 be accompanied by clear and comprehensive documentation which forms the medical practitioner's prescription;

25.4 bear the means of identifying tablets of similar appearance so that, should it be necessary to withhold one tablet (for example Digoxin), it can be identified from those in the container space for the particular time and day;

25.5 be able to be stored in a secure place and

25.6 make it apparent if the containers (be they blister packs or spaces within a container) have been tampered with between the closure and sealing by the pharmacist and the time of administration.

26. While the introduction of a monitored dosage system transfers to the pharmacist the responsibility for being satisfied that the container is filled and sealed correctly so as to comply with the prescription, it does not alter the fact that the practitioner administering the medicines must still consider the appropriateness of each medicine at the time administration falls due. It is not the case, therefore, that the use of a monitored

dosage system allows the administration of medicines to be undertaken by unqualified personnel.

27. It is not acceptable, in lieu of a pharmacist-filled monitored dosage system container, for a practitioner to transfer medicines from their original containers into an unsealed container for administration at a later stage by another person, whether or not that person is a registered practitioner. This is an unsafe practice which carries risk for both practitioner and patient. Similarly it is not acceptable to interfere with a sealed section at any time between its closure by the pharmacist and the scheduled time of administration.

The role of nurses, midwives and health visitors in community practice in the administration of medicines

28. Any practitioner who, whether as a planned intervention or incidentally, becomes involved in administering a medicine, or assisting with or overseeing such administration, must apply paragraphs 8 to 11 of this paper to the degree to which they are relevant.

29. Where a practitioner working in the community becomes involved in obtaining prescribed medicines for patients, she or he must recognise her or his responsibility for safe transit and correct delivery.

30. Community psychiatric nurses whose practice involves them in providing assistance to patients to reduce and eliminate their dependence on addictive drugs should ensure that they are aware of the potential value of short term prescriptions and encourage their use where appropriate in the long term interests of their clients. They must not resort to holding or carrying prescribed controlled drugs to avoid their misuse by those clients.

31. Special arrangements and certain exemptions apply to occupational health nurses. These are described in Information Document 11 and the Appendices of 'A Guide to an Occupational Health Nursing Service; A Handbook for Employers and Nurses'; published by the Royal College of Nursing (4).

32. Some practitioners employed in the community, including in particular community nurses, practice nurses and health visitors, in order to enhance disease prevention, will receive requests to participate in vaccination and immunisation programmes. Normally these requests will be accompanied by specific named prescriptions or be covered by a protocol setting out the arrangements within which substances can be administered to certain categories of persons who meet the stated criteria. The facility provided by the 'Medicines Act 1968' (5) for substances to be administered to a number of people in response to an advance 'direction' is valuable in this respect. Where it has not been possible to anticipate the possible need for preventive treatment and there is not relevant protocol or advance direction, particularly in respect of patients about to travel abroad and requiring preventive treatment, a telephone conversation with a registered

medical practitioner will suffice as authorisation for a single administration. It is not, however, sufficient as a basis for supplying a quantity of medicines.

Midwives and midwifery practice

33. Midwives should refer to the current editions of both the Council's 'Midwives Rules' (6) and 'A Midwife's Code of Practice' (7), and specifically to the sections concerning administration of medicines. At the time of publication of this paper, 'Midwives Rules' sets out the practising midwife's responsibility in respect of the administration of medicines and other forms of pain relief. 'A Midwife's Code of Practice' refers to the authority provided by the 'Medicines Act 1968' and the 'Misuse of Drugs Act 1971' (8), and regulations made as a result, for midwives to obtain and administer certain substances.

What if the Council's standards in paragraphs 8 to 11 cannot be applied?

34. There are certain situations in which practitioners are involved in the administration of medicines where some of the criteria stated above either cannot be applied or, if applied, would introduce dangerous delay with consequent risk to patients. These will include occupational health settings in some industries, small hospitals with no resident medical staff and possibly some specialist units within larger hospitals and some community settings.

35. With the exception of the administration of substances for the purpose of vaccination or immunisation described in paragraph 32 above, in any situation in which a practitioner may be expected or required to administer 'prescription-only medicines' which have not been directly prescribed for a named patient by a registered medical practitioner who has examined the patient and made a diagnosis, it is essential that a clear local policy be determined and made known to all practitioners involved with prescribing and administration. This will make it possible for action to be taken in patients' interests while protecting practitioners from the risk of complaint which might otherwise jeopardise their position.

36. Therefore, where such a situation will, or may apply, a local policy should be agreed and documented which:

    36.1 states the circumstances in which particular 'prescription-only medicines' may be administered in advance of examination by a doctor;

    36.2 ensures the relevant knowledge and skill of those to be involved in administration;

    36.3 describes the form, route and dosage range of the medicines so authorised and

    36.4 wherever possible, satisfies the requirements of Section 58 of the 'Medicines Act 1968' as a 'direction'.

Substances for topical application

37. The standards set out in this paper apply, to the degree to which they are relevant, to substances used for wound dressing and other topical applications. Where a practitioner uses a substance or product which has not been prescribed, she or he must have considered the matter sufficiently to be able to justify its use in the particular circumstances.

The administration of homoeopathic or herbal substances

38. Homoeopathic and herbal medicines are subject to the licensing provisions of the 'Medicines Act 1968', although those on the market when that Act became operative (which means most of those now available) received product licences without any evaluation of their efficacy, safety or quality. Practitioners should, therefore, make themselves generally aware of common substances used in their particular area of practice. It is necessary to respect the right of individuals to administer to themselves, or to request a practitioner to assist in the administration of substances in these categories. If, when faced with a patient or client whose desire to receive medicines of this kind appears to create potential difficulties, or if it is felt that the substances might either be an inappropriate response to the presenting symptoms or likely to negate or enhance the effect of prescribed medicines, the practitioner, acting in the interests of the patient or client, should consider contacting the relevant registered medical practitioner, but must also be mindful of the need not to override the patient's rights.

Complementary and alternative therapies

39. Some registered nurses, midwives and health visitors, having first undertaken successfully a training in complementary or alternative therapy which involves the use of substances such as essential oils, apply their specialist knowledge and skill in their practice. It is essential that practice in these respects, as in all others, is based upon sound principles, available knowledge and skill. The importance of consent to the use of such treatment must be recognised. So, too, must the practitioner's personal accountability for her or his professional practice.

Practitioners assuming responsibility for care which includes medicines being administered which were previously checked by other practitioners

40. Paragraph 10.6 of this paper referred to the unacceptability of a practitioner administering a substance drawn into a syringe or container by another practitioner when the practitioner taking over responsibility for the patient was not present. An exception to this is an already established intravenous infusion, the use of a syringe pump or some other kind of continuous or intermittent infusion or injection apparatus, where a valid

prescription exists, a responsible practitioner has signed for the container of fluid and any additives being administered and the container is clearly and indelibly labelled. The label must clearly show the contents and be signed and dated. The same measures must apply equally to other means of administration of such substances through, for example, central venous, arterial or epidural lines. Strict discipline must be applied to the recording of any substances being administered by any of the methods referred to in this paragraph and to reporting procedures between staff as they change and transfer responsibility for care.

Management of errors or incidents in the administration of medicines

41. In a number of its Annual Reports, the Council has recorded its concern that practitioners who have made mistakes under pressure of work, and have been honest and open about those mistakes to their senior staff, appear often to have been made the subject of disciplinary action in a way which seems likely to discourage the reporting of incidents and therefore be to the potential detriment of patients and of standards.

42. When considering allegations of misconduct arising out of errors in the administration of medicines, the Council's Professional Conduct Committee takes great care to distinguish between those cases where the error was the result of reckless practice and was concealed and those which resulted from serious pressure of work and where there was immediate, honest disclosure in the patient's interest. The Council recognises the prerogative of managers to take local disciplinary action where it is considered to be appropriate but urges that they also consider each incident in its particular context and similarly discriminate between the two categories described.

43. The Council's position is that all errors and incidents require a thorough and careful investigation which takes full account of the circumstances and context of the event and the position of the practitioner involved. Events of this kind call equally for sensitive management and a comprehensive assessment of all of the circumstances before a professional and managerial decision is reached on the appropriate way to proceed.

Future arrangements for prescribing by nurses

44. In March 1992 the Act of Parliament entitled the 'Medicinal Products: Prescription by Nurses etc Act 1992' (9) became law. This legislation is to come into operation in October 1993. The legislation will permit nurses with a district nursing or health visiting qualification to prescribe certain products from a Nurse Prescribers' Formulary. The statutory rules, yet to be completed, will specify the categories of nurses who can prescribe under this limited legislation. The Council will issue further information concerning this important new legislation prior to it becoming operative.

45. Enquiries in respect of this Council paper should be directed to the:

Registrar and Chief Executive
United Kingdom Central Council
for Nursing, Midwifery and
Health Visiting
23 Portland Place
London W1N 3AF

References

1. United Kingdom Central Council for Nursing, Midwifery and Health Visiting, 'Administration of Medicines; A UKCC Advisory Paper; A framework to assist individual professional judgement and the development of local policies and guidelines', April 1986.
2. United Kingdom Central Council for Nursing, Midwifery and Health Visiting, 'The Administration of Medicines', PC 88/05, September 1988.
3. United Kingdom Central Council for Nursing, Midwifery and Health Visiting, 'Code of Professional Conduct for the Nurse, Midwife and Health Visitor', Third Edition, June 1992.
4. Royal College of Nursing, 'A Guide to an Occupational Health Nursing Service; A Handbook for Employers and Nurses', Second Edition 1991.
5. 'Medicines Act 1968', Her Majesty's Stationery Office, London, Reprinted 1986.
6. United Kingdom Central Council for Nursing, Midwifery and Health Visiting, 'Midwives Rules', March 1991.
7. United Kingdom Central Council for Nursing, Midwifery and Health Visiting, 'A Midwife's Code of Practice', March 1991.
8. 'Misuse of Drugs Act 1971', Her Majesty's Stationery Office, London, Reprinted 1985.
9. 'Medicinal Products: Prescription by Nurses etc Act 1992', Her Majestys' Stationery Office, London, 1992.

Appendix 5   Midwives rules[*]

Introduction

The Rules made by the United Kingdom Central Council for Nursing, Midwifery and Health Visiting (referred to as the Council) are legally expressed in the form of Statutory Instruments (SIs). It has been necessary to amend the Statutory Instruments to accommodate change and development and the amendments are referenced throughout this document using footnotes. The main sources of reference are as follows:

1. Part V of the Nurses, Midwives and Health Visitors Rules 1983, SI 1983 No 873 which was repealed. However, the citation and interpretation in this Statutory Instrument, which is also known as the 'principal Rules', remain a relevant part of the Midwives Rules. The numbering of the Midwives Rules commences with Rule 27 which is sequential to Part IV of the principal Rules;

2. SI 1986 No 786 – The Nurses, Midwives and Health Visitors (Midwives Amendment) Rules Approval Order 1986;

3. SI 1989 No 1456 – The Nurses, Midwives and Health Visitors (Registered Fever Nurses Amendment Rules & Training Amendment Rules) Approval Order 1989;

* Originally published as *Midwives Rules*, by the United Kingdom Central Council for Nursing, Midwifery and Health Visiting, November 1993.

4. SI 1990 No 1624 – The Nurses, Midwives and Health Visitors (Midwives Training) Amendment Rules Approval Order 1990;

5. SI 1993 No 1901 – The Nurses, Midwives and Health Visitors (Entry to Examinations and Training Requirements) Amendment Rules Approval Order 1993;

6. SI 1993 No 2106 – The Nurses, Midwives and Health Visitors (Midwives Amendment) Rules Approval Order 1993.

This document draws together Rules relating to the education and practice of midwives to provide a ready reference to the relevant legislation for all midwives.

The Midwives Rules have been approved and made by the Council and are framed in accordance with the recommendations of the Council's Midwifery Committee (as required by Section 4(4) of the Nurses, Midwives and Health Visitors Act 1979) following consultation with the National Boards for Nursing, Midwifery and Health Visiting, the profession and others. The Midwives Rules apply to midwives practising in all parts of the United Kingdom.

Principal Rules

In these Rules, unless the context otherwise requires, 'the principal Rules' means the Nurses, Midwives and Health Visitors Rules 1983 (SI 1983 No 873).

Amendment of the principal Rules

(1) The principal Rules shall be amended in accordance with the following provisions of the Rules as indicated.

(2) The definition of 'student' in Rule 2(1) of the principal Rules shall be deleted and there shall be substituted the following:

> 'Student' means any person whose name is on the index of students maintained by each Board as required under Rule 20, 25(1) and 34 of these Rules.

(3) In Rule 2(1) of the principal Rules:

   (i)   the definition of 'approved educational institution' shall be amended to add 'or a programme of education or both' after 'course of preparation';
   (ii) the definition of 'approved training institution' shall be amended by deleting '10 and';
   (iii) before the definition of 'Registrar' there shall be inserted the following definition:

   > '"programme of education" means a theoretical and clinical programme which meets the requirements of the Council as to its content and standard, the successful completion of which enables an application to be made for admission to Part 10 of the register.' (SI 1990 No 1624).

References for Statutory Instruments

For ease of reference the key Statutory Instruments (SIs) which have amended the Rules have been assigned a footnote letter as follows:

SI 1986 No 786-[a]
SI 1989 No 1456-[b]
SI 1990 No 1624-[c]
SI 1993 No 1901-[d]
SI 1993 No 2106-[e]

Midwives Rules

27 Interpretation[a] (applies to Sections A and B of the Rules)

For the purpose of this part of these Rules, the following expressions have the meanings hereby respectively assigned to them except where the context otherwise requires:

Emergency

means in the context of Rule 40(1) any illness of the mother or baby or any abnormality becoming apparent in the mother and baby during the antenatal, intranatal and postnatal periods;

Health Authority

(a) in relation to England and Wales has the same meaning as in the National Health Service Act 1977[f];
(b) in relation to Scotland means a Health Board constituted under Section 2 of the National Health Service (Scotland) Act 1978[g];
(c) in relation to Northern Ireland means a Health and Social Services Board established under Article 16 of the Health and Personal Social Services (Northern Ireland) Order 1972[h];

Local supervising authority

means a body prescribed by Section 16(1) of the Act as being a local supervising authority for midwives;

---

[f] 1977 chapter 49
[g] 1978 chapter 29
[h] 1972/1265 (NI 14)

Midwives Directive

means Council Directive No 80/155/EEC concerning the co-ordination of provisions laid down by law, regulation of administrative action relating to the taking up and pursuit of activities of midwives as amended by Council Directive No 89/594/EEC[i];

Mother and baby

means a woman and her baby whether before or after birth and a reference to 'mother and baby' shall be a reference to the woman and her unborn baby during the antenatal and intranatal periods and to the mother and her baby during the period from the birth of the baby to the end of the postnatal period and 'mother' and 'baby' shall be construed accordingly;

Postnatal period

means a period of not less than ten and not more than twenty-eight days after the end of labour, during which the continued attendance of a midwife on the mother and baby is requisite;

Practising midwife

means a midwife who attends professionally upon a woman during the antenatal, intranatal and/or postnatal period or who holds a post for which a midwifery qualification is essential and who notifies her intention to practise to the local supervising authority.

Supervisor of midwives

means the person appointed by the local supervising authority in accordance with Section 16(3) of the Act.

Section A Education Rules

28 Midwifery Education leading to a registration in Part 10 of the register

The conditions of a person being admitted to training and the kind and standard of the programme of education shall be in accordance with this section of these rules.[ac]

---

[i] OJ No L33 of 11.2.80 p8 and
OJ No L341 of 23.11.89 p19

29 Age of entry

Persons admitted to a programme of education at an approved educational institution shall be aged not less than 17 years and 6 months on the first day of the commencement of a programme of education except that in exceptional circumstances related to the specific programme of education or individual the Council on the recommendation of a Board may agree to entry earlier but in no circumstances at less than 17 years of age.[ac]

30 Educational requirements

(1) The educational conditions for entry to a programme of education leading to a qualification for admission to Part 10 of the register shall meet any obligations of the Midwives Directive but shall not be less than either:[ac]

(a) a minimum of five subjects, any of which may be obtained in the General Certificate of Secondary Education in England and Wales, grade A, B or C, or at Ordinary level grade A, B or C in the General Certificate of Education of England and Wales, or at grade 1 in the Certificate of Secondary Education, of which one shall be English Language and one shall be a Science subject or[b]

(b) a minimum of five subjects, any of which may be obtained at Ordinary or Standard Grade, grade 1, 2 or 3, or at Ordinary Grade (band A, B or C) in the Scottish Certificate of Education, of which one shall be English and one shall be a Science subject or[b]

(c) a minimum of five subjects, any of which may be obtained in the General Certificate of Secondary Education in Northern Ireland, grade A, B or C, or at grade A, B or C in the Northern Ireland General Certificate of Education at Ordinary level, of which one shall be English Language and one shall be a Science subject or[b]

(d) such other qualifications as the Council may consider the equivalent to those set out in sub-paragraph (a), (b) or (c) of this paragraph or[a]

(e) a specified pass standard in an educational test approved by the Council or[a]

(f) such vocational qualifications as the Council may, from time to time, approve as providing a standard of education appropriate to entry to such programmes of education.[d]

(2) The above requirements shall not apply to a person registered in Part 1 or Part 12 of the register.[ac]

31 Programmes of education[c]

(1) A programme of education shall:

(a) unless sub-paragraph (b) below applies, be not less than 3 years in length, and each year shall contain 45 programmed weeks or

(b) where the student is already registered in Part 1 or Part 12 of the register, be not less than 18 months in length.

(2) A student undertaking a programme of education shall be directed throughout the programme of education by the approved educational institution.

(3) The content of a programme of education shall include one or more periods of practical experience of midwifery of such duration as the Council may from time to time require in relation to any particular approved educational institution.

(4) A student undertaking a programme of education of the length set out in subparagraph (a) of paragraph (1) of this Rule shall have supernumerary status.

(5) In this Rule 'supernumerary status' means, in relation to a student, that she shall not as part of her programme of education be employed by any person or body under a contract of service to provide midwifery care.

32 Interruption in programmes of education[c]

(1) Student midwives having an interruption in a programme of education of:

(a) less than three years should complete the outstanding period of the programme of education;
(b) three years or more should complete the outstanding period of the programme of education and such additional education as the appropriate National Board may determine.

(2) For the purpose of paragraph (1) of this Rule 'interruption' means any absence from a programme of education other than annual leave, statutory and public holidays.

(3) A student midwife may transfer to another approved educational institution subject to any condition that the relevant Board may require, and where the intended transfer is to an approved educational institution which is subject to the approval of another Board, the transfer must be acceptable to the receiving Board and shall be subject to any conditions which that Board may require.

33 Outcomes of programmes of education leading to admission to Part 10 of the register[c]

(1) The content of programmes of education shall be such as the Council may from time to time require.

(2) Programmes of education shall be designed to prepare the student to assume on registration the responsibilities and accountability for her practice as a midwife.

(3) Such programmes of education shall;

(a) meet the requirements of the Midwives Directive and

(b) be provided at an approved educational institution and

(c) enable the student midwife to accept responsibility for her personal professional development and to apply her knowledge and skill in meeting the needs of individuals and of groups throughout the antenatal, intranatal and post-natal periods and shall include enabling the student to achieve the following outcomes:

    (i)   the appreciation of the influence of social, political and cultural factors in relation to health care and advising on the promotion of health;

    (ii)   the recognition of common factors which contribute to, and those which adversely affect, the physical, emotional and social well-being of the mother and baby, and the taking of appropriate action;

    (iii) the ability to assess, plan, implement and evaluate care within the sphere of practice of a midwife to meet the physical, emotional, social, spiritual and educational needs of the mother and baby and the family;

    (iv) the ability to take action on her own responsibility, including the initiation of the action of other disciplines, and to seek assistance when required;

    (v)   the ability to interpret and undertake care prescribed by a registered medical practitioner;

    (vi) the use of appropriate and effective communication skills with mothers and their families, with colleagues and with those in other disciplines;

    (vii) the use of relevant literature and research to inform the practice of midwifery;

    (viii) the ability to function effectively in a multi-professional team with an understanding of the role of all members of the team;

    (ix) an understanding of the requirements of legislation relevant to the practice of midwifery;

    (x)   an understanding of the ethical issues relating to midwifery practice and the responsibilities which these impose on the midwife's professional practice;

    (xi) the assignment of the midwife of appropriate duties to others and the supervision and the monitoring of such assigned duties.

34   Student inde[ac]

(1) Each Board shall keep an index of all student midwives undergoing a programme of education at an approved educational institution under this part of the Rules.

(2) When an applicant has been accepted by an approved educational institution as a student midwife, the educational institution shall submit to the Board, on the appropriate form within thirty days of the commencement of her programme of education, an application for the inclusion of her name on the index of student midwives.

35 Examinations [ac]

To qualify as a person who can apply to be registered in Part 10 of the register under Rule 6, a student midwife shall:

- (a) have her name on the index of students maintained by a Board and
- (b have completed the relevant programme of education for the period required under Rules 31, 32 and 33 of these Rules and
- (c) have passed an examination held or arranged by the Board of the country in which the programme of education has just been completed in accordance with Section 6(1)(c) of the Act which may be in parts and which shall be designed so as to assess the students' ability to undertake the relevant outcomes specified in Rule 33 of these Rules.

Transitional provision [acd]

In their application to any student who commenced training before the date on which these Rules come into force, the principal Rules, except sub-paragraph (4) of Rule 35,* shall have effect as if the amendments made by these Rules had not been made.

Section B Practice Rules

36 Notification of intention to practise [ae]

(1) If a midwife intends to practise in the area of any local supervising authority she shall, subject to paragraph (2) of this Rule, before commencing to practise as a midwife:

- (a) give notice of her intention to do so to each such local supervising authority and thereafter;
- (b) give like notice in respect of each period of 12 months beginning on 1st April, by a date in the month of March, to each local supervising authority where she continues to practise by virtue of employment for which registration as a midwife is essential;

and the date in the month of March referred to in sub-paragraph (b) of this Rule shall be such date as shall be published, under Rule 45(a)(i), by each such local supervising authority for any year.

(2) Notwithstanding the provisions of paragraph (1), the notice referred to in that paragraph may, in an emergency, be given after the time when she commences to practise provided that it is given within 48 hours of that time.

* SI 1986 No 786

(3) Every notice shall contain such particulars as may be required in the form from time to time prescribed by the Council.

(4) The local supervising authority shall inform the Council pursuant to Section 15(2) of the Act, of notices received by it under this Rule by sending the originals of the notices to the Council:

(a) by the 30th of April of each year for those practising midwives who have notified such intention by the end of March or

(b) subject to sub-paragraph (a) above by the 7th day of each month for those practising midwives who have notified such intention during the preceding month.

37 Refresher courses[ae]

(1) Subject to paragraph (2) of this Rule every midwife who gives notice of intention to practise under Rule 36 shall within 12 months of notifying such intention complete a course of instruction or provide evidence of appropriate professional education approved by a Board for the purpose of this Rule.

(2) The requirements of paragraph (1) of this Rule need not be satisfied where a midwife has within a period of five calendar years immediately preceding the year of giving notice of intention to practise:

(a) qualified as a midwife in the United Kingdom or

(b) attended a course of instruction referred to in paragraph (1) or

(c) complied with paragraphs (3) and (4) of this Rule;

and for a midwife qualified overseas and registered in Part 10 of the register without passing the midwifery qualifying examination of a Board, the requirement in respect of sub-paragraph (2)(a) of this Rule shall be registration as a midwife by the Council.

(3) Any midwife who has not notified her intention to practise for a period of five years or more shall, before being eligible to resume practice, attend a course of practical and theoretical instruction of a minimum period of 4 weeks approved by a Board at an approved educational institution. A midwife may not resume practice until such a course has been completed.

(4) A midwife who has notified her intention to practise and has not practised as a midwife for at least the equivalent of 12 working weeks during the preceding five years shall follow a course of instruction as prescribed in paragraph (3) of this Rule.

(5) In the case of a midwife who has not previously given notice of intention to practise, a Board may accept evidence of practice as a midwife outside the United Kingdom in lieu of the requirement to follow the course of instruction described in paragraph 3 of this Rule.

(6) In exceptional circumstances a Board, having regard to the qualifications and experience of a registered midwife who under paragraph (1) of this Rule is due to attend a

course of instruction, may, on the recommendation of the local supervising authority, grant a postponement of attendance at a course of instruction for a specified period of not more than one year.

(7) A midwife who does not attend a course of instruction as provided for in this Rule shall be reported to the supervisor of midwives, whose duty it shall be to report the matter to the relevant Board, which shall thereafter investigate the matter with a view to appropriate action being taken.

38 Suspension from practice by a local supervising authority [ae]

(1) It shall be the duty of the local supervising authority to suspend a midwife from practice when necessary for the purpose of preventing the spread of infection, whether or not she has contravened any of the Rules laid down by the Council.

(2) The local supervising authority may suspend from practice until any proceedings or investigations have been determined:

(a) a midwife against whom it has reported a case for investigation to the Council;

(b) a midwife who has been referred to the Professional Conduct Committee of the Council as defined in the Nurses, Midwives and Health Visitors (Professional Conduct) Rules 1993;*

(c) a midwife who has been referred to the Health Committee of the Council as defined in the Nurses, Midwives and Health Visitors (Professional Conduct) Rules 1993.*

(3) A local supervising authority in discharging any duty imposed on it by Section 16(2)(b) of the Act, or in exercising the power given in paragraph (1) and (2) of this Rule to suspend a midwife from practice shall:

(a) immediately notify the midwife concerned in writing of any decision to suspend her and the reason for such suspension and

(b) in respect of a suspension authorised by paragraph (2) of this Rule forthwith report any such suspension and the grounds thereof to the Council.

39 Duty to be medically examined [ae]

A practising midwife shall, if the local supervising authority deem it necessary for preventing the spread of infection, undergo medical examination by a registered medical practitioner.

---

* SI 1993 No 893

40 Responsibility and sphere of practice[a]

(1) A practising midwife is responsible for providing midwifery care to a mother and baby during the antenatal, intranatal and postnatal periods. In any case where there is an emergency or where she detects in the health of a mother and baby a deviation from the norm, a practising midwife shall call to her assistance a registered medical practitioner and shall forthwith report the matter to the local supervising authority in a form in accordance with the requirements of the local supervising authority.

(2) A practising midwife must not, except in an emergency, undertake any treatment which she has not been trained to give either before or after registration as a midwife and which is outside her sphere of practice.

41 Administration of medicines and other forms of pain relief [ae]

(1) A practising midwife shall not on her own responsibility administer any medicine, including analgesics unless in the course of her training, whether before or after registration as a midwife, she has been thoroughly instructed in its use and is familiar with its dosage and methods of administration or application.

(2) A practising midwife shall not on her own responsibility administer any inhalational analgesic by the use of any type of apparatus unless:

- (a) that apparatus is for the time being approved by the Council as suitable for use by a midwife and
- (b) the midwife has ensured that the apparatus has been properly maintained.

(3) Unless special exemption is given by the Council to enable a particular hospital, or other institution, to investigate new methods, a practising midwife must not administer any form of pain relief by the use of any type of apparatus or by any other means, which has not been approved by the Council other than on the instructions of a registered medical practitioner.

42 Records[a]

(1) A practising midwife shall keep as contemporaneously as is reasonable detailed records of observations, care given and medicine or other forms of pain relief administered by her to all mothers and babies.

(2) The records referred to in paragraph (1) of this Rule shall be kept:

- (a) in the case of a midwife employed by a health authority* in accordance with any directions given by her employer;
- (b) in any other case in a form approved by the local supervising authority.

* or NHS Trust

(3) A midwife must not destroy or arrange for the destruction of official records which have been made whilst she is in professional attendance upon a case (for the purpose of this Rule called 'official records'). If she finds it impossible or inconvenient to preserve her official records safely she must transfer them to the local supervising authority or to her employing authority and details of the transfer must be duly recorded by each party to the transfer.

(4) Immediately before ceasing to practise as a midwife employed by a health authority* a midwife shall transfer her official records to the local supervising authority and details of the transfer must be duly recorded by each party to the transfer.

(5) Immediately before a self-employed midwife ceases to practise she must ensure that her official records are kept in a safe place and she may transfer them to the local supervising authority and details of any such transfer must be duly recorded by each party to the transfer.

43 Inspection of premises and equipment [ae]

(1) A practising midwife shall give to her supervisor of midwives, the local supervising authority and the Council every reasonable facility to inspect her methods of practice, her records, her equipment and such part of her residence as may be used for professional purposes.

(2) A midwife shall use her best endeavours to permit inspection from time to time by a midwifery officer, who shall be a practising midwife, of the Council or of an authority designated by the Council, of all institutional premises in which she practises other than the private residence of the mother and baby.

44 Supervisors of midwives [ae]

(1) A person to be appointed in accordance with Section 16(3) of the Act by a local supervising authority to exercise supervision over midwives in its area shall be a registered midwife and either:
   (a) shall have had three years' experience as a practising midwife of which at least one year shall have been in the period of two years immediately preceding the appointment or
   (b) shall be eligible to practise and shall undertake any further midwifery experience as may be required by the Council.

(2) A person to be appointed a supervisor of midwives shall, unless the Council decides otherwise, have completed a course of instruction not more than three years prior to

---

* or NHS Trust

appointment and shall undertake to receive further instruction at intervals of not more than five years.

(3) In sub-paragraph (2) of this Rule a course means a course approved by a Board for the instruction of a person in the duties of a supervisor of midwives.

45 Discharge of statutory functions by a local supervising authority[e]

Each local supervising authority shall ensure that, in respect of practising midwives within its area, there is published in writing at least once every two years:

   (a) (i) the date in the month of March by which notice of intention to practise under Rule 36(1)(b) must be received by it and

        (ii) the name or office of the person to whom the said notice must be sent;

   (b) the means by which it will:

        (i) investigate any *prima facie* case of misconduct and

        (ii) determine whether to suspend a midwife from practice pursuant to Section 16(2)(c) of the Act;

   (c) (i) a list of the supervisors of midwives whom it has appointed and

        (ii) details of how it will provide midwives with continuous access to a supervisor of midwives;

   (d) details of how the practice of midwives will be supervised;

   (e) all policies which it has formulated affecting the practice of midwives.

The various Rules set out in this document are given under the seal of the Council and signed by:

Dame Audrey Emerton
Chairman of the Council
(to 31 March 1993)

Miss M E Uprichard
President of the Council

Colin Ralph
Registrar and Chief Executive of the Council

November 1993

Appendix 6   The midwife's code of practice

Introduction

1. This 1994 Edition of the Midwife's Code of Practice sets out the Council's standards, other requirements and further information for the professional practice of each midwife. You, as a practising midwife, are subject to this Code regardless of employment circumstances.

2. Each midwife as a practitioner of midwifery is accountable for her[a] own practice in whatever environment she practises. The standard of practice in the delivery of midwifery care shall be that which is acceptable in the context of current knowledge and clinical developments. In all circumstances the safety and welfare of the mother and her baby[b] must be of primary importance.

3. A practising midwife is also subject to the UKCC (the Council) Midwives Rules, Code of Professional Conduct, the Council's Standards documents and other Council documents related to professional practice issued from time to time. It is the midwife's responsibility to familiarise herself with such information.

[a] All references in the female gender include the male
[b] Interpretation of mother and baby is as in the Midwives' Practice Rules, Section 27 (Statutory Instrument 1986 No 786)

The definition of a midwife

4. The definition of a midwife was adopted by the International Confederation of Midwives (ICM) and the International Federation of Gynaecologists and Obstetricians (FIGO), in 1972 and 1973 respectively and later adopted by the World Health Organisation (WHO). This definition was amended by the ICM in 1990 and the amendment ratified by the FIGO and the WHO in 1991 and 1992 respectively and now reads as follows:

> 'A midwife is a person who, having been regularly admitted to a midwifery educational programme, duly recognised in the country in which it is located, has successfully completed the prescribed course of studies in midwifery and has acquired the requisite qualifications to be registered and/or legally licensed to practise midwifery.
>
> She must be able to give the necessary supervision, care and advice to women during pregnancy, labour and the postpartum period, to conduct deliveries on her own responsibility and to care for the newborn and the infant. This care includes preventative measures, the detection of abnormal conditions in mother and child, the procurement of medical assistance and the execution of emergency measures in the absence of medical help. She has an important task in health counselling and education, not only for the women, but also within the family and the community. The work should involve antenatal education and preparation for parenthood and extends to certain areas of gynaecology, family planning and child care. She may practise in hospitals, clinics, health units, domiciliary conditions or in any other service.'

Activities of a midwife

5. The activities of a midwife are defined in the European Community Midwives Directive 80/155/EEC Article 4 as follows.

> 'Member States shall ensure that midwives are at least entitled to take up and pursue the following activities:
>
> 5.1 to provide sound family planning information and advice;
> 5.2 to diagnose pregnancies and monitor normal pregnancies; to carry out examinations necessary for the monitoring of the development of normal pregnancies;
> 5.3 to prescribe or advise on the examinations necessary for the earliest possible diagnosis of pregnancies at risk;
> 5.4 to provide a programme of parenthood preparation and a complete preparation for childbirth including advice on hygiene and nutrition;
> 5.5 to care for and assist the mother during labour and to monitor the condition of the fetus in utero by the appropriate clinical and technical means;
> 5.6 to conduct spontaneous deliveries including where required an episiotomy and in urgent cases a breech delivery;

5.7   to recognise the warning signs of abnormality in the mother or infant which necessitate referral to a doctor and to assist the latter where appropriate; to take the necessary emergency measures in the doctor's absence, in particular the manual removal of the placenta, possibly followed by manual examination of the uterus;

5.8   to examine and care for the new-born infant; to take all initiatives which are necessary in case of need and to carry out where necessary immediate resuscitation;

5.9   to care for and monitor the progress of the mother in the postnatal period and to give all necessary advice to the mother on infant care to enable her to ensure the optimum progress of the new-born infant;

5.10 to carry out the treatment prescribed by a doctor;

5.11 to maintain all necessary records.'

Matters directly related to the Midwives Practice Rules

Notification of intention to practise (Rule 36)

6. In order to comply with this Rule you must submit a notification of intention to practise to the supervisor of midwives in the district[c] in which you intend to work. The supervisor of midwives to whom you have notified your intention to practise acts on behalf of the Local Supervising Authority (LSA), and LSAs are cited at paragraph 44.

7. Where you work in more than one district or LSA, you must notify your intention to practise to the supervisor of midwives in each different district or LSA.

8. You are responsible for notifying any change of name and address to:

8.1 the UKCC and

8.2 the supervisor(s) of midwives to whom you have notified your intention to practise. The supervisor will then inform the LSA.

Refresher courses (Rule 37)

9. Enquiries with regard to appropriate and available refresher courses should be directed to the National Board of the country in which the course is to be undertaken.

10. A supervisor of midwives to whom you have notified your intention to practise as a midwife may be approached for advice and help about the choices and options available that would fulfil refresher course requirements. Consideration should also be given to the need for a clinical skills refresher course option.

---

[c] district means the geographical jurisdiction of the supervisor of midwives

11. Those midwives undertaking midwifery care outside the United Kingdom and who intend to return to practise in the United Kingdom are advised to keep evidence of length, type and place of midwifery experience undertaken outside the United Kingdom, for consideration/verification by a National Board in relation to appropriate refresher course requirements.

12. Requirements for refresher courses under Rule 37 will apply until any new legislation regarding standards for post-registration education and practice is put in place. The Council will ensure timely communication in relation to any forthcoming changes which will not have retrospective requirements.

Responsibilities and sphere of practice (Rule 40)

13. Midwives have a defined sphere of practice and you are accountable for that practice. The needs of the mother and baby must be the primary focus of your practice. The mother should be enabled to make decisions about her care based on her needs, having discussed matters fully with you and any other professionals involved with her care.

14. You should be appropriately prepared and clinically up to date to ensure you are able effectively to carry out emergency procedures for the mother or baby such as resuscitation.

15. The conditions in which midwives practise vary widely, whether in the home, in hospital or elsewhere. The responsibilities of the midwife and the registered medical practitioner are inter-related and complementary and each practitioner retains the clinical accountability for her own practice.

16. The necessary degree of co-operation can only be ensured by mutual recognition of the respective roles of midwives and registered medical practitioners and those others who may participate in the care of mother and babies. Such mutual respect should enhance care and practice must be based upon agreed standards to ensure effective communication and co-operation in care.

17. When you consider that there could be significant risk in the type of care the mother is requesting, you should discuss her wishes with her, giving detailed information relating to her requests, options for care and any risk factors so that the mother may make a fully informed decision about her care. A detailed record should be made of any such discussion. If the mother rejects your advice, you should seek further advice and discussion with your supervisor of midwives. Such advice and information should be recorded and signed by both you and your supervisor. You must continue to give unbiased care to the best of your ability, seeking peer support as necessary.

18. In some instances where risk factors have been identified, or in an emergency, you may require medical assistance for a mother or baby, but the mother or her partner may refuse to have the registered medical practitioner in attendance. If this situation arises you must continue to care for the mother and baby and consult as soon as possible with

your supervisor of midwives, making a detailed record of the circumstances and action taken.

19. It is the duty of the supervisor of midwives to ensure that agreed local policies are easily available to all practising midwives within their supervisory jurisdiction. The local policy should provide you with support in all settings, including home births and the availability of emergency services, to enable the best possible arrangements to be made for the care of the mother and baby.

Responsibility for competency in new skills

20. You are responsible for maintaining and developing the competence you have acquired during your initial and subsequent midwifery education.

21. Some of the developments in midwifery care can become an integral part of the role of the midwife and are then incorporated in the initial preparation of the midwife. It is necessary for you to acquire competence in such new skills, and to achieve this you must ensure that you have received adequate preparation.

22. Other developments in midwifery and obstetric practice may also require you to acquire new skills, but these skills do not necessarily become an integral part of the role of all midwives. In such circumstances each employing authority should have locally agreed policies which observe the Council's requirements and National Board advice and guidance. You should familiarise yourself with the policies of any authority by which you are employed and any other authority in which you may practise.

23. When your practice requires the acquisition of new skills, you should consult with your supervisor of midwives with regard to the requisite preparation and experience.

Medicines including analgesics (Rule 41)

Supply, possession and use of controlled drugs

24. The possession and administration of controlled drugs by midwives is covered by the Misuse of Drugs Regulations 1985 SI (1985 No 2066); the Misuse of Drugs (Northern Ireland) Regulations 1986 (SR 1986 No 52) and the Medicines Act 1968.

25. The Misuse of Drugs Regulations provide for the supply of Pethidine to midwives (and any other controlled drug listed in Schedule 3 Parts I and III of the Medicines (Products Other Than Veterinary Drugs) (Prescription Only) Order 1983, SI 1983 No 1212) and subsequent orders using the supply order procedure. Supply Order forms can be obtained from your supervisor of midwives.

26. The administration of controlled drugs by a midwife working in a hospital/institution should be in accordance with locally agreed policies and procedures. It may be

decided locally that midwives practising in hospitals/institutions may follow the same practice as midwives working in the community.

Destruction of controlled drugs obtained by a midwife through a supply order procedure

27. Regulation 26 of the Misuse of Drugs Regulations contains a procedure for witnessing the destruction of Pethidine (or other controlled drugs approved in accordance with the Medicines Act 1968) which have been supplied to the midwife, but which are no longer required. The destruction is done by the midwife but only in the presence of an 'authorised person' who may be one of the following:

27.1 A supervisor of midwives in England, Wales and Northern Ireland;
27.2 a Regional Pharmaceutical Officer in England;
27.3 Pharmaceutical Adviser, Welsh Office;
27.4 Chief Administrative Pharmaceutical Officer of Health Boards in Scotland;
27.5 in Northern Ireland, an Inspector appointed by the Department of Health and Social Services under the Misuse of Drugs Act 1971;
27.6 Medical Officers of the Regional Medical Services in England, Scotland and Wales;
27.7 an Inspector of the Pharmaceutical Society of Great Britain;
27.8 a police officer and
27.9 an Inspector of the Home Office Drugs Branch.

Surrender of controlled drugs

28. There is a provision within the Misuse of Drugs Regulations for midwives to surrender stocks of unwanted controlled drugs to the pharmacist from whom they were obtained or to an appropriate medical officer, but not to a supervisor of midwives.

Controlled drugs obtained by a woman on prescription from a family practitioner for use in her home birth

29. In the case of controlled drugs supplied directly to the mother on prescription from a family practitioner, the responsibility for destruction of any which are unused is that of the mother to whom in law they belong. You should advise the mother to destroy the drugs and suggest that she does so in your presence. Alternatively you may advise the mother to return the unused drugs to the pharmacist from whom they were obtained. You may not do this for her. The advice you have given and any action taken should

be recorded in the mother's notes, together with details of the nature and amounts of drugs involved.

Prescription only and other medicines used by midwives

30. Certain medicines which are normally only available on a prescription issued by a medical practitioner may be supplied to midwives who have notified their intention to practise for use in their practice under the Medicines Act 1968, either from a retail chemist or hospital pharmacy.

31. These medicines are listed in Schedule 3 Parts I and III of the Medicines (Products Other Than Veterinary Drugs) (Prescription Only) Order 1983, SI No 1212 and any subsequent orders.

32. A midwife in the course of her practice in the community may need to carry antiseptics, sedatives and analgesics, local anaesthetics, oxytocic preparations and approved agents for neonatal and maternal resuscitation. The particular medicines and controlled drugs which a midwife may use will be determined locally in collaboration with the senior midwife and medical and pharmaceutical staff and should be listed in written local policy. A midwife should obtain details from her supervisor of midwives.

33. Return of prescription only medicines to the supplying pharmacist should be receipted and recorded in the midwife's records. Disposal of prescription only and other medicines should be recorded in the midwife's record.

The administration of homoeopathic or herbal substances

34. Homoeopathic and herbal medicines are subject to the licensing provisions of the Medicines Act 1968, although those on the market when that Act became operative, (which applies to most of those substances now available) received product licences without any evaluation of their efficacy, safety or quality. You should ensure that you are familiar with the requirements of Rule 41(1) in relation to the administration of medicines. It is necessary, however, to respect the right of individuals to self-administer substances of their choice.

35. When a mother wishes to receive medicines of this kind and you believe that the substances might either be an inappropriate response to the presenting symptoms or likely to negate or enhance the effect of prescribed medicines, you have a duty to discuss this fully with the mother. The midwife, acting in the interests of the mother and in her full knowledge, should consider contacting the relevant expert practitioner to seek advice, but must also be mindful of the need not to override the woman's rights. (See also paragraph 56 on complementary and alternative therapies, which are not subject to the provisions of the Medicines Act 1968.)

Administration of controlled drugs and medicines and audit of records

36. When administering controlled drugs and other medicines in the NHS, you should comply with locally agreed health authority[d] policies and procedures. In some authorities such policies may include a standing order signed by a consultant registered medical practitioner and a senior midwife authorising the administration of controlled drugs and medicines for the use by the midwife in her practice in an institution. These drugs and medicines would be similar to those carried by a midwife in her practice in the community.

37. If you are practising outside the area of your employing authority or outside the NHS, you should seek advice from your supervisor of midwives regarding any matters related to the supply, administration, storage, surrender and destruction of controlled drugs and other medicines.

38. Supervisors of midwives should periodically audit the records of controlled drugs and prescription only medicines kept by midwives. Any discrepancies must be investigated.

Records (Rule 42)

39. Your records are an essential aspect of your practice and you must comply with Rule 42. To maintain and improve standards of practice, your supervisor of midwives will periodically audit your records. Rule 42 requires that the format of records kept by midwives practising outside the National Health Service should be approved by the LSA.

Retention of maternity records

40. All essential maternity records (such as those recording the case of a mother and baby during pregnancy, labour and the puerperium, including all test results, prescription forms and records of medicines administered) must be retained for 25 years. Decisions concerning those records which are to be regarded as essential must not be made at local level without involving senior midwifery and medical practitioners concerned with the provision of maternity and neonatal services.

41. Those involved in determining policy at local level must ensure that the records retained are comprehensive, including hospital, community midwifery records and those held by mothers during pregnancy and the puerperium. Records must be of a kind which facilitate any investigation which may be required as a result of action brought under the Congenital Disabilities (Civil Liabilities) Act 1976 or as a result of any other complaint requiring investigation.

---

[d] or NHS Trust

Premises and equipment (Rule 43)

42. Your attention is drawn to Rule 43, which states that a practising midwife's methods of practice, her records, her equipment and such part of her residence that may be used for professional purposes may be inspected by a supervisor of midwives, the LSA and the Council.

43. If practising in the community you must be able to satisfy the LSA or the supervisor of midwives on its behalf, that you have the appropriate equipment for your practice as specified by the LSA.

Supervisors of midwives (Rule 44)

44. The Nurses, Midwives and Health Visitors Act 1979 Section 16 makes provision for the supervision of midwives by LSAs. Regional Health Authorities in England, District Health Authorities in Wales, Health Boards in Scotland and Health and Social Services Boards in Northern Ireland are designated as LSAs.

45. The Council has recommended to LSAs that the LSA function should be discharged by a practising midwife. It is for each LSA to determine its organisational arrangements but the Council considers that this function would be best discharged, and the LSA most appropriately served, by this function being assigned to a practising midwife who is professionally experienced in the supervision of midwives. The Council considers that such a practising midwife should be deployed at LSA level as the designated responsible officer and that the relationship between such a midwife, and the Authority's designated chief nursing/midwifery adviser is of particular importance.

46. In accordance with Section 16(4) of the Nurses, Midwives and Health Visitors Act 1979, the National Boards are required to provide the LSAs with advice and guidance in respect of the exercise of their functions. Supervisors of midwives should have access to this information and to any other relevant information that LSAs may hold.

47. The LSAs appoint supervisors of midwives in accordance with Rule 44 of the Midwives Rules. Persons so appointed are selected from experienced midwives within health authorities who meet the criteria stated in Rule 44, and who have been appropriately prepared prior to undertaking this role.

48. The Council has recommended to LSAs that for effective supervision to be achieved, each supervisor should supervise no more than 40 practising midwives. The Council understands that there is variation across the United Kingdom in the supervisor-midwife ratio and that it may take some time for some LSAs to reach the recommended ratio. The Council's annual statistical analysis will enable changes to be monitored. This recommendation is designed to allow both effective supervision and adequate support for midwives practising within and outside the National Health Service.

49. You should contact your supervisor of midwives on all matters as required by the Midwives Rules. You and your supervisor of midwives, through your respective

roles, should work towards a common aim of optimum care for mothers and babies.

50. The supervisor of midwives is concerned with safety in practice and care. You and your supervisor of midwives have a mutual responsibility for effective communication between you in order that any problems can be shared and a resolution achieved at the earliest opportunity. A key and important aspect of the supervisory function is that it enables this process.

51. Your supervisor of midwives should give you support as a colleague, counsellor and advisor. This should be developed in order to promote a positive working relationship which is conducive to maintaining and improving standards of practice and care.

52. Supervisors of midwives should ensure that effective communication links exist between themselves, LSAs, those engaged in determining health service policy and medical staff in order that relevant issues are appropriately addressed and resolved.

Local supervising authorities (Rule 45)

53. Rule 45 is a new Rule and requires LSAs to publish in writing, at least once every two years, all their policies affecting the practice of midwives and the means by which they investigate and determine any allegations of misconduct. Such policies should be communicated to all supervisors of midwives by LSAs within their area.

54. Supervisors of midwives should ensure that they are familiar with, and where possible have been involved in the formulation of, the policies, information and guidance available from LSAs.

Home births

55. When attending a mother having a home birth, you should ascertain whether or not a registered medical practitioner is available for referral, to attend or to be on call if required. The registered medical practitioner should normally be from the obstetric list in those parts of the United Kingdom where such a list is held. When the support of a registered medical practitioner is not available, you should discuss the situation in advance whenever possible with your supervisor of midwives, and agree and record appropriate arrangements to provide advice and support as necessary.

Complementary and alternative therapies

56. Some practising midwives, having gained a qualification in a complementary or alternative therapy, may wish to apply this additional knowledge and skill in their practice. Such practice may involve the use of substances such as essential oils, or specific equipment. It is essential that practice in these respects, as in all others, is based upon sound principles, and all available and current knowledge and skill. The importance of consent

by the mother to the use of such therapies must be recognised. So, too, must the practitioner's personal accountability for her or his professional practice. (Your attention is also drawn to paragraph 22 which refers to other developments in midwifery and obstetric practice).

Arranging for a substitute

57. Section 17(1) of the Nurses, Midwives and Health Visitors Act 1979, as amended by the 1992 Act states that:

> 'A person other than a registered midwife or registered medical practitioner shall not attend a woman in childbirth'.

Neither you nor your employing authority should arrange for anyone to act as the substitute for a midwife other than another registered midwife eligible to practise or a registered medical practitioner.

58. Section 17(3)(b) of the same Act allows a person undergoing training to become either a midwife or a medical practitioner to attend (under supervision) a woman in childbirth, as part of a course of practical instruction recognised by one of the National Boards or by the General Medical Council. In such circumstances the practising midwife or the registered medical practitioner, as appropriate, remain accountable for the care given.

Maternal death, stillbirth or neonatal death

59. You must inform your supervisor of midwives of any maternal death, stillbirth or neonatal death occurring when you are the midwife responsible for the care of that mother and her baby.

Other legislation relevant to the practice of a midwife

60. Attention is drawn in this section to other legislation with which you are required to comply in the course of your practice.

Congenital Disabilities (Civil Liabilities) Act 1976

61. This Act is applicable in England, Wales and Northern Ireland and provides for a child to be entitled to recover damages where he has suffered as a result of a breach in a duty of care owed to the mother or the father unless that breach of duty of care occurred before the child was conceived and either or both parents knew of the occurrence. It follows, therefore, that preservation of records relating to birth requires special consideration and no midwife should take the responsibility for the destruction of such records.

62. In Scotland the Scottish Law Commission in its report 'Liability for antenatal injury', presented to Parliament by the Lord Advocate in August 1973 (Council 5371), considered that existing law and precedents in Scotland made the same provisions as those which were later enshrined in the above legislation for the other three countries of the United Kingdom.

63. It is important that records should be made at the time of each attendance, that they should be clear and contain all the relevant details. Attention is drawn to Rule 42 and paragraphs 39–41 of this document which specifies your responsibility in relation to records made in the course of your professional attendance on a case.

The Data Protection Act 1984

64. This Act applies to the whole of the United Kingdom. Under the Act, information is protected and persons (individuals or organisations) who hold personal data on computer without being registered would be committing an offence. The Act relates only to data capable of being automatically processed. Data subjects have a basic right of access to information held on computer about them.

Access to Health Records Act 1990

65. With effect from 1 November 1991, clients have had the right of access to manual records about themselves made from that date as a result of the Access to Health Records Act 1990 coming into effect. This has brought such records into line with computer-held records which have been required to be accessible to patients since the Data Protection Act 1984 became operative.

66. The Council fully supports the principle of open access to records contained in these Acts and the guidance notes concerning their operation and expects that access will not be unreasonably denied or limited.

67. You must be aware of the rights of the client with regard to access to records pertaining to them. You must exercise discretion in the use of language and terminology in records and the important relationship of trust and confidence between mother and midwife.

Births and Deaths Registration Acts and Public Health Acts

68. Under the Births and Deaths Registration Acts and the Public Health Acts, a midwife must in certain cases notify the Registrar of Births and Deaths and the Appropriate Medical Officer. The following is a summary of your duties under these Acts.

Notification of births

69. Although the duty of notifying a birth (whether the baby is born alive or stillborn) to the appropriate medical officer within 36 hours is laid upon the father or any other person in attendance upon the mother at the birth or within six hours after the birth, it is usually the midwife who does this. You can obtain the proper form of notice free of charge by application to the health authority.

Registration of Births

70. It is the duty primarily of the father or mother to give the Registrar of Births within 42 days[e] after the birth, information about the birth, whether the baby is born alive or stillborn. In default of the father or mother this duty falls upon any person present at the birth, including the midwife.

Certification and burial or cremation of a stillborn baby

71. When a registered medical practitioner is present at a stillbirth or examines the body, it is his statutory duty to give the qualified informant (usually the father or mother) a certificate of stillbirth. If a registered medical practitioner is not present at a stillbirth but arrangements for maternity care have been made with one, the midwife should inform him and ask him to examine the body and complete the certificate of stillbirth. If a registered medical practitioner is not available, you should only complete the certificate if you were present at the delivery of the stillbirth or examined the body. Whenever possible you should state on this certificate the cause of death and the estimated duration of the pregnancy to the best of your knowledge and belief.

72. A stillborn baby may not be buried or cremated until a certificate for burial or cremation has been obtained from the Registrar of Births and Deaths or an Order for Burial has been obtained from the Coroner or, in Scotland, the Procurator Fiscal. In certain circumstances a certificate (which will serve the same purpose) can be obtained from the Registrar that he has received notice of the stillbirth.

Notification of deaths

73. In the case of death it is primarily the duty of the relatives to notify the Registrar, but in default of the relatives the duty falls upon any person present at the death.

74. For the purpose of the registration of births and deaths:

[e] In Scotland 21 days

74.1 a baby born at any stage of pregnancy who breathes or shows other signs of life after complete expulsion from its mother is born alive. If such a baby dies after birth, the birth and the death will both require to be registered;

74.2 a baby who has issued forth from its mother after the 24th week of pregnancy and has not at any time after being completely expelled from its mother breathed or shown any sign of life is a stillborn baby;

74.3 the birth before the 24th week of pregnancy of a baby who did not breathe or show signs of life after complete expulsion from its mother is neither a live birth nor a stillbirth and need not be registered.

Babies born dead before the legal age of viability

75. When a baby is born dead before the legal age of viability, that is before 24 weeks' gestation, the law does not require the birth to be certified or registered.

76. However, parents who decide to hold a funeral for their baby will need a certificate or letter from the doctor or midwife who attended the birth, stating that their baby was born before the legal age of viability and showed no signs of life. Funeral directors will not accept a body of any gestation for cremation or burial without such documentation.

Exemption from Jury Service

77. Practising midwives are exempt from jury service under legislation other than that directly related to midwives. This legislation, which also includes exemption for practising nurses, is:

England and Wales – Juries Act 1974 C1.9 and Part III, Schedule 1
Northern Ireland – Juries (Northern Ireland) Order 1974 SI No 2143
Scotland – Law Reform Act 1980 (Scotland) Group C3 of Schedule 1.2

This Code of Practice will be revised regularly by the Council. Suggestions for any future revisions would be welcome and should be forwarded to the:

Professional Officer, Midwifery
United Kingdom Central Council for Nursing, Midwifery and Health Visiting
23 Portland Place
London W1N 3AF.

Appendix 7   Exercising accountability*

Contents

* A UKCC Advisory Document, originally published as *Exercising Accountability A framework to assist nurses, midwives and health visitors to consider ethical aspects of professional practice* by the United Kingdom Central Council for Nursing, Midwifery and Health Visiting, March 1989.

'Exercising Accountability' is the fourth in a series to supplement the Code of Professional Conduct (Second Edition: November 1984) and is made available free to all persons on the UKCC's professional register to assist them and to stimulate discussion of this important subject.

It should be read in conjunction with the Code of Professional Conduct for the Nurse, Midwife and Health Visitor and other UKCC Advisory Papers.

The Council, through its professional staff, is always willing to respond to individual requests for advice on matters related to professional practice.

458

A Introduction

1. The United Kingdom Central Council for Nursing, Midwifery and Health Visiting regulates the nursing, midwifery and health visiting professions in the public interest.

The UKCC was established by the Nurses, Midwives and Health Visitors Act 1979.

Section 2(1) of the Nurses, Midwives and Health Visitors Act 1979 states that 'The principal functions of the Central Council shall be to establish and improve standards of training and professional conduct'.

Section 2(5) of the same Act moves from the requirement to improve conduct to one of the methods to be employed when it states that 'The powers of the Council shall include that of providing in such manner as it thinks fit, advice for nurses, midwives and health visitors on standards of professional conduct'.

2. The Code of Professional Conduct for the Nurse, Midwife and Health Visitor is the Council's definitive advice on professional conduct to its practitioners. In this extremely important document practitioners on the UKCC's register find a clear and unequivocal statement as to what their regulatory body expects of them. It therefore also provides the backcloth against which any alleged misconduct on their part will be judged.

The Code of Professional Conduct is considered to be

a statement to the profession of the primacy of the interests of the patient or client.

a statement of the profession's values.

a portrait of the practitioner which the Council believes to be needed and which the Council wishes to see within the profession.

3. The Council has already published three advisory documents to supplement the Code of Professional Conduct. Practitioners now seek:

(i)   elaboration of clauses 10 and 11 of the Code and support for their position when doing as these clauses require. These Clauses state that:

'Each registered nurse, midwife and health visitor is accountable for his or her practice and, in the exercise of professional accountability, shall:

10. Have regard to the environment of care and its physical, psychological and social effects on patients/clients, and also to the adequacy of resources, and make known to appropriate persons or authorities any circumstances which could place patients/clients in jeopardy or which militate against safe standards of practice.
11. Have regard to the workload of and the pressures on professional colleagues and subordinates and take appropriate action if these are seen to be such as to constitute abuse of the individual practitioner and/or to jeopardise safe standards of practice'.

(ii) advice and guidance on issues related to consent and the general subject of truth telling.
(iii) advice and guidance on that part of the practitioner's role which concerns advocacy on behalf of patients and clients.

(iv) elaboration of clause 5 of the Code which states that each registered nurse, midwife and health visitor shall:

> 5. 'Work in a collaborative and co-operative manner with other health care professionals and recognise and respect their particular contributions within the health care team'.

(v) advice and guidance on issues related to contentious treatments and conscientious objection.

This document provides a response to those requests, aims to assist professional practitioners to exercise their judgement and reinforces the importance of the Code of Professional Conduct.

B The Code of Professional Conduct and the subject of accountability

1. This new UKCC advisory document has been produced in order to establish more clearly the extent of accountability of registered nurses, midwives and health visitors and to assist them in the exercise of professional accountability in order to achieve high standards of professional practice.

2. The Code begins with an unequivocal statement

> 'Each registered nurse, midwife and health visitor shall act, at all times, in such a manner as to justify public trust and confidence, to uphold and enhance the good standing and reputation of the profession, to serve the interests of society, and above all to safeguard the interests of individual patients and clients'.

This introductory clause indicates that a registered practitioner is accountable for her actions as a professional at all times, whether engaged in current practice or not and whether on or off duty.

In situations where the practitioner is employed she will be accountable to the employer for providing a service which she is employed to provide and for the proper use of the resources made available by the employer for this purpose.

In the circumstances described in the preceding two paragraphs the practitioner has an ultimate accountability to the UKCC for any failure to satisfy the requirements of the introductory paragraph of the Code of Professional Conduct.

The words 'accountable' and 'accountability' each occur only once in the Code, both being found in the stem paragraph out of which the subsequent 14 clauses grow. They do, however, provide its central focus as the Code is built upon the expectation that practitioners will conduct themselves in the manner it describes.

3. Accountability is an integral part of professional practice, since, in the course of that practice, the practitioner has to make judgements in a wide variety of circumstances and be answerable for those judgements. The Code of Professional Conduct does not seek to state all the circumstances in which accountability has to be exercised, but to state important principles.

The primacy of the interests of the public and patient or client provide the first theme of the Code and establish the point that, in determining his or her approach to professional practice, the individual nurse, midwife or health visitor should recognise that the interests of public and patient must predominate over those of practitioner and profession. The second major theme is the exercise by each practitioner of personal professional accountability in such a manner as to respect the primacy of those interests.

4. The Code of Professional Conduct states unequivocally that all practitioners who are registered on the UKCC's register are required to seek to set and achieve high standards and thereby to honour the requirement of Clause 1 of the Code which states that each registered nurse, midwife and health visitor shall:

1. 'Act always in such a way as to promote and safeguard the wellbeing and interests of patients and clients'.

It is recognised that, in many situations in which practitioners practise, there may be a tension between the maintenance of standards and the availability or use of resources. It is essential, however, that the profession, both through its regulatory body (the UKCC) and its individual practitioners, adheres to its desire to enhance standards and to achieve high standards rather than to simply accept minimum standards. Practitioners must seek remedies in those situations where factors in the environment obstruct the achievement of high standards: to start from a compromise position and silently to tolerate poor standards is to act in a manner contrary to the interests of patients or clients, and thus renege on personal professional accountability.

C Concern in respect of the environment of care

1. The dilemma for practitioners in many settings in respect of the environment of care is very real and has been well documented. If practitioners express concern at the situations which obstruct the achievement of satisfactory standards they risk censure from their employers. On the other hand, failure to make concerns known renders practitioners vulnerable to complaint to their regulatory body (the UKCC) for failing to satisfy its standards and places their registration status in jeopardy.

The sections of the Code of Professional Conduct that are particularly relevant to this issue are the introductory paragraphs and clauses numbered 1, 2, 3, 10 and 11. These parts of the Code apply to each and every person on the Council's register. Whether engaged in direct care of the patient or client, or further removed but in a position to exert influence over the setting in which that contact exists, the practitioner is subject to the Code and has an accountability for her actions or omissions.

2. The import of the Sections of the Code referred to is that, having, as part of her professional accountability, the responsibility to 'serve the interests of society and above all to safeguard the interests of individual patients and clients' and to 'act always in such a way as to promote and safeguard the wellbeing and interests of patients/clients', the registered nurse, midwife and health visitor must make appropriate representations about the environment of care:

(a) where patients or clients seem likely to be placed in jeopardy and/or standards of practice endangered;

(b) where the staff in such settings are at risk because of the pressure of work and/or inadequacy of resources (which again places patients at risk); and

(c) where valuable resources are being used inappropriately.

This is an essential part of the communication process that should operate in any facility providing health care, to ensure that those who determine, manage and allocate resources do so with full knowledge of the consequences for the achievement of satisfactory standards. Nurses, midwives and health visitors in management positions should ensure that all relevant information on standards of practice is obtained and communicated with others involved in health policy and management in the interests of standards and safety.

3. Practitioners engaged in direct patient or client care should not be deterred from making representations of their concerns regarding the environment of care simply because they believe that resources are unavailable or that action will not result. The immediate professional manager to whom such information is given, having assessed that information, should ensure that it is communicated to more senior professional managers. This is important in order that, should complaints be made about the practitioners involved in delivering care, the immediate and senior managers will be able to confirm that the perceived inadequacies in the environment of care have been drawn to their attention.

It is clearly wrong for any practitioner to pretend to be coping with the workload, to delude herself into the conviction that things are better than they really are, to aid and abet the abuse and breakdown of a colleague, or to tolerate in silence any matters in her work setting that place patients at risk, jeopardise standards of practice or deny patients privacy and dignity.

In summary, Section C of this document simply restates the UKCC's expectations (set out in the Code of Professional Conduct) that while accepting their responsibilities and doing their best to fulfil them, practitioners on its register will ensure that the reality of their clinical environment and practice is made known to and understood by appropriate persons or authorities, doing this as an expression of their personal professional accountability exercised in the public interest. An essential part of this process is the making of contemporaneous and accurate records of the consequences for patients and clients if they have not been given the care they required.

4. The Code of Professional Conduct applies to all persons on the Council's register irrespective of the post held. Their perspective will vary with their role, but they share the overall responsibility for care. No practitioner will find support in the Code or from the UKCC for the contention that genuinely held concerns should not be expressed or, if expressed, should attract censure.

D Consent and truth

1. It is self-evident that for it to have any meaning consent has to be informed. For the purposes of this document 'informed consent' means that the practitioner involved

explains the intended test or procedure to the patient without bias and in as much detail (including detail of possible reactions, complications, side-effects and social or personal ramifications) as the patient requires. In the case of an unquestioning patient the practitioner assesses and determines what information the patient needs so that the patient may make an informed decision. The practitioner should impart the information in a sensitive manner, recognising that it might cause distress. The patient must be given time to consider the information before being required to give the consent unless it is an emergency situation.

2. In many instances the practitioner involved in obtaining informed consent would be a registered medical practitioner. In those circumstances it is the medical practitioner who should impart the information and subsequently seek the signed consent. Normally, in respect of patients in hospital, there are good reasons why the information should be given and the consent sought in the presence of a nurse, midwife or health visitor. Where the procedure or test is to be performed by a nurse, midwife or health visitor the standards described in the preceding paragraph apply to the consent sought.

3. If the nurse, midwife or health visitor does not feel that sufficient information has been given in terms readily understandable to the patient so as to enable him to make a truly informed decision, it is for her to state this opinion and seek to have the situation remedied. The practitioner might decide not to co-operate with a procedure if convinced that the decision to agree to it being performed was not truly informed. Discussion of such matters between the health professionals concerned should not take place in the presence of patients.

In certain situations and with certain client groups the practitioner's level of responsibility in this respect is greatly increased where she stands *in loco parentis* for a patient or client.

4. There are occasions on which, although the patient has been given information by the medical practitioner about an intended procedure for which he has given consent, his subsequent statements and questions to a nurse, midwife or health visitor indicate a failure to understand what is to be done, its risks and its ramifications. Where this proves to be the case it is necessary for that practitioner, in the patient's interest, to recall the relevant medical practitioner so that the deficiencies can be remedied without delay.

The purpose of this approach is to ensure that all professional practitioners involved in the patient's care respect the primacy of that patient's interests, honour their personal professional accountability and avoid the risk of complaint or charges of assault. The practitioner who properly fulfils her responsibilities in this respect should be recognised by medical colleagues as a source of support and information to improve the overall care of the patient.

5. The concept of informed consent and that of truth telling are closely related. If it is to be believed that, on occasions, practitioners withhold information from their patients the damage to public trust and confidence in the profession, on which the introduction to the Code of Professional Conduct places great emphasis, will be enormous.

6. This is yet another area in which judgements have to be made and introduces another facet of the exercise of accountability. If it is accepted that the patient has a right to

information about his condition it follows that the professional practitioners involved in his care have a duty to provide such information. Recognition of the patient's condition and the likely effect of the information might lead the professionals to be selective about 'what' and 'when' but the responsibility is on them to provide information. There may be occasions on which, after consultation with the relatives of a patient by the health professionals involved in that patient's care, some information is temporarily withheld. If, however, something less than the whole truth is told at a particular point in time it should never be because the practitioner is unable to cope with the effects of telling the whole truth. Such controlled release of information (i.e. less than the whole truth) should only ever be in the interests of the patient, and the practitioner should be able to justify the action taken.

7. It is recognised that this is an area in which there is the potential for conflict between professionals involved in the care of the same patient or client. The existence of good, trusting relationships between professionals concerned will promote the development of agreed approaches to truth telling. This subject should be discussed between all the professional practitioners involved so that the rights of patients are not affected adversely. This should minimise the number of occasions on which, after a patient or client has been given incomplete information, a nurse, midwife or health visitor is faced with a request for the whole truth. Accountability can never be exercised by ignoring the rights and interests of the patient or client.

E Advocacy on behalf of patients and clients

1. The introductory paragraphs of the Code of Professional Conduct, together with several of its clauses, indicate clearly the expectation that the practitioner will accept a role as an advocate on behalf of his or her patients/clients. Opinions vary as to what exactly that means. Some tend to want to identify advocacy as a separate and distinct subject. It is not. It is a component of many professional activities of this and other professions. Some of these professional activities are the subject of other sections of this document.

2. Advocacy is concerned with promoting and safeguarding the wellbeing and interests of patients and clients. It is not concerned with conflict for its own sake. It is important that this fact is recognised, since some practitioners seem to regard advocacy on behalf of patients or clients as an adversarial activity and feel either attracted to it or not able to accept it for that reason. Dictionaries define an advocate as 'one who pleads the cause of another' or 'one who recommends or urges something' and indicates that advocacy is a positive, constructive activity.

3. There are occasions on which the practitioner's advocacy role has to be exercised to 'plead the cause of another' where, in the case of any person incapable of making informed decisions, the parents or relatives withhold consent for treatment which the various practitioners involved believe to be in the best interests of the patient. The parents or relatives, from their knowledge of the patient, will also have an opinion as to what

constitutes his or her best interests. There have been a limited number of cases in which the courts have taken the view that the parents or relatives have not decided in the patient's best interests. Taking the right of decision away from the parents or relatives should only occur in the rarest of cases. The practitioner's advocacy role in situations of this kind requires knowledge of the patient's condition and prognosis, sensitivity to the feelings of the parents or relatives and considerable empathy.

4. To fulfil the Council's expectations set out in the Code is, therefore, to be the advocate for the patient or client in this sense. Each practitioner must determine exactly how this aspect of personal professional accountability is satisfied within her particular sphere of practice. This requires the exercise of judgement as to the 'when' and 'how'. The practitioner must be sure that it is the interests of the patient or client that are being promoted rather than the patient or client being used as a vehicle for the promotion of personal or sectional professional interests. The Code of Professional Conduct envisages the role of patient or client advocate as an integral and essential aspect of good professional practice.

5. Just as the practice of nursing involves the practitioner in assisting the patient with those physical activities which he would do for himself were he able, so too the exercise of professional accountability involves the practitioner in assisting the patient by making such representations on his behalf as he would make himself if he were able.

F Collaboration and co-operation in care

1. Clause 5 of the Code of Professional Conduct requires that 'Each registered nùrse, midwife and health visitor, in the exercise of professional accountability shall work in a collaborative and co-operative manner with other health care professionals and recognise and respect their particular contributions within the health care team'. This clause deliberately emphasises the importance of collaboration and co-operation and, by implication, the importance of the avoidance of dispute and the promotion of good relationships and a spirit of co-operation and mutual respect within the team.

2. It does so because it is clearly impossible for any one profession or agency to possess all the knowledge, skill and resources to be employed in meeting the total health care needs of society. The delivery of full and appropriate care to patients/ clients frequently necessitates the participation of professional practitioners from more than one profession, their efforts often being supplemented by other agencies and persons.

The UKCC recognises the complexity of medical and health care and stresses the need to appreciate the complementary contribution of the professions and others involved.

The delivery of care is therefore often a multi-profession and multi-agency activity which, in order to be effective, must be based on mutual understanding, trust, respect and co-operation.

3. It is self-evident that collaborative and co-operative working is essential if patients and clients are to be provided with the care they need and if it is to be of the quality

required. It is worthy of note that this concept of teamwork is evident in many situations in which the care of patients and clients is a shared responsibility. Unfortunately there are exceptions. Experience has demonstrated that such co-operation and collaboration is not always easily achieved if:

(a) individual members of the team have their own specific and separate objectives; or
(b) one member of the team seeks to adopt a dominant role to the exclusion of the opinions, knowledge and skill of its other members.

In such circumstances it is important to stress that the interests of the patient or client must remain paramount.

4. The UKCC and the General Medical Council agree that there is a range of issues which calls for co-operation between the professions at both national and local level and wish to encourage this co-operation.

5. In spite of acceptance of the importance of co-operation and collaboration, differences can sometimes occur within the team regarding appropriate care and treatment. Such conflict can become an influence for good if it results in full discussion between members of the team. It may prove harmful to the care and treatment of patients or clients unless resolved in a manner which recognises the special contribution of each professional group, agency and individual and ensures that the interests and needs of the patient or client remain paramount.

6. Collaboration and co-operation between health care professionals is also necessary in both research and planning related to the provision or improvement of services. This may sometimes give rise to concern where one professional group is requested to pass information (obtained by its members in the course of professional practice) to a member of another professional group to use for a purpose other than that for which it was obtained and recorded. That level of concern will inevitably rise unless it can be seen that the purpose for which the information is required is valid, the information is made available only to persons bound by the same standards of confidentiality and the means of storage of that information is secure.

This should not present a problem where consent can be obtained from the patients or clients to whom the information relates or from relatives who have been provided with the relevant information. In certain fields, such as care of the elderly and persons with mental illness and mental handicap, the information gathering and research geared to the provision of services for these client groups may need to proceed without specific consent. This should only occur where the individuals receiving care are unable to give informed consent and where there is no close contact with relatives. Those who proceed without consent in these particular circumstances must be satisfied that their activities will not affect the current provision of care adversely and that the activity is directed to the provision of appropriate or improved services for future recipients of care.

It is anticipated that disputes will be avoided by relevant inter-professional discussions in advance of submissions of the projects for approval by the appropriate ethical committees. Where a dispute does arise it should be resolved between colleagues and the ethical committee.

Clause 9 of the Code of Professional Conduct and the UKCC's Advisory Paper on 'Confidentiality' provide further sources of reference for nurses, midwives and health visitors in respect of this aspect of practice.

G Objection to participation in care and treatment

1. Clause 7 of the Code of Professional Conduct states:

   'Make known to an appropriate person or authority any conscientious objection which may be relevant to professional practice'.

2. The law does not provide a general opportunity for practitioners to register a conscientious objection to participation in care and treatment. That right applies in respect of termination of pregnancy only (not the care of the patient thereafter) under the terms of Section 4 of the Abortion Act 1967.

3. Some practitioners choose not to participate in certain other forms of treatment on the grounds of conscience. Since the law provides no basic right to such a refusal it is imperative that any practitioner should be careful not to accept employment in a post where it is known that a form of treatment to which she has a conscientious objection is regularly used. In circumstances where a practitioner finds that a form of treatment to which she objects, but which is not usually employed, is to be used she must declare that objection with sufficient time for her managers to make alternative staffing arrangements and must not refuse to participate in emergency treatment.

   Some practitioners may object to participation in certain forms of treatment, such as resuscitative treatment of the elderly, the transfusion of blood, or electroconvulsive therapy. These practitioners must respect clause 7 of the Code and make their position clear to their professional colleagues and managers, and recognise that this may have implications for their contract of employment.

4. Objection to participation in treatment does not only occur as a product of conscience. It is the Council's stated position that, on each and every occasion a prescribed medication is being administered, the practitioner should ensure that, in her view, the patient is not presenting symptoms that contra-indicate its administration. The practitioner who is concerned about the administration of a particular drug in these circumstances might reasonably ask the prescribing doctor to attend the patient and, if the prescriber still requires it to be given, to request her to administer the medication if not fully reassured. The practitioner involved in such an incident should make a detailed record of the reasons why she felt concern and, if so, why she declined to administer prescribed medication.

5. The principle that applies in the previous paragraph can also be applied in appropriate circumstances to substances that are prescribed for topical use including wound dressings. Where the practitioner attending the patient believes (from knowledge, published research evidence or from previous experience) that the prescribed substance may be harmful, or even more so where it is evident that it is actively harmful, she should make a record of the condition of the wound or site (where appropriate including a photographic record) and ask the prescribing medical practitioner to attend.

If the prescription stands after medical examination the practitioner, having chosen either to respond to the prescription or not, should make a detailed record of the reasons for her expressed concern and subsequent actions.

It is believed that the spirit of co-operation and mutual respect referred to at paragraph F1. of this document should make such situations exceptional.

6. Objections to participation in treatment are not always associated with the nature or form of treatment or its appropriateness in a particular set of circumstances. Some practitioners indicate their wish or active intention to refuse to participate in the delivery of care to patients with certain conditions. Such refusal may be associated particularly with patients suffering from Hepatitis B Infection and those with Acquired Immune Deficiency Syndrome, AIDS Related Complex or who are HIV seropositive but asymptomatic.

Those who seek the UKCC's support for such actual or intended refusal are informed that the Code of Professional Conduct does not provide a formula for being selective about the categories of patient or client for whom the practitioner will care. To seek to be so selective is to demonstrate unacceptable conduct. The UKCC expects its practitioners to adopt a non-judgemental approach in the exercise of their caring role.

H Summary of the principles against which to exercise accountability

1. The interests of the patient or client are paramount.

2. Professional accountability must be exercised in such a manner as to ensure that the primacy of the interests of patients or clients is respected and must not be overridden by those of the professions or their practitioners.

3. The exercise of accountability requires the practitioner to seek to achieve and maintain high standards.

4. Advocacy on behalf of patients or clients is an essential feature of the exercise of accountability by a professional practitioner.

5. The role of other persons in the delivery of health care to patients or clients must be recognised and respected, provided that the first principle above is honoured.

6. Public trust and confidence in the profession is dependent on its practitioners being seen to exercise their accountability responsibly.

7. Each registered nurse, midwife or health visitor must be able to justify any action or decision not to act taken in the course of her professional practice.

Appendix 8   AIDS and HIV infection: a UKCC statement Registrar's Letter, 6 April 1993

Dear Colleague

1. *Acquired Immune Deficiency Syndrome and Human Immunodeficiency Virus Infection (AIDS and HIV Infection)*

2. *Anonymous Testing for the Prevalence of the Human Immunodeficiency Virus (HIV)*

The Council last reviewed, revised and distributed its declared position and policy on the important subjects of AIDS and HIV Infection and Anonymous Testing for the Prevalence of the Human Immuno-deficiency Virus in September 1992.

In view of a number of developments since that date and of the degree of attention given to the subject by the media, the document has again been reviewed. This further revised edition replaces Registrar's Letter 24/1992 which should now be destroyed.

Annexe 1 to this letter sets out the Council's position on the illness and infection generally and elaborates upon and clarifies certain passages of the previous text. This applies particularly to those passages concerning the responsibility of individual registered nurses, midwives and health visitors. This revised text contains nothing that, in principle or fact, contradicts the previous text. In view of the misunderstanding reflected by some of the media coverage, the document also states the Council's opposition to routine testing of health care professionals for HIV infection and gives its reasons.

The central feature of the Council's position – security through safe standards of personal practice supplemented by appropriate re-assignment of infected practitioners whose role involves them in invasive procedures – is found in paragraph 14 of this annexe.

Annexe 2 provides the latest revised edition of the Council's position concerning the specific subject of anonymous testing for the prevalence of the Human Immunodeficiency Virus (HIV) which is performed for epidemiological purposes. This sets out the Council's position and its advice to practitioners, together with a set of principles on which agreement to participate in the unlinked anonymous screening programmes should be based. Provided that these principles are honoured, the Council supports the programme of anonymous testing.

Questions in respect of the contents of these papers should be directed to Mr Reg Pyne, Assistant Registrar, Standards and Ethics, on telephone extension 241 at this address.

Yours sincerely
Colin Ralph
Registrar and Chief Executive

Annexe 1: Acquired Immune Deficiency Syndrome and Human Immuno-deficiency Virus infection (AIDS and HIV infection)

Introduction

1. In March 1988 the Council approved and released a statement on 'AIDS and HIV Infection' to provide information for practitioners on its register. The statement emphasised the importance of good standards of practice in all circumstances and briefed those who employ nurses, midwives and health visitors on the UKCC's position and the management of staff known to be infected with the virus. The statement was also intended to contribute to dispelling the mythology that is associated with this subject.

2. In the light of developments since the statement was issued, particularly the Government decision in respect of anonymous unconsented testing for HIV infection, amendment of the Council's Code of Professional Conduct and the preparation of occupational guidance by the United Kingdom Health Departments, that original 1988 Council statement has been revised on a number of occasions.

3. This latest revision replaces Registrar's Letter 24/1992 which should now be destroyed.

4. This statement, issued as Registrar's Letter 12/1993, has been prepared for the attention and information of nurses, midwives and health visitors, those who employ them and any other interested persons.

Means of transmission

5. The means of transmission of the Human Immunodeficiency Virus (HIV) are well established. Three modes of transmission only have been identified. These are:

*   sexual intercourse (heterosexual or homosexual);
*   blood, blood products, donated organs and semen and
*   mother to child transmission before or during birth and through breast feeding.

There is no evidence to indicate that HIV infection can be transmitted by respiratory or enteric routes, or by casual person-to-person contact in any social, domestic, work, school, hospital, prison or other settings.

The Council's position

6. The 'Code of Professional Conduct for the Nurse, Midwife and Health Visitor' is a statement to the profession of the primacy of the patient's and client's interests. It is for this reason that the introductory paragraph requires each registered nurse, midwife and health visitor to serve the interests of society and, above all, to safeguard the interests of individual patients and clients. It is for the same reason that it goes on to indicate to all persons on the register maintained by the Council that:

'As a registered nurse, midwife or health visitor you are personally accountable for your practice and, in the exercise of your professional accountability, must:

*   act always in such a manner as to promote and safeguard the interests and well-being of patients and clients and
*   ensure that no action or omission on your part, or within your sphere of responsibility, is detrimental to the interests, condition or safety of patients and clients;'

7. Other clauses within the Code are relevant to the subject of this statement, not least Clause 3 with its requirement to improve knowledge and competence, Clause 11 which concerns the environment of care and its physical, psychological and social effects on patients, and any circumstances which could place patients in jeopardy or militate against safe standards of practice and clause 7. The latter clause requires the practitioner, in the exercise of her or his professional accountability to:

'recognise and respect the uniqueness and dignity of each patient and client, and respond to their need for care, irrespective of their ethnic origin, religious beliefs, personal attributes, the nature of their health problems or any other factor.'

8. The Code of Professional Conduct emphasises, therefore, the ethical imperative faced by each individual nurse, midwife and health visitor to serve the interests of patients and clients through all their decisions and actions.

Avoiding infection and the spread of infection

9. Blood and body fluids from all patients pose a potential infection risk and appropriate precautions must be taken.

10. There is only one known authenticated instance of HIV transmission from an infected dentist to a patient. Safety comes through recognising that all practitioners, like all patients, pose a potential infection risk, and all must ensure that high standards of clinical practice are maintained. The promotion of these standards is an important task for in-service education staff and for managers. Such standards require that, if a nurse, midwife or health visitor is infected with HIV, she or he take appropriate precautions to eliminate any possibility of blood or body fluid contamination to a patient. This necessitates the use of well established appropriate precautions to prevent transmission of any infection to a patient and, in some instances, re-assignment of the practitioner to a different area of professional practice.

11. There have been a very limited number of documented incidents of HIV transmission by needle-stick injuries, but the occupational risk of HIV transmission is minimal or even negligible if appropriate practice methods and strategies are diligently followed. These methods of reducing risk, appropriate to the setting, should be introduced and complied with. It must be emphasised, however, that such precautions amount to no more than the good clinical practice which all practitioners have a responsibility to maintain in all situations, irrespective of their serological status and any knowledge they may have of the serological status of their patients.

Security through safe standards

12. Some employers will become aware of a situation in which a nurse, midwife or health visitor has developed AIDS, has an HIV related illness or is HIV positive but not presenting symptoms. In determining their response to such a situation, employers should note the means of transmission stated in paragraph 5 above. Employers should also have regard to the information and guidance contained in the publication 'AIDS – HIV Infected Health Care Workers – Occupational Guidance for Health Care Workers, their Physicians and Employers' issued by the United Kingdom Health Departments in December 1991.

The Council's position in respect of routine HIV testing of health care professionals

13. The Council is opposed to the introduction of routine testing for registered nurses, midwives and health visitors and other health care professionals. Its reasons for such opposition are that:

13.1 it would generate a false sense of security;

13.2 it might lead practitioners to allow standards of personal practice to fall should they, quite falsely, believe no HIV seropositive practitioner to be present and

13.3 given the known sero-conversion time (perhaps 12 or 13 weeks), between acquisition of the infection and the appearance of antibodies in the blood, even frequently repeated testing at great expense could not guarantee that the practitioners involved in the care of patients are not infected, any more than routine testing of patients will provide a guarantee that they are not infected.

14. The Council's position is therefore based on achieving security through safe standards of practice at all times, supplemented by the appropriate re-assignment of practitioners known to be infected with HIV if their role involves the performance of invasive procedures.

The position of occupational health physicians, occupational health departments and employers

15. Occasionally information that such practitioners are infected with HIV will be provided to an employer by an employee. On other occasions practitioners who develop clinical manifestations of HIV infection may consult the Occupational Health Service and a diagnosis of AIDS or HIV related illness may be established and, where deemed absolutely necessary, communicated to the individual's manager in confidence by that service. Given knowledge of the means of transmission, the establishment of such a diagnosis should not automatically lead to dismissal or suspension of the employee on the grounds that they pose an unacceptable infection risk to patients. To simply remove the known HIV positive nurse, midwife or health visitor, or, indeed, any other person in contact with patients, but fail to address the issue of standards promotes a false sense of security and is discriminatory and counter-productive. The particular role and functions of the infected person must be considered. Where she or he is involved in performing invasive procedures re-assignment to an alternative area of practice is necessary.

16. If a practitioner is infected with HIV infection that person must be assessed on an individual basis and regularly. She or he must then act on the advice received, having first sought an urgent specialist second opinion if so desired. As a result, just as re-assignment may be necessary in the interests of patients, the practitioner may require re-assignment in order to protect her or him from opportunistic infections. Such decisions should be made by the Occupational Health Physician and the individual employee's own personal medical advisers with appropriate specialist advice. The obligations of confidentiality owed by Occupational Health staff apply in these circumstances to nurses, midwives and health visitors as they do to other patients. If Occupational Health Departments within Health Service settings share information (other than the conclusion that the employee is either fit or unfit for duty) with managers it will lead to distrust of such services and staff will be likely to avoid using them. The only exception will be that in which the HIV positive practitioner engaged in invasive procedures is not seeking re-assignment voluntarily.

The responsibility of individual practitioners with HIV infection

17. In many situations it should not be regarded as necessary to re-assign such a practitioner deemed fit for work to a different clinical area because, if practising safe

standards that should be practised she or he is not an infection risk to patients. The exception to this must be a situation in which a nurse, midwife or health visitor who is known to be HIV positive is practising in a post which involves contact with sharp instruments or sharp splinters or edges of bone, particularly when the hands are not completely visible. A nurse, midwife or health visitor who knows or suspects herself or himself to be HIV positive must not, therefore, continue to practise in such a situation. She or he must seek specialist medical advice in respect of acceptable areas of practice and must adhere to that advice. Failure to do so will be regarded as a contravention of the Council's Code of Professional Conduct which emphasises the individual's prime responsibility and duty of care to patients.

The responsibility of individual practitioners in respect of other health care professionals known or believed to be infected with HIV

18. In those circumstances in which, for whatever reason, nurses, midwives or health visitors who are infected with HIV do not follow the specialist advice given, the statutory procedures designed to protect patients and clients, including the power to suspend or remove a practitioner's registration, can be brought into operation. Nurses, midwives or health visitors who know or believe a fellow practitioner, whether within their own profession or not, to be infected with HIV but refusing to comply with specialist advice to change her or his area of professional practice should consider the Council's expectations of them set out in the Code of Professional Conduct which apply at all times and in all circumstances. In taking any consequent action they would be fulfilling not only their duty to patients but also their duty to colleagues.

Occupational guidance from the United Kingdom Health Departments

19. Documents available from other sources such as 'AIDS and Employment' from the Department of Employment and the Health and Safety Executive provide useful guidelines. The UK Health Departments' document 'AIDS–HIV Infected Health Care Workers – Occupational Guidance for Health Care Workers, their Physicians and Employers' is an essential source of reference in this context.

The need to disseminate information and avoid discrimination

20. Prevention of the spread of HIV infection is important and is largely dependent on the dissemination of accurate information. Information and education programmes can only succeed if there is a supportive social environment and relevant health services are available. Such a supportive environment includes tolerance and avoids discrimination. Indeed, discrimination will undermine the information and education programme and thus endanger public health.

21. It is the responsibility of every registered nurse, midwife and health visitor to be well informed and equipped to disseminate accurate information and eliminate the mythology surrounding this infection.

22. The Declaration on AIDS Prevention Issues approved by representatives of 149 countries at the conclusion of the World Summit of Ministers of Health on AIDS Prevention held in January 1988 included the following statements:

> 'We emphasise the need in AIDS prevention programmes to protect human rights and dignity. Discrimination against and stigmatisation of HIV infected people and people with AIDS undermine public health and must be avoided.

> We urge the media to fulfil their important social responsibility to provide factual and balanced information to the general public on AIDS and on ways of preventing its spread'.

The Council continues to strongly endorse these important statements.

AIDS – testing, treatment and care of patients and clients

23. On the specific issue of the taking of blood for testing without consent, the Council advises all its practitioners that they expose themselves to the possibility of civil action for damages, of criminal charges of assault or battery or of complaint to their regulatory body (the Council) alleging misconduct if they personally take the blood specimens, and of aiding and abetting an assault or battery if they cooperate in obtaining such specimens. The making of statements aimed at leading patients to believe that blood specimens taken for HIV testing were for some other purpose might also be construed as misconduct in a professional sense. In these respects blood taken for HIV testing is no different from blood taken for other purposes. Consent based on information is regarded as essential where samples of blood are being taken for any laboratory examination.

Justified exceptions to consented testing of patients and clients

24. The Council accepts, however, that there are rare and exceptional circumstances when unconsented testing may legitimately occur. These must be able to be justified as in the interests of the particular patient at the appropriate time, and for no other reason, and only where it is not possible to obtain consent. In adopting this position the Council recognises that improved forms of treatment are now available which, while not offering the prospect of cure, ameliorate the symptoms and assist the quality of remaining life for infected persons.

Anonymous prevalence monitoring

25. The only other exception would be a situation in which, blood having been taken for the purpose of tests ordered by the patient's registered medical practitioner, the

residue of the specimen is rendered anonymous and included in a programme of unlinked testing for HIV approved by the local research ethics committee as part of prevalence testing. Such use of the residue of that specimen could only be regarded as acceptable if the patient (or, where necessary the parent, relative or guardian) had, when able to understand it, been given access to explanatory literature about the anonymous prevalence testing programme, been provided with an opportunity to consider it, assisted where required and had not expressed an objection to the use of the blood for this purpose.

26. In respect of other aspects of the treatment and care of patients known to be or suspected of being infected with the Human Immuno-deficiency Virus, the UKCC reminds those on its register that the first two clauses in its Code of Professional Conduct are a major part of the backcloth against which allegations of misconduct are judged and are not a formula for a practitioner to be selective about the categories of patient for whom he or she will care.

27. Questions in respect of this statement should be directed to the Assistant Registrar, Standards and Ethics, telephone (071) 637 7181, extension 241.

Annexe 2: Anonymous testing for the prevalence of the Human Immuno-deficiency Virus (HIV)

Introduction

1. In November 1988 the Secretary of State for Health announced that a major programme of anonymous unconsented prevalence testing for the Human Immuno-deficiency Virus (HIV) was to take place. This testing programme, co-ordinated by the Public Health Laboratory Service, commenced during 1989.

2. Unconsented anonymous testing means that, blood having been taken for some other specified purpose, the residual specimen is stripped of any identifying factors before being sent for further – in this case HIV – testing. It is unlinked in the respect that the results of the tests will not be able to be associated with an identified patient or client.

3. This annexe sets out the Council's position and provides advice and guidance for all registered nurses, midwives and health visitors on the register. It replaces Council Circular PC89/01 which should now be destroyed. It should be read in conjunction with Annexe 1 to Registrar's Letter 24/1992.

The Council's position and advice to practitioners

4. The Council has determined a set of principles on which agreement to participate in the unlinked anonymous screening programmes should be based. The principles are as follows:

- a specific research protocol for each test group (e.g. pregnant women, newborn infants, G.U.M. clinic patients, etc) must have been approved by the local research ethics committee of the health authority covering the territory within which the blood specimens are to be obtained prior to the commencement of any unlinked anonymous test programme;

- the relevant providers of health care, as an associated part of the research approval, have considered and acted upon any resource implications for their professional staff and pronounced themselves satisfied;
- prior to the commencement of any such approved research programme, those whose blood will or may be used for unlinked anonymous screening have been able to become aware of the monitoring programme (through a general public information campaign supplemented by easily understood posters and leaflets made available in locations where blood will be taken and in the full range of languages appropriate to the known patient/client population) and of their right to state that their blood should not be used for this purpose;
- all registered nurses, midwives and health visitors employed in places from which samples are being obtained for this prevalence testing programme must be made aware of that fact in order:
  (a) that they may answer honestly any questions put to them by patients and clients about the full range of purposes for which blood samples will or may be tested, and
  (b) they may consider how best to act to protect the interests of any patients or clients whose transient or permanent condition results in an inability to consider and/or understand the available information literature.
- that there must be no possible detriment to those whose blood either is or is not screened as part of the unlinked anonymous HIV screening programmes;
- that any patient or client who objects to participation in the test programme should have his or her wishes respected fully and should not:
  (a) be discriminated against in any way;
  (b) be identified as being higher risk than those who have not objected and
  (c) have required treatment withheld or suffer any other detriment.
- The amount of blood taken on any occasion should be only that which would normally be taken for the specific tests ordered by the patient's medical practitioner.

5. The Council hopes this advice will assist nurses, midwives and health visitors. The Council also urges members of local research ethics committees, prior to the approval of the research protocols, to note the contents of the guidance it has provided for nurses, midwives and health visitors in paragraph 4 of this paper and to satisfy themselves that the conditions will be met.

Questions in respect of the contents of this paper should be directed to the Assistant Registrar, Standards and Ethics on telephone (071) 637 7181, extension 241.

Appendix 9 Standards for records and record-keeping*

Introduction

1. The important activity of making and keeping records is an essential and integral part of care and not a distraction from its provision. There is, however, substantial evidence to indicate that inadequate and inappropriate record keeping concerning the care of patients and clients neglects their interests through:

1.1 impairing continuity of care;
1.2 introducing discontinuity of communication between staff;
1.3 creating the risk of medication or other treatment being duplicated or omitted;
1.4 failing to focus attention on early signs of deviation from the norm and
1.5 failing to place on record significant observations and conclusions.

2. For these reasons the Council has prepared this standards paper to assist its practitioners to fulfil the expectations it has of them and to serve more effectively the interests of their patients and clients.

---

* Originally published as *Standards for Records and Record-keeping*, by the United Kingdom Central Council for Nursing, Midwifery and Health Visiting, April 1993.

3. To meet the standards set out in this document is to honour, in this aspect of practice, the Council's expectation (set out in the 'Code of Professional Conduct for the Nurse, Midwife and Health Visitor') (1) that:

'As a registered nurse, midwife or health visitor you are personally accountable for your practice and, in the exercise of your professional accountability, must:

1. act always in such a manner as to promote and safeguard the interests and well-being of patients and clients;
2. ensure that no action or omission on your part, or within your sphere of responsibility, is detrimental to the interests, condition or safety of patients and clients;'

The purpose of records

4. The purpose of records created and maintained by registered nurses, midwives and health visitors is to:

4.1 provide accurate, current, comprehensive and concise information concerning the condition and care of the patient or client and associated observations;
4.2 provide a record of any problems that arise and the action taken in response to them;
4.3 provide evidence of care required, intervention by professional practitioners and patient or client responses;
4.4 include a record of any factors (physical, psychological or social) that appear to affect the patient or client;
4.5 record the chronology of events and the reasons for any decisions made;
4.6 support standard setting, quality assessment and the audit and
4.7 provide a baseline record against which improvement or deterioration may be judged.

The importance of records

5. Effective record keeping by nurses, midwives and health visitors is a means of:

5.1 communicating with others and describing what has been observed or done;
5.2 identifying the discrete role played by nurses, midwives and health visitors in care;
5.3 organising communication and the dissemination of information among the members of the team providing care for a patient or client;
5.4 demonstrating the chronology of events, the factors observed and the response to care and treatment and
5.5 demonstrating the properly considered clinical decisions relating to patient care.

Standards for records: key features

6. In addition to fulfilling the purposes set out in paragraph 4, properly made and maintained records will:

6.1 be made as soon as possible after the events to which they relate;

6.2 identify factors which jeopardise standards or place the patient or client at risk;

6.3 provide evidence of the need, in specific cases, for practitioners with special knowledge and skills;

6.4 aid patient or client involvement in their own care;

6.5 provide 'protection' for staff against any future complaint which may be made and

6.6 be written, wherever possible, in terms which the patient or client will be able to understand.

Standards for records: ethical aspects

7. A correctly made record honours the ethical concepts on which good practice is based and demonstrates the basis of the professional and clinical decisions made.

8. A basic tenet of records and record keeping is that those who make, access and use the records understand the ethical concepts of professional practice which relate to them. These will include, in particular, the need to protect confidentiality, to ensure true consent and to assist patients and clients to make informed decisions.

9. The originator will ensure that the entry in a record that she or he makes is totally accurate and based on respect for truth and integrity.

Standards for records: recording decisions on resuscitation

10. It is essential that the records on the subject of resuscitation accurately and explicitly reflect any wishes of a patient expressed when legally and mentally competent or those of the patient's next of kin or other significant persons when those circumstances do not apply. This is particularly important when a patient has expressed a wish not to be resuscitated. This is to say that the wishes of a patient, made and expressed when she or he was legally and mentally competent, should be respected.

11. Where the views of the patient and/or those of 'significant others' in relationship to them have not been recorded, but a decision not to resuscitate has been made on clinical grounds by the relevant medical staff, this also should be entered in writing in the medical record and the entry must be signed and dated by the responsible registered medical practitioner. Wherever possible this should be a team decision which, though made by the medical staff, would take the informed views of the nursing staff (and, where applicable, midwifery staff) into account. The patient's family or other significant personal carers should, wherever possible, be consulted.

12. Whether the circumstances in paragraph 10 or paragraph 11 apply, the entry must be able to be located easily and quickly in the medical record and must include a time limit for which it is to apply before review. Nursing and midwifery staff must not enter this decision in the nursing or midwifery record unless it has first been entered in the medical record in the way described in paragraph 11 above.

Standards for records: essential elements

13. In order to fulfil the purpose stated in paragraph 4, to be effective and to meet the standards set out above, records must:

13.1 be written legibly and indelibly;

13.2 be clear and unambiguous;

13.3 be accurate in each entry as to date and time;

13.4 ensure that alterations are made by scoring out with a single line followed by the initialled, dated and timed correct entry;

13.5 ensure that additions to existing entries are individually dated, timed and signed;

13.6 not include abbreviations, meaningless phrases and offensive subjective statements unrelated to the patient's care and associated observations;

13.7 not allow the use of initials for major entries and, where their use is allowed for other entries, ensure that local arrangements for identifying initials and signatures exist and

13.8 not include entries made in pencil or blue ink, the former carrying the risk of erasure and the latter (where photocopying is required) of poor quality reproduction.

14. In summary, the record:

14.1 is directed primarily to serving the interests and care of the patient or client to whom the record relates and enabling the provision of care, the prevention of disease and the promotion of health and

14.2 will demonstrate the chronology of events and all significant consultations, assessments, observations, decisions, interventions and outcomes.

15. In hospitals or other institutions providing care, a local index record of signatures should be held. Where initials are regarded as acceptable for any purpose, these also should feature in the index, together with the full name in printed form.

The 'process approach' or 'planned individualised care' approach to nursing and midwifery care

16. Given the nature of care plans and records associated with the planned individual care approach, this important aspect of records must satisfy the criteria specified in paragraphs 4 to 15 above. The 'process' approach assists a systematic approach to practice. It also provides a framework for the documentation of that practice. The term

therefore describes the continuum of distinctly separate yet interrelated activities of practice, assessment, planning, implementation and evaluation of care.

17. Meticulous and timely documentation provides evidence of the practitioner's actions, the patient's or client's response to those actions and the plans and goals which direct the care of the patient or client.

18. The preparation and completion of care plans will, therefore, in addition to satisfying the criteria set out in paragraphs 4 to 15 above, demonstrate that each step in what is a continuing process has been followed and provides the basis for further goal settings and actions.

19. The making of entries will be organised so that:

> 19.1 a measurable, up to date, description of the condition of the patient or client and the care delivered can be easily communicated to others and
> 19.2 the plan and other records complement each other.

20. The practitioner, in applying the process and using the plan, will distinguish between those matters which must be recorded in advance (such as planning and goals) and those which can only be current or slightly retrospective (such as observations and evaluation). Equally, the distinction must be made between entries on papers, (for example, planning forms) which may not be locally retained, and other forms which are part of the clinical nursing or midwifery care records which record changes and events and must be retained.

The legal status of records and its implications

21. Any document which records any aspect of the care of a patient or client can be required as evidence before a court of law or before the Preliminary Proceedings Committee or Professional Conduct Committee of the Council (the UKCC) or other similar regulatory bodies for the health care professions including the General Medical Council, the comparable body to the UKCC for the medical profession.

22. For this, in addition to their primary purpose of serving the interests of the patient or client, the records should provide:

> 22.1 a comprehensive picture of care delivered, associated outcomes and other relevant information;
> 22.2 pertinent information about the condition of the patient or client at any given time and the measures taken to respond to identified need;
> 22.3 evidence that the practitioner's common law duty of care has been understood and honoured and
> 22.4 a record of the arrangements made for continuity of a patient's care on discharge from hospital.

23. Particular care will be exercised and frequent record entries made where patients or clients present complex problems, show deviation from the norm, require more

intensive care than normal, are confused and disoriented or in other ways give cause for concern.

24. In situations where the condition of the patient or client is apparently unchanging, local agreement will be necessary in respect of the maximum time allowed to elapse between entries in patient or client records and the nature of those entries. All exceptional events, however, must be recorded and the Council will expect nurses, midwives and health visitors to exercise suitable judgement about entries in the record.

25. Ownership of the contents of a record would normally be seen as residing with the originator of any particular entry. In practice, however, where the professional practitioner is a salaried employee of the health services, the question of ownership turns on ownership of the document on which the record is made. Ownership does not rest with the patient or client, as the creation of law to grant patient or client access in certain circumstances clearly reveals.

26. Midwives must ensure that they are aware of and comply with the requirements in respect of records set out in the Council's 'Midwives Rules'.

27. It is essential that members of the professions must be involved in local discussions to determine policies concerning the retention or disposal of all or any part of records which they or their colleagues make. Such policies must be determined with recognition of any aspects of law affecting the duration of retention and make explicit the period for which specific categories of records are to be retained. Any documents which form part of the chronological clinical care record should be retained.

Retention of obstetric records

28. All essential obstetric records (such as those recording the care of a mother and baby during pregnancy, labour and the puerperium, including all test results, prescription forms and records of medicines administered) must be retained. Decisions concerning those records which are to be regarded as essential must not be made at local level without involving senior medical practitioners concerned with the provision of maternity and neo-natal services and a senior practising midwife.

29. Those involved in determining policy at local level must ensure that the records retained are comprehensive (in that they include both hospital, community midwifery records and those held by mothers during pregnancy and the puerperium) and are such as to facilitate any investigations required as a result of action brought under the Congenital Disabilities (Civil Liabilities) Act 1976 or any other litigation.

Patient or client held records

30. The Council is in favour of patients and clients being given custody of their own health care records in circumstances where it is appropriate. Patient or client held records

help to emphasise and make clear the practitioner's responsibility to the patient or client by sharing any information held or assessments made and illustrate the involvement of the patient or client in their own care.

31. Evidence from those places where this has become the practice indicates that there are no substantial drawbacks and considerable ethical benefits to be derived from patients or clients having custody of their records. This immediately disposes of any difficulties concerning access and reinforces the discipline that should apply to making entries in records.

32. A small number of instances will inevitably arise, where a system of patient or client held records is in operation, in which the health professional concerned will feel that her or his particular concerns or anxieties (for example about the possibility of child abuse) require that a supplementary record be created and held by the practitioner. To make and keep such a record can, in appropriate circumstances, be regarded as good practice. It should be the exception rather than the norm, however, and should not extend to keeping full duplicate records unless in the most unusual circumstances.

Patient or client access to records

33. With effect from 1 November 1991, patients and clients have had the right of access to manual records about themselves made from that date as a result of the Access to Health Records Act 1990 coming into effect. This has brought such records into line with computer held records which have been required to be accessible to patients since the Data Protection Act 1984 became operative.

34. These Acts give the right of access, but the health professional most directly concerned (which, in certain cases will be the nurse, midwife or health visitor) is permitted to withhold information which she or he believes might cause serious harm to the physical or mental health of the patient or client or which would identify a third party. The system for dealing with applications for access is explained in the 'Guide to the Access to Health Records Act 1990', published by the Government Health Departments (2).

35. The Council fully supports the principle of open access to records contained in these Acts, and the guidance notes concerning their operation, and trusts that access will not be unreasonably denied or limited.

36. All practitioners who create records or make entries in any records must be aware of the rights of the patient or client in this regard, give careful consideration to the language and terminology employed and recognise the positive advantages of greater trust and confidence of patients and clients in the professions that can result from this development.

Shared records

37. The Council recognises the advantages of 'shared' records in which all health professionals involved in the care and treatment of an individual make entries in a single record

and in accordance with a broadly agreed local protocol. These are seen as particularly valuable in midwifery practice. The Council supports this practice where circumstances lend themselves to it and where relevant preparatory work has been undertaken. Each practitioner's contribution to such records should be seen as of equal importance. This reflects the collaborative and cooperative working within the health care team on which emphasis is laid by the Council in its 'Code of Professional Conduct for the Nurse, Midwife and Health Visitor'. The same right of access to records by the patient or client exists where a system of shared records is in use. It is essential, therefore, that local agreement is reached to identify the lead professional to be responsible for considering requests from patients and clients for access in particular circumstances.

Computer held records

38. The application of computer technology should not be allowed to breach the important principle of confidentiality. To say this is not to oppose the use of computer held records, whether specific to one profession or shared between professions. Practitioners must satisfy themselves about the security of the system used and ascertain which categories of staff have access to the records to which they are expected to contribute important, personal and confidential information.

39. Where computer technology is employed it must provide a means of maintaining or enhancing service to patients or clients and avoid the risk of inadvertent breaches of confidentiality. It must not impose a limit on the amount of text a practitioner may enter if the consequence is that it impedes the compilation of a sufficiently comprehensive record. The case for it has to be considered in association with the questions of access, patient or client held records, shared records and audit. Local protocols must include means of authenticating an entry in the absence of a written signature and must indicate clearly the identity of the originator of that entry.

The practitioner's accountability for entries made by others

40. Irrespective of the type of record or the form of medium employed to create and access it, the registered nurse, midwife or health visitor must recognise her or his personal accountability for entries to records made by students or others under their supervision.

Summary of the principles underpinning records and record-keeping

41. The following principles must apply:

    41.1 the record is directed primarily to serving the interests of the patient or client to whom it relates and enabling the provision of care, the prevention of disease and the promotion of health;

41.2 the record demonstrates the accurate chronology of events and all significant consultations, assessments, observations, decisions, interventions and outcomes;

41.3 the record and the activity of record keeping is an integral and essential part of care and not a distraction from its provision;

41.4 the record is clear and unambiguous;

41.5 the record contains entries recording facts and observations written at the time of, or soon after, the events described;

41.6 the record provides a safe and effective means of communication between members of the health care team and supports continuity of care;

41.7 the record demonstrates that the practitioner's duty of care has been fulfilled;

41.8 the systems for record keeping exclude unauthorised access and breaches of confidentiality and

41.9 the record is constructed and completed in such a manner as to facilitate the monitoring of standards, audit, quality assurance and the investigation of complaints.

42. Enquiries in respect of this Council paper should be directed to the:

Registrar and Chief Executive
United Kingdom Central Council
for Nursing, Midwifery and
Health Visiting
23 Portland Place
London
W1N 3AF

References

1. 'Code of Professional Conduct for the Nurse, Midwife and Health Visitor'; UKCC, London, 1992.
2. 'Access to Health Records Act 1990: a Guide for the NHS'; Government Health Departments, 1990.

Appendix 10 The scope of professional practice*

Introduction

1. The practice of nursing, midwifery and health visiting requires the application of knowledge and the simultaneous exercise of judgement and skill. Practice takes place in a context of continuing change and development. Such change and development may result from advances in research leading to improvements in treatment and care, from alterations to the provision of health and social care services, as a result of changes in local policies and as a result of new approaches to professional practice. Practice must, therefore, be sensitive, relevant and responsive to the needs of individual patients and clients and have the capacity to adjust, where and when appropriate, to changing circumstances.

2. Education and experience form the foundation on which nurses, midwives and health visitors exercise judgement and skill, these, naturally, being developed and refined over time. The range of responsibilities which fall to individual nurses, midwives and health visitors should be related to their personal experience, education and skill. This range

* Originally published as *The Scope of Professional Practice*, by the United Kingdom Central Council for Nursing, Midwifery and Health Visiting, June 1992.

of responsibilities is described here as the 'scope of professional practice' and this paper sets out the Council's principles on which any adjustment to the scope of professional practice should be based.

Education for professional practice

3. Just as practice must remain dynamic, sensitive, relevant and responsive to the changing needs of patients and clients, so too must education for practice. Pre-registration education prepares nurses, midwives and health visitors for safe practice at the point of registration. The pre-registration curriculum will continue to change over time to absorb relevant changes in care as advances are made. Pre-registration education is, therefore, a foundation for professional practice and a means of equipping nurses, midwives and health visitors with the necessary knowledge and skills to assume responsibility as registered practitioners. This foundation education alone, however, cannot effectively meet the changing and complex demands of the range of modern health care. Post-registration education equips practitioners with additional and more specialist skills necessary to meet the special needs of patients and clients. There is a broad range of post-registration provision and the Council regards adequate and effective provision of quality education as a pre-requisite of quality care.

Registration and the Code of Professional Conduct for the nurse, midwife and health visitor

4. The act of registration by the Council confers on individual nurses, midwives and health visitors the legal right to practise and to use the title 'registered'. From the point of registration, each practitioner is subject to the Council's Code of Professional Conduct and accountable for his or her practice and conduct. The Code provides a statement of the values of the professions and establishes the framework within which practitioners practise and conduct themselves. The act of registration and the expectations stated in the Code are central to the Council's key role in regulating the standards of the professions in the interest of patients and clients and of society as a whole.

5. Once registered, each nurse, midwife and health visitor remains subject to the Code and ultimately accountable to the Council for his or her actions and omissions. This position applies regardless of the employment circumstances and regardless of whether or not individuals are actively engaged in practice. This position will only change if the decision is made by the Council (through clearly established legal processes related to professional misconduct or unfitness to practise due to illness) to remove a name from the Council's register. This reflects the key, central role which the registration process plays in maintaining standards in the public interest. On the specific question of employment of nurses in the personal social services in general and the residential care sector in particular, the Council recognises that there are ambiguities. These are addressed in paragraphs 20 and 21 of this paper.

The Code of Professional Conduct and the scope of professional practice

6. The Code includes a number of explicit clauses which relate to changes to the scope of practice in nursing, midwifery and health visiting. These clauses are:

'As a registered nurse, midwife or health visitor you are personally accountable for your practice and, in the exercise of your professional accountability, must:

1. act always in such a manner as to promote and safeguard the interests and well-being of patients and clients;
2. ensure that no action or omission on your part, or within your sphere of responsibility, is detrimental to the interests, condition or safety of patients and clients;
3. maintain and improve your professional knowledge and competence;
4. acknowledge any limitations in your knowledge and competence and decline any duties or responsibilities unless able to perform them in a safe and skilled manner.'

7. The Code, therefore, provides a firm bedrock upon which decisions about adjustments to the scope of professional practice can be made. There are, however, important distinctions relating to the scope of practice in nursing, in midwifery and in health visiting. These are described in the paragraphs that follow the Council's principles for adjusting the scope of practice. These principles apply to the practice of nursing, midwifery and health visiting addressed later in this paper and to any application of complementary or alternative and other therapies by nurses, midwives or health visitors.

Principles for adjusting the scope of practice

8. Although the practices of nursing, midwifery and health visiting differ widely, the same principles apply to the scope of practice in each of these professions. The following principles are based upon the Council's Code of Professional Conduct and, in particular, on the emphasis which the Code places upon knowledge, skill, responsibility and accountability. The principles which should govern adjustments to the scope of professional practice are those which follow.

9. The registered nurse, midwife or health visitor:

9.1 must be satisfied that each aspect of practice is directed to meeting the needs and serving the interests of the patient or client;

9.2 must endeavour always to achieve, maintain and develop knowledge, skill and competence to respond to those needs and interests;

9.3 must honestly acknowledge any limits of personal knowledge and skill and take steps to remedy any relevant deficits in order effectively and appropriately to meet the needs of patients and clients;

9.4 must ensure that any enlargement or adjustment of the scope of personal professional practice must be achieved without compromising or fragmenting existing aspects of professional practice and care and that the requirements of the Council's Code of Professional Conduct are satisfied throughout the whole area of practice;

9.5 must recognise and honour the direct or indirect personal accountability borne for all aspects of professional practice and

9.6 must, in serving the interests of patients and clients and the wider interests of society, avoid any inappropriate delegation to others which compromises those interests.

10. These principles for practice should enhance trust and confidence within a health care team and promote further the important collaborative work between medical and nursing, midwifery and health visiting practitioners upon which good practice and care depends.

11. The Council recognises that care by registered nurses, midwives and health visitors is provided in health care, social care and domestic settings. Patients and clients require skilled care from registered practitioners and support staff require direction and supervision from these same practitioners. These matters are directly concerned with standards of care. This paper, therefore, also addresses the matter of the 'identified' practitioner, practice in the personal social services and residential care sector and support for professional practice.

The scope and 'extended practice' of nursing

12. The practice of nursing has traditionally been based on the premise that pre-registration education equips the nurse to perform at a certain level and to encompass a particular range of activities. It is also based on the premise that any widening of that range and enhancement of the nurse's practice requires 'official' extension of that role by certification.

13. The Council considers that the terms 'extended' or 'extending' roles which have been associated with this system are no longer suitable since they limit, rather than extend, the parameters of practice. As a result, many practitioners have been prevented from fulfilling their potential for the benefit of patients. The Council also believes that a concentration on 'activities' can detract from the importance of holistic nursing care. The Council has therefore determined the principles set out in paragraphs 8 to 10 inclusive to provide the basis for ensuring that practice remains dynamic and is able readily and appropriately to adjust to meet changing care needs.

14. The reality is that the practice of nursing, and education for that practice, will continue to be shaped by developments in care and treatment, and by other events which influence it. This equally applies to midwifery and health visiting. In order to bring into proper focus the professional responsibility and consequent accountability of individual practitioners, it is the Council's principles for practice rather than certificates for tasks which should form the basis for adjustments to the scope of practice.

The scope of midwifery practice

15. The position in relation to midwifery practice is set out in the Council's Midwife's Code of Practice. This indicates that it is the individual midwife's responsibility to maintain and develop the competence which she has acquired during her training, recognising the sphere of practice in which she is deemed to be equipped to practise with safety and competence. It also indicates that, while some developments in midwifery become an essential and integral part of the role of every midwife (and are subsequently incorporated into pre-registration education), other developments may require particular midwives to acquire new skills because of the particular settings in which they are practising. The importance of local policies which are in accord with the Council's policies and standards and the guidelines issued by the National Boards for Nursing, Midwifery and Health Visiting is self-evident. The importance of the midwife practising outside the area of her employing authority or outside the National Health Service discussing the full scope of her practice with her supervisor of midwives is emphasised in the Midwife's Code of Practice.

16. It can be seen from this position that it is accepted by the Council that some developments in midwifery care can become an integral part of the role of *all* midwives and other developments may become part of the role of some midwives. The Council believes that the Midwife's Code of Practice, cited above, and the Code of Professional Conduct, together provide key principles to underpin the scope of midwifery practice. These are now supplemented by those stated in paragraphs 8 to 10 inclusive of this paper.

The scope of health visiting practice

17. The position of health visiting differs from that of nursing and midwifery, as there are frequent occasions when the full contribution of health visitors may not find expression where it is most needed. There is, for example, often a concentration on the role of the health visitor in relation to those in the under-five age group at the expense of other groups in the community who need, and would benefit from, the special preparation and skill of health visitors. These circumstances have the effect of constraining practice and limiting the degree to which individuals and communities are able to benefit from the knowledge and skill of health visitors. There is merit in allowing health visitors, where they judge it to be appropriate, to use the full range of their skills in response to needs identified in the pursuit of their health visiting practice. To single out any aspect of practice would be unwise but, where health and nursing need is identified, the health visitor is well placed to determine what intervention may be necessary and able to draw on both her nursing and health visiting education.

18. The community setting of health visiting practice, the relationship between numerous agencies and services and the health visitor's professional relationship with clients and their families are factors which must be taken into consideration. The health visitor,

in all aspects of her practice, is subject to the Council's Code of Professional Conduct and should also satisfy the requirements of paragraphs 8 to 10 inclusive of this paper.

Practice and the 'identified' nurse, midwife and health visitor

19. The Council recognises that, in a growing number of settings, patients and clients will be in the care of an 'identified' practitioner. The practitioner may be identified as the 'named' practitioner or as the primary, associate or sole practitioner providing nursing, midwifery or health visiting care. In such roles, individuals assume key responsibility for coordinating and supervising the delivery of care, drawing on the general and special resources of colleagues where appropriate. Professional practice naturally involves recognising and accepting accountability for these matters. The Council expects that practitioners will recognise the need to provide all necessary support for colleagues and ensure that practice is underpinned by the required knowledge and skill. The Council equally expects that practitioners identified in one of these ways will be fully prepared for, and supported, in this key role.

Practice in the personal social services and residential care sector

20. The Council recognises that the community nursing services have a duty to provide a nursing service to those in need of nursing care in the personal social services and residential care sector. Registered nurses who are employed in this sector, whether in homes or in the provision of other services, remain accountable to the Council and subject to the Council's Code of Professional Conduct, even if their posts do not require nursing qualifications. In this regard, as explained in paragraph 5 of this paper, the position of such nurses is the same as that of nurses engaged in direct professional nursing practice.

21. The Council requires that registered nurses employed in such circumstances will use their judgement and discretion to identify the nursing needs of residents and others for whom they may have responsibility, and will comply with any requirements of the Council. The Council expects that employers will recognise the advantages to the personal social services and residential care sector which result from the employment of registered nurses.

Support for professional practice

22. Nurses, midwives and health visitors require support in their work. In institutional and community settings, a range of support staff form part of the team. The development of the health care assistant role is linked with a form of vocational training. The Council does not have a direct role in this training, but recognises that this

development has an impact upon aspects of care and on the practice and standard of nursing, midwifery and health visiting, for which the Council is responsible.

23. The Council's position in relation to support roles is as follows:

23.1 health care assistants to registered nurses, midwives and health visitors must work under the direction and supervision of those registered practitioners;

23.2 registered nurses, midwives and health visitors must remain accountable for assessment, planning and standards of care and for determining the activity of their support staff;

23.3 health care assistants must not be allowed to work beyond their level of competence;

23.4 continuity of care and appropriate skill/staff mix is important, so health care assistants should be integral members of the caring team;

23.5 standards of care must be safeguarded and the need for patients and clients, across the spectrum of health care, to receive skilled professional nursing, midwifery and health visiting assessment and care must be recognised as of primary importance;

23.6 health care assistants with the desire and ability to progress to professional education should be encouraged to obtain vocational qualifications, some of which may be approved by the Council as acceptable entry criteria into programmes of professional education and

23.7 registered nurses, midwives and health visitors should be involved in these developments so that the support role can be designed to ensure that professional skills are used most appropriately for the benefit of patients and clients.

Conclusion

24. The principles set out in paragraphs 8 to 10 inclusive of this paper should form the basis for any decisions relating to adjustments to the scope of practice. These principles should replace the system of certification for specific tasks. They provide a realistic, effective and rational approach to adjustments to professional practice.

25. This change has consequences for managers of clinical practice and professional leaders of nursing, midwifery and health visiting, who must ensure that local policies and procedures are based upon the principles set out in this paper and in the Council's Code of Professional Conduct. Any local arrangements must ensure that registered nurses, midwives and health visitors are assisted to undertake, and are enabled to fulfil, any suitable adjustments to their scope of practice.

26. This statement sets out the Council's position relating to the scope of professional practice of the professions it regulates, to the 'identified' practitioner, to practice in the residential care sector and to support staff. The Council hopes that this statement, and the principles which it sets out, will provide a clear framework for the logical and desirable development of practice and for the management of practice and care teams. The framework provides for greater flexibility in practice and for enhancing the

contribution to care of nurses, midwives and health visitors. Above all, the framework and the principles reflect the personal responsibility and accountability of individual practitioners, entrusted by the Council to protect and improve standards of care.

27. Enquiries in respect of this Council paper should be directed to the:

Registrar and Chief Executive
United Kingdom Central Council for Nursing, Midwifery and Health Visiting
23 Portland Place
London
W1N 3AF

Appendix 11 Congenital Disabilities (Civil Liability) Act 1976[*]

1 Civil liability to child born disabled

(1) If a child is born disabled as the result of such an occurrence before its birth as is mentioned in subsection (2) below, and a person (other than the child's own mother) is under this section answerable to the child in respect of the occurrence, the child's disabilities are to be regarded as damage resulting from the wrongful act of that person and actionable accordingly at the suit of the child.

(2) An occurrence to which this section applies is one which

   (a) affected either parent of the child in his or her ability to have a normal, healthy child; or
   (b) affected the mother during her pregnancy; or affected her or the child in the course of its birth so that the child is born with disabilities which would not otherwise have been present.

(3) Subject to the following subsections, a person (here referred to as 'the defendant') is answerable to the child if he was liable in tort to the parent or would, if sued in due time, have been so; and it is no answer that there could not have been such liability

[*] 1976 c.28; reproduced by permission of HMSO.

because the parent suffered no actionable injury, if there was a breach of legal duty which, accompanied by injury, would have given rise to the liability.

(4) In the case of an occurrence preceding the time of conception, the defendant is not answerable to the child if at that time either or both of the parents knew the risk of their child being born disabled (that is to say, the particular risk created by the occurrence); but should it be the child's father who is the defendant, this subsection does not apply if he knew of the risk and the mother did not.

(5) The defendant is not answerable to the child, for anything he did or omitted to do when responsible in a professional capacity for treating or advising the parent, if he took reasonable care having due regard to then received professional opinion applicable to the particular class of case; but this does not mean that he is answerable only because he departed from received opinion.

(6) Liability to the child under this section may be treated as having been excluded or limited by contract made with the parent affected, to the same extent and subject to the same restrictions as liability in the parent's own case; and a contract term which could have been set up by the defendant in an action by the parent, so as to exclude or limit his liability to him or her, operates in the defendant's favour to the same, but no greater, extent in an action under this section by the child.

(7) If in the child's action under this section it is shown that the parent affected shared the responsibility for the child being born disabled, the damages are to be reduced to such extent as the court thinks just and equitable having regard to the extent of the parent's responsibility.

2 Liability of woman driving when pregnant

A woman driving a motor vehicle when she knows (or ought reasonably to know) herself to be pregnant is to be regarded as being under the same duty to take care for the safety of her unborn child as the law imposes on her with respect to the safety of other people; and if in consequence of her breach of that duty her child is born with disabilities which would not otherwise have been present, those disabilities are to be regarded as damage resulting from her wrongful act and actionable accordingly at the suit of the child.

3 Disabled birth due to radiation

(1) Section 1 of this Act does not affect the operation of the Nuclear Installations Act 1965 as to liability for, and compensation in respect of, injury or damage caused by occurrences involving nuclear matter or the emission of ionising radiations.

(2) For the avoidance of doubt anything which

    (a) affects a man in his ability to have a normal, healthy child; or
    (b) affects a woman in that ability or so affect her when she is pregnant that her child is born with disabilities which would not otherwise have been present

is an injury for the purpose of that Act.

(3) If a child is born disabled as the result of an injury to either of its parents caused in breach of a duty imposed by any of sections 7 to 11 of that Act (nuclear site licensees and others to secure that nuclear incidents do not cause injury to persons, etc.), the child's disabilities are to be regarded under the subsequent provisions of that Act (compensation and other matters) as injuries caused on the same occasion, and by the same breach of duty, as was the injury to the parent.

(4) As respects compensation to the child, section 13 (6) of that Act (contributory fault of person injured by radiation) is to be applied as if the reference there to fault were to the fault of the parent.

(5) Compensation is not payable in the child's case if the injury to the parent preceded the time of the child's conception and at that time either or both of the parents know the risk of their child being born disabled (that is to say, the particular risk created by the injury).

4 Interpretation and other supplementary provisions

(1) References in this Act to a child being born disabled or with disabilities are to its being born with any deformity, disease or abnormality, including predisposition (whether or not susceptible of immediate prognosis) to physical or mental defect in the future.

(2) In this Act

    (a) 'born' means born alive (the moment of a child's birth being when it first has a life separate from its mother), and 'birth' has a corresponding meaning; and

    (b) 'motor vehicle' means a mechanically propelled vehicle intended or adapted for use on roads.

(3) Liability to a child under section 1 or 2 of this Act is to be regarded

    (a) as respects all its incidents and any matters arising or to arise out of it; and

    (b) subject to any contrary context or intention, for the purpose of construing references in enactments and documents to personal or bodily injuries and cognate matters

as liability for personal injuries sustained by the child immediately after its birth.

(4) No damages shall be recoverable under either of those sections in respect of any loss of expectation of life, nor shall any such loss be taken into account in the compensation payable in respect of a child under the Nuclear Installations Act 1965 as extended by section 3, unless (in either case) the child lives for at least 48 hours.

(5) This Act applies in respect of birth after (but not before) its passing, and in respect of any such birth it replaces any law in force before its passing, whereby a person could be liable to a child in respect of disabilities with which it might be born; but in section 1 (3) of this Act the expression 'liable in tort' does not include any reference to liability by virtue of this Act, or to liability by virtue of any such law.

(6) References to the Nuclear Installations Act 1965 are to that Act as amended; and for the purposes of section 28 of that Act (power by Order in Council to extend the Act to territories outside the United Kingdom) section 3 of this Act is to be treated as if it were a provision of that Act.

5 Crown application

This Act binds the Crown. (*N.B. The Act was passed on 22nd July, 1976)*

Appendix 12 Guidelines for staff on the death of a patient in hospital

Contents

Issued by Cardiff Royal Infirmary and West Wing and reproduced with permission of the Unit Administrator.

1 When death is expected

It is essential that as much warning as possible should be given to relatives if the condition of the patient is causing concern. The name and address and telephone number of the next of kin should have been recorded when the patient was admitted. The Nurse should arrange for Medical Staff to give the next of kin and other relatives full information about the patient's condition. It is the duty of the Doctor to ensure this information is given to relatives.

2 Recording the wishes of a patient

(a) Making a Will

(i) If the patient wishes to make a Will, he should be encouraged to arrange for his own Solicitor to come into hospital. The Administrator should have a list of Solicitors who are prepared to assist patients in the making of Wills, at the patient's expense.

(ii) In situations of urgency, in the absence of a Solicitor, the Administrator should arrange for a Will to be drawn up, signed and witnessed by two independent persons. Doctor's opinion should be obtained on the mental state of the patient at the time of signing the Will to ensure the patient is competent.

Nurses should not be involved in the witnessing of Wills except in extreme emergencies.

(iii) If the patient lacks the competence to make a Will on the grounds of permanent incapacity e.g. Mental Disorder, and the relatives wish one to be made, they should be advised to apply to the Court of Protection.

(b) Donating human organs

A patient can either in writing, or by word of mouth before two or more witnesses during the last illness, express a wish that his body or parts be used for Therapeutic, Medical

Education or research purposes after his death. The Administrator should make appropriate arrangements if this request is made known. *(See also section 3)*

(c) Leaving a body for medical research

A patient who wishes to do this should be told to send a written statement to H.M. Inspector of Anatomy, DHSS, Eileen House, 80–94 Newington Causeway, London SE1. Telephone: 01 703 6380, Ext 3743. A record of this intention should also be kept in the patient's notes.

3 Organ donation and transplant procedure

Where the patient has indicated his wish either in writing or by word of mouth *(see section 2(b))*, the person in lawful possession of the body should check to ensure that he did not withdraw this intention before giving permission for organs to be taken for transplant. It is usually customary to check that the relatives do not object, although there is no legal duty under the Human Tissue Act 1961 in these circumstances.

If the case is one that is reportable to the Coroner or likely to be reportable, his consent must be sought before proceeding with any organ or tissue removal for donation. There may be other situations where the patient has not expressed a view in accordance with the Act, but where certain organs are suitable for transplant, the Medical Staff should approach the relatives with consideration and empathy. The suggestion may come as a consolation in their grief. In these circumstances, the person in lawful possession of the body must make such reasonable enquiry as may be practicable to ensure

(1) The deceased did not express any objection to his body being so dealt with after his death.
(2) The surviving spouse or any surviving relative of the deceased does not object to the body being so dealt with.

A Code of Practice issued by the DHSS in 1979 sets out the procedure to be followed when organs are to be taken for transplant. It covers the procedure to determine whether the patient is clinically dead and specifies that two Doctors must certify brain death of the potential donor and independently complete a check list. One Doctor must be a Consultant or his deputy of at least five years or more since registration, with experience in these cases. Neither of these two Doctors should be a member of the transplant team and the results of the examination should be recorded in the case notes relating to the dead person.

4 When a patient dies

(1) Where death appears to have occurred the Senior Nurse should contact the Doctor and ask the Doctor to attend as soon as possible. The body should not be removed until the Doctor has verified the fact of death.

(2) Next of kin and other relatives should be notified in as considerate a way as possible.

(3) The Doctor should complete where possible, the Medical Certificate of the cause of death. (*See section 12 where this is not possible.*)

5 Caring for the bereaved

(1) The relatives should be given the opportunity to discuss with the Doctor the cause of death.

(2) Privacy and quiet surroundings should be provided for staff to offer sympathy and comfort.

(3) Arrangements should be made, if desired, for relatives to view the body in the Viewing Room of the Mortuary, or in the ward if possible.

(4) Relatives should be given the leaflet 'Advice to the Bereaved' and advised that arrangements can usually be made with Funeral Directors over the weekend and before the Medical Certificate of Cause of Death has been issued.

6 Registration of death

It is the relatives' duty to register the death at the Register Office. The death must be registered in the area where it occurred, not where the person lived. The relative must give the Registrar the following details:

Full name of deceased.
Maiden surname of married lady.
Last known address.
Date of birth.
Place of birth.
Occupation.
Whether in receipt of a pension.
Name, date of birth and occupation of husband of the deceased.
Date of birth of the surviving spouse.

The Registrar will also ask for the Medical Card which can be handed in at the time of registration or sent later (if available).

The Registrar will give the relative a green coloured certificate that should be handed to the Undertaker. The Registrar will issue the Death Certificate and provide copies for a fee on request. The Registrar will issue a free Certificate for DHSS purposes.

The death must be registered within 5 days unless there is an inquest or Post Mortem.

7 Cremation

If a cremation is planned, it is necessary for 2 Doctors to sign a Cremation Certificate. Relatives should be advised to tell the Clerk in the hospital Death Registration Office, that that is the intention, so that she can make the necessary arrangements for the Cremation Certificate to be signed ready for the Undertaker to collect it.

The House Officer should complete Form B of the Cremation Certificate answering all questions otherwise the certificate is ineffective. The second part of the Cremation Certificate Form C, is the Confirmatory Medical Certificate which must be completed by another Doctor, not from the same firm, qualified for not less than 5 years who is not a relative of the deceased or a relative or partner of the Doctor who signed Form B.

The requirement for Form C can be dispensed with where the patient died as an In-Patient in hospital and a Post Mortem examination has been made by a suitably qualified Doctor and the deceased's medical attendant knows the result of the examination, before giving the certificate.

8 Funeral arrangements

It is the duty of the relatives to arrange the disposal of the body. They must give the green form received from the Registrar to the chosen firm of Undertakers. There are several local firms who can be contacted whose names can be found in the Yellow Pages. The Funeral Directors will assist the relatives in arranging the time and place of the funeral. Assistance can also be provided by the appropriate Minister of Religion. Relatives unable to pay for a funeral or transport costs may in certain circumstances receive help from the Health Authority. HM (72) 41.

9 Patients dying without relatives

When a patient with no known next of kin dies, his property and valuables should be taken to the General Office/Cashiers Office for safe keeping. The person responsible for deceased patient's affairs should make a reasonable search for any relatives of the deceased and if necessary inform the police of the death so that the name can be entered on a missing person's list. After allowing a reasonable time for relatives to come forward (approximately 2 weeks), the hospital must then register the death and make arrangements for a contract funeral. It is usual for the hospital to arrange for bodies to be cremated unless there is a particular note in the patient's records to the contrary. Records should be kept of these arrangements in order that subsequent enquiries by the DHSS can be answered promptly. The cost of the funeral can be met from any property owned by the deceased.

10 Specific religious and cultural practices

There are Chaplains of the Church of Wales, Roman Catholic and Welsh Church at this hospital who can advise relatives at this time. The Ward Sister should offer to arrange a meeting.

(1) Christians

Chaplains should be informed by the nursing staff when a patient is dying or receiving terminal care. They should also be told of sudden emergencies such as unforeseen deterioration, cardiac arrest, when the decision is taken to discontinue use of a life support system, or when a patient is seriously ill in the Accident and Emergency Department. After death, Christians are normally clothed in a shroud and wrapped in a cloth or sheet. The arms and hands are placed at the sides. There is no religious objection to Post Mortem or Cremation.

(2) Jews

A Jewish Rabbi is on call in hospital. The local Synagogue should be contacted. Special rites and prayers are given and special facilities are available for Jews to register a death at the local Register Office on Saturdays and for burials on Sunday. If relatives cannot be traced, the Jewish Burial Society or Synagogue should be contacted immediately to make funeral arrangements. Post Mortems are allowed on Jewish patients only by order of the Coroner and only very liberal Jews would permit cremation. The body should not be touched until the views of the relatives' local Synagogue are known.

(3) Moslems

If the death of a Moslem is expected, the Moslem Imam (priest) should be called so that special prayers can be given to the dying patient. Following the death, the body should normally be left untouched. When it is removed to the Mortuary, it should be washed by another Moslem of the same sex and then left uncovered. The body should, if possible, face Mecca (i.e. South East). Prayers which follow the death should preferably be said at the Mosque, and it is therefore important to release the body to the Undertakers as soon as possible. If relatives cannot be traced, the local Mosque should be notified immediately. Post Mortems are against the belief of the Moslem faith, but cannot be refused, if the Coroner orders one.

(4) Sikhs

There are no particular arrangements which should be observed on the death of a Sikh. However Post Mortems are not normally allowed and it is usual for burial to take place rather than cremation.

(5) Hindus

Hindu priests very often wish to perform the last rites but in their absence anyone may read to the patient from the Bhagavad Gita if this is desired by the patient. Although there are no particular rules about Post Mortems, often relatives will refuse consent. It is usual for cremation to take place rather than burial.

(6) Buddhists

There is no particular guidance concerning the death of a Buddhist. Normally the relatives do not object to Post Mortems and arrangements are usually made for the body to be cremated.

(7) Church of Jesus Christ of Latter Day Saints (Mormons)

The Hospital Chaplain should be informed when a member of this Church is admitted to hospital so that he can inform a member of the Church if required. The relatives should usually be asked who they would like to be called in. There are no special observances which should be met, nor strong views about Post Mortems or cremation. A list of local Ministers for all religions should be available in each ward.

11 Procedure in special circumstances

(a) Stillbirths – i.e. birth after 28 weeks' gestation

A Medical Certificate must be completed by the registered Medical Practitioner who attended the mother at the delivery of a still-born child. This certificate must be taken to the Register Office within 42 days of delivery. He will then issue a Certificate of Disposal to permit burial or cremation.

(b) Perinatal or neonatal deaths

When a baby is born alive and subsequently dies (irrespective of the duration of life or the period of gestation), the Medical Practitioner who attended the baby must issue a Medical Certificate giving cause of death. The parents will be required to register both birth and death. They should take to the Register Office the Medical Certificate within 5 days of the baby's death. A green certificate (a Certificate of Disposal) will be issued by the Registrar to permit Burial or Cremation. (For further details on Registration and Disposal see leaflet 'Advice to the Bereaved'.)

(c) Patients dying in Accident and Emergency Department

(a) A patient who is brought to the hospital in a state beyond resuscitation must be certified dead in the ambulance by a member of the medical staff of the Accident and Emergency Department. The body is not brought into the Department but taken straight to the Mortuary. If the body is certified dead in the ambulance, the following rules should be followed:
   (1) The body is not undressed.
   (2) The pockets in any clothes are not emptied.
   (3) A 'Dead on Arrival' form is completed.
   (4) The date and time of arrival is recorded in the admission book in the Accident and Emergency Department.
   (5) Nursing Administration and Medical Staff are informed.
(b) Where a patient admitted to the Accident and Emergency Department dies before being transferred to a ward, the following procedures should be followed:

(1) He should be undressed for medical examination.

(2) His clothes and valuables must be listed and put in a safe place until they can be handed over to General Office/Cashiers.

(3) After certification of death, the body shall be prepared for transport to the Mortuary:

  (a) The feet should be tied together with a name label.

  (b) The body should be wrapped in a Mortuary Sheet.

  (c) The sheet should be tied with a bandage round the neck, waist and ankles with a name label.

  (d) The body should be taken to the Mortuary.

(c) Both Dead on Arrival cases and Death After Admission to Accident and Emergency cases should be reported to the Coroner (*see section 12.*)

(d) Where relatives were not with the patient the police will usually contact them as soon as possible and arrangements should be made for them to identify the body, at any time (not just office hours).

(d) Patients from overseas dying in NHS hospitals

Deaths of persons from overseas must be registered in the usual way. A Medical Certificate of cause of death will be issued and notification made to the Consul of the country concerned that the patient has died. If the relatives wish the body to be transported back to that country for disposal, help should be sought from the appropriate Embassy. The Health Authority cannot give financial help for such transport.

(e) Bodies thought to be contaminated with dangerous pathogens

Post Mortems must be made in cases or suspected cases of infection with category A pathogens. Special arrangements should be made for handling bodies. It is imperative to wear full protective clothing, wrap the body in a special cadaver bag and to make all necessary arrangements to avoid the spread of infection. The cadaver bag should be clearly labelled a 'high risk infectious body'. Any member of staff who thinks he/she had contracted any kind of infection from a deceased person should be referred to the Occupational Health Department. Doctors are asked to make the appropriate information available so that the appropriate precautions can be taken and all those who handle bodies are protected.

12 Notification to the Coroner

The Doctor attending the patient in his last illness has a duty to complete the Medical Certificate of cause of death. If he is unsure of the cause of death, he should not issue the Medical Certificate but should report the death to the Coroner. The following cases should be reported to the Coroner:

1. Every case where the Doctor treating the patient during the past illness cannot give cause of death – acceptable to the Registrar of Births and Deaths.
2. Dies within 24 hours of admission to hospital.
3. When the Doctor attending the patient did not see him or her within 14 days before death.
4. Deaths in public place or persons brought in dead.
5. Unidentified persons.
6. Death not thought to be due to natural causes.
7. Death related to suspicious or criminal actions.
8. Death related to injury however remote or if accidental cause is alleged by relatives or friends.
9. Deaths within 24 hours of operating or administration of an anaesthetic at any time subsequently if cause of death is thought to be related to either.
10. Deaths due to industrial disease, even if only a contributory factor.
11. Deaths occurring as result of industrial injury.
12. Patients dying who were in receipt of War Pensions, Industrial Injuries Pensions or Disability Pension if related to cause of death.
13. Deaths of persons in hospital in legal custody (e.g. serving a prison sentence or under Mental Health Act or other Act).
14. Deaths where there is a question of self neglect or neglect by others.
15. Deaths from Hypothermia.
16. Deaths from illegal termination of pregnancy.
17. Deaths from food poisoning.
18. Deaths related to alcoholism acute or chronic.
19. Deaths related to non-addictive abuse or drugs or to drug addiction.
20. Deaths related to medical mishap or where relatives have criticised hospital, medical or nursing management, if related to cause of death.
21. All patients that are potential organ donors if their death would be reportable to the Coroner.
22. A stillbirth, and if there is any doubt about the child being born alive.

In cases of doubt the Coroner or his Officer are available for you to discuss matters with them.

Where death is reportable to the Coroner, the Doctor should record in the notes if relatives were present at death since this makes it unnecessary for further identification of the body by relatives at a later date.

13 The Coroner's Office

If a death is reported to the Coroner, he may order that a Post Mortem examination of the body be carried out. Relatives cannot oppose this order, but have the right to have a doctor of their own choice present during the autopsy (at their own expense).

The Coroner will issue the certificate either direct to the Registrar or to the relatives of the family to take to the Register Office. If the body is to be cremated the Coroner will provide the Certificate of Cremation.

In certain circumstances the Coroner may require to hold an inquest, which is an enquiry into the circumstances surrounding the death. In these circumstances he will issue an order for Burial or Cremation at the opening of the Inquest, so that the funeral can take place prior to the full Inquest proceedings being completed. In cases where the death has been reported to the Coroner families may contact an Undertaker so that arrangements can be made for the funeral service. However they should advise the Undertaker that the death has been reported to the Coroner, so that any delay in the funeral proceedings can be kept at a minimum. Further details concerning the Coroner can be obtained from the Coroner's Office.

14 The inquest

If the Coroner decides to hold an Inquest he may require staff to provide statements relating to the death. Staff should obtain advice from Senior Staff on the preparation of the statement. The Coroner decides who should be called as a witness to give evidence at the Inquest. The purpose of the inquest is to ascertain:

1. Who the deceased was.
2. How, when and where the deceased came by his death.
3. The particulars required for registration (*see section 6*).

15 Post mortem examinations

Where the Coroner orders a Post Mortem examination, the relatives have no right to stop it proceeding. Sometimes the Medical Staff may wish to know more about the extent of a disease or enhance medical knowledge by carrying out a Post Mortem examination. The consent of the next of kin is required and they should be asked to complete the consent form. Since Post Mortem examinations are very important in evaluating methods of treatment for the benefit of other patients, the next of kin should be advised to give serious consideration to such a request before deciding to refuse it.

Before requesting permission from the relatives the Doctor must be able to complete the certificate as to the cause of death and the matter must not be reportable to the Coroner.

The Howie Report 1978 provides a Code of Practice for safety in clinical laboratories and Post Mortem rooms. It recommends that the Head of Department of Histopathology takes overall responsibility for safety precautions in the Post Mortem room, assisted by the Post Mortem technician and Department Safety Officer. The rules laid down in the report on the safety in the Post Mortem room should be readily available to all staff concerned, and action should be taken to ensure they are implemented.

16 Cardiac pacemakers and radioactive material

Where a patient fitted with a Cardiac Pacemaker has died it is desirable for the Pace-maker to be removed and returned to the Cardiac Department which implanted it for checking and evaluation of its performance so that the knowledge gained can be applied for the benefit of future patients. The consent of the person lawfully entitled to dispose of the body should be obtained before the pacemaker is removed. If the patient is to be cremated it is essential that the Pacemaker is removed, since if heated to high temper-ature, pacemakers are liable to explode and give off toxic fumes which could be hazardous to cremation staff.

17 Procedure for mortuary staff

An Anatomical Technician is responsible for assisting in the Mortuary and Post Mortem room with duties which include opening up and reconstructing bodies, their disposal and care of instruments. She/he is usually also responsible for releasing bodies from the mortuary. A body should not be released unless the Undertakers have a removal order and an authorisation form from the relatives to release the body. Strict proce-dure should be followed to ensure that the correct body is released and the appropriate signature obtained from the Undertakers. The Anatomical Technician is also respon-sible for preparing bodies for identification.

Nurses should accompany relatives to the viewing room. Porters who assist in the Mortuary and collect bodies from the wards should ensure that the correct procedures in relation to identification and property of the deceased are followed.

18 Patients' property and valuables

Patients should be discouraged from bringing valuable items into hospital with them and should be advised to hand over to the safe keeping of the hospital any such items. These should be entered in the Ward Property Book and taken to the Cashiers. Patients admitted unconscious in Accident and Emergency Department should have their prop-erty checked by two nurses, entered in the Accident and Emergency Property Book and given to the Cashier.

When a patient dies the relatives should be asked if they wish the wedding ring to remain on the body of the deceased. This should be noted on the body and in the patient's records. The relatives should also be asked to collect the personal clothing from the Ward Sister. They will be asked to sign an indemnity and a receipt.

The Financial Control System of the authority is as follows:

1. Caution must be taken only to release property, where it does not exceed £1,500 to a person who is bona fide entitled to it. If the property exceeds this amount, then Grant of Probate or Letters of Administration are proof of identity required.
2. Where it is not a person's intention to obtain a Grant of Probate on claiming property, an Indemnity Form must be completed before any property is handed

over to the claimant. Likewise the form has to be completed where the person is named as an Executor in a Will.

3. It should be noted that although a form is being completed, the fullest enquiries must still be made before property is released.

4. Where there is no Will in existence the following points must be strictly complied with:

   (a) Property in excess of £500 in value requires Letters of Administration to be produced.

   (b) If the value of the property held is less than £1,500:

       (i)   The relationship of the claimant to the deceased must be ascertained and that the person is entitled to apply for Letters of Administration.

       (ii) Obtain Authority to hand over property from all persons who could claim in priority to or equally with the claimant.

       (iii) Having complied with the above only hand property over on completion of an Indemnity Form.

   (c) No property should be handed over to persons who have not attained their majority (i.e. under 18 years of age). In such cases, parent(s) or lawful guardian(s) must give the undertaking.

Wills

If the relatives have any queries over a Will or the absence of one, they should be advised to contact the Probate Office.

Property of patients with no known relatives

If a person dies without any known relatives and without a Will, his property is passed to the Crown and is administered by the Treasury Solicitor or the Solicitors of the Duchy of Cornwall or Lancaster, (for residents of Cornwall or Lancaster.) The Administrator should make enquiries to ascertain the existence of relatives and/or a Will and if the results are negative inform the Treasury Solicitor. The Treasury Solicitor will require the following information of the deceased:

Full name.
Permanent address.
Address at which death occurred.
Date of death.
Marital Status and if widowed, name and date and death of husband/wife.
Certificate of birth, marriage and death.
Details of relatives.
Details of enquiries to find relatives.
Age at death.
Place and date of birth.

Occupation and last employer.
Any knowledge of life history or visitors.
Any other identifiable property.
Details of DHSS benefits.

19 Acknowledgements

We wish to record our grateful thanks to those firms whose contribution enabled us to produce this booklet.

Appendix 13 Disclosure of confidential information to the police

The problem

The Health Authority has a duty to preserve the confidentiality of personal information about patients. This duty is enforceable in the civil courts, unless disclosure is justified or authorised by law.

The Police in their investigation of crimes or alleged crimes require information to be made available to them so that offenders can ultimately be successfully prosecuted.

Statutes

Specific powers and duties are set out in the following Acts of Parliament.

Road Traffic Act 1972 S. 168 (2)

Any person shall if required, give any information which it is in his power to give and which may lead to the identification of the driver.

It was held in *Hunter* v. *Mann* 1974 RTR 338 that this provision covers a Doctor who could not claim any privilege against disclosure.

Prevention of Terrorism (Temporary Provision) Act 1984 S.11

Information must be given to the Police in relation to any acts of terrorism.

Police and Criminal Evidence Act 1984

Special provisions are laid down for access to excluded material. S.11 includes personal records and human tissue or tissue fluid taken for purposes of diagnosis or medical treatment where it is held in confidence.

Access may be obtained to excluded material by following the procedures set out in Schedule 1 to Act. This involves an application to a Circuit Judge who may make an order requiring the person in possession of the material to produce it to a Constable for him to take away, or to give a Constable access to it, within a specified period. Access conditions are laid down in paragraph 3 of Schedule 1.

A suggested procedure

If the information required by the Police comes under the 'excluded material' and the access conditions are present, the Health Authority will normally await a Circuit Judge's order before releasing any information or body fluids or samples.

Basic principles for accident and emergency staff

1. No information will be released to the Police without the consent of the Consultant/Senior Doctor in charge at the time.
2. No body fluids or samples can be given or taken by the Police without the consent of the Doctor *and* the consent of the patient. Where body fluids or samples have already been taken for another purpose only a Circuit Judge can order release to the Police.
3. Questioning by Police of a patient is subject to medical clearance on the patient's clinical condition and the consent of the patient.
4. Where the Police wish to effect an arrest, this will be subject to clinical considerations, and the Police presence will not interfere with the workings of the department/ward.
5. Staff should not notify the Police when a patient is about to be discharged unless exceptional circumstances apply.

Appendix 14   Disciplinary policy

Contents

ANNEXES
1. Counselling
2. Roles and responsibilities
3. Suspension from duty
4. Investigation
5. Disciplinary hearing
6. Disciplinary warnings
7. Dismissal
8. Criminal and potentially criminal offences
9. Disciplinary action against accredited representatives
10. Appeals against warnings or dismissal
11. Designated disciplinary responsibilities
12. Levels of dismissal, disciplinary responsibility & delegation (General Managers & Senior Officers)
13. Levels of dismissal, disciplinary responsibility & delegation (other officers)
14. Disciplinary rules

Part I Policy statement

1.1 It is the policy of this Health Authority to promote good industrial relations between the Authority and all its staff. Consequently it attaches the greatest importance to the principle of fair and consistent treatment of all its employees. The Authority recognises the need for the highest standard of conduct of its staff which is fundamental to the purpose of the Authority – the provision of health care services to the public it serves.

1.2 It is the policy of the Authority to ensure that fair and effective arrangements exist for dealing with disciplinary matters and to ensure uniform standards are observed. It is considered that the observance of an agreed procedure is in the interests of both management and staff. It is agreed that managers and staff organisation representatives will be trained in the provisions of this document.

1.3 Disciplinary rules are needed to set a reasonable standard of conduct which, if observed, will ensure the wellbeing of all individuals at work and this is reinforced by the ACAS Code of Practice, and the ACAS advisory handbook 'Discipline at Work'.

1.4 The policy is based on the following principles:

1.4.1 The attainment and maintenance of the required standards of conduct by all staff.

1.4.2 The right of the employee to be treated fairly and consistently in accordance with the principles of natural justice; the right of representation and the right to seek redress.

1.4.3 The right of the manager to exercise the authority delegated to him* by the Health Authority to manage, organise and supervise the work of those for whom he is responsible and to take any disciplinary action, including dismissal, which is necessary and authorised.

Part II Counselling

It is important that, wherever possible, problems relating to unsatisfactory conduct or performance are dealt with as close to the source of the problem as possible. This will ensure the avoidance of unnecessary use of disciplinary action. Provisions for undertaking counselling are contained in Annexe 1.

Part III Disciplinary procedure

Section 1 Application

1.1 This procedure applies to all staff under a contract of service with this Health Authority.

1.2 Under the terms of paragraph 190 of the Hospital Medical and Dental Staffs Whitley Council WHC(82)17, HM(61)112 and SHM/49/1968 hospital medical and dental staff (other than junior staff) are excluded where specific arrangements apply in cases of professional conduct or competence.

1.3 Where disciplinary action has been undertaken against an employee, the matter will be reported to the relevant statutory/registration body by the District General Manager or responsible Senior Officer, if the offence is considered contrary to the relevant code of professional conduct.

1.4 Nothing in this procedure shall supersede any more favourable arrangements constituted under national agreement or statutory enactment.

Section 2 Principles

2.1 Where disciplinary action is contemplated, a number of important principles need to be followed.

2.1.1 The need for any issue to be treated in the strictest confidence
2.1.2 The need for a thorough investigation

* Disclaimer: Reference to employees being male is simply a means of illustration. It is intended that the policy will be applied equally to all male and female employees.

2.1.3 The need to provide the employee with details of complaints against him

2.1.4 The exercise of the right of representation, if required

2.1.5 The opportunity for the employee to state his case

2.1.6 The need to ensure that all warnings are clearly explained and recorded

2.1.7 The exercise of the right of appeal

Section 3 Roles and responsibilities

It is important that the roles and responsibilities of those conducting or participating in any of the activities in accordance with this policy are clearly understood. These are set out in Annexe 2.

Section 4 Suspension from duty

Situations arise from time to time when it becomes necessary to suspend a member of staff, usually when there is need to investigate an incident or occurrence. The provisions relating to suspension are outlined in Annexe 3.

Section 5 Investigation

It is vital that all situations are investigated before any disciplinary action is taken. The purpose of the investigation is to establish whether or not there is a case to answer in a disciplinary hearing. Consequently, the investigation must always be thorough and be carried out with no delay. It is also important that a consistent approach is used when investigating an incident and the appropriate information on this is contained in Annexe 4.

Section 6 Disciplinary hearing

When consideration is given to taking disciplinary action, a proper hearing must always take place before any decision is arrived at or any disciplinary action taken. Details of the preliminaries to the hearing and of how it should be conducted are in Annexe 5.

Section 7 Disciplinary warnings

Depending on the seriousness of the offence, a series of warnings exist which may be administered in appropriate cases. The policy provides for three levels of formal warnings namely:

   oral warning
   written warning
   final written warning

Information on the application of these warnings is given in Annexe 6.

Section 8 Dismissal

The procedure to be followed for dealing with dismissals is the same as that for disciplinary warnings short of dismissal. Dismissal is the most severe sanction and must be considered and, where necessary, carried out, in strict accordance with the provisions of the policy. The special factors relating to dismissal, including alternatives to termination of employment, are detailed in Annexe 7.

Section 9 Criminal and potentially criminal offences

Sometimes incidents arise which are potentially a breach of criminal law as well as being a breach of the contract of employment. Whilst this does not necessarily prevent disciplinary action being undertaken, special consideration needs to be given to certain matters which are described in Annexe 8.

Section 10 Disciplinary action against accredited representatives

Overall, the same standards and provisions apply to representatives of recognised staff organisations as to those for all other employees. However, the issues for particular consideration in relation to this are contained in Annexe 9.

Part IV Appeals procedure

Every member of staff has the right of appeal against disciplinary action or dismissal. The means of exercising this right and the procedure to be followed are given in a detailed description in Annexe 10.

Part V Designated disciplinary responsibilities

Every member of staff has the right to know the identity of the officer who carries responsibility for dismissing him should it become necessary. The arrangements for this and an outline of these responsibilities are contained in Annexe 11. More specific detail will be available from the appropriate personnel manager.

Part VI Disciplinary rules

Reasonable standards of behaviour and conduct are expected of all members of staff. These are described in a set of rules entitled Disciplinary Rules. Any breach of these rules may lead to disciplinary action. A copy of rules will be given to every member of staff.

Annexe 1 Counselling

1. The immediate manager should decide whether the matter warrants disciplinary action or is of a very minor nature not justifying any stage of formal disciplinary warning. If the latter is the case, the appropriate counselling should be carried out.

2. In such circumstances the manager should discuss the matter with the employee on an informal basis with no other party or representative present. Counselling does not constitute disciplinary action or a stage in the formal disciplinary procedure; this should be made clear to an individual at the beginning of the discussion. The purpose is to explain the reasons for management dissatisfaction, to discuss thoroughly the problems and reasons, to obtain the individual's views on these, and to indicate clearly the improvements required. The discussion is treated in the strictest confidence with only a diary entry that it took place.

3. This informal discussion will not be used as a substitute for an investigation as laid down in Section 5.

Annexe 2 Roles and responsibilities

1. Wherever an investigation is warranted an officer will be appointed to undertake this in accordance with the terms of this procedure.

2. The designated disciplining officer shall be identified in accordance with the procedure where it is established there is a case to answer (see Part V). This officer shall not normally have had any involvement in the case. Only in exceptional circumstances where there is no practicable alternative should an officer with prior involvement in the case be responsible for taking and implementing any disciplinary decision.

3. A personnel manager or officer shall participate in every disciplinary hearing as indicated in this procedure.

Annexe 3 Suspension from duty

1. Prior to or during an investigation, it may become necessary to suspend an employee from duty. In such circumstances, the employee will receive normal pay entitlement, i.e. the payment that would be receivable had the period of suspension been worked. Suspension is not disciplinary action and the employee concerned should clearly understand this when being suspended.

2. The main circumstances in which suspension should be considered are where continuing attendance could:

    2.1 compound the offence
    2.2 frustrate or interfere with any investigations
    2.3 jeopardise the employee's safety or wellbeing, or

2.4 be perceived as not being in the interests of, or for the protection of the patients and/or staff.

3. Suspension should not be prolonged and should not last longer than necessary.

4. A decision to suspend should be confirmed in writing no later than the following working day.

Annexe 4 Investigation

When a situation arises which could result in disciplinary action being considered, the undermentioned procedure must be followed:

1. An investigation must be carried out. The employee(s) concerned must be informed that an investigation is to be carried out and must be told of the subject of that investigation.

2. The investigation should be started immediately and completed as soon as is reasonably practicable. The purpose of the investigation is to establish whether or not there is a case to answer.

3. The objective of the investigation is to obtain all relevant information. This will include interviewing all relevant witnesses, taking statements, obtaining documentary evidence (e.g. employment records), and contacting outside agencies, bodies or individuals as appropriate.

4. It is expected that the employee concerned will need to be interviewed during the investigation; in such circumstances he shall be informed of his right to be accompanied by a representative of a Trade Union, professional organisation, or a friend.

5. The investigation should be undertaken by an officer other than the one who carries responsibility for disciplining the employee concerned. Only in exceptional circumstances, where there is no practicable alternative, should an officer carry out an investigation which may lead to disciplinary action for which he is the designated officer responsible.

6. The outcome of the investigation will usually take the form of a written report containing the appropriate recommendations by the investigating officer responsible.

7. The designated disciplining officer must be satisfied that a thorough investigation has been undertaken. If he is satisfied there is a case to answer, the matter should be referred for formal disciplinary hearing.

8. Where it is decided there is no case to answer the individual must be informed accordingly.

Annexe 5 Disciplinary hearing

1. Where it is established there is a case to answer, the employee should be informed in writing of the allegation(s) made against him and should be given adequate notice

of the time and date of the hearing. The notice period must not be subject to unreasonable delay, but must allow reasonable time for preparation of case. He must also be informed of the right of representation. Relevant documentary evidence including statements from witnesses, records and reports (where appropriate or available) should be sent to the employee in advance of the hearing. Where witnesses are required to attend, arrangements should be made by those calling them to ensure their availability at the hearing.

2. There is a duty upon every employee to co-operate with management when required by giving written evidence and/or appearing as a witness. Every effort should be made to release witnesses subject to the exigencies of the service.

3. An appropriate personnel manager/officer will be present at all disciplinary hearings. He will have a full involvement in the disciplinary proceedings and deliberations.

4. The disciplinary hearing itself should normally take the following pattern, requiring the designated disciplinary officer to:

4.1 Introduce those present.

4.2 Explain the purpose of the hearing, i.e. indicate that it is a disciplinary hearing convened in accordance with the Health Authority's Disciplinary Policy to address the allegation(s) as outlined and (where applicable and appropriate) to consider a report concerning the issue(s), together with any other evidence relevant to the case.

4.3 Outline the nature of the hearing, i.e. that the allegation(s) is/are viewed most seriously and may result in disciplinary action, including dismissal, where appropriate.

4.4 Refer to the principles which govern the hearing:
   (i)   that full and fair consideration will be given to all issues pertinent to the case
   (ii) that all relevant evidence will be considered, and
   (iii) that the employee or his representative will have the opportunity to deny, answer or defend himself against the allegation(s).

4.5 Describe the procedure to be followed at the hearing (and ensure this is understood by the individual):
   4.5.1 At any time during the hearing the disciplining officer and personnel manager/officer shall have the right to ask questions of clarification of anyone present.
   4.5.2 The employee or his representative and the investigating officer shall have the right to ask questions of any witness. For this purpose the employee will be counted as a witness.
   4.5.3 The disciplining officer will consider a report (where applicable and appropriate) and documentary evidence.
   4.5.4 The investigating officer shall remain in attendance throughout the hearing. Provided he is not the officer responsible for taking disciplinary action, he shall present the findings of his investigation.

4.5.5   This officer shall answer questions from the employee or his representative, and then from the discipling officer and/or personnel manager.

4.5.6   Any witness called either by the investigating officer or the employee should not be present at the hearing before giving evidence. Witnesses called in support of the allegations shall first be questioned by the investigating officer and thereafter shall answer questions from the employee or his representative and then from the discipling officer and/or personnel manager. Witnesses called by the employee or his representative shall first be questioned by that person and thereafter may be questioned by the investigating officer and then by the discipling officer and/or personnel manager. After giving evidence witnesses may be asked to remain available for clarification purposes, but shall not remain in attendance.

4.5.7   The employee or his representative will be invited to make statements and present evidence, whether oral and/or written, to explain, deny, offer mitigating circumstances or otherwise comment upon the allegation(s).

4.5.8   The employee and/or his representative will then answer questions from the discipling officer and then from the personnel manager.

4.5.9   An opportunity will be given for any other relevant remarks from any party.

4.5.10 All parties, including the investigating officer, shall then withdraw (see also Part V). The discipling officer and personnel manager/officer will then deliberate in private. When a conclusion is reached the former will communicate his decision to the employee in person, and to his representative. If the decision takes the form of any disciplinary action it must be confirmed in writing by the discipling officer within seven working days of the decision. Such written confirmation must detail the right of appeal.

5. In all cases of disciplinary action short of dismissal the advice of the District Personnel Manager (or a representative) on the application of the policy may be sought if required (for dismissal see also paragraph 8.3).

6. When considering the need for disciplinary action the discipling officer must be satisfied that:

6.1 an investigation and hearing have been conducted in accordance with the procedure

6.2 the offence(s) has/have taken place on the balance of probabilities

6.3 the disciplinary rules have been considered and applied

6.4 the action contemplated is reasonable in the circumstances and reflects the seriousness of the offence.

Annexe 6 Disciplinary warnings

1. It is necessary to distinguish between different levels of seriousness of conduct. The level of warning will reflect the seriousness of an offence, together with the

employee's previous disciplinary record, if applicable. Any level of warning may be given for a first offence, i.e. it will not be automatic that a first offence will result in a 'first' warning: a first offence, if sufficiently serious, may result in a 'final' warning. Where disciplinary action is required the following warnings will apply.

2. In deciding upon the appropriate level of disciplinary action, any rules relating to standards of conduct should be taken into account.

3. *Oral warning* This will be applicable in cases of minor misconduct. An Oral Warning issued to an employee will be simultaneously recorded on the personal file for six months.

4. *Written warning* This will be applicable in cases of serious misconduct or minor misconduct where an oral warning has already been issued. A Written Warning issued to an employee will be simultaneously recorded on the personal file for one year.

5. *Final written warning*

   5.1 This will be applicable in cases of very serious misconduct or serious misconduct or minor misconduct where a Written Warning (and, where appropriate, Oral Warning) has already been issued. A Final Written Warning issued to an employee will be simultaneously recorded on the personal file for two years.
   5.2 After one year a compulsory review involving the individual (and his representative where requested) will take place. If the review is satisfactory, the final written warning will be removed from the file.
   If the review is unsatisfactory the final written warning will stand for the remainder of the two year duration. The decision on the review is not appealable.
   5.3 It will be the responsibility of the disciplining officer (or, where applicable, his successor) who made the original disciplinary decision to carry out the review.

6. *Removal of Warnings* Expired warnings will be removed from the personal file, and returned to the employee with written confirmation of removal. No copy of either of these documents will be retained on the personal file.

Annexe 7 Dismissal

1. The officers delegated with the responsibility for dismissal are shown in Part V and a decision to dismiss may only be taken and actioned by the designated dismissing officer or in accordance with the provisions of delegation (see Part V).

2. The procedure to be followed in cases of dismissal will be the same as that outlined in Sections 5 and 6. However, except in cases of gross misconduct, no employee should be dismissed for a first offence. Failure to comply with the terms of a Final Written Warning or gross misconduct which represents a fundamental breach of contract shall be grounds for termination of employment.

3. In every case where dismissal is being considered, the case must be discussed with the District Personnel Manager (or his/her representative) whose advice and guidance

must be obtained before a decision to dismiss is taken. This will relate in particular to the application of, or compliance with, the Authority's policy and procedure.

4. Any dismissal, whether summary or with notice, will be confirmed in writing within seven days of the decision and must detail the date of dismissal, the grounds for the decision and the right of appeal. Dismissal will be summary, i.e. without notice or payment in lieu of notice, in all cases of gross misconduct. In all other cases of dismissal, statutory notice should be given or appropriate payment in lieu made.

5. As an alternative to dismissal, consideration may be given by the dismissing officer to offer downgrading, demotion or transfer to the employee concerned. However, in such cases, the advice of the District Personnel Manager (or his/her representative) must be sought since contractual difficulties can arise in such circumstances. Failure to accept such an offer will result in termination of employment.

Annexe 8 Criminal and potentially criminal offences

1. Certain alleged offences may constitute criminal acts and may lead to police involvement. In such circumstances, management shall not be precluded from undertaking disciplinary action in accordance with Sections 6, 7 and 8.

2. Where a criminal offence has allegedly been committed by an employee inside or outside work, an investigation of the facts and circumstances surrounding the case will be conducted as in Part III Section 5. Where it is established there is a case to answer, a disciplinary hearing will normally be arranged. However, it may be delayed pending the outcome of any police involvement at the discretion of the disciplining officer following discussion with the Unit Personnel Manager and then the District Personnel Manager (or a representative) whichever is the more appropriate. Normally, however, the hearing should proceed within the same timescale as any other disciplinary case.

3. In such cases disciplinary action including dismissal will not be automatic, the main factors to be taken into account in deciding whether or not the (alleged) criminal offence renders the employee unsuitable to continue employment are as follows, although it is stressed that the list is not exhaustive and each case stands on its own merits:

    3.1 the relevance of the offence to the job for which the employee is employed: whether or not it impinges upon the contract of employment

    3.2 seniority of the employee – the expected standards would be the greater the more senior the officer

    3.3 breach of the trust and responsibility vested in the employee in relation to the job for which the individual is employed

    3.4 unacceptability of the employee to work with colleagues

    3.5 potential risk to patients, public, other employees or to the employee himself

    3.6 effect on the image or reputation of the Health Authority.

Annexe 9 Disciplinary action against accredited representatives

Although normal disciplinary standards should apply to their conduct as employees, no disciplinary action should be taken against an accredited representative of a recognised trade union, professional organisation or staff association until the circumstances of the case have been discussed with an appropriate senior representative or full-time officer.

Annexe 10 Appeals against warnings or dismissal

1. Section 40 of the General Whitley Council handbook provides for an employee who is aggrieved by disciplinary action which results in the issue of a formal written warning or a final written warning or in dismissal to have the right of appeal against such action to the employing authority* subject to paragraph 4. below.

2. It is important that appeals should be made and heard quickly. An appeal by the employee should be lodged with the District Personnel Manager within 3 weeks of the date of the written confirmation of disciplinary action/dismissal. The hearing of the appeal by the appeal committee should take place within 3 weeks of the receipt of the appeal by the employing authority. However, by the agreement of both parties, this period may be extended for a further period of up to 5 weeks. The employee shall be given at least 14 days written notice of the date of the hearing.

3. The letter of appeal should indicate whether or not he wishes to be represented at the hearing and if so by whom. The employee should have the right of appearing personally before the appeal committee either alone or accompanied by a representative of his trade union, professional organisation, staff organisation or a friend acting in this capacity. An appellant may elect to be legally represented but, if so, he shall give the name and status of that person and shall be responsible for such costs as he may incur; and in these circumstances, the employing authority may also elect to be legally represented.

4. Not less than 10 days before the date of the hearing each party shall submit a statement of case which briefly states the grounds on which the appeal is based. The statement should also include a chronological breakdown of the events leading up to the appeal, together with an indication of the redress sought.

5. Employees with under 26 weeks service will be allowed the right of appeal against disciplinary action including dismissal to the officer to whom the disciplining officer is responsible.

6. Appeals against oral warning shall be made to and heard by the disciplining officer's appropriate superior officer. This may be the officer to whom the disciplining officer

* Other than employees whose employment may be terminated only by the full Health Authority.

reports or someone more senior, if appropriate. An employee who receives an oral warning must be informed of his right of appeal and the arrangements for making such an appeal including identification of the officer to whom the appeal should be made.

7. The appeal committee will normally consist of three members of the Health Authority. If possible at least one member of the committee should have a special knowledge of the field of work of the employee where this is relevant to the case. Where this is not possible in cases of an appeal against dismissal, the committee shall at the request of the employee or his representative, appoint an assessor who is experienced in the particular discipline of the employee, and who has not been directly involved in the circumstances leading to disciplinary action. The assessor may only advise the committee on any matter arising during the course of the hearing which he feels may be related to the professional conduct or professional competence of the employee.

8. The appeal committee shall not include any member of the Authority or committee or sub-committee of the Authority who has been directly involved in the circumstances leading to disciplinary action. No officer of the Authority who has been directly involved in the circumstances that appeared to indicate the need for disciplinary action at an earlier stage of the disciplinary procedure shall be present at the appeal hearing as Secretary to the appeals committee or in any other capacity except as a witness or as the representative of the employing authority.

9. Those required to be present throughout the hearing shall be the management's presenting officer, the disciplining/dismissing officer, (where these are not one and the same person), and the appellant and his representative (where chosen). Where the disciplining/dismissing officer is not management's representative at the appeal hearing he shall nevertheless be present throughout the hearing.

10. Before the commencement of the hearing the appeal committee should designate a chairman who will preside over the conduct of the appeal.

11. The District General Manager shall act, or nominate his representative to act, as Secretary to the Committee during the hearing. The role of the secretary shall be to advise the members of the Committee on:

   11.1 the conduct of the hearing
   11.2 the relevant regulations relating to the Whitley Councils, statutory and case law, and to those of the Health Authority

   and to:

   11.3 record the salient points of the hearing
   11.4 record the recommendation and ensure it is put to the Health Authority.

12. At the hearing of an appeal before the appeal committee the following procedure shall be observed:

   12.1 The management representative shall state the management's case in the presence of the appellant and his representative and may call witnesses.

12.2   The appellant or his representative shall have the opportunity to ask questions of the management representative and witnesses.

12.3   The members of the appeal committee shall have the opportunity to ask questions of the management representative and witnesses.

12.4   The management representative shall have the opportunity to re-examine his witnesses on any matter referred to in their examination by members of the appeal committee, the appellant or his representative.

12.5   The appellant or his representative shall put his case in the presence of the management representative and may call witnesses.

12.6   The management representative shall have the opportunity to ask questions of the appellant, his representative and his witnesses.

12.7   The members of the appeal committee shall have the opportunity to ask questions of the appellant, his representative and witnesses.

12.8   The appellant or his representative shall have the opportunity to re-examine his witnesses on any matter referred to in their examination by members of the appeal committee or the management representative.

12.9   The management representative and the appellant or his representative shall have the opportunity to sum up their cases if they so wish. The appellant or his representative shall have the right to speak last. *In his summing up neither party may introduce any new matter or evidence.*

12.10 Nothing in the foregoing procedure shall prevent the members of the committee from inviting either party to elucidate or amplify any statement they may have made, or from asking them such questions as may be necessary to ascertain whether or not they propose to call any evidence in respect of any part of their statement, or alternatively, whether they are in fact claiming that the matters are within their own knowledge, in which case they will be subject to examination as a witness under 12.2 or 12.6 above.

12.11 The committee may at its discretion adjourn the appeal in order that further evidence may be produced by either party to the dispute or for any other reason.

12.12 The management representatives, the appellant and his representative, and witnesses shall withdraw.

12.13 The committee with the officer appointed as Secretary to the committee and, where appropriate, the assessor shall deliberate in private only recalling both parties to clear points of uncertainty on evidence already given. If recall is necessary both parties shall return notwithstanding only one is concerned with the point giving rise to doubt.

12.14 No statement of previous acts of misconduct by the employee or the issue of a formal warning or warnings unrelated to the alleged offence(s) on which the disciplinary action is based shall be made until after the committee has reached a decision on the appeal.

13. The committee, as a sub-committee of the Health Authority, shall reach a conclusion and will inform the parties of it. The conclusion will be reported to the Health Authority for approval. The Secretary to the Appeal Sub-Committee will confirm in

writing to the appellant the decision of the Authority which will then be actioned accordingly.

14. Where officers can only be disciplined/dismissed by the Health Authority or Sub-Committee a separate appeal procedure exists which is binding on them and detailed in their contract of employment documentation.

Annexe 11 Designated disciplinary responsibilities

Under the General Whitley Council agreement (Section 40) on Disciplinary Procedure, an employee should be informed in writing on appointment, or as soon as possible thereafter, whether he can be dismissed only by a decision of the full employing authority, or by an officer or committee of officers. In those cases where an employee can be dismissed by an officer or committee of officers, the employee should be informed which officer(s) has/have the power of dismissal delegated to them. In the case of employees whose employment can be terminated only by a decision of the full employing authority, power of dismissal shall not be delegated to any officer or committee of officers. This will include the Authority's more senior graded staff, e.g. senior professional, managerial, administrative or technical staff.

Annexe 12 Officers whose employment may only be terminated by the health authority and other senior officers: levels of dismissal, disciplinary responsibility & delegation

Titles	Dismissal*	Disciplinary action**		Suspension
	Responsibility	Responsibility	Delegation	Responsibility
Top Level				
District General Manager	HA	Chairman		Chairman
First Level				
Deputy District General Manager	HA	Chairman	DGM	DGM
Chief Administrative Nursing Officer	HA	Chairman	DGM	DGM
Chief Administrative Medical Officer	HA	Chairman	DGM	DGM
Director of Finance	HA	Chairman	DGM	DGM
Unit General Manager(s)	HA	Chairman	DGM	DGM
Director of Works and Estate Management	HA	Chairman	DGM	DGM
Director of Planning	HA	Chairman	DGM	DGM
Assistant General Manager	HA	Chairman	DGM	DGM
Chief Administrative Dental Officer	HA	Chairman	DGM	DGM
Chief Administrative Pharmaceutical Officer	HA	Chairman	DGM	DGM
Second Level				
Director(s) of Nursing Services	DGM	UGM		UGM
Unit Administrator(s)	DGM	UGM		UGM
Director of Midwifery Services	DGM	UGM		UGM
Assistant Chief Administrator	DGM	DDGM		DDGM
Chief Ambulance Officer	DGM			
District Building Officer	DGM	DWEM		DWEM
District Engineer	DGM	DWEM		DWEM
Supplies & Commercial Development Manager	DGM	DrF		DrF
Senior Assistant Treasurer(s)	DGM	DrF		DrF
Assistant Chief Administrative Nursing Officer	DGM	CANO		CANO
Director of Nurse Education	DGM	CANO		CANO
Senior Tutor in Midwifery	DGM	CANO		CANO
District Personnel Manager	DGM	AGM		AGM

* includes alternatives to dismissal.
** short of dismissal.

Annexe 13 Levels of dismissals & disciplinary responsibility & delegation (other officers)

	Dismissal*		Disciplinary Action (short of dismissal)		Suspension	
	Responsibility	*Delegation*	*Responsibility*	*Delegation*	*Responsibility*	*Delegation***
Unit Based Staff	Unit General Manager	Appropriate 2nd level officer	Appropriate 2nd level officer	Appropriate 3rd level officer	Appropriate 2nd level officer	Appropriate 3rd level officer
District Based Staff	Chief Officer or Senior Manager	Appropriate 2nd level officer	Appropriate 2nd level officer	Appropriate 3rd level officer	Appropriate 2nd level officer	Appropriate 3rd level officer

Top level officer   District General Manager

1st level officer   (i) Unit General Managers who are members of the Management Board
(ii) Senior Managers – Directors or Chief Officers

2nd level officer   (i) Unit based officers reporting directly to UGM's and who are members of unit management team
(ii) District based officers reporting directly to SM's or CO's and who are Heads of Divisions/Departments

3rd level officer   Unit or District based officers with management responsibilities who are responsible to second (or first) level officers.

*   includes alternatives to dismissal under the policy.

** in certain circumstances, e.g. at night or weekends, the suspension may be undertaken by the most senior officer on duty.

N.B. *The above arrangements are all subject to the overall provisions of Part V of the disciplinary policy.*

Annexe 14 Disciplinary rules

Introduction

The Employment Protection (Consolidation) Act 1978 (Part 1, Section 1, Sub-section 4) states:

> 'Every Statement of terms of employment given to an employee ... shall include a note specifying any disciplinary rules applicable to the employee, or referring to a document which is reasonably accessible to the employee and which specifies such rules.'

The Authority's Written Statement of main terms and particulars of employment (together with the Authority's Disciplinary Procedure) fulfils its legal requirement to refer to a document specifying such rules and indicating where it may be obtained.

This document specifies the disciplinary rules as laid down by this Health Authority. The rules are applicable to all employees of the Authority and it is the Authority's intention that every employee be given a copy of this document.

The need for rules

The need for disciplinary rules is more than just to fulfil a legal requirement. Rules are necessary for promoting fairness and order in the treatment of individuals and in the conduct of industrial relations. They assist the organisation to operate effectively and help to secure the efficient and safe performance of work and the maintenance of satisfactory relationships within the workforce and between employees and managers.

In addition to Authority-wide rules, other local or specific rules may apply, for example in a specific hospital or laboratory and breach of these also could result in disciplinary action including dismissal.

The purpose of rules

Management is responsible for maintaining discipline and the purpose of disciplinary rules is to give a clear indication to every employee of the standards of conduct required of him or her. The rules are the means of setting the standards and do so by indicating clearly the kinds and instances of conduct at work which are regarded as unsatisfactory and which will not be tolerated.

The rules also indicate the degree of seriousness with which management views such breaches of conduct or of duty. In addition, the rules indicate the level of disciplinary action which different offences will incur.

In conclusion, the following disciplinary rules inform the Authority's employees of the conduct required of them by indicating the kinds of offences which management seeks to deter and the consequences of failure to meet the standard set by not complying with the rules.

The rules cannot cover all circumstances and will vary in application according to the type of work, working conditions, environment and size of establishment.

1. *Gross misconduct* The undermentioned offences are regarded by the Authority as constituting gross misconduct. An employee who commits any of these offences will therefore be regarded as having fundamentally breached his or her contract of employment and can expect to be summarily dismissed in accordance with the Authority's Disciplinary Policy. Summary dismissal, which is defined as termination of employment following investigation but without notice or payment in lieu of notice, will be the normal action taken against an employee on the first occasion on which any of these offences is committed.

It is the Authority's policy that a thorough investigation will be carried out in all cases where any disciplinary action may result. Consequently, every case will be considered on individual merit but will also have full regard for the principle of consistent and uniform treatment of every employee. Due consideration will therefore be given to any mitigating circumstances attendant in each case.

The action taken will reflect the seriousness of the offence. The seriousness of the offence (and therefore the culpability of the employee) will depend on the individual circumstances and consequences of each case, but particular consideration will be given to the implications or resultant consequences of the offence; whether the offence is persistent; or whether a previous warning has been issued for the same or related offence(s), for example negligent performance in respect of safety as a first offence may result in a final written warning but where this jeopardises patient care or places others at risk, dismissal may result.

1.1   Theft or unauthorised possession of NHS property or money or patients' property or money or that of a fellow employee or visitor or member of the public.
1.2   Falsification of any document or documentation requiring completion during the course of employment (for example application form, expense claim form or sick note) and which undermines the relationship between the employee and the Authority as his employer.

Any misuse of the time clock (or any time recording system) including clocking in or clocking out any other employee.

Any one of these offences is regarded by the Authority as fraud on the employee's part.
1.3   Unacceptable behaviour towards staff, patients, visitors or public in the course of work or on NHS premises including:
1.3.1 fighting, assault or physical provocation or threat
1.3.2 extreme verbal abuse or insolence
1.3.3 obscene or indecent behaviour in the course of work or on NHS premises.
1.4.   Gross negligence in the performance of duties, for example breach of procedures where loss of money or property results; or offence(s) relating to health and safety practice, procedure or regulations where a person's safety is seriously jeopardised.
1.5   Gross insubordination including:
1.5.1 wilful refusal or failure to carry out a reasonable instruction.

> 1.5.2 behaviour or other display of attitude which seriously undermines management's authority.

1.6 Incapacity for duty whilst at work due to drink or drugs which have been self-inflicted and not prescribed by a person qualified to do so.

1.7 Wilful or malicious damage:

> 1.7.1 to NHS property, premises or equipment
>
> 1.7.2 to the property within Authority premises belonging to patients, visitors or other members of staff or the public
>
> 1.7.3 to any other property or premises in the course of work.

1.8 Unauthorised disclosure of information which is confidential to the Authority. This will apply in particular to information disclosed in relation to a patient, or member of staff or where the relationship of trust between the employee and the Authority as the employer is undermined.

1.9 Receipt of money, goods, favours or excessive hospitality given in an attempt to unfairly influence members of staff in the exercise of their duties for example, bribery directed at obtaining preferential treatment. (See H.M. (62)21).

1.10 Serious professional misconduct.

The foregoing does not represent a comprehensive or exhaustive list of those offences regarded as gross misconduct warranting summary dismissal. Offences other than those listed above may be regarded as gross misconduct and where considered as such will also result in summary dismissal. Furthermore, nothing in these rules absolves staff from the provisions of the Mental Health Acts 1959 and 1983.

2. *Other cases leading to dismissal* The following cases can lead to dismissal although they may not necessarily be offences of gross misconduct. The Authority therefore considers it necessary to bring these to the attention of its employees.

In the following cases it is the Authority's policy that a thorough investigation will precede any hearing from which disciplinary action may result. Consequently, each case will be considered on individual merit but will also have full regard for the principle of consistent and uniform treatment of every employee.

2.1 Withholding information which has a serious bearing on the offer or continuation of employment, for example, a past conviction which an employee fails to disclose.

2.2 Conviction for a criminal offence committed in or out of work which renders the employee unsuitable or unavailable for continued employment.

2.3 Continuation in a post in employment which would result in either the employee or the Health Authority contravening a duty or restriction imposed by law, for example failure to obtain a work permit or professional registration, or disqualification from driving where driving is an essential feature of the job.

2.4 Any incidence of misconduct following a final written warning which has already been issued for misconduct.

3. *Misconduct* The undermentioned offences are regarded by the Authority as misconduct warranting a disciplinary warning in accordance with the Authority's Disciplinary Policy. The severity of disciplinary measure used will depend on the circumstances of the case.

The stage of disciplinary warning issued will reflect the level of seriousness of the offence. The seriousness of the offence (and therefore the culpability of the employee) will depend on the individual circumstances and consequences of the case, but particular consideration will be given to the implications or resultant consequences of the offence(s); whether the offence is persistent, or whether a previous warning has been issued for the same or related offence(s).

Mitigating circumstances and the need for consistent treatment will be given full consideration in every case and in compliance with the Authority's policy every case which may result in disciplinary action will be fully investigated before any decision is taken.

3.1 Unacceptable or unsubstantiated or excessive absence from work. This would include absence where national or local sickness regulations have been abused.

3.2 Unauthorised absence from work without notification within four hours of the normal time of commencement of duty. (See local rules).

3.3 Lateness, unpunctuality, failure to comply with break times, or leaving the expected place of duty without prior permission.

3.4 Unhygienic, improper or unsuitable appearance or condition which can reasonably be expected at work including:

    3.4.1 failure to wear uniform in work

    3.4.2 unauthorised wearing of uniform outside work

    3.4.3 failure to wear protective clothing where issued

    3.4.4 unsatisfactory condition or appearance relating to personal hygiene.

3.5 Negligent performance in respect of:

    3.5.1 Health and Safety Rules

    3.5.2 Safe Food Handling

    3.5.3 Security

    3.5.4 Failure to report an accident or any other untoward occurrence.

3.6 Improper use of working hours or authority equipment or facilities, for example gambling or running a business during working hours.

3.7 The possession in work of dangerous or offensive weapons.

3.8 Sleeping on duty.

3.9 Failure to comply with local or departmental rules, workplace rules (where applicable) relating to performance, safety or conduct.

The foregoing offences do not represent a comprehensive or exhaustive list of those regarded as misconduct. Offences other than those listed above may also be regarded as misconduct.

Reproduced with the permission of Mr Geoff Davies, District Personnel Manager, South Glamorgan Health Authority.

Appendix 15 The Department of Health and the liability for medical and dental staff

Medical negligence: new NHS arrangements

Introduction

1. New arrangements for dealing with medical negligence claims in the hospital and community health services are being introduced from 1 January 1990. Subject to final agreement with the medical defence organisations on the financial arrangements, health authorities will take direct financial responsibility for cases initiated before that date, as well as for new claims. In future, medical and dental staff employed by health authorities (health boards in Scotland and Northern Ireland) will no longer be required under the terms of their contracts to subscribe to a medical defence organisation. However, the health authority indemnity will cover only health authority responsibilities. The Health Departments advise practitioners to maintain their defence body membership in order to ensure they are covered for any work which does not fall within the scope of the indemnity scheme.

Set up below are the Health Departments' replies to some of the questions most commonly asked about the operation of the new arrangements.

2. Why is this change necessary?

Medical defence subscriptions rose rapidly in the 1980s, because of growth both in the number of medical negligence cases and in the size of the awards made by the courts. Subscriptions tripled between 1986 and 1988, and the Doctors' and Dentists' Review Body concluded that to take account of the increase in subscriptions through practitioners' pay would lead to distortions in pay and pensions. The pressure to relate subscription rates to the practitioner's specialty underlined the difficulty of maintaining the system. The Health Departments issued in March 1989 a proposal for a health authority indemnity. The new arrangements follow discussions with the medical defence organisations, the medical profession, health authority management and other interested bodies.

Coverage

3. Who is covered by the health authority indemnity scheme?

Health authorities as employers are liable at law for the negligence (acts or omissions) of their staff in the course of their NHS employment. The legal position is the same for medical and dental staff as for other NHS employees, but for many years doctors and dentists have themselves taken out medical defence cover through the three medical defence organisations (MDOs). Under the indemnity scheme, health authorities will take direct responsibility for costs and damages arising from medical negligence where they (as employers) are vicariously liable for the acts and omissions of their medical and dental staff.

4. Does this include clinical academics and research workers?

Health authorities are vicariously liable for the work done by university medical staff and other research workers under their honorary contracts in the course of their NHS duties, but not for pre-clinical or other work in the university.

5. Is private work in NHS hospitals covered by the indemnity scheme?

Health authorities will not be responsible for a consultant's private practice, even in an NHS hospital. However, where junior medical staff are involved in the care of private patients in NHS hospitals, they would normally be doing so as part of their contract with the health authority. It remains advisable that any junior doctor who might be involved in any work outside the scope of his or her employment should have medical defence (or insurance) cover.

6. Is Category 2 work covered?

Category 2 work (eg reports for insurance companies) is by definition not undertaken for the employing health authority, and will therefore not be covered by the indemnity scheme; medical defence cover would be appropriate.

7. Are GMC disciplinary proceedings covered?

Health authorities should not be financially responsible for the defence of medical staff involved in GMC disciplinary proceedings. It is the responsibility of the practitioner concerned to take out medical defence cover against such an eventuality.

8. Is a hospital doctor doing a GP locum covered?

This would not be the responsibility of the health authority, since it would be general practice. The hospital doctor and the general practitioners concerned should ensure that there is appropriate medical defence cover.

9. Is a GP seeing his own patient in hospital covered?

A GP providing medical care to patients in hospital under a contractual arrangement, eg where the GP was employed as a clinical assistant, will be covered by the health authority indemnity. On the other hand, if the health authority is essentially providing only hotel services and the patient(s) remain in the care of the GP, the GP would be responsible and medical defence cover would be appropriate.

10. Are GP trainees working in general practice covered?

In general practice the responsibility for training and for paying the salary of a GP trainee rests with the trainer (with funds from the FPC). Where the trainee's medical defence subscription is higher than the subscription of an SHO in the hospital service, he or she may apply through the trainer for the difference in subscription to be reimbursed. While the trainee is receiving a salary in general practice it is advisable that both the trainee and the trainer, and indeed other members of the practice, should have medical defence cover.

11. Are clinical trials covered?

The new arrangements do not alter the current legal position. If the health authority was responsible for a clinical trial authorised under the Medicines Act 1968 or its subordinate legislation and that trial was carried out by or on behalf of a doctor involving NHS patients of his, such a doctor would be covered by the indemnity scheme. Similarly, for a trial not involving medicines, the health authority would take financial responsibility unless the trial were covered by such other indemnity as may have been agreed between the health authority and those responsible for the trial. In any case, health authorities should take steps to make sure that they are informed of clinical trials in which their staff are taking part in their NHS employment and that these trials have the required Research Ethics Committee approval.

12. Would a doctor be covered if he was working other than in accordance with the duties of his post?

Such a doctor would be covered by the health authority indemnity for actions in the course of NHS employment, and this should be interpreted liberally. For work not covered in this way the doctor may have a civil, or even in extreme circumstances criminal, liability for his actions.

13. Are doctors attending accident victims ('Good Samaritan' acts) covered?

By definition, 'Good Samaritan' acts are not part of the doctor's work for the employing authority. Medical defence organisations are willing to provide low-cost cover against the (unusual) event of a doctor performing such an act being sued for negligence.

14. Are doctors in public health medicine or in community health services doing work for local authorities covered? Are occupational physicians covered?

Doctors in public health medicine, or clinical medical officers, carrying out local authority functions under their health authority contract would be acting in the course of their NHS employment. They will therefore be covered by the health authority indemnity. The same principle applies to occupational physicians employed by health authorities.

15. Will NHS hospital doctors working for other agencies, eg the Prison Service, be covered?

In general, health authorities will not be financially responsible for the acts of NHS staff when they are working on a contractual basis for other agencies. (Conversely, they will be responsible where, for example, a Ministry of Defence doctor works in an NHS hospital.) Either the agency commissioning the work would be responsible, or the doctor should have medical defence cover. However, health authorities' indemnity should cover work for which they pay a fee, such as domiciliary visits and family planning services.

16. Are retired doctors covered?

The health authority indemnity will apply to acts or omissions in the course of NHS employment, regardless of when the claim was notified. Health authorities will thus cover doctors who have subsequently left the Service, but they may seek their co-operation in statements in the defence of a case.

17. Are doctors offering services to voluntary bodies such as the Red Cross or hospices covered?

The health authority would be responsible for the doctor's actions only if the health authority were responsible for the medical staffing of the voluntary body. If not, the doctors concerned may wish to ensure that they have medical defence cover, as they do at present.

18. Will a health authority provide cover for a locum hospital doctor?

A health authority will take financial responsibility for the acts and omissions of a locum doctor, whether 'internal' or provided by an external agency.

19. Are private sector rotations for hospital staff covered?

The medical staff of independent hospitals are responsible for their own medical defence cover, subject to the requirements of the hospital managers. If NHS staff in the training grades work in independent hospitals as part of their NHS training, they would be covered by the health authority indemnity, provided that such work was covered by an NHS contract.

20. Will academic General Practice be covered?

The Health Departments have no plans to extend the health authority indemnity to academic departments of general practice. In respect of general medical services FPCs will be making payments by fees and allowances which include an element for expenses, of which medical defence subscriptions are a part.

Practical arrangements

21. On what basis will medical defence organisations handle claims for health authorities?

MDOs, in advising on claims for health authorities, will act as their agents; the charging arrangements for such services are for agreement between the MDO and the Authority concerned.

22. Will doctors be reimbursed by MDOs for the 'unexpired' portion of their subscriptions?

This is a matter between each MDO and its members.

23. Will membership of a medical defence organisation continue to be a contractual obligation?

On an individual basis doctors and dentists may wish to continue their membership in order to receive the cover referred to in paragraphs 5–20 above, as well as the other legal and advisory services provided by the MDOs. The Health Departments are advising health authorities that they should no longer require their medical and dental staff to subscribe to an MDO, but a health authority could require a doctor to be a member of an MDO if the doctor were to be carrying out private work on NHS premises. The two-thirds reimbursement of subscriptions will cease at the end of 1989.

24. Will medical defence subscriptions be tax-allowable in future?

The Health Departments understand that medical defence subscriptions will continue to be allowable under income tax rules.

25. What happens if a doctor wishes to contest a claim which the health authority would prefer to settle out of court, eg where a point of principle or a doctor's reputation is at stake?

While the final decision in a case rests with the health authority since it will bear the financial consequences, it should take careful note of the practitioner's view. Health authorities may seek the advice of the relevant MDO on whether a case should be contested, and they should not settle cases without good cause.

26. If a doctor wishes to have separate representation in a case, what would be the extent of his liability?

Since it is the health authority which is sued for the medical negligence of its staff and which will in future be solely financially liable, then it must have the ultimate right to decide how the defence of a case is to be handled. Subject to this, a health authority may welcome a practitioner being separately advised in a case without cost to the health authority. However, if a practitioner claims that his interests in any case are distinct from those of the health authority and wishes to be separately represented in the proceedings, he will need the agreement of the plaintiff, the health authority and the court. If liability is established, he would have to pay not only his own legal expenses but also any further costs incurred as a result of his being separately represented. The health authority would remain liable for the full award of damages to the plaintiff.

27. Will health authorities put restrictions on the clinical autonomy of doctors?

Health authorities have a responsibility to organise services in a manner which is in the best interests of patients. In the past, medical defence organisations have advised doctors and dentists on patterns of practice carrying unacceptable dangers to patients. However, there is no question of health authorities barring certain services which carry risks but are a high priority for patients.

28. Will health authorities be able to secure statements from doctors for the defence of a case of medical negligence?

Health authorities will need co-operation from medical and dental staff if they are to defend cases. As part of this, practitioners should supply such statements or documents as the health authority or its solicitors may reasonably require in investigating or defending any claim. A doctor's refusal without good reason to provide a statement could result in the health authority being unable to defend itself properly and so incurring additional costs.

29. Will health authorities be able to trace doctors who formerly worked for them?

It is accepted that health authorities may have difficulty in tracing the doctors responsible, especially if they were junior medical staff at the time, and in securing statements from them; they may find the MDOs helpful in this respect. Often, however, good medical records kept at the time will be of more value than statements made some years after the event.

30. Will the new arrangements apply to NHS Trust hospitals (self-governing units)?

As employers, NHS Trusts will be vicariously liable for the acts of their employed medical and dental staff, and will take the financial responsibility for negligence. Further guidance will be issued in due course.

Financial effects

31. How can District Health Authorities meet damages which could be as much as £1m for a single case?

RHAs have been asked to make arrangements under which they will provide an element of cost-sharing with Districts for medical negligence costs above a certain level, as most RHAs do for non-medical negligence actions at present. And for a transitional period health authorities will have access (under certain criteria) to some of the reserves of the MDOs.

32. The incidence of medical negligence damages may be uneven as between Regions; how will that be met?

It is quite likely that some Regions will have to pay out more under the new arrangements than they would in reimbursing two-thirds of medical defence subscriptions. The funds from the MDOs will be of some help in the short term, but in the longer run the incidence of medical negligence costs and damages will fall on the Regions where they arise.

UK Health Departments
December 1989

Information to be returned annually, no later than 31 May (starting 31/5/90)

1. The following information should be supplied for the previous financial year:

   i.   The number of claims of medical negligence against the health authority and/or its employees, including the number of cases brought forward from an earlier period;

   ii. The number of such cases settled during the period with the health authority's costs, including damages payable, in the following cost bands:

	Number of cases	£	£
(a)		0	– 100,000
(b)		100,000	– 200,000
(c)		200,000	– 300,000
(d)		over £300,000	

   iii. The total cost of the settlements reached or awards made; distinguishing

   a) the Authority's costs from the payment of the plaintiff's costs and damages; and

   b) an estimate of costs and damages attributable to medical negligence, as distinct from negligence of other staff.

2. Returns to be sent to: FPS1A2
                             Room 426 Portland Court
                             158–176 Great Portland Street
                             London W1N 5TB

Appendix 16 Health service management: Hospital Complaints Procedure Act 1985*

Unless otherwise notified, this Circular but not the directions to which it refers will cease to be valid on 31 May 1993.

Summary

1. This Circular encloses at Annexe A a copy of the directions required by S.1 of the Hospital Complaints Procedure Act 1985 and advises on the procedure to be operated in respect of complaints by hospital patients.

Background

2. The Hospital Complaints Procedure Act received the Royal Assent in July 1985. The Act requires the Secretary of State to issue directions on the complaints

*Health Circular to Regional Health Authorities, District Health Authorities and Special Health Authorities (for action) and Community Health Councils and Family Practitioner Committees (for information), June 1988.

542

procedure to be operated in respect of hospital patients and the steps to publicise the procedure. It came into force on 11 July 1989.

3. Health Authorities were invited in 1986 to comment on proposals for handling complaints. The consultation exercise offered the opportunity to re-examine existing complaints procedures. Many authorities confirmed either that their local practices corresponded already to the proposed procedures or that arrangements were being made to align their procedures accordingly.

4. The directions enclosed at Annexe A confirm the arrangements which health authorities are obliged to make for dealing with complaints and for publicising these. The remainder of this circular advises how authorities may interpret the requirements of the directions.

The need for a complaints procedure

5. Patients are entitled to bring to the attention of health authorities aspects of their care and treatment about which they are unhappy. The Department recognises that suggestions, constructive criticism and complaints can be valuable aids to management in maintaining and developing better standards of health care. It is important that no one (staff or patients) should be inhibited from making valid complaints and that there is full confidence that these will be given full, proper and speedy consideration. Many matters that trouble patients can be dealt with as they arise. Staff should be encouraged to be aware of and to deal with these in a way which reassures the patient and to bring the complaint to the attention of management when this is appropriate.

Procedural requirements

6. The basis of any complaints procedure is good communication. Problems of communication between patients and staff can generate misunderstandings which can result in complaints. Good communications may help defuse awkward situations. However, not all complaints can be dealt with on the spot and in this informal way. Some complaints will be of such concern to the patient that they warrant consideration and a formal response by a senior officer of the authority or it may be that the complaint is comparatively trivial but the patient feels unwilling or unable to discuss the matter with the staff who are directly involved. Again, good communications will be necessary to ensure that the complainant can give full expression to his concerns and that the full facts about the complaint are obtained.

7. The directions outline the mandatory requirements which health authorities must adopt in establishing complaints procedures. They involve

(i)   *A designated officer* Each Health Authority must designate a senior officer for each hospital or group of hospitals for which it is responsible. The designated officer should be located in the hospital for which he is responsible and his where-abouts made known to facilitate contact by patients or those acting on a patient's behalf. The Unit General Manager might be the appropriate person for this task. The designated officer will be the recipient of formal complaints made by or on behalf of patients and will be accountable for the investigation of complaints other than those involving clinical judgement, serious untoward incidents, disciplinary proceedings, physical abuse of patients or criminal offences. Where the designated officer is also the Unit General Manager he may well be directly involved in these particular complaints. But investigation of these may also involve other senior officers, e.g. the Regional Medical Officer (RMO) or the equivalent or the District General Manager (DGM), or members of the Authority (see sub paragraph iv below). The designated officer should not be denied access to relevant records which are essential for the investigation of a complaint. The designated officer should normally be available to assist in cases of minor grievances which the patient feels unable to discuss with e.g. ward staff.

(ii) *Who may complain* Any person who is or has been a patient at the hospital (either as an inpatient or outpatient) is eligible to make a complaint. If the person concerned has died or is otherwise unable to act for himself the complaint should be accepted from a close relative, or friend, or a body or individual suitable to represent him. The designated officer must be satisfied that where the patient is capable, the complaint is being made with his knowledge and consent.

(iii) *Investigating the complaint* In investigating the complaint, the designated officer must ensure that he has a full picture from the complainant of the events complained about. This may involve a preliminary interview to clarify the nature of the complaint or to obtain further information. It may be possible at this stage to resolve the issue to the complainant's satisfaction without taking the matter further. Care must be taken not to prejudice the outcome of any further investigation.

The designated officer, in liaison with other appropriate senior officers, should circulate details of the complaint to the staff concerned for their comments and seek to agree a reply. General complaints about, for example, the hotel services would be sent to the Head of the Department concerned for advice on a reply. Care must be taken not to introduce delays into the system by allowing excessive periods for comment. The aim should be to process the complaint speedily and thoroughly at all stages. The complainant must be kept informed of progress and where appropriate interim replies or holding letters must be sent. Where the designated officer considers that a complaint carries a threat of litigation he should seek legal advice on whether and in what form an investigation might proceed to minimise the risk of prejudicing any civil proceedings. The possibility of legal proceedings should not prevent the officer undertaking the investigations necessary to uncover faults in procedures and/or prevent a recurrence.

(iv) *Further action to certain complaints* Where the complaint concerns:
    (a) the exercise of *Clinical Judgement* which cannot be resolved by discussion with the consultant concerned;

(b) what the authority is satisfied constitutes *a serious untoward incident* involving harm to a patient;

(c) the conduct of hospital medical or dental staff which the Authority considers ought to be the subject of *disciplinary proceedings*;

(d) the alleged *physical abuse of patients*;

(e) a possible *criminal offence*;

the designated officer should bring the matter to his senior officers' attention (or if appropriate the RMO) without delay so that appropriate action can be taken to ensure that the complaint is dealt with promptly in accordance with the Department's guidelines and local procedures.

(v) *Conclusion of an investigation* When an investigation into a complaint has been completed the designated officer must complete a report and send a letter detailing the results of the investigation to the person who made the complaint, to any person who is involved in the complaint and where appropriate to the manager of any Department or service concerned. The letter should be informative both as to the reasons for any failure in service and any steps taken to prevent a recurrence and should contain an apology where appropriate. If the complainant remains dissatisfied he should be advised to refer the matter to the Health Service Commissioner unless the complaint is clearly outside the Health Service Commissioner's jurisdiction or the complainant proposes to take further action through the courts.

(vi) *Monitoring complaints* Health Authorities must monitor the arrangements. The purpose of this requirement is to ensure that health authorities monitor trends in complaints and can direct that appropriate action is taken. The designated officer should therefore provide summaries of complaints for the health authority. These summaries should be anonymised to preserve confidentiality of patients. The monitoring role must be undertaken by the authority itself, a committee of the authority or specified authority members. Progress in dealing with complaints should be kept under review by the District General Manager who should report to the Authority at quarterly intervals about any cases outstanding.

(vii) *Publicity* Publicity must be given to the procedure. This is an essential part of improving the public perception of the complaints procedure. Health authorities should consider giving publicity to the procedures using:

(a) *Admission booklets* Information about making a complaint should be given in the hospital booklet issued to patients on or prior to admission to hospital and available in hospital outpatient departments. It is essential for the location of the designated officer to be included.

(b) *Leaflets* A leaflet explaining the complaints procedure and including a reference to the Health Service Commissioner's role in investigating complaints should be available for all patients. In addition to explaining the procedure in straightforward terms, the leaflet should give the location of the designated officer. Authorities should consider the need to make leaflets available in ethnic minority languages.

(c) *Notices* These should be displayed in health authority premises including reception areas. Notices should give the location of the designated officer to whom appropriate comments, suggestions and complaints should be addressed.

(d) *CHCs* Publicity material should be available to CHCs for information and issue to the public.

(e) *Staff training* All staff will need to be made aware of the complaints procedure and to know the name and location of the designated officer to enable them to refer patients. Training will be needed to ensure that staff attitudes are positive and do not deter legitimate complaints.

Additional procedures

8. In considering their procedures health authorities are asked to take the following elements, which are not requirements under the directions, into account.

(i) *Form of complaint* It is not a requirement that a complaint should be in writing. But it is important that a note be made in cases where the complaint is not readily settled and where a dispute as to the precise nature of the complaint might arise. This is particularly so when a formal investigation is likely. Where the complainant is unable to put the formal complaint in writing the designated officer should ensure that a record of the complaint is made and ask the complainant to sign it. A refusal to sign by the complainant should not delay investigation of the complaint.

(ii) *Time limits* Complaints should be made and dealt with as quickly as possible. The longer the delay the more memories fade and less fruitful the investigation of the complaint. It is reasonable to expect that complaints should be made within three months of the incident giving rise to the complaint and publicity should encourage this. However there may be circumstances in which this recommended time limit may not be appropriate and the directions provide the designated officer with the discretion to extend the period if it is considered that the complainant has good reason for delay.

(iii) *Complaints about the Community Health Services* Complaints about the Community Health Services do not come within the scope of the procedures to be laid down in the directions under the Hospital Complaints Procedure Act 1985. Health Authorities are asked to consider that the procedure directed for the handling of general complaints about hospital services should also be adopted in respect of the community health services.

Investigation by statutory authorities

The Health Service Commissioner

9. Section 1 (2) of the Hospital Complaints Procedure Act provides that nothing in the procedure promulgated in the directions shall preclude investigation by the Health

Service Commissioner. The Health Service Commissioner may therefore investigate a complaint about health authority services or maladministration if a complainant is not satisfied with the conduct or outcome of the health authority's own investigations. The Health Service Commissioner cannot investigate complaints relating to actions taken solely in consequence of the exercise of clinical judgement. Whether the action is taken solely in consequence of the exercise of clinical judgement will be determined by the Health Service Commissioner.

The Mental Health Act Commission

10. Section 120(1) of the Mental Health Act empowers the Mental Health Act Commission to investigate any complaint which a detained patient thinks has not been dealt with satisfactorily by the hospital managers. Nothing in the directions preclude such investigation by the Mental Health Act Commission.

The Police

11. The District General Manager must be consulted where it appears that a criminal offence may have been committed. Where the allegation is serious and substantial the police must be notified immediately.

Complaints about clinical judgement

12. The current procedures for dealing with complaints relating to the exercise of clinical judgement by hospital medical and dental staff are subject to an agreement with the medical profession. The procedures were outlined in circular HC(81)5 Annex Part III (A copy is attached as Annexe B).

13. The procedures provide for the complainant to be accompanied by a relative or personal friend. It is for the complainant to decide who the friend is. Such a person is there to help and support the complainant and not to act as an advocate nor in a way which detracts from the clinical nature of the consultation. The friend may sometimes help a less articulate complainant explain their concerns but this should not be allowed to create an adversarial situation.

Cancellation of circulars

14. The guidance contained in HN(78)39, HC(81)5, HN(83)31 and DA(86)14 is hereby withdrawn and those circulars should be regarded as cancelled.

Action

15. Health Authorities are asked to consider this guidance and to ensure that the directions enclosed with this circular are complied with. Regional Health Authorities are asked to confirm by 26 August 1988 to the address below that the required procedures are in place.

From:
Health Services Division (HSIC),
Alexander Fleming House, Elephant and Castle, London SE1 6BY
Tel. 01 407 5522 Ext 6682

Further copies of this Circular may be obtained from DHSS Store Health Publications Unit, No 2 Site, Manchester Road, Heywood, Lancs OL10 2PZ quoting code and serial number appearing at top right hand corner.

Annexe A Directions on hospital complaints procedures

The Secretary of State for Social Services in exercise of the powers conferred on him by Section 17 of the National Health Service Act 1977, hereby directs:

(i) each district health authority in England or Wales; and each of the following special health authorities:
  Each of the Authorities for the London Postgraduate Teaching Hospitals;
  The Board of Governors of the Eastman Dental Hospital;
  Broadmoor Hospital Board;
  Moss Side and Park Lane Hospitals Board;
  Rampton Hospital Board;
to make arrangements, as specified or described in the following paragraphs of these directions, for dealing with complaints made by, or on behalf of, persons who are or have been patients at any hospital for the management of which that authority is responsible and for monitoring the effectiveness of, and for publicising, the arrangements made for dealing with such complaints; and

(ii) that such arrangements should be made and brought into force not later than 29th July 1988.

1. In these Directions:
'authority' means any district health authority or special health authority to whom these directions are given;
'complainant' means a person who is or who has been a patient at a hospital or the person acting on behalf of any such patient in making a complaint in relation to such hospital;
'designated officer' means a person who has been designated by a health authority

as having responsibility for dealing with complaints made in relation to that hospital or group of hospitals.

2. (1) For each hospital or group of hospitals for which an authority has responsibility, there must be an officer designated by the authority as having responsibility for dealing with complaints made in relation to that hospital or group of hospitals.

(2) The duties of a designated officer must include responsibility for receiving, and seeing that action is taken upon, any formal complaint made at the hospital or hospitals for which he is given responsibility and, where the complainant had indicated a wish for him so to do, assisting in dealing with a complaint that is likely to be able to be dealt with informally.

(3) Except to the extent that the subject matter of a complaint falls within any of the categories specified in the next sub-paragraph of these directions the duties of the designated officer must include responsibility for investigating and reporting on the investigation of any formal complaint to the complainant, to any person involved in the complaint, and to such other persons as the authority may require.

(4) To the extent that the subject matter of any complaint made at a hospital or group of hospitals for which a designated officer is responsible:
   (a) concerns the exercise of clinical judgement by a hospital doctor or dentist and cannot be resolved by discussion with the consultant concerned; or
   (b) relates to what the authority is satisfied constitutes a serious untoward incident involving harm to a patient; or
   (c) relates to the conduct of hospital medical or dental staff which the authority considers ought to be the subject of disciplinary proceedings; or
   (d) gives reasonable grounds for inviting a police investigation as to whether a criminal offence may have been committed;
   the duties of the designated officer in accordance with arrangements made pursuant to these directions shall not involve responsibility for investigating the complaint but the designated officer shall be required to bring the matter to the attention of his authority who shall in the case of a matter specified in (a), (b) or (c) of this sub-paragraph, secure that the matter is promptly dealt with in accordance with the appropriate procedure laid down in guidance issued to authorities by the Department of Health and Social Security in respect of England and by the Welsh Office in respect of Wales.

(5) Arrangements made may include provision for a designated officer to have the assistance of other officers of the authority in carrying out his duties under those arrangements and, with the agreement of the designated officer, such other officers may act on his behalf in the performance of those duties.

3. Each authority shall secure that arrangements are made for staff at any hospital for which that authority is responsible to seek to deal informally to the satisfaction of the complainant with any complaint made at that hospital and to advise any complainant, whose complaint cannot be so dealt with to his satisfaction, to make a formal complaint to the designated officer for that hospital.

4. Arrangements for making formal complaints should secure that such complaints are made or recorded in writing. Such complaints should normally be made within three months of the matter complained of arising although the designated officer ought to have a discretion to allow a longer period if satisfied that the complainant had good cause for not having made the complaint earlier. Arrangements made should secure that formal complaints are investigated promptly and that both the complainant and any hospital staff involved are afforded an opportunity to bring to the attention of the designated officer any information or comments they wish to make that are relevant to his investigation of the complaint.

5. Each authority must monitor arrangements made for dealing with complaints at hospitals for which it is responsible. Arrangements must be made for reports to be prepared at quarterly intervals for use by the authority in monitoring progress on the procedure for dealing with complaints, for considering trends in complaints and for taking remedial action on complaints as appropriate.

6. Each authority shall take such steps as are necessary to ensure that any patients at, or visitors to, any hospital for which the authority is responsible as well as the staff working at the hospital, and any Community Health Council covering an area served by that hospital, are fully informed of the arrangements for dealing with complaints made at the hospital and are informed of the identity and location of the designated officer for such hospital.

Signed by authority of the Secretary of State for Social Services

M A Harris
An Assistant Secretary of
the Department of Health
and Social Security

ANNEXE B Memorandum of an agreement for dealing with complaints relating to the exercise of clinical judgement by hospital medical and dental staff (first issued as part of circular HC(81)5)

First stage

18. As explained in Paragraph 5 of Part 1, a complaint may initially be made, and dealt with, orally or in writing. Complaints concerning clinical matters may be made direct to the consultant concerned, or to a health authority or one of its officers. In either case it is the responsibility of the consultant in charge of the patient to look into the clinical aspects of the complaint. This must be the first step in handling the complaint at the *first stage*.

---

[1] In this Memorandum the terms 'medical' and 'doctor' include 'dentists' in appropriate cases.

19. If another member of the medical[1] staff is involved the consultant should discuss the complaint with the doctor concerned at the outset and at all later stages in this procedure. It may be helpful to discuss the complaint with the patient's general practitioner. The consultant should try to resolve the complaint within a few days preferably by offering to see the complainant[2] to discuss the matter and seek to resolve his anxieties. If there is any delay, he should get in touch with the complainant and explain the reason. When the consultant sees the complainant, he should make a brief, strictly factual, record in the hospital notes.

20. Where a complaint is made which involves hospital medical staff other than consultants, the consultant in charge of the patient and the doctor concerned should both be involved in the handling of the complaint at all stages.

21. If the consultant feels the risk of legal action is significant, he should at once bring the matter to the notice of the district administrator.[3] Where there are non-clinical aspects to a complaint made direct to a consultant, the consultant should inform the district administrator, who will arrange for these aspects of the complaint to be considered by an appropriate member of staff.

22. Where a complaint which has a clinical element is made to the authority or one of its officers, the district administrator should show the complaint to the consultant concerned and refer the clinical aspects to him.

23. The normal practice will be for the district administrator to send a written reply to the complainant on behalf of the authority. Any reference to clinical matters in the reply, whether interim or final, should be agreed by the consultant concerned. Sometimes it may be appropriate to confine this to mentioning that the clinical aspects had been discussed between the consultant and the complainant. On occasion, the consultant may wish to send the complainant a written reply direct covering the clinical aspects.

Second stage

24. Where a complainant is dissatisfied with the reply he has received at the first stage, he may renew his complaint either to the authority, one of its administrators or to the consultant. In any case, if he has not so far put his complaint in writing, he should now be asked to do so before his complaint is considered further. The next step, *in this second stage*, is for the Regional Medical Officer (RMO) to be at once informed; this should be done by the consultant, informing the district administrator that he has done so. The RMO will discuss the matter with the consultant.

---

[2] The doctor's first responsibility is to the patient, hence this Memorandum is concerned with complaints made by patients. It applies also to complaints made by parents or guardians of minors, and relatives of those patients with physical or mental disability limiting their competence to deal with the matter themselves, and of deceased patients. The term 'complainant' is used to cover all such cases.
[3] References made to 'district administrator' should be substituted with the words 'district general manager'.

25. At this point, the consultant may indicate to the RMO that he also wishes to discuss the matter with his professional colleagues. After these discussions, he may consider that a further talk with the complainant might resolve the complaint. If this fails, or if the consultant feels that such a meeting would serve no useful purpose, the RMO should discuss with the consultant the value of offering to the complainant the procedure – outlined more fully below – whereby the RMO would arrange for two independent consultants to see the complainant jointly to discuss the problem. If in the light of his discussion with the consultant and – where necessary – the complainant, the RMO considers it appropriate, the procedure of the *third stage* should be set in motion.

Third stage: independent professional review

26. The procedure at the third stage is intended to deal with complaints which are of a substantial nature but which are not *prima facie* (and in the light of legal advice where appropriate) likely to be the subject of more formal action either by the health authority or through the courts. The procedure is intended for use in suitable instances as an alternative to the inquiry procedures provided in HM(66)15, though these will remain available for use when necessary. It would not be appropriate if legal powers such as subpoena seem likely to be required. Nor is it intended that the new procedure should be invoked for complaints of a trivial nature.

27. Arrangements should be made by the RMO for all aspects of the case to be considered by two independent consultants in active practice in the appropriate specialty or specialties. They should be nominated by the Joint Consultants Committee. At least one should be a doctor working in a comparable hospital in another Region. These 'second opinions' should have the opportunity to read all the clinical records. They should discuss the case with the consultant concerned and any other member of the medical staff involved as well as with the complainant. The meeting between the two independent consultants and the complainant should be in the nature of a medical consultation. The consultant who had been in charge of the patient at the time of the event giving rise to the complaint should not be present at the meeting, but should be available if required. The complainant should, if he wishes, be accompanied by a relative or personal friend and might wish to ask the general practitioner to be present.

28. 'Second opinions' should discuss the clinical aspects of the problem fully with the complainant. In cases in which it is their view that the clinical judgement of the medical staff concerned has been exercised responsibly, they should endeavour to resolve the complainant's anxieties. The view they have reached and the outcome of the discussion with the complainant should be reported to the RMO on a confidential basis.

29. In other cases the 'second opinions' might feel that discussion with the medical staff concerned would avoid similar problems arising in the future. When they had held such a discussion they would inform the complainant and would explain to him, as far as appropriate, how it was hoped to overcome the problems which had been identified. They should not provide a detailed report for the complainant but they should report the action they had taken to the RMO. The 'second opinions' would also consider whether

there were any other circumstances which had contributed to the problems in the case and on which they could usefully make recommendations, which they would include in their report to the RMO. These might include matters requiring action by the health authority, for example the workload carried by the medical or nursing staff.

30. In exceptional cases it may appear to the 'second opinions', at any stage of an investigation, that the particular case is not appropriate to the second opinions procedure and that the complaint would be best pursued by alternative means. In this event they should report to the RMO accordingly.

Concluding action by the health authority

31. The district administrator will on completion of the review by the 'second opinions', write formally to the complainant on behalf of the authority, with a copy to the consultant. The district administrator will, where appropriate, explain any action the authority has taken as a result of the complaint but, where clinical matters are concerned, he will follow the RMO's advice regarding the comment which would be appropriate. So far as the authority is concerned the matter will remain confidential unless previous or subsequent publicity makes it essential for the authority to reply publicly, in which case comment on clinical matters will be confined to the terms of the district administrator's letter.

The Health Service Commissioner

32. Complaints relating to clinical judgement remain outside the responsibility of the Health Service Commissioner. However, it will be possible for him to advise complainants whose complaints contain elements of clinical judgement of the availability of the procedure described in this part of the Memorandum.

Appendix 17 Redundancy, reorganisation and the NHS

1. N.B. Redundancy arrangements are *contractual* not statutory. The Redundancy Provision of the Employment Protection (Consolidation) Act 1978 does *not* apply to NHS employees who come under the Whitley Council: General Council Conditions of Service – Section XXV (June 1975).

2. *Remedy* is to the Industrial Tribunal only after compliance with the requirements of the General Circular (*Pearce* v. *Epsom Group Hospital Management Committee* 1967 1.T.R. 328).

3. *Redundancy* is defined according to the statutory definition: (Sect 45(i) of G.C. handbook S.81(2) E.P. (C) A.1978) dismissal by reason of redundancy if the dismissal is attributable wholly or mainly to

(a) The fact that his employer has ceased, or intends to cease, to carry on the business for the purposes for which the employee was employed by him, or has ceased, or intends to cease, to carry on the business in the place where the employee was so employed or

(b) the fact that the requirements of that business for employees to carry out work of a particular kind, or for employees to carry out work of a particular kind in the place where he was so employed, have ceased or diminished or are expected to cease or diminish.

Case Law would be followed in the interpretation of this definition: e.g. work place disappears = contractual place of work NOT geographical area, *Rowbotham* v. *Arthur Lee* 1974; work disappears = contractual work, *O'Neill* v. *Merseyside Plumbing Co. Ltd*. 1973 (*Lee* v. *Notts. C.C.* 1980 C.A. – employee knew work running down when commenced; entitled to R.P.)

4. *Conditions of eligibility*
   1. Qualifying Service – not less than 104 weeks reckonable service (16 hours + per week or 8 hours for 5 years), in the National Health Service in Great Britain.
   2. Employee within purview of the Whitley Councils for the Health Service (Great Britain).
   3. Not come within excluded category – i.e.
   (a) is employed on a fixed term contract and completes the term of that contract;
   (b) is dismissed for reasons of misconduct, with or without notice;
   (c) is aged 65 or over (male) or 60 or over (female);
   (d) obtains without a break or with a break not exceeding 4 weeks suitable alternative employment with the same or another Health Service Authority in Great Britain;
   (e) unreasonably refuses to accept or apply for suitable alternative employment with the same or another Health Service Authority in Great Britain;
   (f) leaves his employment before expiry of notice.

5. There must be *a dismissal* – onus on employee to show this. Once employee has proved he was dismissed, then that dismissal is presumed for the purposes of 1.T. proceedings to have been by reason of redundancy unless the contrary is proved. Dismissal includes constructive dismissal.

6. Redundancy is a statutory reason for dismissal, but the employer must show he acted reasonably. Failure to do so will enable employee to apply for remedy for UNFAIR DISMISSAL.

7. Contractual NHS scheme must incorporate the Detailed CONSULTATIONS required by the statutory scheme S.99 and E.P.A. 1975 (NHS is not excluded). Code of Practice 1972 should be followed.

8. Contractual NHS scheme does provide for a trial period for the suitable alternative employment (like statutory provisions).

9. Time Off for seeking a job or arranging training (S.31. E.P. (C) A78) applies to NHS employees. Employee must have been continuously employed for 2 years or more and must be given notice of dismissal by reason of redundancy. Employee is entitled to reasonable PAID time off.

Suitable alternative employment – definition from Section 45 General Conditions of Service, Whitley Council

8. 'Suitable alternative employment', for the purposes of paragraph 7, refers to both the place and to the capacity in which the employee would be employed. The following

considerations shall be applied in deciding whether a post is suitable alternative employment and whether it was unreasonably refused:

8.1 *Place* A post is normally suitable in place if it involves no additional travelling expenses or is within 6 miles of the employee's home. If the new post is at a greater distance, the fact that assistance will be given with extra travelling expenses (see paragraph 6 of Section 23) will normally outweigh any added difficulties in travel, but exceptionally an employee's special personal circumstances will be considered in comparison with the travel undertaken by other employees in comparable grades. If the post is too far for daily travel, it will be reasonable, since removal expenses will be payable, to require staff (other than those who can be expected to seek employment in their neighbourhood) to move home unless they can adduce special circumstances such as age.

8.2 *Capacity* Suitable alternative employment may not necessarily be in the same grade; the employment should be judged in the light of the employee's qualifications and ability to perform the duties. Nor need it be at exactly the same pay. A post carrying salary protection for the employee should on that fact alone be treated as suitable in capacity.

Glossary

actus reus the physical elements which make up the definition of a crime.

bailee a person who undertakes to care for the property of another.

bailment the transfer of property from a bailor to a bailee.

bailor one who leaves property in the care of another.

burden of proof the task of establishing the facts.

case citation the reference to an earlier reported case made possible because of the reference system, e.g. 1981 1 All ER 267 means the first volume of the All England Reports for 1981 at Page 267 which is the reference for the case of *Whitehouse* v. *Jordan*. Where Whitehouse is the plaintiff, Jordan the defendant and 'v' stands for versus, i.e. against. Other law reports include:

AC   Appeals Court
QB   Queens Bench Division
WLR   Weekly Law Reports.

civil refers to matters which are non-criminal, i.e. they pertain to the civil courts.

committal proceedings the hearing which takes place in the Magistrates Court to determine if the case should go to the Crown Court for trial.

criminal refers to matters which pertain to the criminal courts.

damage harm which has occurred.

damages compensation payable as the result of a tort or civil wrong.

ex gratia without admitting liability (usually refers to a payment by a prospective defendant).

HC Health Circular issued by DHSS, e.g. HC(77)22.

indictable can be tried on an indictment.

judiciary judges.

mens rea the mental element required in most crimes. Crimes which do not require this mental element are known as crimes of strict liability.

plaintiff the person bringing the action in a civil case.

precedent an earlier case which may be binding upon the judge.

prima facie at first sight.

res ipsa loquitur the thing speaks for itself.

standard of proof the level that the party who has the burden of proof must satisfy, e.g. on a balance of probabilities or beyond all reasonable doubt.

statute an Act of Parliament cited by year and chapter, e.g. Congenital Disabilities Act 1976 c.28.

summary relating to the proceedings before magistrates.

tort civil wrong excluding breach of contract.

trustee one who holds property in trust for another, e.g. has duties to care for it.

void is invalid or not legally binding.

voidable can be made void.

Useful addresses

Association of British Paediatric Nurses
Central Nursing Office, Hospital for Sick Children, Great Ormond Street, London WC1N 3JY

Association of Community Health Councils
362 Euston Road, London NW1 3BL

Association of Nurse Administrators
13 Grosvenor Place, London SW1X 7EN

Association of Supervisors of Midwives
Mrs Guest, Maternity Unit, Northgate Hospital, Great Yarmouth

British Medical Association
BMA House, Tavistock Square, London WC1H 9JP

Charity Commission
Ryder Street, London SW1Y 6AH

Confederation of Health Service Employees
Glen House, High Street, Banstead, Surrey SM7 2LH

English National Board for Nursing, Midwifery and Health Visiting
Victory House, 170 Tottenham Court Road, London W1P 0HA

Family Planning Association
27–35 Mortimer Street, London W1N 7RJ

Health and Safety Commission
Regina House, 259 Old Marylebone Road, London NW1 5DT

Health Service Commissioner for England, Scotland and for Wales
Church House, Great Smith Street, London SW1 3BW
11 Melville Crescent, Edinburgh EH3 7LU
Fourth Floor, Pearl Assurance House, Greyfriars Road, Cardiff CF1 3AG

Health Visitors Association
36 Eccleston Square, London SW1V 1PF

Mind
22 Harley Street, London W1N 2ED

National and Local Government Officers Association
1 Mabledon Place, London WC1H 9AJ

National Association of Theatre Nurses
22 Mount Parade, Harrogate, Yorkshire

National Board for Nursing, Midwifery and Health Visiting for Northern Ireland
123–137 York Street, Belfast BT15 1AB

National Board for Nursing, Midwifery and Health Visiting for Scotland
22 Queen Street, Edinburgh EH2 1JX

National Childbirth Trust
9 Queensborough Terrace, London W2 3TB

National Union of Public Employees
Civic House, 20 Grand Depot Road, Woolwich, London SE18 6SF

Patients Association
Room 33, 18 Charing Cross Road, London WC2H 0HR

Royal British Nurses' Association
94 Upper Tollington Park, London N4 4NB

Royal College of Midwives
15 Mansfield Street, London EH1 3HU

Royal College of Nursing of the United Kingdom
20 Cavendish Square, London W1M 0AB

Royal National Institute for the Blind
224 Great Portland Street, London W1N 6AA

Royal National Institute for the Deaf
105 Gower Street, London WC1E 6AH

Royal National Pension Fund for Nurses
Burdett House, Buckingham Street, London WC2N 6ED

Royal Society for Mentally Handicapped Children and Adults
National Centre, 123 Golden Lane, London EC1Y 0RT

Royal Society for the Prevention of Accidents
Cannon House, The Priory, Queensway, Birmingham B4 6BS

United Kingdom Central Council for Nursing, Midwifery and Health Visiting
23 Portland Place, London W1A 1BA

Welsh National Board for Nursing, Midwifery and Health Visiting
Floor 13, Pearl Assurance House, Greyfriars Road, Cardiff CF1 3AG

Women's Royal Voluntary Service
17 Old Park Lane, London W1Y 4AJ

Recommended further reading

ACAS, *Discipline at Work Advisory Handbook*, 1987

Appelbe, G.E. and Wingfield, J. (eds), *Dale and Appelbe's Pharmacy: Law and Ethics*, 5th edn, The Pharmaceutical Press, 1993

Beauchamp, T.L. and Childres, J.F., *Principles of Biomedical Ethics*, 3rd edn, Oxford University Press, 1989

Beddard, R., *Human Rights and Europe*, 3rd edn, Grotius Publications, Cambridge, 1992

Brazier, Margaret, *Medicine, Patients and the Law*, Penguin, 1992

Brazier, Margaret (ed.), *Street on Torts*, Butterworth, 1993

Campbell, A.V., *Moral Dilemmas in Medicine*, Churchill Livingstone, 1984

Clarkson, C.M.V. and Keating, H.M., *Criminal Law: Text and Materials*, 2nd edn, Sweet and Maxwell, 1990

Department of Health, *AIDS/HIV Infected Health Care Workers*, April 1993

Dimond, B.C., *Accountability and the Nurse*, Distance Learning Pack, South Bank University, 1992

Dimond, B.C., *Patients' Rights, Responsibilities and the Nurse*, Central Health Studies, Quay Publishing, 1993

Ellis, Norman, *Employing Staff*, 5th edn, British Medical Journal, 1994

English National Board, *Preparation for Supervisors of Midwives*, Open Learning Programme, 1992

Faulder, C., *Whose Body Is It?*, Virago, 1985

Finch, John (ed.), *Speller's Law Relating to Hospitals*, 7th edn, Chapman and Hall Medical, 1994

Gann, Robert, *The NHS A to Z*, 2nd edn, The Help for Health Trust, 1993

Glover, J., *Causing Death and Saving Lives*, Penguin, 1984

Glover, J., *What Sort of People Should There Be?*, Penguin, 1984

Ham, Chris, *The New National Health Service*, NAHAT, 1991

Hoggett, Brenda, *Mental Health Law*, 3rd edn, Sweet and Maxwell, 1990

Hunt, Geoffrey and Wainwright, Paul (eds), *Expanding the Role of the Nurse*, Blackwell Scientific Publications, 1994

Jones, Michael, *Medical Negligence*, Sweet and Maxwell, 1991

Jones, Richard, *Mental Health Act Manual*, 4th edn, Sweet and Maxwell, 1994

Kennedy, I. and Grubb, A., *Medical Law and Ethics*, Butterworth, 1994

Kidner, Richard, *Blackstone's Statutes on Employment Law*, 3rd edn, Blackstone Press, 1993

Kloss, Diana, *Occupational Health Law*, 2nd edn, Blackwell Scientific Publications, 1994

Mason, David and Edwards, Peter, *Litigation: A Risk Management Guide for Midwives*, Royal College of Midwives, 1993

Mason, J.K. and McCall-Smith, A., *Law and Medical Ethics*, Butterworth, 1987

Miers, David and Page, Alan, *Legislation*, 2nd edn, Sweet and Maxwell, 1990

Morgan, Derek and Lee, Robert G., *Human Fertilisation and Embryology Act 1990*, Blackstone Press, 1991

National Association of Theatre Nurses, *The Role of the Nurse as First Assistant in the Operating Department*, 1993

Nurse's Handbook of Law and Ethics, Springhouse Corporation, 1992

Pearse, P. *et al.*, *Personal Data Protection in Health and Social Services*, Croom Helm, 1988

Pyne, R.H., *Professional Discipline in Nursing, Midwifery and Health Visiting*, 2nd edn, Blackwell Scientific Publications, 1991

Royal College of Midwives, *Examples of Effective Midwifery Management*, 1993

Royal College of Midwives, *The Midwife: Her Legal Status and Accountability*, 1993

Royal College of Nursing, *Focus on Restraint*, 2nd edn, 1992

Rowson, Richard, *An Introduction to Ethics for Nurses*, Scutari Press, 1990

Rumbold, Graham, *Ethics in Nursing Practice*, 2nd edn, Bailliere Tindall, 1993

Salvage, J., *Nurses at Risk: Guide to Health and Safety at Work*, Heinemann, 1988

Salvage, J. and Rogers, R., *Health and Safety and the Nurse*, Heinemann, 1988

Selwyn's Law of Employment, 8th edn, Butterworth, 1993

Selwyn's Law of Safety at Work, Butterworth, 1982

Smith, K. and Keenan, D., *English Law*, 10th edn, Pitman, 1992

Social Security Inspectorate, Department of Health, *No Longer Afraid: Safeguard of Older People in Domestic Settings*, HMSO, 1993

Steiner, Josephine, *Textbook on EC Law*, 3rd edn, Blackstone Press, 1992

Thompson, Robin and Thompson, Brian, *Dismissal: A basic introduction to your legal rights*, Robin Thompson and Partners and Brian Thompson and Partners, 1993

Thompson, Robin and Thompson, Brian, *Equal Pay*, Robin Thompson and Partners and Brian Thompson and Partners, 1993

Thompson, Robin and Thompson, Brian, *Health and Safety at Work*, Robin Thompson and Partners and Brian Thompson and Partners, 1993

Thompson, Robin and Thompson, Brian, *Injuries at Work and Work-related Illnesses*, Robin Thompson and Partners and Brian Thompson and Partners, 1993

Thompson, Robin and Thompson, Brian, *Women at Work*, Robin Thompson and Partners and Brian Thompson and Partners, 1993

Tschudin, Verena and Marks-Maran, Diane, *Ethics: A Primer for Nurses*, Bailliere Tindall, 1993

Vincent, Charles *et al.*, *Medical Accidents*, Oxford University Press, 1993

Walters, T.C. and O'Connell, M.A., *The Police and Criminal Evidence Act 1984*, Blackstone Press, 1985

White, Richard, Carr, Paul and Lowe, Nigel, *A Guide to the Children Act 1989*, Butterworth, 1991
Young, Ann P., *Legal Problems in Nursing Practice*, Harper & Row, 1989
Young, Ann P., *Law and Professional Conduct in Nursing*, 2nd edn, Scutari Press, 1994

Reference should also be made to the many articles on different legal aspects of nursing, health visiting and midwifery practice which can be found in *Nursing Times*, *Nursing Standard*, *British Journal of Nursing*, *Senior Nurse*, *Modern Midwife*, *British Journal of Midwifery*, *Midwives Chronicle*, *Midwifery Matters*, *Midwife Community Care*, *Nursing the Elderly*, *Practice Nurse* and similar journals for registered practitioners in general. The *British Medical Journal*, the *Lancet* and the *Journal of Medical Ethics* and other medical journals also include articles on the legal and ethical issues that are of relevance to nurse practitioners. The Midwives Information and Resource Service (MIDIRS) provides an extremely useful guide to articles relevant to midwifery published in other journals (Institute of Child Health, Royal Hospital for Sick Children, St Michael's Hill, Bristol BS2 8BJ, Tel. 0272-251791).

A bibliography of general and specialist books on midwifery, nursing and medical books is available from Meditec, Nursing Book Service, York House, 26 Bourne Road, Coldersworth, Lincs., NG33 5JE.

Index

complaints
answers sought, 373
from the community, 375–6
handling
on clinical matters, 382, 543–5, 550–53
on failure of communication, 373–6
on non-clinical matters, 374–7, 542–8
procedures, 4, 542–53
relevant authorities, 374, 378–81, 546–7
motives, reasons behind, 373
reasons for refraining from, 374
complementary therapies, 428, 453–4
confidentiality
advisory paper (UKCC), 119, 123, 406–13
and abortions, 118, 243
and abuse/neglect of children, 215, 272–3
and community nursing, 325, 335
and proper disclosure of information,
111–12, 113–23, 412–13, 512–13
basis of duty, 3–4, 11–12, 110–11
breach
classified as misconduct, 533
defined, 410
in accident and emergency departments, 304,
306–7, 513
in genito-urinary medicine, 310–11
in reproductive medicine, 314, 318
problems posed by AIDS, 97–8, 113, 115, 117,
119–20, 311, 360, 367–70
consent
and adequate information, 88–98, 102–3,
462–4
forms for giving, 89–97
to abortion, request by child/minor, 243–4
to treatment/research
after premedication for surgery, 263–4
and accountability, 4, 462–4
and actions for trespass, 88–101
and blood transfusion, 88–99, 208, 212,
264–5
and vaccination, 338, 340–1
basic principles, 88, 97–8
in pregnancy, childbirth, 220, 222–4
of children, 205–7, 208–13
of elderly, 276–8, 279–80, 296–7
of mentally disordered, 100, 285, 293,
294–7, 325, 332
of minors, 205–8
of unconscious patient, 100–1
overruling parental decision, 210–11
problems posed by AIDS, 97–8, 359–61,
362–3, 367–9, 475
responsibility of tutors, 269, 273–4
surgery refused, 260, 264–5

withholding, by parents, 212–13
to use of organs, tissue, for transplants,
211–12, 233–4, 255–7, 501
see also **information**
contraception *see* **family planning, sterilisation**
contract, breach of *see* **employment, contracts of**
contributory negligence, 72, 80–2, 187
coroner
inquests, 396, 398–400, 508
report of death to, 255, 396, 397–8, 506–7
role, and accountability of nurse, 5
corporal punishment, legality challenged,
216–17
costs, in civil action, 74, 76
counselling, in disciplinary policy, 516, 519
County Councillors, complaints to, 373
cremation *see* **body (of deceased)**
crime
and disciplinary policies, 518, 524
reporting of, to police, 123
suspicions of community nurse, 325, 335
see also **crimimal law**
Criminal Injuries Compensation Board, 199,
200–2
criminal law
accountability in, 3–5, 5–7, 11–12
and death of patient, 250–2
charges brought under
and elements of crime, 15, 22–3
available defences, 15, 23–6
jurisdiction of courts, 17–18
offences classified, 17
rights of appeal, 22
sentencing, 18, 22
stages in proceedings, 15–22
civil law distinguished, 11–12
in context of childbirth, 220, 221–2, 225
Crown, the, immunity withdrawn from health
authorities, 188, 190, 192
Crown Court, procedure in, 15, 18–22
Crown Prosecution Service, 17
custom and practice, terms in contract of
employment derived from, 142, 146

damages
deduction of social security benefits, 78
determination by judge, 76
general, 77–9
interest payable, 78
special, 77
data protection, 4, 106–9, 116–17, 411
death
and accountability, 4–6, 36, 250
and switching off life support, 252–3

death (*continued*)
and transplant surgery, 255–7, 500–1
and withholding of resuscitation, 253–5
dealing with relatives, 396, 397, 500, 502
determination of, 248–50
importance of time of, 250–1
in accident/emergency departments, 505–6
law and procedures
for patients from overseas, 506
in absence of relatives, 503, 510–11
on certification, registration, 395–7, 454, 455, 456–7, 501–2
on dealing with property of deceased, 396, 400, 509–11
on disposal of body, 233, 397, 456, 457, 502–3
on funeral arrangements, 503–5
on inquests, 396, 398–400, 508
on post-mortem, 396, 397, 508
on report to coroner, 255, 396, 397–8, 506–7
religious aspects, 503–5
unexpected, subject of complaint, 343
see also **wills**
defamation, action for
defences available, 139
privileged situations, 139
statements giving rise to, 12, 138–9
defects
in equipment, 193–6
in premises, problem for community nurse, 325, 329–30
relative to product liability, 193–6
defence organisations, membership of, by medical staff, 69, 535
defences
in civil case, 73, 79–86, 126, 139, 274–5
in criminal law, 15, 23–6
demotion, as disciplinary measure, 10
Department of Health and Social Services, codes of practice, 11
diminished responsibility, a defence in criminal law, 24–5
discharge
from hospital, 373
from treatment, 100
discipline
designated responsibility, 516–17, 528
disiplinary policy, 514–34
of children in hospital, 216–17
powers of employer, rights of employee, 8, 10
rules, 531–4
discovery, in civil case, 72–4
discrimination (by race/sex/religion)

and rights to equal pay, 142, 164
and segregation, 163
and victimisation, 162–3
direct, defined, described, 162
exceptions to laws against, 163, 164
indirect, 162
diseases, notifiable, 117
dismissal
as disciplinary action, 10, 22, 518, 523–4, 532–4
of student nurses, 271
unfair
and redundancy, 552–4
appeal against, 10, 518, 525–8
employees' rights, 22, 142, 149–53, 156–60
procedures, 158–9
remedies, 158–9
doctors *see* **medical practitioners**
documentation, documents
legal, defined, 135
required, in police work, 15–16
see also **medical records**
Down's syndrome, consent to treatment, 213
drugs
addiction, addicts
notification required, 393
prescription for, 393
responsibilities of nurses, 392–3, 426
administration
conflict with prescriber, 388–9
exceptional circumstances, 427
in domestic setting, 424
in hospital, 423–4
in theatre nursing, 260, 265–6
principles summarised, 49–50, 388, 420, 421–3
self-, by patients, 392, 424–5
sources of information, 389, 429–30
supervision necessary, 391–2
to mentally disordered, 332
UKCC advisory policy, 384, 389, 391–2, 418–30
and accountability, 4–6
and product liability, 393
classification, 385–6
destruction of controlled, 451
dispensing, 421
homoeopathic and herbal medicines, 428, 450
misuse, disclosure, 111, 118
prescription
by nurses, not permitted, 392–3
by telephone, 420
by word of mouth, 390–1, 420

Mental Health Act Commission, 299–300,
      380–1, 547
mentally disordered patients
   and aggression towards nurse, 198–200
   care in the community, 298–9
   compulsory removal, 299–300, 332, 333–4
   consent to treatment, 100, 285, 293, 294–7,
      325, 332
   exempt from law on time limits, 86
   guardianship, 297–8
   holding powers, 285, 286–7, 287–9
   in community nursing, 298–9, 325, 332–4
   nearest relatives
      defined, 287, 291
      responsibilities, 288–9, 291
      right to information, 291, 292–3
   responsibilities of
      doctors, 284–7, 288–90
      management, 284–7, 288–9, 292–3, 300
      social workers, 285–9, 290–3, 299
   responsibility for property, of, 349–54
   review tribunals, 285, 288–9, 292–3, 300, 301
   right to information, 285, 290–1, 293
   safeguards in brain surgery, 296
mentally handicapped
   abortion of, 244–5
   sterilisation, 210–11, 212–13, 245–6
midwifery/midwives
   administration of drugs, 392, 393–4, 426–7,
      441, 448–51
   and accountability, 3–4
   and AIDS, 220, 234, 365
   and law against sexual discrimination, 164,
      165
   dealing with opposition, 220–1, 223–4
   defined, 445
   duty towards unborn, 221, 228
   EC directive, 434, 445–6
   education and training, 435–8
   future developments, 234
   legal relationship with doctors, 220, 226–7,
      453
   matters of compulsion/consent, 219–24
   notifications required, 455–6
   power to compel admission to hospital, 220,
      222–3
   professional standards, 220, 228–9
   record-keeping, 226–7, 441–2, 451–2, 483
   rules/codes of practice, 219–21, 403–5,
      431–43, 444–57, 491–2
   statutory controls, 166–70, 448–53, 454–5,
      457
   supervision, 442–3, 452–3
   welfare of baby

   and liabilities of mother, 220, 224–5,
      229–30, 496
   in community nursing, 220, 227–8, 446
   in midwifery departments, 220, 226, 231
   in nurseries, 220, 231
   in special care baby units, 220, 231
minors
   abortion of, 243–4
   consent to treatment, 205–8
   defined, 205
   exempt from law on time limitation, 86
   family planning advice, 338, 341–2
   sterilisation, 245–6
misconduct
   a ground for striking off, 167, 170–1
   conduct amounting to, 59, 167, 173, 175–6,
      532–3
   judicial review, 8
   responsibility for inquiry into, 168
mistake, a defence in criminal law, 24, 25
mortuary staff, procedures for, 509
mothers
   consent to treatment, 220, 222–4
   legal liabilities, 220, 224–5, 229–30, 496
murder, significance of time of death in
      relation to, 250–1

National Boards (of UKCC), 166–9
National Health Service Trusts
   and Crown immunity 188, 190, 192
   as defendants in civil action, 73
   complaints to, 373, 376
   direct liability, 53–8, 67–9
   disclaimers of liability, 83
   law on product liability, 194–5
   'no fault' liability, 8, 83, 274
   vicarious liability, 8, 53–4, 60–7, 183, 186, 199
national security, protection of, a ground for
      dismissal, 159
**National Society for the Prevention of Cruelty
      to Children**, principle of confidentiality,
      273
necessity, a defence in criminal law, 24, 25
neglect of children *see* **children**
negligence
   and accountability
      in civil law, 3–5, 8, 11–12
      in criminal law, 3–5, 5–7, 11–12
      in criminal/civil law distinguished, 11–12
      professional standards, 3–5, 7–8
      to employer, 3–5, 8, 10
   civil liability for
      and extended role of nurse, 45–8, 260, 262,
         343, 395–7